Reading Virgil

Virgil's *Aeneid*, an epic which tells the story of Aeneas' flight from burning Troy, his adventures on the high seas and eventual arrival in Italy, thereby founding the Roman race, is one of the most influential works of Roman literature. This edition of the first two books is designed for those who have completed an introductory course in Latin and aims to help such users to enjoy one of Latin literature's greatest masterpieces. The text is accompanied by a running vocabulary, learning vocabulary, full grammatical help and notes. Essays at the end of each passage are designed to encourage appreciation of Virgil's plot-handling, poetic art and rich understanding of humanity, and there are references throughout to the most helpful modern thinking about the poem and its significance. No other intermediate text is so carefully designed to provide all the help that is needed to make reading Virgil a pleasure.

PETER JONES was Senior Lecturer in Classics at the University of Newcastle upon Tyne until his retirement. He has written many books for the student of Latin and Greek, most recently *Reading Ovid* (Cambridge University Press, 2007) and (with Keith Sidwell) the Reading Latin textbook series. He is also the author of *Vote for Caesar* (Orion, 2008).

Frontispiece. The Tiepolo Aeneas and Venus on the shores of Carthage.

Reading Virgil

Aeneid I and II

PETER JONES

CAMBRIDGE
UNIVERSITY PRESS

CAMBRIDGE
UNIVERSITY PRESS

University Printing House, Cambridge CB2 8BS, United Kingdom

Cambridge University Press is part of the University of Cambridge.

It furthers the University's mission by disseminating knowledge in the pursuit of education, learning and research at the highest international levels of excellence.

www.cambridge.org
Information on this title: www.cambridge.org/9780521171540

© Peter Jones 2011

First published 2011
Reprinted 2013

A catalogue record for this publication is available from the British Library

ISBN 978-0-521-76866-5 Hardback
ISBN 978-0-521-17154-0 Paperback

Contents

Illustrations

Maps

Preface

This book follows the same pattern as my *Reading Ovid* (Cambridge University Press 2007). It assumes readers have done a year of Latin and have a grasp of basic grammar and vocabulary at about the level of *Reading Latin* (Jones and Sidwell, Cambridge University Press 1986) or *Wheelock's Latin* (New York 2000). Line-by-line help with grammar and vocabulary is generous to start with, and regular learning vocabularies specify what must now be learned because it will not feature in the glossing again (though the total vocabulary set to be learned is contained at the back, pp. 302–15).

It is important to stress, however, that each book is glossed from scratch as if it were a separate entity. So if you are reading Book 2, the glossing will assume you have not read Book 1, and *vice-versa*. The line-by-line help also contains notes on names, places, customs, literary devices, rhetoric and so on. At the end of each passage, an embellished paraphrase summarises and draws out some of the wider implications of the passage. At the end of each major *Section*, **Study Sections** suggest ways in which students can think about the passages just read. An *Appendix* contains five alternative accounts of the sacking of Ilium.

Virgil is not easy. The text, therefore, is split into quite small passages to start with to encourage careful reading, gradually extending in length. Comment, too, on almost any line of the *Aeneid* could run to pages. But this is a book for beginners, and one can do only so much. Further, I do not take the view that, for this audience, Virgil is best served as a means for exploring modern literary theories of e.g. gender. So, as with the Ovid, the comment concentrates on elucidating the surface meaning and expanding primarily on poetry, plot and character, touching briefly on other issues as they arise, as far as they relate to Books 1 and 2 alone; but, inevitably, Virgil being the poet he is, comment is denser than it was with Ovid. As for Virgil's use of earlier poets, occasional reference is made to e.g. Apollonius Rhodius, Ennius and Lucretius, but mainly to Homer. One difference from most editions of this scale: the frequent quotations from Servius, the fourth-century AD commentator on Virgil. However occasionally misleading, he has much of great interest to say.

My debts to the commentaries of J. Henry, J.P. Conington, T.E. Page, R.G. Austin and R.D. Williams will be obvious on every page. N.M. Horsfall's arrived too late for any but brief consultation. I am most grateful to R.D. Dawe for permission to quote from his extremely accurate prose translation of Homer's *Odyssey*, here printed as verse for ease of reference (from R.D. Dawe, *The*

Odyssey: Translation and Analysis (Lewes 1993), available from the Hellenic Bookservice, London). Translations of the *Iliad* come from E.V. Rieu, *Homer: The Iliad*, revised and updated by Peter Jones and D.C.H. Rieu (Harmondsworth 2003), and referred to in the text as 'Rieu-Jones'.

I am most grateful to Jeannie Cohen for making Servius' commentary on Book 1 available to me; to Alan Beale for commenting on draft versions and then testing them in the University of Sunderland's excellent Centre for Lifelong Learning and their summer school at Durham; to an anonymous American referee whose detailed and perceptive comments significantly improved much of the book; and to Andrew Morley for the maps.

My purpose throughout is, as with the Ovid, to make reading Virgil a pleasure, since I can think of no other reason for reading him.

Peter Jones
Newcastle on Tyne, October 2009

Abbreviations and other conventions

1f., 2m., etc. refer to the declension and gender of a noun
1/2/3/4 and 3/4 (which some grammars call 5) refer to the conjugation of a verb

abl.	ablative	*loc. cit.*	*locō citātō*, the passage/
abs.	absolute		author just cited
acc.	accusative	m.	masculine
act.	active	n.	neuter
adj.	adjective	neg.	negative
ad loc.	*ad locum*, at the relevant	nom.	nominative
	place	obj.	object
adv.	adverb	*OLD*	*Oxford Latin Dictionary*
cf.	*cōnfer*, 'compare'	part.	participle
comp.	comparative	pass.	passive
Cong.	Conington (1858) in	perf.	perfect
	Bibliography	pl.	plural
conj.	conjugation, conjugated	plupf.	pluperfect
dat.	dative	p.p.	principal part
decl.	declension	prep.	preposition
dep.	deponent	pres.	present
dir.	direct	prim.	primary
f.	feminine	pron.	pronoun
ff.	following	q.	question
fut.	future	rel.	relative
gen.	genitive	s.	singular
imper.	imperative	sc.	*scīlicet*, 'presumably'
impf.	imperfect	sec.	secondary
ind.	indicative	seq.	sequence
indecl.	indeclinable	sp.	speech
indir.	indirect	subjunc.	subjunctive
inf.	infinitive	sup.	superlative
intrans.	intransitive	tr.	translate
irr.	irregular	trans.	transitive
lit.	literally	vb	verb
local	used of abl. meaning 'in/	voc.	vocative
	at/on'		

Introduction: Virgil and the *Aeneid*

Life of Virgil

1   The life of Virgil is a controversial topic. Instead of constructing yet another second-hand 'life', I here quote some of the less controversial excerpts from the lives of Virgil composed by Donatus (*Introduction* Sections 1–9 = *Intro* [1–9]) and Servius (*Intro* [10]), both fourth century AD, on which all modern constructions of his life are based:[1]

Early life, looks, health

'Publius Vergilius Maro was a native of Mantua . . . born in 70 BC on 15 October, in the village called Andes, not far from Mantua[2] . . . Virgil passed the first years of his life at Cremona, until he assumed the *toga* of manhood which he did in his seventeenth year . . . But he moved from Cremona to Milan and shortly after that to Rome.[3] He was tall and well-built, with a swarthy complexion and the look of a countryman. His health was mixed; he commonly had problems with his throat and stomach, suffered from headaches, and often spat up blood. He ate and drank little.'

---

[1]   Notes to the early life of Virgil are mainly based on chapter 2 of L.P. Wilkinson, *The Georgics of Virgil* (Cambridge 1969). Much of the information collected in the footnotes to this *Introduction* comes from a collection of short poems called *Catalepton* ('small-scale') ascribed to Virgil, some of which are thought actually to have been composed by him. The statements contained in accounts of ancient 'lives' are notoriously difficult to assess for accuracy. This one is no different. R.J. Tarrant 'Poetry and Power: Virgil's Poetry in Contemporary Context' in Martindale (1997: 169–87) has much of interest to say on Virgil's life and Rome in Virgil's day. Note that our convention is to spell his name 'Virgil'. In Latin he is *Vergilius*. The translation is based on W.A. Camps, *Virgil's* Aeneid (Oxford 1969) 115ff.

[2]   Julius Caesar was aged 30 at the time, and the republican system already falling apart.

[3]   These moves, the last to Rome in 52 BC, were presumably for educational reasons. He learned rhetoric and, we are told, medicine and mathematics, probably including astronomy and astrology. At this time Caesar was conquering Gaul, and Rome was in increasing turmoil (see [12] below). Virgil was probably sympathetic to Caesar.

Retiring nature

2   'He was so respectable in life, speech and mind that in Naples[4] he was
     usually called Parthenias ("Virginia"/"Maiden");[5] and if anyone recognised
     him in Rome (where he rarely went), he would escape those following and
     pointing at him by taking refuge in the nearest house . . . He had a house on
     the Esquiline, next to the Gardens of Maecenas,[6] though he spent most of
     his time well out of sight in homes in Campania and Sicily . . . He argued a
     case in court once, and once only. According to Melissus[7] he was slow of
     speech, as if he had not been properly trained.'
     (There follow details of his early poetic efforts.)

Summary of writings: Aeneid *and Rome's origins*

3   'He tried to write on Roman history, but found the subject uncongenial,
     and turned to pastoral poetry in his *Eclogues*[8] . . . Next he wrote the *Georgics*[9]
     in honour of Maecenas . . . Last of all he began the *Aeneid*, a complex and
     diverse story, a sort of counterpart of the *Iliad* and *Odyssey* combined,
     involving both Greek and Roman places and characters and designed
     (Virgil gave special attention to this) to cover the origins of both Rome and
     Augustus.'

Compositional technique

4   'When he was writing the *Georgics* he is said to have dictated a large number
     of lines early in the day, and spent the rest of it working them over and
     reducing them to a very few, saying that he produced his poetry like a she-
     bear gradually licking her cubs into shape. He first made a prose sketch of
     the *Aeneid* and divided it into twelve books, and then, as the fancy took
     him, and not following any particular order, turned them bit by bit into
     poetry. Further, not wishing to lose momentum, he left some passages

---

[4] Where he lived after abandoning rhetorical education. He went to Naples to study under the Epicurean
     philosopher Siro.
[5] Since the Greek for 'virgin' is *parthenos*, this name may simply be Vergilius (cf. *uirgō*) in Greek.
[6] Maecenas was the future emperor Augustus' agent and general fixer. Virgil was drawn into Augustus'
     'circle' by Maecenas soon after publishing *Eclogues* and became rich on the strength of it. Augustus is said
     to have given him 10 million sesterces.
[7] An ex-slave of Maecenas.
[8] Greek *eklogē* 'short poem' or 'selections'; also known as *Bucolics* (Greek *boukolika* 'To do with
     herdsmen'). *Eclogues* consists of ten short poems.
[9] Four books ostensibly on farming (Greek *geōrgos* 'farmer'). See on **1.148–56**.

unfinished, and propped up others with temporary verses, joking that they were struts to hold the work up until the solid columns were delivered.'

Recitations

5   'He finished the *Eclogues* in three years,[10] the *Georgics* in seven,[11] and the *Aeneid* in eleven.[12] The *Eclogues* were so successful that they were soon regularly recited on stage. He read the *Georgics* aloud to Augustus on four successive days when the emperor was on his way back to Rome after the victory at Actium[13] and resting at Atella with a throat infection. Whenever Virgil's voice gave up and he had to stop, Maecenas took over. Virgil recited poetry sweetly and with a wonderful charm.'

Augustus' keen interest

6   'Even when the *Aeneid* was hardly begun, the reports were such that Sextus Propertius [a contemporary poet] did not hesitate to declare:

"Give way, you poets of Rome and Greece:
Something greater than the *Iliad* is in the making."[14]

When Augustus was away on his campaign against the Cantabriges,[15] he rather browbeat the poet with a combination of entreaties and joking threats to send him (in Augustus' own words) "either the first sketch or any specimen". Much later, when the work was essentially finished, Virgil *did* recite just three books – the second, fourth and sixth. This last had a notable effect on the listening Octavia, who is said to have fainted at the verses referring to her son *tū Marcellus eris* and been revived only with difficulty.'[16]

Death

7   'When Virgil was 52 and intending to put the finishing touches to the *Aeneid*, he decided to retire to Greece and Asia and do nothing for three

---

[10] c. 38 BC.

[11] 29 BC.

[12] Unfinished at his death in 19 BC.

[13] In 31 BC. See [12] below.

[14] 2.34.66. Some commentators have seen this as sarcastic.

[15] c. 26 BC.

[16] Marcellus died in 23 BC, aged 20. He was the son of Augustus' sister Octavia. Augustus had adopted him as his son and successor in 25 BC and married him to his daughter Julia. The reference is to *Aeneid* 6.883.

years except revise, so that he could leave the rest of his life free for philosophy. But on his way to Athens he met Augustus on his way back to Rome
from the East and determined to accompany him. But on a very hot day on
a sight-seeing visit to the nearby town of Megara, he became ill. He wors-
ened the condition by refusing to abandon his journey and was seriously ill
by the time he reached Brundisium. There he died a few days later, on 21
September.'[17]

Virgil's wishes ignored

8   'Before he left Italy, Virgil had tried to get Varius to agree to burn the
Aeneid if anything should happen to himself, but Varius had firmly refused
to do any such thing. So on his death-bed Virgil repeatedly demanded the
box containing the manuscript, intending to burn the poem himself, but no
one gave it to him . . . On Augustus' orders Varius published it, but it was
revised only cursorily, so that any unfinished lines remained unfinished.'[18]

Critical reactions

9   'M. Vipsanius[19] spoke of Virgil as inventor, with the encouragement of
Maecenas, of a new kind of artificiality, neither extravagant nor affectedly
simple, but based on common words and for that reason unobtrusive . . .[20]
Asconius Pedianus in the book which he wrote against the detractors of
Virgil cites only a few complaints against him, and those mostly relating to
matters of fact or to his borrowings from Homer, and says that Virgil used
to rebut the charge of plagiarising Homer with the following remark: "Why
don't they try to do the same themselves? They would soon realise that it is
easier to steal his club from Hercules than a line from Homer." Nevertheless
(says Asconius) he had planned to retire abroad and wrap the whole poem
up to satisfy even his most hostile critics.'

---

[17] 19 BC.

[18] The unfinished lines (e.g. 1.534, 2.720) are clear evidence that the poem is unfinished. There are more
unfinished lines in Book 2 than any other Book.

[19] Presumably the soldier and politician Agrippa, a close friend and supporter of Augustus.

[20] L.P. Wilkinson 'The Language of Virgil and Horace' in S.J. Harrison (1990: 418–20), using statistics from
A. Cordier *Études sur le vocabulaire épique dans l'Énéide* (Paris 1939), points out that Virgil's use of
archaic, rare and compound words is extremely sparse: archaic words, one every forty lines; rare words,
one every thirty lines; compound words not used in everyday speech, one every hundred lines. One
proviso, however: Cordier does not take repeated incidents of the same word into account.

Servius on the nature of the Aeneid and its praise of Augustus' parentage

10   'It is clear what sort of poem it is: it is in the heroic metre, and the format is composite, with the poet himself speaking and introducing other speakers too. It is heroic because it consists of human and divine characters, mixing truth with fiction. For it is obvious that Aeneas came to Italy, but it is agreed that Venus' conversation with Jupiter[21] and Mercury's mission [to Dido][22] are invented. The style is lofty, consisting as it does of refined speech and noble sentiments . . . Virgil's purpose is to imitate Homer[23] and praise Augustus in respect of his parentage.[24] For Augustus is the son of Atia, who is the daughter of Julia, the sister of Julius Caesar, whose name "Julius" derives from Aeneas' son Iulus, as Virgil himself confirms in "a name handed down from great Iulus".'[25]

Rome in the first century BC

Rome's rise to power

11   Romans were intensely proud of their 'constitution' which they claimed could be traced back almost 500 years to the moment when the Etruscan kings were thrown out and, virtually overnight (they believed), Rome turned into a republic. That constitution lay at the heart, they felt, of Rome's dramatic rise to power, which put them in control of Italy by the 270s BC and, after the conquest of that other great western power, Carthage, in the three Punic wars, made them masters of an expanding empire. By the middle of the first century BC, Rome's provinces spread round the Mediterranean – Spain, Gaul, Greece, much of the Near East and north Africa.[26]

---

[21] 1.229–96.

[22] 1.297–304.

[23] Virgil also imitates the *Argonautica* by the Greek epic writer Apollonius from Rhodes (third century BC). This tells of the adventures of Jason and his Argonauts in their efforts to get the Golden Fleece from Phasis (the eastern coast of the Black Sea) and bring it back to Greece. Jason is helped by Medea, the daughter of Aeetes, king of Phasis. Virgil models aspects of Dido (with whom Aeneas will have an affair when he arrives in Carthage) on Medea.

[24] Cf. [3].

[25] *Aeneid* 1.288.

[26] Jones and Sidwell (1997: sections 26–44).

The end of the republic and rise of Octavian/Augustus

12   But that proud confidence in what it meant to be Roman was almost completely destroyed by the nightmare of the destruction of the republican system. It started in 133 BC, when the senate refused to accept Tiberius Gracchus' sensible reforms designed to help ordinary Romans own land on which to farm and support themselves. Tiberius ignored the senate and forced the legislation through via the people's assemblies, but the traditional concord between senate and people had broken down. A vicious 'Social War' over political rights was then fought between Romans and Italians (91–87 BC), while internal conflict sprang up between powerful Romans, such as Marius, Sulla, Pompey, Crassus and Julius Caesar, with private armies at their back, fighting among themselves to gain power in defiance of every age-old and hallowed constitutional procedure. Caesar appeared to have come out on top in 49 BC when he defeated Pompey; but he was assassinated on the Ides of March 44 BC, unleashing the dogs of yet further bloody civil war. This culminated in a stand-off between Marc Antony and Caesar's nominated heir, his adoptive great-nephew Octavian (later Augustus), which was settled in Octavian's favour in 31 BC at the battle of Actium.[27] Rome held its breath. Horace had talked of this period as the result of inherited sin, going back to Romulus killing his twin brother Remus, and of the need for a saviour to appear.[28] Virgil described the battle of Actium in terms of Mars raging, Furies descending from the skies, Discord triumphant and Bellona (goddess of war) cracking her whip.[29] What was to happen to Romans after all *that*?

Maecenas' wooing of Virgil

13   Virgil, born in 70 BC, lived through this terrible period. But it did not stop poets going about their work; indeed, it was poetically the most brilliant period in the whole of Rome's history. Lucretius, Catullus and Horace worked throughout it; Propertius and Ovid were soon to spring on the scene. Horace and Virgil in particular became engaged on Octavian's side through the offices of Octavian's trusted friend and agent Gaius Maecenas, a supreme fixer who made it his business to develop a circle of broadly sympathetic poets (those were the days when the views of poets could be seen as politically significant). Virgil's *Eclogues*, probably appearing about 38 BC,

[27]   Jones and Sidwell (1997: sections 70–80).
[28]   *Epodes* 7 and *Odes* 1.2.
[29]   *Aeneid* 8.700–3.

refer in parts to the confiscations of land that took place during the civil wars to pay off soldiers.

Virgil's hopes of Octavian/Augustus

14   As his next poem *Georgics* shows, Virgil was impressed by what Octavian might achieve. He says there:

> Gods of our fathers, local gods, Romulus and mother Vesta,
> Who guard Tuscan Tiber and the Roman Palatine,
> At least do not prevent this young man from saving a world
> Turned upside down. For quite long enough now have we paid
> The price of Trojan Laomedon's perjury;
> For quite long enough, Caesar, has heaven
> Begrudged you to us.[30]
>
> Georgics 1.498–504

Further, at the end of *Georgics* he talked of Octavian 'giving laws to a willing people and setting out on the road to Olympus' (i.e. deification).

And so it gradually came to be. In the years following Actium, it did indeed become clear that Virgil's and others' hopes might be fulfilled, and Octavian might, just might, be able to restore much-needed peace and security to a war-torn Rome. In 27 BC, he had himself re-named Augustus and declared the republic officially restored. It was nothing of the sort, of course. The machinery had been restored, but everyone knew it was being worked by Augustus who had become, to all intents and purposes, Rome's first emperor. The Romans, nevertheless, seemed to acquiesce in this new settlement.

Virgil's early plans for an epic

15   That said, peace was not signed and sealed. Augustus' experiment had only just begun. At such a time of transition, no one could possibly tell how it would all turn out. An assassin's knife (think Julius Caesar) could end it at a stroke. So Virgil and others may have had high hopes, but hopes were all they were. As a result, if Virgil *was* planning an epic with Augustus at the heart of it, he would have to plan extremely carefully. The opening of

---

[30] Laomedon (Priam's father) had commissioned Neptune to build the walls of Troy but had not paid him for his efforts. Romans were descended from Trojans, and Virgil talks here as if they had inherited an ancestral curse from those times (cf. [12]). Octavian had also taken the name 'Caesar' from Julius Caesar, who had adopted him.

Georgics 3 suggested one possibility, where Virgil, rejecting the 'hackneyed' themes of mythology, says that he must find a way to rise above such 'common ground' and hints at building a great temple to Augustus with him as god in the middle, featuring (among much contemporary history) a beginning in Troy and 'the offspring of Assaracus [Priam's grandfather] . . . Tros [Assaracus' father] and . . . Apollo [a founder of Troy]'. In the event, the *Aeneid* would turn out to be something completely different.

The *Aeneid* and its forerunners

Homer

16   Virgil was facing a monumental task in composing a Roman epic at all, let alone one culminating in Augustus. The epics that everyone looked back to were those of Greece's most famous poet, Homer (c. 700 BC), composer of the *Iliad* and *Odyssey*.[31] The *Iliad* means 'tale about Ilium', the city in the region of Troy ruled by king Priam, which the Greeks were besieging in order to win back Helen. She was wife of the Greek king Menelaus, and had been seduced to Troy by Paris, Priam's son. Paris had won her as a reward for giving the golden apple inscribed 'to the most beautiful' to Aphrodite/ Venus (goddess of sex), thus incurring for the Trojans the everlasting enmity of the two rejected goddesses, Athena/Minerva and Hera/Juno. The *Iliad* does not deal directly with the seduction of Helen, nor with the final capture of Ilium, but took as its theme one event from the ten-year war – the consequences of the anger of the greatest Greek fighter, Achilles, who was insulted by the leader of the Greek expedition to Troy, Agamemnon, and withdrew from the fighting. The *Odyssey* told the story of the return of the tricky Greek hero Odysseus after the war to his home on Ithaca (Virgil calls him *Ulixēs*, derived from a dialect form Olysseus, cf. our Ulysses). After three years of adventures at sea and seven years held by the sea-nymph Calypso on her island, he reached home only to find 108 suitors effectively besieging his palace, demanding Penelope marry one of them. These mighty epics had not been designed as nationalistic statements – but that is what they became. They were to have a lasting influence on subsequent Greek and Roman literature.

[31] See [10] and footnote 23. There is debate about the date of Homer (anywhere between 750 and 650 BC), and whether he was in fact sole author of the *Iliad* and *Odyssey*.

Virgil's use of Naevius' 'Punic War' epic

17   Romans had been in contact with Greeks for hundreds of years through Greek settlements in southern Italy, before they conquered Greece in 146 BC and turned it into a province. They saw themselves as culturally backward by comparison and, captivated by Greek artistic and literary culture, began to look to Greek models to see how to do it. Naevius, who was not Roman but came from the south of Italy, where Greek influence was strong (thanks to its colonising from the eighth century BC), made the first serious attempt at a Roman epic, composing a *Bellum Pūnicum* (the first Punic war fought by Rome against Carthage over Sicily, 264–241 BC, in which Naevius himself had served). The very few fragments from it survive only because they were quoted by later authors, e.g. Servius [51]. They indicate that Naevius mentioned Anchises and his son Aeneas leaving Troy (we have references to Anchises seeing an omen, women fleeing, etc.); a storm at sea; and their arrival in Latium, where Romulus (Aeneas' grandson in this version) was born and Rome was founded. This seems to have been integrated somehow or other into the narrative of the Punic war. But how? Since in Book 1 the Roman consul Valerius is mentioned as going to Sicily, and there is also a reference to the temple of Zeus at Agrigentum where the capture of Troy was depicted, it may be (this is controversial) that the consul or one of his men was described seeing a depiction of Aeneas there and told his story.[32] If so, Virgil lifted the idea at 1.450–93, where Aeneas sees depictions of the Trojan war in Juno's temple in Carthage. However, we can be fairly sure that in Naevius Aeneas did not play any part in starting the eternal enmity between Rome and Carthage by having a disastrous affair with the local queen Dido, as in Virgil (though Naevius does mention Dido).[33] But the result was the first 'national' epic – celebrating a nation's historical achievements.

Naevius' use of Aeneas

18   An important move on Naevius' part was to focus on Aeneas. He was a great Trojan hero, destined (Homer tells us) to survive the war and rule Troy (*Iliad* 20.294–308). Naevius, however, picks up the tradition (reported in Greek historians in the fifth century BC) that Aeneas came to Italy and founded the Roman race. The great advantage of Aeneas was that he could

---

[32]   See Goldberg in Boyle (1993: 28–9).

[33]   See Horsfall 'Dido in the Light of History' in S.J. Harrison (1990: 139–44) for the argument that there was enough in Naevius to *prompt* Virgil's new conception of Dido.

bring with him a range of myths and gods, an authentic Homeric ancestry and a justification for a Roman attack on Greece (Troy, as it were, having its revenge, which happens in the second century BC: see on **1.278–88**). As Hainsworth puts it, 'he was the Roman passport to membership in the civilised world'.[34] Aeneas brought with him a slight problem, of course, because Greek Eratosthenes had dated the fall of Troy to 1184 BC, while Romulus and Remus founded Rome in 753 BC. But myth was ever flexible. As a result of later juggling of dates (of which Virgil took advantage), Aeneas was portrayed settling down and dying in Lavinium south of Rome, while his son Ascanius subsequently moved to Alba Longa; over 300 years later, his descendants Romulus and Remus actually founded Rome itself (see 1.265–74). The idea that Carthage and Rome were of equal age was, of course, a complete invention, but necessary for nationalistic purposes.

Naevius' use of Venus

19   Of equal importance was the role Naevius assigned to Venus, who at that time was coming to be recognised – how, we do not know – as the 'mother' of the Roman race. Macrobius (c. AD 430) reports that, early on in Naevius' epic, 'when the Trojans are in trouble because of the storm, Venus complains to Jupiter, and there follow words of Jupiter comforting his daughter with hope for the future'. Venus may well have begun with a line quoted by the historian Festus (c. AD 350) *summe deum rēgnātor, quianam mē genuistī?* 'Greatest ruler of the gods, why did you beget me?' (Cf. especially 1.223–96.) Venus was to loom large in Virgil's plans.

Ennius imitates Homer: a nation's destiny

20   Ennius (239–169 BC), from south Italy like Naevius, dramatically developed this nationalistic, epic genre with his eighteen-book epic *Annālēs* (note the technical title, used of priestly records). He did this by consciously adopting the metre – the hexameter – and much of the style of Homer (who at the beginning of the epic, he claims, appeared to him in a dream). To do this in Latin at this time was no mean feat. Ennius has Books 1–3 deal with the early kings of Rome (starting, of course, with Aeneas); 4–6 with the conquest of Italy and the defeat of the Greek chieftain Pyrrhus who had come to help the largely Greek-colonised southern Italian states; 7–9 with the Punic wars (at the end of which the hostile pro-Carthage Juno yields to Jupiter);

[34] (1991: 78).

10–12 with affairs in Greece and Roman victories in Spain; and 13–18 with further Roman adventures in Greece and the east, down to about 170 BC.

These were the years of Rome's seemingly unstoppable rise to dominance in the Mediterranean, and Ennius had the vision to see it and expound it as destiny, ordained at the gods' command (our fragments contain six scenes on Olympus where the destiny of Rome is discussed). He bestows heroic status on the historical participants, treating Roman soldiers as Homeric figures.[35] But the true hero at the heart of it all is the Roman people – *mōribus antīquīs rēs stat Rōmāna uirīsque*, as he put it ('the Roman state stood firm on its ancient traditions and its men'), a national epic indeed.

Ennius' use of the present tense

21   Importantly, as Hainsworth points out,[36] it was Ennius who also made a major contribution to epic style by consistently adopting the *present* tense for the narrative, giving it a new immediacy, an almost visual impact. Hainsworth offers the following (and very eloquent) example, with only the final verb in the past:

> *incēdunt arbusta per alta, secūribu(s) caedunt,*
> *percellunt magnās quercūs, excīditur īlex,*
> *fraxinu(s) frangitur atque abiēs cōnsternitur alta,*
> *pīnūs prōcērās peruortunt: omne sonābat*
> *arbustum fremitū siluāī frondīsāī.*
> Skutsch (1985: 175–9)

> They advance through deep forests, hew with axes,
> topple great oaks, the holm is sliced down,
> the ash is split apart and tall pine laid low,
> they overturn high firs: the whole forest
> was ringing with the crash of leafy trees.

All subsequent epic authors imitated him.

Post-Ennian epic: battles in verse

22   Here, then, was a 'Homeric' Roman epic, a national celebration of Rome's greatest historical achievements, and (even better) in a Latin adapted to Homeric metre. It was a bit rough-hewn, but had real dignity and grandeur.

---

[35] Dominik in Boyle (1993: 48–51).
[36] (1991: 82).

That was something to be proud of. But none of the attempted epics that followed Ennius for the next 150 years – a dreary sequence of versified battles – was to come anywhere near it. As the satirist Petronius (died AD 66) said of the genre, 'simply versifying events is beside the point. Historians do it better' (*Satyricon* 118). So where was Virgil to turn, faced not with great triumphs anyway but only the bloodstained history of Roman civil strife in the first century BC? He could hardly argue that the upheaval had all been worth it because it resulted in Augustus. And what if Augustus suddenly died – or was assassinated?

Virgil's epic brand: Romanised history, myth, morals and politics

23   How Virgil actually thought his way into the *Aeneid* is impossible to construct.[37] All we can do is look at the result and see what he has done. Broadly he has constructed an epic that works on five levels – historical (the founding of Rome), mythical (the divine involvement), allegorical (the trials of Rome's founding father Aeneas as a way of thinking politically about contemporary Rome), moral (the Roman virtues) and aetiological (explaining the reason – Greek *aition* – for many contemporary Roman institutions, customs, etc.).[38]

The most important decision Virgil took was to locate the epic in the deep 'Homeric' past, gods and all, and then to *historicise* that mix. The result is a sense of historical and divine inevitability and rightness about the founding of Rome, made specific in two important ways: first, in the visions of the largely glorious, Jupiter-backed, future, culminating in the present day, that are vouchsafed to readers throughout the course of the epic; and second, in the assertion that Aeneas' divine mother Venus had been ensuring throughout that Rome's destiny would not be thrown impossibly off-course. Since Rome's new leader Augustus (not to mention his adopting father Julius Caesar) was in direct descent, through Aeneas, Romulus and Remus, from *her*, Rome, it could be argued, had reached its divinely ordained, historic moment. Not that Rome's destiny ground to a halt with Augustus: its world-wide empire was guaranteed by Jupiter for all time to come (see 1.278–9). Augustus' reign was, then, both culmination and fresh starting-point after the horrors of civil war.

---

[37] Symmachus quotes a letter from Virgil to Augustus in which Virgil regrets taking on the epic: 'but so huge is the subject I have started out on that I seem to myself to have embarked on it almost in a moment of mental weakness' (Macrobius, *Saturnalia* 1.24.10–12).

[38] Cf. Johnson (1976: 19).

But as well as historicising the past, Virgil also *Romanised* it. Aeneas may be a Trojan, but his reflexes are increasingly Roman. He displays many of those virtues with which Romans liked to associate themselves (see [29]). He becomes responsible for the adoption or invention of various customs and institutions that continued down to Virgil's day (see e.g. **1.254–66, 1.289–96, 2.692–704**). At the same time, he is responsible (in Roman eyes) for the most dramatic revolution the world had ever seen – the foundation of the Roman state – and has to go through fire to achieve it. Here is another important sense in which Aeneas' story works for Virgil. As A.D. Nuttall says, 'all future history is *implicit*' in the *Aeneid*.[39] Past and present are indissolubly connected, the one forming a sort of allegorical template against which the other can be viewed. The many anachronisms to be found in the poem help to reflect this sense of the connection of, and continuity between, the historic and the contemporary.[40]

The advantages of Virgil's epic concept

24   There were many technical advantages to Virgil's scheme. First, given that his encomium of Rome and Augustus was to be at a very general 'culmination of history' level, the death of Augustus would not wreck the whole thing. The argument about the origins of and necessity for Rome's dominion would still stand, and Virgil had not said anything about Augustus that had not already been achieved (he does not e.g. look into *Augustus'* personal future). Second, while the use of Aeneas was not new – he had featured in both Naevius and Ennius ([16–22]), and Livy introduces his history of Rome with him (1.1–2) – he was not a widely exploited hero (Hainsworth points out that in all his voluminous writings Cicero, who was murdered in 43 BC, never mentioned Aeneas once). If that is so, Virgil had few expectations of the audience to meet and therefore pretty much *carte-blanche* to make of his hero whatever he wished. For example, the whole Dido episode that dominates the first third of the epic seems to have been Virgil's invention.[41] Third, because the story was set in the deep past, he could be selective about his praise of Augustus – who was intensely interested in Virgil's work[42] – and from that perspective provide a more oblique, and possibly more demanding, panegyric that it would be all the harder to

[39] Martindale (1984: 76).
[40] See Sandbach 'Anti-antiquarianism in the *Aeneid*' in Harrison (1990: 449–65).
[41] E.g. Livy, a contemporary of Virgil, makes no mention of her in his summary of Aeneas' travels, *Histories* 1–2. Presumably he dismissed Virgil's account as invention. (See [25], [30] below.)
[42] See [5–8] above.

live up to ([29]); likewise, he could gloss over the nasty truth about many aspects of Augustus' rise to power after the Ides of March, e.g. the illegality of his career, his march on Rome, proscription of innocent citizens and so on.[43] Finally, because Virgil chose to bring the whole panoply of his poetic arts to bear upon the imaginative reconstruction of what was to combine both a historical *and a mythical* past, shaped to his own requirements, gods and all, he opened the way to becoming for Rome what Homer had been for the Greeks. No wonder Romans were agog at the prospect – that a *Roman* could ever become a Homer, the most revered poet of the ancient world! No wonder Virgil's contemporary Propertius reacted as he did ([6] above, but with footnote). The consequence was that Virgil became *the* poet, known to everyone from schoolboys up and endlessly quoted, from the walls of Pompeii (sixty-seven quotations in all) to Britain. *arma uirumque canō* (*Aeneid* 1.1) and *conticuēre omnēs* (*Aeneid* 2.1) both occur thirteen times in Pompeii; *Aeneid* 1.1 occurs twice in the Vindolanda tablets, probably part of a writing exercise.[44] So much for the big picture. A closer look at Books 1 and 2 will reveal more of the detail.

Book 1: Rome, Troy and Carthage

25   Ennius indicated his debt to Homer by claiming that Homer had appeared to him in a dream ([20] above). Virgil goes one better, by unambiguously shaping the introduction to his *Aeneid* ('proemium' is the technical term) on the openings of the *Iliad* and *Odyssey*,[45] and then plunging straight into the story (1.12 'There was an ancient city . . .'), as Homer too had done. But there was, perhaps, something of a shock value to 1.12. The audience may well have expected the story to begin in a besieged Ilium (as Naevius and Ennius had done). In the event, the story begins in Carthage, picking up

---

[43] Griffin (2001: 57); Jones and Sidwell (1997), 74.

[44] In his *Dialogus*, Tacitus makes a playwright contrast the anxiety-ridden life of the orator with that of Virgil:

> I prefer the secluded life of Virgil, calm and untroubled, in which he still retained the favour of Augustus and the acclaim of the Roman people. We know this from the letters of Augustus, and the response of the people. For when they heard lines from Virgil quoted during a theatrical performance at which he himself happened to be present, they rose to their feet as one and acclaimed him in the same way as they would Augustus.

See Griffin (2001: 102–7) for a brief summary of Virgil's 2000-year-old influence on the classical tradition, taking the story down to T.S. Eliot and Mussolini; and on the larger scale, Williams and Pattie (1982) and Martindale (1984). Ziolkowski and Putnam (2008) is a vast source-book, all Latin translated, demonstrating in minute detail Virgil's influence from his own times to the fifteenth century.

[45] 1.1–11; see **1.1–7, 1.8–11**. See Jones (1999: 103–5).

and developing the theme of Juno's wrath signalled in the proemium at 1.4. Carthage was clearly going to be of central importance in this epic – and every Roman knew what Carthage meant: it meant the Punic wars. Again, whatever motive Naevius had for the subsequent storm that followed in his epic ([17] above), or wherever it took the Trojans, Virgil links it to the wrath of Juno and ensures the Trojans are thereby driven to land in Carthage. Romans might already be wondering – what about the siege? Are we not going to get the fall of Ilium? And some of them might be reflecting that in the *Iliad* Homer does not describe the fall of Ilium either (the *Iliad* ends before it happens). The fall was in fact told in other epics, notably the *Iliou persis* ('Sack of Ilium') by Arctinus (*Appendix* 1–2). Already Virgil is in new, uncharted and rather interesting waters.

The storm, Neptune and Venus

26 They become more interesting (and aquatic) yet when Virgil subjects Aeneas' men to a violent storm (81–123, as happened too in Naevius) but does not send Venus to save them. He brings Neptune on the scene to calm the storm, lever the ships off the sandbanks and thus enable Aeneas to land safely in Carthage (124–79). Why? The sea is, of course, Neptune's domain. That may be the answer. Even so, there is no reason Virgil should not have depicted Venus asking Neptune to intervene. Perhaps the reason is that, since Venus does not want Aeneas anywhere near Carthage, it would be awkward for her to 'save' them by landing them on what she knew to be hostile (because Juno-worshipping) soil. But in fact Virgil has other plans for the goddess. Instead of appealing to Neptune for help, she goes straight to the top and appeals to Jupiter (223–96).

Jupiter: Rome's national god

27 Naevius did this too: Jupiter consoled Venus, we are told ([19]), and offered her hope for the future. What form that hope took we do not know, but Naevius' elevation of Jupiter to personal protector of the *Roman* state above all others marked a dramatic shift away from the *persona* of Greek Zeus, who as a pan-Hellenic god was and remained above national interests.[46] Virgil takes full advantage of this in a scene of the very highest importance ([26]), since it sketches out the track of the *Aeneid*'s whole argument (and,

---

[46] Feeney (1991: 113–15). At *Iliad* 4.44–9, for example, Zeus claims that Ilium is his favourite city – which Romans must have liked – but is perfectly happy to plan its destruction.

incidentally, confirms its claim to be a true national epic): for the king of the gods assures Venus that it is fated for Aeneas to become a god, for Rome to be founded and control an empire without end, and for Augustus, descendant of Venus, to restore peace and prosperity to a shattered world. In other words, Virgil makes the target of divine goodwill *the present day* – but without having to 'heroise' hordes of contemporary Romans, as Ennius did ([20]).

Virgil and Augustus (i)

28   This raises an important, and much-debated, question: how far is the *Aeneid* an exercise in adulation of Augustus? Donatus ([3] above) and Servius ([10] above) did not seem to think it was except in a limited sense. They both say that one of the purposes was to praise Augustus' *lineage*. This Virgil certainly does, especially by making Venus a key player.[47] Further, Aeneas' outstanding characteristic is his *pietās*, which was a central feature of Augustus' self-image.[48]

But does Virgil go any further? In Books 1 and 2 it is hard to see how any Roman would immediately see Augustus, or the situation in contemporary Rome, reflected through the figure of Aeneas. If Augustus is (as he boasted) the re-founder of Rome after the horrors of the civil war,[49] there is no direct parallel with Aeneas, who did not found Rome at all (see [18] above) but merely laid the groundwork for it. Indeed, if Aeneas founded anywhere, it was Rome's great enemy Carthage, in the course of his liaison in Book 4 with Dido; and this, paradoxically, is one of the things Augustus actually *did* do, sending colonists there in 29 BC to rebuild the city after the Romans had destroyed it in 146 BC! (See on 1.20.)

Further, those passages that do look directly forward to the glories of Rome under Augustus take the form of digressions from the main theme (a discussion on Olympus in Book 1, a prophecy from Aeneas' father in Book 6 and a work of art in Book 8), usually occurring at moments when the future of Rome is in doubt. For example, at 1.283–96 Jupiter associates Augustus with the future greatness of Rome and refers to him closing the Gates of War (and so on), which Augustus actually did, but in the context of Venus' concern that Aeneas will never reach Rome in the first place. Nor, in fact, do these actions have any *direct* connection with the person of Aeneas,

[47] Zanker (1988: 192ff.).
[48] Zanker (1988: 96ff.).
[49] Zanker (1988: 167ff. especially 201–10).

except through lineage (Aeneas–Romulus–Augustus); and the prophecies themselves do not always sing from the same hymn-sheet.[50]

Finally, the *Aeneid* is not a monolithic epic driven from a single standpoint, but one in which different points of view are treated.[51] In the course of the epic, Virgil sees into and sympathises with a wide variety of characters, both pro- and anti- Aeneas and Rome. Dido is an outstanding example; and since Carthage was being *rebuilt* by Augustus in Virgil's time (and would in time become the third largest city in the Mediterranean after Rome and Alexandria), might Virgil have been trying to prompt a degree of sympathetic understanding about its past?

Many commentators have tended to see Virgil's broad sympathies as indicative of an underlying 'ambivalence' to his material. It is perfectly true that the *Aeneid* is far from outright panegyric, and Virgil does not hesitate to stress that the founding of Rome exerts a high price in death and destruction. Further, Virgil is never more moving than when describing the pointless loss that battle entails (e.g. the death of Priam in Book 2). But the idea that Virgil is thereby subtly 'subverting' the idea that Rome was A Good Thing is unlikely. Since good and evil are fundamentals of the human condition and co-exist quite normally in the real world, Virgil was merely being a realist. He certainly knew that every human endeavour, however noble in principle, took its toll. After everything that had happened in the previous hundred years to the republic, Romans did too. The *Aeneid* in this respect is simply being true to Roman experience.

Virgil and Augustus (ii)

29 Augustus took an intense interest in Virgil's work. This is not surprising, since (as we have seen) Augustus was keen to rebrand himself as the virtuous founder of the 'New Rome'. To this end, after the bloodshed of the civil wars in which he was an especially brutal operator, he developed a kinder, gentler image of himself – a man working to build *cōnsēnsus* among the Romans, on the model of the earlier republic's *Concordia* – as well as pouring vast sums of money into his rebuilding programme.

But if there are to be comparisons between Augustus and Aeneas, it seems to me that, apart from the three bursts of fervently patriotic prophecy, they work for the most part on a very general level. But one feature does stand out. Aeneas–Augustus looks both back and forward, to the past

[50] See Zetzel 'Rome and its Traditions' in Martindale (1997).
[51] As Conte (1986: 141–84) points out at excessive length.

and the future: Virgil presents Aeneas as 'old Roman' with the old Roman's ethical (republican) virtues – *uirtūs, disciplīna, fidēs, pietās* – but also as the impending *pater patriae*, the father (founder) of his new Roman fatherland, the title which became associated with the emperor and one-man rule. In this respect the *Aeneid* attempts to reach some sort of compromise over the major problem inherent in the political and social revolution taking place in contemporary Rome – i.e. that, in establishing the new (essentially monarchic) order, Augustus seemed to be destroying the old (republican) one. To the extent that the *Aeneid* emphasises the supremacy of the Julian *gēns*, it is a very pro-monarchic text; but in its harking back to the 'old values', it strongly promotes the republican ethos.

But whatever Virgil was trying to do, it certainly worked: its ecstatic reception (see [24]) demonstrates that. There was an immediate, contemporary, quasi-allegorical *resonance* to this new national epic, rich in ideas and images in a story round which the Romans felt they could unite, as if it held up a mirror to their world where they could seek their own face and, on the whole, like what they found.[52] Many modern scholars do not, but the Roman world and its values are not ours.

What is not clear, however, is how far any emperor would want to be saddled, so early in his reign, with e.g. a prophecy in Book 6.791–5 that promised the founding of a golden age.[53] Was that a challenge on Virgil's part, that Augustus live up to the prophecies of future Roman glory which he would find emanating from the mouths of men and gods in the *Aeneid*? As Griffin points out,[54] 'Augustus would be shown an image of heroic splendour, moral elevation, true patriotism. Judicious praise – praise of the virtues of a ruler – could be a form of pressure on him to exhibit those very virtues.'

Aeneas and Dido: old Troy, new Carthage

30   To return to the story. Satisfied by Jupiter that Rome's future is secure, Venus can arrange matters so that Aeneas will come to no harm – as indeed she does, meeting him disguised as a huntress, alerting him to Dido's situation, assuring him that his fleet has come to no harm, and making him and his companion Achates invisible to ease their way into Carthage (314–414).

---

[52]   So W.H. Auden was wrong: 'No, Virgil, no: / Not even the first of the Romans can learn / His Roman history in the future tense, / Not even to serve your political turn; / Hindsight as foresight makes no sense' ('Secondary Epic' in *Collected Shorter Poems, 1927–57* (London) 1926).

[53]   Unless *condō* here means not 'found' but 'bury', as Thomas (2001: 3–7) argues.

[54]   (2001: 57).

It is at once clear from Venus' description of Dido and from Aeneas' first sight of Carthage and of Dido that the two have much in common. Both are exiles, needing to find a new life elsewhere; but while Aeneas is still searching, Dido has found her home, and her city is rising from the ground, bearing under her guidance all the hallmarks both structurally and institutionally of a proper 'Roman' town (420–49). Further, both are connected by the Trojan war: for Aeneas sees and draws comfort from the scenes of the war which he finds depicted on the temple which Dido has had constructed in honour of Juno, goddess of the Carthaginians (450–93). Already, then, it is clear that Carthage is going to feature large in Virgil's account of Aeneas' travels and, at this moment at any rate, does not appear such a hostile place as Roman readers might have been expected to find it.

Aeneas and his men

31   The impression is reinforced by the arrival of some of the men Aeneas thought had been lost at sea. Still invisible, Aeneas watches Ilioneus appeal to Dido to be allowed peaceful access to land so that they can repair their ships and, if Aeneas is still alive, make their way to Italy, but if not, return to Sicily (where they last landed *en route* from Troy, 509–60). Ilioneus pays handsome, unforced tributes to Aeneas in the course of this speech. Dido's reply is warm and welcoming; indeed, she would like them to settle in Carthage if they wanted to, and prepares to send out search parties to look for Aeneas, about whom she knows and of whom she is clearly in some awe (561–78). At this the cloak of invisibility is removed from Aeneas and Achates, Aeneas modestly introduces himself, and compliments and thanks her (586–612). An amazed Dido can hardly believe it, welcomes Aeneas and his men as fellow-sufferers and exiles into the palace and prepares a feast (613–30).

Aeneas and Dido: immigrant co-founders of Carthage?

32   What Juno thinks of all this Virgil does not tell us, but the fact is that Dido too appreciates the common (mis)fortune that binds them. Clearly Aeneas is among friends, and while Dido prepares a banquet to celebrate their arrival (631–42), Aeneas sends Achates to the ships to bring him his son Ascanius and select for Dido appropriate guest-gifts saved from Troy (643–56). It looks as if their luck has turned at last. But Venus is not persuaded. She still fears Juno, and decides to ensure that Dido will not change her mind about the Trojan arrivals. She does so by sending her son Cupid,

disguised as Ascanius, to make the queen fall hopelessly in love with Aeneas (657–756). By this time Roman readers must have been thoroughly intrigued at what was going on. Had they thought that the *Aeneid* would be a straightforward series of triumphs for a great hero sweeping all before him, they must have realised that they were now in for something very different and much more stimulating. Nor can one imagine many of them at this stage thinking that Aeneas was a sort of *alter*-Augustus.

But this is not all that is going on here. Roman historians depicted Rome as a city of immigrants. When Romulus founded it 300 years after Aeneas' arrival in Italy, it was desperately short of bodies. So he not only opened it to Italian 'asylum-seekers' (anyone who wanted to swell the population of the burgeoning city) but also seized Sabine women to provide them with wives.[55] Virgil builds this into the *Aeneid*. Aeneas' Trojans were immigrants from Troy to Italy, who would in time[56] become fully integrated with local Latins. Further, the question of the integration of outsiders into Rome was a hot one in Virgil's time. The Romans had recently fought a nasty Social War against Italians over Italian rights to citizenship (see [12] above), but the wounds were still not healed. Will Aeneas and his men integrate with – Carthaginians, their oldest and bitterest enemy?! That seems quite likely after their arrival and warm reception in Carthage in Book 1, but Jupiter has already indicated that the Roman race will be a *toga*-wearing one (*Aeneid* 1.282). That is the last thing an Aeneas settled in Carthage would be.[57]

Book 2: Sources for the Trojan war

33 Virgil now replays the narrative device of Homer's *Odyssey* Books 9–12, when Odysseus, in the comfort of the banqueting hall of the Phaeacians where he has arrived on his journey home to Ithaca, is invited to tell the story of his journey from Troy. But the motivation for Aeneas' story is very different – for he is invited to tell it after the banquet by an increasingly love-sick Dido, hanging on his every word. She begs him to tell the whole story, but Aeneas ignores the reasons for, and ten years of, the Trojan war and starts with the fall of Ilium. This occupies Book 2; and in Book 3 Aeneas will tell of his and his men's circuitous travels around the Mediterranean taking in Thrace (northern Greece), Crete, Epirus (north-western Greece)

[55] Livy 1.8–9.
[56] As Virgil emphasises, *Aeneid* 12.830–40.
[57] See Dench (2005: 102–3, 276–7).

and Sicily as they search increasingly desperately for their new home. (In *Aeneid* 1 we are introduced to Aeneas and his men just after they have left Sicily, 1.34.)

As we have seen, Homer did not describe the fall of Ilium. But it was obviously a popular subject with later writers, and Virgil had a large number of versions on which to draw. In the *Appendix* (pp. 298–301) there is a selection of some of the versions that survive – the summary of Arctinus' *Sack of Ilium* (**1–2**), the summary of Lesches' *Little Iliad* (**3**), and relevant extracts from the *History* of Virgil's contemporary Dionysius (**4–8**), the later handbook of myths compiled by Apollodorus (**9–17**) and the historian Diodorus' account of Aeneas' *peaceful* departure from Troy (**18**). (We have the works of Arctinus and Lesches only in summaries made by later writers.)

Aeneas heroised

34   When the Roman historian Livy described the early history of Rome, he talked of Aeneas and another Trojan hero Antenor in what might seem rather odd terms: 'First of all there is general agreement that, when Troy was captured, revenge was taken on the rest of the Trojans but not on Aeneas and Antenor. The Greeks spared those two because of long-standing personal connections and because they had consistently advocated peace and the return of Helen' (1.1, cf. *Appendix* **18**) – Aeneas the practical man. Other sources were outright hostile, e.g. Menecrates, who claimed Aeneas actually betrayed the Trojans out of hatred of Paris (*Appendix* **8**). So Virgil had work to do if he was to present Aeneas in a favourable light – which he could hardly not do, since it was Aeneas himself who was telling the story.

The tragic dimension of the Aeneid

35   Book 2 contains some of the most powerful and emotionally charged writing in the whole of Latin literature – which is saying something. *sunt lacrimae rērum* indeed (see the famous line 1.462). It prepares the way for an increasing sense of the *tragic* dimension of the *Aeneid*, of which the gullibility of the Trojans in believing the treacherous Greek Sinon (2.195–8, 234–49) and the Priam episode (2.506–58) are powerful examples, as well as the general divorce between what humans know and what the omniscient narrator knows (generating pathos and irony). Such tragic notes will be sounded more and more frequently as the *Aeneid* progresses. Virgil, of

course, had access to many Greek and Latin tragedies depicting tragic situations, e.g. the fall of a city, and tragic figures, e.g. Cassandra, Andromache, Palamedes, and he calls upon them in *Aeneid* 2.[58] But as Plato knew (*Republic* 598d), Homer actually invented tragedy,[59] and Virgil draws on Homer too. There was nothing novel about the tragic in epic.

The structure of Book 2

36   Book 2 falls into three sections. In the first, Aeneas describes how the Trojans were deceived by the Greek Sinon into bringing the horse into the city (13–249). It is not at all clear how far Aeneas was an active party to this decision. He uses 'we' occasionally, but for the most part reports what 'they' (the Trojans) did or did not do. In the second part, Aeneas becomes more personally involved, describing his part in the battle and attempts to save Ilium, culminating in his helpless observation of the death of king Priam. That signals the end of the city (250–558). In the third part, he describes his flight with his father, son and others, but loss of his wife Creusa (559–804). But there is a major issue here: are we to understand Book 2 only as the words of a character in the plot, with his necessarily partial, fragmented and personally 'focalised' (see **Glossary of literary terms**) knowledge and understanding of what is going on, or as the words of the master-poet, who gives us the definitive picture of what really happened, through an Aeneas who is nothing but a poetic mouthpiece? To take one example, do any of the similes that Aeneas uses in Book 2, many rich with Homeric and other associations (e.g Ilium falling like a felled ancient ash-tree, 2.624–33), tell us about his human (or literary) sensitivities?

Aeneas' account: absolving a losing hero

37   Virgil's selection of episodes, the spin he puts on them and the picture of Aeneas that emerges throughout his first-person account make for a fascinating study. First, as the commentator Servius endlessly points out, it must not be thought that the Trojans were beaten by their own stupidity or any lack of valour. Aeneas therefore goes out of his way to stress the brilliant persuasiveness of Sinon's act of deceit, contrasting foul Greek treachery with wholesome Trojan trust in someone who claims to have been

---

[58] Cf. Hardie in Martindale (1997: 312–26) and Horsfall (2008: xviii–xxii), starting with a very useful two-page summary of *all* sources.

[59] Cf. Jones (2003: 222–4) on the tragedy of *Iliad* 16.

grotesquely treated by his own people (e.g. 195–8). The result is that the Trojans are beaten before the battle has ever begun. Second, Aeneas emphasises the role of the gods/fate in forwarding Greek designs (e.g. 54–6, 602–3). For example, the priest Laocoon, who understands that the wooden horse is a Greek trick, is killed with his children by serpents that emerge from the sea and then take refuge in Minerva's shrine in Ilium. Aeneas does not say the serpents were sent by her, but the implication is clear enough (199–233).

Aeneas: some questions

38   As for valour in battle, if the odds and gods are stacked heavily against the Trojans, there is still no doubt about the intensity of Aeneas' commitment as he launches himself again and again into the attack (e.g. 336–8). That said, Virgil never makes things simple, and we are occasionally invited to wonder whether Aeneas has got his tactics right (to be discussed below, [42–3]), e.g. should he have ignored the advice of the dead Trojan hero Hector who appeared to him in a dream before he joined the battle (268–95)? Should he not have taken more care of Creusa (710–11, 738–40)? And so on. However that may be, we are left in no doubt at all that, despite some traditions, Aeneas did not betray his people.

Aeneas

Not a modern hero

39   Our first description of Aeneas is as a man of *pietās* (1.10). The unhappy association of our 'piety' with a rather smug, complacent superiority makes it difficult for a reader to warm to Aeneas, but that is to misunderstand the importance of the word for a Roman, for whom it indicated someone out-standing in his sense of duty towards man, gods and family. In this context, it is worth stressing that the house, even the humblest, was a holy place for Romans, with its household gods (*Lārēs*, *Penātēs* and *Genius locī*, the spirit of the family's tribe – *gēns* – in the place), its rituals, and its hearth, thresh-old, door and lintel especially under divine protection, all generating strong emotional feelings. So it is with Aeneas' *pietās* that Venus confronts Jupiter, challenging him to justify treating such a man so badly (1.253). That said, it is clear that a man for whom familial, civic and religious duty overrides all other considerations is far removed from the sort of character one would

expect to meet in a TV drama or modern novel, where issues like happiness, relationships, lifestyle and 'being yourself' dominate the conversations, and characters tend to be constructed in terms of their 'right' to self-fulfilment and to behave in accordance with their own emotions and desires.

The ethical hero

40   Ancient authors do not generally share that view of life. They tend rather to use their characters to explore the demands made upon them by communal interests and how they do – or do not – meet them. Consequently, those agreed values expressed in ethical terms that make for social cohesion – such as mercy, justice, duty, moderation and so on – are usually at stake. *Pietās* is a good example: how does a man fulfil the demands that gods, family and others make upon him in the circumstances in which he finds himself, in Aeneas' case, as a citizen suddenly thrust into the position of a leader with a mission to found a new nation? It is, then, a consistent feature of ancient *character* that a man is uninterested in his 'rights', as a 'member of the human race', on 'this Planet Earth' or any other one. If you asked him whether he had a '*right* to happiness' (different from *wanting* to be happy), he would have thought you unhinged. In these circumstances, there would be little point in Virgil setting the scene in a backstreet taverna where Aeneas discusses with his companions whether he would have more success with girls if he changed his hairstyle.

The stoic Aeneas: a man of few words

41   Of the 333 speeches in the *Aeneid*, 135 receive no reply in words.[60] The conclusion is that Aeneas is 'aloof, repressed in speech, devoid of close friends', an isolated figure in private (cf. his meeting with Venus at 1.314–417), however effective his *public* utterances can be. That raises the stimulating question whether terms like 'repression' and the 'need for close friends' are relevant to ancient concepts of character.

It is certainly true that, compared with Homeric heroes, Aeneas is a man of relatively few words. Further, when he does have the stage to himself (as in Book 2), many scholars suggest that he seems to be giving more of an objective account, as if Virgil is reporting the story himself in the third person, and Aeneas is merely his mouthpiece (cf. [36]). The result is that,

---

[60] Feeney 'The Taciturnity of Aeneas' in S.J. Harrison (1990: 167–90); cf. Heinze (1914: 404/315).

for long stretches (it is argued), we do not get an intimate sense of a man talking and, in the process, revealing his inner thoughts. There is *some* truth in this. Frustrating as such single-mindedness may be to the modern mind – we long to see Aeneas 'lighten up' and reveal his sparkling personality by describing how he got drunk and stole a traffic-cone – it may be that Virgil intended it that way. The distinction between a man of words and a man of action is a classical one, and Aeneas veers towards the latter. He is a man on whom fate/the gods have imposed a task of massive communal responsibility – the resettlement of a people who will one day rule the world. To that extent his burden is far heavier than one ever borne by Odysseus or Achilles in Homer.[61] All Aeneas' energies are devoted towards his mission, at whatever personal price; and the tones in which he does speak, tinged with foreboding, are the mark of a man who is carrying a burden which he is not sure that he can sustain. He is primarily a doer and a leader, not a talker; and when he does talk, he is business-like and to the point (cf. [34]). His account of the fall of Ilium in Book 2 shares these qualities, which lend it an 'objective' air. But Aeneas the man still emerges through it (see [44]).

It may be that we sense an element of the Stoic in Aeneas. Stoicism was a philosophy, much favoured by many Romans, that made heavy demands on its adherents: all that counted was *uirtūs* and reason, and the emotions/passions were not to be trusted. The paradox is that Aeneas' particular *uirtūs*, *pietās*, seems to count for nothing in an eternally hostile world (cf. 1.2–5, 8–10, 33).[62]

Aeneas: no superman (i)

42   There is much to be said for using this as a starting-point – no more – for thinking about the *Aeneid*'s hero. The reason is that, once it is understood that Aeneas is not constructed like twenty-first-century man, the reader becomes more sensitive to how he *is* constructed. To draw the broader picture, what emerges in Book 1 is a man under severe pressure (e.g. 1.195–209, 1.595–9), doing all he can to further his mission, and with a particular care for his son Ascanius (646) who will continue it (267–71). He is deeply envious of Dido (with whom he has much in common) since she has already settled in Carthage (as was fated) and is building her own city

---

[61]   See Nuttall in Martindale (1984: 78–9), 'In the whole of the *Iliad* no military leader ever pauses to consider the responsibility he carries *prospectively*, as a burden of office'. Hector at *Iliad* 6.492–3 gets close to the idea.

[62]   On this see Bowra, 'Aeneas and the Stoic Ideal' in S.J. Harrison (1990: 363–77) and Lyne, 'Vergil and the Politics of War' in S.J. Harrison (1990: 316–38).

(1.437); and he feels let down by his divine mother Venus (1.405–9) – reasonably, given all his sufferings and failed attempts to locate his final destination. If she will not play fair by him, who will? At the same time, he is aware that suffering is endemic, but men's sufferings touch the hearts of others (the famous line 1.462). Consequently, as he says, he can feel a degree of hope when he sees the Trojan war depicted in Juno's temple (1.450–2): the Carthaginians are, like him, men who know what suffering means. Ilioneus' handsome tribute to Aeneas makes it clear what he means to his men (1.544–58), and Dido is fascinated by him before she has ever seen him (1.565–6, 575–8). His tactful reply to her illustrates a mastery of diplomacy (1.595–610). He is clearly a leader of men.

Aeneas: no superman (ii)

43   In Book 2, the same eloquent sense of despair and tragic waste hangs over him (e.g. 2.3–13, 195–8, 234–9, 361–9, 554–8) – the powerful emotions that surface as he tells the story do not suggest a cold, distant automaton – but he still emerges as a warrior leader too.[63] The disaster of the sack of Troy is not his fault; he rallies his men constantly (e.g. 2.353–4); he acts with high courage throughout (e.g. 2.359–60); and he earns the right to lead the Trojans into exile (e.g. Hector's speech 2.289–97; cf. 2.797 and note). That said, it has been argued that no Stoic hero (if such he is) should yield to *furor* or *īra* (cf. [40]), a key word in the *Aeneid* (and used of Aeneas right at its end, 12.946); while Aeneas' refusal to follow Hector's advice and determination to plunge at once into battle (2.314–17: note *furor* 316 and cf. 2.594–5) have raised questions about his control of his emotions and ability to exert reason over them (*āmēns, sat ratiōnis* 314); compare the Trojans at 2.244, Dido at 1.659, Cassandra at 2.345, Neoptolemus at 2.499, Aeneas again at 2.745 (cf. 2.776) and the note on the text at 2.771.

Against that, however, it must be stressed that it is Aeneas *himself* who is admitting to all this. It is not, in other words, an objective judgement in the mouth of the master-narrator Virgil, but Aeneas' personal feelings about his actions, many years after the event; and, while he does not flinch from the admission, what would *you* do when the city and people you love, and for which you feel responsible, are being destroyed before your very eyes?

Further, Virgil is an epic poet, and passion is at the heart of the epic hero's motivations (the *Iliad* begins with the poet announcing the theme: Achilles' *rage*, the first word of western literature). Stoic philosophers may

---

[63]   See Nisbet '*Aeneas Imperator*' in Harrison (1990: 378–89).

have disapproved, but Virgil is not composing a treatise on Stoic philosophy (at *Aeneid* 10.714 he talks of *iūsta īra*). When, for example, Priam yields to *īra* at the sight of the merciless slaughter of his son (2.534), only the most purblind Stoic could disapprove. Virgil does not see life in the black-and-white terms that Stoicism demands. He understands too much about, and sympathises too deeply with, humanity's contradictions. That said, an unalterable disposition towards anger was in no one's interests (cf. [28] above). Aeneas certainly does not exhibit that (see on **2.735–51**). Arguably, in the *Aeneid* that is a trait characteristic only of gods, especially Juno.[64]

The hero who obeys

44   Likewise, questions have been asked about Aeneas' failure to protect Creusa, where further loss of control seems to be in evidence (*āmēns* 745, *īnsānō dolōrī* 776). The problem is considered in the discussions covering the passages from 2.705–804, but I feel this is all of a piece with a hero who, when instant action had to be taken, takes full responsibility for it, does all he can to retrieve the situation and is man enough to admit to failure. When Creusa is lost, he movingly describes the grief that overwhelms him, so severe that, despite the divine sign that he has just received, he is prepared to risk all to find her.

It has been well said that 'the sort of moral qualities that Aeneas is called upon to display are not the best material for the dramatic characteriser; subordination does not translate itself into theatre so well as vast, egoistic passions do'.[65] Aeneas is a man who must learn to *submit* to the will of the gods, a response wholly at odds with much of today's 'culture' which insists that following the devices and desires of one's own heart represents the very zenith of human achievement. But it is precisely here that the man of *pietās* becomes so extraordinarily interesting, especially when he has to balance its demands (community – family – gods) against each, e.g. fighting to save Ilium now or protecting his family (594–8, cf. his search for Creusa 749–51); weighing the prospect of a future Troy against the present Troy (664–70).

In all of this, it is worth pointing out that Aeneas was, as a matter of fact, a son of the goddess of sex and therefore a brother of Cupid (1.667). For

---

[64]   See Wright '*Ferox uirtus*: anger in Virgil's *Aeneid*' in Braund and Gill (1997). Wright points out that, in a military context, 'anger' can be a healthy biological survival mechanism, as Aristotle recognised. For divine disposition to anger, especially in Juno, see in particular Wright 174–5.

[65]   Lyne (1987: 149).

obvious reasons, Virgil was not over-keen to associate his hero too closely with that side of his immediate family's particular interests (see on **1.402–9**).

Gods and fate

Gods: what the poet makes of them

45 Cicero said that, if anyone asked him what god is or what he is like, he would take the Greek poet Simonides as his authority. Simonides was asked by Hiero, tyrant of Syracuse, the same question, and requested a day to think about it. Next day Hiero demanded the answer, and Simonides begged for two more days. Still no answer. Continuing to double up the days, Simonides was eventually asked by Hiero what the matter was. He replied, 'The longer I think about the question, the more obscure the answer seems to be.'[66]

It is a frequent assumption that any ancient writer who has things to say about 'The Gods' has all the answers to deep and important mysteries. Not true. For any epic writer, the gods are (on one level, at least) part of the furniture, to be handled as he sees fit. So his picture of the gods, like that of fate, will be whatever he wants it to be (he cannot, of course, break free from his own cultural assumptions), and most of all the picture will be a literary creation, serving the literary purposes of his work. Nor will his views subject him to censure, since Romans did not have divinely inspired scriptures, policed by religious authorities, telling him what to believe or write on the subject, or else. The only constraint on the poet, then, is that his picture of divine activity had to make sense to his readers. This, incidentally, is the view that Aristotle took of fiction: 'a convincing impossibility is preferable to something unconvincing, however possible'.[67] It is the poet who makes it convincing.

'Dignifying Rome's foundation'

46 In this respect, Virgil had it easy, since he made the decision to locate the story in the deep past, allowing him to combine history (Aeneas' founding of the Roman people was history for Romans) with myth. That meant he had the example and divine framework of Homer at his disposal; and

[66] *On the Nature of the Gods* 1.60.
[67] *Poetics* 61b 9; cf. Feeney (1991: 29).

Homer, as we have seen, was universally admired. The gods *belonged* in epic.[68] So it was a matter of redeploying that framework convincingly in its new, Roman context. Nor was there any particular problem about that approach. The Roman historian Livy, for one, thoroughly approved:

> One can forgive the ancients for drawing no hard line between the human and the supernatural. They did so to dignify their cities' foundations. Further, if any nation should be allowed to sanctify their origins and put them down to divine intervention, the military glory won by Romans is such that every nation on earth might as well accept Rome's claim that Mars was indeed their first father, and father of their founder Romulus, as they accept Rome's dominion. (*Histories*, Preface 7)

Gods human and divine

47   We can therefore jettison any idea that the gods in Virgil are not somehow 'real', or that they stand for something other than themselves. They are as real as only fiction can permit them to be. And a great relief that is too; for the performance of this 'plurality of partial and capricious gods'[69] on the page of the *Aeneid* is as vivid and believable as that of any god in Homer. The key to understanding them is that, as in Homer, they are anthropomorphic (Greek *anthrōpos* 'human', *morphē* 'shape') i.e. behaving like humans. So when Virgil says Juno is angry, she is angry all right (1.36–50), and demonstrates it at once by bribing and flattering Aeolus – characterised as a keen-to-please and easily bribable minor divinity (1.64–80) – into unleashing thoroughly Homeric storm winds with thoroughly Homeric results (1.81–123). It requires an equally angry Neptune to come down and sort it all out, before majestically racing off back home again (1.124–56). Likewise Jupiter, who is very worried about events on earth when we first see him, laughs up his sleeve at the sulking Venus and gives her a paternal kiss before assuring her that everything will be just fine (1.254–96). At the same time, as in Homer too, these gods can be bizarre and implausible; and they can, at the other end of the spectrum, become distant, awesome, mysterious powers, going incomprehensibly about their dreadful work. Aeneas is granted privileged sight of this – and horrific it is too – at 2.604–23, especially that last, terrifying, unfinished line *nūmina magna deum . . .*

---

[68] Feeney (1991: 42).
[69] Lyne (1987: 65).

The gods' commitment to Rome

48   The gods in Virgil, in other words, have their parts to play in the drama of
the *Aeneid*, and they play them to the full: a drama which results in Rome.
Gods too, Virgil suggests, were part of that historical process. The point
here is that Virgil is not using sacred texts or personal spiritual insights in
an attempt to penetrate the mysteries of divine activity in the world and
reach 'the ultimate truth'. For example, no god or power, even Jupiter, represents a fixed, authoritative point from which the action can be viewed and
judged. Jupiter is father of Venus, god of Rome, husband of Juno etc., and
responds to each accordingly: their different viewpoints are in constant
competition.[70] This is because all the gods are wrapped up in the events as
interested individuals with their own priorities and biases (just like
Homeric gods). So at 1.39 Juno claims it is 'fate' that prevents her diverting
the Trojans away from Italy; at 2.602–3 Venus argues that it is the gods that
have destroyed Ilium. Both blame other powers for their own failures.
Meanwhile Jupiter at 2.617–18 helps personally with the ruthless destruction of Troy; but a few lines later (689–704) he is helping the Trojans on
their way to found a new city.

Making the incredible credible: the poet's art

49   All this is Virgil's choice. The whole action, in other words, human and
divine, is the will of the poet, and the ultimate aim of the epic was to persuade its readers that, ultimately, and for all the suffering entailed (not to
mention demonstrations of divine anger), the picture of a Rome founded at
the command of destiny was accurate. To persuade us of that, he can do
what he likes with gods, fate, history and myth. The only question is: does
the result persuade? Does it work? Or does it just seem silly? In a world
where it was taken for granted that the whole apparatus of the epic world –
from gods to heroes – made sense, it all depended on the poet's skill *as poet*.
It seems transparent to me that, in the context of this Romano-Homeric
epic, the poet's skill sees him through.[71] That does not mean that the
Romans believed in the objective existence of gods as they were depicted in
Virgil (let alone that they were required to), any more than we believe in the
characters in a James Bond story. We believe in them in so far as they make
sense in the context of the story.

---

[70] Feeney (1991: 155).
[71] Contrast Coleman 'The Gods in the *Aeneid*' in McAuslan and Walcot (1990: 58–60).

Fate as historical process

50   If, however, one needs distance and mystery in one's sense of the supernatural, 'fate' provides it. The key to its success as an artistic device is that, as in Homer, it is not given human form. It cannot therefore be given emotions or feelings. It cannot be angry or feel pity; it does not have children or favourites to worry about. It is simply *there*, an indefinable force or power, another arrow in the poet's quiver, which Virgil deploys as he sees fit to give the reader the *objective* sense that, in the *long* term, everything has already turned out, or will turn out, as it should – in the case of the *Aeneid*, in the foundation and triumph of Rome. *Fātum*, in other words, wins out over 'historical process'; it *becomes* historical process, assuring the reader that the line leading from Venus will reach its fulfilment in Augustus and that from Aeneas in the Roman people.

It is fate's inherent objectivity that makes it such a useful card to play. The result for the poet is that, the more men and gods get themselves into the most terrible tangles, the more the 'fate' card can be produced to assure the reader (and sometimes the characters) that everything will ultimately be all right. This card therefore *allows* the poet to create those tangles – tangles involving gods as much as men – and so to demonstrate on the page that humans (and gods too) are not simply puppets but engaged in a tremendous struggle to reach the goal in the foundation of Rome (1.33). Admittedly, there does seem to be some sense of alignment between fate and the will of Jupiter, but Virgil does not make explicit the precise power relationship of the two.[72] For 'fate' is objective and inevitable; but anthropomorphised gods, even Jupiter, get thrown into the mix of life, in heaven as on earth, as much as humans do. If therefore even the gods do not always seem to get things right, if even they do not quite seem to understand what is going on, or even if they kick against fate (cf. Juno at 1.18–23), one cannot be surprised. It is no coincidence that Stoic philosophy imagined fate as an ox-drawn cart pulling a dog on a long lead. There is no doubt that the cart will go from A to B, and the dog with it – ultimately. But on its long lead, the dog has a degree of flexibility about its actual route, though not its final destination. 'Fate' is Virgil's get-out card, for men and gods.

In fine, Virgil's achievement was to invest the myth/history of Aeneas with such significance that it became the definitive explanation of why things were as they were in the time of Augustus.[73]

---

[72] See Coleman 'The Gods in the *Aeneid*' in 'McAuslan and Walcot (1990: 53ff.).
[73] Feeney (1991: 185).

Servius

51   Servius, who taught in Rome c. AD 400, composed *in tria Virgiliī Opera Expositiō* a commentary on Virgil's *Eclogues*, *Georgics* and *Aeneid*. It comes to us in two different manuscript traditions. There is Servius' version, designed for school use, watered down from a much larger scholarly commentary by the critic Donatus. This 'school' version has two out of every three notes consisting of grammatical comment and only one in seven on broader historical and literary topics.[74] Then there is the second, enlarged Servius version (*Servius auctus* or *DServius*, because the manuscript was first published by the French scholar Danielis in the sixteenth century). This was written about the same time and preserves the original Servius but with additional comments by Donatus brought back into it. This enlarged Servius discusses grammar and syntax, the meaning of words, difficult word-order, etymology (nearly all sheer fantasy, e.g. *Parcae* 1.22, though not, of course, to the Romans), proper names, references to mythology, reflections on other poets' works, ancient customs and traditions, history, religion, etc. Beginners with Virgil should be heartened by this. Even in Servius' time, schoolboys did not know the meaning of some Latin words and needed help with constructions, parsing, word-order and so on. The whole commentary makes for a wonderful *pot-pourri* of views and information, much like today's commentaries. Indeed, commentaries on Virgil ever since have unwittingly drawn much of their comment from him.

I have quoted liberally from it, not distinguishing Servius from non-Servius. It is of great interest to compare what we think with what intelligent people made of Virgil at a time when their cultural world had not changed all that dramatically from what it was in Virgil's day, and raises teasing questions, e.g. did Virgil compose his text with the actual etymological word-plays in mind that Servius comes up with? After all, Romans loved word-play, and presumably Virgil regarded Roman etymological principles as scientifically grounded, as Servius did. Again, Servius seems excessively committed to the notion that Aeneas as a hero must, by definition, be noble, bold and true (and *pius*), in control of his emotions all the time (see on 1.196). As you read the *Aeneid*, you may wonder whether this is actually true of Virgil's picture.

---

[74]   Kaster (1988: 170).

Glossary of literary terms

Alliteration: any repetition of the same sound or syllable in two words or more which produces a notable effect, e.g. the *i*, *m* and *c* of *illī indignantēs magnō cum murmure montis / circum claustra fremunt*, 'they [the winds] protesting with loud roar rage round the bolted gates of the mountain' (1.54–5).

Anaphora: a figure of speech in which a sequence of phrases or clauses begins with the same word(s), e.g. the *tū* in *tū mihi, quodcumque hoc rēgnī, tū scēptra Iouemque/conciliās, tū dās epulīs accumbere dīuum*, 'You grant me this little kingdom, you the sceptre and Jupiter's favour, you the right to dine with the gods' (1.78–9). It is often, as in this example, in the form of a **tricolon** and accompanied by **asyndeton**.

Aposiopesis: when a speaker breaks off in mid-sentence, e.g. *quōs ego – sed mōtōs praestat compōnere flūctūs*, 'As for you [lit. 'whom'], I'll –! But first I had better calm the stormy seas' (1.135).

Apostrophe: a figure of speech in which a third person narrative reverts to the second person, e.g. 'A did this, and B did this and *you, C, said*', e.g. *Troiaque nunc stārēt, Priamīque arx alta manērēs*, '[If fate had not been against us,] Troy would now be standing and you, high citadel of Priam, would remain' (2.56).

Assonance: repeated vowels/syllables, e.g. the *a/ad/ent* sounds in *suādentque cadentia sīdera somnōs*, 'the setting stars entice [us to] sleep' (2.9, here combined with alliteration of *s*).

Asyndeton: the absence of a linking word (e.g. 'and') in a series of parallel utterances (see the example in **anaphora** above).

Captātiō beneuolentiae: lit. 'the striving for the goodwill (of the listeners)', i.e. the ingratiating sentiments with which speeches often begin. See e.g. 1.520ff.

Chiasmus: two corresponding pairs of words or phrases placed 'criss-cross', i.e. in the order ABBA, or ABC[C]BA, etc., e.g. (A) *spem* (B) *uultū* (C) *simulat*, (C) *premit altum corde* (B) *dolōrem* (A), lit. 'hope in the face he pretends, he suppresses in the heart deep grief' (1.209).

Dramatic irony: a plot device in which a character does not understand the true significance of his beliefs or behaviour, e.g. Aeneas' constant sense that the gods/fate are against him; or the Trojans' excitement at welcoming the Trojan horse into the city, thinking their troubles are over (2.234–49).

Ecphrasis: often used, in the modern sense, of the literary description of a work of art, but ancients seem to have thought of it as the technique of extended, lively and detailed literary description of an object or place, real or imaginary, e.g. Aeneas' landing-place (1.158–69).

Ellipsis/ellipse: the unexpected omission of a word, frequently part of the verb 'to be' e.g. *dux fēmina factī*, 'the leader of the action [was] a woman' (1.364).

Focalisation: or 'viewpoint', 'interpretation'; through whose eyes a narrator – Virgil or one of his characters – may suggest that an action be viewed, e.g. 1.470 – how could a picture tell you that Rhesus has *just* fallen asleep? This comment is Aeneas' interpretation. This raises a major question about the whole of Book 2: how far is Aeneas to be seen as simply the poet's 'definitive' mouthpiece, or a fallible human giving his own fallible account of what happened?

Genre: very basically, a term used to help to classify or categorise the content of any composition, especially literary and musical. 'Epic', 'tragic', 'comic' etc. are all different genres (Latin *genus* 'class, variety, kind, type').

Golden line: line of poetry in which two nouns, each with an adjective in agreement, and a verb are placed in the order A B (verb) A B or A B (verb) BA, e.g. (A) *aspera tum* (B) *positīs* (C) *mītēscent* (A) *saecula* (B) *bellīs*, 'Then the harsh ages soften, war being laid aside' (1.291).

Hendiadys: a figure of speech in which a single idea is expessed by two nouns or a noun + adjective, *mōlemque et montīs*, 'mass and mountains' = 'massive mountains' (1.61). It comes from the Greek *hen-dia-dis* 'one-through-two'. That said, one cannot always be certain that Virgil was not thinking of two separate features.

Hiatus: 'Hiatus' ('yawning gap') is the term applied when elision is not observed. An example is at 1.405, where the final *a* of *dea* in *dea ille* is not elided and is thus 'in hiatus'.

Hypallage (also called **transferred epithet**): a figure of speech in which an adjective applied to one word applies more logically to another, e.g. 'The ploughman homeward plods his <u>weary</u> way' (it is the ploughman who is weary). Cf. *fortia corpora* (1.101). Should the corpses of the dead be 'strong', or should the adjective really apply to the men?

Metonymy: a figure of speech in which one word is substituted for another closely related to it. Thus Vulcan, god of fire, often means 'fire' (2.311); Ceres, goddess of grain, can mean 'grain' or 'bread' (1.177).

Oxymoron: an apparently contradictory use of words, producing a paradoxical fusion (e.g. '*Wisest fool* in Christendom'; *dōnum exitiāle*, 'a *deadly present*' (2.31).

Pathetic fallacy: the act of crediting nature with human feelings, e.g. Virgil's description of 'silent' waters, 'living' rock and 'tired' ships at 1.164–8.

Proemium: or proem. The introductory survey of the main theme of and background to an epic, before the story actually starts, e.g. 1.1–32.

Proleptic: applying to some future happening, e.g. describing Dido as *miserae* at 1.719. She is not *misera* yet; but she will be.

Syncope: an abbreviation, e.g. *tenuēre = tenuērunt* (3rd pl. perf. act.).

Synecdoche: a figure of speech in which the part expresses the whole, e.g. *carīna* means 'keel' but at 2.23 stands for 'ship' (Greek *sun-ek-dochē* 'together-out-picking', i.e. selecting one feature to stand for the whole feature).

Transferred epithet: see **hypallage**.

Tricolon: a unit of words, phrases or clauses repeated three times; often 'rising' (each element getting longer), sometimes 'decreasing', and regularly used with asyndeton (e.g. 'Friends, Romans, countrymen') and anaphora. See the example under **anaphora** above.

Notes for the reader

In general, the text has been over-punctuated in an attempt to clarify word-groups.

Macra (s. macron; i.e. syllables pronounced long) are marked throughout, e.g. *ā*, *ē*, etc. *hūīc* and *cūī* are treated as one syllable, *hūīus* and *cūīus* as two syllables.

Please note:

(a) Words to be taken together for translation purposes (almost always because they agree) are linked A^ . . . ^B.
(b) When more than two words are so linked, the sequence continues A^ . . . ^B . . . ^C . . . ^D, etc.
(c) When other words agree inside the ^ . . . ^ pattern, or in circumstances where different sorts of interlocked word-order occur, A* . . . *B is used. Thus:

arma uirumque^ canō, Troiae ^quī prīmus ab ōrīs
Ītaliam fātō ^profugus Lāuīniaque uēnit*
*lītora, multum ^ill̲e̲ et terrīs ^iactātus et altō,
uī superum saeuae^ memorem* ^Iūnōnis ob *īram

i.e. (1) *uirum* is picked up by *quī* which agrees with (2) *profugus*, (3) *ille* and *iactātus*; (2) *Lāuīniaque* agrees with (3) *lītora*; (4) *saeuae* agrees with *Iūnōnis*; and *memorem* agrees with *īram*. The sequence A^ . . . ^B . . . C^ . . . ^D would mean that A agrees with B, and C agrees with D. Note that these linking-marks are gradually phased out.

An underlined vowel or -*m* ending is to be disregarded for the purpose of scansion:

lītora, multum̲ ^ill̲e̲ et terrīs ^iactātus et altō

The -*um* of *multum* and the *e* of *ille* are to be disregarded. This underlining too will be phased out.

Help with the text

A line-by-line commentary accompanies each passage, consisting of vocabulary, grammar and notes (*VGN*). It cross-refers users to the Grammars of three commonly used Latin books:

RL = Peter Jones and Keith Sidwell, *Reading Latin: Grammar, Vocabulary and Exercises* (Cambridge University Press 1986). A plain number, e.g. **RL**88, refers to sections of the Running Grammar (marked at the top of every page); letter + number, e.g. **RL**A4, refers to the Reference Grammar at the back.

W = F. M. Wheelock, *Wheelock's Latin* (sixth edition, rev. R. A. LaFleur, New York 2000). The number, e.g. **W**38, refers to the grammatical chapters; Suppl. syntax = Supplementary syntax in the *Appendix.*

M = James Morwood, *Latin Grammar* (Oxford 1999). References are to page numbers.

It is assumed that students will know the meaning of those words which **RL** and **W** *between them* share as set to be learned (so if any word appears for learning in **RL** but not in **W**, and *vice-versa*, it will not be assumed that it has been learned). All those shared words are in the *Total learning vocabulary* at the back of this book (pp. 302–15) and are not glossed in the running *VGN* that accompanies each passage. All other words are glossed in the running *VGN*.

In Book 1.1–656 and Book 2.1–633, words marked with an * in the running *VGN* must be learned because they will not appear in the *VGN* again. These words are listed after each passage's *VGN* in alphabetical order under the heading **Learning vocabulary** (e.g. p. 61). At the end of each larger *Section*, all the words listed under **Learning vocabulary** for that *Section* are repeated as **Learning vocabulary for Section** (e.g. p. 68). All these words have also been added to the *Total learning vocabulary* (pp. 302–15).

The line-by-line *VGN* for both books does *not* assume that you have read the other Book. So if you read only *Aeneid* 2, you will receive exactly the same level of help with vocabulary and grammar as if you had begun with *Aeneid* 1. If you read both Books, you will therefore find a degree of repetition of help in the second book you read.

At the end of each line-by-line *VGN* and **Learning vocabulary**, there is an embellished paraphrase/discussion of the passage just read. That paraphrase/ discussion is marked and cross-referred to throughout in **bold**, e.g. **1.1–7**.

At the very end of every *Section*, again headlined and numbered in bold, is a Study section (e.g. **Study section for 1.1–33**), containing suggestions for further study.

Grammar

Here a few of the regular features of Virgilian poetry that distinguish it (for the most part) from prose are listed and described:

(a) Genitive plurals of 2nd declension in *-um* not *-ōrum* e.g. 1.4 *super(ōr)um* 'of the gods', 2.14 *Dana(ōr)um* 'of the Greeks'; and some third declension nom. and acc. plurals in *-īs*, not *ēs*, e.g. 1.93 *duplicīs*, not *duplicēs*

(b) Abbreviated perfect forms, especially:
    (i) *-ērunt* replaced by *-ēre*, e.g. 1.12 *tenuēre = tenuērunt* 'they held'; 2.1. *conticuēre = conticuērunt* 'they fell silent'
    (ii) suppression of *-ui-, -ue-* e.g. *seruāuissent* becomes *seruāssent*

(c) Verb-forms (especially perfect participles) which would normally be translated as passive translated as 'middle', in two senses:
    (i) Reflexively/intransitively 'doing X to oneself', e.g. 1.155 *inuectus* not 'being driven' but 'driving himself', 'driving'
    (ii) with a direct object, as if active, e.g. 1.228 *oculōs . . . nitentīs suffūsa* not 'filled as to her shining eyes' but 'filling her shining eyes'. Venus is doing this intentionally

(d) Acc. of respect, e.g. 1.320 *nūda genū* 'naked in respect of her knee', 'with naked knee'; 2.57 *manūs iuuenem . . . reuīnctum* 'a young man bound in respect of his hands', 'with hands bound' – the young man has had the action done to him

(e) Ellipsis (i.e. omission) of the verb 'to be', e.g. 1.364 *dux fēmina factī* 'the leader of the action [was] a woman'; 2.2. *ōrsus [est]* 'he began'; 1.22 *uenturum [esse]* '[that] it would come'

(f) Ellipsis of prepositions, e.g.
    (i) *in/ab/ex* + abl. becomes plain abl., e.g. 1.3 *terrīs* ' by/on land'; 2.33 *arce* 'in the citadel' (both the 'local' abl.); 1.375 *Troiā antīquā* 'from ancient Troy'; 2.8 *caelō* 'from the sky'
    (ii) *in/ad* + acc. becomes plain acc., e.g. 1.2 *Ītaliam* 'to Italy'
    (iii) 'to' of motion sometimes expressed by the dat. e.g. 1.6 *Latiō* 'to Latium', 2.36 *pelagō* 'into the sea'

(g) Note also the very wide range of uses of the plain abl., all common in prose too:
    (i) abl. of cause, e.g. 1.2 *fātō* 'because of fate', 2.13 *bellō fātīsque* 'because of the war and the fates'

    (ii) abl. of manner, e.g. 1.73 *cōnūbiō stabilī* 'in a stable marriage', 2.208 *uolūmine* 'in a coil/spiral'

   (iii) abl. of instrument/means, e.g. 1.4. *uī* 'by means of violence', 2.15 *dīuīnā arte* 'by means of the divine skill'

   (iv) abl. of description, e.g. 1.71 *praestantī corpore* 'with a lovely body'

    (v) abl. of respect, e.g. 1.10 *īnsignem <u>pietāte</u>* 'distinguished in respect of/for his piety', 2.21 *nōta <u>fāmā</u>* 'known in respect of/for its fame'

   (vi) abl. of association, e.g. 1.75 *pulchrā prōle* 'in association with fine offspring'

  (vii) abl. of origin, e.g. 1.582 *nāte <u>deā</u>* 'born from/son of a goddess'

(h) Plural nouns where prose would write singular, and *vice-versa*, e.g. 1.11 *īrae* 'anger'

(i) Figures of speech: see **Glossary of literary terms**.

Metre and verse in the *Aeneid*

Heavy and light syllables

(a) In Latin prose and verse, **vowels** – a, e, i, o, u – always retain their natural sound, long or short. Short *a* is always pronounced as in 'h<u>a</u>t', long *ā* as in 'r<u>a</u>ther'. In *amat* the two *a*s are short and will always be pronounced short, but in *amāmus* the second is long and will always be pronounced long. You have to learn whether a vowel is long or short, though there are some rules, e.g. vowels before *ns* and *nf* are always pronounced long, e.g. *īnfāns*, but *īnfantem*.

(b) But the shape of Latin verse is determined *not* by vowels but by *syllables*. A syllable is a single sound, either a vowel or vowel + consonant. *īnfantem* has three syllables: *īn-fan-tem*. *Every* syllable counts in the metre, as either 'heavy' or 'light'.

Heavy syllables consist of:

(a) vowels that are *pronounced* long, e.g. *Rōmānī* – three vowels pronounced long and therefore three heavy syllables.

(b) vowels that are followed by two consonants or a double consonant (x, z, qu, see p. 42(d)) e.g. *ingentēs* – the first two syllables are heavy as each is followed by two consonants, the last vowel is pronounced long and the syllable is therefore heavy. Observe that the rule holds even if words are divided. For example, *et* is light, but would become heavy in *et fugit*, because *e* is then followed by two consonants, *t* and *f*. Note that the quantity of the vowel, its pronunciation, does not change. The *e* of *et* will be *pronounced* short in both instances. It is just that, in the second, it will *count* as heavy for the purposes of the metre.

(c) [Observe the rule for the formation of syllables: (i) a syllable divides between consonants *if it can*, e.g. the three syllables of *ingentes* are *in-gen-tēs* (not e.g. *ing-ent-ēs*). This means that, *technically speaking*, a syllable ending in a consonant is heavy, because (by the rule) if a syllable *ends* in a consonant, the next syllable must *begin* with a consonant. (ii) if a syllable cannot divide between consonants, it starts after a vowel and before a consonant, e.g. *Ci-ce-ro*. However, since it is difficult to remember the strict rule for the formation of syllables, it is usually best to think in terms of a heavy syllable being a combination of vowel + 2 consonants.]

(d) a short vowel followed by a mute consonant (p, b, ph, f; t, d, th; k, c, qu, g, ch) + l or r may remain light or become heavy. Thus at 2.663 we find side by side *patris, patrem* – in the first instance with a light *a*, in the second with a heavy *a*!

(e) diphthongs, e.g. *sēū* – a diphthong, therefore heavy. Latin diphthongs are *ae, au, ei, eu, oe* and *ui*.

All other syllables are light, e.g. *arma uirumque canō* – *ar-* heavy (*a* followed by consonant), *-ma* light, *ui-* light, *-rum-* heavy, *-que* light, *ca-* light, *-nō* heavy.

x (ks), *z* (ds) and *qu* (kw) count as *two* consonants.

h does not count as a consonant for metrical purposes. So *et* in *et habuit* scans light.

i and *u* sometimes count as vowels, sometimes as consonants like the English y and w. Thus for metrical purposes *Iūnō = Yūnō, Iuppiter = Yuppiter, iungō = yungō, Lāuīnia = Lāwīnya*, etc. So too *saeuus = saewus*, where the first *u* is consonantal *w*, and the second the vowel *u*. *hēū*, meanwhile, counts as a diphthong.

Some vowels admit of alternative lengths. For example, both vowels in *mihi, tibi* and *sibi* are usually pronounced short, but can be pronounced short-long, where they will be so marked (*mihī, tibī* and *sibī*).

Elision

If a word *ends* in a vowel or *-m* and is followed by a word *beginning* with a vowel or *h*, the final vowel is *elided* (lit. 'crushed') and does not count for the purpose of the metre. Observe:

(a) *ego et tū* for metrical purposes = *eg et tū*
(b) *quam et* for metrical purposes = *qu et*
(c) *cum habēs* for metrical purposes = *c abēs*

'Hiatus' ('yawning gap') is the term applied when elision is not observed. An example is at 1.405, where the final *a* of *dea* in *dea ille* is not elided and is thus 'in hiatus'.

Pronunciation

Just to repeat: the *pronunciation* of a syllable is affected *only* by whether the vowel is long or short, *not* by whether it is heavy or light. That length is fixed and has to be learned. You have to *know* that e.g. the Latin for 'muse', *Musa*, is in fact *Mūsa*. Conversely, *et* is short. It is therefore pronounced short. If it becomes heavy because it is followed by a consonant, e.g. *et fugit*, it is still *pronounced* short. There are no circumstances in which you would ever pronounce it long, *ēt*. Thus, in this text, all vowels *pronounced* long are *marked* long (and therefore automatically count heavy for scansion purposes). All *other* vowels are pronounced *short*, though (like *et* in *et fugit*) they may be heavy for the purposes of scansion.

Exercise

Read the first eighteen lines of Book 1 and/or the first twenty of Book 2, pronouncing all syllables short except where they are *marked* as long.

The hexameter

The *Aeneid* is composed in hexameters ('six metra/feet'). This consists of a metron/foot called a 'dactyl' (heavy-light-light, -u u, tum-ti-ti) and a metron/foot called a 'spondee' (heavy-heavy, - -, tum-tum), on the following pattern:

1	2	3	4	5	6
tum-ti-ti	tum-ti-ti	tum-ti-ti	tum-ti-ti	tum-ti-ti	tum-tum
- u u	- u u	- u u	- u u	- u u	- - *or* - u
or	*or*	*or*	*or*		
tum-tum	tum-tum	tum-tum	tum-tum		
- -	- -	- -	- -		

In other words, the first four 'feet' can be a dactyl or a spondee. Foot 5 is virtually always a dactyl, and foot 6 a spondee, though the last syllable is allowed to be light.

Caesura

There is nearly always a division between words in the third or fourth foot of the hexameter. This is called 'caesura' (from *caedō*, 'I cut'), e.g.

arma uirumque canō // Troiae quī prīmus ab ōrīs

There are useful statistics relating to Virgil's use of dactyls and spondees in the first four feet of his hexameters. Of the eight most frequent patterns of dactyl and spondee (thirty-two feet in all), twenty are spondees and twelve are dactyls:

they are (i) DSSS (ii) DDSS (iii) DSDS (iv) SDSS (v) SSSS (vi) DDDS (vii) SSDS (viii) SDDS. But there is no regularity about the feel and rhythm of Virgil's hexameters. Elision is relatively frequent; and sense groups regularly run over the caesura, and over the line into the next line (enjambement). This is difficult to appreciate at first in Latin; it is easier to understand in English. We shall come to this on pp. 45–8.

Exercises

A. Examine carefully the opening lines of Books 1 and/or 2 ('long' pronunciation marks removed), here scanned for you. Underlined vowels are elided and do not count for the purpose of scansion; caesuras are marked //. Make sure you understand why they are scanned as they are.

Book 1
arma uirumque cano // Troiae qui primus ab oris
Italiam fato // profugus Lauiniaque uenit
litora, mult<u>um</u> ill<u>e</u> // et terris iactatus et alto,
ui superum saeuae // memorem Iunonis ob iram,
multa quoqu<u>e</u> et bello // passus, dum conderet urbem,   5
inferretque deos // Latio, genus unde Latinum,
Albanique patres, // atqu<u>e</u> altae moenia Romae

Book 2
conticuer<u>e</u> omnes // intentiqu<u>e</u> ora tenebant.
inde toro pater Aeneas // sic orsus ab alto:
'infandum, regina, // iubes renouare dolorem,
Troianas ut opes // et lamentabile regnum
eruerint Danai, // quaequ<u>e</u> ipse miserrima uidi,   5
et quorum pars magna // fui. quis talia fando
Myrmidonum Dolopumu<u>e</u> // aut duri miles Vlixi*
temperet a lacrimis? // et iam nox umida caelo
praecipitat, suadentque // cadentia sidera somnos.

*V = capital U

B. Now scan the following lines. Hints:

(a) Every *new* foot must begin -.
(b) If a foot *begins* -u, the *next* syllable must be u and the *next* -.
(c) The last five syllables of a line will virtually always scan - u u - - or - u u - u.
(d) Check for elisions.
(e) Mark caesuras in the third or fourth foot.

urbs antiqua fuit, Tyrii tenuere coloni,
Karthago, Italiam contra Tiberinaque longe
ostia, diues opum studiisque asperrima belli;
quam Iuno fertur terram magis omnibus unam
posthabita coluisse Samo; hic illius arma,
hic currus fuit; hoc regnum dea gentibus esse,
si qua fata sinant, iam tum tenditque fouetque.

Aeneid 1.12–18

incipiam. fracti bello fatisque repulsi
ductores Danaum, tot iam labentibus annis,
instar montis equum, diuina Palladis arte,   15
aedificant, sectaque intexunt abiete costas;
uotum pro reditu simulant; ea fama uagatur.
huc, delecta uirum sortiti corpora, furtim
includunt caeco lateri, penitusque cauernas
ingentis uterumque armato milite complent.

Aeneid 2.13–20

Verse and sentence structure

Consider the following passages of poetry and ask: how does the sentence structure relate to the verse-line?

A. John Milton, *Paradise Lost* 4.492–505
In the Garden of Eden, before the fall, Eve innocently embraces her husband Adam, while the Devil looks enviously on:

So spake our general mother, and with eyes   492
Of conjugal attraction unreproved*
And meek surrender, half embracing leaned
On our first father, half her swelling breast   495
Naked met his under the flowing gold
Of her loose tresses hid. He, in delight
Both of her beauty and submissive charms,
Smiled with superior love, as Jupiter
On Juno smiles, when he impregns the clouds   500
That shed May flowers; and pressed her matron lip
With kisses pure. Aside the devil turned
For envy, yet with jealous leer malign
Eyed them askance, and to himself thus plained,
'Sight hateful, sight tormenting! . . .'   505

---

* i.e. honourable, irreproachable

B. Alexander Pope, *Essay on Man* 2.1–18
It is not man's business to study God, but himself – and to understand that he has great strengths and great weaknesses:

Know then thyself, presume not God to scan,
The proper study of mankind is man.
Placed on this isthmus of a middle state,
A being darkly wise and rudely great:
With too much knowledge for the sceptic side,   5
With too much weakness for the stoic's pride,
He hangs between; in doubt to act, or rest;
In doubt to deem himself a god, or beast;
In doubt his mind or body to prefer;
Born but to die, and reasoning but to err;   10
Alike in ignorance, his reason such,
Whether he thinks too little, or too much:
Chaos of Thought and Passion, all confused;
Still by himself abused or disabused;
Created half to rise, and half to fall;   15
Great lord of all things, yet a prey to all;
Sole judge of truth, in endless error hurl'd:
The glory, jest, and riddle of the world!

The answer is that, in Milton, there is no relationship between verse-line and sentence; in Pope there is an absolute relationship, each verse-line either being a complete sentence or a single syntactical unit. To make an extremely crude generalisation: Milton is to Virgil as Pope is to poets before Virgil (with the stern proviso that poets before Virgil were not nearly as rigorously line-restrained as Pope chose to be).

Latin prose in the first century BC was developing into a highly complex and sophisticated 'periodic' structure, i.e. long sentences with lots of sub-clauses. Virgil tended not to subordinate, but to add, i.e. not 'when she had done this, having done that, because she had done the other, she . . .' but 'she did this and she did this and she did this . . .' (the so-called 'paratactic' style).[1] But by that addition Virgil did introduce the long sentence into verse in a way that had never been done before. The result is that, instead of a complete phrase or clause occupying the whole line (with an inevitable sense-break or, if one prefers, syntactical pause, at the end of the line), phrases and clauses now spread themselves

---

[1] From the Greek *parataktikos* 'drawn up alongside', used of men drawn up side by side in battle formation! It is typical of the style of Homer – another example of Virgil's use of him.

over series of lines, the sense-breaks or syntactical pauses appearing in whatever part of the line Virgil chose, just like Milton. Result: the hexameter became an infinitely flexible and mobile verse-form.

I repeat: the story is not quite as black-and-white as all that, but look at the following brief examples, chosen (admittedly) to make this specific point:

A. Ennius, *Annales* 1.34–42 (Skutsch)
Note: early verse may ignore final *s* for scansion purposes.
Ilia describes to her half-sister how she dreamt that Mars raped and left her and how she tried to find her half-sister but could not:

et cita quom tremulīs anus attulit artubu(s) lūmen,
tālia tum memorat lacrumāns, exterrita somnō:
'Euridicā prognāta, pater quam noster amāuit,
uīrēs uītaque corpu(s) meum nunc dēserit omne.   35
nam mē uīsus homō pulcher per amoena salicta
et rīpās raptāre locōsque nouōs; ita sōla,
postillā, germāna soror, errāre uidēbār,
tardaque uestīgāre et quaerere tē, neque posse
corde capessere; sēmita nūlla pedem stabilābat.'   40

And when the old woman, limbs trembling, had quickly brought a light,
Then [Ilia] spoke as follows, crying, frightened out of sleep:
'Daughter of Eurydice [wife of Aeneas] whom our father loved,
Strength and life now leave my whole body.   35
For a handsome man [Mars] seemed, through pleasant thickets
And banks and new places, to drag me off; so on my own,
half-sister, I later seemed to wander,
and slowly to track and look for you, and not to be able
to reach you in my heart; no path steadied my foot.'   40

Most lines contain a complete syntactical unit, to which there is a natural pause at the end. To which lines does this not apply?

B. Catullus, 64.241–5
Aegeus sees that his son Theseus' ship has black, not white, sails and, assuming he is dead, hurls himself from the cliff:

at pater, ut summā prospectum ex arce petēbat,   241
anxia in assiduōs absūmēns lūmina flētūs,
cum primum īnflātī cōnspexit lintea uēlī,
praecipitem sēsē scopulōrum ē uertice iēcit,
āmissum crēdēns immītī Thēsea fātō.   245

But his father, as he scanned the view from the top of the Acropolis,   241
Exhausting his worried eyes in constant tears,
As soon as he saw the canvas of the billowing sail,
Hurled himself headlong from the top of the rocks,
Believing Theseus was lost by cruel fate.   245

Each line is a self-contained syntactical unit, and there are strong natural pauses at the end of each.

C. Virgil, *Aeneid* 1.1–7
arma uirumque canō, Troiae quī prīmus ab ōrīs
Ītaliam, fātō profugus, Lāuīniaque uēnit
lītora, multum ille et terrīs iactātus et altō
uī superum, saeuae memorem Iūnōnis ob īram,
multa quoque et bellō passus, dum conderet urbem,   5
īnferretque deōs Latiō, genus unde Latīnum,
Albānīque patrēs, atque altae moenia Rōmae.

War and the man I sing, who first from Troy's shores
To Italy, exiled by fate, came to the Lavinian
Shore, he having been much buffeted by land and sea,
By the violence of the gods, because of the unforgetting anger of savage Juno,
And suffering much too in war, till he should found a city   5
And bring his gods to Latium, whence the Latin race,
The Alban fathers and the walls of high Rome.

Here there is a single sentence, of some syntactical complexity, running over the lines and with very little relationship between line-end and sense-pause; indeed, there are sense-pauses all over the place. All very Miltonic, in fact.

Stress and ictus

One final feature of all verse must now be mentioned: stress. Go back to the Milton (p. 45). It is composed in pentameters, i.e. five feet to the line, each foot consisting of u -. The metric stress lands on the -. The question is – where does the natural stress of any word land? You will soon find out by reading the Milton aloud, heavily emphasising the metrical stress. Here the metrically stressed syllable is in capitals:

So SPAKE our GEN'ral MOther, AND with EYES   492
Of CONjugAL attrACtion UNreprOV'd
And MEEK surRENder, HALF embrACing LEANED
On OUR first FAther, HALF her SWElling BREAST   495

NakED met HIS undER the FLOWing GOLD
Of HER loose TRESses HID. He, IN deLIGHT

Now read it as you would normal English. You will often find the 'normal' stress in a quite different place. Line 496 is a good example, with two very violent stress contrasts. The point is that, if natural stress and metric stress coincided exactly, it could sound very boringly repetitive, especially if each word is a complete foot in itself (the Pope extract on p. 46 runs that risk occasionally). The clashes give the verse rhythmical interest, variety and tension.

We call the metrical stress *ictus* (Latin 'beat') and the natural stress 'accent', and the *ictus*/accent clash is an important feature of all verse. Shakespeare also composed in pentameters, and you can have fun working out the *ictus*/accent clash in one of his most famous lines:

'Friends, Romans, countrymen, lend me your ears'

One desperately wants to stress 'Friends', and in speech one would, but that is not where the verse *ictus* lies. Later on in the speech, one finds:

'I come to bury Caesar, not to praise him'

where almost complete harmony of *ictus* and accent is in evidence (again, the first word 'I' is the problem).

In Virgil's hexameter, the *ictus* fall on the first beat of the foot, e.g. TUM-ti-ti TUM-tum TUM-tum TUM-ti-ti TUM-ti-ti TUM-tum. But our English examples tell us what the rule is: you must read the verse paying attention to the *natural accent* of the spoken word, or you torture the verse to death. Then you can enjoy hearing the metrical *ictus* either clashing or coinciding underneath. In Virgil, they nearly always coincide in the fifth and sixth foot.

Rules of word-accent

The rules of word-accent in Latin are as follows:

(a) A two-syllable word accents on the *first* syllable (technically the 'penultimate', *paene* 'almost', *ultimus* 'last'), e.g. *ámat, séruīs, mónēs*.

(b) A three-syllable word also accents on the penultimate if that syllable is heavy, e.g. *amámus, seruórum, fecístis, monébat, ingéntem, mandáre* ('entrust').

(c) Otherwise, a three-syllable word accents on the *first* syllable (the antepenultimate 'before-almost-last'), e.g. *óptimus, péssimo, fáciunt, mándere* ('chew').

(d) Treat words with more than three syllables as if they had just the three final syllables, e.g. *Itáliam, impúlerit, inimíca*.

(e) Note that the addition of e.g. *-que* (etc.) alters the *ictus*. So *uírum*, but *uirúmque*; *inférret* but *inferrétque*.

The following lines show the *ictus* in **bold** and the *accent* with an áccent. The elisions are indicated by -:

hís accénsa súp**er**, iac**tá**tos áequore tóto
Tróas, **re**líquias **Dá**na- **á**tqu- im**mí**tis Achílli,   30
ar**cé**bat lónge Láti**o**, múlt**o**sque per ánnos
er**rá**bant, ácti fátis, mári- ómnia cír**c**um.
tán**t**ae mólis érat Románam cón**d**ere gén**t**em.

Aeneid 1.29–33

Exercise
Read all the above lines, first stressing the **bold** metrical *ictus* throughout, then the nátural áccent. Note the struggle between *ictus* and accent in 31–2 and the almost complete coincidence in 33 – might this reflect the meaning?

Notes on Virgil's style

As observed above (p. 46), Virgil's style is not 'periodic' but 'paratactic', i.e. the 'adding' style. To that extent it is, for the most part, structurally fairly simple; and Virgil uses remarkably common words (see *Intro* [9], footnote 20). Its complexity lies in the magical, but often unexpected, *word-order*, and the tight *relationship* between individual words. As a result, you must pay the very closest attention to the form of every word (especially the *case* of nouns and adjectives) and see how each word plays off against other words in terms of (i) its grammatical relationship and (ii) its position in the line.

Take, for example, the following lines. Queen Dido, abandoned by Aeneas, prepares to die on a funeral pyre, and utters a curse on him as he sails away (4.661–2):

hauriat	*hunc^*	*oculīs*	*^ignem*	*crūdelis^*	*ab*	*altō*
Let-him-drink	this	with-his-eyes	fire	heartless	from	the-deep
^Dardanus,	*et*	*nostrae^*	*sēcum*	*ferat*	*ōmina*	*^mortis.*
Trojan,	and	of-our	with-himself	let-him-carry	the-omens	of-death

Literally, it means 'Let the heartless Trojan on the high seas drink in with his eyes this fire, and carry with him the omens of my death.' The contemptuous *Dardanus* (meaning 'Aeneas'), subject, is held and spat out at the beginning of the second line to complete the meaning, though already glossed with *crūdelis*. *oculīs* knocks against *ignem* (he is going to see the fire) and *ignem* against *crūdelis* (the fire will be cruel to me/him?); but *grammatically ignem* construes with *hunc* and *crūdelis* with *Dardanus*. *crūdelis* likewise feeds into *ab altō* (he is heartless *because* he is sailing away). *nostrae* construes with *mortis*, but *nostrae sēcum* puts 'me' and 'with him' together. The words are plain, the grammar simple, but the word-order is complex and rich in suggestiveness.

Since it is important to get used to this style as quickly as possible, 'crunch' exercises (working on the cerebral rather than abdominal six-pack) are added at regular points, where you will be asked to carry out the above sort of analysis. This will entail:

(a) defining accurately the *grammatical* relationship of each of the words – case, agreement, function, etc.
(b) considering the effect of the *word-order* (e.g. the 'shadow' that one word casts on the next, the holding back of key words, etc.)
(c) examining how the utterance is shaped to the line of the verse.

Observe some other stylistic features, some mentioned already, others to appear:

(a) Use of the present tense, *Intro* [21]
(b) Simple language, *Intro* [9] footnote 20
(c) Paratactic style, pp. 46–7
(d) Expansion/repetition, see on **2.132–44**
(e) Flexibility of verse patterns, see pp. 45–8 and on **1.78**.

Suggestions for further reading

Note: this is not a recommended reading-list; it refers to the books cited in the course of the commentary.

Anderson, W.S. (1969) *The Art of the* Aeneid (Englewood Cliffs N.J.)

Austin, R.G. (1964) *Aeneidos Liber Secundus* (Oxford)

— (1971) *Aeneidos Liber Primus* (Oxford)

Bowie, A.M. (1990) 'The Death of Priam: Allegory and History in the *Aeneid*', *Classical Quarterly* New Series 40 (470–81)

Bowra, C.M. 'Aeneas and the Stoic Ideal', *Greece and Rome* 3 (1933–4: 8–21) (in S.J. Harrison 1990: 363–77)

Boyle, A. J. (ed.) (1993) *Roman Epic* (London)

Braund, S.M. and Gill, C. (eds.) (1997) *The Passions in Roman Thought and Literature* (Cambridge)

Camps, W.A. (1969) *An Introduction to Virgil's* Aeneid (Oxford)

Clausen, W.V. (1987) *Virgil's* Aeneid *and the Tradition of Hellenistic Poetry* (Berkeley)

— (2002) *Virgil's* Aeneid: *Decorum, Allusion and Ideology* (Leipzig)

Coleman, R. 'The Gods in the *Aeneid*', *Greece and Rome* (October 1982) (in McAuslan and Walcot 1990: 39–64)

Commager, S. (ed.) (1966) *Virgil: A Collection of Critical Essays* (Englewood Cliffs, N.J.)

Conington, J. P. (ed.) (1858) *Vergili Maronis Opera* vol. II (London)

Conte, G.B. (1986) *The Rhetoric of Imitation* (Ithaca, N.Y.)

Dawe, R.D. (1993) *The Odyssey: Translation and Analysis* (Sussex)

Dench, E. (2005) *Romulus' Asylum* (Oxford)

Feeney, D.C. 'The Taciturnity of Aeneas', *Classical Quarterly* New Series 33 (1983: 204–19) (with corrections, in S.J. Harrison 1990: 167–90)

— (1991) *The Gods in Epic* (Oxford)

Fowler, D. (2000) *Roman Constructions* (Oxford)

Goold, G.P. 'Servius and the Helen Episode', *Harvard Studies in Classical Philology* 74 (1970: 101–68) (in S.J. Harrison 1990: 60–126)

Gransden, K.W. 'The Fall of Troy', *Greece and Rome* (April 1985) (in McAuslan and Walcot 1990: 121–33)

— (1990) *Virgil*: The Aeneid (Cambridge)

Griffin, J. (1985) *Latin Poets and Roman Life* (Oxford)

— (2001) *Virgil* (Bristol)

Hainsworth, J.B. (1991) *The Idea of Epic* (Berkeley)

Hardie, P. (1986) *Virgil's* Aeneid: *Cosmos and Imperium* (Oxford)

— (1998) *Virgil* (*Greece and Rome*: New Surveys in the Classics no. 28) (Oxford)

Harrison, E.L 'Divine Action in *Aeneid* Book 2', *Phoenix* 24 (1970: 320–32) (revised, in S.J. Harrison 1990: 46–59)

Harrison, S.J. (1990) *Oxford Readings in Vergil's* Aeneid (Oxford)

Heinze, R. (1914) *Virgil's Epic Technique* (third edition), tr. H. and D. Harvey and F. Robertson (second edition, Bristol, 1999) (Note: two references are given, e.g. 26/16–17, the first indicating the original German edition, the second the translation)

Henry, J. (1873) *Aeneidea*, vol. I (London)

— (1878) *Aeneidea*, vol. II (Dublin)

Horsfall, N.M. 'Dido in the Light of History', *Proceedings of the Virgil Society* 13 (1973–4: 1–13) (in S.J. Harrison 1990: 127–44)

— (ed.) (1995) *A Companion to the Study of Virgil* (Leiden)

— (ed.) (2008) *Virgil,* Aeneid 2: *A Commentary* (Leiden)

Hunt, J.W. (1973) *Forms of Glory: Structure and Sense in Virgil's* Aeneid (Carbondale, Ill.)

Jackson Knight, W.F. (1966) *Roman Vergil* (Harmondsworth)

Jenykns, R. (1998) *Virgil's Experience* (Oxford)

Johnson, W.R. (1976) *Darkness Visible* (Berkeley)

Jones, P. (1988) *Homer's* Odyssey: *A Commentary to the Translation of Richmond Lattimore* (Oxford/Carbondale, Ill.)

— (1999) *An Intelligent Person's Guide to Classics* (Oxford)

— (2003) *Homer's* Iliad: *A Commentary on Three Translations* (Oxford)

— (2007) *Reading Ovid* (Cambridge)

Jones, P. and Sidwell, K. (eds.) (1997) *The World of Rome* (Cambridge)

Kaster, R. (1988) *Guardians of Language* (Berkeley)

Kenney, E.J. '*Indicium transferendi*: Virgil, *Aeneid* 2. 469–505 and its antecedents' (in West and Woodman 1979: 103–20)

Knauer, G.N. 'Vergil's *Aeneid* and Homer', *Greek, Roman and Byzantine Studies* 5 (1964: 61–84) (in S.J. Harrison 1990: 390–412)

Knox, B.M.W. 'The Serpent and the Flame: The Imagery of the Second Book of the *Aeneid*', *American Journal of Philology* 71 (1950): 379–400 (in Commager 1966: 124–42)

Lyne, R.O.A.M. 'Vergil and the Politics of War', *Classical Quarterly* New Series 33 (1983: 188–203) (in S.J. Harrison 1990: 316–38)

— (1987) *Further Voices in Vergil's* Aeneid (Oxford)

— (1989) *Words and the Poet: Characteristic Techniques of Style in Vergil's* Aeneid (Oxford)

Martindale, C. (ed.) (1984) *Virgil and his Influence* (Bristol)

— (1997) *The Cambridge Companion to Virgil* (Cambridge)

McAuslan, I. and Walcot, P. (eds.) (1990) *Virgil* (Greece and Rome Studies) (Oxford)

Miles, R. (2010) *Carthage Must Be Destroyed* (Harmondsworth)

Nelis, D. (2001) *Vergil's* Aeneid *and the* Argonautica *of Apollonius Rhodius* (Oxford)

Nisbet, R.G.M. '*Aeneas Imperator*: Roman Generalship in an Epic Context', *Proceedings of the Virgil Society* 18 (1978–80: 50–61) (in S.J. Harrison 1990: 378–89)

— (1995) *Collected Papers on Latin Literature*, ed. S.J. Harrison (Oxford)

Nuttall, A.D. 'Virgil and Shakespeare' (in Martindale 1984: 71–93)

O'Hara, J.J. (1996) *True Names* (Ann Arbor)

— 'Virgil's Style' (in Martindale 1997: 241–58)

OLD, The Oxford Latin Dictionary (1982) ed. P.G.W. Glare (Oxford)

Otis, B. (1964) *Virgil: A Study in Civilised Poetry* (Oxford)

Page, T.E. (ed.) (1894) *The* Aeneid *of Virgil Books I–VI* (London)

Pöschl, V. (1970) *The Art of Vergil* (Ann Arbor)

Quint, D. (1993) *Epic and Empire: Politics and Generic Form from Virgil to Milton* (Princeton)

Reed, J.D. (2007) *Virgil's Gaze: Nation and Poetry in the* Aeneid (Princeton)

Rieu-Jones (2003) *Homer:* The Iliad, tr. E.V. Rieu, revised and updated by Peter Jones with D.C.H. Rieu (Harmondsworth)

Ross D.O. (2007) *Virgil's* Aeneid: *A Reader's Guide* (Oxford)

Rudd, N. (2005) *The Common Spring* (Bristol)

Sandbach, F.E. 'Anti-antiquarianism in the *Aeneid*', *Proceedings of the Virgil Society* 5 (1965–6: 26–38) (with corrections, in S.J. Harrison 1990: 449–65)

Schlunk, R.R. (1974) *The Homeric Scholia and the* Aeneid (Ann Arbor)

Skutsch, O. (1985) *The* Annals *of Quintus Ennius* (Oxford)

Stahl, H.-P. (1981) 'Aeneas, an Unheroic Hero?', *Arethusa* 14, 1 (157–86)

Thomas, R.F. (2001) *Virgil and the Augustan Reception* (Cambridge)

West, D.A. 'Multiple-correspondence Similes in the *Aeneid*', *Journal of Roman Studies* 59 (1969: 40–9) (in S.J. Harrison 1990: 429–44)

— (1990) *Virgil: The Aeneid*, tr. David West (Harmondsworth)

West, D. and Woodman, T. (1979) *Creative Imitation and Latin Literature* (Cambridge)

— (1984) *Poetry and Politics in the Age of Augustus* (Cambridge)

Williams, R.D. 'The Pictures on Dido's Temple (*Aeneid* 1.450–93)', *Classical Quarterly* New Series 10 (1960: 145–51) (in S.J. Harrison 1990: 37–45)

Williams, R.D. (ed.) (1972) *The* Aeneid *of Virgil Books 1–6* (London)

Williams, R.D. and Pattie, T.S. (1982) *Virgil: His Poetry through the Ages* (London)

Zanker, P. (1988) *The Power of Images in the Age of Augustus* (Ann Arbor)

Ziolkowski, J.M. and Putnam, M.C.J. (2008) *The Virgilian Tradition: The First Fifteen Hundred Years* (New Haven, Conn.)

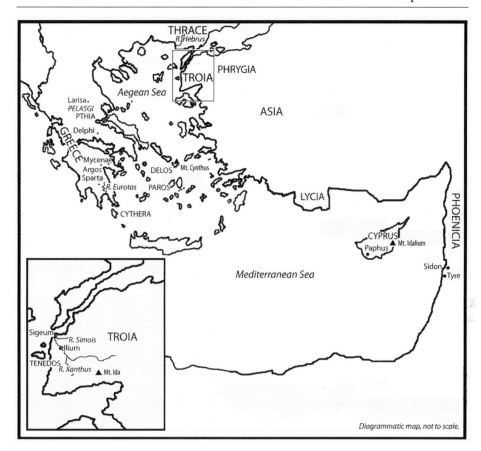

Map 1 The Greek World

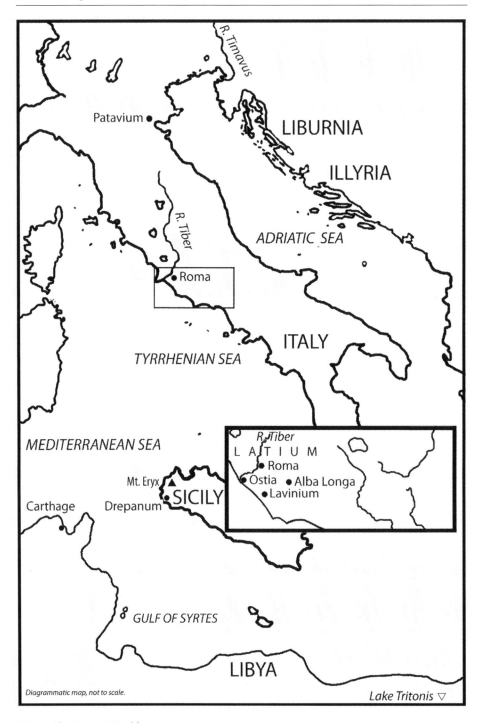

Map 2 The Roman World

Book 1
Aeneas' mission: from storm to refuge

In Book 1, Aeneas and his men have just left Sicily on the last leg of
their journey to their new home in Italy (*Introduction*, section 33 =
Intro [33]). But the goddess Juno, who loves Carthage and hates
Trojans, ensures that they are blown off course, and nearly wrecked.
With the intervention of the sea-god Neptune, they manage to make it
to Carthage in Libya on the north African coast (1–222). There Aeneas'
mother, the goddess Venus, having been assured by Jupiter that
Aeneas' mission will be completed, reassures him (223–417). He makes
for Carthage, envies its rapid development, is encouraged by depictions
of the Trojan war in a temple and meets the queen Dido, where he is
also re-united with men he thought lost in the storm (418–656). At a
feast laid on for the Trojans' benefit, Venus makes Dido fall in love
with Aeneas (657–756). See *Intro* [25–32].

1.1–33: Introduction – Juno's anger and the founding of Rome

In this Section, *Virgil introduces the themes that will dominate the* Aeneid: *the trials of Aeneas (1–7); Juno's anger (4, 8–11) and its reasons (19–28); the role of fate (2, 18, 22); Aeneas'* pietās *(10); his and his men's sufferings (3, 5, 28–33); Carthage (12ff.); and, most important of all, the promise of the eventual founding of Rome (5–7, 33)*

1.1–7: *My theme – a much-travelled, long-suffering Trojan on a mission to found a city and the Roman race*

arma uirumque^ canō, Troiae ^quī prīmus ab ōrīs
Ītaliam fātō ^profugus Lāuīniaque* uēnit

1 *arma*: the fourth-century AD commentator Servius (henceforward S., see *Intro* [51]) comments that by *arma*, Virgil (hence forward V.). means *bellum*

uirumque: the linking device looks forward to *quī* '[the man] . . . *who*'. On *-que* see p. 50(e)

canō 3 I sing (of, about); not meant literally. V. is referring to the convention of Greek heroic epic, where the bards actually *did* sing. S. points out that *canō* can also mean 'I extol' and 'I prophesy'

*Troi-a ae 1f. Troy, the area in which the city of Ilium was located, from which Aeneas and his men fled; take with *ab ōrīs* 'from the shores of Troy'

quī: the man referred to here will remain the subject of the sentence and its adjs. *prīmus* (**1**), *profugus* (**2**), *ille* (**3**) and participles *iactātus* (**3**), *passus* (**5**) up to **6**

prīmus: see on 242 for the (apparent) arrival of Trojan Antenor before Aeneas (*Intro* [34]); *prīmus* can also mean 'earliest in respect of some action' (*OLD* 3c, 4) – the action of founding Rome

*ōr-a ae 1f. shore

2 *Ītaliam*: acc. of motion after *uēnit*, so understand *ad*, as also *Lāuīniaque . . . lītora* (S. comments 'it is well known that authors decide for themselves whether to include or omit prepositions' – as you will frequently see!). *Ītaliam* is in a 'strong' position at the start of a line, linking 'from Troy' closely with the great climax 'to Italy'. Right at the start of the epic, V. juxtaposes the two – the heart of his epic

fāt-um ī 2n. fate, destiny; here abl. of cause, 'as a result of fate' (see *Intro* [45–50] and on 2.777). With *fātō*, V. is already assuring us that the events of his epic are not random (S. adds that it must not be thought Aeneas fled Troy on a criminal charge or lusting for new worlds to conquer). But does it go with *profugus* or *uēnit* – or what? S. has no doubt: 'it applies to both his flight and his arrival in Italy'

profug-us ī 2m. exile; i.e. Aeneas did not want to leave Troy. He had no option

Lāuīni-us a um of Lavinium; note that the second *-i-* is treated as a consonant, 'y' (as if *Lāuīnyus*, p. 42). This is the territory of Lavinia, the princess of Latium (roughly modern Lazio – the area surrounding Rome). Aeneas will eventually marry her and settle his men there in the new town of Lavinium, c. 20 miles south of Rome, which he will rule till he dies. See on **1.267–77**

uēnit: note the long *ē*. What does *uenit* mean?

1.1–7: There is a great deal going on here in the first half of the proem (Greek *prooimion*, Latinised into *proemium* – the technical term for the brief opening statement of the theme of an epic):

*lītora, multum ^illē et terrīs ^iactātus et altō,
uī superum saeuae^ memorem* ^Iūnōnis ob *īram,
multa quoquē et bellō passus, dum conderet urbem,   5
īnferretque deōs Latiō, genus^ unde ^Latīnum,
Albānīque patrēs, atque altae moenia Rōmae.

3 *lītus lītor-is 3n. coast, coast-line (here pl. used for s., a common poetic device). Aeneas will arrive by sea, not overland

multum: here an (irregular) adverb, 'much'. See RL79, W32, M23 (see p. 37 for these references)

ille: focusing sharply on *that* man

terrīs . . . altō: abl. of place (local abl.), 'by/on land . . . sea' (for altō cf. English 'the deep'); Aeneas' sufferings will not be restricted to the sea (see lītus above) – hence et terrīs first, for emphasis. terrīs indicates that Aeneas will visit many lands in his travels

*iactō 1 I throw/toss about (used of troubles on land as well as sea); hurl/toss out

4 uī: abl. of instrument, with iactātus. fātō (2) is (broadly) benign; uī certainly is not. S. comments that this shows the Trojans did not deserve their sufferings; it was all the gods' doing

*super-ī ōrum 2m. pl. gods, powers above; superum here = super(ōr)um 'of the gods'. This contraction, a mark of epic style, is very common, especially with e.g. de(ōr)um/dīu(ōr)um 'of the gods', Dana(ōr)um, Argīu(ōr)um 'of the Greeks', uir(ōr)um 'of men', etc. Aeneas is under the whip – the rest of the line tells us whose (and it will turn out to be one god alone)

*saeu-us a um savage, cruel, vicious; follow carefully the linking devices in the rest of this line

*memor -is mindful, unforgetting

*Iūnō Iūnōn-is 3f. Juno, wife of king of the gods Jupiter. Note the first I- counts for scansion purposes as a consonant, 'y' (Yūnō – of course you do; see on 2 above). As a result, the -em of memor-em is not elided

*ob + acc. on account/because of; this holds the key to the whole saeuae . . . īram phrase

*īr-a ae 1f. anger, wrath

5 multa: acc. pl. n., obj. of passus – an expansion of multum . . . (3), pointed up by quoque

bellō: in addition to Aeneas' trials while travelling by land and sea (cf. arma, 1). The bella will come in the second half of the Aeneid when Aeneas finally arrives in Italy

condō 3 I found; note that it is subjunc., like īnferret (6) – giving what meaning to dum? (For the construction, see RL165.2, M119, 124–5)

urbem: i.e. Lavinium

6 īnferō īnferre 3 I introduce, bring in

deōs: i.e. the penātēs (Roman household gods) that Aeneas brings with him from Troy (cf. 2.293–5)

*Lati-um ī 2n. Latium (see on Lāuīniaque, 2); S. notes that Latiō is dat. of place to, whereas prose would write in Latium. There is also perhaps a touch of 'to Latium's advantage', dat. of advantage, RLL(e)1(ii), W38, M10

genus unde: take in order unde genus. Note the ellipsis of e.g. 'came/arose' as the main verb in 6–7. 'Ellipsis/ellipse' – omission of a word – is very common in poetry

*Latīn-us a um Latin, from Latium

7 *Albān-us a um Alban, from Alba, i.e. relating to Alba Longa, the city that Aeneas' son Iulius/Ascanius will found when Aeneas dies (cf. on Lavinium, 2 and 265–71). Alba Longa is about 12 miles south-east of Rome

patrēs: probably = senators, noble families

altae: S. suggests the description because Rome was built on seven hills or had tall buildings; but it also means 'high' in the sense of 'exalted', 'glorious'

*moeni-a um 3n. pl. (defensive) walls; fortified town

Rōmae: observe the sequence: Lavinium/Latins – Alba Longa – and finally, with its great walls, Rome (last word, founded last from these earlier

(a) In general, note the economic sketch of the story-line: Aeneas flees Troy for Italy (1–2) and, after much trouble in his travels (3), reaches Latium (6), where battles too await (5); but he does finally found Lavinium (2), whence Alba Longa (7) and Rome (7). The hero, his sufferings, the hand of the gods (destiny [2] and Juno [4]), his piety (resettling his penātēs [6]) and his eventual triumph (7) are all there.

(b) V. sets up expectations in the reader: 'arms and a man' (1) make for a dramatic opening – what wars are these, and who is this one man? What exactly are Aeneas' troubles by land, sea and in war? What exactly did Juno remember that made her

foundations, and the grand climax!). Dryden (1697) translates 'From whence the Race of *Alban* Fathers come / And the long Glories of Majestick *Rome*' – a thrilling second line, bearing little relation to the Latin, but one poet responding to another

Learning vocabulary

Albān-us a um Alban, from Alba
fāt-um ī 2n. fate, destiny
iactō 1 I throw/toss about; hurl/toss out
īr-a ae 1f. anger, wrath
Iūnō Iūnōn-is 3f. Juno, wife of king of the gods Jupiter

Latīn-us a um Latin, from Latium
Lati-um ī 2n. Latium
lītus lītor-is 3n. coast, coast-line
memor -is mindful, unforgetting
moeni-a um 3n. pl. (defensive) walls; fortified town
ob + acc. on account/because of
ōr-a ae 1f. shore
super-ī ōrum 2m. pl. gods, powers above; *superum* = gen. pl. *super(ōr)um*
saeu-us a um savage, cruel, vicious
Troi-a ae 1f. the region where Ilium, the city destroyed by Greeks, was situated

angry? And how did Aeneas manage to overcome all this and fulfil his mission? Where one might have expected tub-thumping triumphalism, a far more subdued note is *currently* being heard.

(c) V. alludes to Homer's *Iliad* and *Odyssey* throughout this opening (see *Intro* [10, 16, 25]): *arma* remind us of the wars of the *Iliad*, *uirum* of Odysseus (*andra*, 'man', is the first word of the *Odyssey*), whose trials by land and sea reflect an Odysseus who 'suffered much at sea' (*Odyssey* 1.4). Odysseus, however, struggled to return home; Aeneas *cannot* return home: he must found a new one. The 'land and sea' formula is regularly used to express Rome's control over the whole world. Aeneas may find himself in trouble by land and sea at the moment (cf. 1.280, 598, 756, 2.780–1); but when Rome is founded, it is Rome that will control, and therefore possess, it in its entirety (cf. Venus at 1.235–6).

But *canō* raises a question: Homer appealed to the Muse to sing the story *through* him; V. ('I') does it all himself – or does he? See 8

(d) The fluid word-order of Latin allows a master-poet like V. to play the most wonderful word-games. Enjoy e.g. the emphasis of *Troiae* (1), grammatically 'out of position' but where the epic in fact 'starts', and the blossoming of *Ītaliam*, first word of the next line, the target of the mission, followed at once by *fātō*; the way *īram* is held till the end of 4 – so *that* is what 'savage Juno' is all about; and the sonorous build-up of 6–7, climaxing in *Rōmae*, superbly caught by Dryden. When you have translated the Latin, it is always revealing to go back and ask 'why these words in *this* order?' and appreciate the tension, and sometimes dissonance, between the grammatical structure and apparent displacing of words that allows one word to 'play off' against its neighbours.

See: Otis (1964: 232) on Aeneas' new home; and Hardie (1986: 302ff.) on the 'land and sea' formula.

Crunch (See p. 51): 1–4

1.8–11: *Muse, why did Juno make such a good man suffer?*

Mūsa, mihī causās memorā, quō nūmine laesō,
quidue dolēns, rēgīna deum tot^ uoluere ^cāsūs
īnsignem^ pietāte ^uirum, tot^ adīre ^labōrēs   10
impulerit. tantaene^ animīs caelestibus ^īrae?

8 *Mūs-a ae* 1f. Muse, daughter of Memory (one of the nine Muses in Greek mythology) – but was not V. singing the song himself (1)?

mihī: the last syllable of *mihi* scans long or short (so too *tibi*, *sibi*. See p. 42)

*memorō 1 I say, tell, mention, narrate

quō . . . quidue (**9**): two ind. qs. after *causās* 'because of what . . . or what?'

*nūmen nūmin-is 3n. divine power, godhead, majesty

*laedō 3 *laesī laesum* I damage, injure, offend, wrong; *quō nūmine laesō* is an abl. of cause, '[because of] what majesty [of Juno's] having been offended'

9 *quidue dolēns*: *dolēns* is nom. part., referring to the subject of the ind. q. (*rēgīna de[ōr]um*), and *quid* its obj., 'or grieving *at what*' (for the construction, see **RLR3**, **W**30, **M**94). Note *-ue*

**-ue* or

*rēgīn-a ae 1f. queen

deum = *deōrum*, cf. *superum*, **4**. The 'queen of the gods' is Jupiter's wife, Juno; she has been offended, or is grieving at something. We wait to find out what. The vb. she controls will be a long time coming – *impulerit* (**11**), '[why] did [she]

drive/force'; the object is *īnsignem^ pietāte ^uirum* (**10**), whom she drives to do two things, (i) *tot^ uoluere ^cāsūs*, and (ii) *tot^ adīre ^labōrēs*

*uoluō 3 *uoluī uolūtum* I roll through; set in motion; unfold, relate. Aeneas has to unroll the scroll of destiny, as it were

10 *īnsign-is e famous, distinguished (with reference to, + abl.)

*pietās pietāt-is 3f. respect for gods, men and family; sense of duty; piety; goodness. S. comments on the paradox that if Aeneas is a good man, why does he labour under the hatred of the gods? That is what V. calls on the Muses to explain. *pietās* is the source of our 'pity'; this feeling will be much in evidence as Aeneas attempts to fulfil his mission. See *Intro* [39–42]

11 *impellō 3 *impulī impulsum* I drive, force; here perf. subjunc. in the indir. q. beginning at **8**

animīs caelestibus: dat. of possession, **RL**48.2, **W**Suppl. syntax, **M**10

īrae: poetic pl. for s. Ellipsis of e.g. 'Can there be/Is there such . . . ?' Juno has been offended (**8**); she grieves (**9**); and her grief turns to anger. But we still do not know why

1.8–11: This epic is a fusion of myth with heroic history to uncover the origins of the Roman race (S. says that some ancients called the poem the *gesta populī Rōmānī* – 'deeds of the Roman people'). The 'historian' V. therefore personally sings (1) the outline of what happened – the facts. But no mere historian is privy to the mind of the gods. To solve that problem, V. needs the help of the (divine) Muse. Hence his appeal to her to enable him to explain the *reasons* for it all (*causās*, 8). The result is hard history – the Latin race, the Alban fathers and Rome (6–7). See *Intro* [23]. Observe that V. is getting one up on Homer here. Homer too appealed to the Muse at the start of both his epics, but to tell him absolutely *everything*.

Further vital information is signalled in this part of the proem. Juno has been offended by someone or something; Aeneas is a man of *pietās*; and he has been compelled to confront both *cāsūs* (the products of chance or accident) and *labōrēs* (perhaps in the sense of the labours of Hercules, i.e. disagreeable tasks he cannot evade?). *Pietās* is an important word: it covers 'the right relationship that exists beween a human being and (1) the gods, (2) his family, (3) other human beings; and a man's public responsibilities as citizen or political leader'.

The question at the end of the proem (11) is pure V. – can divinities *really* be so consumed with anger? (Cf. Milton *Paradise Lost* 6.788 'In heavenly spirits could such per-

1.12–18: *Carthage, a city loved by the goddess Juno, was her kingdom, while fate allowed*

urbs antīqua fuit, Tyriī^ tenuēre ^colōnī,
Karthāgō,^ Ītaliam contrā Tiberīnaque* longē
*ōstia, ^dīues opum studiīsque_ ^asperrima bellī;

Learning vocabulary

impellō 3 *impulī impulsum* I drive, force
īnsign-is e famous, distinguished (for/in + abl.)
laedō 3 *laesī laesum* I damage, injure, offend, wrong
memorō 1 I say, tell, mention, narrate
nūmen nūmin-is 3n. divine power/majesty, godhead
pietās pietāt-is 3f. respect for gods, men and family; sense of duty; piety; goodness
rēgīn-a ae 1f. queen
-ue or
uoluō 3 *uoluī uolūtum* I roll through; set in motion; unfold, relate

12 *antīqu-us a um* ancient (often with overtones of 'noble', 'venerable'); it will be 'new' when we first meet it at 417ff. See next note
Tyri-us a um Tyrian, from Tyre. Tyre was one of the most powerful cities in an area the ancients called Phoenicia (roughly modern Lebanon: see on 1.302), famous throughout the Bronze Age for its fleet of trading vessels that transported luxury goods and raw materials for whoever wanted them (e.g. the Israelite King Solomon). This brought Tyre its wealth and influence, but also made it susceptible to powerful land-based

imperialists like the Assyrians, who could blackmail it into serving them. It was to buy off the Assyrians that Tyre had sent its fleet westwards in search of precious metals from the ninth century BC. Spain was a main target, but they settled likely places as stopping-off points *en route*. One such was Carthage, in modern Tunisia (*Āfrica* to the Romans). Its name derives from semitic Qart Hadasht, 'New City', latinised by the Romans into *Karthāgō* (see on 1.366, 522). In time it developed into a powerful city in its own right
colōn-us ī 2m. settler, colonist
13 *Karthāgō Karthāgin-is* 3f. Carthage
contrā . . . longē (adverbial) = 'facing . . . a long way away' (i.e. with much sea between) + acc. (*Ītaliam* and *Tiberīna . . . ōstia*); but (significantly) *contrā* also means 'against', 'in opposition to'
Tiberīn-us a um of the (river) Tiber
14 *ōsti-um ī* 2n. mouth (of a river); here pl. for s. Ostia was the name of Rome's harbour town on the Tiber
dīu-es dīuit-is wealthy, rich
opum: gen. of respect, 'in [respect of] wealth', **RL**L(d)7, **M**9
studiīs: abl. of respect, **RL**L(f)5

---

verseness dwell?') This is not the sort of question Homer in his role as all-knowing, third-person narrator asks (though his characters can ask it). Is it simply rhetorical, i.e. not really expecting an answer? Or is the sophisticated V. putting down a moral or even theodicean 'challenge' here ('theodicy' is a theory about divine justice)? That gods could be prey to unpredictable, all-too-human emotions was taken for granted in Homeric epic, but was not an idea that appealed to Roman philosophers such as the Stoics (who thought the divine rational spirit was good) and Epicureans (who thought gods had no interest in men at all), cf. *Intro* [43] in particular, and [45–50].

See: Anderson (1969: 21) on *pietās*.

1.12–18: V. the 'historian' now fills in the historical background to explain Juno's wrath – that Carthage was her favourite city (15–17), rich and war-like (14), and she was determined it should become the ruler of all nations (17–18), if fate was to allow it (18). We can see the way the argument is about to go, and it is beautifully prompted by the significant juxtaposition of words at 13 – *Karthāgō* immediately followed by *Ītaliam*! Put Carthage and Italy opposite each other and *contrā*, and every Roman would be thinking

quam^ Iūnō fertur ^terram magis omnibus ^ūnam   15
posthabitā* coluisse *Samō; hīc illius arma,
hīc currus fuit; hoc rēgnum dea gentibus esse,
sī quā fāta sinant, iam tum tenditque fouetque.

15 *quam* (picking up Carthage) . . . *ūnam* (= 'alone')
. . . *terram*: obj. of *coluisse*, itself perf. inf. after
Iūnō fertur; *terrīs . . . omnibus* is abl. of
comparison after *magis* (**RL**J5, **W**26/Suppl.
syntax, **M**14); *posthabitā Samō* (**16**) is abl. abs.
(abl. of circumstances; **RL**150–1, **W**24, **M**79–80)
*feror (pass. of *ferō*): I am said (to + inf.)
16 *posthabeō* 2 *posthabuī posthabitum* I hold
inferior, make second
Sam-os f. Samos, a Greek island housing a large,
very old and famous temple of Hērā (Greek name
for Juno). Since *h* at the start of a word does not
count for scansion purposes, one would expect
the *ō* of *Samō* to be elided. But here there is no
elision. The technical term is 'hiatus'. See p. 34
above
hīc: i.e. in Carthage. S. pedantically comments that
V. should have said *illīc*
illius: 'of her (Juno)', 'belonging to her'. Juno is a
military goddess (as is obvious in the *Aeneid*;
images of her regularly feature a spear and
shield). She therefore needs weapons and a
chariot in which to ride to battle. She has to keep
them somewhere
17 *curr-us ūs* 4m. chariot
fuit: acts as the main vb for both *arma* and *currus*.
Multiple subjects commonly take s. vbs in poetry;
S. comments that, where agreement is at stake,
the *nearest* word tends to take precedence (as
here). Note also that, since *h* at the start of a word

does not count in scansion, the *-it* of *fuit* remains
short
hoc . . . esse: acc. and inf. after *dea . . . tenditque
fouetque*. These two vbs. suggest Juno's thoughts
on the matter, expressed in the acc. and inf., i.e.
'this [city] to be a *rēgnum gentibus*', i.e. 'a seat-of-
sovereignty for/over the nations'. Note the tenses
of *tenditque fouetque* – present. V. commonly
uses the present in place of the more logical past
tense (*Intro* [21])
*rēgn-um ī 2n. kingdom, kingship, control,
dominion, territory
18 *quā somehow, by any route; where, by which
route
sinō 3 I allow, permit; note subjunc., representing
more of Juno's thoughts in indirect speech
(**RL**R4, **W**Suppl. syntax, **M**83–4)
tendō 3 I aim, strive (for)
foueō 2 I nurture, cherish

Learning vocabulary

antīqu-us a um ancient (often with connotations of
'noble', 'venerable')
feror I am said (to + inf.): pass. of *ferō*
quā somehow, by any route; where, by which route
rēgn-um ī 2n. kingdom, kingship, control,
dominion, territory
tenuēre = *tenuērunt*
Tyri-us a um Tyrian, from Tyre

'The Punic wars'. The first was fought over control of wealthy Sicily, and mostly at sea
(264–241 BC); the second (218–201 BC) largely in Italy, when Hannibal, whose base was
in mineral-rich southern Spain, famously crossed the Alps. The Punic wars were Rome's
defining moment as a Mediterranean power (Jones and Sidwell [1997]: sections 29–33).
After them, Rome was the master of the western Mediterranean, had the finest citizen
army in the ancient world and made Sicily (241 BC) its first province in an empire
which, at its peak some 350 years later, would stretch from Britain to Syria, the Rhine–
Danube to Egypt and north Africa. Carthage had that ambition (15–18); Rome will
achieve it.

    But what has Roman Juno/Greek Hera got to do with Phoenician Carthage? It was
common in the ancient world to see one's own gods as identical with the gods of other
nations ('syncretism' is the technical term for associating one god with another), and
Juno was associated with Phoenician Tanit. Hannibal made the link, and so did the
Romans. Indeed, during the Punic wars the Romans frantically tried to placate Juno, as
if she had turned against them in favour of Carthage. The earlier epic poet Ennius,

1.19–28: *Juno had heard that a man of Trojan descent would destroy Carthage; and she hated the Trojans anyway, after Paris had insulted her*

prōgeniem* sed enim Troiānō^ ā ^sanguine dūcī
audierat, Tyriās^ ōlim *quae uerteret ^arcēs;   20
hinc populum^ lātē ^rēgem bellōque ^superbum
^uentūrum excidiō Libyae: sīc uoluere Parcās.

19 *prōgeni-ēs ēī* 5f. breed, offspring (i.e. in time, the Romans)
sed enim 'but nevertheless (despite all her hopes/ efforts)'
*Troiān-us a um Trojan
*sangu-is -inis 3m. blood
dūcī: pass. inf. in an acc. (*prōgeniem*) and inf. after *audierat* (**20**) (**RL**98–9, **W**25, **M**82–4)
20 *audierat*: = *audīuerat*. S. approves of the use of *audiō* on the grounds that it gives Juno a reason to believe that things could be changed
*ōlim one day; at some time; long ago
*uertō 3 *uersī uersum* I turn, turn upside down, overthrow; *uerteret* is subjunc. of purpose 'to . . .', regularly introduced with the relative pronoun, **RL**145.3, **M**97.5. When in 29 BC Augustus decided to rebuild Carthage (*Intro* [28]), the top of the city needed to be flattened to provide the base for the new city. The Romans physically sliced off the top of the hill and shovelled down the hillside over 136,000 cubic yards of earth and rubble, as we can tell from the later material spread down it (the evidence is archaeological). *uerteret* indeed!
arcēs: pl. for s.
21 *populum*: subject of continuing acc. and inf. (*uentūrum*, **22**)

*lātē far and wide, broadly (*lāt-us a um* broad, wide)
*rēx rēg-is 3m. king, ruler; here used more as an adj., 'ruling'
*superb-us a um proud, haughty, glorying in (+ abl. of respect). This often has pejorative overtones, especially when referring to people. S. thinks it means 'outstanding, glorious' here. Is this what Juno would say of Romans?
22 *uentūrum* (*esse*): the *esse* of the fut. inf. and perf. pass. inf. is often dropped in poetry (see 'Ellipsis', p. 34 above)
excidi-um ī 2n. destruction; here dat. of purpose 'for the destruction of', 'to destroy' (**RL**88.6, **W**Suppl. syntax)
*Liby-a ae 1f. Libya (= North Africa), used here for 'Carthage'
uoluere: continuing the acc. (*Parcās*) and inf. after what Juno *audierat* (**20**); here used intransitively
Parc-ae ārum 1f. pl. Fates. These were originally goddesses of childbirth (*pariō* 'I bear'), but then (wrongly) identified with the Greek word for Fates, *Moirai*. S. claims that *Parcae* derives from *parcō* 'I spare' on the principle of contradiction, i.e. because they did *not* spare anyone, in the same way that *bellum* (he claims) derives from *bellus*

---

whom V. is following here, also made Juno hostile to Rome (see *Intro* [20]). It is worth adding that Juno had connections too with Italian tribes hostile to Rome in its early years (fourth century BC), e.g. the Veii (Livy 5, 21.3–22.7).

sī quā fāta sinant (18) raises another big issue – the role of 'fate' in the *Aeneid*. V. here reminds us that Juno, divinity though she is, is still subject to it but can do her best to subvert it. See *Intro* on fate generally [45–50] and especially [50].

See: Miles (2010: 24–95) for the rise of Carthage.

Crunch: 12–14

1.19–28: V. has given us the Roman angle on his epic in 1–11 in a proem which hints at Homeric epic; the Carthaginian angle in 12–18 (with nods to Ennius); and now he expands further on the reasons for Juno's wrath by giving us the Trojan angle, i.e. the Trojan war. It is not really a *Homeric* angle, because none of the incidents mentioned in

id metuēns, ueterisque^ memor Sāturnia* ^bellī^,
*prīma ^quod ad Troiam prō cārīs^ gesserat ^Argīs –
necdum etiam causae īrārum saeuīque dolōrēs   25
exciderant animō: manet altā mente repostum^
^iūdicium Paridis sprētaeque^ iniūria ^fōrmae,
et genus inuīsum, et raptī Ganymēdis honōrēs.

because war is *not* beautiful. This is etymological rubbish, like most of S.'s forays into this area, but is significant because it shows how interested the ancients were in what words 'really' meant and where they came from. V. took such word-plays very seriously (see *Intro* [51])

23 *metuō 3 metuī metūtum* I fear, am afraid of (Juno is the subject)

Sāturni-a ae 1f. daughter of Saturn(us), i.e. Juno

24 *prīma quod*: take in order *quod prīma*, and treat *prīma* as 'foremost [enemy]' of the Trojans; *quod* picks up *bellī* and refers to the Trojan war

ad Troiam: 'at Troy'

cār-us a um dear, beloved

Arg-ī ōrum 2m. pl. Argos, an important Greek city, housing (like Samos, **16**) an impressive temple to Juno. V., following Homer, uses 'Argos' and 'Argive' to mean 'Greek', as here. We would now expect to read something like '. . . the furious Juno decided to make life hell for Aeneas and his men'. Instead, we get a long parenthesis (to 28, *honōrēs*) detailing the additional insults she feels she has been paid by the Trojans, detailed in 27–8. See appended discussion, and on 29

25 *necdum* not yet

īrārum . . . dolōrēs: more poetic pl. for s.

26 *excidō 3 excidī* I fall from (+ abl.), escape, slip out

manet: s., but has four subjects in **26–7**!

altā mente: local abl., 'in . . .'

repost-us a um stored away (syncopated form of *repositus*, 4th p.p. of *repōnō*)

27 *iūdici-um ī* 2n. judgement

Paris Parid-is 3m. Paris; the young Trojan prince who, asked to choose the most beautiful of Juno (Hera), Minerva (Athena) and Venus (Aphrodite), selected Venus (Aeneas' mother)

and incurred the undying fury of the two other divinities (*Intro* [16])

spernō 3 sprēuī sprētum I spurn, reject

iniūri-a ae 1f. insult, injustice

fōrm-a ae 1f. beauty, shape, form; a genitive of respect

28 *inuīs-us a um* hated, loathed, despised. This may be because the Trojan race was sprung from Dardanus, a son of Jupiter not by Juno but by Electra; or it might be a general exclamation of disgust on Juno's part – 'how I hate them all!' (Henry (1873))

Ganymēd-ēs is 3m. Ganymede, the handsome young Trojan youth snatched up (*raptī*) by Jupiter to be his cup-bearer in heaven

honōrēs: i.e. the honouring of Ganymede (instead of Juno) by Jupiter

Learning vocabulary

Arg-ī ōrum 2m. pl. Argos, an important Greek city; Greece

cār-us a um dear, beloved

excidō 3 excidī I fall from, escape, slip out (+ abl.)

inuīs-us a um hated, loathed, despised

lātē far and wide, broadly (*lāt-us a um* broad, wide)

Liby-a ae 1f. Libya (= North Africa)

metuō 3 metuī metūtum I fear, am afraid of

ōlim one day; at some time; long ago

rēx rēg-is 3m. king, ruler

sangu-is -inis 3m. blood

Sāturni-a ae 1f. daughter of Saturn(us), i.e. Juno

superb-us a um proud, haughty, glorying in (often pejorative)

Troiān-us a um Trojan

uertō 3 uersī uersum I turn, turn upside down, overthrow

27–8 are central to Homer's version of the war in the *Iliad*. The reason is that the war is being seen through the narrowed eyes of Juno, whose interests are not Homeric. She is concerned about the resentments the war generated in her, in particular, the insults paid to her sexual attractiveness. Indeed, the parenthesis at 25–8, especially *memor*, seems almost to represent her own unfolding thoughts and rising fury, climaxing with the observation that Jupiter even prefers a *boy* to her, and a Trojan one at that – and she, wife of the king of the gods (cf. 46–7)! The point is that, fearful as she is for her beloved

1.29–33: *So she harried the Trojans constantly, making the founding of Rome a tremendous struggle*

hīs accēnsa super, iactātōs^ aequore tōtō

^Trōas, ^rēliquiās Dana<u>um</u> atque immītis Achillī,   30

arcēbat longē Latiō, multōsque^ per ^annōs

29 *hīs . . . super*: 'by these things . . . on top of everything else'. We now return from the parenthesis to Juno's fears at 24 and the consequences

accendō 3 *accendī accēnsum* I inflame, set on fire

super in addition (adverbial)

*aequor -is 3m. sea, ocean (often calm, cf. *aequus*); local abl., 'over . . .'

30 *Trōs Trojan (Greek declension: *Trōas* here is acc. pl., obj. of *arcēbat* **31**)

rēliqui-ae ārum 1f. pl. remnants, survivors; in apposition to *Trōas*

*Dana-ī ōrum 2m. pl. Greeks; note gen. pl. *Dana(ōr)*

um, with *reliquiās* meaning 'those remnants/ survivors of, i.e. left by, the Greeks'. Danaus was an Egyptian, father of fifty daughters (the Danaids). They all fled to Argos in Greece so that his daughters could escape marriage to their fifty cousins. We do not know exactly how *Danaoi* (Greek)/*Danaī* came to mean 'Greeks'. Aeschylus' tragedy *Supplices* ('Suppliants', Greek *Hiketides*) treats the story

immīt-is is cruel, merciless

**Achill-ēs is/ī* 3m. Achilles, the most powerful and terrifying Greek hero of the Trojan war

31 *arceō 2 *arcuī* I keep at a distance, ward off

Latiō: abl. of separation, 'from'

Carthage (*metuēns* 23), at least she might be able to do something about that (cf. *sī quā* 18). But she can do nothing about these old insults – they are a matter of record, stored up *altā mente* (26) and still fiercely felt (*īra, saeuus, dolor*, 25). Only revenge will satisfy her. That, at least, is a very Homeric motif. Juno is *memor* indeed (4). Nevertheless, she will not win: Rome *will* overcome Carthage, as *sīc uoluere Parcās* (22) makes clear. Rome will eventually fulfil its *historical* destiny.

See: Lyne (1987: 62–5) for 'Homeric' revenge; and Horsfall 'Dido in the Light of History' in S.J Harrison (1990: 130) on Rome's historical destiny.

Crunch: 19–22

1.29–33: So ends the prologue to the *Aeneid*. In sketching the final destination (Rome), V. has established the great theme. In sketching the route (Lavinium – Alba Longa – Rome), he has reconciled myth with history (see *Intro* [18]). In sketching the background, he has both introduced the Carthaginian and Trojan/Homeric dimension and established the reason for the struggle – Juno's anger (summarised in the magnificent, sonorous final line of the prologue *tantae mōlis . . .*, a *mōlis* brought about by Juno's anti-historical determination that Rome will never emerge). Meanwhile, it is made clear that the whole enterprise is being shaped by *fātum* (*Intro* [50]) and that the man at the centre of it is distinguished for his *pietās*.

In these last five lines, V. summarises the main strands of the action and brings us up to the point where the narrative can begin – Juno's anger (*accēnsa*), Ilium's destruction and Trojan exile (*rēliquiās*), Juno's determination to do what she can to frustrate *fātum* (*arcēbat*), resulting in the Trojans wandering (*errābant*), but doing so under fate's control (*āctī fātīs*) i.e. all part of the *ultimate* divine plan, whatever Juno's interventions. The last line points to the massive burden one man will bear. Will a man of *pietās* be up to it? Will *pietās* be enough?

errābant, āctī fātīs, maria omnia circum.
tantae mōlis erat Rōmānam^ condere ^gentem.

---

32 *errābant*: Trojans are the subject

*circum + acc. around (here controlling *maria omnia*)

33 **mōl-ēs is* 3f. undertaking, burden; huge structure; mass, lump. Here the gen. is one of general value or cost: 'To found the Roman race was [at the cost of] such a huge burden', cf. RLL(d)5, **M**9

*condō 3 *condere condidī conditum* I found, build, bury

Learning vocabulary

Achill-ēs is/ī 3m. Achilles

aequor -is 3m. sea, ocean (often calm)

arceō 2 *arcuī* I keep at a distance, ward off

circum + acc. around

condō 3 *condere condidī conditum* I found, build, bury

Dana-ī ōrum 2m. pl. Greeks

mōl-ēs is 3f. undertaking, burden; huge structure; mass, lump

Trōs Trojan (Greek declension: *Trōes* nom. pl., *Trōas* acc. pl.)

Further, V. has brought into play some of the key nations who will be part of the mostly eastern, and so to a Roman slightly worrying, 'mix' that, over a thousand years or so, will emerge as noble 'Romans': Trojans, Carthaginians, Greeks and Italians.

See: on the peoples that will eventually make up Rome, Reed (2007: 8–10).

Learning vocabulary for Section 1.1–33

Achill-ēs is/ī 3m. Achilles

aequor -is 3m. sea, ocean

Albān-us a um Alban, from Alba

antīqu-us a um ancient (often with overtones of 'noble, 'venerable')

arceō 2 *arcuī* I keep at a distance, ward off

Arg-ī ōrum 2m. pl. Argos, an important Greek city; Greece

cār-us a um dear, beloved

circum + acc. around

condō 3 *condere condidī conditum* I found, build, bury

Dana-ī ōrum 2m. pl. Greeks

excidō 3 *excidī* I fall from, escape, slip out (+ abl.)

fāt-um ī 2n. fate, destiny

feror I am said (to + inf.): pass. of *ferō*

iactō 1 I throw/toss about; hurl/toss out

impellō 3 *impulī impulsum* I drive, force

īnsign-is e famous, distinguished (for/in + abl.)

inuīs-us a um hated, loathed, despised

īr-a ae 1f. anger, wrath

Iūnō Iūnōn-is Juno, wife of king of the gods Jupiter

laedō 3 *laesī laesum* I damage, injure, offend, wrong

lātē far and wide, broadly (*lāt-us a um* broad, wide)

Latīn-us a um Latin, from Latium

Lati-um ī 2n. Latium

Liby-a ae 1f. Libya (= north Africa)

lītus lītor-is 3n. coast, coast-line

memor -is mindful, unforgetting

memorō 1 I say, tell, mention, narrate

metuō 3 *metuī metūtum* I fear, am afraid of

moeni-a um 3n. pl. (defensive) walls; fortified town

mōl-ēs is 3f. undertaking, burden; huge structure; mass, lump

nūmen nūmin-is 3n. divine power/majesty, godhead

ob + acc. on account/because of

ōr-a ae 1f. shore

pietās pietāt-is 3f. respect for gods, men and family; sense of duty; piety; goodness

quā somehow, by any route, where, by which route

rēgīn-a ae 1f. queen

rēgn-um ī 2n. kingdom, kingship, control, dominion, territory

*rēx rēg-is 3m. king, ruler

saeu-us a um savage, cruel, vicious

sangu-is -inis 3m. blood

Sāturni-a ae 1f. daughter of Saturn(us), i.e. Juno

superb-us a um proud, haughty, glorying in (often pejorative)

super-ī ōrum 2m. pl. gods, powers above; *superum*
  = gen. pl. *super(ōr)um*
tenuēre = *tenuērunt*
Troi-a ae 1f. Troy, the region of Ilium, the city
  destroyed by Greeks
Troiān-us a um Trojan
Trōs Trojan (Greek declension: *Trōes* nom. pl.,
  Trōas acc.)

Tyri-us a um Tyrian, from Tyre
-ue or
uertō 3 *uersī uersum* I turn, turn upside down,
  overthrow
uoluō 3 *uoluī uolūtum* I roll through; set in motion;
  unfold, relate

Study Section for 1.1–33

1. *memorem . . . īram* (4) – demonstrate the full significance of this point, with examples.
2. *tantae mōlis . . .* how far do 1–33 support this claim?
3. *canō* (1) also means 'I prophesy'. Can that meaning have any intelligible resonance here?
4. Scan 29–33.
5. Here are the proems of Homer's *Iliad* and *Odyssey*, sources or models on which V. drew heavily. But *how* heavily? Use the appended questions to explore similarities and differences:

Wrath – sing, goddess, (the wrath) of Peleus' son Achilles,
Accursed (wrath), that placed unnumbered agonies on the Greeks,
And dispatched to Hades many mighty souls
Of heroes, and made them prey for dogs
And a feast for birds, and Zeus's plan was fulfilled,   5
From when the two first split in conflict –
Agamemnon, lord of men, and godlike Achilles.
Which, then, of the gods brought the two together to fight?
Leto's and Zeus's son, Apollo. For he, angered at the king,
sent an evil plague throughout the army, and the people perished . . .   10
Homer, Iliad 1.1–10

The man – tell me, Muse of (the man) of many turns, who very far
Was driven, when he had sacked Troy's holy citadel.
Many men's cities he saw, and knew their minds,
Many agonies he suffered at sea in his heart,
Trying to win his life and return of his companions.   5
But even so he did not save his companions, though desiring to:
For they destroyed themselves by their own recklessness,
Fools, who consumed the cattle of Hyperion the sun
And he removed from them their day of return.
From some point, goddess, daughter of Zeus, tell us these things too.   10
Homer, Odyssey 1.1–10

(a) The first word of the *Aeneid* is *arma*. To what extent does that actually hint at the proem of the *Iliad*, if at all? Look at Achilles and consider whether an Iliadic start would be appropriate for the *Aeneid*.

(b) Trace the correspondences between the proem of the *Odyssey* and *Aeneid* 1–11. Is the *Aeneid* more Odyssean than Iliadic at this point? If so, why?

(c) How different in tone is the *Aeneid* proem? Consider e.g. pathos, politics, death/experience/suffering.

(d) Both Homeric proems and *Aeneid* 1.1–33 concern a man and god(s): what is the difference between what they are all trying to do? Consider the 'theology' involved, especially 'fate'.

See: Jones (1988) on *Odyssey* 1.1–10, and Jones (2003) on *Iliad* 1.1–7.

6. The magnificent proem to Milton's *Paradise Lost*, talking of Adam and Eve's sin (1–4) and Christ's redemption (4–5), is deeply influenced by classical proems – what are the similarities and differences?

> Of man's first disobedience, and the fruit
> Of that forbidden tree, whose mortal taste
> Brought death into the world, and all our woe,
> With loss of Eden, till one greater man
> Restore us, and regain the blissful seat,   5
> Sing, heavenly muse . . .
> [*More detail here of the nature of the Christian muse and its inspiration*]
> Say first, for heaven hides nothing from thy view,
> Nor the deep tract of hell, say first what cause
> Moved our grand parents in that happy state,
> Favoured of heaven so highly, to fall off   30
> From their creator, and transgress his will
> For one restraint, lords of the world besides?
> Who first seduced them to that foul revolt?
> The infernal serpent; he it was, whose guile . . .

Milton, Paradise Lost 1.1–6, 27–34

See: Jones (1999: 103–12), where Homer's and Virgil's proems and Milton's proem to *Paradise Lost* are discussed, with Pope's *Rape of the Lock*.

1.34–123: Storm at sea

In this Section, Juno decides to destroy Aeneas' fleet. She bribes the wind-god Aeolus to unleash storm-force gales, which sink one ship and scatter the rest of the fleet.

1.34–41: *As the Trojans leave Sicily, Juno remembers how Minerva treated her beloved Greeks, and decides to act*

uix ē cōnspectū Siculae tellūris in altum
uēla dabant laetī, et spūmās salis aere ruēbant,　　　　　　　　35
cum Iūnō, aeternum^ seruāns sub pectore ^uulnus,
haec sēcum: 'mēne^ inceptō dēsistere ^uictam,
nec posse Ītaliā Teucrōrum^ āuertere ^rēgem?

34 *uix* scarcely, hardly
cōnspect-us ūs 4m. sight
Sicul-us a um Sicilian. See *Intro* [33] for Aeneas' travels after the fall of Troy
tellūs tellūr-is 3f. land
35 *uēl-a ōrum* 2n. pl. sails, canvas; *uēla dō* 1 I set sail
laetī: 'the happy [men]', subject
spūm-a ae 1f. foam, froth
sal -is 3m. salt, sea; hear the hissing in *spūmās salis*
aes aer-is 3n. bronze; this refers to the bronze-covered prow of the ship (an anachronism: Homeric ships did not have them, but Roman ships did; cf. on 182 and see *Intro* [23]). '(Churning the foam) of the salt with the bronze' is typical 'poetic' diction, using prosaic words in a special sense (metonymy)
ruō 3 *ruī rutum* I drive ahead, churn; rush
36 *cum*: 'inverted' *cum* ('when') clause, **RLT**(e)3, **M**122, cf. **W**31

aetern-us a um eternal
pectus pector-is 3n. chest, breast
37 *haec sēcum*: ellipsis of 'said', 'thought'
mē . . . dēsistere: acc. and inf., used to express outrage, shock or desperation, as if the speaker had begun 'Who would think *that* I (*mē*) should *dēsistere* . . .'
-ne attached to *mē* turns it into a question
incept-um ī 2n. attempt, plan, designs
dēsistō 3 I abandon, give up on (+ abl. of separation)
38 *nec posse*: continuing the acc. and inf. '. . . and not be able'
Ītaliā: i.e. *dē Ītaliā* (S.)
Teucr-ī ōrum 2m. Trojans; Teucer was one of the first kings of Troy
āuertō 3 *āuertī āuersum* I divert X (acc.) from Y (abl.), turn back/away
rēgem: Aeneas. S. comments that Juno would feel she was honouring someone so inferior to herself by naming him

---

1.34–41: The narrative begins with things apparently going very well for Aeneas' men (*laetī*, 35). They have left Sicily and are on the last leg 'home' for Italy; the ship is racing along (35); they are clearly revelling in their apparent control of nature (*ruēbant*: they are not actually *doing* this, only causing it to be done – but it *feels* to them as if they are). But always be on the look-out when V. says things are going well. They can have a way of turning nasty fairly soon and in this case, very soon – with *cum Iūnō* 36, 'Gathering her brows like gathering storm, Nursing her wrath (*seruāns*) to keep it warm' (Burns, *Tam O'Shanter*, 11–12). Juno is determined not to be baffled by fate (cf. 18, 22) – having

quippe uetor fātīs. Pallasne̲ exūrere classem
Argīuu̲m atque̲ ipsōs potuit summergere pontō,   40
ūnius^ ob ^noxa̲m et furiās Aiācis Oīle̅ī?'

1.42–9: 'Minerva smashed Ajax's ships and killed him – is no one left to worship me, queen of the gods?'

'ipsa^ Iouis rapidum* ^iaculāta̲ e̅ nūbibus *ignem,
disiēcitque ratēs, e̅uertitque̲ aequora uentīs,

39 *quippe* of course! The reason is that! (used here with indignant irony)
uetō 1 I forbid, prevent
Pallas Pallad-is/os* 3f. Pallas Athena, (Roman) Minerva; she is subject of *potuit* (40**). 'Pallas' is an epithet used forty-seven times of Athena by Homer, but it is not clear what it means: perhaps 'lady/mistress'
exūrō 3 *exussī exustum* I burn up, destroy by fire
**class-is is* 3m. fleet
40 **Argīu-ī ōrum* 2m. pl. the Greeks (see on *Argī*, 24); here gen. pl. *Argīu(ōr)um* cf. note on *superōrum*, 4
ipsōs: i.e. the Greeks themselves
**summergō* 3 *summersī summersum* I sink, submerge X (acc.) under Y (abl.)
**pont-us ī* 2m. sea
41 *ūnius*: i.e. Ajax
nox-a ae 1f. guilt
furi-ae ārum 1f. pl. mad passion; it explains *noxam*
Aiāx Oīleus, Aiāc-is Oīlē̅ī 3m. Ajax, son of Oileus; he raped the Trojan prophetess Cassandra at the shrine of Minerva in Ilium where she was seeking protection (see on 2.403)

Learning vocabulary
aes aer-is 3n. bronze
aetern-us a um eternal, everlasting
Argīu-ī ōrum 2m. pl. the Greeks
āuertō 3 *āuertī āuersum* I divert X (acc.) from Y (abl.), turn back/away/round (trans. and intrans.)

class-is is 3m. fleet
cōnspect-us ūs 4m. sight
Pallas Pallad-is/os 3f. Pallas Athena, (Roman) Minerva
pectus pector-is 3n. chest, breast
pont-us ī 2m. sea
ruō 3 *ruī rutum* I drive ahead, churn; rush
sal -is 3m. salt, sea
summergō 3 *summersī summersum* I sink, submerge X (acc.) under (+ abl.)
tell-ūs ūris 3f. land
Teucr-ī ōrum 2m. pl. Trojans
uēla dō 1 *dedī datum* I set sail
uēl-a ōrum 2n. pl. sails, canvas
uix scarcely, hardly

42 *ipsa*: Minerva. S. emphasises the *ipsa*, pointing out that revenge served up by your own hand is very sweet (as it was here for Minerva), but Juno will have to use Aeolus to smash Aeneas' fleet (50ff.)
Iouis: famed for his thunderbolt
**rapid-us a um* violent, swift, consuming (cf. *rapiō*)
iaculor 1 dep. I throw (understand *est*)
**nūb-ēs is* 3f. cloud (ancients thought lightning came from the collision of clouds, S.)
43 **disiciō* 3 *disiēcī disiectum* I scatter, shatter, disperse. Note the first *i = y*, as if *disyēcit* (hence the scansion)
rat-is is 3f. raft, ship (a demeaning word, S.)
**ēuertō* 3 *ēuertī ēuersum* I churn up; overthrow

begun, *inceptō* 37, she will finish – and justifies herself with reference to Minerva, who smashed her beloved Greeks (cf. *cārīs* 24) because of Ajax's *noxa* and *furiae* (41). Since Ajax's crime was sexual, it fits her case neatly; presumably she is thinking in particular of Paris' treatment of her (27). Anything Minerva can do, she can do better.

See: on Juno, Feeney (1991: 130–5).

Crunch: 34–7

1.42–9: Minerva took revenge on Ajax son of Oileus for insulting her shrine, and took it when he was at sea. Juno describes how she did it: enlisting Jupiter's help with his

illum exspīrantem trānsfīxō pectore flammās,
turbine corripuit, scopulōque^ īnfīxit ^acūtō.   45
ast ego, quae dīuum incēdō rēgīna, Iouisque
et soror et coniūnx, ūnā^ cum ^gente tot annōs
bella gerō! et quisquam nūmen Iūnōnis adōrat
praetereā, aut supplex ārīs impōnet honōrem?'

44 *illum*: Ajax, obj. of *corripuit* (**45**)

exspīrō 1 I breathe X (acc.) out from Y (abl.)
  (*flammās* is the obj. – he is on fire!)

trānsfīgō 3 *trānsfīxī trānsfīxum* I impale

45 **turbō turbin-is* 3m. whirlwind

*corripiō 3 *corripuī correptum* I snatch up, seize

*scopul-us ī 2m. rock (local abl.)

īnfīgō 3 *īnfīxī īnfīxum* I impale (understand 'Ajax' as
  obj.)

acūt-us a um sharp

46 *ast* but

*dīu-ī ōrum 2m. gods (*dīuum = dīu(ōr)um*)

rēgīna . . . soror (**47**) *. . . coniūnx*: all in apposition to
  ego. Juno indicates how dishonoured she feels
  that Minerva should get her way while she, for all
  her status and authority, cannot

*incēdō 3 *incessī incessum* I move, come, advance
  (often connotes stately entry)

47 **soror -is* 3f. sister

*coniūnx coniug-is 3f., m. wife, husband

ūnā . . . gente: i.e. the Trojans

tot annōs: acc. of time throughout

48 *quisquam*: careful – this is not *quis* (**RL176**,
  M28)

Iūnōnis: prouder than 'my' (and so suggesting the
  greater loss of dignity and respect that her failure
  will entail)

adōrō 1 I worship

49 *praetereā* besides, in the future

*supplex supplic-is 3m. suppliant, one coming to
  supplicate/beg help from (here in apposition to
  quisquam)

ārīs: local abl.

*impōnō 3 *imposuī impositum* I lay, place (careful
  with the tense!). Some manuscripts write *adōret*
  (**48**) and *impōnat*. What forms are they, and what
  difference would (hint!) they make? Do you
  prefer them? Think of Juno's current state of
  mind

Learning vocabulary

coniūnx coniug-is 3f., m. wife, husband

corripiō 3 *corripuī correptum* I snatch up, seize

disiciō 3 *disiēcī disiectum* I scatter, shatter

dīu-ī ōrum 2m. gods

ēuertō 3 *ēuertī ēuersum* I churn up, overthrow

impōnō 3 *imposuī impositum* I lay, place (on)

incēdō 3 *incessī incessum* I move, come, advance
  (often used of stately entry)

nūb-ēs is 3f. cloud

rapid-us a um violent, swift, consuming

scopul-us ī 2m. rock

soror -is 3f. sister

supplex supplic-is 3m. suppliant, one coming to
  supplicate/beg help from

turbō turbin-is 3m. whirlwind

lightning/thunderbolt (42), burning and smashing the Greek fleet (43) and targeting Ajax for special treatment (44–5). This is not how *Odyssey* 4.499–511 originally described the incident, but Juno is not a Homerist and has her own agenda in describing Minerva's action as she does (cf. Euripides *Trojan Women*, 77) – for she plans to do roughly the same. Her resentments at the treatment of one of her divine status (cf. on **1.19–28**) rise to the surface again (46–7 are especially grand; note the 'stately . . . majesty of movement' of *incēdō* 46, Page (1894)); again she justifies her behaviour, this time by arguing that (i) unlike Minerva, who was basically pro-Greek and simply engaged in a one-off assault on them, she had been waging war against the Trojans for years (*tot annōs* 47), and (ii) her inability to demonstrate her power by imposing her will would result in a collapse of her worship (48–9). Ancient gods survived only as long as their cult was maintained.

Crunch: 42–5

1.50–7: *Juno reaches Aeolia, where Aeolus keeps the howling storm winds under control*

tālia flammātō^ sēcum dea ^corde uolūtāns,   50
nimbōr̲um̲ in patriam, loca fēta furentibus Austrīs,
Aeoliam uenit. hīc uastō^ rēx Aeolus ^antrō
luctantēs uentōs tempestātēsque sonōrās
imperiō premit ac uinclīs et carcere frēnat.
illī̲ indignantēs magnō cum murmure montis   55
circum claustra fremunt; celsā^ sedet Aeolus ^arce
scēptra tenēns, mollitqu̲e̲ animōs et temperat īrās.

50 *flammō* 1 I inflame
*cor cord-is 3n. heart
uolūtō 1 I turn over, revolve
51 **nimb-us ī* 2m. cloud
loc-a ōrum 2n. pl.: a common form of *locus*, often suggesting 'region'
*fēt-us a um teeming, fertile, pregnant
*furō 3 *furuī* I rage
*Auster Austr-ī 2m. south wind; used here to represent not any wind but *storm* winds of particular ferocity (abl. of association)
52 *Aeoli-a ae* 1f. Aeolia (= *in Aeoliam*)
*uast-us a um huge, vast
*Aeol-us ī 2m. Aeolus, lord of the winds
antr-um ī 2n. cave(rn) (local abl.)
53 *luctor* 1 dep. I struggle, brawl
*tempestās tempestāt-is 3f. storm, tempest
sonōr-us a um loud, howling
54 **uinc(u)l-um ī* 2n. chain, binding
carcer -is 3m. prison
frēnō 1 I restrain, control
55 *indignor* 1 dep. I complain, protest
*murmur -is 3m. murmuring, humming

56 **claustr-a ōrum* 2n. cage, prison; bolts, bars
*fremō 3 *fremuī fremitum* I roar, howl, rage
cels-us a um high (local abl.)
57 **scēptr-um ī* 2n. sceptre, rod (often = power, kingdom; here pl. for s.)
molliō 4 I soothe
temperō 1 I moderate, control

Learning vocabulary

Aeol-us ī 2m. Aeolus, lord of the winds
Auster Austr-ī 2m. south wind
claustr-a ōrum 2n. cage, prison; bolts, bars
cor cord-is 3n. heart
fēt-us a um teeming, fertile, pregnant
fremō 3 *fremuī fremitum* I roar, howl, rage
furō 3 *furuī* I rage
murmur -is 3m. murmuring, humming
nimb-us ī 2m. cloud
scēptr-um ī 2n. sceptre, rod (= power, kingdom)
tempestās tempestāt-is 3f. storm, tempest
uast-us a um huge, vast
uinc(u)l-um ī 2n. chain, binding

1.50–7: As Minerva summoned Jupiter's help to deal with Ajax (42), Juno will summon that of the wind-god, Aeolus, to deal with Aeneas. One wonders what hold she has on him, if any. Juno's heart (*flammātō* 50) seems also as transfixed by fire as poor Ajax's (44) – though her fiery nature is already evident (29) – and a place where the storm-winds rage (51) seems especially appropriate to her mood (Robert Burns' 'gathering storm' indeed); so is the storm-winds' frustration at being kept locked up and unable to wreak the damage they crave. Commentators remark on the alliterative and metrical effects of 53–6 – the 'massy' power of the struggling spondees of 53 and 55 (Page (1894)), and the alliteration of *i*, *m* and *c* in 54–6. The winds seem almost like wild animals in a cage, roaring and howling, needing control and soothing (57); an image of horses at the starting-gates eager for the off has also been suggested (see on 63), or of prisoners in prison (see further on **1.58–64** below).

Aeolus is king of the winds (not storm-winds) in Homer (*Odyssey* 10.1–79) and, far from sitting guard like a despot over the winds making sure they behave (56, see Cong.,

1.58–64: *Destruction would have ensued had Jupiter not put Aeolus in charge to keep them in check*

nī faciat, mari̯a ac terrās caelumque profundum
quippe ferant rapidī, sēcum uerrantque per aurās.
sed pater omnipotēns^ spēluncīs abdidit ātrīs,   60
hoc ^metuēns, mōlemqu̯e et montīs īnsuper altōs
imposuit, rēgemque dedit, quī^ foedere certō
et premer̯e et laxās* scīret dare ^iussus *habēnās.
ad quem tum Iūnō supplex hīs uōcibus ūs̯a est:

58 *nī = nisi*; note subjunc. *faciat*. (See **RL**139, 173, **W**33, **M**115–17)

profund-us a um deep

59 *quippe* surely, otherwise (take with *nī faciat*)

ferant: note subjunc. and cf. *faciat*

rapidī: nom. pl. m.; understand 'winds'

uerrō 3 I sweep along (objects in **58**); note mood again

aur-a ae 1f. heaven, upper air; breeze; breath

60 *omnipotēns omnipotent-is* all-powerful (i.e. Jupiter)

spēlunc-a ae 1f. cave (local abl.)

*abdō 3 abdidī abditum I hide, conceal

*āter ātr-a um black, dark

61 *mōlem et montīs*: 'a mass and mountains', hendiadys (see **Glossary of literary terms**) = 'massive mountains'

62 *foedus foeder-is* 3n. charter, condition, treaty (abl. of cause)

63 *lax-us a um* free, loose

scīret: subjunc. of characteristic after *quī* (**62**), '[the sort of person] who should know . . .' (**RL**140.1, **RLQ**2(a), **W**38, **M**100); *sciō* + inf. (*dare*) = 'know how to'

dare: the final *e* does not elide because *iussus = yussus*

iussus: 'having been ordered' – but by whom? This will become an important issue

habēn-a ae 1f. rein (cf. *habeō*, 'I hold') – the winds are metaphorically thought of as a team of horses

Learning vocabulary

abdō 3 *abdidī abditum* I hide, conceal

āter ātr-a um black, dark

nī = nisi

Page (1894)), he is a most civilised fellow. He entertains Odysseus and his men for a whole month, and gives him the winds tied up in a leather bag to help them home – all except the west wind which will blow him gently on his way. They are almost within sight of home (cf. 34–5) when the men, thinking the bag contains treasure, open it up, the winds leap out and drive them and a despairing Odysseus back to Aeolus, who refuses to help them any more. This offers a good example of the way V. takes a story in Homer and completely re-works it: the only points of comparison are that in both epics Aeolus is the god of winds, put in charge by Zeus/Jupiter.

See: on 54–6, Williams (1972) and Cong. *ad loc.*; Jones (1988: 90) on the civilised Aeolus.

Crunch: 55–7

1.58–64: Aeolus is sitting, as it were, on a volcano, a natural force of such tremendous power that it could sweep away heaven and earth (58–9). To point up the potential danger of the situation, V. explains that even Jupiter was terrified of the winds (*metuēns* 61) and therefore placed them underground, heaping a huge mountain over them. That suggests an image of the monstrous giants buried deep under the earth by Zeus, with mountains heaped on top, in punishment for taking the side of Zeus's father Cronus in the battle to decide who was to be king of the gods (cf. Hesiod *Theogony* 853–80 on the giant Typhoeus, source of ferocious winds, 'creating havoc for

1.65–70: 'My enemies are sailing for Italy; smash them'

'Aeole – namque tibī dīuum pater atque hominum rēx   65
et mulcēre dedit flūctūs et tollere uentō –
gēns^ inimīca mihī Tyrrhēnum nāuigat aequor,
Īlium in Ītaliam ^portāns uictōsque penātēs:
incute uim uentīs summersāsque^ obrue ^puppēs,
aut age dīuersōs, et dissice corpora pontō.'   70

65 *Aeole*: it is flattering to be personally named by a god so superior (S., see on *rēgem* 38)

tibi; indir. obj. after *dedit* (**66**) 'granted [to] you [the power/duty] to . . .' *Did* he?

dīuum = dīu(ōr)um

66 **mulceō* 2 I calm

dedit: 'granted [the power to]' + inf.

*flūct-us ūs 4m. wave

67 *Tyrrhēn-us a um* Tyrrhenian, Etruscan (the sea is to the immediate west of Italy)

68 **Īli-um ī* 2n. Ilium; this is the name of the town besieged by the Greeks (hence Homer's *Iliad*); *Troia* is strictly the name of the region or its inhabitants/people

portō 1 I carry. The tone is contemptuous, almost suggesting 'carting'

*penāt-ēs um 3m. Penates, Roman household gods. Note that Juno says they are *uictōs* – so Aeolus need have no fear of them (S.); since Aeneas is also carting Ilium into Italy, he is also upsetting the 'natural' order of things

69 *incutiō* 3 I strike, hurl, throw X (acc.) into Y (dat.)

*obruō 3 I overwhelm, bury, sink

*pupp-is is 3f. stern, poop; ship

70 *age dīuersōs*: 'drive [understand 'the sailors', acc. pl. m.] [so that they are] *dīuersōs*'

*dīuers-us a um scattered

dissice: imper. from *disiciō*

pontō: local abl.

See: on *portō*, Lyne (1989: 60).

Learning vocabulary

dīuers-us a um scattered

flūct-us ūs 4m. wave

Īli-um ī 2n. Ilium (the town besieged by the Greeks; *Troia* is the region or the inhabitants/people)

mulceō 2 *mulsī mulsum* I calm

obruō 3 *obruī obrutum* I overwhelm, bury, sink

penāt-ēs um 3m. Penates, household gods

pupp-is is 3f. stern, poop; ship

---

men as they rush across the misty sea, evil, raging'). Further, Aeolus was placed in charge by Jupiter on strict conditions (*foedere certō* 62) – to release them only when ordered (*iussus* 63). One assumes Jupiter means 'when ordered *by Jupiter*' – but that is not what it says. The point, however, is this: these are not your ordinary winds. They are Beaufort scale 12 hurricanes which Aeolus cannot simply unleash when the whim takes him.

But Juno needs Aeolus' help. So, having just expressed the wish that more humans should supplicate her (49), she prepares to supplicate him (64). Even Juno is prepared to abase herself if it means she can get what she wants.

See: on Typhoeus, Hardie (1986); and Jones (2003) on *Iliad* 2.783.

1.65–70: As S. points out, Juno must do four things to get her way: show her request is possible (64–5), give a satisfactory reason for it (66–8), make the demand (69–70) and offer a bribe (71–5). Juno starts with a flattering lie: Jupiter has granted Aeolus the power to raise and calm storms. This is not true: as we have already seen, he can do so only when *iussus* – by someone else (*presumably* Jupiter). But Juno is softening Aeolus up. At 65–6 she tells Aeolus her problem, inviting his sympathy (all ancients understood about revenge) and suggesting that Aeneas is an easy target (see notes *ad loc.*). Then

1.71–5: 'I shall give you Deiopea as your wife'

'sunt mihi bis septem praestantī corpore nymphae,
quārum quae fōrmā pulcherrima Dēiopēa,
cōnūbiō^ iungam ^stabilī propriamque dicābō,
omnīs^ ut tēcum meritīs prō tālibus ^annōs
exigat, et pulchrā^ faciat tē* ^prōle *parentem.'   75

---

71 *sunt mihi*: 'there are to me' i.e. I have (**RL**48.2, **RL**88.1(b); **W**Suppl. syntax; **M**10)

**bis* twice

praestāns praestant-is outstanding (abl. of description)

**nymph-a ae* 1f. young woman, nymph

72 *quārum . . .*: take in order *quārum Dēiopēa, quae pulcherrima fōrmā [est] . . .*

Dēiopē-a ae 1f. name of a nymph (five syllables)

73 *cōnūbi-um ī* 2n. marriage. Treat the noun for metrical purposes here as *cōnūbyum*. Note that *cōnūby-ō* does not lose its final -ō because the initial *i-* of *iungam* is consonantal (*yungam . . .* cf. 'junction').

iungō* 3 *iūnxī iūnctum* I join, yoke, unite (in + abl.). The obj. is *Dēiopēa* (so what case and form should she be?). She has been attracted into the nom. by the *quae* clause of **72. V. is playing on the name

Iūnō here. She was goddess of marriage, and her name was often taken by the ancients to be connected with *iungō*

stabil-is e steady, permanent, firm (abl. of manner)

propri-us a um (one's) own; here '[her] your own/as yours', obj. of *dicābō*. Note the *o* of *propriamque* scans light; see p. 42(d)

dicō 1 I assign, pronounce

74 *merit-um ī* 2n. service

75 *exigō* 3 I pass, live; subjunc. like *faciat* **76**, indicating that *ut* **74** means – what?

prōl-ēs is 3f. offspring (abl. of means)

Learning vocabulary

bis twice

iungō 3 *iūnxī iūnctum* I join, yoke, unite

nymph-a ae 1f. young woman, nymph

---

comes the crunch: she *orders* him to sink the ships and scatter the dead all over the ocean. Note: she does not say from whom the orders have come. As S. comments, if Juno cannot block fate, she can at least do all in her power to keep the Trojans away from Italy (see *Intro* [48, 50]).

Crunch: 65–8

1.71–5: To clinch the deal, Juno offers Aeolus a bribe – marriage to the best of the pick of fourteen of her nymphs (presumably her attendants). V. lifts the trick from Homer (Rieu-Jones, *Iliad* 14.243–76), where Hera (Juno), wishing to send Zeus to sleep (so that the Greeks can start winning the battle against the Trojans again), begs the help of the Sleep-god. At first Sleep refuses, on the grounds that experience tells him it is dangerous to cross Zeus. So Hera bribes him with marriage to one of her attendant *Kharites* ('Graces') and agrees to give him Pasithea, whom he says he has lusted after all his days. Note that Juno insists Aeolus' will be a marriage which will be (as S. points out) legitimate (*cōnūbiō*), long (*stabilī* and cf. 74), free of any suspicion of adultery (*propriam*) and productive of children (75), thus removing any hint that she is appealing to Aeolus' baser instincts – in contrast with Homer. Homer was occasionally criticised by the ancients for, at times, lowering the 'dignity' of epic. Not Virgil. He read Homer with commentary in hand, noting what critics said about him and trying to avoid his 'mistakes'.

See: Jones (2003) *ad loc.* on the scene in Homer.

1.76–80: *Aeolus: 'Agreed, for thanks to you I have my seat among the gods'*

Aeolus haec contrā: 'tuus^, ō rēgīna, quid optēs
explōrāre ^labor; mihi iussa capessere fās est.
tū mihi, quodcumque hoc rēgnī, tū scēptra Iouemque
conciliās, tū dās epulīs^ accumbere ^dīuum,
nimbōrumque facis tempestātumque potentem.'   80

76 *Aeolus*: ellipse of 'said'

tuus: note emphatic position; picked up by equally
emphatic *mihi* (**77**). With *tuus . . . labor* (**77**)
understand *est*

rēgīna: Aeolus respectfully calls his superior not by
name but by title (S.)

*optō 1 I wish, desire, want (it is subjunc. in indir. q.
after *explōrāre*)

77 *explōrō* 1 I decide, ascertain

*iuss-um ī 2n. ('your') order

capess-ō 3 I carry out, undertake

*fās n. duty, divine law (for X + dat. to Y + inf.)

78 *tū . . . tū . . . tū*: rising (lengthening) tricolon
(group of three similar grammatical units) with
anaphora (repeated word, here *tū*) and asyndeton
(no 'and'). V. brilliantly negotiates between the
regular pauses imposed by the hexameter
(particularly at e.g. the caesura and the end of the
line) and the freedom required by the sweep of
elegant sentence structure. This passage is a fine
example, in which the flowing rhetoric of the
rising tricolon is not compromised or its effect
lessened by the hexametric form: **76** runs over
into **77**, closing effectively at the end of the line
with two single vowels *fās est*; **78** launches out
into a tricolon that spreads over three lines, each
element of varied length, the last line a grand
four-worder (**80**)

mihi: take after *conciliās*

quodcumque . . . rēgnī: 'whatever [part/tiny sort] of
kingdom' (**RLL**(d)2, **W**15, **M**8); then understand
est and take in order *quodcumque rēgnī hoc est*

79 *conciliō* 1 I win, secure X (acc.) for Y (dat.); win
the favour of (+ acc.). This last meaning explains
Iouem

dās: understand '[you grant] *me*' [the right to]

accumbō 3 I recline at (+ dat.)

*epul-ae ārum 1f. pl. feast

dīuum: case?

80 *nimbōrum . . . tempestātum*: gens. of respect after
potentem

facis . . . potentem: i.e. 'you make me *potentem*'

*potēns potent-is powerful, i.e. *mē potentem*

See: Camps (1969: 66–7) on the superb sentence
structure.

Learning vocabulary

epul-ae ārum 1f. pl. feast
fās n. duty, divine law
iuss-um ī 2n. order
optō 1 I wish, desire, want
potēns potent-is powerful

1.76–80: Aeolus not only does not wrangle, as Sleep did in Homer, he also ignores the
bribe completely, and goes off on quite another tack – the duty he owes to Juno for past
favours, in particular, her help in giving him the power and authority he now holds and
therefore the right to dine with the gods. He sets this up very tactfully by saying that
Juno must decide to do what *she* wants (75–6), but *his* duty (*fās*) is to obey her. In other
words, he has been *iussus* – her orders are his orders.

One would like to know where Aeolus gets his assertion that he owes his power to
Juno (78–80). There is nothing about it in any sources (though S. points out that Juno is
'goddess of the air'). But that may not be relevant. The point is that a flattered and
grateful Aeolus clearly wants to please Juno; and his assertion *suggests* that (to his mind)
Juno and Jupiter see eye to eye on the matter (cf. *Iouemque / conciliās* 78–9). As a result,
he feels fully confident that it is right for him to release the winds, *iussus* by Juno. He is

1.81–91: *The storm breaks: huge waves, men scream, rigging shrieks, darkness, thunder and lightning, death everywhere*

haec ubi dicta, cauum^ conuersā cuspide ^montem
impulit in latus: ac uentī, uelut agmine factō,
quā data porta, ruunt, et terrās turbine perflant.
incubuēre marī, tōtumque ā sēdibus īmīs
ūnā Eurusque Notusque ruunt, crēberque^ procellīs   85
^Āfricus, et uastōs^ uoluunt ad lītora ^flūctūs.
īnsequitur clāmorque uirum strīdorque rudentum.
ēripiunt subitō nūbēs caelumque diemque
Teucrōrum ex oculīs; pontō nox^ incubat ^ātra.
intonuēre polī, et crēbrīs^ micat ^ignibus aethēr,   90
praesentemque^ uirīs intentant omnia ^mortem.

---

81 *dicta*: ellipsis of *sunt*; so with *data* **83**
*cau-us a um hollow
*conuertor 3 *conuersus* I turn round, convert, change
cuspis cuspid-is 3f. spear; *conuersā cuspide* i.e. the butt of the spear (abl. of instrument)
82 *latus later-is 3n. side. The action seems an odd way to open the *claustra* (**56**) of the *carcer* (**54**) in the *latus* of the mountain – is he smashing the doors open? – but is certainly dramatic
**uelut(ī)* just as
*agmen agmin-is 3n. battle-line, line
83 *perflō* 1 I blow over (like *ruunt*, historic pres.; cf. **85, 86**)
84 *incumbō 3 *incubuī incubitum* I lean on, fall on (+ dat.); what form is *incubuēre*? (**RLA4, W12** (footnotes))
tōtumque: understand 'sea' (obj. of *ruunt* **85**, here trans. 'raise, churn up')
*sēd-ēs is 3f. seat
*īm-us a um deepest, bottom-most
85 *ūnā all together, as one
*Eur-us ī 2m. east wind

*Not-us ī 2m. south wind
procell-a ae 1f. storm, blast (abl. of reference)
86 *Āfric-us ī* 2m. south-west wind
87 *īnsequor 3 dep. *īnsecūtus* I follow closely on, pursue
*clāmor -is 3m. cry, shout
uirum: case?
strīdor -is 3m. howling, shrieking
rudēns rudent-is 3m. rope
88 *ēripiō* 3 I rip X (acc.) *ex* Y (abl.)
diem: i.e. daylight
89 *incubō* 1 I brood on (+ dat.)
90 *intonō* 3 *intonuī* I thunder
*pol-us ī 2m. pole, sky
*micō 1 I flash, sparkle
*aether -is 3m. upper air, heaven
91 *praesēns praesent-is* instant, present
intentō 1 I threaten X (acc.) on Y. (dat.), i.e. Y (dat.) with X (acc.)
omnia: nom. pl. n.

(Learning vocabulary over page)

---

not to know that Juno, a consummate liar (**130**) in the *Aeneid* (like Venus), has been setting him up. He just swallows her story hook, line and sinker.

It is significant that Aeolus says nothing about the marriage offer. Presumably his opening words, that he must obey whatever orders she gives, are a politely oblique way of accepting Juno's offer without going into the details. As we have seen (**1.71–5**), V. has gone out of his way to evade the charge that (in contrast with Homer) Juno was tempting Aeolus with sexual favours. But that still raises the question: does this sort of dealing between deities trivialise the gods?

At any rate, Juno has got her way.

1.81–91: No epic of travel by sea is complete without a ferocious storm (*Intro* [17, 26]). In his *Odyssey*, Homer describes eleven in all, the most extensive at 5.291–332, 12.403–25, 14.301–13; you will be invited to compare and contrast Homer and Virgil in the

1.92–101: *Aeneas despairs: 'Why could I not have died at Troy with Hector and all the rest?'*

extemplō Aenēae soluuntur frīgore membra:
ingemit, et duplicīs^ tendēns ad sīdera ^palmās

92 *extemplō* immediately, at once
Aenēās (Aenēān acc., *Aenēae* gen.) Aeneas – the first
    mention by name of the hero
*soluō 3 *soluī solūtum* I loosen, dissolve, release; pay,
    perform
frīgus frīgor-is 3n. cold, chill
membr-um ī 2n. limb
93 *ingemō* 3 I groan
duplex duplic-is both, double
*palm-a ae 1f. palm (of hands)

Learning vocabulary

aether -is 3m. upper air, heaven
agmen agmin-is 3n. battle-line, line

cau-us a um hollow
clāmor -is 3m. cry, shout
conuertor 3 *conuersus* I turn round, convert, change
Eur-us ī 2m. east wind
īm-us a um deepest, bottom-most
incumbō 3 *incubuī incubitum* I lean on, fall on
īnsequor 3 dep. *īnsecūtus* I follow closely on, pursue
latus later-is 3n. side
micō 1 I flash, sparkle
Not-us ī 2m. south wind
pol-us ī 2m. pole, sky
sēd-ēs is 3f. seat
uelut(ī) just as
ūnā all together, as one

Study Section for 1.34–123. Aeolus reacts immediately to Juno's commands and is so keen to please her that he does not even bother to undo the bolts of the prison where the winds are kept: he (apparently) smashes them down with his spear-butt. The winds are likened to troops lining up and pouring out into battle (82–3) from the gates of a camp (83); *turbō* (83) is used of tornados or whirlwinds, but also of rushing crowds. The '*s*' sounds of 84–6 imitate the shrieking gale (cf. *strīdor* 87) and the alliterative *uastōs uoluunt* (causing the mouth to open) creates a sense of the size and power of the waves. V. immediately paints the *effect* on the men and the rigging (87) before switching our attention to the heavens – all is sudden blackness, which seems to settle over the sea (88–9); then we are hit with the sound – echoing thunder (first half of 90) and crackling lightning (second half) – closing with the looming consequence in a resounding line: wherever the men look (*omnia*), no escape from death (91). This is highly dramatic scene-painting, with its swift changes of perspective and combination of sight and sound effects – *iactātus et altō* (3) indeed.

Crunch: 87–91

1.92–101: Our first sight of Aeneas, and one is tempted to say 'Him? A *hero*?' Far from rising to the challenge of the elements, he (literally) freezes (92). We may at least expect him to raise his hands to the gods to ask for help; instead, he calls a blessing on those who died in Troy (94–6) and wonders why he had not been one of them (97–8). Further, he is a man who recognises bravery (96–7) in an enemy, and looks emotionally, almost longingly, back to the place where old, brave companions died (98–101). This – a man with a *mission*? It is clearly all too much for him. He is not up to the job.

Wrong. S. explains, saying that Aeneas is groaning not in fear of death ('for he says thrice and four times blessed [sc. are those who died . . .]') but at the type of death to which he thinks he is going to be subjected. So he is not a hero 'in despair' or 'frightened of the elements'. He simply reflects on what a truly heroic death would have meant, i.e. one on the battlefield – of which he is worthy, since he survived when the great Hector

tālia uōce refert: 'ō terque quaterque beātī,
quīs ante ōra patrum, Troiae sub moenibus altīs,   95
contigit oppetere! ō Danaum fortissime^ gentis
^Tȳdīdē! mēne Īliacīs^ occumbere ^campīs
nōn potuisse, tuāque^ animam hanc effundere ^dextrā,
saeuus^ ubi Aeacidae tēlō iacet ^Hector, ubi ingēns
Sarpēdōn, ubi tot^ Simoīs* ^correpta sub undīs   100
^scūta uirum galeāsque et fortia corpora *uoluit?'

94 *tālia* n. pl., obj. of *refert*; *uōce* abl. of means
referō referre rettulī relātum I bring/carry back,
   return; recall, recount. The speech introduced by
   refert is as beautifully articulated as Aeolus' above
   (see on 78)
ter three times
quater four times
beāt-us a um happy, blessed
95 *quīs = quibus*, with *contigit* **96**
ōs ōr-is 3n. face, mouth, speech – Aeneas' deep
   attachment to his home is evident
96 *contingit* (impersonal) 3 *contigī* it comes to
   pass for X (dat.) (with the idea of a happy chance)
oppetō 3 (understand *mortem*) I meet death
Danaum: case?
97 *Tȳdīdē*: Greek voc. of *Tȳdīdēs* (Greek *Tūdeidēs*),
   lit. 'son of Tydeus', i.e. Diomedes, one of the great
   Greek warriors at Troy. He crippled Aeneas with
   a rock and would have killed him had Aphrodite/
   Venus not first protected Aeneas and then carried
   him away to safety (*Iliad* 5.297–317)
mē-ne: compare note on 37, here expressing
   desperation: 'Why could I (*mē*) . . .' + acc. and inf.
Īliac-us a um of Ilium
occumbō 3 I fall, lie
camp-us ī 2m. plain (local abl.)
98 *anim-a ae* 1f. life, soul, spirit
effundō 3 I pour out
dextr-a ae 1f. right hand (abl. of instrument)
99 *ubi . . . ubi . . . ubi* (**100**): a moving and passionate
   rising anaphora (repetition, here of *ubi*), as Aeneas
   remembers his dead companions, individuals and

masses alike. Austin finds the speech 'markedly
   dactylic, a rush of anguished utterance'
Aeacidae: gen. s. of *Aeacidēs* (Greek *Aiakidēs*) lit.
   '[grand]son of Aeacus', i.e. Achilles
tēl-um ī 2n. spear (abl. of instrument)
iacet: i.e. lies dead
Hector m. Hector, greatest Trojan fighter, killed by
   Achilles (*Iliad* 22.131–366)
100 *Sarpēdōn* m. Sarpedon, warrior fighting for
   Troy killed by Achilles' close companion
   Patroclus. Significantly for Aeneas, he was
   especially honoured in death by being removed
   from the battlefield by Sleep and Death (on Zeus's
   orders) and buried in his homeland (*Iliad* 16.477–
   507, 666–83)
Simoïs: three syllables, nom. of river Simois (also
   called Xanthus) in Troy, blocked with bodies
   from Achilles' ferocious onslaught in pursuit of
   Hector (*Iliad* 21.1–26)
101 *scūta . . . galeāsque . . . corpora*: all objects of
   uoluit
scūt-um ī 2n. shield
uirum: case?
gale-a ae 1f. helmet
fortia corpora: if one feels *fortia* really describes the
   men, not their bodies, this is an example of
   hypallage, or transferred epithet, i.e. the epithet
   fortia should be transferred from *corpora* to *uirum*
   (S.). One might feel the same about *tot* (**100**). Cf.
   'The ploughman homeward plods his weary way.'

(**Learning vocabulary** over page)

and Sarpedon did not (99–101). Achilles has similar thoughts at *Iliad* 21.272–83, where, threatened with being drowned by the river Scamander 'like a boy in charge of pigs who is swept away by a mountain stream he has tried to cross in winter' (Rieu-Jones), he wishes he had died a proper death in battle at the hands of Hector.

The passage also establishes major themes that will run through the *Aeneid*: (i) the dead heroes fell *ante ōra patrum* (95) – we touch on the long ancestry of Aeneas' people and the closeness Aeneas feels to them; (ii) the dead lie in their own land (95), or are taken into the bosom of their own river Simois (100–1). So Aeneas, though all (indeed) at sea, remembers people grounded in history, embedded in their own soil. The themes of land, history and nation will be of high importance throughout the *Aeneid*.

1.102–7: *Aeneas' ship is badly damaged, others thrown about on the waves*

tālia iactantī, strīdēns∧ Aquilōne ∧procella
uēl̲u̲m̲ ∧aduersa ferit, flūctūsqu̲e̲ ad sīdera tollit.
franguntur rēmī; tum prōr̲a̲ āuertit, et undīs
dat latus; īnsequitur cumulō praeruptus∧ aquae ∧mōns.   105
hī summ̲ō̲ in flūctū pendent; hīs unda dehīscēns
terr̲a̲m̲ inter flūctūs aperit; furit aestus harēnīs.

Learning vocabulary

Aenēās (Aenēān acc., *Aenēae* gen.) Aeneas
contingit (impersonal) 3 *contigī* it comes to pass for
   X (dat.) (with the idea of a happy chance)
dextr-a ae 1f. right hand
effundō 3 *effūdī effūsum* I pour out
Hector m. Hector, greatest Trojan fighter, killed by
   Achilles
Īliac-us a um of Ilium
ōs ōr-is 3n. face, mouth, speech
palm-a ae 1f. palm (of hands)
quater four times
referō referre rettulī relātum I bring/carry back,
   return; recall, recount
soluō 3 *soluī solūtum* I loosen, dissolve, release; pay,
   perform
tēl-um ī 2n. spear
ter three times

102 *iactantī*: here used of speech. It is dat. s. part.,
   referring to Aeneas 'to/for him throwing out
   tālia'; a dat. of disadvantage? Ethic dat. (**RL**88.4,
   W38, **M**10)? It is almost the equivalent of an abl.
   abs.
strīdō 3 *strīdī* I howl, shriek; whirr
Aquilō -nis 3m. north wind
procell-a ae 1f. squall
103 *feriō* 4 I strike, hit, break, pierce
104 *frangō* 3 *frēgī frāctum* I break, smash
rēm-us ī 2m. oar
prōr-a ae 1f. prow

āuert-ō 3 I turn round (intrans. here, but usually
   trans.), divert
105 *cumul-us ī* 2m. mass, pile, heap (here abl. of
   manner, 'in a mass')
praerupt-us a um sheer, giddy
aquae mōns: the single syllable at the end of the line
   (rare in V.) creates the effect of 'the heavy fall of
   the mass of sea-water' (Page). In this line, there is
   no coincidence between *ictus* and accent (pp.
   48–50 above)!
106 *hī . . . hīs*: 'these [men]'
pendō 3 *pependī pēnsum* I hang
hīs: 'for these . . .'
und-a ae 1f. wave
dehīscō 3 I gape, yawn, split
107 *aperiō* 4 I open (up), reveal
aest-us ūs 4m. seething (water), swell, tide; heat
harēn-a ae 1f. sand

Learning vocabulary

aest-us ūs 4m. seething, swell, tide; heat
aperiō 4 I open (up), reveal
āuertō 3 *āuertī āuersum* I turn round (trans. and
   intrans.), divert
feriō 4 I strike, hit
frangō 3 *frēgī frāctum* I break, smash
harēn-a ae 1f. sand
strīd(e)ō (2)3 *strīdī* I howl, shriek, creak; whirr
pendō 3 *pependī pēnsum* I hang
und-a ae 1f. wave

See: Stahl (1981: 157–77) on Aeneas' prayer; and Jenkyns (1998: 61) on the land/
   history/nation theme.

Crunch: 97–101

1.102–7: Almost as if the winds have heard Aeneas' prayer, they hit his ship with the sort of sudden, ferocious blast that every sailor fears. The reaction of the ship indicates the consequences. It is travelling north from Sicily, and the north wind slams straight into it. Whatever the detailed effect of the wind slamming into a sail *aduersa*, the ship would immediately lose way, especially in the mountainous seas (103); add the smashing of the

1.108–23: *Three ships hit a reef, three run aground on the Syrtes, another sinks*

trīs^ Notus ^abreptās in saxa latentia torquet –
saxa^ uocant Italī mediīs* ^quae in *flūctibus 'Ārās' –
dorsum immāne marī summō; trīs Eurus ab altō   110
in breuia et Syrtīs urget, miserābile uīsū,
inlīditque uadīs atque aggere cingit harēnae.
ūnam, quae Lyciōs fīdumque^ uehēbat ^Orontēn,
ipsius ante oculōs ingēns^ ā uertice ^pontus

108 *abripiō* 3 *abripuī abreptum* I seize, snatch away;
   abreptās refers to the ships
*lateō 2 I lie hidden; I escape the notice of
*torqueō 2 *torsī tortum* I twist, rotate, hurl, bend; cf.
   117
109 *sax-um ī 2n. rock, stone
Ital-ī ōrum 2m. Italians (note the alternative
   scansion; cf. *Ītaliam*, 2)
quae: understand *sunt*
Ār-ae ārum 1f. pl. 'Altars'; unknown rocks so
   named, here in apposition to *saxa*, as is *dorsum
   immāne*
110 *dors-um ī* 2n. back, ridge, spine
*immān-is e huge, vast; savage, brutal
marī summō: '*on* the surface of the water' (the rocks
   are normally hidden, **108**, but emerge as the sea
   heaves up and down)
*trīs = *trēs* (understand 'ships'), object of *urget*
   111
111 *syrt-is is* 3f. sandy flats, sandbanks (the Gulf of
   Syrtes is the name given to a coastal stretch off
   Libya, 400 miles south-east of Carthage; its
   modern name, Sidra, derives from Syrtes)

urgeō 2 I squeeze, push, thrust
miserābil-is e pitiful, pathetic
uīsū: abl., lit. 'with reference to sight', i.e. 'to see'.
   This form is often called the 'supine', but is in fact
   the abl. of a noun based on the supine
112 *inlīdō* 3 *inlīdī inlīsum* I strike, drive X (acc.,
   nauēs understood) against (dat.)
*uad-um ī 2n. shallow(s), sea-bed, depth(s), ford
agger -is 3m. heap, mound, rampart
*cingō 3 *cīnxī cīnctum* I surround, encircle, block in
113 *ūnam*: i.e. *nauem*, object of *ferit*
Lyci-ī ōrum 2m. men from Lycia (in Turkey = Asia
   Minor), Lycians (Trojan allies)
fīd-us a um faithful, loyal (generating pathos at
   Orontes' death, S.)
*uehō 3 *uēxī uectum* I carry, bear, transport; cf.
   uectus **121**
Orontēn: Gk. acc. of *Orontēs*
114 *ipsius*: i.e. of Aeneas himself
*uertex uertic-is 3m. peak (i.e. from high above,
   plunging straight down), head, summit;
   whirlpool, eddy (its meaning at **117**)

oars (*franguntur rēmī* 104), and it is now uncontrollable, at the mercy of the elements. The ship swings round (*prōra āuertit* 104) and presents itself side-on ('beam on' in technical terms) to the waves (*et undīs dat latus* 104–5), wallowing helplessly in the trough. The ship would eventually come round, stern or bow first, into the waves, but before it can a great precipice of a wave smashes *into* it (105, not 'down on top of it'). The rest of the fleet find themselves in the same plight, some swept up onto the crest of the waves (106), others plunged so deep into the trough that they can see the *terram* (sea-bed), while the water boils with sand (106–7). This is not epic exaggeration; since they are near sandbanks (111–12), it is perfectly possible. (Thanks to Cate Trend, an experienced Atlantic-going yachtswoman, for the personal nautical observations, confirmed by others I have consulted.)

1.108–23: Three ships are swept onto sandbanks (110–12), Orontes' ship is sucked into a whirlpool (113–17: much alliteration and swirling rhythm to the lines), three others spring leaks (120–3); we are not told what happened to Aeneas'. 118–19 are remarkable: the heavy spondees of 118 generate a sense of useless (and therefore pathetic) struggle

in puppim ferit: excutitur prōnusque magister   115
uoluitur in caput; ast illam ter flūctus ibīdem
torquet agēns circum, et rapidus^ uorat aequore ^uortex.
adpārent rārī nantēs in gurgite uastō,
arma uirum, tabulaeque, et Trōia gāza per undās.
iam ualidam^ Īlioneī ^nāuem, iam fortis Achātae,   120
et quā uectus Abās, et quā grandaeuus Alētēs,
uīcit hiems; laxīs^ laterum ^compāgibus, omnēs
accipiunt inimīcum imbrem, rīmīsque fatīscunt.

115 *in puppim*: a rare example of V. adding an
   unnecessary prep. (S.)!
ferit: *ferō* or *feriō*?
excutitur . . . caput: take in order *magister excutitur*
   prōnusque uoluitur in caput
*excutiō 3 excussī excussum I throw/shake off, shake
   out
prōn-us a um face down
magister magistr-ī 2m. helmsman, master, teacher
116 *in caput*: give full weight to *in* – 'onto'
ast but
illam: = *nauem*
ibīdem in that very spot/instant
117 *uorō* 1 I devour, engulf
118 **appāreō 2 appāruī appāritum* I appear; it has
   four subjects – *nantēs, arma, tabulae, gaza*. S.
   wonders how they can 'appear' in the darkness
   (89); he is likewise worried about how arms (etc.)
   can float (**119**) – perhaps, he speculates, because
   the storm is so fierce?
rār-us a um here and there
nō 1 I swim
gurges gurgit-is 3m. ocean, flood, whirlpool
119 *uirum*: form? (p. 39 ((a)) above)
tabul-a ae 1f. spar
Trōi-us a um Trojan
gāz-a ae 1f. treasure. Much Trojan treasure had been
   taken by the Greeks (2.763–6); now more is lost,
   but not all (1.647–56)
120 *iam . . . hiems* **122**: *uīcit hiems* is the subj. and vb
   of this sentence; *nauem* is to be understood as the
   obj. throughout, i.e. *iam ualidam^ Īlioneī*
   ^nāuem, iam [nauem] fortis Achātae, et [nauem]

quā uectus [est] Abās, et [nauem] quā [uectus est]
   grandaeuus Alētēs. 'Ellipsis', the technical term for
   an omitted word, is in full evidence here
*ualid-us a um strong
*Īlioneī: gen. s. of *Īlioneus*, a ship's captain
Achātae: gen. s. of *Achātēs*
121 *Abās . . . Alētēs*: names of other captains
grandaeu-us a um old, aged
122 **hiems hiem-is* 3f. storm, winter
lax-us a um loosened
compāgēs compāg-is 3f. framework, structure
omnēs: i.e. ships
123 *imber imbr-is* 3m. water, rain
rim-a ae 1f. chink, crack (local abl.)
fatīscō 3 I gape, spring leaks (of timbers)

Learning vocabulary
appāreō 2 appāruī appāritum I appear
cingō 3 cīnxī cīnctum I surround, encircle, block in
excutiō 3 excussī excussum I throw/shake off, shake
   out
hiems hiem-is 3f. storm, winter
Īlioneus a ship's captain
immān-is e huge, vast; savage, brutal
lateō 2 I lie hidden; escape the notice of
sax-um ī 2n. rock, stone
torqueō 2 torsī tortum I twist, rotate, hurl, bend
trīs = trēs
uad-um ī 2n. shallow(s), sea-bed, depth(s), ford
ualid-us a um strong
uehō 3 uēxī uectum I carry, bear, transport
uertex uertic-is 3m. peak, head, summit; whirlpool,
   eddy

for the doomed men (so few of them too, *rārī* 118) in the vast expanse of ocean, the
dactyls of 119 suggest glimpses of the inanimate flotsam of the ship bobbing about in the
waves, all that will survive of these men's hopes. *miserābile uīsū* (111) and *ipsius ante
oculōs* (114) – Aeneas' eyes – underline the expedition's and its leader's helplessness: all
they can do is witness the disaster unfolding in front of them. So much for Jupiter's plan.
Juno has won. It is the end.

Crunch: 113–19

Learning vocabulary for Section 1.34–123

abdō 3 *abdidī abditum* I hide, conceal
Aenēās (*Aenēān* acc., *Aenēae* gen.) Aeneas
Aeol-us ī 2m. Aeolus, lord of the winds
aes aer-is 3n. bronze
aest-us ūs 4m. swell, tide; heat
aetern-us a um eternal
aether -is 3m. upper air, heaven
agmen agmin-is 3n. battle-line, line
aperiō 4 I open (up), reveal
appāreō 2 *appāruī appāritum* I appear
Argīu-ī ōrum 2m. pl. the Greeks
āter ātr-a um black, dark
āuertō 3 *āuertī āuersum* I divert X (acc.) from Y
   (abl.), turn back/away/round (trans. and intrans.),
   divert
Auster Austr-ī 2m. south wind
bis twice
cau-us a um hollow
cingō 3 *cīnxī cīnctum* I surround, encircle, block in
clāmor -is 3m. cry, shout
class-is is 3m. fleet
claustr-a ōrum 2n. pl. cage, prison; bolts, bars
coniūnx coniug-is 3f., m. wife, husband
cōnspect-us ūs 4m. sight
contingit (impersonal) 3 *contigī* it comes to pass for
   X (dat.) (with the idea of a lucky chance)
conuertor 3 *conuersus* I turn round, convert,
   change
cor cord-is 3n. heart
corripiō 3 *corripuī correptum* I snatch up, seize
dextr-a ae 1f. right hand
disiciō 3 *disiēcī disiectum* I scatter, shatter,
   disperse
dīu-ī ōrum 2m. gods
diuers-us a um scattered
effundō 3 *effūdī effūsum* I pour out
epul-ae ārum 1f. pl. feast
ēuertō 3 *ēuertī ēuersum* I churn up, overthrow
Eur-us ī 2m. east wind
excutiō 3 *excussī excussum* I throw/shake off, shake
   out
fās n. duty, divine law
feriō 4 I strike, hit
fēt-us a um teeming, fertile, pregnant
flūct-us ūs 4m. wave
frangō 3 *frēgī frāctum* I break, smash
fremō 3 *fremuī fremitum* I roar, howl, rage
furō 3 *furuī* I rage
harēn-a ae 1f. sand
Hector m. Hector, greatest Trojan fighter, killed by
   Achilles
hiems hiem-is 3f. storm, winter
Īliac-us a um of Ilium

Īlioneus a ship's captain
Īli-um ī 2n. Ilium (the town besieged by the Greeks;
   Troia is the region)
immān-is e huge, vast; savage, brutal
impōnō 3 *imposuī impositum* I lay, place (on)
īm-us a um deepest, bottom-most
incumbō 3 *incubuī incubitum* I lean on, fall on
īnsequor 3 dep. *īnsecūtus* I follow closely on,
   pursue
iungō 3 *iūnxī iūnctum* I join, yoke, unite
iuss-um ī 2n. order
lateō 2 I lie hidden; escape the notice of
lat-us -eris 3n. side
micō 1 I flash, sparkle
mulceō 2 *mulsī mulsum* I calm
murmur -is 3m. murmuring, humming
nī = nisi
nimb-us ī 2m. cloud
Not-us ī 2m. south wind
nūb-ēs is 3f. cloud
nymph-a ae 1f. young woman, nymph
obruō 3 *obruī obrutum* I overwhelm, bury, sink
optō 1 I wish, desire, want
ōs ōr-is 3n. face, mouth, speech
Pallas Pallad-is/os 3f. Pallas Athena, (Roman)
   Minerva
palm-a ae 1f. palm (of hands)
pectus pector-is 3n. chest, breast
penāt-ēs um 3m. Penates, household gods
pendō 3 *pependī pēnsum* I hang
pol-us ī 2m. pole, sky
pont-us ī 2m. sea
potēns potent-is powerful
pupp-is is 3f. stern, poop; ship
quater four times
rapid-us a um violent, swift, consuming
referō referre rettulī relātum I bring/carry back,
   return; recall, recount
ruō 3 *ruī rutum* I drive ahead, churn; rush
sal -is 3m. salt, sea
sax-um ī 2n. rock, stone
scēptr-um ī 2n. sceptre, rod (= power, kingdom)
scopul-us ī 2m. rock
sēd-ēs is 3f. seat
soluō 3 *soluī solūtum* I loosen, dissolve, release; pay,
   perform
soror -is 3f. sister
strīd(e)ō (2)3 *strīdī* I howl, shriek, creak
summergō 3 *summersī summersum* I sink, submerge
   X (acc.) under (+ abl.)
supplex supplic-is 3m. suppliant, one coming to
   supplicate/beg help from
tellūs tellūr-is 3f. land

tēl-um ī 2n. spear
tempestās tempestāt-is 3f. storm, tempest
ter three times
Teucr-ī ōrum 2m. pl. Trojans
torqueō 2 *torsī tortum* I twist, rotate, hurl, bend
trīs = trēs
turbō turbin-is 3m. whirlwind
uad-um ī 2n. shallow(s), sea-bed, depth(s), ford
ualid-us a um strong
uast-us a um huge, vast

uehō 3 *uēxī uectum* I carry, bear, transport
uēla dō 1 *dedī datum* I set sail
uēl-um ī 2n. sail, canvas
uelut(ī) just as
uertex uertic-is 3m. peak, head, summit; whirlpool,
    eddy
uinc(u)l-um ī 2n. chain, binding
uix scarcely, hardly
ūnā all together, as one
und-a ae 1f. wave

Study Section for 1.34–123

1. Compose a character-study of Juno from what you have read about her so far.
2. How good is Virgil at describing natural forces at work?
3. Scan 93–101.
4. Compare V.'s description of the storm with the following one from Homer's *Odyssey*. Consider (i) the details of the storm (ii) the role of the gods (iii) the response of Odysseus/Aeneas (iv) the role of fate. What are the major differences that V. makes, and why?

Odysseus has sailed on his raft away from the cave of the demi-goddess Calypso (300). His enemy the sea-god Poseidon, being royally entertained by Ethiopians while the gods debated the fate of Odysseus (286–7), sees him.

Notes: Danaoi (306) and Achaians (311) = Greeks; when Achilles was killed in battle, shot in the heel by Trojan Paris, there was a tremendous battle over his body (310).

See: Pöschl (1970: 34–6), Otis (1964: 231–2).

. . . Poseidon was deeply enraged,	
And shaking his head said to himself:	285
'Well, I'll be – ! The gods have really changed their minds	
About Odysseus while I was away with the Ethiopians.	
There he is, near the land of the Phaeacians, where it is fated	
For him to escape the misery that presently assails him.	
But I can promise I'll give him his fill of trouble yet.'	290
With these words he gathered the clouds and stirred up the sea,	
Holding the trident in his hands. He whipped up all the blasts	
Of all kinds of winds, and in clouds covered up	
Land and sea alike. Night rushed down from the sky.	
East and South winds fell to, the evil West	295

And bright-born North rolling huge waves.
Then Odysseus' knees and spirit collapsed,
And in despair he said to his great heart:
'Unhappy man that I am! What finally is going to become of me?
I fear the goddess spoke the whole truth   300
When she said that, at sea, before I reached my native land,
I would have my fill of troubles. And now they are all happening.
In such clouds is Zeus wreathing the broad heaven;
He has stirred up the sea, and blasts come rushing down
Of all kinds of winds. Now my instant destruction is certain.   305
Thrice and four-times blessed are the Danaoi, who lost their lives then
In broad Troy, as a favour to the sons of Atreus.
Would that I had died and met my fate
On that day when a host of Trojans hurled
Their bronze spears at me over the body of dead Achilles.   310
Then I would have earned my burial rites and the Achaians granted me everlasting glory.
As it is, I am fated to die a pitiful death.'
As he spoke a gigantic wave drove down from a height,
A fearful onslaught, and whirled round his craft.
Far from the craft he landed, letting the tiller   315
Fall from his hands . . .

Odyssey 5.284–316 (Dawe 1993)

5. Hardie (1986: 103, 107) argues that 'Aeneas (and by implication the destiny of Rome) is exposed to these mighty forces, but is as yet powerless to act towards the preservation of order' and the winds 'are envisaged as Gigantic forces that threaten the cohesion of the cosmos itself'. Do you agree? Cf. Anderson (1969: 13) '[Juno] represents the forces of disorder in the *Aeneid* . . . anger . . . irrational thinking and action, destructivity of others and self . . . and such symbolic occurrences as storms'.

1.124–222: Neptune's intervention, and landfall

In this Section, Neptune comes to the rescue, freeing the ships and calming the storm like a wise statesman calming a mob. Aeneas' men find land and prepare food. Aeneas, looking for the other ships which he assumes lost, kills seven deer for the men to eat. He attempts to rally them, they eat and mourn lost comrades.

1.124–31: *Neptune senses the disturbance, rises up and summons the winds*

intereā magnō^ miscērī ^murmure pontum,
ēmissamque hiemem sēnsit Neptūnus^, et īmīs*   125
stāgna refūsa *uadīs, grauiter ^commōtus; et altō
prōspiciēns, summā^ placidum caput extulit ^undā.
disiectam^ Aenēae tōtō* uidet *aequore ^classem,
flūctibus oppressōs Trōas caelīque ruīnā,
nec latuēre dolī frātrem Iūnōnis et īrae.   130
Eurum ad sē Zephyrumque uocat, dēhinc tālia fātur:

124 *misceō 2 miscuī mistum/mixtum I mix, disturb, confuse, scatter; miscērī, ēmissam (esse) (125) and refūsa (esse) (126) are all infs. in acc. and inf. construction after sēnsit (RL98–9, W25, M82–4)
125 ēmittō 3 ēmīsī ēmissum I release, eject, send out
īmīs . . . uadīs: ex or ab omitted
126 stāgn-um ī 2n. lake, pool
refundō 3 refūdī refūsum I pour back, drain
grauiter seriously
commoueō 2 commōuī commōtum I move, disturb, stir up
altō: local abl., cf. tōtō . . . aequore 128
127 *prōspiciō 3 prōspexī prōspectum I look out
summā . . . undā: cf. on īmīs . . . uadīs 125
*placid-us a um peaceful, calm, cool
*efferō efferre extulī ēlātum I raise/lift up, bring out; carry off

128 disiectam: as Juno had ordered (69–70), as too 129; see on 43 for scansion
Aenēae: gen. s. of Aeneas
129 Trōas: acc. pl. m. of Greek Trōes
*ruīn-a ae 1f. wreck, ruin, collapse (cf. ruō)
130 *dol-us ī 2m. trick, treachery; dolī and īrae are subjects of nec latuēre (form? Here transitive in meaning). Note the clever position of Iūnōnis: Neptune is the frāter of Juno, but it is also Juno's tricks and anger that he perceives
frātrem = Neptune
131 Zephyr-us ī 2m. west wind. But this wind (which would have taken Aeneas' men to Italy, S.) did not feature at 102–10. S. says that 'it expresses Neptune's anger when he reprimands a wind that had not even been there'
dēhinc next (scans as one syllable)
*for 1 dep. fātus I speak, talk, say

1.124–31: Neptune, being god of the sea (see on 139), does not take kindly to having his realm invaded by storms of which he knows nothing. Enjoy the alliterative *m*'s in 124 that alert Neptune to what is going on up above, and note that for Neptune the vast oceans are but *stāgna* – lakes, pools (126). *Grauiter commōtus* he may be – literally and metaphorically (S.) – but the head he raises up to scan his 'lake' is masterful in its coolness (*placidum*, 127) – a graceful line – immediately contrasted with *disiectam*, first word of 128. Precisely

1.132–41: 'Have you dared to act without my orders? Tell Aeolus to keep to his own realm'

'tantane^ uōs generis* tenuit ^fidūcia *uestrī?
iam caelum terramque meō^ sine ^nūmine, uentī,
miscēre, et tantās^ audētis tollere ^mōlēs?
quōs ego – sed mōtōs^ praestat compōnere ^flūctūs.   135
post mihi nōn similī poenā commissa luētis.
mātūrāte fugam, rēgīque^ haec dīcite ^uestrō:
nōn illī imperium pelagī saeuumque tridentem,

Learning vocabulary

dol-us ī 2m. trick, treachery
efferō efferre extulī ēlātum I raise/lift up, bring out; carry off
for 1 dep. *fātus* I speak, talk, say
misceō 2 *miscuī mistum/mixtum* I mix, disturb, confuse, scatter
placid-us a um peaceful, calm, cool
prōspiciō 3 *prōspexī prōspectum* I look out
ruīn-a ae 1f. wreck, ruin, collapse

132 *generis*: the winds were offspring of the Dawn (S.)
*fidūci-a ae 1f. trust, confidence, faith in (+ gen.)
134 *miscēre . . . tollere*: controlled by *audētis*. To 'mix heaven and earth' was a proverb expressing universal confusion (Cong.). Since Neptune's interest is the sea, *mōlēs* must refer to the gigantic waves the winds have stirred up
135 *quōs ego . . .*: 'whom I . . .', referring to the *uentī*. Neptune is about to threaten the winds with something horrible, when he realises he has more urgent priorities. This figure of speech is known

as 'aposiopesis', Greek for 'breaking off (*apo*) in silence' (*siōpaō*, 'be silent')
praestat: 'it is preferable/more important'
*compōnō 3 *composuī compositum* I settle, arrange, compose, construct; lay to rest
136 *post*: adverbial 'in the future'
nōn similī poenā: i.e. not like the winds' current punishment, a severe telling-off. Neptune's immediate priority is to sort out the situation (135); so he warns them that he will punish them properly *post* (S.).
commissa: lit. '[things] committed', 'what you have done'
luō 3 *luī lūtum* I pay, atone for
137 *mātūrō* 1 I hasten
138 *illī*: i.e. Aeolus, to be contrasted with *mihi* (139)
imperium . . . tridentem: acc. and inf. after *dīcite* ('that not to him . . .'). The inf. is *datum (esse)* (139)
*pelag-us ī 2n. (note gender!) sea
*tridēns trident-is 3m. trident (Neptune's and other sea gods' traditional implement)

how he knows this is the work of Juno is a nice question. V. does not always make things absolutely explicit, but Juno's hatred of the Trojans was well-known among the gods, Neptune was, after all, her brother (130), and this storm has come out of the blue.

Crunch: 124–7

1.132–41: Ancient gods are status-conscious creatures, and winds are very small beer compared with an Olympian god like Neptune – a point Neptune impresses on them from the very start (132). He is equally scathing about Aeolus, mockingly referring to his home as a huge pile of uncouth rocks (139), ironically referring to his *aula* as nothing better than a prison (140–1). We now realise how insignificant Aeolus really is in the great sum of things, how pitiful his gratitude to be allowed to dine with *real* gods (79), how absurdly over-inflated his view of his 'power' (80) and how pathetically easily he has been duped by Juno. *meō sine nūmine* (133) may seem contradictory, given that we know Jupiter has put himself in charge of the winds (61–3), but Neptune has the right to run his own realm, i.e. the sea, and he will have no one interfering there without his permission – let alone Juno. But it is worth noting that he has no special interest in Aeneas.

sed mihi sorte datum. tenet ille immānia saxa,
uestrās, Eure, domōs; illā^ sē iactet in ^aulā   140
Aeolus, et clausō^ uentōrum ^carcere rēgnet.'

1.142–7: *Neptune, with help, calms the waves and rescues the ships . . .*

sīc ait, et dictō citius tumida aequora plācat,
collēctāsque^ fugat ^nūbēs, sōlemque redūcit.
Cȳmothoē simul et Trītōn adnīxus acūtō^
dētrūdunt nāuīs ^scopulō; leuat ipse tridentī   145
et uastās^ aperit ^Syrtīs, et temperat aequor,
atque rotīs^ summās* ^leuibus perlābitur *undās.

139 *sors sort-is* 3f. lot(tery), chance. When the world was divided up between the gods (by lot), Zeus/Jupiter drew the sky, Poseidon/Neptune the sea and Hades/Pluto the underworld (*Iliad* 15.189–93): the earth and Olympus remained common among them all. 138–9 (up to *datum*) were later used of Nelson, expressing his total mastery at sea over *illī*, i.e. Napoleon

140 *uestrās*: one might expect *tuās*, since only Eurus is being addressed; but Neptune is talking about the homes of all the winds
sē iactet: jussive subjunc. (as *rēgnet* **141**) 'let him . . .' (**RL**152, **W**28, **M**34, 89); the picture is one of Aeolus swaggering about
aul-a ae 1f. royal residence (irony)
141 *claudō* 3 *clausī clausum* I close, shut
carcer -is 3m. prison
rēgnō 1 I rule, reign

Learning vocabulary

claudō 3 *clausī clausum* I close, shut
compōnō 3 *composuī compositum* I settle, arrange, compose, construct; lay to rest
fidūci-a ae 1f. trust, confidence, faith (in + gen.)
pelag-us ī 2n. sea
sors sort-is 3f. lot(tery), chance
tridēns trident-is 3m. trident (Neptune's traditional implement)

142 *ait*: scans as two shorts
dictō: 'orders' (lit. 'the thing said'; 'what he said'), abl. of comparison after *citius* (**RL**J5, **W**26/Suppl. syntax, **M**14)
citius more quickly
tumid-us a um swelling
plācō 1 I calm, settle, cf. 126–7
143 *collēct-us a um* gathered; note that **143** reverses 88
fugō 1 I disperse, put to flight
144 *Cȳmothoē*: Greek nom. s. Cymothoe ('wave-swift'), a sea-nymph, daughter of the god Ocean
*simul at the same time, together
Trītōn: Greek nom. s. Triton, a sea-god (named after the nearby Libyan lake Triton)
adnītor 3 dep. *adnīxus* I lean forward
acūt-us a um sharp
145 *dētrūdō* 3 I push X (acc.) off Y (abl.)
leuō 1 I lever up, lift, lighten
ipse: Neptune
tridentī: note the abl. in -*ī*
146 *aperit*: i.e. opens up a way through
Syrt-is is 3f. treacherous sandbanks off the coast of north Africa, between Carthage and Cyrene
temperō 1 I restrain, soothe
147 *rot-a ae* 1f. wheel (of chariot)
leu-is e light
perlābor 1 dep. I skim through, across

It is his own authority that concerns him. Does this, again, threaten to trivialise the gods? (See on **1.76–80** above.)

This interpretation may raise questions about the views of Hardie (1986), who sees the storm as one that threatens to wreck the whole cosmos (**1.58–64** above).

Crunch: 137–41

1.142–7: Neptune gets to work, and very graphic it is too: his helpers push the three ships off the rocks (144–5, cf. 108), while he uses his trident to lever the three others off

1.148–56: . . . *like a great man calming a noisy, seditious rabble*

ac uelutī magnō̲ in populō cum saepe coorta̲ est
sēditiō, saeuitque̲ animīs ignōbile uulgus,
iamque facēs et saxa uolant – furor arma ministrat;   150
tum, pietāte grauem̲^ ac meritīs sī forte ^uirum ^quem
cōnspexēre, silent, arrēctīsque̲ auribus astant;
ille regit dictīs animōs, et pectora mulcet, –
sīc cūnctus^ pelagī cecidit ^fragor, aequora postquam
prōspiciēns genitor, caelōque̲^ inuectus ^apertō,   155
flectit equōs, curruque^ uolāns dat lōra ^secundō.

Learning vocabulary

leu-is e light
leuō 1 I lever up, lift, lighten
simul at the same time, together
temperō 1 I restrain, soothe

148 *uelutī*: a simile starts here: 'Just as often, when
[mob description] . . . so *sīc* **154** [Neptune
mastered the elements]'
cum: picked up by *tum* **151**
saepe: here = 'as often happens'
coorior 4 dep. *coortus* I arise
149 *sēditiō -nis* 3f. civic riot, disorder
saeuiō 4 I run riot
animīs: *animus* (pl.) often means 'anger' (as it does
at **153**)
ignōbil-is e common, low
*uulg-us -ī 2n. (m.) crowd, mob
150 *fax fac-is* 3f. torch (Roman mobs use torches to
set fire to buildings)
*furor -is 3m. passion, (irrational) fury – a key word
in the *Aeneid* (*Intro* [43])
ministrō 1 I provide
151 *tum . . . sī forte*: take in order *sī forte cōnspexēre
uirum quem grauem . . .*
grauem: *pietāte* and *meritīs* (abl.) describe in what
respect he is *grauis*
merit-um ī 2n. service (to the state)
quem: *sī quis* means 'if anyone' **RL**139(i), **W**33,

M117; so 'if they see *uirum quem*' = 'any man', i.e.
quem is not a relative
152 **cōnspiciō* 3 *cōnspexī cōnspectum* I catch sight
of, see
*sileō 2 I fall silent
*arrēct-us a um raised, pricked up
aur-is is 3f. ear
astō 1 I stand still
153 **regō* 3 *rēxī rēctum* I rule, control
154 **cūnct-us a um* all
fragor -is 3m. noise, sound, crashing
aequora: object of *prōspiciēns* (**155**)
155 **genitor -is* 3m. father (Neptune)
caelō . . . apertō: abl. abs.; S. comments 'driving not
across the sky, but across the sea, under a clear
sky'
inuehō 3 *inuēxī inuectum* I carry, drive, convey; here
the passive is used in a 'middle' reflexive sense, i.e.
not 'being driven' but 'driving himself' or simply,
as we say in English, 'driving' (intrans.). This is
very common in V. and will be noted. See p. 39
((c)(i)) above
156 *flectō* 3 I turn, guide, bend
*curr-us ūs 4m. chariot; *currū* here is the syncopated
form of the dat. *curruī*
uolō 1 I fly, race
*lōr-um ī 2n. whip, rein
*secund-us a um willing, obedient; cf. 147

---

the sandbanks and cut a channel through for them (145–6, cf. 110–11), racing across the sea in his magnificent horse-drawn chariot which simply skims the surface, like Poseidon in *Iliad* 13.23–31.

1.148–56: Homer's epics were famed for their extended similes, and V. now produces one of his own, unlike almost anything in Homer because it reverses the usual pattern. In Homer, a human situation is usually likened to one from nature, e.g. men running for it *like fawns*, two men fighting *like lions over a dead stag* and men rushing for the ships from an assembly like *rollers at sea being driven by a high wind* (*Iliad* 2.144–9). Here a

1.157–69: *Aeneas' men make for Libya and find a threatening-looking, but easy, safe anchorage*

dēfessī Aeneadae, quae proxima lītora, cursū
contendunt peter̯e, et Libyae uertuntur ad ōrās.

Learning vocabulary	
arrēct-us a um raised, pricked up	**157** **dēfess-us a um* exhausted
cōnspiciō 3 *cōnspexī cōnspectum* I catch sight of, see	*Aeneadae*: Greek nom. pl., 'sons/companions of Aeneas'
cūnct-us a um all	*quae . . . lītora*: take in order *contendunt petere* (**158**) *lītora quae proxima* [*erant*]
curr-us ūs 4m. chariot	*cursū*: abl. of manner; the ships get to land as fast as they can
furor -is 3m. passion, fury	
genitor -is 3m. father	**158** *contendō* 3 *contendī contentum* I hurry, strain, fight, strive
lōr-um ī 2n. whip, rein	
regō 3 *rēxī rēctum* I rule, control	*uertuntur*: 'middle' reflexive usage, i.e. they turn themselves, or just 'turn'; see p. 39 ((c)(i)) above
secund-us a um willing	
sileō 2 I fall silent	
uulg-us -ī 2n. (m.) crowd, mob	

phenomenon of nature is likened to a human one – a storm at sea being calmed *like a mob being brought under control by a statesman*.

The content of the image has wide application to the *Aeneid*, preparing the reader for a number of major themes, in particular, the opposition between *furor* (irrational, destructive, 150, a word with strong negative connotations in the *Aeneid* used widely to indicate that something has gone wrong), characteristic of riots in Rome during the collapse of the republic, and the need for men of *pietās* to control it (151). The order of the natural world, in other words, 'stands for' right order in the political world – a theme which V. had developed in his earlier treatise on farming, the *Georgics*. So the simile alerts us to the possibility of a political dimension to the *Aeneid*. It also signals a general 'order-disorder' theme, e.g. Jupiter's ordering of nature (1.255) and Augustus' ordering of peace (1.291–6). The simile is, strictly, anachronistic; but V.'s anachronisms are a test of the extent to which he wants to make this ancient 'Homeric' epic a commentary on the contemporary Roman world (cf. *Intro* [23]).

It is possible that, in composing this simile, V. had in mind an incident from Roman history in 54 BC when Cato the Younger silenced an angry mob. Worried about bribery at elections, he had demanded that the candidates submit accounts of their election finances. This did not go down well, and he was shouted at, sworn at, assaulted and man-handled when he tried to address the people. Eventually he made the platform: 'Standing up there, unflinching and looking the mob in the eye, he asserted his authority over the rioters and stopped the shouting. Matching words to the occasion, he was listened to in peace and brought the whole riot to an end' (Plutarch, *Cato the Younger* 44.3–4).

The image may also have another resonance, since Octavian was 'commonly depicted in . . . works of art in the style and role of Neptune'.

See: Pöschl (1970: 23) on 'order'; Otis (1964: 229–30) on *pietās*; Camps (1969: 8) on Octavian's image; and West 'Multiple-correspondence Similes in the *Aeneid*' in S.J. Harrison (1990: 429–44) on Virgilian similes in general.

1.157–69: When we first met Aeneas (34), he had just left Drepanum, the western-most tip of Sicily (3.707) and was on his way due north for Italy – a straight run. The storm,

est in sēcessū longō locus: īnsula portum
efficit obiectū laterum, quibus omnis^ ab altō   160
frangitur inque sinus* scindit sēs̲e̲ ^unda *reductōs.
hinc atqu̲e̲ hinc uastae rūpēs geminīque minantur
in caelum scopulī, quōrum sub uertice lātē
aequora tūta silent; tum siluīs scaena coruscīs

159 *est*: first word, 'there is'. S. comments 'this is an invented harbour, in accordance with poetic licence, but so as not to depart too far from reality, V. is thought to have described the harbour of New Carthage in Spain. However, it is agreed this place exists nowhere in Africa.' This is an 'ecphrasis' (see **Glossary of literary terms**). The Greek historian Polybius describes the Spanish harbour in terms remarkably similar to V.'s. See Austin (1971) for discussion

sēcess-us ūs 4m. secluded place; V. is describing a place approached by a long *sēcessus* – we might say 'fjord' or 'sound'. The *locus* is the place where they will land (*hūc*, **170**). Note the alliterative *s* sounds

160 *obiect-us ūs* 4m. blocking off, barrier (see on 43 for scansion); here abl. 'because of the barrier-effect, *laterum*, of its sides' i.e. this long sound is blocked off by an island, protecting it and making it into a harbour. Aeneas' men will sail round the island, down the sound and disembark in the safety of the bay at the end (**170**)

quibus omnis . . . unda: '(sides of the island) by which every wave (subject) . . .'
161 **sin-us -ūs* 4m. inlet, gulf; (perhaps) ripple
**scindō* 3 I divide, cut
reduct-us a um recessed, deep; (perhaps) retreating; the idea seems to be that the waves are broken up by the sides of the island, and *either* divide themselves into (*scindit sēse in*), i.e. split up and travel into, the various 'deep inlets' round the shore, *or* divide themselves into 'retreating ripples'
162 **rūp-ēs -is* 3f. cliff (forming the sides of the sound)
**gemin-us a um* twin; i.e. two tall peaks at the head of the sound
**minor* 1 dep. I loom up; threaten
164 *siluīs . . . umbra* (**165**) *. . . scopulīs* (**166**): abl. of description
scaen-a ae 1f. backdrop, background (ellipsis of *est*); a striking word, lifted from the theatre – after the horrors of the storm, is this setting almost too good to be true?
**corusc-us a um* tremulous, shimmering; note the rustling *s* sounds again

however, whatever detours it has taken him on, has blown him 120 miles west as the crow flies to . . . Carthage! The very last place Aeneas would want to find himself, if he knew what Juno had in mind for him. This destination will not be revealed till 338 (we are just told it is Libya, i.e. north Africa, at 158), but will be greeted by him without comment because he does not know any better. He is just relieved to be on land again. This point is worth making here, however, because of what V. does *not* tell us – i.e. how *Juno* reacted to the present turn of events. Her plan to destroy Aeneas has, obviously, been foiled; but at least the inevitable (i.e. the founding of Rome) has been delayed (better than nothing), and now by happy chance Aeneas seems to be about to leap out of the frying pan into the fire. Not that she planned it, let alone that it was fated; it was just one of those *cāsūs* (9), well allowed for by a flexible destiny (see *Intro* [48–50]).

Aeneas and the six other surviving ships (seven in all) make for the nearest shore and sail up a long sound whose entrance is protected by an island (159). The sound is flanked on either side by long cliffs (162–3), and their destination at the end of it features woods (164–5) and a cave with a spring of fresh water (166–8). It is secure (164) and no anchors are needed (168–9). The description – whether it bears any relation to New Carthage or not (see note on 159) – is partly based on Homer where Odysseus after his twenty years of fighting at Troy and journeying finally arrives home in Ithaca:

There is a harbour of Phorcys, the old man of the sea,   96
in Ithaca, with two projecting headlands,

dēsuper, horrentīqu̲e̲ ātrum nemus imminet umbrā.   165
fronte sub aduersā scopulīs pendentibus antrum,
intus aquae dulcēs, uīuōque sedīlia saxō,
nymphārum domus: hīc fessās nōn uincula nāuīs
ūlla tenent, uncō nōn alligat ancora morsū.

---

165 *dēsuper* from above
*horrēns horrent-is quivering, awe-inspiring;
   bristling; *horreō* 2 I shudder
*nemus nemor-is 3n. grove
immineō 2 I overhang
166 *frōns front-is* 3f. cliff-face (*aduersā* i.e. 'straight
   ahead')
antr-um ī 2n. cave
167 **intus* inside
uīuō: i.e. natural (not cut out by men)
sedīl-e is 3n. seat
168 **fess-us a um* tired (as tired as the men, **157**)
169 *unc-us a um* hooked
alligō 1 I hold fast
ancor-a ae 1f. anchor. Another anachronism:
   Homeric ships moored with stones
mors-us ūs 4m. bite, grip

Learning vocabulary

corusc-us a um tremulous, shimmering
dēfess-us a um exhausted
fess-us a um tired
gemin-us a um twin
horrēns horrent-is quivering, awe-inspiring;
   bristling; *horreō* 2 I shudder
intus inside
minor 1 dep. I loom up; threaten
nemus nemor-is 3n. grove
rūp-ēs -is 3f. cliff
scindō 3 I divide, cut
sin-us -ūs 4m. inlet, gulf, ripple

---

craggy cliffs, looming out over the harbour,
which provide shelter from the great waves made by the winds
outside. Inside, without cables, rest   100
the well-benched ships when they reach the mooring-place.
At the head of the harbour is a long-leafed olive-tree
and near it a lovely, shadowy cave
holy to the nymphs, who are called Naiads.
                    Odyssey 13.96–104 (Dawe 1993)

One may well ask why V. cannot be a little more original. But Homeric epic revels in details of e.g. food and landscape. This may seem rather trivial subject-matter for so great an enterprise, but he makes it all work. So, therefore, must V. That, however, is where the similarity ends. First, V. is doing it in Latin, and he has to show that Latin is equipped to do the job as well as, if not better than, the legendary Homer. So he intentionally takes on Homer, and on Homer's terms (*Intro* [23–4]). Second, he never simply translates. He transforms, deepens and enriches. Unlike the straightforwardly descriptive Homer, V. infuses the scene with a sense of the numinous (i.e. the mysterious, the divine, the awe-inspiring). *uastae* and *minantur* (162, cf. *imminet* 167) give a sense of desolation and threat; *horrentī* (165) reinforces the idea of the numinous (cf. *coruscīs* 164), while *ātrum* and *umbra* (165) add to the general apprehension. At the same time, the 'pathetic fallacy' is at work, i.e. inanimate nature has feelings just like man. The waters *silent* (164, also rather sinister in this context); the rock is *uīuō* (167); the ships are *fessās* (168). The climax comes with the information that nymphs live here, so the numinosity of the place is not accidental. There is, in other words, a unique (for its time) 'proto-romantic feeling about nature' in V., a picture that 'belongs to the wonderful

1.170–9: *The crew of the seven remaining ships disembark, light a fire and prepare to eat*

hūc septem^ Aenēās ^collēctīs ^nāuibus omnī*   170
ex *numerō subit; ac, magnō^ tellūris ^amōre,
ēgressī optātā^ potiuntur Trōes ^harēnā,
et sale tābentīs artūs in lītore pōnunt.
ac prīmum silicī scintillam excūdit Achātēs,
succēpitque ignem foliīs, atque ārida^ circum   175
^nūtrīmenta dedit, rapuitque in fōmite flammam.
tum Cererem corruptam undīs Cereāliaque arma
expediunt fessī rērum, frūgēsque receptās
et torrēre parant flammīs et frangere saxō.

170 *hūc to here
septem . . . nāuibus: abl. abs. (twenty ships left Troy
   with him, 381)
171 *subeō subīre subī(u)ī subitum* I put in, seek
   shelter; come up to/under, undergo
amōre: abl. of cause
173 *tabeō* 2 I corrode, waste, decay; here 'caked'? Or
   'dripping', in the way that something rotten
   liquefies?
art-us ūs 4m. limb
174 *silex silic-is* 3f. flint
scintill-a ae 1f. spark
excūdō 3 I strike X (acc.) out of Y (dat.). This is the
   first stage of fire-lighting – get a spark
Achātēs: nom., Achates, a loyal companion of
   Aeneas, busy at a mundane task. No real hero did
   such things – a feature of V.'s 'decorum'
175 *succipiō* (also *suscipiō*) 3 *succēpī* (*suscēpī*)
   susceptum I keep X (acc.) going
foli-um ī 2n. leaf. Now Achates builds up the spark
   into a proper fire

ārid-us a um dry
176 *nūtrīment-um ī* 2n. twig, kindling
rapiō = I 'catch' [a flame]
fōmes fōmit-is 3m. wood chips
177 *Cer-ēs -is* 3f. grain, corn (Ceres was goddess of
   grain: here the word for the goddess is used to
   describe her attribute – 'metonymy')
corrupt-us a um tainted
Cereāl-is e lit. relating to Ceres, i.e. bread-making
   (with *arma* = bread-making equipment)
178 *expediō* 4 I get ready
rērum: gen. after *fessī* (cf. 'tired *of*')
frūx frūg-is 3f. fruits, i.e. the grain
receptās: i.e. rescued from the waves
179 *torreō* 2 I roast (ancients roasted/dried grain
   before milling and baking it, cf. our coffee beans)
frangere: here 'to mill'

See: Clausen (2002) on Achates 174.

realm of heroic myth and speaks to a feeling for nature that we can share . . . both alien
. . . and something that we know'. And quite unHomeric.

See: Jenkyns (1998: 63–72) on the landscape; R.D. Williams, *The Nature of Roman
   Poetry* (Oxford 1970: 140–2) on 'unHomeric' V.

Crunch: 162–5

1.170–9: 174–9 offer an example of the way that an epic poet deals with technicalities. It is not brilliant, suggestive writing of the sort used to sketch the landing-place, but nevertheless competent, and epic enough. 171–2, however, are typical of the Virgilian reflex, i.e. man's need 'to fix himself, to be rooted, to be based solidly on some particular portion of the earth'. Aeneas has lost his homeland, Troy, for ever. Where and when will he find his new native land? Heaven only knows, but after their recent buffeting at sea, his and his men's immediate need is the security of solid land *somewhere*, and at last

1.180–6: *Aeneas climbs a rock. He can see no other ships, but spots some stags*

Aenēās scopulum intereā cōnscendit, et omnem   180
prōspectum lātē pelagō petit, Anthea^ sī ^quem
^iactātum uentō uideat Phrygiāsque birēmīs,
aut Capyn, aut celsīs^ in ^puppibus arma Caīcī.
nāuem^ in cōnspectū ^nūllam, trīs lītore ceruōs^
prōspicit ^errantīs; hōs tōta armenta sequuntur   185
ā tergō, et longum^ per uallīs pāscitur ^agmen.

Learning vocabulary

art-us ūs 4m. limb
Cer-ēs -is 3f. grain, corn (Ceres was goddess of
    grain)
hūc to here
subeō subīre subī(u)ī subitum I come up to, come
    under, seek shelter, undergo

180 *cōnscendō* 3 I climb
181 *prōspect-us ūs* 4m. view, prospect
pelagō: local abl., as is *lītore* **184**
Anthea: Greek acc. of Antheus, one of his lost ship's
    captains
quem: 'any', agreeing with *Anthea*, i.e. any sign of
    (cf. on 151)
182 *Phrygi-us a um* Trojan (Phrygia is an area north
    of Troy)
birēm-is is 3f. ship with two banks of oars, bireme
    (an anachronism: Homer knew of no such

ship, but V. did, and that is good enough for
    him)
183 *Capyn*: Greek acc. of *Capys*
cels-us a um high
Caīcī: three syllables, gen. of *Caīcus*, presumably a
    helmsman who would have had his shield etc.
    with him on the stern
184 *ceru-us ī* 2m. stag
185 *arment-um ī* 2n. herd
186 **ā tergō* in the rear, from behind; *terg-um ī* 2n.
    back, hide (also *tergus terg-oris* 3n.)
uall-is is 3f. valley (pl. for s.)
*pāscor 3 *pāstus* I graze, feed (trans. *pāscō* 3)

Learning vocabulary

ā tergō in the rear, from behind
pāscor 3 *pāstus* I graze, feed (trans. *pāscō* 3)
terg-um ī 2n. back, hide
tergus tergor-is 3n. back, hide

---

they find it. *magnō tellūris amōre* and *optātā . . . harēnā* make the point about the men's emotional needs; *potiuntur* exudes a sense of relief, but there is irony here as well: this is north Africa, the *wrong* place to be, and in Book 4 Aeneas will be ordered by Mercury to leave it. So, *fessī rērum* as they are (178), they set about the business of lighting a fire and drying out after the storm (much needed after shipwreck) and cooking food (badly tainted though it is from their trials at sea, 177, cf. 173). Or rather, that is what the *men* do. Aeneas has other concerns.

See: Jenkyns (1998: 60) on 'rootedness'.

Crunch: 170–3

1.180–6: Austin says that *intereā* (180) 'does not mean that Aeneas missed his meal'; it just means 'and now'. But we know Aeneas did not miss his meal because he and the men do not eat till 210. It means, as usual, 'meanwhile', to emphasise that Aeneas has better things to do (as S. says, great men should not bother themselves with trivia). The point is that Aeneas is a leader for whom the safety of his men takes priority over everything else, even, or especially, after the frightful battering at sea. So while the men dry out and cook, he (as we know from 188) summons Achates (who has got the fire going; the men do the rest, 177–9) and climbs a hill to see if he can catch sight of any of his lost companions. No

1.187–97: *Aeneas returns with seven stags, divides them up and shares out Acestes' wine*

cōnstitit hīc, arcumque manū celerīsque sagittās
corripuit, fīdus^ quae tēla gerēbat ^Achātēs.
ductorēsque ipsōs^ prīmum, capita alta ^ferentīs
cornibus arboreīs, sternit; tum uulgus et omnem^   190
miscet agēns tēlīs nemora* inter *frondea ^turbam;
nec prius absistit, quam septem ingentia^ uictor
^corpora fundat humī, et numerum cum nāuibus aequet.
hinc portum petit, et sociōs^ partītur in ^omnēs.
uīna, bonus^ quae dēinde cadīs onerārat ^Acestēs*   195
lītore Trīnacriō dederatque abeuntibus *hērōs,
dīuidit, et dictīs maerentia pectora mulcet:

187 *arc-us ūs* 4m. bow
188 **fīd-us a um* faithful
*tēl-um ī 2n. weapon (and **191**); *tēla* is in
apposition to *sagittās* (**187**); take in order *tēla
quae* ...
Achātēs: nom., Achates, Aeneas' ever-loyal
companion, cf. on 174
189 **ductor -is* 3m. leader
capita alta: not '[their] high heads' but '[their] heads
high'
190 *arbore-us a um* tree-like, branching; with
cornibus abl. of description
sternō 3 *strāuī strātum* I lay low, flatten
191 *miscet*: i.e. breaks up the herd, and then drives it
(*agēns*) into the wood
fronde-us a um leafy
192 *absistō* 3 I stop
*uictor -is 3m. conqueror, winner; triumphant
193 *fundō* 3 I stretch out; note subjunc. (and *aequet*)
after *prius ... quam*, indicating that he did not
stop until he *should have* hit seven – which in fact
he did, **RLT**(c), **M**118–21
humī on the ground

*aequō 1 I make equal
194 *partior* 4 dep. I divide up (i.e. the deer)
195 *uīna*: object of *dīuidit* (**197**!); take in order *dēinde
[Aenēās] dīuidit uīna quae bonus Acestēs* ...
dēinde then, next (two syllables)
cad-us ī 2m. wine-jar
*onerō 1 I load, stow (= *onerāuerat*)
Acestēs: Greek nom. s., Acestes, the Sicilian king
whom Aeneas had just left
196 *Trīnacri-us a um* Sicilian (lit. 'three-cornered'),
here local abl.
abeuntibus: 'to [them] departing' (dat. pl.)
hērōs m. Greek nom. s., hero (i.e. Acestes was a
generous, bounteous host). S. here defines the
hero as a man 'brave, demi-god and superhuman'
(*Intro* [51]). Put a comma after *abeuntibus*, and it
would describe Aeneas as the understood subject
of *dīuidit* (**197**)
197 *dīuidō* 3 I share out
maereō 2 I grieve

See: Clausen (2002: 15–17) on Achates 188.

luck, but he does see three stags. V. knows about their behaviour: leaders at the front, at the head of a long line of deer stretched out along the valley, cropping away (184–6). (But *are* there deer in Africa? Are they 'really' antelopes? Does it matter?)

This is a small but important scene. Aeneas has responsibilities. Whatever blows fate deals him, whatever his feelings, he has to fulfil them. This is the first of many such moments in the *Aeneid*.

1.187–97: This is a lucky strike for which Aeneas was not prepared, since that was not his purpose in climbing the hill: so, seeing the main chance, he has to respond at once, and snatches his bow from Achates who is carrying it, 188. A crack marksman (of course), he brings down the three leaders (189–90) and scatters the rest of the panicking

1.198–207: *Aeneas rallies his men: 'You have suffered worse; be of good heart; Troy will rise again in Latium'*

'ō sociī – neque̱ eni̱m ignārī sumus ante malōrum –
ō passī grauiōra, dabit deus hīs quoque finem.
uōs et Scyllaeam rabiem penitusque sonantīs^   200
accēstis ^scopulōs, uōs et Cyclōpia saxa

Learning vocabulary

aequō 1 I equal, divide up equally
ductor -is 3m. leader
fīd-us a um faithful
onerō 1 I load, stow
tēl-um ī 2n. weapon
uictor -is 3m conqueror, winner

198 *sociī*: Aeneas is immediately on the side of his men – they are all in this together, without distinction, as one (S.)
ignār-us a um ignorant (of + gen.)
sumus: 'we have been (and still are) . . .'
ante: adverbial, 'previously'
199 *passī*: '[you] having suffered/who have suffered'
grauiōra: n. pl. acc. S. comments that this is extremely clever: 'Aeneas wants them to remember worse times in order to alleviate the present'

hīs: presumably *malīs*
*fin-is is 3m. end, boundary, limit
200 *Scyllae-us a um* of Scylla, Homer's female sea-monster (*Odyssey* 12.235–59), in some traditions girded with dogs; in his account in Book 3 of his adventures after leaving Troy, Aeneas tells how they were warned off her (3.424ff.) and avoided her (3.558ff.)
rabi-ēs ēī 5f. ferocity, savagery (maintaining the canine imagery)
*penitus from deep within (i.e. the barking dogs echoing in Scylla's cavern); far away
*sonō 1 sonuī I sound, echo, thunder
201 *accēstis = accēssistis (accēdō)*. See p. 39 (b (ii)) above
Cyclōp-ius a um of Cyclops (Homer's one-eyed monster, *Odyssey* 9.181–564); Aeneas' men have a brush with him at *Aeneid* 3.569ff., but do not enter his cave or have rocks thrown at them

---

herd (190–1). When he has picked off seven in all, one for each ship, he is satisfied. V. does not tell us how he got the animals back to the ship (contrast Homer, in the **Study Section**). Some wine given by Acestes when they were in Sicily is laid out to accompany the venison. Things are looking up? Not really. On land they may be, but for all their relief at being saved from the sea, the loss of their friends and the true significance of their situation sink in as they prepare the food – food that only they, the survivors, will enjoy. Aeneas feels the need to offer comfort before they eat.

All this is, again, very Odyssean. You will have the chance to compare and contrast later in the **Study Section for 1.124–222**.

1.198–207: Aeneas consoles his men with two *proofs* from the past: (i) you have suffered worse than this and survived (198–9, exemplified by 200–2; note the emphatic anaphora of *uōs et . . . uōs et . . .*); therefore the gods will help us out now (199); and (ii) *fātum* – it is destiny for us to reach our goal (205–6). It is interesting that V. has decided they should not be aware that the gods have already saved them from the storm, but this is typical of V.'s tactics. We, the readers, may know what has happened, but we are in a privileged position. In *real* life, who can say when or whether deities have intervened or not? Part of the epic strength of the *Aeneid* resides in the sense that nothing is easy for Aeneas; he may feel that destiny is on his side, and we *know* it is (dramatic irony), but he does not. At every turn, he is assailed by contrary evidence, the recent storm being another example. His strength is that he manages to keep the faith, as he does here (cf. *Intro* [35]).

expertī: reuocāte animōs, maestumque timōrem
mittite: forsan et haec ōlim meminisse iuuābit.
per uariōs cāsūs, per tot discrīmina rērum
tendimus in Latium, sēdēs^ ubi fāta ^quiētās   205
ostendunt; illīc fās rēgna resurgere Troiae.
dūrāte, et uōsmet rēbus^ seruāte ^secundīs.'

202 *experior* 4 dep. *expertus* I experience (ellipsis of *estis*)
*reuocō 1 I summon up, recall
animōs: the pl. can mean 'anger' (see on 149) but also 'courage, spirits', as here
*maest-us a um tearful
203 *forsan* perhaps. *forsan . . . iuuābit* is a very famous sentiment
204 *discrīmen discrīmin-is* 3n. fluctuation, difference. S. comments that Aeneas does well to talk of *cāsūs* and *discrīmina* in order to minimise the seriousness of their past troubles ('for he does not say *perīcula*')
205 *Latium*: elsewhere in the epic, Aeneas is never exactly sure where fate is supposed to be leading them

quiēt-us a um peaceful
206 *illīc* there
fās: ellipsis of *est*, followed by acc. and inf.
resurgō 3 I rise again
207 *dūrō* 1 I endure, hold out
uōsmet = *uōs* (acc., object of *seruāte*); *-met* adds urgency

Learning vocabulary
fīn-is is 3m. end, boundary, limit
ignār-us a um ignorant (of + gen.)
maest-us a um tearful
penitus (from) deep within, far away
reuocō 1 I summon up, recall
sonō 1 *sonuī* I sound, echo, thunder

This is important in the context of the start of the epic: they *will* find their *sēdēs* – a place to settle – and despite the trials and tribulations (204), it will eventually be *quiētās* (205) and it will be their real home, a resurrection of Troy (206). What is required is *endurance* (a particular characteristic of Odysseus in Homer's *Odyssey*), until these assertions come good (207). One may add: but if Carthage turns out to be a *sēdēs quiēta*, what then? In all this, Aeneas is presenting us with his picture of what it means to be a hero on a mission.

Christianity was to show much respect for Virgil and Aeneas (and much less, generally, for Homer's self-seeking Achilles and Odysseus). One can see why. V. has constructed a hero on a mission 'quite without apparent precedent in Greek and Latin literature' – of a man 'called to serve a high purpose in history at the behest of heaven'. Cf. Abraham, the founding father of Judaism, Christianity and Islam, told by God 'Get thee out from thy country, and from thy kindred, and from thy father's house, unto a land that I will show thee: And I will make of thee a great nation, and I will bless thee, and make thy name great' (*Genesis* 12.1–4). And so, according to one tradition, Abraham leads his people from Haran (N. Syria) into Canaan (Palestine). Cf. on 2.780.

Aeneas' confident speech contrasts with his inability to do anything in the face of the storm (94–101). It is rhetorically effective: note the doublets, or variations, at 198–9, 200–2, 202–3, 204, 207; note too the emphatic position of key words (especially *Troiae* 206, the climax to the whole argument, though S. notes that it is the *rēgna* of Troy that will rise again, not Troy itself). He is a real leader after all.

See: Jenkyns (1998: 62) on the importance of this speech; Otis (1964: 232) on a hero's mission; Camps (1969: 22–3) on the Abraham parallel.

Crunch: 204–7

1.208–15: *Aeneas hides his misery; his men prepare the food, eat and drink*

tālia uōce refert, cūrīsque ingentibus aeger
spem uultū simulat, premit altum corde dolōrem.
illī sē praedae accingunt dapibusque futūrīs.   210
tergora dīripiunt costīs et uīscera nūdant;
pars in frusta secant ueribusque trementia figunt;
lītore aēna locant aliī, flammāsque ministrant.
tum uictū reuocant uīrēs, fūsīque per herbam
implentur ueteris Bacchī pinguisque ferīnae.   215

208 *tālia . . . refert*: see on 94 (as if V. is drawing attention to that earlier passage? Or is it simply a repetition typical of Homer and V.?)

*aeger aegr-a um sick, ill

cūrīs: abl. of cause. S. (absurdly) informs us that *cūra* derives from *cor ūrat* 'it burns the heart'. See O'Hara (1996)

209 *uult-us ūs* 4m. face

*simulō 1 I imitate, pretend; note the fine contrasting chiasmus here – *spem* (1) *uultū* (2) *simulat* (3), *premit* (3) *altum corde* (2) *dolōrem* (1) – that *altum* the only word upsetting the balance, and all the more effective for it. Note the 'subjective' description of Aeneas' feelings here (see **1.208–15** below)

210 **praed-a ae* 1f. game, booty (the seven deer)

*accingō 3 *accīnxī accinctum* I prepare (myself) for (+ dat.); get down to (+ dat.); gird myself with

daps dap-is 3f. feast, banquet

211 *dīripiō* 3 I tear, part

cost-a ae 1f. rib; abl. of separation

uīscer-a um 3n. pl. flesh ('beneath the skin', S.)

nūdō 1 I lay bare, strip

212 *pars*: i.e. of the men, contrasted with *aliī* in **213**

frust-um ī 2n. bit, piece

secō 1 cut (understand *uīscera* as obj.)

uer-ū ūs 4n. spit. Homeric heroes kebabbed their food

*tremō 3 I quiver (referring to the *frusta, trementia* because freshly slain meat is very soft. S. says 'still quivering'!)

*figō 3 *fixī fixum* I fix, skewer

213 **aēn-us a um* bronze; here n. pl. = cauldrons. Presumably these were for (anachronistically) boiling the meat, but that is odd, given that V. mentions skewers as if the meat was being kebabbed (as it always is in Homer). S. explains that, in accordance with Homeric decorum, the men are using the cauldrons to wash in before eating

*locō 1 I place

ministrō 1 I tend to, see to

214 *uict-us ūs* 4m. food (victuals)

*fūs-us a um sprawled, spread; *fundō* 3 *fūdī fūsum* pour out, shed, scatter; rout

herb-a ae 1f. grass

215 *impleor* 1 I take my fill of + gen.; a 'middle' reflexive use of the pass. of *impleō* 'I fill', cf. p. 39 ((c)(i)) above

Bacch-us ī 2m. Bacchus, god of wine; wine

pingu-is is rich, fat

ferīn-a ae 1f. game, venison

See: Clausen (2002: 23) on washing 213.

1.208–15: Perhaps not so confident a speech after all? A leader must keep the faith in front of his men and suppress his private feelings, but his feelings are as black as theirs. This is a hero with a difference. He cannot bring himself to believe that destiny is on his side, cf. *tantae mōlis . . .* (33).

These lines show what can be done by a master-poet working outside the Homeric tradition. Here V. does not narrate 'objectively' in the third person as Homer does, i.e. reports what he sees and leaves the characters to speak for themselves about their feelings, motivation and so on. Instead, he peers into and reports the inner workings of the minds of his subjects (feelings, etc.) – the interpretative, psychological 'subjective' style.

1.216–22: *Food eaten and tables cleared, they grieve for lost comrades*

postqu<u>am</u> exēmpta famēs epulīs, mēnsaeque remōtae,
āmissōs^ longō* ^sociōs *sermōne requīrunt,
spemque metumqu<u>e</u> inter dubiī, s<u>eū</u> uīuere crēdant,
sīu<u>e</u> extrēma patī nec <u>iam</u> exaudīre uocātōs.
praecipuē pius Aenēās nunc ācris Orontī,   220
nunc Amycī cāsum gemit, et crūdēlia^ sēcum
^fāta Lycī, fortemque Gyān, fortemque Cloanthum.

Learning vocabulary

accingō 3 *accīnxī accīnctum* I prepare (myself) for
(+ dat.); get down to (+ dat.); gird myself with
aeger aegr-a um sick, ill
aēn-us a um bronze
figo 3 *fixī fixum* I fix, skewer
fundō 3 *fūdī fūsum* I pour out, shed, scatter; rout
fūs-us a um sprawled, spread
locō 1 I place
praed-a ae 1f. game, booty
simulō 1 I imitate, pretend
tremō 3 *tremuī* I quiver

216 *eximō* 3 *exēmī exēmptum* I remove, take out,
free; ellipsis of *est* with *exēmpta* and *sunt* with
remōtae
fam-ēs -is 3f. hunger, famine
*mēns-a ae 1f. table, meal; *mēnsa* often refers to
courses, not the tables on which they were placed
remoueō 2 I remove, clear away
217 *requīrō*: here meaning 'I lament the loss of'
218 *inter*: take with *spem* and *metum*
*seu, sīue whether/or
uīuere: inf. in acc. (understand *sociōs* 217 as subject)
and inf. after *crēdant* (itself an indir. deliberative
subjunc. after *dubiī sēū*, 'doubtful, whether they
were to believe . . .'; **RL**152, **M**34)

219 *sīue*: 'or [whether they were to believe that their
sociōs] *patī* . . . *exaudīre*'
nec: scans long because *iam = yam*
extrēma: n. pl., lit. 'last/final things'. These are all
ways of suggesting someone is dead without
actually saying it
uocātōs: referring to the *sociōs*, i.e. 'being/when they
were/called'; this refers to the Roman funeral
custom of calling on a person by name to see if
they will answer
220 **praecipuē* especially, in particular
Orontī: gen. s. of Orontēs (dependent on *cāsum*
221), the only one who has in fact been lost to the
waves (113–17)
221 *Amyc-us ī* 2m. Amycus
gemō 3 I lament, mourn
sēcum: i.e. in his own special grief (Cong.)
222 *Lyc-us ī* 2m. Lycus
Gyān: acc. s. of Gyas
Cloanth-us ī 2m. Cloanthus

Learning vocabulary

mēns-a ae 1f. table, meal
praecipuē especially, in particular
seu, sīue whether/or

And so, at last, to food and the busy 'Homeric' detail of cooking and eating it: the meat is stripped off the bones (211); the men wash (or do they boil the food?), and wine is taken with the venison (214); then the men spread themselves out over the grass as if reclining at a Roman banquet. They arrived *fessī rērum* (178); their strength is now restored (214, S.), perhaps with their morale after Aeneas' speech. But V. makes no comment on that issue.

See: Otis (1964: 49ff.) on the 'subjective' style.

1.216–22: There is something most human about this scene. The men are safe, and fed (216); their doubts eased by Aeneas' encouragement; their trial temporarily over. Now their thoughts can turn away from themselves and their needs to those who are lost. Without certain knowledge of what has happened to their friends (*dubiī*), they have only belief (*crēdant* 218), and some are more optimistic than others (*spem metumque*). 219 is beautifully tactful: as they go round and round the subject (*longō . . . sermōne* 217), they seek euphemisms to avoid having to use the word 'dead'. Aeneas, a man of few words (*Intro* [41]), is still a man of deep feeling, and is not afraid to let it show – no dissimulation or 'stiff upper lip' this time (220–2, cf. 208–9).

Crunch: 216–19

Learning vocabulary for Section 1.124–222

ā tergō in the rear, from behind
accingō 3 *accīnxī accīnctum* I prepare (myself) for (+ dat.); get down to (+ dat.); gird myself with
aeger aegr-a um sick, ill
aēn-us a um bronze
aequō 1 I equal, divide up equally
arrēct-us a um raised, pricked up
art-us ūs 4m. limb
Cer-ēs -is 3f. grain, corn (Ceres was god of grain)
claudō 3 *clausī clausum* I close, shut
compōnō 3 *composuī compositum* I settle, arrange, compose, construct, lay to rest
cōnspiciō 3 *cōnspexī cōnspectum* I catch sight of, see
corusc-us a um tremulous, shimmering
cūnct-us a um all
curr-us ūs 4m. chariot
dēfess-us a um exhausted
dol-us ī 2m. trick, treachery
ductor -is 3m. leader
efferō efferre extulī ēlātum I raise/lift up, bring out; carry off
fess-us a um tired
fidūci-a ae 1f. trust, confidence, faith (in + gen.)
fīd-us a um faithful
figo 3 *fīxī fīxum* I fix, skewer
fīn-is is 3m. end, boundary, limit
for 1 dep. *fātus* speak, talk, say
fundō 3 *fūdī fūsum* I pour out, shed, scatter; rout
furor -is 3m. passion, fury
fūs-us a um sprawled, spread
gemin-us a um twin
genitor -is 3m. father
horrēns horrent-is quivering, awe-inspiring; bristling
horreō 2 I shudder
hūc to here
ignār-us a um ignorant (of + gen.)
intus inside
leu-is e light
leuō 1 I lever up, lift, lighten
locō 1 I place

lōr-um ī 2n. whip, rein
maest-us a um tearful
mēns-a ae 1f. table, meal
minor 1 dep. I loom up; threaten
misceō 2 *miscuī mistum/mixtum* I mix, disturb, confuse, scatter
nemus nemor-is 3n. grove
onerō 1 I load, stow
pāscor 3 *pāstus* I graze, feed (trans. *pāscō* 3 *pāuī pāstum*)
pelag-us ī 3n. sea
penitus (from) deep within, far away
placid-us a um peaceful, calm, cool
praecipuē especially, in particular
praed-a ae 1f. game, booty
prōspiciō 3 *prōspexī prōspectum* I look out
regō 3 *rēxī rēctum* I rule, control
reuocō 1 I summon up, recall
ruīn-a ae 1f. wreck, ruin, collapse
rūp-ēs -is 3f. cliff
scindō 3 I divide, cut
secund-us a um willing
seu, sīue whether/or
sileō 2 I fall silent
simul at the same time, together
simulō 1 I imitate, pretend
sin-us -ūs 4m. inlet, gulf, ripple
sonō 1 *sonuī* I sound, echo, thunder
sors sort-is 3f. lot(tery), chance
subeō subīre subī(u)ī subitum I come up to, come under, seek shelter, undergo
tēl-um ī 2n. weapon
temperō 1 I restrain, soothe
terg-um ī 2n. back, hide
tergus tergor-is 3n. back, hide
tremō 3 *tremuī* I quiver
tridēns trident-is 3m. trident (Neptune's traditional implement)
uictor -is 3m conqueror, winner
uulg-us -ī 2n. (m.) crowd, mob

Study Section for 1.124–222

1. Is the harbour a sinister place? Are we worried that Aeneas has landed there?
2. What image of Aeneas does V. create for us in this *Section*? Compare and contrast 92–101 with 198–209.
3. Scan 198–203.
4. The hunting episode and Aeneas' speech at 198–207 are based on two separate incidents in Homer's *Odyssey* (note that in these passages Odysseus is talking in the first person).What has V. done with them to make them his own? Consider especially Odysseus' and Aeneas' analyses of the problems they face and their hopes and in whom their hopes lie, and in particular, V.'s comment on Aeneas' feelings at 209–10 (see Schlunk (1974: 50–5)).

A. *After the Aeolus incident* (see above, **1.50–7**), *Odysseus describes how he arrives at an unknown island, and sets out to explore:*

'I took my spear and sharp sword and went up	145
smartly from the ship where one could look all round,	
in the hope of seeing some work of mortals, and hearing their sounds.	
I went up to a rocky vantage point and stood,	
and smoke appeared before me, rising from the widely-spreading ground,	
in the palace of Circe, through the dense thickets of the wood.	150
I then deliberated in my mind and heart	
about going and finding out, now that I had seen the fiery smoke.	
As I thought, this seemed to me the better course,	
first to go to the fast ship and the sea shore,	
and give my comrades dinner and send them on to find out.	155
When I was quite close on my way to the rolling ship,	
then one of the gods took pity on me as I was alone:	
he sent a big stag with high antlers right into my path.	
It was coming down to the river from the pastures of the wood,	
to drink: it was feeling the strength of the sun.	160
I struck it as it came out, full in the body along the spine;	
the thrown spear passed right through it.	
It fell in the dust with a cry, and its spirit flew from it.	
Standing on it, I pulled the bronze spear from the wound.	
This I then laid down on the ground and left.	165
I dragged brushwood and osiers,	
and weaving them together into a well-twisted rope about six feet long,	
I bound together the feet of the enormous beast at both ends,	
and went carrying it over my shoulders to the black ship,	
leaning on my spear – because it was impossible to carry it over my shoulder	170
with one hand: it really was a huge animal.	

I threw it down in front of the ship, and woke up my comrades,
each one of them, with words like honey, standing close.
"My friends, not yet are we to sink down, for all our sorrow,
into the house of Hades; not before our fated day comes.   175
So come now, while there is something to eat and drink in the fast ship,
let us think of food and drink and not let ourselves be weakened by hunger."'

Odyssey 10.145–77 (Dawe 1993)

B. *Odysseus and his men have just escaped from the Sirens, when they see smoke
and heaving waters and hear strange sounds ahead of them. They are terrified,
drop their oars, and the ship comes to a halt:*

'I went through the ship and encouraged my comrades,   206
each one of them, with words like honey, standing close.
"My friends, we are not by any means without experience of hardships.
This hardship that is on us now is no greater than when the Cyclops
kept us shut in his hollow cave by main force.   210
But we escaped even from there by my courage, advice and intelligence,
and I shall not, I think, forget these."'

Odyssey 12.206–12 (Dawe 1993)

1.223–304: Jupiter's promise

In this Section, *Venus demands to know what Aeneas has done to make Jupiter break all his promises about the future glory of Rome. Jupiter reassures her, outlining what fate holds in store for Aeneas and the Roman people.*

1.223–33: *Jupiter turns his attention to Libya, and Venus asks him why he is causing such suffering for her son Aeneas*

et iam fīnis erat, cum Iuppiter,^ aethere summō
^dēspiciēns mare uēliuolum terrāsque iacentīs
lītoraque̠ et lātōs populōs, sīc uertice caelī   225
cōnstitit, et Libyae dēfīxit lūmina rēgnīs.
atque̠ illum,^ tālīs* ^iactantem pectore *cūrās,
trīstior^ et lacrimīs oculōs* ^suffūsa *nitentīs
adloquitur ^Venus: 'ō quī rēs hominumque deumque

223 *fīnis*: of what? The story-telling, or the day, or their hunger, or food or troubles suggests S.; the episode from 157ff., suggests Austin

cum: does not elide with *Iuppiter* because *Iuppiter* begins with consonantal 'y'

224 *dēspiciō* 3 I look down on (acc.: there are four obj. in all) from (abl.)

uēliuol-us a um flying with sails (he is looking down over the whole world)

225 *uertice*: local abl.

226 *dēfīgō* 3 I fix

*lūmen lūmin-is 3n. light; eye

rēgnīs: dat. = *ad rēgna*

227 *illum*: i.e. Jupiter, obj. of *Venus adloquitur* (**229**)

cūrās: i.e. the sufferings of Aeneas and his men

228 *trīstior*: comp.? Or 'rather sad/saddened'?

*lacrim-a -ae 1f. tear

oculōs . . . nitentīs suffūsa: here is a *second* 'middle' use of what is technically a pass. part., i.e. not reflexive (cf. on 155 for the reflexive 'middle'

usage) but taking a dir. obj., in this case *oculōs . . . nitentīs*, as if *suffūsa* were an act. part., 'filling her shining eyes'. This is very common in V., and must be distinguished from the acc. of respect (**RL**6.3, L(c)5). The distinction is that the acc. of respect construction indicates that the subject is not taking an active role in any sense (see on 2.57 for a clear example); the dir. obj. construction indicates that the subject is taking an active role and intentionally doing something – as Venus is here. See p. 39 ((c)(ii)) above

suffundō 3 *suffūdī suffūsum* I fill, cover

niteō 2 I shine

229 *adloquor* 3 dep. I address

quī: '[you] who'; *rēs* is object of *regis* (**230**). Venus is no rhetorical amateur; she begins flatteringly by saying that Jupiter controls everything and everyone (**229–30**), and then punches low – so what about the plight of my son Aeneas?

1.223–33: We have here a radical change of direction: from Aeneas in Libya to Venus and Jupiter in the heavens. V. is always careful to round off a scene and leave the reader with the sense that it has reached a 'natural break' before moving on to the next. Thus

aeternīs^ regis ^imperiīs, et fulmine terrēs,   230
quid^ meus Aenēās in tē committere ^tantum,
quid Trōes potuēre, quibus^, tot fūnera ^passīs,
cūnctus^ ob Ītaliam terrārum clauditur ^orbis?'

---

230 *fulmen fulmin-is* 3n. thunderbolt; having the
right to give orders (*imperiīs*) is one thing –
enforcing them is another (ancient gods
were not gods of 'love' in our sense: they
imposed themselves, by force if
necessary)

231 *quid . . . tantum*: 'what so great [thing] = crime?
offence?', obj. of *committere*

committere: understand *Aenēās potuit* (from *potuēre*
232), and with *Trōes potuēre* understand
committere. Venus is wondering what Aeneas
and/or the Trojans could possibly have done to
Jupiter to warrant their present situation

(especially as the Trojans were not a match even
for the Greeks, S.)

232 *quibus*: 'from whom [**233**] *orbis clauditur*' ('is
closed off')

*fūnus fūner-is 3n. death

233 *ob Ītaliam*: i.e. to stop them reaching Italy

*orb-is is 3m. globe, orb, world

Learning vocabulary

fūnus fūner-is 3n. death
lacrim-a ae 1f. tear
lūmen lūmin-is 3n. light; eye
orb-is is 3m. globe, orb, world

Aeneas and his men are safe and have eaten. When we return to them, they are all asleep
– apart from Aeneas (305).

In Homer's *Iliad*, Zeus is far from the serene lord of the universe: his squabbling
family see to that. Indeed, Zeus's first words in western literature are (roughly para-
phrased) 'My wife is going to *kill* me . . .' (*Iliad* 1.518–19). In V., there is a much greater
sense of Jupiter's mastery, *Intro* [27]. In our first sight of him at work, he is calmly surveying the whole world – sea, land and all its peoples (224–5). *aethere summō* (223) and
uertice caelī (225) emphasise his world-wide perspective. But his attention is drawn to
the situation off the Libyan coast (226), and it clearly concerns him (*pectore* 227). See
Intro [47–8]. So Venus sees her chance.

In Homer, Venus is Aphrodite, goddess of sex, often and most aptly described as
'smile-loving Aphrodite' ('fun-loving' might be a fair translation). Our first sight of her
in the *Aeneid* is quite the reverse: *trīstior* (228), far less fun-loving than usual, and in
tears, a sure way to Jupiter's heart. Venus is no slouch when it comes to getting her way.
See *Intro* [19]. First, she flatters Jupiter's authority. *imperium* (230) is a key word in
Roman politics, meaning the 'right to give orders' (with the implication 'and to be
obeyed'). *imperium* was the power with which you were invested in order to govern, but
on earth it was only temporary, unless you were emperor – and even emperors died. For
Jupiter, it is *aeternus*. Second, she flatters his might. On earth, men with *imperium* had
their power to enforce merely symbolised, by rods (*fascēs*) and an axe; Jupiter has the
thunderbolt (230). Venus now wonders what Aeneas and the Trojans could have done
to cross Jupiter so dramatically (231–2) and deserve (i) mass slaughter (232) and (ii)
denial of access to land anywhere, let alone Italy (233). Note *meus Aenēās* (231) – an
emotional touch from a mother fearing for her son.

But how much of 232–3 is actually true? How much *is* Jupiter's fault? *Have* the
Trojans been denied Italy? See *Intro* [48–50].

See: Heinze (384/304) on natural breaks; Jones and Sidwell (1997: sections 119–34) on
imperium (especially 127 on Augustus).

Crunch: 223–6

1.234–41: 'You promised they would found Rome; that was my consolation. When will their trials end?'

'certē hinc Rōmānōs ōlim, uoluentibus annīs,
hinc fore ductōrēs, reuocātō ā sanguine Teucrī,   235
quī mare, quī terrās omnīs diciōne tenērent,
pollicitus – quae^ tē, genitor, ^sententia uertit?
hōc equidem occāsum Troiae trīstīsque ruīnās
sōlābar, fātīs contrāria fāta rependēns;
nunc eadem fortūna uirōs^ tot cāsibus ^āctōs   240
īnsequitur. quem^ dās ^fīnem, rēx magne, labōrum?'

234 *hinc*: i.e. from Aeneas and the Trojans
Rōmānōs: acc. in an acc. and inf. after *pollicitus* [*es*]
   237, referring to Jupiter
235 *fore*: fut. inf. of *sum*, cf. **RLE1**
ā sanguine: 'from the blood-line'
Teucer Teucr-ī 2m. Teucer, one of the founders of
   Troy
236 *quī . . . quī*: picking up the Romans
diciō -nis 3f. dominion, power. In the text printed,
   omnīs agrees with *terrās*; S. prefers *omnī*, agreeing
   with *diciōne*. Do you have a preference? Ask
   yourself what is at stake in the argument here –
   Rome's world-wide dominion, or their total
   control over all aspects of power, i.e. (S.) 'peace,
   laws, war'?
237 *polliceor* 2 dep. *pollicitus* I promise
238 *hōc*: i.e. 'with this promise'

equidem (I) for my part
occās-us ūs 4m. fall, eclipse; west, sun-set
239 *sōlor* 1 dep. I console myself for (+ acc.)
contrāri-us a um opposite
rependō 3 I balance, weigh ('fates contrary to fates',
   i.e. one destiny against another quite different
   one). Venus, knowing what Jupiter had
   apparently promised, used to reconcile herself to
   the fall of Troy with the prospect of the re-
   founding of Troy in Rome
240 *eadem*: i.e. the same as before
fortūna: i.e. *mis*fortune!

Learning vocabulary

equidem (I) for my part

1.234–41: Venus now reviews Jupiter's promise (*pollicitus* 237, qualified by the accusatory *certē* with which she starts) – not just that Troy's line would be restored (235) in Rome (234), but that these same Romans would also be world rulers by land and sea (236, cf. on 1.1–7[c]) – and asks if he has changed his mind (237). Note the rhetorical doublets in *hinc . . . hinc . . ., Rōmānōs . . . ductōrēs . . ., quī . . . quī . . .*; the breaking off at *pollicitus* (was V. trying to suggest that her voice was cracking, as if it was all becoming too much for her?); and the final question (237). So Jupiter, according to Venus, has made promises that he has broken. But note, with S., that she does not cast the blame where she should, i.e. on Jupiter's wife Juno. That would not have been tactful (cf. Jupiter's reply at 260).

   Now Venus moves the point of attack, reverting to the effect all this is having on *her* and the dashing of *her* hopes (239), with more rhetorical doublets (*occāsum . . . ruīnās* 238 and *fātīs . . . fāta . . .* 239), the comparison of past with present (*nunc* 240) and, again, a final question (241). This question challenges Jupiter to do something about it: when is it all going to end?

1.242–53: 'Trojan Antenor was allowed to escape the Greeks and found Patavium; but Aeneas is betrayed, his obedience unrewarded'

'Antēnor* potuit, mediīs^ ēlāpsus ^Achīuīs,
Illyricōs^ penetrāre ^sinūs atque intima^ *tūtus
^rēgna Liburnōrum, et fontem superāre Timāuī,
unde per ōra nouem, uastō cum murmure montis,   245
it mare prōruptum et pelagō^ premit arua ^sonantī.
hīc tamen ille urbem Pataui sēdēsque locāuit

242 *Antēnor -is* 3m. Antenor, a Trojan hero. The historian Livy says (1.1) that 'Antenor ... came to the inmost bay of the Adriatic ... and took possession of the lands ... where the people are called the Veneti' (the origin of the name Venice, founded in the seventh century AD). In making that journey he would have gone up the east side of the Adriatic, passing by the region of Illyria (**243**), Liburnia (roughly Croatia) and the mouth of the river Timavus (**244**, modern Timava), before rounding the Adriatic at the north end and finally settling at Patavium on the far north-west of the Adriatic (**247**, modern Padua, where V. was born, c. 20 miles due west of Venice). Antenor's activities would seem to contradict V.'s *prīmus* at 1; but S. explains that, at that time, Padua was a part of Gaul, not Italy. Some traditions made Antenor a traitor, spared for betraying Troy; other traditions say the same about Aeneas, claiming that he betrayed Troy because of his feud with Paris. Cf. *Intro* [34] and *Appendix* **8**
potuit: controls *penetrāre* (**243**) and *superāre* (**244**)
**elābor* 3 dep. *ēlāpsus* I escape, slip away from + abl.
**Achīu-ī ōrum* 2m. Greeks
243 *Illyric-us a um* Illyrian
penetrō 1 I pass by; its objects are *sinūs* and *rēgna*

intim-us a um inmost
244 *Liburn-ī ōrum* 2m. pl. Liburnians
fōns font-is 3m. spring, fountain, source
superāre: used here to express the difficulty Antenor experienced. This part of the world was notorious for its storms at sea (cf. Aeneas' current plight) and pirates
Timāu-us ī 2m. river Timavus; the *fōns Timauī* seems to be the place where the river, having travelled underground, emerges in numerous springs (*ōra nouem* **245**) and finally reaches the Adriatic. The *arua* are the fields flooded by the springs (Cong. on **244**)
245 *nouem* nine
murmure: perhaps the noise of the underground springs surging along beneath the mountain?
246 *it*: 'there emerges'; *mare* is subject (the river is meant, as it is by *pelagō*), a way of describing the effect of the *fōns*
prōrupt-us a um bursting up (*prōrumpō*)
premit: i.e. 'floods'
**aru-um ī* 2n. fields
247 *hīc*: i.e. in this general area
ille: Antenor
Pataui-um ī 2n. Patavium (Padua). Note the compressed gen. s. *Pataui* for *Patauiī*

1.242–53: Good rhetoric always offers examples. Having dealt with Jupiter's broken promises and their effect on her, Venus offers an example of a Trojan who did make good after the fall of Troy – Antenor. *potuit* (242) contrasts pointedly with *potuēre* (232). Three rising clauses supposedly illustrate the increasing difficulties he faced (243–4) – note *tūtus* (243) in marked contrast to the Trojans – which Venus emphasises with the excited description of 246–7. It is hard to see what has made this journey to a distant land so extraordinarily difficult, demanding *tamen* (but he *made* it!) at 247; nor is it necessary for Venus to argue for its difficulty. Her point is one of principle. Antenor could do it; so Jupiter has nothing against Trojans establishing their line in that part of the world; so what has Jupiter got against Aeneas? The picture of Antenor in 247–9 corresponds exactly to what Aeneas longs to do: found a city as a permanent *sēdēs* for the Trojans (247, cf. on **1.92–101** and 171–2), give it a Trojan name and finally put his feet up – or in this case, his *arma*, signifying the end of one's labours (248) – and take it easy, in peace at last (249).

Teucrōrum, et gentī nōmen dedit, armaque^ fixit
^Trōia; nunc placidā^ compostus ^pāce quiēscit.
nōs^, tua prōgeniēs, caelī ^quibus adnuis arcem,   250
nāuibus (īnfand<u>um</u>!) āmissīs, ūnīus ob īram
prōdimur, atqu<u>e</u> Italīs^ longē disiungimur ^ōrīs.
hic pietātis honōs? sīc nōs in scēptra repōnis?'

248 *armaque fixit*: on retirement one dedicated
one's armour to the gods as a mark of gratitude,
usually hanging it up in a temple
249 *Trōia*: three syllables
compōnō 3 composuī compos(i)tum I settle, arrange,
adjust
quiēscō 3 I live quietly
250 *prōgeni-ēs ēī 5f.* off-spring. Venus was a
daughter and Aeneas therefore a grandson of
Jupiter
caelī . . . arcem: i.e. a place in Olympus. Venus is
referring to Aeneas
adnuō 3 I grant
251 *nāuibus*: something of an exaggeration (S.),
since only one was sunk (Orontes', 113–17). But
Venus is (as usual) lying for effect. Aeneas left
Troy with twenty ships (381) and after the storm
seven that he knows of (including his own)
survive, while Orontes' was sunk. The twelve
others (not mentioned during the storm) will be
found to have been scattered to the winds, but to
have regrouped and be safe after all (509ff.; cf.
1.387–401)

*īnfand-us a um unspeakable, accursed
ūnīus: i.e. Juno. Venus is careful not to name her in
front of her husband
252 **prōdō 3 prōdidī prōditum* I betray
Ital-us a um Italian
disiungō 3 I debar. The *i*- of *iungō* counts as
consonantal y
253 *in scēptra*: i.e. to power
pietātis: Aeneas', of course: she began with him
(231), and ends with him
repōnō 3 I restore, replace. Venus is referring to her
power lost in Troy which she had expected to see
restored in Italy

Learning vocabulary

Achīu-ī ōrum 2m. Greeks
aru-um ī 2n. field
compōnō 3 composuī compos(i)tum I settle, arrange,
adjust
ēlābor 3 dep. ēlāpsus I escape, slip away from
īnfand-us a um unspeakable, accursed
prōdō 3 prōdidī prōditum I betray

The conclusion Venus now draws is tremendous (250–3), beginning with a sharp triplet: (1) the emphatic first word *nōs* (250) – she takes it, as they say, personally. (2) Then *tua prōgeniēs* (as opposed to Antenor's) argues that Jupiter has a responsibility to her and Aeneas (ancients divided people into friends you supported and enemies you attacked, and there were no greater friends than family). The claim that Venus is Jupiter's daughter is at least true in one Greek tradition, where Aphrodite is daughter of Jupiter and Dione. However, the more common tradition is that she sprang from the seed spurting from the severed genitals of Uranus falling into the sea. (3) Finally, *caelī . . . arcem*, reminding Jupiter of his assurances, completes the triplet. In other words – Jupiter, you have obligations to us.

Then come three accusations spat out – ships lost (with outraged interjection); one woman responsible (251, cf. 4); and Venus/Trojans betrayed by Jupiter, who makes no objection to seeing the Trojans kept away from Italy (252). In other words – Jupiter, you are not meeting those obligations.

She ends, as before, with questions (253), two of them, summarising her complaint. They ask whether Jupiter pays his debts or keeps his word – a serious accusation in the ancient world where friends and family are concerned. Note that *nōs* again. It brings the speech to a brilliant close.

Crunch: 250–3

1.254–66: *Jupiter, smiling, replies 'Fear not: it will all happen, Aeneas will win his battles in Italy and reign for three years'*

ollī subrīdēns hominum sator atque deōrum

uultū quō caelum tempestātēsque serēnat,   255

ōscula lībāuit nātae, dēhinc tālia fātur:

'parce metū, Cytherēa: manent immōta^ tuōrum

^fāta tibī; cernēs urb<u>em</u> et prōmissa^ Lauīnī

^moenia, sublīmemque^ ferēs ad sīdera caelī

^magnanimum ^Aenēān; neque mē sententia uertit.   260

hic (tibi fābor enim, quandō haec^ tē ^cūra remordet,

longius et uoluēns fātō<u>rum</u> arcāna mouēbō)

---

254 *ollī* = an archaic form of *illī*
subrīdeō 2 I smile, laugh at (+ dat.)
sator -is 3m. sower, planter
255 *uult-us ūs 4m. face, look; here 'with the look', after *subrīdēns*
serēnō 1 clear, soothe. This splendid image is strongly reminiscent of Ennius, *Annālēs* 1.446–7: *Iuppiter hīc rīsit, tempestātēsque serēnae/rīsērunt omnēs rīsū Iouis omnipotentis* 'Jupiter smiled at this, and the glorious weathers/all smiled with the smile of all-powerful Jove'. Jupiter is, first and foremost, god of the sky and therefore of the weather
256 *lībō 1 I graze, touch lightly; pour (a libation)
*nāt-us a um born of; *nātus* = son, *nāta* = daughter
dēhinc then (scanned as one syllable)
257 *metū*: the old form of *metuī* (*parcō* takes the dat.; cf. on 156). As S. says, when one is being accused, it is important to clear the ground immediately. *Parce metū* does just that

Cytherē-a ae 1f. Venus; often named after the island of Cythera. After she was born in the sea, she was said to have touched on that island, before finally reaching her destination at Paphos in Cyprus
immōt-us a um unchanged
tuōrum: i.e. of your own people
258 *tibī*: 'ethic' dat., i.e. 'to your comfort' (Cong.). RL88.4, W38, M10
cernō 3 I see
prōmiss-um ī 2n. promise
Lauīni-um ī 2n. Lavinium (cf. 2)
259 *sublīm-is e* raised up
260 *magnanim-us a um* great-hearted
uertit: probably perf.
261 *hic*: Aeneas
fābor: word-play with *fātōrum* (262) – what Jupiter says (*for fārī*) is *fātum*. See O'Hara (1996) for a discussion of such word-plays, and 2.777
remordeō 2 I bite, torment, nag away at
262 *longius*: 'in more detail', 'at greater length'
arcān-a ōrum 2n. pl. secrets
mouēbō: here 'I shall bring to light'

1.254–66: That *subrīdēns*! The glorious smile of Jupiter playing on that all-powerful face (255) makes such a contrast with Venus (see on **1.223–33** and on *trīstior* 228), and is followed by a kiss (256). Is that smile meant to console? To reassure? To suggest that he has seen through her rhetoric (this is S.'s solution)? Or that he approves of the calming of the storm (see on 255)? Amusingly, he calls her *Cytherēa* (see note on 257), suggesting that he is contradicting her claim that she is his daughter (250); but then Virgil does call Venus *nātae* (256)!

But Jupiter begins with the unconditional, triple assurance that fate is on track: it is *immōta* (257), the *prōmissa* will be fulfilled (258, cf. 2) and Aeneas will become a god (259–60: note *magnanimum* in emphatic position in the line, matched by *sublīmem* in emphatic first position in the clause, and contradicting Venus at 250). Result: Jupiter can deny Venus' main charge (260, cf. 237). Further, Jupiter, as master of fate, will now unroll its secrets in detail (262) in order to reassure her (261). It will take three years for

bellum ingēns geret Ītaliā, populōsque ferōcēs
contundet, mōrēsque uirīs et moenia pōnet,
tertia^ dum Latiō rēgnantem uīderit ^aestās,   265
ternaque^ trānsierint Rutulīs* ^hīberna *subāctīs.'

1.267–77: 'His son Ascanius/Iulus will reign for thirty years, and build a new city in Alba Longa which will last 300 years; then Romulus will be born and build Rome'

'at puer Ascanius, cūi^ nunc cognōmen ^Iūlō
additur (Īlus erat, dum rēs^ stetit ^Īlia rēgnō),

263 *Ītaliā*: local abl.
ferōx ferōc-is fierce, warlike
264 *contundō* 3 I crush, blunt
265 *dum* until (+ fut. perf.), **RLT**(c), **M**118–21
*rēgnō 1 I rule; the participle refers to Aeneas
aestās aestāt-is 3f. summer
266 *tern-ī ae a* three each
trānseō trānsīre trānsi(u)ī I pass
Rutul-ī ōrum 2m. pl. the Rutulians (local tribe in Latium, whose leader Turnus was Aeneas' main adversary when he finally arrived in Italy)
hībern-a ōrum 2n. pl. winter quarters, winters in camp
subagō 3 *subēgī subāctum* I crush, defeat, subject

See: Skutsch (1985: 111, 604) on Ennius.

Learning vocabulary
lībō 1 I graze, touch lightly; pour (a libation)
nāt-us a um born of; *nātus* = son, *nāta* = daughter
rēgnō 1 I rule
uult-us ūs 4m. face, look

267 **Ascani-us ī* 2m. Ascanius or Iulus, son of Aeneas. S. observes that Jupiter tactfully leaves out any reference to Aeneas' death
*cūi: scans as one long syllable
cognōmen cognōmin-is 3n. cognomen, i.e. surname of a family, usually derived from some special characteristic, connection, achievement, etc. V. now elucidates the connection that explains the name Iulus
*Iūl-us ī 2m. Iulus (three syllables); dat. to agree with *cūi*
268 **addō* 3 I add, receive
Īl-us ī 2m. Ilus, the earlier name of Iulus (V. now explains why)
Īli-us a um relating to Ilium (the town in Troy besieged by the Greeks); *rēs Īlia* is formed like *rēspūblica*, i.e. the kingdom/rule of Ilium
rēgnō: vb or noun?

Aeneas to win his battles in Latium (265–6), but in doing so he will lay two sorts of foundations (264): physical (*moenia*) and moral (*mōrēs*). As Page well notes, *mōrēs* include 'not only laws but all customs and institutions'. In other words, there will be a complete makeover for the people of Latium; the arrival of the Trojans announces the end of a *ferōcēs* people (263) who need hammering down (*contundet* 264) and the start of a civilising mission, one (as the *Aeneid* will later explain) committed to peace and the rule of law. Note, however, that Aeneas knows none of this. He will have to discover it for himself, slowly and painfully. It may be destined, but that does not mean it will be easy for those charged with fulfilling it.

Crunch: 254–6

1.267–77: A simple chronology, therefore: 3 years (Aeneas rules, creating 'Latins') + 30 years (Ascanius rules Lavinium) + 300 years (rule from Alba Longa, the *Albānī patrēs* of 1.7) = 333 years, and Rome is then founded by Romulus. Ascanius is quickly given a new name Iulus to link him back to Troy (Ilus – Ilium, 268) and forward (Ilus – Iulius) to Julius Caesar/Augustus (267). This binding of the deep past to the present day is of great

trīgintā^ ^magnōs uoluendīs mēnsibus ^orbīs,
imperiō explēbit, rēgnumque ab sēde Lauīnī   270
trānsferet, et Longam^ multā uī mūniet ^Albam.
hīc iam ter centum tōtōs^ rēgnābitur ^annōs
gente^ sub ^Hectoreā, dōnec rēgīna sacerdōs^,
Mārte ^grauis, geminam* partū dabit ^Īlia *prōlem.
inde lupae^ fuluō* ^nūtrīcis *tegmine laetus   275
Rōmulus excipiet gentem, et Māuortia^ condet
^moenia, Rōmānōsque suō^ dē ^nōmine dīcet.'

269 *uoluendīs*: i.e. in the (future) turning of the years. Enjoy the heavy spondees in this line
mēns-is is 3m. month
orbīs: *orbis* here means a year
270 *imperiō*: 'with his rule/kingdom'
*expleō 2 I complete, fulfil, satisfy
Lauīnī: cf. 2, and note the changed scansion. See also on 109
271 *trānsferō trānsferre* 3 I transfer
mūniō 4 I fortify
272 *rēgnābitur*: an impersonal usage here, lit. 'it shall be ruled' (= 'men shall rule') Cf. **RL**154, F2, **W**2, **M**106–7
273 *Hectore-us a um* of Hector (Troy's chief hero, killed by Achilles)
*dōnec until (here with indic., to indicate it did/ would actually happen) **RL**T(c), **M**118–21
*sacerdōs sacerdōt-is 3m./f. priest(ess); her name is Ilia (274), maintaining the Trojan connection
274 **Mārs Mārt-is* 3m. Mars, god of war
grau-is e pregnant (by + abl.)
*gemin-us a um twin
part-us ūs 4m. birth

Īli-a ae 1f. Ilia (also known as Rhea Silvia, mother of Romulus and Remus)
prōl-ēs is offspring
275 *inde* from there, then
lūp-a ae 1f. wolf
fulu-us a um tawny
nūtrīx nūtrīc-is 3f. nurse (i.e. 'that nursed him')
tegmen tegmin-is 3n. hide, covering; abl. of cause
laetus: describing Romulus' pleasure at wearing the hide. This refers to Romulus and Remus being exposed to die, but found and suckled by a wolf
276 *Rōmul-us ī* 2m. Romulus
excipiet: 'will take over'
Māuorti-us a um of Mars (*Māuors* was the ancient name for Mars)
277 *dīcet*: 'will call [them]'

Learning vocabulary
addō 3 *addidī additum* I add, receive
Ascani-us ī 2m. Ascanius or Iulus, son of Aeneas
cūi scans as one long syllable
dōnec until
expleō 2 *explēuī explētum* I complete, fulfil, satisfy

importance in this epic: history is replaying itself, and that in itself 'justifies' Rome's position in the world, cf. *Intro* [23]. The gods would not allow it otherwise. All this is well in line with ancient critics' view of one of the purposes of the *Aeneid* – to praise Augustus' family line (*Intro* [3, 10]).

Jupiter now winds remote pre-history fast forward (see *Intro* [18] for the chronological problems involved in integrating the Aeneas legend with the Romulus and Remus myth). After 30 years ruling Lavinium, Ascanius will relocate in Alba Longa (270–1), and 300 years after that, Romulus and Remus will be born to – Ilia, another name for Rhea Silvia and another Trojan connection (274–5). The union of Rome (through Mars, the Roman god of war) with Troy (through the name Ilia and over 300 years of pre-history) will produce the new, destined people. Jupiter emphasises the point about Rome with the *Rōmulus–Rōmānus* name play (276–7). But the Trojan connection is not yet forgotten: *gente sub Hectoreā* (273) keeps it alive – for Hector, having been killed in Troy, is associated with nowhere else. Note: neither Aeneas nor Ascanius will be *Romans* (nor rule empires) – that will come much later.

See: Jenkyns (1998: 394–6) on Ascanius.

1.278–88: 'Rome will rule for ever, and Juno will be won over. Romans will conquer Greece, and Julius Caesar will be born'

'hīs ego nec mētās rērum nec tempora pōnō;
imperium sine fīne dedī. quīn aspera Iūnō,
quae mare nunc terrāsque metū caelumque fatīgat,   280
cōnsilia in melius referet, mēcumque fouēbit
Rōmānōs, rērum dominōs gentemque togātam.
sīc placitum. ueniet lūstrīs lābentibus aetās,
cum domus Assaracī Pthīam clārāsque Mycēnās
seruitiō premet, ac uictīs^ dominābitur ^Argīs.   285
nāscētur pulchrā^ Troiānus ^orīgine Caesar^,
imperium Ōceanō, fāmam ^quī terminet astrīs –
Iūlius, ā magnō^ dēmissum nōmen ^Iūlō.'

gemin-us a um twin
Iūl-us ī 2m. Iulus (three syllables)
Mārs Mārt-is 3m. Mars, god of war
sacerdōs sacerdōt-is 3m./f. priest(ess)

278 hīs: 'on these [Romans]'
mēt-a ae 1f. bound, limit (rērum suggests spatial limits, to contrast with tempora)
279 quīn what's more
280 metū: abl. of cause, probably the fear she feels for Carthage (S., cf. 23)
caelumque: said through gritted teeth. It is bad enough that Juno is creating havoc by land and sea – but in heaven too!
fatīgō 1 I harass
281 referet: here, 'will change'
*fouēō 2 I nurture, nourish, grow
282 togāt-us a um wearing the toga
283 *lūstr-um ī 2n. sacred season. This was a uniquely Roman measurement of time (five years). Jupiter even speaks Roman! (See Intro [27])
284 domus Assaracī: i.e. the descendants of Assaracus, subject of premet

Assarac-us ī 2m. Assaracus (grandfather of Aeneas' father Anchises)
Pthī-a ae 1f. Pthia (Achilles' home)
*Mycēn-ae ārum 1f. pl. Mycenae (palace of Agamemnon, brother of Menelaus)
285 seruiti-um ī 2n. slavery
*dominor 1 dep. I rule over (+ dat.)
286 *nāscor 3 dep. nātus I am being born
*orīgō orīgin-is 3f. stock, source, origin
Caesar -is 3m. Caesar – but which one? Julius Caesar, or his adopted son and first Roman emperor, Augustus Caesar (who also became a Julius)? See **1.289–96**
287 Ōcean-us ī 2m. Ocean. S. comments that Roman mastery over the Ocean was demonstrated by their conquest of the Britons
terminō 3 I establish the boundaries of X (acc.) by Y (abl.); this vb. (subject quī = Caesar) controls as objs. both imperium and fāmam. terminet is subjunc., indicating a sense of purpose, 'destined to . . .' (Cong.; see **RL**145.3, **M**97.5)
astr-um ī 2n. star, sky
288 Iūli-us ī 2m. Julius (scanned as if Yūlius)
*dēmittō 3 dēmīsī dēmissum I hand/pass/send down

1.278–88: 278–82 are magnificent lines, designed to warm any Roman's heart – the vision of the Eternal City: for this is what Jupiter has promised them. Even aspera Juno will come on-board (S. comments that aspera is the most Jupiter can get away with to describe his wife). Note in particular dedī (279); Jupiter is making all sorts of promises for the future, but here he makes it quite clear that he has already granted Romans imperium sine fīne – an assumption that every Roman took for granted. 282 is pointed: Rome will be master of the world (militarily), while 'the toga-wearing race' sums up everything it meant to be Roman in civil life. But as Jenkyns again makes clear, Rome will not lose its Trojan connections. Assaracus is the grandfather of Aeneas' father Anchises, taking us even further back in Trojan history; and here Jupiter says that Assaracus' offspring

1.289–96: 'Caesar will be received into heaven, justice will prevail, war will end and Strife be locked up'

'hunc^ tū ōlim caelō, spoliīs Orientis ^onustum,
accipiēs sēcūra; uocābitur hic quoque uōtīs.   290

Learning vocabulary	
dēmittō 3 *dēmīsī dēmissum* I hand/pass/send down	*caelō*: local abl.
dominor 1 dep. I rule over (+ dat.)	**spoli-a ōrum* 2n. pl. spoils, booty, plunder; but what
foueō 2 I nurture, nourish, grow	spoils are these? See **1.289–96** below for
lūstr-um ī 2n. sacred season	discussion
*Mycēn-ae ārum 1f. pl. Mycenae (palace of	*Oriēns Orient-is* 3m. East, daybreak
Agamemnon, brother of Menelaus)	*onust-us a um* loaded, heaped
nāscor 3 dep. *nātus* I am being born	**290** *secūr-us a um* not anxious (here, 'any more',
orīgō orīgin-is 3f. stock, source, origin	because Juno will no longer be hostile); carefree,
	unconcerned
	hic quoque: i.e. Julius Caesar/Augustus will become
289 *hunc*: Caesar (we are still not sure whether this	a god too, like Aeneas (S.; in V.'s time, Caesar was
is Julius or Augustus), obj. of *tū . . . accipiēs*	already a god)
tū: Jupiter now addresses Venus directly, foretelling	*uōt-um ī* 2n. prayer, vow
Caesar's deification	

(i.e. the Romans) will conquer three of Greece's most famous Homeric-heroic towns (see notes on Pthia and Mycenae; Argos was home of Diomedes, 284–5). Jupiter is referring here to Rome's conquest and provincialisation of Greece in the second century BC – as if the Trojans are fighting back against Greece and finally getting their revenge in a second 'Trojan war'! (See *Intro* [18].) So V. adds another layer of history to the seamless sequence: contemporary Rome with its world-wide empire, second-century BC Rome, the Troy of the Trojan war, and Troy three generations earlier.

In three resounding lines, *Troiānus Caesar* (286) confirms the link between the imperial household and Troy, while *Iūlius* (288) takes us back to the Trojan origin of the name *Iūlus* (288, cf. 267), the Trojan origins elevated with *pulchrā* (286) and *magnō* (288). In between the historical name-games of 286 and 288, the achievement of this Trojan Caesar is predicted in the scope of both his *imperium* (cf. Venus' flattery of Jupiter at 230, and note) and his *fāma* (cf. 259–60).

Is this all a little too 'pat'? V. usually has a keen sense of historical process and of the price that 'destiny' and 'empire' extract. Here it is easy to feel that 'In these places [i.e. 278–82 particularly] the demands of patronage and panegyric have overridden the historical sense.'

See: Jenkyns (1998: 395) on Roman connections with Troy, and (121) on the price of empire; Jones and Sidwell (1997: sections 34–44) on Rome's conquest of Greece.

Crunch: 286–8

1.289–96: So, at last, in the person of Caesar, 'Troy is subsumed in Rome, and the names that reverberate in the final sentence – *cāna Fidēs, et Vesta, Remō cum frātre Quirīnus* – are Roman: Roman to the core.' So too is the history, which Jupiter assures Venus will happen 'at some time' (*ōlim*). It had, of course, happened in V.'s day, and points to the conclusion that the 'Caesar' being referred to at 286 is not Julius Caesar, but Augustus. The 'spoils of the East' (289) refer to the triumph of Octavian (Augustus) over Marc Antony and Cleopatra at the sea-battle off Actium (31 BC) when Egypt fell to Rome, and Octavian marched through the Near East – Judea, Syria and Asia Minor – before triumphing in

asperaᐱ tum positīs* mītēscent ᐱsaecula *bellīs;
cāna Fidēs, et Vesta, Remōᐱ cum ᐱfrātre Quirīnus,
iūra dabunt; dīraeᐱ ferrō et compāgibus artīs
claudentur Bellī ᐱportae; Furorᐱ impius intus,
saeua* ᐱsedēns super *arma, et centum* ᐱuīnctus *aēnīs   295
post tergum *nōdīs, fremet horridus ōre cruentō.'

291 *mītēscō* 3 I am softened, ripen, mellow; a 'golden line' (i.e. two nouns qualified by two adjs. with a vb keeping them apart). In this line, the order is AB vb. AB; AB vb. BA (chiasmus) is also used
*saecul-um ī 2n. age
292 *cān-us a um* grey
Fidēs: here deified. These four deities are chosen as 'typical of the primitive and golden age of Rome' (Cong.)
*Vest-a ae 1f. goddess of the hearth and family
Rem-us ī 2m. Remus
Quirīn-us ī 2m. (another name for) Romulus
293 **dīr-us a um* fearful, horrible (hypallage (see on 101), i.e. transferred epithet, really referring to *bellī*?)
compāg-ēs is 3f. fastening (*ferrō . . . compāgibus*: hendiadys? See **Glossary of literary terms**)
*art-us a um tight

294 *Bellī portae*: what are these gates? See discussion below
*impi-us a um unholy, godless (V. has civil war in mind)
295 *uinciō* 4 *uīnxī uīnctum* I bind, tie
296 **nōd-us ī* 2m. knot
horrid-us a um hideous, ghastly
*cruent-us a um bloody, bloodthirsty

Learning vocabulary
art-us a um tight
cruent-us a um bloody, bloodthirsty
dīr-us a um fearful, horrible
impi-us a um unholy, godless
nōd-us ī 2m. knot
saecul-um ī 2n. age
spoli-a ōrum 2n. pl. spoils, booty, plunder
Vest-a ae 1f. goddess of the hearth and family

Rome in 29 BC; the end of war prophesied in 291 is realised in 293–4, when the gates of the temple of Janus, closed only when peace reigned, were shut by Octavian in 29 BC, and again in 25 BC; while 292 and *Furor* in 294–6 refer to the disastrous and, to Romans who prided themselves on the solidity of their state, utterly traumatic civil war, now brought to an end and (they hoped) banished for ever by Octavian's victory. The ghastliness of the *Furor* that brought the war about is chillingly portrayed by V. at 294–6 in all its bloody savagery; note *impius* – the opposite of everything *pius Aenēās* stands for. *Fidēs* – 'truth, honour, loyalty' – is a famous old-fashioned Roman virtue, hence *cāna*, and personified as a deity here; *Vesta*, Roman goddess of the hearth, conjures up a picture of the nation as one huge family gathering; and Romulus and Remus now join them to impose laws (292–3), instead of fighting each other (Romulus killed Remus in a dispute over the walls of Rome). See *Intro* [12, 28–9]; Page's notes on these lines are well worth consulting.

If one compares this whole scene with the proem at 1–11, the same concerns emerge throughout: Aeneas' travels and suffering, his *pietās*, the role of fate, the rivalry with Carthage, the foundation of Rome, the enmity of Juno, etc. In other words, the 'programme' laid out for Aeneas in 1–11 matches the view of Rome's historic destiny confirmed by Jupiter here. It is just a matter of when and how it will all turn out. There will be plenty of room for tragedy and despair on the way, but one can argue that that does not necessarily 'subvert' V.'s overall design (cf. [28]). What one can say is *tantae mōlis . . .* (33): destiny commands a price.

See: Jenkyns (1998: 396) on Troy and Rome; Horsfall (1995: 101–5) on the proem connections.

Crunch: 292–6

1.297–304: *Maia's son Mercury is sent to prepare Dido and the Carthaginians to welcome Aeneas and the Trojans*

haec ait, et Maiā genitum dēmittit ab altō,
ut terrae, utque nouae^ pateant Karthāginis ^arcēs
hospitiō Teucrīs, nē fātī nescia Dīdō
fīnibus arcēret: uolat ille per āera magnum   300
rēmigiō ālārum, ac Libyae citus astitit ōrīs.
et iam iussa facit, pōnuntque ferōcia^ Poenī

297 *Mai-a ae* 1f. Maia, mother of Mercury (Hermes)
genit-us a um [one] born from, son/daughter of
 (+ abl.)
298 *pateō 2 I am accessible, lie open; am
 revealed
299 *hospiti-um ī 2n. welcome, entertainment,
 hospitality; here dat. 'for a welcome, to be a
 welcome'
nesci-us a um ignorant of (+ gen.)
*Dīdō Dīdōn-is 3f. Dido, queen of Carthage. At 340,
 S. says that her name was in fact Elissa, and she
 was named Dido only after her death, the Punic
 for 'virago'. The reason was that, after the loss of
 her first husband, she was forced into a marriage
 she did not want. She therefore committed
 suicide on a pyre she had constructed in pretence
 of appeasing the shade of her first husband. Her
 man-like qualities will be very evident in V.'s
 telling of her story, which will take a very different

turn: Dido will commit suicide because Aeneas
 leaves her (Book 4)
300 *arcēret*: understand 'the Trojans from' + abl.
*āēr āer-is 3m. air (*āer-a*, three syllables, is the Latin
 acc. s.)
301 *rēmigi-um ī* 2n. (abl. of instrument) oarage,
 rowing; flying was often described in terms of
 rowing with wings
āl-a ae 1f. wing
cit-us a um quick(ly), speedy
astō 1 *astitī* I alight at, reach, stand by
302 *et*: scans long because *iam = yam*
*Poen-ī ōrum 2m. Carthaginians. Greeks called this
 people, who came from roughly modern
 Lebanon, *Phoinikes*, Greek *phoinos*, 'red',
 probably after the luxury purple dye produced
 there by crushing shell-fish (the Bible calls them
 Canaanites). Romans latinised their name into
 Poen-us and *Pūnic-us* (see on 1.366 for 'Carthage')

1.297–304: To show that he means what he says (to a still doubtful Venus?), Jupiter follows his words with immediate action: he sends Mercury to prepare the way for the arrival of Aeneas in Carthage. Page (on 299) suggests that it is odd for V. to say that Jupiter was worried 'lest Dido *nescia fātī* should keep them away', since Aeneas' visit will mean her death, i.e. it is only thanks to her ignorance of fate that she lets them in! But that is to look too far ahead. As S. says, the *fātum* referred to is not Dido's. All Jupiter means is that it is fated that Aeneas should arrive in Carthage (whatever happens later on there), and he does not want Dido preventing that first step. Given that her people possess *ferōcia corda* (302), this looks distinctly possible; cf. 539–41, where the Trojan arrivals complain at their treatment, and 563–4, where Dido explains that a new city has to be especially careful to guard its frontiers. *Fātum*, in other words, can use a local helping hand now and again.

But it may be that V. means exactly what he says, i.e. that Mercury's aim *is* to deceive Dido 'in order to further the Roman mission. Dido's ignorance of destiny . . . has been divinely assured (*uolente deō* 303) and the god's gift to Dido of inner peace and human kindness (303–4) ensures from the beginning her own madness and death. Can this be viewed as anything but divine cruelty?'

In Apollonius Rhodius' *Argonautica*, as soon as Jason arrives in Phasis to get the golden fleece, Aphrodite/Venus sends down her son Eros/Cupid to make Medea fall in

^corda, uolente de<u>ō</u>; in prīmīs rēgīna quiētum^
accipit in Teucrōs ^animum mentemque benignam.

303 *in prīmīs* especially
quiēt-us a um peaceful, gentle, relaxed
304 *in Teucrōs*: i.e. towards the Trojans
benign-us a um friendly, kind

Learning vocabulary

āēr āer-is 3m. air
Dīdō Dīdōn-is 3f. Dido, queen of Carthage

hospiti-um ī 2n. welcome, entertainment,
   hospitality
pateō 2 I am accessible, lie open; am
   revealed
Poen-ī ōrum 2m. Carthaginians

---

love with Jason at once (see *Intro* [10] footnote 23). V. delays this moment. See **Study Section for 1.657–756** where the Apollonius passage is quoted in full.

See: Ross (2007: 108–9) on the deception of Dido; Nelis (2001: 73–9) on Apollonius.

Learning vocabulary for Section 1.223–304

Achīu-ī ōrum 2m. Greeks
addō 3 *addidī additum* I add, receive
āēr āer-is 3m. air
art-us a um tight
aru-um ī 2n. field
Ascani-us ī 2m. Ascanius or Iulus, son of Aeneas
compōnō 3 *composuī compos(i)tum* I settle, arrange,
   adjust
cruent-us a um bloody, bloodthirsty
cūī scans as one long syllable
dēmittō 3 *dēmīsī dēmissum* I hand/pass/send down
Dīdō Dīdōn-is 3f. Dido, queen of Carthage
dīr-us a um fearful, horrible
dominor 1 dep. I rule over (+ dat.)
dōnec until
ēlābor 3 dep. *ēlāpsus* I escape, slip away from
equidem [I] for my part
expleō 2 *explēuī explētum* I complete, fulfil, satisfy
foueō 2 *fouī fōtum* I nurture, nourish, grow
fūnus fūner-is 3n. death
gemin-us a um twin
hospiti-um ī 2n. welcome, entertainment,
   hospitality
impi-us a um unholy, godless

īnfand-us a um unspeakable, accursed
Iūl-us ī 2m. Iulus
lacrim-a ae 1f. tear
libō 1 I graze, touch lightly; pour (a libation)
lūmen lūmin-is 3n. light; eye
lūstr-um ī 2n. sacred season
Mārs Mārt-is 3m. Mars, god of war
Mycēn-ae ārum 1f. pl. Mycenae (palace of
   Agamemnon, brother of Menelaus)
nāscor 3 dep. *nātus* I am being born
nāt-us a um born of (+ abl.); *nātus* = son, *nāta* =
   daughter
nōd-us ī 2m. knot
orb-is 3m. globe, orb, world
orīgō orīgin-is 3f. stock, source, origin
pateō 2 I am accessible, lie open; am revealed
Poen-ī ōrum 2m. Carthaginians
prōdō 3 *prodidī proditum* I betray
rēgnō 1 I rule
sacerdōs sacerdōt-is 3 m./f. priest(ess)
saecul-um ī 2n. age
spoli-a ōrum 2n. pl. spoils, booty, plunder
uult-us ūs 4m. face, look
Vest-a ae 1f. goddess of the hearth and family

Study Section for 1.223–304

1. To what extent does Venus bring emotional pressure to bear on Jupiter?
2. Is Venus' primary concern for Aeneas, or for her own plans for Rome? Or are the two indistinguishable?

3. Why is V. so insistent that Trojan history must be linked to Roman?
4. How could you use Jupiter's speech to argue that V. was a propagandist for Augustus' regime?
5. Scan 254–60.

1.305–417: Encounter with Venus

In this Section, *as Aeneas and Achates explore the terrain, Venus, disguised as a huntress, meets Aeneas and tells him the story of Dido's arrival in Carthage and informs him that his men are safe. He recognises her as she leaves.*

(Note: from now on till the end of Book 1, elisions will not be marked, and linking devices will be more sparingly used. You can also choose your own passages to *crunch*.)

1.305–13: *In the morning Aeneas and Achates set out to explore the land*

at pius Aenēās, per noctem plūrima uoluēns,	305
ut prīmum lūx alma data est, exīre locōsque	
explōrāre nouōs, quās uentō accesserit ōrās,	
quī teneant (nam inculta uidet) hominēsne feraene,	
quaerere cōnstituit, sociīsque exācta referre.	
classem^ in conuexō nemorum, sub rūpe cauātā,	310
arboribus ^clausam circum atque horrentibus umbrīs	

306 *ut prīmum* as soon as
*alm-us a um kindly, fostering
exīre . . . explōrāre (**307**) *. . . quaerere* (**309**) *. . . referre* (**309**): all the infins. are dependent on *cōnstituit* (**309**)
307 *explōrō* 1 I investigate, reconnoitre
quās . . . ōrās: '[to] what shores'; the first of two indir. qs. (the other is *quī . . . feraene* **308**) after *quaerere cōnstituit* (**309**). See **RLR3, W30,M94**
308 *incult-us a um* uncultivated, rough (here n. pl. acc.)
uidet: *-et* here counts as long, an occasional feature of the first beat of a foot when it is followed by a

caesura, especially if there is a pause after it (as there often is); but there are many unexplained such lengthenings which do not seem to follow any 'rule'
hominēs-ne ferae-ne [*sint*]: *-ne* here means 'whether . . . or'
fer-a ae 1f. wild animal
309 *cōnstituō* 3 *cōnstituī cōnstitūtum* I decide
exāct-us a um precise (n. pl. acc., i.e. details)
310 *classem*: obj. of *occulit* (**312**)
conuex-us a um overarching, covering. Treat here as a noun with *nemorum*, lit. 'in the covering of [i.e. offered by] the grove'
cauāt-us a um hollow

1.305–13: *pius* 305 reminds us of Aeneas' outstanding quality: devotion to duty. It is illustrated here by a sleepless night, Aeneas deep in thought on *plūrima*. But that does not mean he can indulge himself: *ut prīmum . . .* (306) and he is up at once, examining the terrain and deciding on action. It looks such a wasteland he wonders whether people actually inhabit it (308). Carthage will dispel all that. Since his fleet is the only means of escape if danger looms, he ensures it is well enough hidden by natural means – covering trees under a rocky overhang (310–12) – before setting off with Achates, and two spears for defence. This hero has foresight.

occulit; ipse ūnō graditur comitātus Achāte,
bīna manū lātō^ crispāns hastīlia ^ferrō.

1.314–24: *Aeneas' mother Venus, dressed as a Spartan girl or Thracian huntress, meets him and asks if he has seen her fellow huntresses*

cuī māter^ mediā sēsē tulit ^obuia siluā,
uirginis ōs habitumque ^gerēns, et uirginis^ arma   315
^Spartānae, uel quālis^ equōs ^Thrēissa fatīgat
^Harpalycē, uolucremque fugā praeuertitur Hebrum.
namque umerīs dē mōre habilem suspenderat arcum
uēnātrīx, dederatque comam diffundere uentīs,
nūda genū, nōdōque sinūs collēcta fluentīs.   320

312 *occulō* 3 I conceal, cover up; presumably 'leaving the fleet hidden' rather than actually hiding it. 164–5 suggest the harbour offered automatic cover
ūnō = 'only, alone'
*gradior 3 dep. *gressus* I walk, step
*comitor 1 dep. I accompany (+ abl.)
Achāte: abl. of *Achātēs*
313 *bīn-us a um* twin
*lāt-us a um broad (referring to the spears' head)
crispō 1 I balance, grasp
hastīl-e is 3n. spear

Learning vocabulary
alm-us a um kindly, fostering
comitor 1 dep. I accompany (+ abl.)
gradior 3 dep. *gressus* I walk, step
lāt-us a um broad

314 *cuī*: i.e. Aeneas, dat. after *obuia*. Another example of Latin starting a sentence with a relative that picks up something from the previous sentence
māter: Venus
*sēsē = *sē*
obui-us a um in the way of, to meet (+ dat.)
315 *habit-us ūs* 4m. look, appearance, condition
gerēns: 'with' is the easiest translation
316 *Spartān-us a um* Spartan (renowned for their hard training)

uel quālis: lit. 'or [being] of what sort *Thrēissa Harpalycē fatīgat* . . .', i.e. 'like *T H* when she . . .'
Thrēiss-us a um from Thrace
fatīgō 1 I wear out, i.e. outlast (because she is faster than the horses)
317 *Harpalycē*: nom., Harpalyce, daughter of the Thracian king Harpalycus, suckled by heifers and mares when her mother died and raised as a warrior princess. When her father lost his throne, she lived in the wilds, plundering herds
uolucr-is e swift
praeuertor 3 I outstrip
Hebr-us ī 2m. Hebrus (a river in Thrace)
318 *dē mōre*: 'according to custom'
habil-is e ready, fit
*suspendō 3 *suspendī suspēnsum* I hang
arc-us ūs 4m. bow
319 *uēnātrīx uēnātric-is* 3f. huntress; here 'as a huntress'
*com-a ae 1f. hair. Take *uentīs* (dat.) next, and then explain what the wind is doing to it with *diffundere*, an 'epexegetic' – i.e. explanatory – inf., more common in Greek than Latin
diffundō 3 I scatter, blow about
320 *nūd-us a um* naked, stripped
gen-ū ūs 4n. knee (here acc. of respect after *nūda*)
collēcta: the 'middle' usage with *collēcta* active in meaning, controlling the dir. obj. *sinūs fluentīs*.

1.314–24: V. chooses to make Venus appear to Aeneas in a wood, alone and in disguise (it is the Virgilian convention, shared by Homer in the *Odyssey* but not in the *Iliad*, that gods virtually never appear in their own person to humans). *sēsē tulit obuia* exudes her sense of purpose. But V. must then motivate her appearance in what is an odd location for a woman – nice girls stayed at home in the ancient world and certainly did not wander round woods, let alone on their own – and chooses to make her a huntress. V. gives her the appearance of a young girl of virginal appearance (an ironic touch: Venus

ac prior, 'hēus' inquit 'iuuenēs, mōnstrāte meārum^
uīdistis sī quam* hīc *errantem forte ^sorōrum,
*succīnctam pharetrā et maculōsae tegmine lyncis,
aut spūmantis aprī cursum clāmōre *prementem.'

1.325–34: *Aeneas, convinced she is a goddess, asks for help, promising her sacrifices*

sīc Venus; et Veneris contrā sīc filius ōrsus: 325
'nūlla tuārum^ audīta mihī neque uīsa ^sorōrum –

collēcta means 'having gathered' in the sense of 'fastened'; see p. 39 ((c)(ii)) above. Her dress would normally reach her feet, but since she is a huntress she has caught it up above the knee for ease of movement.

**fluō* 3 *flūxī flūxum* I flow, ebb (away)

321 **prior* *-is* first, earlier, former (i.e. before Aeneas can speak)

heūs hey! (a colloquial, familiar usage)

**mōnstrō* 1 I show, point out

meārum . . . sorōrum (322): take in order *sī forte uīdistis quam* ('any' (f. acc. s.); see on 151) *meārum sorōrum errantem hīc*

322 **forte* perhaps, by chance

323 *succīnct-us a um* girded with (+ abl.), i.e. having (the abl.) hanging from her belt

**pharetr-a ae* 1f. quiver

maculōs-us a um spotted

tegmen tegmin-is 3n. covering

lynx lync-is 3f. lynx, lynx-skin

324 **spūmō* 1 I foam

aper apr-ī 2m. boar

cursum . . . prementem: i.e. chasing hard

See: Jones (2007: 7–8) for mythical women turning to hunting.

Learning vocabulary

com-a ae 1f. hair

fluō 3 *flūxī flūxum* I flow, ebb (away)

forte perhaps, by chance

mōnstrō 1 I show, point out

pharetr-a ae 1f. quiver

prior -is first, earlier, former

sēsē = sē

spūmō 1 I foam

suspendō 3 *suspendī suspēnsum* I hang

325 *ōrdior* 4 dep. *ōrsus* I begin. Ellipsis of *est* here and in the next line

326 *mihī*: dat. of agent after *audīta* (common after perf. pass.; **RLL**(e)1(iv), **W**24, **M**111); *audīta* picks up *clāmōre* (324)

is goddess of sex). But she sports all the right hunting gear (318–19) and is racily clothed (dress hitched up, showing a leg, 319–20), with hair flying in the wind. She is out with a troupe of other girls (!) and, before Aeneas can speak, hails him in what seems like distinctly convivial tones. Since it was the job of hunters to search for prey and then give chase, it was presumably easy to become separated from the group (hence 321–4). Is there something 'troubling . . . sinister and slithery' about this 'sexy, virginal mother'. Or amusing? What one would expect from a slippery character like Venus? Might it have brought to the mind of the Roman reader Venus' affair with the handsome young Adonis, for whom she abandoned Olympus to join him in hunting in the woods (Ovid *Metamorphoses* 10.519–739, cf. Jones (2007: 228–49))? Perhaps the fact that she is hunting with other *girls* is designed to allay that suspicion.

See: Jones (1988) on *Odyssey* 1.105 for Homeric gods; Jenkyns (1998: 391) for a 'troubling' Venus.

1.325–34: *Venus . . . Veneris filius* is a neat ironic touch. But *pius* Aeneas can spot a god when he has to (he has no doubts about the matter, *certē* 328); so when he has answered

ō quam tē memorem, uirgō? namque haud tibi uultus
mortālis, nec uōx hominem sonat: ō, dea certē,
(an Phoebī soror? an nymphārum sanguinis ūna?)
sīs fēlīx, nostrumque leuēs, quaecumque, labōrem,   330
et, quō sub caelō tandem, quibus orbis in ōrīs
iactēmur, doceās. ignārī^ hominumque locōrumque
errāmus, uentō hūc uastīs et flūctibus ^āctī.
multa^ tibi ante ārās nostrā cadet ^hostia dextrā.'

1.335–42: *Venus denies it, saying she is an ordinary Tyrian girl in a city where Dido now rules. She tells the story*

tum Venus: 'haud equidem tālī mē dignor honōre;   335

327 *ō*: Aeneas breaks off in bewilderment – he
realises this is no ordinary huntress
quam tē memorem: *memorem* is deliberative
subjunc. *quam* (from *quis*) agrees with *tē*, lit. '[as]
whom/what you am I to . . .?' (See **RL**152,
M34.) He is groping for the right identity to
apply to a woman who he is confident is a goddess
(S.)
327 *tibi*: dat. of possession; ellipsis of *est*
328 **mortāl-is e* mortal, human
sonat: 'has the ring of'; *hominem* (as usual) means
'human', not 'male'
329 **Phoeb-us ī* 2m. (Phoebus) Apollo (his sister is
Diana, goddess of hunting). Note ellipsis of *es*
(twice). Aeneas blurts out flustered questions
nymphārum: i.e. Diana's nymphs (the Oreades)
sanguinis: i.e. family
330 *sīs*: jussive subjunc. (see **RL**152, **W**28, **M**34, 89);
so too *leuēs* and *doceās* (**332**)

fēlīx fēlīc-is propitious, happy, fortunate, successful;
the *sīs fēlīx* formula is regularly used when a
human is asking for divine help
quaecumque: ellipsis of *es*
331 *tandem*: often in commands and questions,
'please/I beg you'
332 **doceō* 2 *docuī doctum* I teach, inform
locōrumque: very occasionally V. elides a vowel at
the end of the line before a vowel in the next line
334 *multa*: 'many a'
cadet: tense?
host-ia ae 1f. sacrificial animal

Learning vocabulary
doceō 2 *docuī doctum* I teach, inform
mortāl-is e mortal, human
Phoeb-us ī 2m. Phoebus (Apollo)

335 *dignor* 1 dep. I count X (acc.) worthy of (+ abl.)

her question, he has no idea how to name her. *uirgō* is the best he can do as he breaks off
(327). His guess at 329 is informed enough (the huntress god Diana/Artemis is sister of
Apollo, always attended by her nymphs), but it is only a guess. The point of all this is that
it is extremely important to get the right name of the god if you want the god to help
you. In prayers, you always specify the god on whom you are calling, and list his/her
attributes; otherwise, you call on 'any other god who may be listening' (*quaecumque*,
330). Aeneas now goes into the typical *quid prō quō* prayer sequence – after naming the
god, ask for help (330–2); explain the need (332–3); and end with the promise of sacrifice if the god grants the request (334). Further, it is a very modest request – only for
information (*labōrem* 330 referring to Aeneas' present exploration of his surroundings,
made explicit in the questions at 331–2). Does the elided *-que* at the end of 332 suggest a
'catch in [Aeneas'] voice' to indicate despair (Williams (1972))?

See: Jones (2003: 29–30) for Homeric prayers.

1.335–42: Venus' opening disavowal (335) and explanation of her gear (336–7) make it

uirginibus Tyriīs mōs est gestāre pharetram,
purpureōque altē sūrās uincīre cothurnō.
Pūnica rēgna uidēs, Tyriōs et Agēnoris urbem;
sed finēs Libycī, genus intractābile bellō.
imperium Dīdō^ Tyriā regit urbe ^profecta,   340
germānum ^fugiēns. longa est iniūria, longae
ambāgēs; sed summa sequar fastīgia rērum.'

1.343–52: 'Dido's beloved husband Sychaeus was killed by her evil brother Pygmalion for Sychaeus' gold; he kept the deed secret from her'

'huīc coniūnx Sychaeus erat, dītissimus agrī
Phoenīcum, et magnō miserae dīlēctus amōre,

336 gestō 1 I wear, carry
pharetr-a ae 1f. quiver
337 purpure-us a um purple. This famous, and very
expensive, dye – a mark of power and status in
Rome (cf. our 'born to the purple') – originated
from shell-fish, crushed and treated, found
especially off the coast of Tyre, and therefore
likely to feature on a Carthaginian inhabitant
(1.12)
altē: i.e. high up the leg
sūr-a ae 1f. calf (of the leg)
uinciō 4 I bind
cothurn-us ī 2m. boot
338 Pūnic-us a um Carthaginian, Punic
Agēnor -is 3m. Agenor, an ancestor of Dido from
Tyre
339 finēs: this refers to the surrounding territory, the
hinterland
*Libyc-us a um Libyan
intractābil-is e difficult to handle
340 imperium: not 'empire'; rather 'power'
urbe: i.e. (from) Tyre
341 *germān-us ī 2m. brother; germān-a 1f. sister
iniūri-a ae 1f. crime, wrong (here, 'the story of the
wrongs done to her')

342 ambāg-ēs um 3f. pl. twists and turns
*fastīgi-a ōrum 2n. pl. outlines (lit. 'headings,
peaks'); heights, tips

Learning vocabulary
fastīgi-a ōrum 2n. pl. outlines; heights, tips
germān-a 1f. sister
germān-us ī 2m. brother
Libyc-us a um Libyan

343 huīc: i.e. Dido (dat. of possession)
Sychae-us ī 2m. Sychaeus. Note the alternative
scansion at **348**. This is fairly common with
proper names (cf. Lauīnium/Lāuīnium, Italus/
Ītalus, etc.)
dīs dīt-is rich in (+ gen., here agrī)
agrī: all the manuscripts write agrī, but since the
Phoenicians were a commercial people and there
is much talk of gold in this passage (**349**, 359,
363), it may be that aurī is preferable
344 Phoenīc-ēs um 3m. pl. Phoenicians (with
dītissimus)
miserae: dat. of agent, 'by the unfortunate [woman]',
i.e. Dido
dīligō 3 dīlēxī dīlēctum I hold dear

---

clear that she is not about to reveal who she is. But she is clearly satisfied with Aeneas' reply
because she proceeds to answer his request. Pūnica rēgna (338) sends no shivers down
Aeneas' spine – why should it? – while Venus offers further comfort by implying that it is
not a warlike place, in contrast with the surrounding territory (339). So far, so good. Her
introduction to Dido's story is also well-calculated to catch Aeneas' keen attention: for Dido
is an exile from Tyre (340) who, wronged and after many adventures (341–2), has founded a
new city abroad – neatly matching Aeneas' story (so far) and his hopes for the future.

1.343–52: Dido's marriage was a love-match – one senses her one, true love (344–6,
351–2). Venus prepares us for the murderous activity of Dido's brother in 347 and 348

cūi pater intāctam dederat, prīmīsque iugārat   345
ōminibus. sed rēgna Tyrī germānus habēbat
Pygmaliōn, scelere ante aliōs immānior omnēs.
quōs inter medius uēnit furor. ille^ Sychaeum*
^impius ante ārās, atque aurī ^caecus amōre,
clam ferrō *incautum superat, ^sēcūrus amōrum   350
germānae; factumque diū cēlāuit, et aegram^,
multa malus simulāns, uānā spē lūsit ^amantem.'

1.353–64: 'Sychaeus revealed all in a dream and, telling Dido where his gold was, persuaded her to flee, which she did, with companions'

'ipsa^ sed in somnīs inhumātī* uēnit ^imāgō
*coniugis, ōra modīs ^attollēns pallida mīrīs,

345 *cūi*: i.e. to Sychaeus
pater: i.e. of Dido
intāct-us a um virgin, untouched (ellipsis of 'her')
iugō 1 I join, unite (ellipsis of 'her to him'); *iugāuerat* = *iugārat*
346 *ōmen ōmin-is* 3n. auspices (taken in the course of any serious business); here = marriage omens; *prīmīs* indicates it was Dido's first marriage
Tyr-us ī 2f. Tyre
347 *Pygmaliōn -is* 3m. Pygmalion, Dido's brother (do not confuse with the Pygmalion who fell in love with the statue he had made, Ovid *Metamorphoses* 10.243–97)
scelere: 'in villainy', abl. of respect with *immānior*
ante: = *quam*
348 *quōs inter* = *inter quōs*
medius: i.e. coming between, alienating
ille: Pygmalion
349 *caecus a um* blind
350 *clam* in secret
incaut-us a um off one's guard
sēcūr-us a um unconcerned about (+ gen.)

351 *diū* for a long time
cēlō 1 I hide
352 *uān-us a um* empty, illusory, vain
amantem: note powerful position, held till the end

See: Jones (2007: 222–7) on Ovid's Pygmalion.

Learning vocabulary

ōmen ōmin-is 3n. auspices (taken in the course of any serious undertaking)
uān-us a um empty, illusory, vain

353 *ipsa*: referring to *imāgō*
inhumāt-us a um unburied (it was a great wrong to leave a body unburied; such souls were thought to wander the world, haunting and disturbing the living)
imāgō imāgin-is 3f. image, likeness, appearance, ghost
354 *ōra*: from *ōs* (pl. for s., as *pectora* 355)
mod-us ī 2m. way, method (pl. for s., abl. of manner)
attollō 3 I raise, lift up
pallid-us a um pale, wan

(*furor*). In 349 she puts *impius* in emphatic position and immediately explains it by *ante ārās* (349) (was Sychaeus sacrificing there? Or seeking refuge from the unexpected – *incautum* 350 – assault?). Defiant of gods, motivated by blind greed (349), secretive and scheming (350, 351), Pygmalion is also defiant of duty to family, uncaring about his sister and cruelly deceiving her (350–2) – *miserae* (344) and *aegram* (351) indeed, and about to become yet *miserior* and *aegrior*. For she will fall in love with Aeneas, and he too will deceive and abandon her in Book 4, leading her to commit suicide.

1.353–64: *inhumātī* (353) compounds Pygmalion's wickedness, as do the *crūdēlēs ārās* (355) which would normally have been expected to protect a man, but could not when

crūdēlēs ārās trāiectaque pectora ferrō   355
nūdāuit, caecumque domūs scelus omne retēxit.
tum celerāre fugam patriāque excēdere suādet,
auxiliumque uiae ueterēs^ tellūre reclūdit
^thēsaurōs, ignōtum argentī pondus et aurī.
hīs commōta, fugam Dīdō sociōsque parābat: 360
conueniunt, quibus aut odium crūdēle tyrannī
aut metus ācer erat; nāuīs, quae forte parātae,
corripiunt, onerantque aurō: portantur auārī
Pygmaliōnis opēs pelagō; dux fēmina factī.'

1.365–71: 'So they sailed to Carthage and measured out their territory with bull's hide. But who are you?'

'dēuēnēre locōs, ubi nunc ingentia cernēs   365
moenia surgentemque nouae Karthāginis arcem,

355 *trāiciō* 3 *trāiēcī trāiectum* I transfix; throw across
356 *nūdō* 1 I reveal, lay bare
caec-us a um secret
domūs: gen. s.
retegō 3 *retēxī retēctum* I uncover, reveal
357 *celerō* 1 I speed
*excēdō 3 *excessī excessum* I depart (from + abl.)
suādeō 2 I urge, advise
358 *auxiliumque uiae*: in apposition ('as a . . .') to *ueterēs thēsaurōs*
tellūre: abl. of place from, 'from the earth'
reclūdō 3 I reveal, uncover
359 *thēsaur-us ī* 2m. treasure
*ignōt-us a um unknown, incalculable
pondus ponder-is 3n. weight
360 *hīs*: i.e. by all these things
commoueō 2 *commōuī commōtum* I move, disturb, astonish
361 **conueniō* 4 *conuēnī conuentum* I meet, assemble, agree (understand as subject 'people *quibus* (dat. of possession) . . .')
*odi-um ī 2n. hatred
tyrann-us ī 2m. tyrant

362 *parātae*: understand *erant*
363 *auār-us a um* greedy
364 *opēs*: as S. comments, what greater punishment is there for a greedy man than to lose the wealth he had criminally procured?

Learning vocabulary
attollō 3 I raise, lift up
conueniō 4 *conuēnī conuentum* I meet, assemble, agree
excēdō 3 *excessī excessum* I depart (from + abl.)
ignōt-us a um unknown, incalculable
imāgō imāgin-is 3f. image, likeness, appearance, ghost
odi-um ī 2n. hatred, loathing

365 *dēueniō* 4 *dēuēnī dēuentum* I reach
*cernō 3 *crēuī crētum* I see. Some manuscripts prefer *cernis*. Do you agree? Consider *nunc* (but does it really qualify the vb.?), and see also 310–14, 321–4; 418ff.
366 *nouae Karthāginis*: *Karthāgō* is the Latinised form of the Punic *Qart Hadasht*, 'New City'. *nouae* amusingly reinforces the point. See 1.12

faced with someone as godless as Pygmalion. The ghost points out the location of the hereditary treasures (*ueterēs* 358) that (presumably) Pygmalion had buried to enjoy himself when the time came, 363–4. So, like Aeneas taking Troy's household gods with him into exile (378–9), Dido takes with her tokens of her past. From *parābat* to the closing, powerfully epigrammatic *dux fēmina factī*, she is all action – a responsible, decisive and courageous leader of men. And Aeneas . . .?

1.365–71: Once again Aeneas is reminded of what might be the case for him in the future: a rising *noua* city with its *nunc ingentia* walls (365–6: nice tension between *nunc*

mercātīque solum, factī dē nōmine "Byrsam",
taurīnō quantum possent circumdare tergō.
sed uōs quī tandem, quibus^ aut uēnistis ab ^ōrīs,
quōue tenētis iter?' quaerentī tālibus, ille   370
suspīrāns īmōque trahēns ā pectore uōcem:

1.372–9: 'The story would be too long; we are Trojans driven ashore here and I am Aeneas'

'ō dea, sī prīmā repetēns ab orīgine pergam,
et uacet annālis nostrōrum audīre labōrum,

---

367 *mercor* 1 dep. I purchase, buy (ellipsis of *sunt*)

*sol-um ī 2n. ground (note the short *o* and cf. *sōlus a um* 'alone' and *sōl sōl-is* 3m. 'sun'); the obj. of *mercātīque* [*sunt*]

factī dē nōmine: 'from the name of the deed'. The *factum* in question is explained in the *quantum* clause below

Byrs-a ae 1f. Byrsa (here in apposition to *solum*), the name of the walled citadel (probably Akkadian *birtu*, 'fortress')

368 *taurīn-us a um* of a bull

quantum: 'as much ground as . . .' This clause explains the derivation of the name *Byrsa. Birtu* was misunderstood as Greek *bursa* 'bull's hide'; hence the story that the arrivals, granted as much land as a *bursa* would enclose, cut it up into very thin strips and enclosed a huge area

possent: this is subjunc. because it reports part of what the natives said: '[Yes, you can buy land] as much as you can enclose . . .' etc. (**RLR**4, **W**Suppl. syntax, **M**83–4)

*circumdō 1 I surround, enclose

369 *uōs quī*: a question (note ellipsis of *estis*), followed by two more

tandem: see on 331

370 *quaerentī*: 'to her asking'

tālibus: ellipsis of *uerbīs*

371 *suspīrō* 1 I sigh; ellipsis of e.g. *dīxit* as main vb

*trahō 3 *trāxī tractum* I drag, draw

Learning vocabulary

cernō 3 *crēuī crētum* I see

circumdō 1 *circumdedī circumdatum* I surround, enclose

sol-um ī 2n. ground

trahō 3 *trāxī tractum* I drag, draw

372 *dea*: Aeneas does not accept Venus' disavowals of divinity

*repetō 3 I begin from (*ab* 'from'), return to, recall

pergō 3 I continue, proceed; note *sī* and the mood of *pergam* (subjunc., not fut.), *uacet* (**373**) but also the mood of the main vb *compōnet* (**374**). See **RLS**2(c)6, 173, **W**33

373 *uacat*: 'there is time' (*uacō* 1)

annāl-ēs ium 3m. (anachronistic) annals, yearly register of events (indicating a slight weariness of tone on Aeneas' part?)

---

and *cernēs*). So does Aeneas sigh not just at the memory of his trials, but at the contrast with Dido's success who, having started from just as terrible a position (perhaps worse, having had her life destroyed by her own family), has now fulfilled ambitions he too longs to match? And how kind was it of Venus to ask the questions at 369–70, to which she well knows the answer? But it is all part of her disguise: it would be very odd of her not to ask them of a 'stranger'.

1.372–9: The reason for Aeneas' sighs emerges at once: the sheer length of time it would take to tell his whole story (and, indeed, it will in fact take Books 2 and 3). So he summarises that part of the story with which we ourselves are acquainted to date: the flight from Troy, the storm and the arrival in Libya (376–7). He then introduces himself as *pius* (378), frequently condemned as a smug, sanctimonious and rather repellent self-description.

ante diem clausō compōnet Vesper Olympō.
nōs^ Troiā antīquā, sī uestrās forte per aurīs   375
Troiae nōmen iit, dīuersa per aequora ^uectōs
forte suā Libycīs tempestās appulit ōrīs.
sum pius Aenēās^, raptōs ^quī ex hoste penātīs
classe uehō mēcum, fāmā super aethera ^nōtus.'

1.380–6: 'My mother showed me the way to Italy, but I have lost many ships and arrived here'

'Ītaliam quaerō patriam et genus ab Ioue summō.   380
bis dēnīs^ Phrygium cōnscendī ^nāuibus aequor,

374 *ante*: here adverbial, 'before then'
clausō . . . Olympō: the sky closes at night and opens again next morning
compōnet: note mood and tense; it indicates greater certainty than the subjunc.
Vesper -is 3m. evening (star); west
Olymp-us ī 2m. sky, heavens; Olympus, home of the gods
375 *nōs*: obj. of *appulit* (377), with *tempestās* (377) subject
Troiā antīquā: abl. of place from (dependent on *uectōs* 376)
aur-is is 3f. ear
377 *suā*: agrees with *forte*, referring to the storm, 'by its own chance/at its whim'
appellō 3 *appulī appulsum* I drive, bring to shore

Learning vocabulary

repetō 3 *repetī(u)ī repetītum* I begin (from), return to, recall

380 *genus*: V. tells us (3.167) that Dardanus, one of the founders of the Trojan race, originally came from Italy, and was also a son of Jupiter
381 *dēn-ī ae a* ten each
Phrygi-us a um Phrygian (Phrygia was to the centre and west of Asia Minor; *Phrygius* is used poetically to = Trojan; the Hellespont is meant, S.)
cōnscendō 3 *cōnscendī cōnscēnsum* I embark on; climb

This is quite wrong. First, Aeneas thinks he is addressing a *god*, and an unknown one at that. How best does one win the favour of an unknown god? By showing that you are yourself the sort of person for whom the gods are a priority, i.e. *pius*. By immediately saying that he saved the *penātīs* from the enemy and brings them with him (378–9), Aeneas does just that, offering clear proof that he is as *pius* as he claimed to be (S.). But that is not all. He follows that with the claim that his fame goes 'beyond the skies' (379 – reaching the gods?). But what fame? He has produced no evidence for it at all – except his salvation of the *penātīs*, which he has, evidently, *snatched* from his enemies (*raptōs* 378: a heroic exaggeration, given that he is presumably handed them by Panthus. See on **2.318–35**). This must be the reason for his claim to *fāma*.

The comparison with Homer confirms it. When Odysseus informs the listening Phaeacians of his identity, he says, 'I am Odysseus, son of Laertes, who, for my tricks / am on the minds of all men, and my fame reaches heaven' (*Odyssey* 9.19–20 (Dawe 1993)). Odysseus is known for trickery, which brings him his fame. Aeneas, however, claims he is known for his sense of duty to gods and family, which brings him his. What better way to win the favour of a mysterious deity (and upstage Odysseus)?

1.380–6: Aeneas now proceeds, all unknowing, to lay into his mother to her face (!), and one cannot help feeling she deserves it. 382 is particularly heartfelt: he (as a

mātre deā mōnstrante uiam, data fāta secūtus;
uix septem, conuulsae undīs Eurōque, supersunt.
ipse ignōtus, egēns, Libyae dēserta peragrō,
Eurōpā atque Asiā pulsus – '. nec plūra querentem   385
passa, Venus mediō sīc interfāta dolōre est:

1.387–401: *Venus says he has reached Carthage and should seek the queen; his ships are safe, to judge by a bird omen she has seen*

'quisquis es^, haud, crēdō, ^inuīsus caelestibus aurās
uītālīs carpis, Tyriam ^quī aduēneris urbem.
perge modo, atque hinc tē rēgīnae ad līmina perfer,
namque tibī reducēs sociōs classemque^ ^relātam   390

383 *uix*: take with *supersunt*
*conuellō 3 conuellī conuulsum I shatter
supersum superesse superfuī I survive
384 **dēsert-a ōrum* 2n. pl. wilderness (*dēserō 3*
   dēseruī dēsertum I desert, abandon)
peragrō 1 I wander
385 *Eurōp-a ae* 1f. Europe (abl. of place from)
pellō 3 pepulī pulsum I drive out, banish; push
plūra querentem: 'him (Aeneas) complaining at
   more [things]' i.e. yet further, obj. of [*Venus*] *nec*
   passa ('enduring, putting up with')
386 *mediō . . . dolōre*: abl. of time when
interfor 1 dep. interfātus I interrupt

Learning vocabulary

conuellō 3 conuellī conuulsum I shatter
dēserō 3 dēseruī dēsertum I desert, abandon
dēsert-a ōrum 2n. pl. wilderness

387 *quisquis es*: Venus too ignores Aeneas' self-
   identification (cf. 372). *Haud crēdō* coming next

makes it (briefly) seem that she does not
believe him at all! (Remember that the
Aeneid would not originally have had any
punctuation)
haud: emphatic position, to be taken with *inuīsus*.
   In **387–8** Venus attempts to justify herself
   in the face of her son's (unknowing) attack on
   her
aur-a ae 1f. breath, breeze
388 *uītāl-is e* of life, vital
carpō 3 I take, gather
quī: causal 'since' (hence the subjunc. *aduēneris*);
   RL140.2
adueniō 4 I reach, arrive at
389 *perge*: go/carry on! (also **401**)
*līmen līmin-is 3n. threshold
390 *redux reduc-is* returning (also **397**); *reducēs . . .*
   relātam is an acc. and inf. (ellipsis of *est*) after
   nūntiō **391**

demonstration of his *pietās*) is following strict instructions from his mother – 'also' a
goddess! – and look what has happened. He angrily reels off a catalogue of disasters – *bis
dēnīs . . . septem conuulsae supersunt . . . ignōtus, egēns . . . dēserta peragrō . . . Eurōpā
atque Asiā pulsus* (383–5) – until it all becomes too much even for Venus, who is forced
to break in and stop him in mid-assault.

1.387–401: Venus still maintains her human *persona*, claiming to 'believe' Aeneas is not
hated by the gods (387) and to 'hope' her parents have taught her augury properly (392);
quisquis (387) is surely a cruel irony. But she finally brings herself to do what one might
have expected of a mother all along: tell him the truth and give him reason to hope
(389–91), though even so she still maintains the fiction of her human *persona* (392). One
really does wonder what all this unfeeling play-acting has achieved. The augury is carefully worked out. Swans are sacred to Venus. The twelve swans = the twelve lost ships
(seven survived, while the thirteenth, Orontes', was sunk, 113–17; see on 1.251). Once
thrown into confusion by an eagle in the open air (394–5) = ships wrecked by storm in

nūntiō, et in tūtum uersīs Aquilōnibus ^āctam,
nī frūstrā augurium uānī docuēre parentēs.
aspice bis sēnōs laetantīs agmine cycnōs,
aetheriā quōs lāpsa plagā Iouis āles apertō^
turbābat ^caelō; nunc terrās^ ōrdine longō   395
aut capere, aut ^captās iam dēspectāre uidentur:
ut reducēs illī lūdunt strīdentibus ālīs,
et coetū cīnxēre polum, cantūsque dedēre,
haud aliter puppēsque tuae pūbēsque tuōrum
aut portum tenet aut plēnō subit ōstia uēlō.   400
perge modo, et, quā tē dūcit uia, dērige gressum.'

1.402–9: *Venus departs, but Aeneas recognises her and complains that she will not even acknowledge him*

dīxit, et āuertēns roseā ceruīce refulsit,
ambrosiaeque comae dīuīnum uertice odōrem

391 *Aquilō Aquilōn-is* 3m. north (wind)
392 *auguri-um ī* 2n. the art of prophecy
393 **aspiciō* 3 *aspexī aspectum* I see, observe
sēn-ī ae a six each
laetor 1 dep. I rejoice
cycn-us ī 2m. swan
394 **aetheri-us a um* ethereal, high in the heavens;
take in order *cycnōs quōs āles Iouis, lāpsa plagā aetheriā, turbābat apertō caelō*
plag-a ae 1f. open expanse (here, of sky); abl. of place from
āles ālit-is 3f. bird (here *Iouis*, i.e. eagle)
apert-us a um open; local abl.
395 **turbō* 1 I scatter, confuse, confound
396 *captās*: i.e. the birds are seen (*uidentur*) either to be capturing *capere* (i.e. landing on) the ground or looking down on land already captured *captās* (to identify a place to land themselves)
dēspectō 1 I look down on
397 *ut*: introduces the comparison – 'as the birds . . ., *haud aliter* (399) . . .'
āl-a ae 1f. wing
398 *coet-us ūs* 4m. flock, group, formation

cīnxēre . . . dedēre: forms?
cant-us ūs 4m. song
399 **pūb-ēs is* 3f. manpower, youth
400 **port-us ūs* 4m. harbour
ōsti-um ī 2n. harbour entrance
401 *dērigō* 3 I direct
*gress-us ūs 4m. steps, feet

Learning vocabulary
aetheri-us a um ethereal, high in the heavens
aspiciō 3 *aspexī aspectum* I see, observe, catch sight of
gress-us ūs 4m. steps, feet
līmen līmin-is 3n. threshold
port-us ūs 4m. harbour
pūb-ēs is 3f. manpower, youth
turbō 1 I scatter, confuse, confound

402 *āuertēns*: note the intrans. use (cf. 104)
rose-us a um rosy
*ceruīx ceruīc-is 3f. neck; abl. of means
*refulgeō 2 *refulsī refulsum* I shine out
403 *ambrosi-us a um* ambrosial. Ambrosia is the perfume (and food) of the gods; at *Iliad* 1.529

open sea, the swans have either landed or are looking for a place to land (395–8) = Aeneas' ships having landed or approaching harbour (cf. *reducēs* 390/397; does *plēnō uēlō* 400 = *strīdentibus ālīs* 397?).

1.402–9: Gods can be recognised in a variety of ways in Homer, and so too in V. The rosiness of the neck (402), the fragrance (403), the sudden change in the dress (now

spīrāuēre, pedēs uestis dēflūxit ad imōs,
et uēra incessū patuit dea. ille ubi mātrem   405
agnōuit, tālī fugientem est uōce secūtus:
'quid nātum totiēns, crūdēlis tū quoque, falsīs
lūdis imāginibus? cūr dextrae iungere dextram
nōn datur, ac uērās audīre et reddere uōcēs?'

Zeus's locks are *ambrosiai*. Gods are often
recognised by their fragrance
diuīn-us a um divine, heavenly
uertice: abl. of place from
odor -is 3m. scent, fragrance
404 *spīrō* 1 I breathe
*uest-is is 3f. dress, clothes
dēfluō 3 *dēflūxī dēflūxum* I flow down
405 *incess-us ūs* 4m. walk, gait
dea. ille: a very rare example of hiatus (absence of
elision), indicating a strong pause and perhaps
Aeneas' astonishment (Page (1894)) – for, after all
the play-acting, the truth (*uēra*) has emerged at
last. Venus is not just a goddess (which Aeneas
knew already) but *mātrem* (emphatic position)
too!
406 **agnōscō* 3 *agnōuī agnōtum* I recognise
fugientem: i.e. Venus as she sped off
407 *quid* why . . .? (acc. s. n. of *quis*, lit. 'in relation to
what?')
nātum: obj. of *lūdis* **408**
totiēns so often. Aeneas was clearly used to this sort
of treatment

*fals-us a um deceitful, treacherous
408 *dextr-a ae* 1f. right hand. This may seem a cold,
unloving request (no embrace?), but Aeneas
wishes to join hands, not (in our sense) shake
them. He will want to do the same with his 'lost'
comrades (1.514, 611), and also with his father
Anchises in the underworld, prior to hugging him
(6.697–8). S. remarks that the right hand was a
marker of high esteem: joining right hands is a
warm, welcoming gesture
409 *datur*: 'it is granted/allowed'

See: Jones (2003) on *Iliad* 5.340 and 14.172 for
divine fragrance.

Learning vocabulary
agnōscō 3 *agnōuī agnōtum* I recognise
ceruīx ceruīc-is 3f. neck
fals-us a um deceitful, treacherous
refulgeō 2 *refulsī refulsum* I shine out
uest-is is 3f. dress, clothes

ankle-length, 404) and the gait (405) all make Venus recognisable as a deity. And, as a
deity, she must look as she is – Aeneas' mother. But she has no intention of allowing her
son the privilege of even a moment with her: she is off (*fugientem* 406) even as he speaks.
Clearly, Aeneas has come to expect this kind of cruel (*crūdēlis* 407) and deceitful (*lūdis*
408) treatment from his mother (*totiēns*, 407) and the gods in general (*quoque* 407, presumably referring to e.g. Juno (S.)); but it remains unclear why Venus in particular
should behave like this towards her son. Is it to demonstrate the nature of the goddess of
sex (sex always led people badly astray, in the ancient view)? Or that, as goddess of sex,
Venus makes a rather dangerous mother for someone like Aeneas to become especially
close to (consider how she uses Aeneas' brother Cupid (!, 1.667) at 1.657–722, cf. *Intro*
[45])? Or to heighten the sense that Aeneas is utterly alone (contrast the meeting
between Odysseus and Athena in the **Study Section for 1.305–417**)? There is something
of a contrast here with Homer, where gods do not treat their favourites so coldly.
Anderson (1969: 27) says, 'Gods do help men, but rarely are men able to perceive this
assistance or to feel it as special personal benevolence.' Cf. Ross (2007: 22–3): '[Venus]
shows little if any concern for Aeneas' suffering and despair . . . her son is but the means
to her own future glory'; and Griffin (2001: 78): 'The gods care for Aeneas because the
plans of destiny need him; his own happiness does not seem to concern them. The
favoured hero is lonely and comfortless' (see *Intro* [41–2]).

1.410–17: *Venus conceals them in a cloud and herself leaves for her sanctuary on Paphos (frontispiece)*

tālibus incūsat, gressumque ad moenia tendit.   410
at Venus obscūrō gradientēs āere saepsit,
et multō nebulae circum dea fūdit amictū,
cernere nē quis eōs, neū quis contingere posset,
mōlīrīue moram, aut ueniendī poscere causās.
ipsa Paphum sublīmis abit, sēdēsque reuīsit   415
laeta suās, ubi templum illī, centumque^ Sabaeō
tūre calent ^ārae, sertīsque recentibus hālant.

410 *tālibus*: see on 370
incūsō 1 I criticise, blame (ellipsis of *eam/Venerem* as obj.)
411 **obscūr-us a um* thick, obscuring, dark
gradientēs: obj., ellipsis of 'them'
*saepiō 4 *saepsī saeptum* I enclose, surround
412 **nebul-a ae* 1f. cloud
circum . . . fūdit: i.e. *circumfūdit*, *gradientēs* understood as obj. *circum . . . fūdit* is an example of tmēsis (Greek 'cutting'), the term used to describe a vb separated from its prefix, a very common feature of Homeric language
amict-us ūs 4m. cloak
413 *cernere nē quis*: take in order *nē quis posset cernere . . .* **413–14** contain three more infs. dependent on *posset*. On *nē quis*, see **RL**145.2, cf. **W**28, **M**96
*contingō 3 I come into contact with
414 **mōlior* 4 dep. I construct, build; strive, labour at
*poscō 3 *poposcī* I demand, beg
415 *Paph-us ī* 2f. Paphos (see on 257)
sublīm-is e soaring, high (in the air)

*reuīsō 3 I return
416 *laeta*: at least *she* is happy – but because she is about to be worshipped!
illī: i.e. to Venus
Sabae-us a um from Sheba (south-western Arabia); Arabian
417 *tūs tūr-is* 3n. incense
caleō 2 I warm
sert-a ōrum 2n. pl. wreaths of flowers
*recēns recent-is fresh
hālō 1 I am fragrant

Learning vocabulary

contingō 3 *contigī contāctum* I touch, reach, influence; happen
mōlior 4 dep. I construct, build; strive, labour at
nebul-a ae 1f. cloud
obscūr-us a um thick, obscuring, dark
poscō 3 *poposcī* I demand, beg
recēns recent-is fresh
reuīsō 3 I return
saepiō 4 *saepsī saeptum* I enclose, surround

1.410–17: 'Spitting nails, Aeneas stomped off' might be quite a good translation of the curt 410. Nor does he ever make the sacrifice he had promised Venus at 334. Strangely for a god (gods are very sensitive on this issue), Venus does not hold it against him, even though she has fulfilled her side of the bargain by giving Aeneas the information he asked for (330–2). It is all a game to her. But at least she gives him and Achates further help by disguising their approach to Carthage. This is a solidly Homeric touch. Odysseus has landed on Scheria and badly needs help. 'And then Odysseus set off for the city. Around him / Athena shed much mist, thinking kindly thoughts towards Odysseus, / in case any of the great-hearted Phaeacians on meeting him / should address insulting words to him and ask him who he was' (*Odyssey* 7. 14–17 (Dawe 1993); in the *Argonautica* 3.210–12 Hera/Juno casts a mist over the whole *city* so that Jason can arrive unseen). See also **1.430–40**. Venus' departure for Paphos is also Homeric. At *Odyssey* 8.362–4, after a court poet has just described how Aphrodite/Venus was embarrassingly caught in bed with her lover Ares (Mars), he tells how she fled the scene: 'Aphrodite, goddess of smiles, came to Cyprus, / to Paphos, where she had a holy place and fragrant altar. / There the Graces washed her and rubbed oil all over her . . .' V. outdoes Homer again in the grandeur of her shrine – one hundred altars, incense, flowers.

See: Nelis (2001: 80) on *Argonautica*.

Learning vocabulary for Section 1.305–417

aetheri-us a um ethereal, high in the heavens
agnōscō 3 *agnōuī agnōtum* I recognise
alm-us a um kindly, fostering
aspiciō 3 *aspexī aspectum* I see, observe, catch sight of
attollō 3 I raise, lift up
cernō 3 *crēuī crētum* I see
ceruīx ceruīc-is 3f. neck
circumdō 1 *circumdedī circumdatum* I surround, enclose
com-a ae 1f. hair
comitor 1 dep. I accompany (+ abl.)
contingō 3 *contigī contāctum* I touch, reach, influence; happen
conuellō 3 *conuellī conuulsum* I shatter
conueniō 4 *conuēnī conuentum* I meet, assemble, agree
dēserō 3 *dēseruī dēsertum* I desert, abandon
dēsert-a ōrum 2n. pl. wilderness
doceō 2 *docuī doctum* I teach, inform
excēdō 3 *excessī excessum* I depart (from + abl.)
fals-us a um deceitful, treacherous
fastīgi-a ōrum 2n. pl. outlines; heights, tips
fluō 3 *flūxī flūxum* I flow, ebb (away)
forte perhaps, by chance
germān-a 1f. sister
germān-us ī 2m. brother
gradior 3 dep. *gressus* I walk, step
gress-us ūs 4m. steps, feet
ignōt-us a um unknown, incalculable
imāgō imāgin-is 3f. image, likeness, appearance, ghost

lāt-us a um broad
Libyc-us a um Libyan
līmen līmin-is 3n. threshold
mōlior 4 dep. I construct, build; strive, labour at
mōnstrō 1 I show
mortāl-is e mortal, human
nebul-a ae 1f. cloud
obscūr-us a um thick, obscuring, dark
odi-um ī 2n. hatred, loathing
ōmen ōmin-is 3n. auspices (taken in the course of any serious business)
pharetr-a ae 1f. quiver
Phoeb-us ī 2m. Phoebus Apollo
port-us ūs 4m. harbour
poscō 3 *poposcī* I demand, beg
prior -is first, earlier, former
pūb-ēs is 3f. manpower, youth
recēns recent-is fresh
refulgeō 2 *refulsī refulsum* I shine out
repetō 3 *repetī(u)ī repetītum* I begin (from), return to, recall
reuīsō 3 I return
saepiō 4 *saepsī saeptum* I enclose, surround
sēsē = *sē*
sol-um ī 2n. ground
spūmō 1 I foam
suspendō 3 *suspendī suspēnsum* I hang
trahō 3 *trāxī tractum* I drag, draw
turbō 1 I scatter, confuse, confound
uān-us a um empty, illusory, vain
uest-is is 3f. dress, clothes

Study Section for 1.305–417

1. From Venus' description, what sort of woman does Dido seem? Would she appeal to Aeneas?
2. 'Aeneas is here being "warmed up" for erotic interest in the huntress Dido, albeit by his own mother' (Stephen Harrison). Discuss.
3. What purpose might V. have had in making Venus so hard-hearted towards her son?

4. Scan 402–6.

5. Odysseus has been deposited, with his gifts (see 230), sound asleep, in Ithaca by the friendly Phaeacians. But he does not know he is home because there is a thick fog around. So his patron goddess Athena comes to help him. Discuss the structure and tone of the exchanges between them, especially the disguise-and-deceit element, and the character's response to it. What are the major differences with the *Aeneid* scene?

. . . But Athena came up to him,	221
with her body looking like a young man, a shepherd of flocks,	
all soft in the way that the children of princes are,	
having round her shoulders a well-made mantle of double thickness.	
She had sandals on her sleek feet and a spear in her hands.	225
Odysseus was happy at seeing her and came face to face,	
and spoke to her with these winged words:	
'My friend, as you are the first person I have come across in this place,	
good day to you. I hope your meeting me will be without any bad intent;	
so keep these things safe and keep me safe: you see, to you I	230
am praying as to god, and come a suppliant to your knees.	
And tell me this truly, so that I can know it well:	
what land is this, what people, what sort of men live here?	
Is it one of the islands, seen from afar? Or is it some shore	
of fertile mainland that lies resting against the sea?	235
The goddess, grey-eyed Athena, said to him in reply:	
'You are being silly, stranger, or you have come from far away,	
if you are really asking . . .	

[Athena now describes the island in glowing terms]

'That is why, stranger, the name of Ithaca has reached even Troy,	248
which they say is far from the Greek land.'	
So she spoke, and the long-suffering divine Odysseus felt happy,	250
delighting in his home land, according to what	
Pallas Athena, the daughter of Zeus said . . .	

[Odysseus now tells a long false tale about where *he* has come from]

So he spoke, and the goddess, grey-eyed Athena, smiled	287
and caressed him with her hand. In her body she became	
like a fine big woman with splendid accomplishments,	
and spoke to him with these winged words:	290
'It would be one with an eye to profit and a thief who could go beyond you	
in all tricks, even if a god met him.	
Hard man, subtle of thought, insatiable in trickery, evidently you were not,	
even when you were in your own land, going to give up deceptions	
and trick stories, which are fundamentally dear to you.	295
But come, let us speak on this no longer, since both of us know	
all about taking profit: you are far the best of all mortals	

in making plans and using words, and I am well known among all gods
for my shrewdness and taking profit. Even you did not recognise me,
Pallas Athena, the daughter of Zeus, who always   300
stand by and watch over you in all your troubles
and also made you a friend of all the Phaeacians.
Now, this time, I have come here to weave a scheme with you
and hide the goods which the proud Phaeacians
gave you as you went home by my thoughtful planning   305
and tell you all the troubles which fate requires you
to endure in your well-made house. You are to be steadfast even under duress,
and not to reveal to any of the men and women,
all of them, that you have in fact come home on your wanderings; but
                                                           [in silence
you are to suffer much that will be painful, accepting men's
                                               [violent treatment of you.'   310
To her in reply the resourceful Odysseus said:
'It is hard, goddess, for a mortal who meets you to recognise you,
even a very intelligent one; you make yourself look like everyone.
But I do know this well enough, that in the past you were kind to me
while we sons of the Greeks were fighting at Troy.   315
But when we had sacked the sheer city of Priam
and went in our ships, and a god scattered the Greeks,
I did not see you any more after that, daughter of Zeus, or notice
you setting foot on my ship to keep suffering away from me.
No: it was always with a ravaged heart in my chest   320
that I went wandering, until the gods set me free from misfortune,
before in the rich town of the Phaeacian men
you encouraged me with your words and took me to the city yourself.
But now I implore you in the name of your father – for I do not think
I have come to sunny Ithaca, but am moving around   325
on some other land: I think by way of provocation
you said what you did to me, to deceive my mind –
tell me if I really have come to my own home land.'
To him then replied the goddess, grey-eyed Athena:
'Always that is what the thought in your breast is like;   330
that is why I cannot abandon you in your unhappy state
seeing that you are polite and sharp of mind and sensible . . .'
                                             Odyssey 13.220–332 (Dawe 1993)

Note: Schlunk (1974: 55–8) finds different *comparanda*, i.e. the Nausicaa meeting
at *Odyssey* 6.148ff. and Odysseus' speech to the Phaeacians at *Odyssey* 9.1ff.

1.418–519: Arrival in Carthage

In this Section, the disguised Aeneas arrives in Carthage, envies the work in progress and is heartened by the reliefs of the Trojan war that he sees on the temple. Queen Dido arrives, and Aeneas is amazed to see some of his 'lost' shipmates petitioning her.

1.418–29: *They reach Carthage and admire the work – gates, streets, walls, buildings, government, harbours, and theatres*

corripuēre uiam intereā, quā sēmita mōnstrat.
iamque ascendēbant collem, quī plūrimus urbī
imminet, aduersāsque aspectat dēsuper arcēs.   420
mīrātur mōlem Aenēās, māgālia quondam,
mīrātur portās strepitumque et strāta uiārum.
īnstant ārdentēs Tyriī: pars dūcere mūrōs
mōlīrīque arcem et manibus subuoluere saxa,
pars optāre locum tēctō et conclūdere sulcō.   425
iūra magistrātūsque legunt sānctumque senātum;
hīc portūs aliī effodiunt; hīc alta theātrīs

418 *sēmit-a ae* 1f. track, trail	dependent on the idea of desire inherent in
419 *ascendō* 3 I climb	*īnstant*
coll-is is 3m. hill	*dūcere*: here 'build'
plūrimus: used of the great size of the hill	**mūrus ī* 2m. wall
420 *immineō* 2 I loom over (+ dat.)	**424** *subuoluō* 3 I roll up
aspectō 1 I gaze at	**425** **tēct-um ī* 2n. building (dat.)
*dēsuper from above	*conclūdō* 3 I enclose, surround
421 **mīror* 1 dep. I wonder, am amazed at	*sulc-us ī* 2m. trench, furrow (abl.)
māgāli-a um 3n. pl. huts (a Punic word)	**426** *magistrāt-us ūs* 4m. government official
quondam once upon a time	*legunt*: here 'they choose'
422 *strepit-us ūs* buzz, bustle, hum	*sānctum*: this epithet was a description of the
strāt-um ī 2n. paving	Roman senate
423 **īnstō* 1 I press on (+ dat., sc. 'with the work');	**427** *hīc . . . hīc . . .*: these continue the sense of 'buzz'
urge on	at the work going on everywhere
*ārdeō 2 *ārsī ārsum* I burn, am keen/fiery	*effodiō* 3 I dig out (the harbour at Carthage, which
dūcere . . . mōlīrī (**423**) . . . *subuoluere* (**423**) . . .	can be seen today, was artificial)
optāre (**424**) . . . *conclūdere* (**424**): infinitives	*theātr-um ī* 2n. theatre

1.418–29: 'No people on earth love their cities as much as the Romans do', said the ancient historian Procopius (c. AD 540), and Aeneas here witnesses a Carthage being built that anachronistically replicates the buildings and institutions, and commands the

[135]

fundāmenta locant aliī, immānīsque columnās
rūpibus excīdunt, scaenīs decora alta futūrīs.

1.430–40: *They are busy like bees working round the hive; Aeneas is impressed and envious*

quālis^ apēs, aestāte nouā, per flōrea rūra,   430
exercet sub sōle ^labor, cum gentis adultōs
ēdūcunt fētūs, aut cum līquentia mella
stīpant et dulcī distendunt nectare cellās,

428 *fundāment-um ī* 2n. foundation
column-a ae 1f. column
429 *excīdō* 3 I quarry, cut out from (+ abl.) (cf.
  excidō and the *caedō/cadō* distinction)
scaen-a ae 1f. backdrop
*decus decor-is 3n. ornament, decoration; honour,
  distinction. Most Roman theatres have a tall,
  pillared stage backdrop. This is highly
  anachronistic.

Learning vocabulary
ārdeō 2 *ārsī ārsum* I burn, am keen/fiery
decus decor-is 3n. ornament, decoration; honour,
  distinction
dēsuper from above
īnstō 1 *īnstitī* I press on (with + dat.); urge on
mīror 1 dep. I wonder, am amazed at
mūrus ī 2m. wall
tēct-um ī 2n. building

430 *quālis . . . labor*: introduces a simile, lit. 'of what
  sort the activity (*labor*) *exercet apēs*', i.e. 'like the
  activity which *exercet apēs*'
ap-is is 3m. bee
aestās aestāt-is 3f. summer (here abl. of time)
flōre-us a um flowery
rūs rūr-is 3n. countryside, land
431 *exerceō* 2 I keep (acc.) busy, exercise
cum: 'when', + indic., **RL**T(d), **W**31, **M**122–3
adult-us a um grown, adult
432 *ēdūcō* 3 I bring on
fēt-us ūs 4m. offspring
līquēns līquent-is melting, oozing
mel mell-is 3n. honey (and **436**)
433 *stīpō* 1 I pack, compress
distendō 3 I swell
nectar -is 3n. nectar, sweet honey
cell-a ae 1f. cell

same work-ethic, as V.'s contemporaries must have thought went into the building of a
great city like Rome (*Intro* [23]), or, indeed, Augustus' rebuilding of Carthage (*Intro*
[28]). The defensive structure of the city comes first to Aeneas' eyes: gates and streets
(421) – but no less the hustle and bustle (*strepitum* 421), arising from the enthusiasm
(*īnstant ārdentēs*) with which building work is going on all round the site – then the walls
and citadel (423–4: Romans *literally* removed the top half of the citadel when they rebuilt
Carthage: see on 1.20). Aeneas then observes homes, not yet built but already marked
out (425), a harbour (427) and a theatre (427–9), one of the Romans' favourite pastimes
(alongside gladiatorial contests and races). But not just structures: he notes law-making,
officials and a 'holy' senate too, just like Rome (426 – another significant anachronism).
These stand for 'order'. They must be in place before any city can be said to be civilised
and properly ruled and its people secure to enjoy the blessings of civilisation in the future
(*futūrīs* 429).

See: Jenkyns (1998: 547) on the building of Rome.

1.430–40: Order . . . and V. at once turns to bees to exemplify it. V.'s earlier poem
Georgics is ostensibly about farming but in fact about man's place in the

aut onera accipiunt uenientum aut, agmine factō,
ignāuum fūcōs pecus ā praesēpibus arcent: 435
feruet opus, redolentque thymō frāgrantia mella.
'ō fortūnātī, quōrum iam moenia surgunt!'
Aenēās ait, et fastīgia suspicit urbis.
īnfert sē saeptus nebulā, mīrābile dictū,
per mediōs, miscetque uirīs, neque cernitur ūllī.   440

---

434 *uenientum*: i.e. the bees coming in with their
   load
435 *ignāu-us a um* idle, lazy
fūc-us ī 2m. drone (non-working, male honeybee,
   whose main purpose in life is to mate with the
   queen-bee. Otherwise, they sit around feeding
   their faces)
pecus pecor-is 3n. herd; *ignāuum pecus* is in
   apposition to *fūcōs*
praesēp-e is 3n. hive, stall
436 *feruēo* 2 I seethe
redoleō 2 I give off a smell
thym-us ī 2m. thyme

frāgrō 1 I am fragrant
437 *fortūnāt-us a um* lucky
438 *suspiciō* 3 I look up to (i.e. Aeneas has now
   come down the hill)
439 *mē īnferō* 3 I move, betake myself
*mīrābil-is e wonderful
dictū: see on 111
440 *mediōs*: ellipsis of e.g. *uirōs*
miscet: ellipsis of *sē* from **439**
ūllī: rare dat. of agent after the present

Learning vocabulary
mīrābil-is e wonderful

---

world, especially his capacity to control nature and the connection between the *uirtūs*
engendered by working close to nature on the farm (the 'traditional' Roman way of life)
and happiness. In that poem, bees are taken as a paradigm, in a limited sense, of the
perfect society – a hard-working, patriotic, thrifty, disciplined community of the like-
minded all working towards a single, noble end, 'that teach / the act of order to a peopled
kingdom' (Shakespeare, *Henry V* i.2). V. applies it here to the Carthaginians, bitter
enemies of Rome, and makes Aeneas immensely envious of their luck (437), for they are
nearly finished (438 – he looks at the *fastīgia* of the city).

   It may seem odd to us that V. feels the need to cloak his hero and companion in a
mist so that no one will see, delay or question them (413–14). But we live in a different world, in which very large towns are the norm, travel from one place to another is
an everyday matter and it is taken for granted that one is surrounded by people one
does not know nor will ever see again (cf. Venus' questioning of Aeneas). Only in
(increasingly rare) remote village life is it possible today, even marginally, to dupli-
cate the sense of interest, or threat, aroused by the arrival of a stranger in the villages
and small towns of the ancient world. If Aeneas and Achates, then, are realistically
(to V.'s mind) to be able to make their way from the woods into Carthage without
being endlessly delayed and questioned (cf. on Odysseus and Athena at **1.410–17**), V.
must hide them from sight. On the other hand, there is an advantage: when they
reach Carthage, the still-invisible Aeneas can 'objectively' witness and assess the
whole situation and (as we shall see) bathe in the compliments paid him by his men,
especially Ilioneus (all of whom he will find Neptune has saved, 142–7, cf. Venus at
390–400).

See: Griffin (1985: 163–7) on bees.

1.441–52: *In a grove Dido was having built a temple to Juno –* *in which Aeneas saw his first signs of hope*

lūcus in urbe fuit mediā, laetissimus umbrā,
quō^ prīmum, iactātī* undīs et turbine, *Poenī
effōdēre ^locō signum, quod rēgia Iūnō
mōnstrārat, caput ācris equī; sīc nam fore bellō
ēgregiam et facilem uīctū per saecula gentem.   445
hīc templum^ Iūnōnī ^ingēns Sīdōnia Dīdō
condēbat, dōnīs ^opulentum et nūmine dīuae,
ā̆erea cūī gradibus surgēbant līmina, nexaeque
ā̆ere trabēs, foribus cardō strīdēbat aēnīs.
hōc prīmum in lūcō noua rēs oblāta timōrem   450

441 *lūc-us ī* 2m. grove; S. comments that these are usually sacred places

442 *quō . . . locō*: lit. '[in] which place', 'where' (**450**)

prīmum: i.e. when the colonists from Tyre reached Carthage in the first place

iactātī: the initial *i-* counts as *y*

443 *effodiō* 3 *effōdī* I excavate, dig up

444 *mōnstrārat*: = *mōnstrāuerat*

equī: Juno told them to look for a horse's head buried in the site they chose. That would guarantee prosperity (horses may not signal 'extreme wealth' to us, but they did to the ancients)

fore: inf. of implied acc. and inf. after *mōnstrārat*. Juno had pointed out where the head would be, and 'that . . .'; *gentem* (**445**) is the acc.

445 *ēgregi-us a um* outstanding (in + abl. of respect, as *uīctū*)

*uīct-us ūs 4m. way of life; provisions, food

446 *Sīdōni-us a um* from Sidon (Sidon in fact founded Tyre, so also = 'Carthaginian'; V. uses either)

447 **dōn-um ī* 2n. gift, offering

opulent-us a um rich

448 *ā̆ere-us a um* of bronze, brazen

cūī: refers to the temple, 'for which/whose', whose grand entrance (*līmina* etc.) is now described

grad-us ūs 4m. step

līmina: here, the whole entrance to the temple

nectō 3 *nexī nexum* I bind (the beam[s] is/are 'bound' with bronze [plates], to look as if made of bronze)

449 **trabs trab-is* 3f. beam, timber, girder (i.e. the single cross-beam across the top of the door; or the door-posts; or the timbers holding up the whole roof)

*for-ēs um 3f. pl. doorway

*cardō cardin-is 3f. door-socket (see on 2.480); turning-point

strīdēbat aēnīs: S. comments that, after the Capitol had been betrayed by Tarpeia in a war between Romulus and the Sabines, door-sockets were made of bronze to act as an alarm system since their noise on opening would be heard by everyone (anachronism)!

450 *noua rēs oblāta*: 'a strange/new sight brought before [his eyes]'; *oblāta* from *offerō*

timōrem: i.e. Aeneas' fear. S. wonders why, after Venus' help, he should be fearful: because he did not believe Venus? Because she had said nothing about the ways of Africans (cf. Aeneas' relief at 459–63)? Or because V. wanted to show that Aeneas was his own man and not a puppet on his mother's string?

1.441–52: Further parallels emerge between Aeneas and the locals: the Carthaginians too had been storm-driven on their way to the land that the god(dess) had in mind for them (442–4), where their future was to be assured as a people that could defend themselves and live easily (444–5). Dido, therefore, has been building a temple to Juno in the very spot where they landed (441, 446). And a magnificent temple it is turning into as well (447–9): the more the offerings and the greater the opulence, the more respect it shows for the deity. Dido, too, is *pia*.

But there is also something unexpected about it (450), easing Aeneas' fears (450),

lēniit, hīc prīmum Aenēās spērāre salūtem
ausus, et adflīctīs melius cōnfidere rēbus.

1.453–63: *Aeneas sees depictions of the Trojan war and is comforted that their sufferings are known even there – so there is hope*

namque sub ingentī lūstrat dum singula templō,
rēgīnam opperiēns, dum quae fortūna sit urbī
artificumque manūs inter sē operumque labōrem   455
mīrātur, uidet Īliacās ex ōrdine pugnās,
bellaque^ iam fāmā tōtum ^uulgāta per orbem,
Atrīdās, Priamumque, et saeuum ambōbus Achillem.

451 *lēniō* 4 I relieve, calm
452 *adflict-us a um* crushed, battered (*adflīgō*)
cōnfīdō 3 I have confidence in, trust (+ dat.); i.e.
   Aeneas can now begin to feel more confident in
   his *fortūna/fātum* which, so far, had been wholly
   adverse

Learning vocabulary

cardō cardin-is 3f. door-socket, turning-point
dōn-um ī 2n. gift, offering
for-ēs um 3f. pl. doorway
trabs trab-is 3f. beam, timber, girder
uīct-us ūs 4m. way of life; provisions, food

453 *namque*: we now get the explanation for what
   this unexpected thing is and why it brings hope;
   take *dum* next
*lūstrō 1 I survey, study
singul-ī ae a individual, each (n. acc. pl.)
454 *opperior* 4 dep. I await. But why did Aeneas
   expect her to arrive? Because of the hustle and
   bustle of the workers (S.)? Because he was trying
   to bring a meeting about (S.)? Or was he waiting
   in the hope of encountering her?

dum: with *mīrātur* (**456**)
quae: an indir. q. after *mīrātur* (**456**), which has as
   its objs. *manūs* and *labōrem* (**455**)
455 *artifex artific-is* 3m. craftsman
manūs: i.e. skill
inter sē: i.e. working together
labōrem: i.e. the work put into *operum*
456 *ex ōrdine*: i.e. in order, one after the other. The
   technical term for the detailed and extended
   literary description of any object, real or
   imaginary, is 'ecphrasis'. An ecphrasis of scenes
   from the Trojan war occupies 456–93
457 *uulgō* 1 I make public, broadcast, spread. S.
   comments 'Europe started it, Asia suffered it, now
   Africa depicts it'
458 *Atrīdās*: acc. pl. of *Atrīd-ae ārum, 'sons of
   Atreus', i.e. Agamemnon (leader of the expedition
   against Troy) and Menelaus (his brother, whose
   wife was Helen)
*Priam-us ī 2m. Priam, king of Troy
ambōbus: i.e. Priam *and* the Atridae, since in the
   course of a dispute Agamemnon took possession
   of Achilles' war-captive Briseis, causing the
   furious Achilles to walk out of the fighting (*Iliad*
   1; see Jones (2003: 53))

---

letting him dare hope that he will be well received by the Carthaginians (451) and giving
him greater confidence in the future (452), despite everything that has happened – a
lovely unfolding progression of thought. We wait to see what it is, but note the typical
feature of Virgilian style: never say once what you can explore, enrich and deepen by
saying two or three times (see O'Hara (1996) on **2.132–44**).

1.453–63: It is argued that there is a paradox here – fame, on the one hand, brings
salvation (463), but at the same time, it generates tears in the spectator (459, 462, 465,
cf. *gemitum* 485). 'What the poet suggests is the hollowness of fame as a value.' But is
this true? The basic meaning of *fāma* is not 'fame' but 'what is reported' (cf. 457
uulgāta). To follow the priorities of the *OLD*, *fāma* means 'news, tidings, report,

cōnstitit, et lacrimāns, 'quis iam locus', inquit 'Achātē,
quae regiō^ in terrīs nostrī nōn ^plēna labōris?   460
en Priamus! sunt hīc etiam sua praemia laudī;
sunt lacrimae rērum et mentem mortālia tangunt.
solue metūs; feret haec^ aliquam tibi ^fāma salūtem.'

---

459 *lacrimō* 1 I weep
Achātē: voc. of Achates
460 *regiō regiōn-is* 3f. region, area. **460** is an
example of V.'s capacity to coin 'original
expressive phrases' out of extremely simple
words. See on **462**, and cf. *Intro* [9], footnote
20
461 *en*! look! S. comments 'as if it really *were* Priam'
and suggests Aeneas' fears were about African
ways, here assuaged (**463**, cf. on 450 and see also
509)
sua praemia: 'its own rewards' (*suus* here = *proprius*,
'one's own, special')
laus laud-is 3f. praise, behaviour worthy of praise,
merit. Presumably Aeneas is looking at the
famous scene depicted at 487, where Priam risks
all begging Achilles for the return of the body of
his son Hector. Priam came to epitomise all
human suffering
462 *rērum*: here = human actions (= 'history'? –
Griffin); the gen. is one of source (**RL6.5**), i.e.
'*lacrimae* arising from/caused by what men do',
i.e. in the very nature of things. This brings about

a reaction of pity in men (*mentem mortālia
tangunt*). *Sunt lacrimae rērum* is a superb
example of V.'s ability to take simple words and
invest them with new meaning
mortālia: n. pl. as noun, 'mortal sufferings/destinies'.
This line, probably the most famous in Latin
literature, expresses the idea that people
everywhere sympathise with others' sufferings.
Dido sympathises with the Trojans', as we shall
see (627–30), where we also learn how she had
come to know about the Trojan war (619–26)
463 *haec . . . fāma*: i.e. the fact that we are known
here

See: Camps (1969: 63) on V.'s original use of words.

Learning vocabulary

Atrīd-ae ārum 2m. pl. sons of Atreus (Agamemnon
and Menelaus)
lacrimō 1 I weep
lūstrō 1 I survey, study
Priam-us ī 2m. Priam, king of Troy
regiō regiōn-is 3f. region, area

---

slander, hearsay, story, opinion and reputation, good *or* bad'. Aeneas' argument is that the Trojan war and the sufferings of the Trojans are known all over the world (459–60). Men must therefore feel sympathy for human sufferings, otherwise why would they bother to depict them (462)? So the *report* of their sufferings will win them sympathy and salvation (463, cf. 565–6). In other words, these depictions explain why V. made Aeneas feel that there was still hope (450–2). There is, of course, irony here: in the Punic wars, Carthage will bring Rome endless suffering (and as a result, some scholars are hostile to the view that Romans might have seen Dido as a sympathetic figure).

Further, these reflections about suffering will come to be seen as a typical response of Aeneas to his divinely imposed 'mission'. In Troy, he was rightly and properly warding off attack; but in Italy (when he gets there) he will be leading the attack – in accordance with fate (for Rome must be founded), but therefore rightly and properly? Far from being a blood-crazed warrior, he will emerge in the course of the *Aeneid* as a man who understands what it means to suffer, and from time to time struggles to reconcile himself to the human price that has to be paid for the founding of Rome. See *Intro* [17] for the suggestion that the idea for this scene *may* have come from Naevius.

See: Boyle (1993: 100) on 'hollow' fame; Horsfall 'Dido in the Light of History' in S.J
Harrison (1990: 137–8) on Dido as 'unsympathetic'.

1.464–78: *Tearfully, he sees Greeks fighting Trojans – Greek Achilles and Diomedes, and Trojan Troilus dragged to his death by his horses*

sīc ait, atque animum pictūrā pāscit inānī,	
multa gemēns, largōque ūmectat flūmine uultum.	465
namque uidēbat, utī bellantēs Pergama circum	
hāc fugerent Graiī, premeret Troiāna iuuentūs,	
hāc Phryges, īnstāret currū cristātus Achillēs.	
nec procul hinc Rhēsī niueīs tentōria^ uēlīs	
agnōscit lacrimāns, prīmō ^quae ^prōdita somnō	470
Tȳdīdēs^ multā uastābat caede ^cruentus,	
ārdentīsque āuertit equōs in castra, prius quam	
pābula gustāssent Troiae Xanthumque bibissent.	
parte aliā fugiēns āmissīs Trōilus armīs,	
īnfēlīx puer atque impār congressus Achillī,	475

464 *pictūr-a ae* 1f. scene, picture
inān-is e empty, insubstantial, unreal (also **476**); another wonderful line, the sum invoking more than its very simple parts
465 *gemō* 3 I groan, lament
larg-us a um copious, abundant
ūmectō 1 I moisten, soak
flūmine: of tears
466 *utī* how, followed by an indir. q. construction (**RLR3, W30, M94**)
bello(r) 1 (dep.) I fight; *bellantēs* describes all the subsequent subjects
*Pergam-a ōrum 2n. pl. Pergama, the citadel of Ilium, or Ilium itself (with *circum*)
467 *hāc . . . hāc* (**468**) *. . . nec procul hinc* (**469**) *. . . parte aliā* (**474**): all these give a sense of Aeneas moving in amazement from panel to panel of the picture, almost re-telling the story to himself
*Grai-us ī 2m. Greek
**iuuentūs iuuentūt-is* 3f. youth, young men
468 *Phryges*: (Greek nom. pl.) Phrygians/Trojans; they are fleeing (like the Greeks in **467**), while Achilles pursues (like the Trojans in **467**)
cristāt-us a um helmeted, plumed
469 *procul* far
Rhēs-us ī 2m. Rhesus, a Trojan ally from Thrace, killed for his divine horses in a night raid by Odysseus and Diomedes (*Iliad* 10.474–514)

niue-us a um snowy, white (with *uēlīs*, abl. of description)
tentōri-um ī 2n. tent
470 *prīmō . . . somnō*: i.e. soon after he had fallen asleep. Could this actually be *depicted*, or is it Aeneas' 'focalisation' i.e. viewpoint?
quae . . . prodita: obj. of *Tȳdīdēs . . . uastābat*
471 *Tȳdīdēs: nom. s. of Tydides, son of Tydeus, i.e. Diomedes
uastō 1 lay waste, destroy
*cruent-us a um bloodthirsty, bloody
472 *prius quam before (+ subjunc.) **RLT(c)**, **M118–21**
473 *pābul-um ī* 2n. fodder
gustō 1 I taste; note the (contracted) subjunc. (cf. *bibissent*), indicating that they did *not* taste it
Xanth-us ī 2m. river Xanthus/Simois in Troy
474 *Trōil-us ī* 2m. Troilus, a young Trojan warrior; there was a tradition that he was ambushed when he was unarmed
475 *infēlīx infēlīc-is* unhappy, unlucky. This adjective and *impār* suggest a 'point of view' on Aeneas' part; it is hard to see how they are objective descriptions of the relief
impār unequal (to + dat.)
congredior 3 dep. *congressus* I close with, meet (in battle)

1.464–78: Aeneas has taken in the broad scope of the depictions (the main action in the sequence of battles (456), and some of the main players in the Atrides, Priam and Achilles (458, 461)). Now he weeps over the Trojan sufferings entailed (464–5). Some have concluded from this sentiment, especially *pictūrā . . . inānī*, that art is 'meaningless', a 'betrayal', and Aeneas is 'delusional'. But one may argue in reply that the sentiment has nothing to do

fertur equīs, currūque haeret resupīnus inānī,
lōra tenēns tamen; hūic ceruīxque comaeque trahuntur
per terram, et uersā puluis īnscrībitur hastā.

1.479–93: . . . Trojans supplicating Minerva, Achilles selling the body of dead Hector, and pro-Trojan Eastern warriors like Memnon, the Amazons and Penthesilea

intereā ad templum nōn aequae Palladis ībant
crīnibus Īliades^ passīs peplumque ferēbant,   480

476 *haereō 2 haesī haesum I am entangled with, cling/stick to; linger, am unable to move
resupīn-us a um on his back, fallen back
477 *lōra tenēns tamen*: Troilus was known as an expert horseman. He tries to retain control even as he is dragged along behind
478 *puluis puluer-is* 3m. dust (note final syllable -*is* is lengthened here; cf. note on *uidet* 308, but in **478** there is no pause to account for it)
īnscrībō 3 I inscribe, write in, i.e the spear-point seems to 'write' in the dust. Austin reckons Troilus is still holding his own spear, S. that the spear is the one with which Achilles transfixed him
hast-a ae 1f. spear

See: Williams 'The Pictures in Dido's Temple' in S.J. Harrison (1990: 37–42) for an ambushed Troilus.

Learning vocabulary
cruent-us a um bloodthirsty, bloody
Grai-us ī 2m. Greek
haereō 2 haesī haesum I am entangled with, cling/stick to; linger, am unable to move
hast-a ae 1f. spear
iuuentūs iuuentūt-is 3f. youth, young men
Pergam-a ōrum 2n. pl. Pergama, the citadel of Ilium, or Ilium itself
prius quam before (+ subjunc.)
puluis puluer-is 3m. dust
Tȳdīdēs nom. s. of Tydides, son of Tydeus, i.e. Diomedes

480 *crīn-is is* 3m. hair. 479–82 are taken from *Iliad* 6.297–311. The Trojan women are trying to placate Minerva by placing a precious robe in her sanctuary in Ilium, in order to stop Diomedes'

with 'art': it is pointing out the paradox (endlessly discussed in Plato, Aristotle and so on) that a mere representation can have a powerful effect on the emotions – in Aeneas' case, because he was feeding (*pāscit*) his soul on what he saw, but he had lived through the *reality*, and his reaction to these depictions makes it clear that it is still all too real to him, *pictūra inānis* though it is. Throughout this scene, 'Aeneas is all but overwhelmed by a sense of displacement and loss. Nowhere else is his grief so powerfully expressed.'

Now Aeneas' view focuses on and selects some of the specifics. First, he picks out scenes where now the Greeks, now the Trojans are winning (466–8). But more and more he focuses on the individual disasters: Rhesus, only just arrived in Troy with his famous horses (469–73); the youthful Troilus, no match for Achilles and, like Hector, brutally mangled (474–8). These two reliefs depict people whose fortune was intimately linked with prophecies about the fall of Troy. An oracle said that Troy would not fall if Rhesus' horses tasted Trojan grass or water (472–3) or if Troilus reached 20. Is there some specific reason the reliefs should enact scenes relevant to the themes of the fate of Troy and of Greek cruelty to Trojans?

See: Johnson (1976) on art as delusion; Clausen (1987: 17) on Aeneas' grief; Williams 'The Pictures on Dido's Temple' in S.J. Harrison (1990: 42–3) on the theme of the reliefs.

1.479–93: Was it the enmity of the gods that sealed Troy's fate? Aeneas lingers on the incident which clearly demonstrated that Minerva at any rate had no time for the Trojans

suppliciter ^trīstēs et ^tūnsae pectora palmīs;
dīua solō fīxōs oculōs āuersa tenēbat.
ter circum Īliacōs raptāuerat Hectora mūrōs,
exanimumque aurō corpus uēndēbat Achillēs.
tum uērō ingentem gemitum dat pectore ab īmō,   485
ut spolia, ut currūs, utque ipsum corpus amīcī,
tendentemque manūs Priamum cōnspexit inermīs.
sē quoque prīncipibus permixtum agnōuit Achīuīs,
Ēōāsque aciēs et nigrī Memnonis arma.
dūcit Amazonidum lūnātīs agmina peltīs   490

rampage. Minerva rejects the offering (**482**; hence *nōn aequae* **479**)

Īliad-es 3f. pl. women of Ilium (short *e*: this is a Greek nom. pl.)

pass-us a um spread, unbound (*pandō* 3 *pandī passum*)

pepl-um ī 2n. robe (in imitation of the robe specially woven and offered every four years to Athena at the Athenian festival of the Great Panathenaea; see *Iliad* 6.92)

481 *suppliciter* in suppliant fashion

tundō 3 *tutudī tūnsum* beat, pound: here the pass. is used as if act. – the 'middle' sense described at p. 39 (c (ii)) above – with *pectora* as its obj.

483 *raptō* 1 I drag off. Note the plupf.: this is not depicted, but Aeneas' 'focalised' commentary on the background to the incident; *uēndēbat* (**484**) shows what is really happening in the picture.

483–7 summarise the events of *Iliad* 24.14–18 and 24.478ff. In *Iliad* 24.14–18, Achilles drives his chariot, with Hector's body dragging behind, three times round the *tomb* of his beloved Patroclus, whom Hector had killed in battle; but V. follows a later version in which Achilles drags Hector round the *walls*, cf. Euripides *Andromache* 105. In *Iliad* 24.478ff., Priam comes to Achilles' tent by night to beg for the return of Hector's body in exchange for a great ransom

Hectora: acc. s.

484 *exanim-us a um* dead, lifeless

aurō: abl. of price

uēndō 3 I sell (very cynical: not Homer's view)

485 **gemit-us ūs* 4m. groan

486 *ut*: here 'as' (+ indic.)

spolia . . . currūs: presumably Hector's armour and Achilles' chariot. S. comments how touching *amīcī* (instead of *Hectoris*) is. This word is 'focalised' through Aeneas' eyes – his comment rather than V.'s third-person description

487 *inerm-is e* unarmed

488–93 summarise events from the Trojan war that take place after Homer's *Iliad* ends, from the epic sequence known as *Aethiopis* ('Ethiopian story': this was probably current in Homer's time, but in the *Iliad* Homer had chosen a different, earlier chunk of the war to concentrate on). *Aethiopis* (which survives only in summary) deals with the arrival of the Amazons to fight for the Trojans, the deaths of the Eastern warriors mentioned here in V. and the death of Achilles

488 *permixt-us a um* joined in battle with (*permisceō* 2). Note the ambiguity: either 'in company with' or 'against'. S. comments that the picture of Aeneas *permixtum* with the Greeks recalls the traditions that made him a traitor (see on 242)

489 *Ēō-us a um* eastern

Memnōn Memnon-is m. Memnon, a black warrior from Ethiopia, killed by Achilles

490 *Amazonid-ēs um* 3f. Amazons (female warriors)

lūnāt-us a um crescent-shaped

pelt-a ae 1f. shield; here abl. of description with *agmina*

(482). The pluperfect *raptāuerat* of 483 suggest the scene of Hector's death was not depicted, and these words are Aeneas' thoughts ('focalisation') as he looks at the depicted scene in which, as a result of his slaughter of Hector, Achilles *uēndēbat* (imperfect) the body. Aeneas' feelings are especially roused by this scene (485), the rising tricolon of 486 reaching its climax in 487 with the pathetic depiction of old Priam able only to stretch out his *unarmed* (emphatic position) hands in supplication to the man who had killed, and now held the body of, his son. Even when Aeneas sees himself (488), he finds no reason to linger on his own performance in battle. There is no rejoicing in heroism here.

Penthesilēa furēns, mediīsque in mīlibus ārdet,
aurea subnectēns exsertae cingula mammae,
bellātrīx, audetque uirīs concurrere uirgō.

1.494–504: *Dido appears, looking like the huntress Diana among her followers*

haec dum Dardaniō Aenēae mīranda uidentur,
dum stupet, obtūtūque haeret dēfīxus in ūnō,   495

491 *Penthesilēa*: nom. s., Penthesilea, the Amazon
leader at Troy, killed by Achilles
mīlibus: abl. pl. of *mīlle*
492 *subnectō* 3 I bind, buckle X (acc.) under Y (dat.)
exsert-us a um protruding, bare
cingul-um 2n. band, support
mamm-a ae 1f. breast
493 *bellātrīx bellātrīc-is* 3f. female warrior
concurrō 3 I join battle with (+ dat.)

Learning vocabulary

crīn-is is 3m. hair
gemit-us ūs 4m. groan

494 *haec*: n. pl. subject
*Dardani-us a um Dardanian/Trojan
(Dardanus was a founding father of the
Trojans, depictions of whose destruction
Aeneas has just been observing). *Dardaniō
Aenēae* is dat. of agent, **RLL**(e)1(iv), **W**24,
M111
495 **stupeō* 2 I am stunned, astonished
obtūt-us ūs 4m. contemplation, gaze; *ūnō* = 'one
[long/unbroken]'
dēfīx-us a um astounded

Exotic Trojan allies from the East fared no better, even Penthesilea, who is depicted dressing for battle with a breast-girdle. Most warriors put on armour; Aeneas acknowledges her spirit (491) and outstanding courage as a woman who is a match for men (493). We may now be hoping that Aeneas will soon be reacting to the depiction of the fall of Troy (if we can assume that too was on the relief, cf. **1.748–56**), but that does not occur at this point because Dido is about to come in). V., however, will not let us down: he is saving the sack for Aeneas himself to describe in Book 2 as he personally experienced it.

It is worth observing that the scenes which Aeneas views emphasise Greeks defeating Trojans. Should we understand this merely to be reflecting Aeneas' selection of what interested him? Or is it what we should expect in a temple dedicated to the Trojan-hating Juno (and it is, of course, a victory monument)? After all, it was a Greek who had fought at Troy who told Dido all about the war (Teucer, 619–24). Whatever the answer, V. tells us that the scenes brought Aeneas *hope* (450–2; wonder and astonishment too, as we shall see at 494–5), which Aeneas explains in terms of men's sympathy with the suffering of others (459–63). Fowler (2000: 77–81) would like to believe it is 'not impossible' that V. is doing more than simply reporting what Aeneas saw: V. is suggesting that some of these scenes represent Aeneas' actual thought-processes as he looks at them (i.e. they are being 'focalised', to use the technical term, through Aeneas' eyes). This looks the case at e.g. 470 *prīmō . . . somnō*; 475 *īnfēlīx puer atque impār*; 486 *amīcī*.

1.494–504: Aeneas is rooted to the spot (*haeret dēfīxus*). Naturally moved by these depictions – for he was one of those who suffered – he also feels wonder and amazement (*mīranda, stupet*). Enter in royal style (*incessit*, cf. Juno 46, Venus 405) *fōrmā pulcherrima* Dido, surrounded by a retinue of young men! Why are Dido's supporters 'young men' in particular? V. does not say. Is it a political point (important Romans paraded the streets of Rome followed by their bands of supporters, *clientēs*)? Is V. inviting

rēgīna ad templum, fōrmā pulcherrima Dīdō,
incessit, magnā iuuenum stīpante cateruā.
quālis^ in Eurōtae rīpīs aut per iuga Cynthī
exercet ^Dīāna chorōs, ^quam mīlle secūtae
hinc atque hinc glomerantur Orēades; illa pharetram   500
fert umerō, gradiēnsque deās superēminet omnīs
(Lātōnae tacitum pertemptant gaudia pectus) –
tālis erat Dīdō, tālem sē laeta ferēbat
per mediōs, īnstāns operī rēgnīsque futūrīs.

496 *fōrm-a ae* 1f. beauty, shape, form (abl. of
respect with *pulcherrima*)
497 *stīpō* 1 I press round
cateru-a ae 1f. crowd, throng
498 *quālis . . . Dīāna*: this starts a simile 'Of what
sort / Just as Diana *exercet . . .*', to be picked up at
503 *tālis Dīdō* 'Of such a sort / So Dido *erat . . .*'
The simile is taken from Homer's *Odyssey* 6.102–
9, describing the young, virgin princess Nausicaa.
See **Study Section for 1.418–519**
Eurōtae: gen. s. of Eurotas, a river in Sparta (*Eu-*
counts as a single long syllable)
rīp-a ae 1f. bank
iug-um ī 2n. ridge, yoke
Cynth-us ī 2m. a ridge on the Greek island of Delos,
where Leto gave birth to Apollo and Diana
499 *exerceō* 2 I drill, lead
Dīān-a ae 1f. Diana (Greek Artemis), goddess of
hunting
chor-us ī 2m. band of (singing and dancing)
nymphs
500 *glomerō* 1 I throng round

Orēades: Greek nom. pl. (note short final *e*),
Oreades, mountain nymphs
illa: Diana
501 *superēmineō* 2 I rise above, am taller than
502 *Lātōn-a ae* 1f. Latona (Greek Leto), Diana's
mother
tacit-us a um silent
pertemptō 1 I thrill, excite
503 *tālem sē*: obj. of *ferēbat*
504 *operī rēgnīsque futūrīs*: hendiadys? (see
Glossary of literary terms)

Learning vocabulary
cateru-a ae 1f. crowd, throng
Dardani-us a um Dardanian/Trojan (Dardanus was
a founding father of the Trojans)
fōrm-a ae 1f. beauty, shape, form
glomerō 1 I throng round
incēdō 3 *incessī incessum* I enter, arrive
iug-um ī 2n. ridge, yoke
stupeō 2 I am stunned, astonished
tacit-us a um silent

speculation that she is a desirable woman (*fōrmā pulcherrima*, 496)? Or may he be
subtly proposing a comparison with Penthesilea, whom Aeneas has just been contemplating, a warrior who is a match for men but doomed to fall to one?

But V. at once likens Dido to Diana, the virgin huntress (any significance to the fact
that this was how Aeneas' mother Venus, goddess of sex, was disguised when she met
him in the wood, 315–20?). Diana walks (501 *gradiēns*, cf. Dido 497 *incessit*, 503 *sē
ferēbat*), is surrounded by her mountain nymphs (500 *glomerantur*, cf. Dido 497 *stīpante
cateruā* – a congruence S. denies), is taller than all of them (501 *superēminet*, cf. Dido
506 *altē*), wears a quiver (500–1 *pharetram*, cf. Dido 506 *armīs*) and brings joy to her
nearest and dearest (502 *gaudia*, cf. Dido 503 *laeta*). We can transfer all this to the
impression that Dido herself makes (note *tālis . . . tālem* 503) – should that include happiness in Aeneas' heart (like Latona's)? Further, she too has the happiness (*laeta*) and
urgency of the Carthaginians (*īnstāns* 504, cf. *īnstant* 422). *dux fēmina factī . . .* (364) –
no ordinary woman, Dido. See *Intro* [17].

See: Anderson (1969: 28) on Penthesilea; West 'Multiple-correspondence Similes in the
Aeneid' in S.J. Harrison (1990: 435–6) on Dido; Pöschl (1970: 67) on Latona.

1.505–19: *As Dido legislates from the temple, Aeneas is amazed to see appearing the men he had thought lost at sea, and longs to question them*

tum foribus dīuae, mediā testūdine templī,   505
saepta armis, soliōque altē subnīxa, resēdit.
iūra dabat lēgēsque uirīs, operumque labōrem
partibus aequābat iūstīs, aut sorte trahēbat:
cum subitō Aenēās concursū accēdere magnō
Anthea Sergestumque uidet fortemque Cloanthum,   510
Teucrōrumque aliōs^, āter ^quōs aequore turbō
dispulerat penitusque aliās āuēxerat ōrās.
obstipuit simul ipse, simul percussus Achātēs

505 *dīuae*: i.e. of Juno; the *foribus* (local abl.) are the doors of the *cella* (shrine, the room situated in the middle of the temple) in which the statue of Juno was placed
testūdō testūdin-is 3f. central vault of a temple
506 *saepta . . . subnīxa*: i.e. Dido, the subject of the sentence
armīs: i.e. armed men
soli-um ī 2n. throne
subnīx-us a um propped up (on + abl.)
resīdō 3 *resēdī* I settle down
507 *iūra dabat*: S. comments (at 446) that Romans in olden times used temples for the transaction of public business (anachronism); that *dabat* is well said, because it was a later people that invented *written* laws; and it redounds to Dido's praise that she legislates for men (*uirīs*)
508 *partibus . . . iūstīs*: 'by fair division'
trahēbat: here 'she assigned'
509 *concurs-us ūs* 4m. crowd (abl. of

accompaniment); this huge accompanying crowd of locals, S. suggests, is another example of Aeneas' fear about African ways, made clear at **513–14** (cf. on 450) – what did it mean?
accēdere: inf. of an acc. and inf. after *uidet* (510)
510 *Anthea Sergestumque . . . Cloanthum*: acc. of Antheus, Sergestus and Cloanthus, three of Aeneas' captains whom he had assumed to be among the (thirteen) ships lost at sea cf. 181, 222 (see on 251)
511 *aequore*: local abl.
turbō turbin-is 3m. whirlwind
512 *dispellō* 3 *dispulī dispulsum* I disperse
āuehō 3 *āuēxī āuectum* I carry away
513 **obstipēscō* 3 *obstipuī* I am astounded, dumbfounded
percutiō 3 *percussī percussum* I strike forcibly, shock

1.505–19: Dido, under guard (the *armīs* carried by the same young men of 497?), takes her high seat in the middle of the temple (the *sānctus* (426) Roman senate often met in temples), and proceeds with the work of government, advancing legislation *uirīs* (507, a pointed insertion) and fairly apportioning the building work (507–8). This is (quite anachronistically) the way monarchical Roman emperors worked (cf. Jones and Sidwell (1997: section 156)) – daily receiving petitions on, and making decisions about, every matter under the sun, from bids for building contracts to requests to overturn legal judgements (Julius Caesar was assassinated when surrounded by a throng of petitioners). It was clearly a rowdy business (519). And suddenly (509), among the petitioners crowding forward with their requests, Aeneas spots – his lost comrades, and representatives of all of them too (*cūnctīs* 518)! One can understand his and Achates' powerful, fluctuating emotions (513–14), desperate desire to make themselves known (514–15) and eagerness to find out what has been going on (517–19) but fear about what *is* going on (*metūque* 514). Caution prevails, and the two take advantage of their cloak of invisibility (515–16).

laetitiāque metūque; auidī coniungere dextrās
ārdēbant; sed rēs animōs incognita turbat.   515
dissimulant, et nūbe cauā speculantur amictī,
quae fortūna uirīs, classem quō lītore linquant,
quid ueniant; cūnctīs nam lēctī nāuibus ībant,
ōrantēs ueniam, et templum clāmōre petēbant.

514 *laetiti-a ae* 1f. joy, happiness (at his men's
safety, but concern too, *metūque*)
auid-us a um greedy, eager
coniungō 3 I join (cf. on 1.408 for the significance of
this)
dextr-a ae 1f. right hand
515 *incognit-us a um* unknown, incomprehensible;
with *rēs*, 'their ignorance of the situation'
(explained by **517–18**)
516 *dissimulō* 1 I conceal (here, their feelings)
speculor 1 dep. I search out, observe
amict-us a um cloaked, veiled (*amiciō* 4)
517 *quae . . . quō . . . quid* (**518** 'why'): indir. qs. after
speculantur

linquō 3 I leave
518 *cūnctīs* 'from all the ships': a great relief for
Aeneas – it looks as if the whole fleet is safe
lēctī: 'picked (men)'
519 *ueni-a ae* 1f. favour (so here, as S. says, in
relation to the burning of their ships, raised at
525ff.); pardon

Learning vocabulary

laetiti-a ae 1f. joy, happiness
obstipēscō 3 *obstipuī* I am astounded,
dumbfounded

Learning vocabulary for Section 1.418–519

ārdeō 2 *ārsī ārsum* I burn, am keen/fiery
Atrīd-ae ārum 2m. pl. sons of Atreus (Agamemnon
and Menelaus)
cardō cardin-is 3f. door-socket, turning-point
cateru-a ae 1f. crowd, throng
crīn-is 3m. hair
cruent-us a um bloodthirsty, bloody
Dardani-us a um Dardanian/Trojan (Dardanus was
a Trojan founding father)
decus decor-is 3n. ornament, decoration; honour,
distinction
dēsuper from above
dōn-um ī 2n. gift, offering
for-ēs um 3f. pl. doorway
fōrm-a ae 1f. beauty, shape, form
gemit-us ūs 4m. groan
glomerō 1 I throng round
Grai-us ī 2m. Greek
haereō 2 *haesī haesum* I am entangled with, cling/
stick to; linger, am unable to move
hast-a ae 1f. spear
īnstō 1 *īnstitī* I press on (with + dat.); urge on

iug-um ī 2n. ridge, yoke
iuuentūs iuuentūt-is 3f. youth, young men
lacrimō 1 I weep
laetiti-a ae 1f. joy, happiness
lūstrō 1 I survey, study
mīrābil-is e wonderful
mīror 1 dep. I wonder, am amazed at
mūrus ī 2m. wall
obstipēscō 3 *obstipuī* I am astounded, dumbfounded
Pergam-a ōrum 2n. Pergama, the citadel of Ilium,
or Ilium itself
Priam-us ī 2m. Priam, king of Troy
prius quam before (+ subjunc.)
puluis puluer-is 3m. dust
regiō regiōn-is 3f. region, area
stupeō 2 I am stunned, astonished
tacit-us a um silent
tēct-um ī 2n. building
trabs trab-is 3f. beam, timber, girder
Tȳdīdēs nom. s. of Tydides, son of Tydeus, i.e.
Diomedes
uīct-us ūs 4m. way of life; provisions, food

Study Section for 1.418–519

1. What lessons, if any, can be drawn from the reliefs that Aeneas inspects? In what sense does Aeneas see them as a reason for hope? Or with Boyle (1993: 101) would you rather see them as 'a poetic self-critique . . . about the power of his own artefact to affect the Roman world . . . [signalling Virgil's] awareness of his didactic impotence'?

2. Do you think that V. 'focalises' the reliefs through Aeneas' eyes (see on **1.479–93**)?

3. What picture of Dido does V. paint? Does she seem to present a threat to Aeneas at this stage?

4. Given that Dido will fall hopelessly in love with Aeneas but he will abandon her and she will commit suicide (*Aeneid* 4), why does V. compare Dido to the virgin goddess Diana/youthful unmarried princess Nausicaa at this moment?

5. 'Aeneas' gaze at Dido/Diana at 1.498ff. presents him as a sort of Actaeon.' Find out who Actaeon is (Ovid *Metamorphoses* 3.138–252) and discuss.

6. Scan 459–63.

7. Here is the scene in which Nausicaa is described, before a grimy Odysseus, shipwrecked on the shore, encounters her and begs her help. How does V. add or develop it? What correspondences (i.e. points in the simile picked up outside the simile) does V. make specifically that Homer did not make?

> When the servants and the girl herself had had their pleasure in eating,
> they began to play with a ball, casting aside their veils,   100
> and Nausicaa of the white arms led them in the exercise.
> As Artemis, the shooter of arrows, goes over the mountains,
> either over the long <range of> Taygetos or Erymanthos,
> taking her pleasure in <the hunt for> boars and swiftly-running deer,
> and with her Nymphs, the daughters of Zeus the aegis-carrier,   105
> denizens of the field, join in the sport, and Leto is happy in her heart,
> and she (Artemis) holds her head and countenance over all of them
> and is easily distinguishable – and all of them are beautiful –
> so she (Nausicaa), the unwedded maiden, stood out among the girls who attended her.
>
> Homer, *Odyssey* 6.99–109 (Dawe 1993)

8. Now compare Apollonius' simile, referring to Medea hurrying through the city to the temple to meet Jason, carrying a drug to help him get the Fleece:

> She herself took the reins and grasped the well-fashioned whip
> in her right hand. She drove through the city, and the other maidservants,
> holding on to the back of the wagon-car,
> ran along the broad road, holding up
> their fine tunics as far as their white thighs.   875
> As when after bathing at the sweet waters,

of the Parthenios or in the river Amnisos,
the daughter of Leto [Artemis] stands in her golden chariot
and drives her swift deer through the hills
to accept a distant offering of rich sacrifice,   880
and with her go her companion nymphs, some gathering
from the very spring of Amnisos, others leaving
the groves and the mountain-peaks with their many streams; around her
the wild beasts whimper and fawn in fear.
Like this did they hasten through the city, and all around the people   885
made way for them, avoiding the eyes of the royal maiden.

Apollonius, Argonautica 3.871–86

Nelis (2001: 83–5) finds links between V. and Apollonius here, e.g. both Medea and Dido are moving with a retinue through the city; both are going to a temple; etc. He finds differences too, e.g. Dido as queen, Medea as witch; but suggests that there is enough in V. recalling Apollonius to hint that Dido's love affair with Aeneas may be as fatal as Medea's was with Jason; cf. **Study Section for 1.520–656**, 5., on Dido-as-Circe, and see also Clausen (2002: 34ff.).

1.520–656: Dido's welcome

In this Section, *after Ilioneus has begged Dido for help (which she willingly grants), Aeneas appears from the cloud and thanks and compliments Dido. She replies in surprise and delight and prepares a feast for them all; Achates goes back to the ships to fetch Ascanius and bring presents.*

1.520–33: *Ilioneus appeals for help: they have not come to plunder the city but to reach Italy*

postquam intrōgressī et cōram data cōpia fandī,   520
maximus Īlioneūs placidō sīc pectore coepit:
'ō rēgīna^, nouam ^cūi condere Iuppiter urbem
iūstitiāque dedit gentīs frēnāre superbās,
Trōes tē miserī, uentīs maria omnia uectī,
ōrāmus, prohibē īnfandōs ā nāuibus ignīs,   525
parce piō generī, et propius rēs aspice nostrās.
nōn nōs aut ferrō Libycōs populāre penātīs
uēnimus, aut raptās ad lītora uertere praedās;

520 *intrōgredior* 3 dep. *intrōgressus* enter; understand *sunt*
*cōram face to face
cōp-ia ae 1f. ability, means; resources, plenty; understand *est*
521 *maximus*: i.e. oldest
placidō: as befits an orator, who speaks as he wishes to be received (S.)
522 *cui . . . Iuppiter . . . dedit* (523): 'to whom J. granted [the power] to', followed by *condere* and *frēnāre* (523)
nouam . . . urbem: for the word-play, see on 366

523 *iūstiti-a ae* 1f. justice
frēnō 1 I bridle, rein in (see on 339)
524 *maria omnia*: i.e. 'over . . .', a sort of cognate acc. after *uectī*
525 *īnfandōs*: presumably Carthaginians were treating them as pirates (527–8) and threatening to burn their ships
526 **pi-us a um* pious, god-fearing
propius more favourably (lit. 'nearer, more closely')
527 *populō* 1 I devastate, ravage (here an inf. expressing purpose)
penātēs: i.e. house and home

1.520–33: Despite their noisy entrance, the Trojans wait their turn for permission to speak (520) – one assumes there is a queue – and the oldest (and therefore by ancient thinking the wisest) begins to speak; and he is speaking peace (*placidō* 521). He begins with two lines of flattery: the *captātiō beneuolentiae* typical of the start of a speech, especially when help was required. Jupiter, he says, has clearly blessed Dido's enterprise in founding a city (522) and reining back hostile tribes, but justly (523) (more irony – here in alien Carthage, Ilioneus is innocently foreseeing the way future Romans will

nōn ea uīs animō, nec tanta superbia uictīs.
est locus – "Hesperiam" Grāī cognōmine dīcunt –   530
terra antīqua, potēns armīs atque ūbere glaebae;
Oenōtrī coluēre uirī; nunc fāma minōrēs
"Ītaliam" dīxisse, ducis dē nōmine, gentem.'

1.534–50 *'But suddenly a storm arose; now we are being attacked and have lost our leader Aeneas'*

'hic cursus fuit:
cum subitō adsurgēns flūctū nimbōsus Orīōn   535

529 *superbi-a ae* 1f. pride
uictīs: 'for the defeated' (as the Trojans must feel at the moment)
530 *Hesperi-a ae 1f. Hesperia, western land
Grāī = Graiī
cognōmen cognōmin-is 3n. name
531 *ūber -is* 3n. richness (abl. of respect)
glaeb-a ae 1f. soil
532 *Oenōtri-us a um* Oenotrian, an early (originally south) Italian people, whose king was said to be *Ītalus* (= *ducis* of **533**)
fāma: ellipsis of *est*, followed by acc. and inf.
minōr-ēs um 3m. pl. descendants

Learning vocabulary
cōram face to face

Hesperi-a ae 1f. Hesperia, western land
pi-us a um pious, god-fearing

534 *hic cursus fuit*: this is one of over fifty incomplete lines in the *Aeneid*, three in this book (here, 560 and 636). Since we know that Virgil did not finish the epic – on his death-bed he wanted the manuscript burned (*Intro* [8–9]) – he would have dealt with them had he been given the chance
535 *subitō*: with *flūctū*
adsurgō 3 I rise
nimbōs-us a um full of rain clouds; stormy
Orīōn -is 3m. Orion, a constellation associated with stormy weather; subject of *dispulit* (**538**)

understand the foundation of Rome). Only a woman respected by Jupiter would have done so well; only a woman who was *iūsta* would act *iūstitiā*. He now introduces the Trojans (note *miserī*, demanding sympathy), how far (*omnia*) they have *been* carried (it was not intentional), and explains that they are being badly treated (525). For they are *piō* (526, like her) and doing no wrong (suggesting they are *iūstī*), as he explains in 527–8 (more irony: Rome will, of course, destroy Carthage in 146 BC). In 529 he enlarges: they are *uictī* anyway, and not like that at heart (*animō*). To put Dido's mind yet further at rest, he now begins to explain where they had *intended* to go (530–3). Ilioneus comes over strongly as a good man, with a mission that does not involve Carthage. Note that a *land* cannot be meaningfully described as *antīqua* (531); only a place of habitation or a *gēns* can be that. It is as if Ilioneus is thinking of Italy as Roman already. Or does *antīqua* simply mean *nōbilis* (S.)?

   As S. says, this is a fine rhetorical four-part opening, followed by expansion: (i) 522–3 winning over the addressee, (ii) 524 saying who they are, (iii) 524 explaining what their situation is and (iv) 525–6 asking for relief. Then 527–9 explain what they are not at Carthage for, and 530–3 what their plans in fact are.

See: Reed (2007: 88) on Rome's foundation and (139–40) on the land as *antīqua*.

1.534–50: So why are the Trojans here? Ilioneus explains with a description of the storm

in uada caeca tulit, penitusque procācibus Austrīs
perque undās, superante salō, perque inuia saxa
dispulit; hūc paucī uestrīs adnāuimus ōrīs.
quod genus hoc hominum? quaeue^ hunc tam ^barbara mōrem
permittit ^patria? hospitiō prohibēmur harēnae;   540
bella cient, prīmāque uetant cōnsistere terrā.
sī genus hūmānum et mortālia temnitis arma,
at spērāte deōs memorēs fandī atque nefandī.
rēx erat Aenēās nōbīs, quō iūstior alter

536 *caec-us a um* unseen, blind
procāx procāc-is fierce, lively, vicious
Austrīs: abl. of instrument
537 *superante*: abl. abs., ellipsis of 'us' as obj.
sal-um ī 2n. waves, billows
inui-us a um uncharted
538 *dispellō* 3 *dispulī* I scatter ('us' as obj.)
adnō 1 I drift to (+ dat.)
539 *quod*: goes with *genus* 'what race . . .?' (ellipsis of *est*); so too *quaeue* with *tam barbara . . . patria*. If it meant 'What is this race?' it would be *quid*
hoc: *hic, hoc* 'this' often scans as if long (i.e. as if *hocc*; originally it was *hodce*); so too *hic* (as if *hicc*)
barbar-us a um barbarian, savage (see on 525 above). Note that Ilioneus distances Dido from this slur (S.)
540 *permittō* 3 I allow, permit
hospitiō: (abl. of separation) a nice touch: there is

little enough *hospitium* in a beach, but they are kept away even from that!
541 *cieō* 3 I provoke, stir up ('they' are the locals)
prīmā: i.e. border, edge
uetō 1 I forbid (ellipsis of 'us' as object)
542 *temnō* 3 I despise
543 *at*: 'still . . .'
spērāte: 'expect'
deōs memorēs: ellipsis of e.g. *fore* as an acc. and inf. after *spērāte*. S. comments that *memorēs* warns them that gods *will* punish wrong-doing, even if they do not do so at once
fand-um ī . . . nefand-um ī 2n. right, wrong (cf. *nefandus* 525)
544 *erat*: S. comments that, had the poet said *fuit*, it would suggest Ilioneus had abandoned all hope of Aeneas' survival
quō: 'than whom'
alter/nec i.e. no other one

and its power. Note *caeca* (536), *inuida* (537) – they have no idea where they are – and *dispulit* (538), preparing for *hūc paucī* (they are a remnant) and the helplessness of the verb *adnāuimus*. Their honest credentials established, Ilioneus can now question from the moral high ground why they are being treated so badly by the natives where they have landed. The contrast between a *iūsta* Dido and the treatment meted out by the locals – not that we have heard of any such thing except from Ilioneus – makes a powerful rhetorical point, and the question format demands an answer. Again, Ilioneus moves on to explain what he means by *barbara* in 540–1. Note *hospitiō*: there were 'rules' about how strangers should be treated in the civilised Roman world (more anachronism), and Ilioneus is suggesting Dido's countrymen are not acquainted with these basic civilised standards. Since it was believed these rules were overseen by gods, 543 makes the point, contrasting *fandum* with *nefandum* and reminding *pia* Dido that the gods never forget. *spērāte* is an ironic understatement, meaning 'you can be absolutely certain'. Note that the first half of the *Aeneid* is often called 'Odyssean': a major theme of Homer's *Odyssey* relates to the treatment of strangers. Ilioneus is challenging Dido to live up to Roman standards of such treatment.

Aeneas is introduced here as both an example and a threat. He is Dido's equal in *pietās* and *iūstitia* (544–5) but also in battle. 546–7 are typical Virgilian repetition/ expansion (see discussion on **2.132–44**), and the conclusion (548–9) is designed to reassure Dido that he is also a man of whom she has no need to feel afraid. By suggesting

nec pietāte fuit, nec bellō māior et armīs.   545
quem^ sī fāta ^uirum seruant, sī uēscitur aurā
aetheriā, neque adhūc crūdēlibus occubat umbrīs,
nōn metus; officiō nec tē certāsse priōrem
paeniteat. sunt et Siculīs regiōnibus urbēs
armaque, Troiānōque ā sanguine clārus Acestēs.'   550

1.551–8: 'Help us to reach Italy, or if Aeneas is dead, at least to return to Sicily'

'quassātam uentīs liceat subdūcere classem,
et siluīs aptāre trabēs et stringere rēmōs –

545 *pietāte*: abl. of respect, as are *bellō* and *armīs*

546 *quem . . . uirum*: i.e. this man
uēscor 2 dep. I live on, feed on (+ abl.)
aur-a ae 1f. air

547 **aetheri-us a um* of heaven
occubō 1 I lie dead

548 *nōn metus*; i.e. we have nothing to fear, for Aeneas will either protect us (if necessary) or repay you (Dido) if you help us (Austin)
*certō 1 I contend, fight

549 *paenitet* it repents X (acc.) to (+ inf.); lit. 'nor would it repent you (= would you repent, be sorry) to have contended as a leader (*priōrem* in apposition to *tē*) in *officiō*', i.e. you would not regret having taken the lead in
et: if Aeneas is dead, there is help *too* in Sicily
Sicul-us a um Sicilian

550 *Acestēs* Acestes, the friendly king of Sicily (see on 195)

Learning vocabulary

aetheri-us a um of heaven
certō 1 I contend, fight
hic, hoc often scan long, as if *hicc, hocc*

551 *quassō* 1 I shake, batter
liceat: i.e. 'for us'; note jussive subjunc. (**RL**152, **W**28, **M**34, 89)
subdūcō 3 I draw up, beach

552 *siluīs*: local abl.
*aptō 1 I prepare, fit
*trabs trab-is 3f. tree-trunk, beam
stringō 3 I shave, trim, strip (i.e. the trees to make new *rēmōs*)
rēm-us ī 2m. oar

that Dido would benefit from doing her duty to strangers, Ilioneus is suggesting Aeneas would know what *his* duty – *officium*, a word rich in moral and political associations – was. But even if Aeneas is dead – and therefore, by implication, there is less chance of making their primary goal – they still do not intend to stay, for they have a friend in Sicily. All this is designed to allay any fears Dido may have, while quietly asserting the obligation she has to treat them in the traditional, civilised manner (hiding an even quieter threat of 'or else', especially in *arma*, 550 (S.)).

1.551–8: Assuming now that Dido is persuaded, Ilioneus gets to the point: they must be allowed to repair their ships and leave for one or other of the two possible destinations. There is no doubt, however, that Italy is a destination possible only if Aeneas, or his son Iulus, is still alive (553, 555–7). Aeneas, in other words, is central to their mission. Sicily is second best. Do not forget that Aeneas is listening to this speech. We have not yet heard how his men feel about him. We have now. The cloak of invisibility has served an important literary purpose in allowing Aeneas himself to witness their true feelings about him. Everything Ilioneus says (especially 544–9 and 555–6) is high praise indeed. The contrast with Odysseus' men in the *Odyssey* – always causing trouble – is marked.

See: Jones (1988: 113D) on Odysseus' men.

sī datur Ītaliam, sociīs et rēge receptō,
tendere – ut Ītaliam laetī Latiumque petāmus;
sīn absūmpta salūs, et tē, pater optime Teucrum,   555
pontus habet Libyae, nec spēs iam restat Iūlī,
at freta Sīcaniae saltem sēdēsque parātās,
unde hūc aductī, rēgemque petāmus Acestēn.'

1.559–78: *Dido greets them, explains the behaviour of her guards and says everyone knows of the Trojans; they will be safe here and she will try to find Aeneas*

tālibus Īlion͞eūs; cūnctī simul ōre fremēbant
Dardanidae.   560
tum breuiter Dīdō, uultum dēmissa, profātur:

553 *rēge*: i.e. Aeneas (so too *pater* 555)	**Learning vocabulary**
554 *ut*: (let us equip our ships) so that (if it is granted, *datur . . .*) *petāmus* (**554**, **558**)	*aptō* 1 I prepare, fit
555 **sin* but if	*fret-um ī* 2n. seas, straits
absūmō 3 *absūmpsī absūmptum* I lose	*restō* 1 I remain, am left (over); survive from
556 **restō* 1 I remain, am left (over); survive from	*sin* but if
Iūlī: (hope) in Iulus (Aeneas' son, who would be lost with his father)	*trabs trab-is* 3f. tree-trunk, beam
557 *at* 'at any rate'	**559** *tālibus* cf. on 370, 410
*fret-um ī 2n. seas, straits (with *sēdēsque* **557** and *rēgemque Acestēn* **558**, obj. of *petāmus*)	*ōre*: i.e. 'aloud', cf. 614
Sīcani-a ae 1f. Sicily	**560** *Dardanidae*: nom. pl., sons of Dardanus, i.e Trojans. Another unfinished line (see on 534)
saltem at least	**561** *breuiter* briefly
558 *unde hūc aductī*: ellipsis of *sumus* (see 34)	*uultum*: *dēmissa* is used in a 'middle' sense with *uultum* as obj. See on 228; also p. 39 ((c)(ii)) above
	profor 1 dep. I speak out

1.559–78: Clearly Dido has felt the force of Ilioneus' speech, as *uultum dēmissa* (her sense of embarrassment or shame) and the subsequent speech make clear. She moves immediately to put them at ease (562) and then answers each of Ilioneus' criticisms in turn: (i) she explains their bad treatment (563–4, cf. 525–9), (ii) she assures them she knows they are men of honour (*uirtūtēs* 566, cf. 526, 544–5; compare also the hopes raised in Aeneas by the reliefs of the Trojan war in her temple, 461–3) and (iii) she asserts that Carthaginians are civilised people (567–8, cf. 539–40 and compare Aeneas' sense that they were sympathetic to human suffering, 462–3). Moreover she will grant their request and do all she can to advance it (569–71); furthermore, if they do prefer to stay she will actively welcome them (572–4: note the collocation of *Trōs Tyriusque* – as if they were etymologically linked?). A colonist herself, she knows a good thing when she sees it – fine men from a fine background who would add immeasurably to her fledgling city. That offer leads her on to wish that Aeneas himself were there (irony again) and to promise to search for him. This is an overwhelmingly generous and humane offer, but there is nothing surprising about it. Dido understands the Roman political language of reciprocal obligations and is deploying it as any leader of a newly

'soluite corde metum, Teucrī, sēclūdite cūrās.
rēs dūra et rēgnī nouitās mē tālia cōgunt
mōlīrī, et lātē fīnīs custōde tuērī.
quis genus Aeneadum, quis Troiae nesciat urbem,   565
uirtūtēsque uirōsque, aut tantī incendia bellī?
nōn obtūnsa adeō gestāmus pectora Poenī,
nec tam auersus equōs Tyriā^ Sōl iungit ab ^urbe.
sēū uōs Hesperiam magnam Sāturniaque arua,
sīue Erycis fīnīs rēgemque optātīs Acestēn,   570
auxiliō tūtōs dīmittam, opibusque iuuābō.
uultis et hīs mēcum pariter cōnsīdere rēgnīs?
urbem quam statuō, uestra est; subdūcite nāuīs;
Trōs Tyriusque mihī nūllō discrīmine agētur.
atque utinam rēx ipse, Notō compulsus eōdem,   575
adforet Aenēās! equidem per lītora certōs
dīmittam, et Libyae lūstrāre extrēma iubēbō,
sī quibus^ ēiectus ^siluīs aut ^urbibus errat.'

562 *corde*: 'from your heart'
sēclūdō 3 I cast off, put away
563 *dūr-us a um* hard, demanding, difficult
nouitās nouitāt-is 3f. newness
564 *custōde*: s. for pl.
*tueor 2 dep. I watch over, protect; view, scan;
    preserve
565 *quis . . . quis*: 'who . . . who . . .', subjects of
    nesciat (potential subjunc., 'could be . . .') **RL**153.2
Aeneadum: gen. pl., 'of the sons/followers of Aeneas'
566 *uirtūtēsque uirōsque*: word-play on *uir* 'man';
    see on 1.261
incendia: metaphorical, war likened to a
    conflagration
567 *obtūns-us a um* blunted, dulled (*obtundō*)
adeō to such an extent, so
gestō 1 I harbour, carry
568 *auersus . . . ab*: '[the sun] turned away', i.e. 'so
    far from'; the expression denies that Carthage is
    'miles from nowhere'
570 *Eryx Eryc-is* 3m. Eryx, a town in Sicily, named
    after another of Venus' sons and boasting a
    magnificent temple of Venus
Acestēn: Acestes (acc.); *rēgem* is in apposition
571 *auxiliō tūtōs* (understand *uōs*): '[you] guarded
    with help/an escort'

iuuō 1 I help (initial *i* = 'y')
572 **pariter* equally, on an equal footing
cōnsīdō 3 I settle
573 *urbem*: one would expect *urbs* (subject of *est*),
    but *urbs* is attracted into the case of the relative
    quam (cf. on 1.72)
*statuō 3 *statuī statūtum* I establish, found; resolve,
    decide. There is irony in Dido saying to Aeneas
    that Carthage will be his. It will indeed – when
    Rome destroys it in 146 BC
subdūcō 3 I draw up
574 *mihī*: dat. of agent, or of interested party ('in my
    eyes')
discrīmen discrīmin-is 3n. distinction
agō 3 = 'I treat'
575 *utinam* would that! (+ subjunc.) ('showing her
    humanity and desire for Aeneas', S.); **RL**153
*compellō 3 *compulī compulsum* I force, drive
576 *adforet*: 'future' subjunc., based on the fut. inf.
    (*ad*)*fore* rather than the usual pres. inf. (*ad*)*esse*.
    RLE1, 130.2
certōs: ellipsis of 'men'
578 *sī*: 'in case'
quibus: 'from any'
ēiciō 3 *ēiēcī ēiectum* I throw out/ashore

founded city would: to work to its advantage. But . . . what sort of a threat would this
pose to the foundation of *Rome*? Cf. *Intro* [32] for Romulus' welcome of local 'asylum-
seekers' into Rome.

See: Reed (2007: 88–90) on asylum-seekers.

1.579–93: *Aeneas and Achates long to reveal themselves; their cloud disperses and Aeneas is revealed, looking like a god*

hīs animum arrēctī^ dictīs, et ^fortis Achātēs
et ^pater Aenēās iamdudum ērumpere nūbem   580
ārdēbant. prior Aenēān compellat Achātēs:
'nāte deā, quae nunc animō sententia surgit?
omnia tūta uidēs, classem sociōsque receptōs.
ūnus abest, mediō in flūctū quem uīdimus ipsī
summersum; dictīs respondent cētera mātris.'   585
uix ea fātus erat, cum circumfūsa repente
scindit sē nūbēs et in aethera pūrgat apertum.
restitit Aenēās clārāque in lūce refulsit,
ōs umerōsque deō similis; namque ipsa^ decōram
caesariem nātō ^genetrīx lūmenque iuuentae   590
purpureum et laetōs oculīs adflārat honōrēs:
quāle^ manūs addunt eborī ^decus, aut ubi flāuō
argentum Pariusue lapis circumdatur aurō.

Learning vocabulary

compellō 3 *compulī compulsum* I force, drive
pariter equally, on an equal footing
statuō 3 *statuī statūtum* I establish, found; resolve, decide
tueor 2 dep. I watch over, protect; view, scan; preserve

579 *arrēct-us a um* aroused, excited (*animum* acc. of respect; p. 39 ((d)) above; **RL**6.3)
580 *iamdūdum* (now) for a long time
ērumpō 3 I break out from (+ acc.)
581 *compellō* 1 I address (cf. *compellō* 3!)
582 *nāte deā*: '[man] born (voc.) of a goddess' (also 614)
584 *ūnus abest*: Orontes; see 113–17, and cf. *uīdimus ipsī* with 114 *ipsius ante oculōs* (S.)
585 *respondent*: 'respond to, agree with'
586 *circumfūs-us a um* surrounding, lit. 'poured round' (*circumfundō*)
*repente suddenly
587 **scindō* 3 *scidī scissum* I split
pūrgō 1 I disperse (subject still *nūbēs*, understand *sē*)
apert-us a um open, clear

589 *ōs umerōsque*: accs. of respect with *similis*
decōr-us a um graceful, handsome
590 *caesari-ēs ēī* 5f. flowing hair
genetrīx genetrīc-is 3f. mother
iuuent-a ae 1f. youth
591 *purpure-us a um* glowing, radiant, rosy
adflō 1 I breathe X (acc.) into Y (dat.); i.e. by breathing on Aeneas, Venus had bestowed on him . . . (*adflārat = adflāuerat*)
honōrēs: i.e. brightness, sparkle
592 *quāle . . . decus*: introduces a simile 'what sort of grace/beauty/charm', 'the sort of grace which'; cf. 316, 430, 498
manūs: i.e. a craftsman's hands (subject)
ebur ebor-is 3n. ivory
flāu-us a um yellow
593 *Pari-us a um* from Paros (a Greek island, site of very fine marble)
lapis lapid-is 3m. stone
circumdatur aurō: i.e. when silver or marble is gilded

Learning vocabulary

repente suddenly
scindō 3 *scidī scissum* I split

1.579–93: After all Aeneas' trials, it looks at last as if his luck has changed. As Achates points out, everything is turning out as his mother had said. Venus has finally proved her worth (585, cf. 387–401). Even better, when the cloud in which she had enwrapped them dissolves, she glorifies Aeneas, spotlighting him (588) and making him look godlike (589), aristocratic (long hair was such a mark – presumably he has it already, so she

1.594–612: *Aeneas explains who he is and praises Dido for her generosity*

tum sīc rēgīnam adloquitur, cūnctīsque repente
imprōuīsus ait: 'cōram, quem quaeritis, adsum,   595
Trōius Aenēās, Libycīs ēreptus ab undīs.
ō sōla^ īnfandōs Troiae ^miserāta labōrēs,
^quae nōs^, ^rēliquiās Danaum, terraeque marisque
omnibus ^exhaustōs iam cāsibus, omnium ^egēnōs,
urbe, domō sociās, grātēs persoluere dignās   600
nōn opis est nostrae, Dīdō, nec quidquid ubīque est
gentis^ Dardaniae, magnum ^quae sparsa per orbem.
dī tibi, sī qua^ piōs respectant ^nūmina, sī quid
usquam iūstitiae est et mēns sibi cōnscia rēctī,
praemia digna ferant. quae^ tē tam ^laeta tulērunt   605

594 *sīc*: S. refers this not to Aeneas' words but to his looks
adloquor 3 dep. I address
595 **imprōuīs-us a um* unexpected (with *cūnctīs*, dat. of agent)
quem: '[I] whom . . .'
597 *miseror* 1 dep. I pity; here the voc. of the perf. part., referring to Dido ('you having/who have . . .')
598 *quae*: the start of a long rel. clause '(you) who . . . sociās' (**600**)
rēliqui-ae ārum 1f. remnants
599 *exhaust-us a um* drained, exhausted (*exhauriō* 4)
egēn-us a um in need of (+ gen.)
600 *urbe, domō*: i.e. a public and private welcome (S.)
sociō 1 I give X (here ellipsis of 'us') a share in (abl.)
grātēs persoluō 3 I give thanks (dependent on the main vb *nōn opis est* etc.)

601 *nōn opis est nostrae . . . nec gentis Dardaniae* (**602**): 'it is not in/of our power . . . nor in/of the power of the Trojan people'
quidquid ubique est: 'whatever there is [of the Trojan people] everywhere/anywhere'. We have already met e.g. Antenor (1.242) in Italy
*ubīque everywhere
602 *spargō* 3 *sparsī sparsum* I scatter, spread (ellipsis of *est*)
603 *qua = quae* (indef.) 'any', with *nūmina*
respectō 1 I regard, have thought for
quid . . . iūstitiae 'any[thing of] justice'
604 **usquam* anywhere
sibi: 'in itself'
*cōnsci-us a um conscious, inwardly aware of (+ gen.)
rēct-um ī 2n. right
605 *ferant*: subjunc., expressing a wish for the future (**RL**153, L–V(a)4, **M**34)

ensures it is looking its best (*decōram*, cf. *decus* 592) after years at sea), youthful (battering at sea takes its toll) and with sparkling eyes. Ancients often say that it is through the eyes that one falls in love. Venus is advancing her scheme already. A brief simile describes the richness of the whole glowing effect – like polished marble, or gold-embossed silver or marble, from the island of Paros (the best in the Mediterranean). When Venus comes through, she really comes through – in her own interests, naturally. See **1.402–9**.

1.594–612: *imprōuīsus* emphasises the utter astonishment which has greeted this revelation (even more astonishing to his own men, who cannot have expected their leader to have had a makeover either). More astonishing, perhaps, is that his first words are to the queen; only at the end does he greet his companions, the immediate reaction one might have expected. But Aeneas knows what he is doing. He knows his men are safe. It is Dido that needs to be won over. He rises brilliantly to the rhetorical challenge of capping Ilioneus' speech while building on Dido's. Aeneas is a diplomat as well as a leader.

^saecula? quī^ ^tantī tālem genuēre ^parentēs?
in freta dum fluuiī current, dum montibus umbrae
lūstrabunt conuexa, polus dum sīdera pāscet,
semper honōs nōmenque tuum laudēsque manēbunt,
quae^ mē ^cumque uocant ^terrae.' sīc fātus, amīcum   610
Īlionēa petit dextrā, laeuāque Serestum,
post aliōs, fortemque Gyān fortemque Cloanthum.

1.613–30: *The amazed Dido can hardly believe it is Aeneas, mentions her links with him through Greek Teucer and welcomes them all*

obstipuit prīmō aspectū Sīdōnia Dīdō,
cāsū deīnde uirī tantō, et sīc ōre locūta est:
'quis^ tē, nāte deā, per tanta perīcula ^cāsus   615

606 *gignō* 3 *genuī* I bear; praise of parentage is a common rhetorical device

607 *fluui-us ī* 2m. river

*currō 3 *cucurrī cursum* I run

608 *conuex-a ōrum* 2n. pl. curves (of valleys)? Slopes (of mountains)?

pāscet: the sky 'feeds' the stars, as fields sheep

609 *tuum*: qualifies all three nouns in this line

610 *quae . . . cumque* = *quaecumque* 'whatever'

611 *Īlionēa*: acc. of Īlioneus

*dextr-a ae . . . *laeu-a ae 1f. right hand . . . left hand, cf. on 1.408

612 *post*: adverbial, 'afterwards'

Gyān: acc. of Gyas

Learning vocabulary

cōnsci-us a um conscious, inwardly aware of (+ gen.)

currō 3 *cucurrī cursum* I run

dextr-a ae 1f. right hand

imprōuīs-us a um unexpected

laeu-a ae 1f. left hand

ubīque everywhere

usquam anywhere

613 *aspectū . . .* **614** *cāsū*: abl. of cause, explaining why she was struck dumb. The questions that follow, as S. points out, are not really questions but expressions of admiration

614 *ōre*: i.e. aloud

He makes the right start. Despite Ilioneus' warm words, Aeneas does not announce himself in the heroic terms that he had e.g. to Venus (378–9). He is (first word) Trojan – that is his identity – and what else? Saved from drowning. That is all. No heroism there. The rest of the speech is dedicated to Dido – what she has done for them (597–600; cf. on **1.1–7**[c]), how impossible it is to thank her enough (600–2) and his hopes for her due reward among gods (603–5) and men (607–9), a cause he will support wherever he finds himself (610 – more irony). Note the powerful collocation of *sōla īnfandōs* (597, heightened by the elision), the emphasis on Dido's pity for them (*miserāta*) – his travels have so far been pretty pitiless – the expansiveness of 598–9, the punchy *urbe, domō sociās* and back to the grateful thanks of the whole Trojan people (600–2: irony). Note again how he emphasises her piety and justice (603–4 picking up Ilioneus' encomium at 522–3, cf. 544–5). Routine praise of the age and parents that bore her is followed by further rolling rhetoric with triplets (river, mountain, sky 607–8 and *honōs, nōmen, laudēs* 609). Aeneas' rhetoric is as overwhelming as Dido's was.

1.613–30: Dido's reaction of bewildered but excited amazement speaks for itself and Virgil explains it: it is due, first, to the very sight of him – no wonder she calls him *nāte deā* after Venus' transformation (588–93) – and then to his story (*cāsū* 614, cf. *cāsus* 615)

īnsequitur? quae uīs immānibus applicat ōrīs?
tūne ille Aenēās, quem Dardaniō Anchīsae
alma Venus Phrygiī^ genuit ^Simoentis ad undam?
atque equidem Teucrum^ meminī Sīdōna uenīre
fīnibus ^expulsum patriīs, noua rēgna ^petentem   620
auxiliō Bēlī; genitor tum Bēlus opīmam
uastābat Cyprum, et uictor diciōne tenēbat.
tempore iam ex illō cāsus mihi cognitus urbis
Troiānae nōmenque tuum rēgēsque Pelasgī.
ipse, hostis, Teucrōs īnsignī laude ferēbat,   625
sēque ortum antīquā Teucrōrum ā stirpe uolēbat.

616 *immānibus*: does Dido feel guilty at the way Ilioneus' men were treated (cf. 525–9, 539–43)?
applicō 1 I join X (acc.: understand 'you' as object) to Y (dat.)
617 *tūne ille*: note the admiration (S.)
Dardaniō: the final ō does not elide (hiatus); note also that the fifth foot is a spondee (very rare in V.)
Anchīsae: dat. s. of Anchises, Aeneas' father
618 *gignō* 3 *genuī genitum* I bear
Simoentis: gen. s. m. of Simois, a river near Ilium. Myth generally identified Mount Ida (south of Troy) as the location for Aeneas' conception
619 *Teucer Teucr-ī* 2m. Teucer, a Greek from Salamis. He was half-brother of the great fighter Ajax, but was unable to prevent Ajax's suicide. When Achilles died, the army decided to give his armour to Odysseus, not Ajax. Ajax went mad and committed suicide. So when Teucer returned home after the war, he was thrown out by his father (*expulsum* **620**) and wandered the Mediterranean till settling in Cyprus. He told Dido all about the Trojan war (**623–4**)
Sīdōna: acc. s. ('to') Sidon, Dido's homeland

620 *expellō* 3 *expulī expulsum* I throw out, reject
621 *Bēlī*: gen. s. of Belus (Baal), presumably Dido's father. If he is the same as Belus king of Egypt (2.82), Dido is in a line of Greek mythical figures, including Io, Europa and the Danae! But he is more likely the Belus who founded the dynasty (729–30)
opīm-us a um rich, wealthy
622 *uastō* 1 I lay waste
Cypr-us ī 2f. Cyprus
diciō diciōn-is 3f. jurisdiction
623 *cāsus*: S. suggests this means specifically 'fall, destruction'
624 *Pelasg-us a um* of the Pelasgi, a northern Greek tribe allied with the Trojans
625 *ipse hostis*: Teucer, as a Greek, was obviously an enemy of the *Teucrī*. But *hostīs* is metrically possible. What is the difference? Do you have a defensible preference?
Teucrōs: here, *Teucrī* = 'Trojans' (see on 38)
ferēbat: 'told of' – high praise indeed, as it emerges, of the Trojans
626 *ortum*: ellipsis of *esse*
stirps stirp-is 3f. line(age), stock

which has clearly affected her. She can hardly believe it is him; her question expands in growing wonder as she ticks off his lineage (617–18: note the collocation of *Dardaniō Anchīsae* with *alma Venus*). (Cf. 495, where Aeneas has the same reaction of bewildered amazement to the reliefs of the Trojan war that – presumably (?) – Dido commissioned.) Her story of Teucer replays the story common to her and Aeneas: exile and the search for a new country (620). It also explains how she knows him and, presumably, why the reliefs in the temple were put up (450–93) – surely a mark of what the Trojan people meant to her, explaining her astonishment that the quasi-mythical figure of Aeneas should now stand before her in the flesh. So she welcomes the Trojans warmly (627) and ends by associating her fortunes with theirs (628–9) and confirming the compassion with which Aeneas credited her (630). This assimilation of Carthage to Troy is one example of the ways in which V. plays with the *idea* of Aeneas/Trojans as foreigners fusing into a brand-new and quite different identity – a fusion that will never happen with Carthage, of

quāre agite, ō tēctīs, iuuenēs, succēdite nostrīs.
mē^ quoque per multōs similis fortūna labōrēs
^iactātam hāc^ dēmum uoluit cōnsistere ^terrā.
nōn ignāra^ malī, miserīs succurrere ^discō.'   630

1.631–42: *Sacrifices are prepared and the palace arranged for a magnificent banquet*

sīc memorat; simul Aenēān in rēgia dūcit
tēcta, simul dīuum templīs indīcit honōrem.
nec minus intereā sociīs ad lītora mittit
uīgintī taurōs, magnōrum^ horrentia centum
terga ^suum, pinguīs centum cum mātribus agnōs,   635
mūnera laetitiamque deī.
at domus interior rēgālī splendida luxū
īnstruitur, mediīsque parant conuīuia tēctīs:
arte labōrātae uestēs ostrōque superbō,
ingēns argentum mēnsīs, caelātaque in aurō   640

627 *agite*: 'come!'
succēdō 3 I come under (the shelter of)
628 *similis fortūna*: subject, vb *uoluit* (**629**), obj. *mē*
629 *dēmum* in particular (with *hāc . . . terrā*)
630 *discō* 3 I learn, am learning (how to + inf.)
631 *in rēgia dūcit/tēcta*: S. comments that here, as in what follows, there seems to be an omen of marriage. Note the irony that the groom would normally lead (*dūcit*) the bride into *his* home
632 *indīcō* 3 I appoint
honōrem: here = 'special sacrifice'
633 *nec minus*: no less – warmly? generously? The context must decide
sociīs: i.e. Aeneas' companions left behind by Ilioneus on his mission
634 *uīgintī* 20
*taur-us ī 2m. bull
635 *sus su-is* 3m./f. pig, sow

pingu-is e fat, rich
agn-us ī 2m. sheep
636 *diī*: another unfinished line. The mss. have *deī* 'of the god', i.e. Bacchus = wine to go with the food. But ancient authors say that *DII* is the reading, and interpret it as *die* = *diēī*, i.e. 'for the day'. All very difficult
637 *interior -is* inner
rēgāl-is e royal
splendid-us a um glittering
lux-us ūs 4m. luxury, splendour
638 **īnstruō* 3 *īnstrūxī īnstrūctum* I prepare, ready, draw up
conuīui-um ī 2n. feast
639 *labōrō* 1 I work at
ostr-um ī 2n. purple
640 *ingēns*: i.e. a great weight of
caelāt-us a um engraved (*caelō* 1)
in aurō: i.e. on gold cups, plate etc.

course, but will with the local Latins, when they arrive in Italy. So too Romulus will welcome 'asylum-seekers' and other outsiders when he founds Rome (*Intro* [32]).

See: Reed (2007) in general, particularly (87–92), on Dido and foreigners.

1.631–42: Dido moves Aeneas and her men from the temple into the palace (632), while thoughtfully sending supplies to his men still left on the beach (634–6, cf. 518, where we are told only representatives of Aeneas' men arrived at Dido's palace). A magnificent reception is planned, with the best of everything. Note how important history is

fortia facta patrum, seriēs^ ^longissima rērum
per tot ^ducta uirōs, antīquā ab orīgine gentis.

1.643–56: *Aeneas sends Achates to fetch his son Ascanius and gifts saved from Troy for the queen*

Aenēās (neque enim patrius^ cōnsistere mentem
passus ^amor) rapidum ad nāuīs praemittit Achātēn,
Ascaniō ferat haec, ipsumque ad moenia dūcat;   645
omnis^ in Ascaniō cārī stat ^cūra parentis.
mūnera praetereā, Īliacīs ērepta ruīnīs,

641 *seri-ēs ēī* 5f. sequence. A *longa seriēs* would impress a Roman
642 *ducta*: 'traced'
antīquā: some manuscripts offer *antīquae*. What is the difference? Do you have a preference?

Learning vocabulary
taur-us ī 2m. bull
īnstruō 3 *īnstrūxī īnstrūctum* I prepare, ready, draw up
643 **patri-us a um* paternal, ancestral

644 *passus*: ellipsis of *est* (*mentem* is obj.)
praemittō 3 I send ahead
Achātēn: acc. s., Aeneas' loyal companion Achates (nom. *Achātēs*, **656**)
645 *ferat*: note subjunc. of indir. command ('for him to . . .'), **RL**134, **W**36, **M**89–91
haec: i.e. 'news'
646 *cārī*: note that *cārus* means 'dear' and 'loving'
647 **praetereā* moreover, further (and **653**)
ērepta: S. comments that this must show how valuable they were

to Dido: the deeds of her fathers are engraved in gold plate from long ago (640–2; was this plate part of what she took with her from Tyre, 359–64?). The past is always present with Dido, who comes from an ancient city rich in history – another point of contact with Aeneas. (S. suggests that this is why the deeds of the Greeks and Trojans were displayed in Juno's temple – because the deeds of the Phoenicians were already on display in this superb gold plate.) All these reminders of the pasts of great cities like Tyre/Sidon and Carthage might equally have prompted reflection by Romans on the destruction of those cities – Tyre by Alexander the Great (332 BC), Carthage by the Roman Scipio (146 BC).

The groundwork for Dido's affair with Aeneas (Book 4) is laid in Book 1. Note in particular (i) Venus' appealing portrait of Dido, generating pity and admiration (338–68), (ii) Aeneas' envy at her new, growing city (420–37), (iii) Aeneas' feeling that there is security here (463), (iv) Dido's first, impressively grand entrance and control of her city (494–508), (v) Aeneas' men's praise for and reliance on him (544–58), (vi) Dido's immediate welcome for the men, knowledge of Aeneas and desire for his safety (565–78), (vii) Aeneas' youthful appearance (588–93), (viii) Dido's amazed welcome of Aeneas and admiration and sympathy for him (613–30), (ix) and the generosity of the banquet she prepares for the Trojans (631–42).

See: Heinze (119–25/95–9) on V.'s preparation for the Aeneas–Dido relationship.

1.643–56: Dido's concern for Aeneas' men is matched by Aeneas for his son. Since Ascanius'/Iulus' role in the future of Rome is as important as Aeneas' (267–71, cf. Ilioneus at 556), it is not surprising that he should now be at the centre of Aeneas' thoughts (646). Aeneas wants to use him to confirm his bond with Dido, and exchange of

ferre iubet, pallam signīs aurōque rigentem,
et circumtextum croceō uēlāmen acanthō –
ōrnātūs^ Argīuae Helenae, ^quōs illa Mycēnīs,   650
Pergama cum peteret inconcessōsque hymenaeōs,
extulerat, mātris Lēdae mīrābile dōnum;
praetereā scēptrum^, Īlionē* ^quod gesserat ōlim,
*maxima nātārum Priamī, collōque monīle
bācātum, et duplicem gemmīs aurōque corōnam.   655
haec celerāns iter ad nāuīs tendēbat Achātēs.

648 *pall-a ae* 1f. cloak
rigēns rigent-is stiff, thick (*rigeō*)
649 *circumtext-us a um* woven
croce-us a um yellow
uēlāmen uēlāmin-is 3n. dress
acanth-us ī 2m. acanthus (a plant, the model for decorative elements on the capital of a 'Corinthian' column)
650 *ōrnāt-us ūs* 4m. adornment (acc. pl., in apposition to *pallam* and *uēlāmen*)
Helen-a ae 1f. Helen (of Troy); so too *illa*
Mycēn-īs: abl. of place from (actually the home of Agamemnon rather than of Helen's husband Menelaus; presumably used here to mean 'Greece' in general, cf. V.'s use of e.g. *Argiuus*, lit. 'from Argos', to mean 'Greek'). For the implied value of the garments, see on **647**
651 *peteret*: long final *e*: see on 308, though no obvious pause here
inconcess-us a um forbidden

hymenae-ī ōrum 2m. pl. marriage (rituals)
652 *Lēd-a ae* 1f. Leda, Helen's mother by Zeus disguised as a swan
653 *Īlionē* nom. s. f. Ilione, wife of Polymestor, king of Thrace. They did not make a model family. Polymestor murdered her brother Polydorus; she (in different versions) murdered Polymestor and committed suicide
654 *maxima*: see on 521
monīl-e is 3n. necklace, choker
655 *bācāt-us a um* of pearl
duplex duplic-is double
gemm-a ae 1f. jewel
corōn-a ae 1f. crown, coronet
656 *celerō* 1 I hurry to do

Learning vocabulary
patri-us a um paternal, ancestral
praetereā moreover, further

gifts was the way that heroes did this, the richer the better (cf. Homer *Iliad* 6.212–36, where the Greek hero Diomedes finds that his opponent Glaucus on the battlefield is of the same family as an old family friend, so refuses to fight him. They maintain that relationship by exchanging armour). Austin (1971) points out that the stories behind these gifts – the robe, specifically linked with Helen's adultery (651) and Ilione's background history (see notes) – make one wonder whether they are the most tactful possible. But when men indulge in such gift-selection, they often make slips (see on 752); or is V. dropping a dark hint about the future of the Aeneas–Dido relationship? On the other hand, Odysseus' son Telemachus, visiting Menelaus in the *Odyssey* to enquire after his 'lost' father, did not reject gifts made by Helen for his (future) marriage (*Odyssey* 15.104–30). If one also wonders how these treasures could have been saved and preserved over seven long years of travel (cf. 119, and see 679, 755–6), the explanation must be that these inanimate objects, as records of a glorious, heroic Trojan past, were supremely precious, as loaded with significance for the Trojans as Dido's treasure was for her (cf. 357–64).

Learning vocabulary for Section 1.520–656

aetheri-us a um of heaven
aptō 1 I prepare, fit
certō 1 I contend, fight
compellō 3 *compulī compulsum* I force,
     drive
cōnsci-us a um conscious, inwardly aware of (+
     gen.)
cōram face to face
currō 3 *cucurrī cursum* I run
dextr-a ae 1f. right hand
fret-um ī 2n. seas, straits
Hesperi-a ae 1f. Hesperia, western land
hic, hoc 'this' often scan long, as if *hicc,*
     hocc
improuīs-us a um unexpected
īnstruō 3 *īnstrūxī īnstrūctum* I prepare, ready, draw
     up
laeu-a ae 1f. left hand

Mycēn-ae ārum 1f. pl. Mycenae, palace of
     Agamemnon, brother of Menelaus
pariter equally, on an equal footing
patri-us a um paternal, ancestral
pi-us a um pious, god-fearing
praetereā moreover, further
repente suddenly
restō 1 I remain, am left (over); survive from
scindō 3 *scidī scissum* I split
sin but if
statuō 3 *statuī statūtum* I establish, found; resolve,
     decide
taur-us ī 2m. bull
trabs trab-is 3f. tree-trunk, beam
tueor 2 dep. I watch over, protect; view, scan;
     preserve
ubīque everywhere
usquam anywhere

Study Section for 1.520–656

1. How successfully does V. prepare the ground for the impending affair between Dido and Aeneas? Consider Aeneas' words and actions as well as Dido's.
2. How is our picture of Aeneas as a leader of men developed in this *Section*?
3. Aeneas and his men are Trojans. They are about to join forces with Carthaginians. To what extent does V. make us feel that they are all really Romans?
4. Scan 627–32.
5. In Homer's *Odyssey*, the witch Circe, after failing to turn Odysseus into a pig, attempts to lure him into her bed. In her response to Aeneas, Dido is said to have something in common with Circe. Compare 613–27 with the following words of Circe:

> 'Who are you, and who are you descended from? Where is your city, and your parents?   325
> I am amazed that you have not been charmed on drinking these drugs.
> No other man has withstood these drugs
> who has drunk them, once they have passed the fence of his teeth;
> but you have some sort of mind that cannot be laid under a spell in your breast.
> Are you the versatile Odysseus, whom   330
> the slayer of Argos with the golden staff [Hermes] was always saying would come,
> returning from Troy with his fast black ship?
> Come now, put your sword in its sheath, and let the pair of us after this
> climb into our bed, so that we may join
> in loving union, with trust in each other.'   335

> *Odyssey* 10.325–35 (Dawe 1993)

Is the comparison a sound one? Would you want to argue that our image of Dido is influenced by it? See Knauer 'Vergil's *Aeneid* and Homer' in Harrison (1990: 399–401).

6. How far does Nicolas Verkolye reflect this scene in the *Aeneid*? (See Figure 1.)

Figure 1 As Ilioneus appeals to Dido, Aeneas bursts on the scene.

1.657–756: Falling in love

In this Section, *Venus plans for her son Cupid, disguising himself as Ascanius, to make Dido fall in love with Aeneas. When the feast is over and the drinking starts, Dido begs Aeneas to tell her his story.*

(Note: there will be no **Learning vocabularies** for the remainder of Book 1. Vocabulary not listed in the *Total learning vocabulary* will be glossed in the text.)

1.657–76: *Venus, fearful of Carthage and Juno, decides to replace Ascanius briefly with her son Cupid and orders him to make Dido fall in love with Aeneas*

at Cytherēa nouās artēs, noua pectore uersat
cōnsilia ut, faciem mūtātus^ et ōra, ^Cupīdō
prō dulcī Ascaniō ueniat, dōnīsque furentem
incendat rēgīnam, atque ossibus implicet ignem;   660
quippe domum timet ambiguam Tyriōsque bilinguīs;
ūrit atrōx Iūnō, et sub noctem cūra recursat.
ergō hīs āligerum dictīs adfātur Amōrem:

657 *Cytherē-a ae* 1f. Venus (see on 257)
uersō 1 I keep turning over, considering
658 *fac-iēs ēī* 5f. look, appearance
mūtātus: since Cupid is doing this himself
(689–90), *faciem* and *ōra* are dir. objs. of a
'middle' *mūtātus* which is used in an act. sense
(see on 228)
Cupīdō Cupīdin-is 3m. Cupid (Venus' son,
and therefore brother of Aeneas; see
667)
659 *prō*: here, 'in place of'
furentem: i.e. who would become *furēns* (with mad
passion for Aeneas) as a result
660 *incendō* 3 I set fire to, inflame (for 'fire of love'
references, see on 713)
oss-a um 3n. pl. bones
implicō 1 I enfold, wrap X (acc.) round Y (abl.). S.
comments that this is used of disease ('for love

too is a disease'). Might it also hint at Dido's
eventual suicide on a funeral pyre?
661 *quippe* the reason is that, for; the subject of
timet is Venus
ambigu-us a um untrustworthy, suspect; *Pūnica
fidēs* 'Punic faith' signalled 'treachery' to a Roman
bilingu-is e (speaking) with forked tongue
662 *ūrō* 1 I burn, chafe (ellipsis of 'Venus' as obj.)
atrōx: angry, cruel
Iūnō: ellipsis of 'the thought of . . .'
sub + acc. under cover of
cūra: i.e. Venus' concern. S. (absurdly to us) suggests
that there is word-play on the etymology of *cūra*
from *cor ūrat*. See on 208
recursō 1 I keep on returning; S. comments that
worries always seem more acute at night
663 *āliger -a um* winged
adfor 1 dep. I address; say farewell to

1.657–76: Venus' plans are *noua* in two senses: first, because Venus has just thought of them; second, because no other poet has made Aeneas have a relationship with Dido, with all the trouble that will entail for him – and her (see *Intro* [17]). Venus' method of

[165]

'nāte – meae uīrēs, mea magna potentia – sōlus^,
nāte, patris summī ^quī tēla Typhōea temnis,   665
ad tē cōnfugiō et supplex tua nūmina poscō.
frāter^ ut ^Aenēās pelagō ^tuus omnia circum
lītora iactētur odiīs Iūnōnis acerbae,
nōta tibi, et nostrō doluistī saepe dolōre.
hunc Phoenissa tenet Dīdō blandīsque morātur   670
uōcibus; et uereor, quō sē Iūnōnia uertant
hospitia; haud tantō cessābit cardine rērum.
quōcircā capere ante dolīs et cingere flammā
rēgīnam meditor, nē quō sē nūmine mūtet,
sed magnō Aenēae mēcum teneātur amōre.   675
quā facere id possis, nostram nunc accipe mentem.'

664 *potenti-a ae* 1f. power, might; Cupid represents
the power of Venus to make people fall hopelessly
in love, usually by shooting them with his arrows.
His power is also depicted by images of him
trampling on Jupiter's thunderbolt, as here
665 *patris summī*: take with *tēla*
Typhōe-us a um that dealt with Typhoeus (a giant
whom Jupiter burnt to ashes with his
thunderbolt): note *Typhōea* is four syllables
temnō 3 I mock, despise
666 *cōnfugiō* 3 I have recourse to
supplex: here in apposition to 'I'
667 *ut*: how (indir. q. after *nōta* **669**)
668 *iactētur*: note the unexpected long *u*, and see on
308
669 *nōta* (n. nom. pl.) sc. *sunt*: 'these things are well
known'
670 *Phoeniss-a ae* f. adj. Phoenician
bland-us a um charming, ingratiating, alluring
moror 1 dep. I delay, hold back
671 *uereor* 2 dep. I fear (+ subjunc.); **RL**S2(d), **W**40,
M102–3

quō sē . . . uertant: lit. 'to where it may turn itself', i.e.
what it will result in
Iūnōni-us a um of Juno
672 *hospiti-um ī* 2n. welcome, hospitality (pl.
for s.)
cessō 1 I give up (Juno is the subject)
cardine: 'at [such a] . . .' S. comments that the image
is 'drawn from a door which can be pushed this
way and that by the movement of the *cardō*'
673 *quōcircā* therefore
ante: adverbial, i.e. before Juno can act
flammā: i.e. of love. *capere, dolīs, cingere* and
flammā all suggest an image of a siege (*dolīs* for
example, like undermining walls)
674 *meditor* 1 dep. I intend, devise
quō . . . nūmine: 'by some power/deity' (Venus is
thinking of Juno)
sē . . . mūtet: Dido is the subject
675 *mēcum*: i.e. 'on my side'
676 *quā*: 'how'; a deliberately prosaic line, as of a
'commander briefing a lieutenant' (Austin
1971)

doing so – using Cupid to act the part of Ascanius – gives V. the chance to explore the
psychology of the situation: Dido falling in love by reacting to (and innocently holding
and feeling 717–18) the man in the son, so much more affecting than the usual mechani-
cal shot from Cupid's bow followed by instant passion. At the same time, Venus' move,
ruthlessly exploiting the warm-hearted and generous Dido in the interests of her son,
generates a sympathy for the innocent queen that imbues her suicide in Book 4 with a
powerful sense of tragedy: this is not a woman we feel deserves to be inflamed (*incendat*)
to madness (*furentem* 659) with a passion that is none of her doing (660). But that is
Venus for you: as unfeeling about Dido as she was earlier about Aeneas (cf. on **387–401**).

V. now explains the situation to Cupid, and very rhetorically too (S.). She combines
flattery, explanation of the situation and praise of Cupid's powers with instructions on
whose behalf he must act, what the problems are, how he will achieve Venus' ends and
so on. Her opening words to her son (*nāte* 664) are both flattering (note the 'power'

1.677–94: 'I shall send Ascanius to sleep and remove him; you act his part and breathe your fire of love into her'

'rēgius,^ accītū cārī genitōris, ad urbem
Sīdoniam ^puer īre parat, mea maxima cūra,
dōna ferēns, pelagō et flammīs restantia Troiae:
hunc ego sōpītum somnō super alta Cythēra   680
aut super Īdalium sacrātā sēde recondam,
ne quā scīre dolōs mediusue occurrere possit.
tū^ faciem illīus, noctem nōn amplius ūnam,
^falle dolō, et nōtōs puerī puer indue uultūs,
ut, cum tē gremiō accipiet laetissima Dīdō   685

---

677 *accītū* at the summons
678 *Sīdoni-us a um* Sidonian, i.e. Carthage (see on 446). It usually scans *Sīdōnius* (see on 343)
puer: i.e. Ascanius (Achates is bringing him, 643–5)
679 *restantia*: + dat. or abl., 'surviving from'
680 *hunc ... sōpītum*: obj. of *recondam* (**681**)
sōpīt-us a um drowsy, stupefied (*sōpiō* 4 I overcome with sleep)
super + acc. on top of, above
Cythēr-a ōrum 2n. Cythera, Venus' island (see on 257)
681 *Īdali-um ī* 2n. a mountain in Cyprus; also *Īdali-a ae* 1f. (**693**)
sacrāt-us a um holy
recondō 3 I hide away
682 *quā* somehow or other

medius: 'in the middle of things' (Ascanius is the subject)
occurrō 3 I turn up, appear; become involved, visible ('blunder in' is the rough idea)
683 *faci-ēs ēī* 5f. look, appearance
amplius more than
684 *fallō* 3 I counterfeit; trick, deceive (also **688**)
nōt-us a um familiar
puer: 'as a boy'
induō 3 I put on, adopt
685 *ut*: two *cum* clauses (+ indic., **RLT**(d), **W**31, **M**122–3) intervene before the *ut* clause is completed (**688**). V. does not often subordinate like this (p. 46 above); it makes the climax in **688** all the more effective (Williams (1972))
gremi-um ī 2n. lap, bosom (also **692**)

---

rising triplet at 664–5) and grovelling (*supplex ... poscō* 667). They turn the emotional screw by referring to Aeneas as Cupid's *frāter* (667) – every Roman knew what 'family' meant – and involving Cupid in her *dolor* (669). The situation, she explains, is now on a knife-edge ('door-socket, turning-point' is V.'s image at 672). Aeneas is in Carthage, 'enemy' – worse, Juno's – territory. Venus does not trust Juno anyway (662, 668, 671–2), and fears that the treacherous Carthaginians, now so welcoming (670–1), may turn hostile and so pose a threat to Aeneas and his men (661–2; Carthaginians were notorious in Roman eyes for their treachery – what Romans ironically meant by *Pūnica fidēs*). She uses the image of military warfare to describe the attack she is to launch on Dido (673–4). Ironically, Aeneas' reciprocal feelings for Dido (not, presumably, part of Venus' plan) will pose just as much of a threat, but that is all in the future. Gods cannot anticipate everything (see *Intro* [11, 17, 50]).

Explanations over, the scheme is adumbrated: before Juno can wreck things, Dido must fall in love with Aeneas (673–6).

1.677–94: Humour and viciousness combine in Venus' cynical plan: humour in her determination that Ascanius must not barge in and wreck things (682) and in Cupid's delight (*gaudēns*) in practising to look like Ascanius (690); viciousness in her open acknowledgement that this is all a trick (*dolō* 684) and Cupid will be poisoning (*uenēnō* 688) the gloriously happy (*laetissima* – irony: 685) Dido who will know nothing of

rēgālīs inter mēnsās laticemque Lyaeum,
cum dabit amplexūs atque ōscula dulcia figet,
occultum īnspīrēs ignem fallāsque uenēnō.'
pāret Amor dictīs cārae genetrīcis, et ālās
exuit, et gressū gaudēns incēdit Iūlī.   690
at Venus Ascaniō placidam per membra quiētem
inrigat, et fōtum gremiō dea tollit in altōs
Īdaliae lūcōs, ubi mollis^ ^amāracus illum
flōribus et dulcī ^aspīrāns complectitur umbrā.

1.695–711: *The Trojans arrive and sit at table, the Carthaginians admire the gifts and 'Ascanius'*

iamque ībat, dictō pārēns^, et dōna ^Cupīdō   695
rēgia portābat Tyriīs, duce ^laetus Achātē.
cum uenit, aulaeīs iam sē rēgīna superbīs
aureā composuit spondā mediamque locāuit.
iam pater Aenēās et iam Troiāna iuuentūs

686 *rēgāl-is e* royal
latex latic-is 3m. liquid (and 736)
Lyae-us a um of Bacchus
687 *amplex-us ūs* 4m. embrace
688 *occult-us a um* secret
īnspīrō 1 I breathe in; subjunc. after *ut* (**685**)
uenēn-um ī 2n. poison
689 *pāret*: which vb?
genetrīx genetrīc-is 3f. mother (cf. **677**)
āl-a ae 1f. wing
690 *exuō* 3 I shed, take off
gaudeō 2 semi-dep. I rejoice, take delight in (+ abl.)
692 *inrigō* 1 I water
fōtum: understand *Ascanium*
gremiō: referring to Venus

693 *lūc-us ī* 2m. grove
moll-is e soft
amārac-us ī 2m. marjoram
694 *aspīrō* 1 I breathe on (understand *illum* as object of *aspīrāns* and *complectitur*)
complector 3 dep. I embrace

695 *Cupīdō Cupīdin-is* 3m. Cupid, son of Venus
696 *portō* 1 I carry
duce . . . Achātē: an abl. abs.
697 *aulae-us a um* curtains, overhanging the couches
698 *spond-a ae* 1f. couch
mediamque: understand 'herself'

what is happening to her (*occultum . . . ignem* 688) as she lovingly hugs and kisses him during the feast (687). 'Mercy' is not in Venus' vocabulary when it comes to those who may stand in her way; but for those who are her *maxima cūra* (678), 'luxurious cosseting' is (680–1 and the wonderfully soporific 691–4). While Dido will innocently embrace Cupid and be fed fire and poison (687–8, cf. 673), Venus takes Ascanius to her bosom (692), soothes him (691) and embraces him with flowers and sweet shade. Dreadful irony here: Venus traditionally surrounds lovers with flowers and sweet shade in their private *locus amoenus* ('delightful location'); they will never encircle Dido and Aeneas.

See: Jones (2007: 8) on the *locus amoenus*.

1.695–711: Dido, all ignorant of what was to befall her, was (ironically) *laetissima* (685); Cupid, meanwhile, is unironically *laetus* (696), happily and brilliantly acting out the

conueniunt, strātōque super discumbitur ostrō.   700
dant famulī manibus lymphās, Cereremque canistrīs
expediunt, tōnsīsque ferunt mantēlia uillīs.
quīnquāgintā intus famulae, quibus ōrdine longam^
cūra ^penum struere, et flammīs adolēre penātīs;
centum aliae totidemque parēs aetāte ministrī,   705
quī dapibus mēnsās onerent et pōcula pōnant.
nec nōn et Tyriī, per līmina laeta frequentēs,
conuēnēre; torīs iussī discumbere pictīs,
mīrantur dōna Aenēae, mīrantur Iūlum
flagrantīsque deī uultūs simulātaque uerba,   710
pallamque et pictum croceō uēlāmen acanthō.

---

700 *strāt-us a um* laid

discumbō 3 I recline, stretch myself out on (also **708**); here impersonal pass., **RL**155, **M**106. Another very Romanising touch – Romans reclined at banquets

ostr-um ī 2n. purple

701 *famul-us ī* 2m. slave (and *famul-a ae* 1f. **703**)

lymph-a ae 1f. water

canistr-um ī 2n. basket

702 *expediō* 4 I provide

tōns-us a um shorn, smooth

mantēl-e is 3n. serviette, napkin

uill-us ī 2m. nap

703 *quīnquāgintā* fifty

intus: i.e. in the kitchen

quibus: take with *cūra* (**704**) and note ellipsis of *erat*; the infins. depend on *cūra*

704 *pen-us ūs* 4f. (household) food, provisions; it is *longam* because there is a long succession of dishes to bring in

struō 3 I arrange

adoleō 2 I honour, magnify; the *penātēs*,

etymologically connected with *penus*, were usually kept over the fire or hearth. 'Honouring the *penātēs* with fire' is a poetic way of saying 'keeping the fires burning'. See Page (1984) on this passage

705 *totidem* as many (this line refers to the waiters and waitresses at table)

aetāte: abl. of respect after *parēs*

minister ministr-ī 2m. waiter, servant

706 *quī*: note the mood of the vbs – telling you what? **RL**145.3, **M**97.5

daps dap-is 3f. banquet

pōcul-um ī 2n. cup

707 *nec nōn*: = 'moreover'

frequēns frequent-is thronging, crowded

708 *tor-us ī* 2m. couch

iussī: i.e. the Carthaginians (subject)

pict-us a um embroidered (also **711**)

710 *flagrāns flagrant-is* radiant, glowing

deī: because it is really Cupid (this is the poet's comment, as is *Iūlum* and *simulāta*)

simulāta: i.e. as if spoken by Ascanius

711 *pallam . . . acanthō*: see 648–9

---

part of Ascanius (710), the beginning of Dido's impending tragedy. When Ascanius arrives with Achates from the ships, all is ready. Dido settles herself in the middle, the mistress of proceedings (697–8), as does the Trojan company. V. carefully distinguishes table-layers (701–2) from cooks (703–4) from wine- and food-waiters (705–6). Politely, their Carthaginian hosts come in last of all (707–8), admiring two things: Aeneas' gifts and the glowing looks and words of the counterfeit Ascanius (709–11). And well, indeed, might they admire him.

This is a very (anachronistic) Roman meal, complete with e.g. reclining (Homeric heroes sit) and napkins (there are no napkins in Homer). It is described richly (697, 700, 708) and elaborately (all those bustling slave and courses 701–6) – no skimping on her guests for Dido. What a joyful, glorious occasion for everyone! But . . .

Figure 2 Aeneas presenting Cupid disguised as Ascanius to Dido.

1.712–22: *Dido is entranced by Cupid/Ascanius, who slowly makes her forget her previous husband and turns her heart to new love*

praecipuē īnfēlīx^, pestī ^dēuōta futūrae,
explērī mentem nequit ārdēscitque tuendō
^Phoenissa, et pariter puerō dōnīsque mouētur.
ille ubi complexū Aenēae collōque pependit   715
et magnum falsī implēuit genitōris amōrem,

712 *īnfēlīx īnfēlīc-is* unfortunate, unhappy (Dido): the whole line heavy with impending disaster
pest-is is 3f. plague, destruction
deuōt-us a um given up to, doomed
713 *expleor* 2 I have my fill of, satisfy; here 'middle' with dir. obj.; see p. 39 ((c)(ii)) above *mēns* is used of the emotional as well as intellectual faculties

nequeō (as if *neque* + *eō*) I am unable
ārdēscō 3 I take fire (for fire of love imagery cf. 660, 673, 688)
714 *Phoeniss-a ae* 1f. Phoenician woman (Dido)
715 *ille*: note the change of subject
complex-us ūs 4m. embrace
716 *impleō* 2 *implēuī implētum* I fulfil, satisfy; fill (see 729). Note the 'golden' line: AB verb BA

1.712–22: *laetissima* at 685, *īnfēlīx* at 712, *miserae* at 719, already in the inescapable grip (*dēuōta*) of the disease (cf. *uenēnō* 688) that will (*futūrae*) kill her, already helpless (*nequit*), already on fire (713 *ārdēscit* cf. *incendat . . . ignem* 660, 673, 688) – the

rēgīnam petit. haec oculīs, haec pectore tōtō
haeret et interdum gremiō fouet, īnscia Dīdō,
īnsīdat quantus miserae deus. at, memor ille
mātris Acīdaliae, paulātim abolēre Sychaeum
incipit, et uīuō temptat praeuertere amōre
iam prīdem residēs animōs dēsuētaque cordā.

720

717 *haec . . . haec*: note the emotional repetition, climaxing with *īnscia Dīdō* (**718**) and the superb **719**

718 *interdum* now and then

gremi-um ī 2n. lap, bosom

īnsci-us a um ignorant, not knowing (controlling the indir. q. *quantus*)

719 *īnsīdat . . . deus*: four simple, breathtaking words, which seem to hang in the air; prosaically, *quantus deus īnsīdat miserae* (sc. Dido). She is not *misera* yet; but she will be (adjectives used in this way are called 'proleptic')

īnsīdo 3 I settle (into), possess, insinuate into (+ dat.) (used of diseases as well as military occupation)

ille: i.e. Cupid

720 *Acīdali-us a um* Acidalian, apparently referring to a spring of that name in Greece, sacred to Venus

paulātim slowly, gradually

aboleō 2 I destroy, blank out (the memory of)

Sychae-us ī 2m. Sychaeus, Dido's murdered husband (see 340–64)

721 *uīuō . . . amōre*: abl. of instrument

temptō 1 I try

praeuertō 3 I preoccupy, overtake

722 *iam prīdem* long since

reses resid-is stagnant, inert (S. comments that Dido had not remarried)

dēsuēt-us a um unused, out of practice

foundations of Dido's tragedy are laid. Cupid is doing his work on the queen already (714), and when he has longingly hugged his deceived father (715–16: Cupid is very keen on deception), in two bare, forked words – *rēgīnam petit* (717) – he has at the queen (*petit* is a word of attack, bristling with intention). Dido, who is childless, takes him to her bosom (cf. Venus and the real Ascanius 691): note the combination of emotional (*haec oculīs, haec pectore tōtō / haeret*) and physical (*gremiō fouet*) feelings. She is as *īnscia* as ever (718), but of – what? There follow four precisely calculated, simple, terrible words – *īnsīdat quantus miserae deus*, that final *deus* exploding like a bombshell. Meanwhile Cupid goes on his merry, care-free way, proving *quantus deus* he is, obeying his mother, obliterating Dido's memories of Sychaeus and creating a living love in a heart where it had long been absent (and therefore all the more prepared for its revival – *uīuō* 721).

Here V., peering into Dido's heart, works the 'subjective' style to the full (see on 1.208–15). Here is a woman in the grip of secret passion – something of a change from the virginal Diana/Nausicaa of her first appearance (498–502) and more like the Circe (perhaps?) of **Study Section 1.520–65**

1.723–35: *After the food, drink is brought in and Dido toasts the occasion, praying for a happy outcome*

postquam prīma quiēs epulīs, mēnsaeque remōtae,
crātērās magnōs statuunt et uīna corōnant.
fit strepitus tēctīs, uōcemque per ampla uolūtant   725
ātria; dēpendent lychnī laqueāribus aurēīs
incēnsī, et noctem flammīs fūnālia uincunt.
hīc rēgīna grauem^ gemmīs aurōque poposcit
implēuitque merō ^pateram, quam Bēlus et omnēs
a Bēlō solitī; tum facta silentia tēctīs: 730
'Iuppiter, hospitibus nam tē dare iūra loquuntur,
hunc laetum Tyriīsque diem Troiāque profectīs
esse uelīs, nostrōsque huius meminisse minōrēs.
adsit laetitiae Bacchus dator, et bona Iūnō;
et uōs, ō, coetum, Tyriī, celebrāte fauentēs.'   735

723 *epul-ae ārum* 1f. pl. banquet, feast (ellipsis of *fuit*)
remoueō 2 remōuī remōtum I remove (ellipsis of *sunt*)
724 *crātēr-a ae* 1f. mixing bowl (in which the wine was mixed with water); it was a classical Greek and Roman custom to bring out the drink when the eating was over
corōnō 1 I garland
725 *strepit-us ūs* 4m. clamour, noise
ampl-us a um large, wide: one simple word like this points up a sense of the spaciousness of the palace through which the sound is echoing
uolūtō 1 I send echoing; a lovely observation of the way conversation grows louder with the drink, filling a huge room with sound
726 *ātri-um ī* 2n. main room, house, palace
dependō 3 I hang from X (abl.)
lychn-us ī 2m. lamp
laquear -is 3n. panelled ceiling
727 *fūnāl-e is* 3n. torch
728 *hīc*: at this point

gemm-a ae 1f. jewel
729 *mer-um ī* 2n. unmixed wine
pater-a ae 1f. bowl (and 739)
Bēl-us ī 2m. Belus, founder of the Tyrian dynasty (cf. 621)
730 *solitī*: ellipsis of *implēre*, of which *quam* is the obj.
silenti-um ī 2n. silence (for the prayer)
732 *profectīs*: 'for those having set out from'
733 *uelīs* subjunc. expressing a wish
huius: i.e. 'day'
734 *Bacch-us ī* 2m. Bacchus, god of wine
dator -is 3m. giver
Iūnō: Juno was also goddess of marriage . . . but *bona* for whom?
735 *coet-us ūs* 4m. union, coming together; it has precisely the same derivation as Latin *coitus* (sexual intercourse)
celebrō 1 I celebrate
faueō 2 I am favourable, well-disposed

See: Camps (1969: 65) on **725** *amplus*.

1.723–35: Food and tables cleared, the serious drinking can begin (724). Noise levels rise (725–6: note the anachronistic panelled ceilings and lamps hanging from them) as the drink takes hold and the day slowly dies (727). The queen demands unmixed wine (*merum* 729, even more serious drinking) for the toast: that this day be remembered by Trojans and Carthaginians alike for ever (733 – and, presumably therefore, together: more irony). She wants happiness – that *laet-* stem again – and Juno to be present (734, goddess of Carthage – and marriage), and calls on the company to celebrate the *coetus* – innocently, this gathering; less so, this unification of peoples; even less so, this (sexual) liaison (735: V. had many other words he could have chosen had he not wanted those

1.736–47: *All partake of the toast; then the singer Iopas entertains them with songs of the origins of the universe*

dīxit, et in mēnsam laticum lībāuit honōrem,
prīmaque, lībātō, summō tenus attigit ōre,
tum Bitiae dedit increpitāns; ille impiger hausit
spūmantem pateram, et plēnō sē prōluit aurō;
post, aliī procerēs. citharā crīnītus Iōpās   740
personat aurātā, docuit quem maximus Atlās.
hic canit errantem lūnam sōlisque labōrēs;
unde hominum genus et pecudēs; unde imber et ignēs;
Arctūrum pluuiāsque Hyadas geminōsque Triōnēs;
quid tantum Ōceanō properent sē tingere sōlēs   745
hībernī, uel quae tardīs mora noctibus obstet.
ingeminant plausū Tyriī, Trōesque sequuntur.

736 *latex latic-is* 3m. liquid
honōrem: a mark of honour i.e. offering, to the
   gods
737 *lībātō*; abl. abs., lit. 'it having been libated'
tenus just as far as (+ abl.)
attingō 3 *attigī* I touch
738 *Biti-ās ae* m. Bitias, a courtier who shares his
   name with a historical admiral of the
   Carthaginian fleet
increpitō 1 I scold (Dido is playfully telling him to
   drink up)
impiger impigr-a um brisk, vigorous
hauriō 4 I drain
739 *spūmō* 1 I foam
prōluō 3 I soak, drench
aurō: we would say 'glass', but it is a gold goblet
740 *procer -is* 3m. nobleman
cithar-a ae 1f. lyre
crīnīt-us a um long-haired
Iōpās nom. s. Iopas, a singer
741 *person-ō* 1 I play, make music
aurāt-us a um gilded, golden
Atlās nom. s. Atlas. His mountain, on which the
   universe was poised, was in Africa, and he seems

to have been connected with astronomy. Iopas'
   song reflects his teacher's cosmic interests
743 *pecus pecud-is* 3f. animal
imber imbr-is 3m. rain
744 *Arctūr-us ī* 2m. the star Arcturus, near the Great
   Bear
pluui-us a um rainy
Hyad-as: Greek acc. (short *a*) of the Hyades
   ('Rainers'), a group of five stars associated with
   wet weather
Triōn-ēs um 3m. pl. the Great and Little Bear
   constellations
745 *quid*: 'why'
Ōcean-us ī 2m. Ocean
properō 1 I hurry
tingō 3 I immerse
746 *hībern-us a um* of winter
obstō 1 I block, hold back (+ dat.); the days in winter
   seem to race by (**745–6**) but the nights to crawl
   (**746**)
747 *ingeminō* 1 I redouble (with), i.e. do it again and
   again
plaus-us ūs 4m. applause

connotations to be present, the last because Dido is already drinking deep of *amor*, 749, as Venus had intended). It is ironic that Venus' plans for Aeneas to found Rome would fall apart completely if he actually went along with *coetus* in all its meanings; and it is ironic that in Book 4 he does, until called sharply back to duty and abandoning the despairing Dido. The best-laid plans of gods and men . . .

1.736–47: Dido modestly just sips the unmixed wine (737–8), but challenges her fellow diners to soak themselves in it, which they duly do (738–40). This is hospitality Carthaginian style: they are showing the Trojans that they need not restrain themselves.

1.748–56: *Dido, transfixed with love, questions Aeneas about Troy and demands he tell his story*

nec nōn et uariō noctem sermōne trahēbat
īnfēlīx Dīdō, longumque bibēbat amōrem,
multa super Priamō rogitāns, super Hectore multa;   750
nunc quibus Aurōrae uēnisset fīlius armīs,
nunc quālēs Diomēdis equī, nunc quantus Achillēs.
'immō age, et ā prīmā dīc, hospes, orīgine nōbīs
īnsidiās,' inquit, 'Danaum, cāsūsque tuōrum,

---

748 *uariō*: any and all conversation will do for Dido to keep Aeneas engaged, as 750–2 demonstrate

749 *longumque bibēbat amōrem*: an appropriate image amid the drinkers at the feast. The two imperfs. *trahēbat . . . bibēbat* play off against each other, conjuring up a picture of Dido reinforcing her growing love with her demand for conversation, her demand for conversation with her growing love

750 *super* concerning (+ abl.). Note the chiastic shape of the line: *multa* A *super Priamō* B – *rogitāns* C – B *super Hectore* A *multa*
rogitō 1 I repeatedly ask

751 *Aurōrae fīlius* 'son of Dawn', i.e. Memnon (see on 489)
uēnisset: i.e. had come to Troy (subjunc. of indir. q. after *rogitāns* 750)

752 *Diomēdis*: gen. s. of Diomedes, a great Greek warrior. This could be a deliciously tactless question: these were enviable horses, the stock of a gift from Zeus (*Iliad* 5.265–73), that Diomedes had taken from Aeneas in battle (*Iliad* 5.297–393)! As Page (1894), who was clearly a world expert, so sagely observes: 'when ladies indulge in such enquiries they often make slips'. On the other hand, they could refer to the horses of Rhesus which Diomedes stole, depicted in the reliefs (469–73)

753 *immō age* 'no, rather, come' (i.e. changing the direction of the enquiry)
ā prīmā . . . orīgine: but Aeneas will begin not with e.g. Paris and Helen but near the end, with the fall of Troy (S.)

754 *īnsidi-ae ārum* 1f. pl. ambush, treacherous

Enter a bard, the traditional accompaniment of the feast from Homer onwards (see e.g. *Odyssey* 8, where Odysseus is being entertained by the Phaeacians and the local blind bard Demodocus strikes up three times: 73ff., 266ff., 499ff.). Iopas' song is taken partly from Apollonius Rhodius *Argonautica* 1.496ff., where Orpheus sings to the Argonauts after their meal on the beach. His subject is how earth, heavens and sea split apart to form the world (in the beginning they were fused together in one solid, indistinguishable mass, cf. Ovid *Metamorphoses* 1.5–31); how the stars, moon and sun had their paths fixed in the sky; and how the gods fought each other for power. Hesiod, a near-contemporary of Homer, sang a similar sort of song in his *Theogony*, the story of the birth of the cosmos. So this is a good (anachronistic) subject for epic song. V. himself had considerable interest in understanding such things. In his farming manual *Georgics* 2.477ff. (see on **1.430–40**), he expressed a desire to know about the paths of the stars, eclipses, earthquakes, tides and the sun; the Roman poet Lucretius devoted a whole work to these matters, *Dē rērum nātūrā* 'On the Nature of the Universe'.

S. comments that Iopas' philosophical subject-matter is appropriate for a queen 'chaste up to this point'. He may be thinking of the bard Demodocus in *Odyssey* 8, who sings three songs at a feast for Odysseus, one featuring the love-affair of Ares (Mars) and Aphrodite (Venus), a popular topic when drink was flowing.

1.748–56: Dido, unlike the rest of the company, is hanging on every word of Aeneas, spinning the night out as long as she can (*trahēbat* 748), asking every question she can

errōrēsque tuōs; nam tē iam septima^ portat   755
omnibus errantem terrīs et flūctibus ^aestās.'

attack (the wooden horse trick). S. comments that	*portō* 1 I carry
Dido does not want it to appear that the Trojans	**757** *aestās aestāt-is* 3f. summer
were defeated by superior bravery	
755 *septim-us a um* seventh	

imagine about what happened in the Trojan war. She was fascinated by it anyway
(565–6), but now she wants only one thing: to keep him talking to her. Presumably she
has already heard many stories from Teucer (623–6), as the reliefs on the temple indicate; after all, she already knows about Memnon (489) and her question about
Diomedes (751) might not be so 'tactless' (see note) but in fact refer to the Rhesus
episode depicted there (469–73). Whatever the answer, she is a woman in love and
that is all that counts. Note the excited *multa . . . multa . . .* and the varied tricolon
quibus . . . quālēs . . . quantus. She must keep her man engaged, even if it requires
asking questions to which she already knows the answer. Note too the 'subjective'
bibēbat: the company was drinking deep of the wine, but she of love (*longum*, 749), a
love which Venus had turned into *uenēnum* (688, cf. *īnfēlīx* 749). When she has
drained Aeneas dry of what he and she (perhaps) already know about others, she
addresses him – more intimately? – as *hospes* (753), turns to what she does not know
– how Troy fell and how he reached Carthage – and invites Aeneas himself to tell *his*
story. But is it true she did not know how Troy fell? (Aeneas is silent on whether the
reliefs on the temple to Juno at 456–93, 623–4 depicted the scene.) Or does she just
want *his* version, to keep him talking?

Book 2, then, will consist of a 'flashback', a device used by Homer. When Odysseus
arrived in Phaeacia, he too was entertained and then invited to tell all about his travels
from Troy to the Phaeacian court (*Odyssey* 9–12). It gives the poet the opportunity to
go back over the past while keeping the story in the present, at the same time as revealing much about the character of the speaker. Aeneas describes the fall of Troy in Book 2
and his travels from there *en route* to Carthage in Book 3 (the point at which Book 1
began).

Study Section for 1.657–756

1. Trace the stages by which Dido falls/is made to fall in love.
2. To what extent is Venus looking after Aeneas' interests here?
3. Scan 715–22.
4. In the following passage from Apollonius' *Argonautica* (the story of Jason's adventure to get the Golden Fleece), Eros/Cupid makes the king's daughter Medea fall in love with Jason, so that she can help him fulfil his 'impossible' mission. Eros has been bribed into this by his mother (Aphrodite/Venus), at the behest of the two pro-Jason goddesses, Hera/Juno and Athena/Minerva. Compare and contrast this passage with V.'s depiction of Dido falling in love with Aeneas. Does Apollonius look sympathetically into Medea's heart, or simply report the event? (There is a lengthy discussion of these passages in Johnson (1976: 36–45).)

Meanwhile Eros came invisibly through the clear air,	275
all action like the gadfly which attacks young heifers . . .	
By the door-post in the entrance to the hall he quickly strung his bow,	
and selected a new arrow from his quiver – one laden with grief.	
Then, looking sharply about him, he raced across the threshold,	280
quite unseen. Crouching low at Jason's feet,	
he fitted the arrow-notch to the bowstring,	
bent the bow full stretch and let fly	
at Medea – speechless, heart-struck Medea.	
He darted back up out of the high-roofed palace,	285
chuckling away to himself; but his arrow, like a flame,	
burned deep in her heart. She shot	
sparkling glances full on at Jason, sick with love,	
all thoughts of restraint gone from her,	
everything forgotten as the ecstatic agony flooded her heart.	290
Like a poor woman, a wool-worker,	
who heaps up twigs around a burning brand	
to light her humble dwelling at night,	
huddling up close to it, and from this tiny brand	
a fierce flame flares up, consuming all the twigs	295
– so destructive love crouched, unseen,	
and blazed up in her heart. Her cheeks now pale,	
now flushed, she had lost all self-control.	

Apollonius Rhodius, Argonautica 3.275–98

Topics for extended essays on Book 1

1. How successfully in Book 1 does Virgil use Homer?
2. With what qualities does Virgil invest Aeneas in Book 1 that may make him a convincing founder of the Roman people?
3. Do you see any problems in Virgil's presentation of divine activity in Book 1?
4. Write an appreciation of any scene in Book 1 that particularly appeals to you.
5. Are the human actors in Book 1 mere puppets in the hands of the gods?
6. On what grounds would you reject or support the suggestion that Aeneas is not a very interesting hero?
7. If you were Virgil, what changes would you have made to Book 1 of the *Aeneid* during your three-year sojourn in Greece (*Intro* [7])?
8. To what extent and to what purpose does Virgil invest Book 1 with a sense of *Rōmānitās*? Does it work in the context of the story?

Book 2
Aeneas' account of the destruction of Ilium

Book 2 falls into three sections: (i) 13–249, how the Trojans were tricked into bringing the wooden horse into Ilium (the city in Troy they were defending); (ii) 250–558, Aeneas' efforts to defend the city; and (iii) 559–804, Aeneas' escape with the gods of Troy, his father, son and followers into whatever the future holds. The story is narrated by Aeneas, which raises the question 'Is Aeneas' account nothing more than an objective report of what really happened, placed in Aeneas' mouth by the definitive master-narrator Virgil, or is it to be understood as Aeneas' personal version of events, revelatory of him as a partial, fallible human?' See *Introduction* sections 33–44 (= *Intro* [33–44]).

2.1–56: The Greeks' 'departure', and the wooden horse

In this Section, a reluctant Aeneas describes how the Greeks appeared to decamp, leaving a wooden horse on the shore. As the Trojans debate what to do about it, the priest Laocoon tells them it is a Greek trick and hurls a spear into it.

2.1–13: As all fall silent, Aeneas introduces the pitiable fall of Troy (see Figure 2), at which even Greeks would weep; but despite his reluctance, he will begin

conticuēre omnēs intentīque ōra tenēbant.
inde torō^ pater Aenēās sīc ōrsus ab ^altō:
'īnfandum^, rēgīna, iubēs renouāre ^dolōrem,
Troiānās^ ut ^opēs et lāmentābile rēgnum
ēruerint Danaī, quaeque^ ipse ^miserrima uīdī,   5

1 *conticeō 2* I fall silent. Cf. the end of Book 1, a rowdy, drink-laden feast. Note the perf.: it happened instantly. *It is common to shorten the -(*u*)*ērunt* ending of the perf. to -(*u*)*ēre*; so *conticuēre* is the shortened form of *conticuērunt*. See p. 39 ((b)(i)) above
intent-us a um attentive, concentrating
***ōs ōr-is* 3n. face; mouth, speech
tenēbant: i.e. as the impf. tense suggests, they were concentrating their *ōra* on Aeneas and keeping them concentrated – a neat contrast with the perfect *conticuēre*. They were all eyes and ears on Aeneas, in other words, as the ancient commentator Servius says (see *Intro* [51]. Servius will henceforth be called S.)
2 **inde* from there, then
tor-us ī 2m. couch, where Aeneas was reclining at the banquet with which Book 1 ended (and – *altō* – in a position of honour, 1.700, next to Dido in the middle 1.698)
***Aenēās* (acc. *Aenēān*, gen. *Aenēae*) Aeneas
ōrdior 4 dep. *ōrsus* I begin; **it is common to omit *est* and other forms of *sum* in perf. tenses
3 ***īnfand-us a um* unspeakable, past words; monstrous, accursed. It is all too dreadful to be

told ('because it is a mark of grief and shame for a strong man to admit defeat', S.). The sound of the line is heavy with grief – note the emphatic positions of *īnfandum* and *dolōrem* – while sorrowful words fill the whole passage (as well they might; see Aeneas' reaction to depictions of the Trojan war at 1.459–65, 494–5)
***rēgin-a ae* 1f. queen, i.e. Dido, queen of Carthage, where the storms at sea have driven Aeneas and his men
iubēs: ellipsis of *mē* as obj. Note that the *i* is consonantal *y*, like *iam* (*yam*) at 8
renouō 1 I renew, bring to life
4 ***Troiān-us a um* Trojan
ut: = 'how' + indir. q., **RL**R3, **W**30, **M**94 (see p. 37 for these references)
lāmentābil-is e mournful, arousing lamentation. The use is 'proleptic', i.e. it foresees what is to happen. The kingdom is not of itself *lāmentābile*; it will become *lāmentābile* when the Greeks have overthrown it
***rēgn-um ī* 2n. kingdom
5 **ēruō 3 ēruī* I overthrow; perf. subjunc. in an indir. q. after *ut*

2.1–13: It is not just some who are listening, but *omnēs* (1). Everyone in the vast dining hall, where there was such a *strepitus* before (1.725), thinks Aeneas' story is worth hearing.

Figure 3 The sack of Troy.

et quōrum pars magna fuī. quis tālia fandō
Myrmidonum Dolopumue_ aut dūrī^ mīles ^Vlixī†

**_Dana-us a um_ Greek; _Dana-ī ōrum_ 2 m.pl. Greeks
(descendants of Danaus; see on 1.30)
quaeque . . . (**6**) _quōrum_: 'and the _miserrima_ things
[n. pl.] which . . . and of which'. Aeneas is not
here responding to Dido's request to tell all, but
referring to his own personal experience. So this
is no longer an indir. q. in answer to Dido, but a
rel. clause; hence the inds. _uīdī . . . fuī_
ipse . . . uīdī: Aeneas is to give a personal, eye-
witness account, relating (i) what he actually _saw_
– these events he merely reports, not necessarily
associating himself with the decisions involved
(13–249); and (ii) what he actually _had a hand in_
(250ff.). One wonders to what extent will Aeneas
absolve himself of responsibility for what he
simply _saw_ – e.g. the admission of the horse into
the city?
6 **_for_ 1 dep. _fātus_ I speak, talk, say; _fandō_ is here a
gerund (**RL**175, N, **W**39, **M**109) in the abl. 'by/in

. . .', with _tālia_ as obj. Aeneas continues to argue
that the story is _īnfandum_
quis: take with _Myrmidonum Dolopumue_ ('of the
. . .', partitive gen. **RL**31, **W**15, **M**8)
7 *_Myrmidon-es um_ 3m. pl. Myrmidons,
Achilles' soldiers (short _-es_ is the Greek nom.
pl.)
*_Dolop-es um_ 3m. pl. Dolopes, the soldiers of
Pyrrhus (Achilles' brutal son)
**_-ue_ or
dūr-us a um hard, pitiless, cruel; S. points out the
contrast with Homer, where he is 'much-
enduring'
*_Vlix-ēs ī/is/eī_ 3m. Ulysses (Greek Odysseus: see
Intro [16]), renowned in the _Aeneid_ for his
mercilessness and deceitfulness (traits already
apparent in Greek tragedy)

† V= capital U

Rightly. They know of the story of the Trojan war because it had been depicted on reliefs
in Juno's temple (1.453ff.); now they have the chance to hear it first hand from one who

temperet ā lacrimīs? et iam nox ūmida caelō
praecipitat, suādentque cadentia sīdera somnōs.
sed sī tantus amor cāsūs^ cognōscere ^nostrōs   10
et breuiter Troiae suprēmum^ audīre ^labōrem,
quamquam animus meminisse horret lūctūque refūgit,
incipiam.'

8 **_temperō_ 1 I refrain, restrain, soothe; note
subjunc., as if in a 'potential' ('could') or fut.
conditional (**RL**153.2, **W**33, **M**115)
**_lacrim-a ae_ 1f. tear
et iam: another reason not to tell the story. Note that
_et_ scans long because _iam_ = _yam_. So too at 14, 34,
70 etc. See p. 42 above
ūmid-us a um dewy
caelō: Roman poets often omit preps., here _ā/ab_. See
12 _lūctū_, and p. 39(f).
9 *_praecipitō_ 1 I hurry (down from + abl., _caelō_);
speed/drive (on); throw headlong. See on 250 for
the way the sky was thought of as 'turning'
overhead. It is now past midnight
suādeō 2 I encourage, urge; the start of a liltingly
dactylic clause, with repeated _s_ and -_ant_-/-_ent_-
('assonance') and the words falling dreamily away
10 _tantus amor_: understand _est tibi_ ('is for you', i.e.
'you have', **RL**48.2, **W**Suppl. syntax, **M**10). **The
vb 'to be' is often omitted from main clauses, as it
is in perf. tenses
11 _breuiter_: more reluctance on Aeneas' part (Dido
had asked him to tell all from the very beginning,
1.753–5)

**_Troi-a ae_ 1f. Troy, the region in which Ilium was
located
suprēm-us a um final, last (used of the last rites paid
to the dead); this is what Aeneas will tell Dido
about Troy, omitting anything earlier (S.)
12 _meminisse_: note that the final _e_ elides because _h_ at
the start of a word does not count for scansion
purposes (see p. 42 above)
**_horreō_ 2 I shudder
*_lūct-us ūs_ 4m. grief; here probably _ā lūctū_
refugiō 3 _refūgī_ I recoil, start back. Note that the _ū_ is
long, and this is therefore the perf. It indicates
Aeneas' instant, first reaction to the request (as we
saw at **3**, _īnfandum_), while _horret_ indicates his
continuing perception of the task
13 *_incipiō_ 3 _incēpī inceptum_ I take in hand, embark,
make a start, begin. This is not an unfinished line
(see on 1.534), but marks the pause before the
story starts – and a very dramatic pause too, right
at the start of the line when one would expect it,
perhaps, at the end. But such variety of stop-
points within the hexameter is typical of Virgil.
See pp. 45–8 above

was actually there and survived it. So the stage is all set. But will Aeneas talk? Aeneas is a
man of very few words anyway (see _Intro_ [41–3]). In Book 1 he speaks a mere 69 lines out
of 756. He is not nearly as loquacious as e.g. Achilles in the _Iliad_ or Odysseus in the
Odyssey. So intense is the effect of the memory of the disaster on himself (3, 4, 8 – even the
Greeks would weep at it! – 11, 12) that it takes a tremendous effort to gear himself up to
speak about it at all (cf. his tears as he views the reliefs at 1.459–65); indeed, so reluctant is
he that he even points out the lateness of the hour (8–9). But after 10–12 – four clauses
that seem 'unwilling ever to reach the point' – he finally takes the plunge with one word –
incipiam – and off he at once goes. Is the rather more reluctant 'take in hand [the story]'
– a primary meaning of _incipiō_ – a translation preferable to 'begin'? Book 2 will continue
to reflect Aeneas' sense of his horror and grief at the whole experience. It is therefore
essential to bear in mind that Aeneas is not simply a mouth-piece by means of which V.
can tell the story of the fall of Ilium; it is _Aeneas the man_ who is speaking (_Intro_ [36, 43]).

See: Rieu-Jones (2003: xxxi ff.) for speeches in Homer; Jenkyns (1998: 330) on Aeneas'
reluctance to begin.

Crunch (see p. 51 above): 3–6

2.13–20: 'After years of failure, the Greeks with Minerva's help constructed a wooden horse, filling it with armed men'

'[incipiam]. frāctī^ bellō fātīsque ^repulsī
^ductōrēs Danaum, tot iam lābentibus annīs,
īnstar montis equum, dīuīnā^ Palladis ^arte,   15
aedificant, sectāque̲^ intexunt ^abiete costās;

Learning vocabulary

Aenēās (acc. *Aenēan*, gen. *Aenēae*) Aeneas
Dana-us a um Greek
Dana-ī ōrum 2m. pl. Greeks
Dolop-es (-ēs) um 3m. pl. Dolopes, Pyrrhus' (Achilles' brutal son) men
ēruō 3 *ēruī* I overthrow
for 1 dep. *fātus* I speak, talk, say
horreō 2 I shudder
incipiō 3 *incēpī inceptum* I begin
inde from there, then
īnfand-us a um unspeakable, past words; monstrous, accursed
lacrim-a ae 1f. tear
lūct-us ūs 4m. grief
Myrmidon-es (-ēs) um 3m. pl. Myrmidons, Achilles' soldiers
ōs ōr-is 3n. face, mouth, speech
praecipitō 1 speed/drive (on); hurry (down from + abl.); throw headlong
rēgin-a ae 1f. queen
rēgn-um ī 2n. kingdom
temperō 1 I refrain, restrain, soothe
Troi-a ae 1f. Troy, the region in which Ilium was located
Troiān-us a um Trojan
-ue or
Vlix-ēs ī/is/eī 3m. Ulysses (Greek Odysseus)

13 **frangō* 3 *frēgī frāctum* I break, smash. The story starts with two thunderously spondaic lines, and a brief (bitter?) note of triumph in Aeneas' voice
***fāt-um ī* 2n. fate, destiny
repellō 3 *reppulī repulsum* I beat back, spurn. Note the ABBA shape of *frāctī . . . repulsī* – participle noun, noun part. ('chiasmus' see **Glossary of literary terms**)
14 ***ductor -is* 3m. commander (used with an alliterative sneer by Aeneas; a word with more of a ring to it than *dux*). These commanders are the subject of *aedificant* (16)
***Danaum*: = *Dana(ōr)um*, a common 'epic' gen. pl.

form; see p. 39 ((a)) above. The initial *ds* of the first two words of this line hammer out Aeneas' contempt for them
tot . . . annīs: an abl. abs., in the pres. (**RL**150–1, **W**24, **M**79–80). Aeneas recounts the story as if it is unfolding before the audience's very eyes
tot: ten, actually, but *tot* is what it must have seemed like (Aeneas suggests) to the Greeks who, *frāctī* by men and *repulsī* by the fates, had taken such a hammering
lābor 3 dep. I pass by, slip by
iam lābentibus annīs: increasing Aeneas' picture of the Greeks' sense of their own helplessness – it was all slipping away from them. Time, then, for a final, desperate throw of the dice
15 *īnstar is* 3n. equivalent (in size) of, as big as, with *montis*; in apposition to *equum*. It had to be big to hold enough Greek soldiers; it is the first thing Aeneas observes about it
dīuīn-us a um divine, heavenly; spoken sarcastically or bitterly? Or ironically, given that it was Ulysses' idea? (185, but obviously on Ulysses' instructions, cf. 44, 164.)
***Pallas Pallad-is/os* 3f. Pallas (Athena) = (Roman) Minerva. The horse was Ulysses' idea, and constructed by Epēos (264). As one of the deities rejected by Paris for the prize of the golden apple (Juno was the other one), Minerva was hostile to the Trojans (see *Intro* [16])
16 *aedificō* 1 I build, construct (a word like *secō*, *intexō*, *costa* and *cauerna* with ship-building connotations). Note that V. tends to keep to the pres. tense throughout (see *Intro* [21])
secō 1 *secuī sectum* I cut
intexō 3 I interweave, put together
abiēs abiet-is 3f. fir, pine; here scanned dactyl, as if *abyete*, cf. 442 *pariete* = *paryete*, 492 *ariete* = *aryete*. At 112 Sinon says it was made of maple; elsewhere it is said to be made of *rōbur* 'oak', but that can also mean any hard wood – as if Aeneas cared
cost-a ae 1f. rib

2.13–20: S. comments 'This book serves two purposes: that no shame should attach to Troy, despite defeat, and to Aeneas, despite flight.' Aeneas therefore makes it clear

uōtum prō reditū simulant; ea fāma uagātur.
hūc, dēlēcta^ uirum sortītī ^corpora, fūrtim
inclūdunt caecō laterī, penitusque cauernās^
^ingentīs uterumque armātō mīlite complent.'   20

17 *uōt-um ī* 2n. votive offering; ellipsis of *eum esse* 'it
    to be . . .' after *simulant*
redit-us ūs 4m. return, i.e. 'for a [safe] return'. This is
    technical terminology: *V S Pro Red* (*uōta suscepta
    prō reditū*) is found on coins expressing the wish
    for an emperor's safe return. So it is something of
    an anachronism (see *Intro* [23])
**simulō* 1 I imitate, pretend
fāma: no Trojan really knew what the horse was for;
    the story just got about, Aeneas says (excusing
    himself, S.), that it was an offering to guarantee
    the Greeks a safe return to Greece
uagor 1 dep. I (am) spread abroad
18 ***hūc* (to) here, i.e. *caecō laterī* (19)
dēligō 3 *dēlēgī dēlēctum* I choose, pick (used of
    levying soldiers)
uirum: case? (See 14 above)
sortior 4 dep. I select, choose by lot
fūrtim in secret
19 *inclūdō* 3 I shut X (acc., ellipsis of *eōs*) into (+
    dat.)
**caec-us a um* blind, hidden, dark
***latus later-is* 3n. side
***penitus* (deep) within; far away
cauern-a ae 1f. hollow, hold
20 **uter-us ī* 2m. womb, belly; cf. 38, 52. S.
    comments that the 'pregnant' image recurs at 238,
    fēta armīs. V. says 'vast hollows and the belly'; we
    would say 'of the vast belly'. V. often puts two

nouns into the same case, where we would
subordinate one of them. This figure of speech is
called 'hendiadys' (Greek *hen-dia-dis* 'one-
through-two': see **Glossary of literary terms**) –
but perhaps V. really was thinking of two separate
features, not one. One cannot always be certain
**armāt-us a um* armed
mīlite: *'collective' s. for pl. ('an armed complement
    of men')
compleō 2 I fill. Note how 19–20 say basically the
    same thing in three different ways. This is a
    typical feature of V.'s style; but the question is
    exactly how similar? See discussion at 2.132–44

Learning vocabulary

armāt-us a um armed
caec-us a um blind, hidden, dark
Danaum = Dana(ōr)um
ductor -is 3m. leader
fāt-um ī 2n. fate, destiny
frangō 3 *frēgī frāctum* I break, smash
hūc (to) here
latus later-is 3n. side
Pallas Pallad-is/os 3f. Pallas (Athena) = (Roman)
    Minerva
penitus (deep) within; far away
simulō 1 I imitate, pretend
uter-us ī 2m. womb, belly

---

that the Greeks could never win in a fair fight, since after all those years of failure, they
are a broken army (13–14). So the Greeks had to resort to trickery with the help of
divine *ars* (15), engage in pretence (*simulant*, 17), secrecy (*fūrtim*, 18), mystery (a
horse?!) – *caecō* adds to the sense of mystification – and stir up *fāma* (17) but nothing
else (*uagor* has connotations of vague drifting). See *Intro* [37–8]. After the event,
Aeneas knows what was going on (18–20); but at the time, no one had the faintest
idea. Most of all, no one thought there was anything *sinister* about it. Aeneas is hinting
at what trusting people the Trojans had been, a hint that will be further developed.
The first day of peace that had dawned for ten years will become Troy's last. Note the
twin description of the horse's belly: as inanimate *cauerna* but also living, pregnant
uterus.

See: Clausen (1987: 34) on the image of the horse.

Crunch: 18–20

2.21–30: *'They then left to hide in the nearby island of Tenedos. We, imagining them gone, came out to explore their camp and the battlefield, where it had all happened'*

'est in cōnspectū Tenedos,^ ^nōtissima fāmā
^īnsula, ^dīues opum Priamī^ dum ^rēgna manēbant,
nunc tantum sinus et statiō male fida carīnīs.
hūc sē prōuectī dēsertō^ in ^lītore condunt;
nōs abiisse ratī et uentō petiisse Mycēnās.   25
ergō omnis^ longō* soluit sē ^Teucria *lūctū;

21 **cōnspect-us ūs 4m. sight (i.e. of the mainland);
Tenedos is now about 4 miles out to sea
Tenedos (nom. s. f.) Tenedos, an island near Troy
*nōt-us a um well-known, famous. This is Aeneas'
comment: as a Trojan, he knew all about Tenedos
and its past glory-days
fāmā: an abl. of respect; see p. 39(g) above for the
wide range of the uses of the 'unmarked' abl.
in V.
22 *īnsul-a ae* 1f. island
dīues dīuit-is rich, wealthy (in respect of + gen.)
**Priam-us ī 2m. Priam, king of Troy, who came to
epitomise great wealth, great power and great
suffering – the tragic fall from supreme felicity to
utter catastrophe
dum: takes the indicative, and therefore means . . .?
See **RL**165.2, **M**119, 124–5
23 *tantum* (adv.) only
**sin-us ūs 4m. inlet, gulf; ripple. *sinus* and *statiō* are
in apposition to *Tenedos*
statiō station-is 3f. anchorage
male badly (take with *fida*, i.e. hardly trustworthy at
all!); *male* is explained by *dēsertō in lītore* (**24**) –
the place was rich at one time (**22**), but now
disused because of the war. S. comments that it
was *fida* enough in Greek eyes
**fīd-us a um faithful, trustworthy
carīn-a ae 1f. lit. keel, here = 'ship'. Using a part to
express a whole is a figure of speech called
synecdoche (Greek *sun-ek-doche* 'together-out-
picking', i.e. selecting one feature to stand for the
whole feature)

24 *prōuehor* 3 *prōuectus* I advance, carry
myself. Note that what is technically a pass.
form (of *prōuehō*) is used in a 'middle'
reflexive sense, i.e. not 'I am carried' but 'I
carry myself'. This 'middle' reflexive usage
of the pass. is very common. See p. 39 ((c)(i))
above
**dēsert-us a um deserted, lonely, abandoned (and
28)
līt-us lītor-is 3n. coast, coast-line (and **28)
**condō 3 *condidī conditum* I hide; found, build;
bury (*sē* is its obj.)
25 *abiisse . . . petiise*: for *abī(u)isse* and *petī(u)isse*.
See p. 39 ((b)(ii)) above
rat-us a um thinking; note the ellipsis of *sumus*, and
of *Danaōs* in the two acc. and infs., 'that [the
Greeks] *abiisse . . . petiisse*', **RL**98–9, **W**25,
M82–4
uentō: all ancient ships used the wind as much as
they could, especially on long journeys
*Mycēn-ae ārum 1f. pl. Mycenae, home of the Greek
king Agamemnon
26 *omnis longō*: emphatic; the line is heavily
spondaic, as of a great weight being lifted (Page)
or a 'long, deep sigh of relief' (Williams (1972));
longō . . . lūctū (last word) makes for an effective
alliteration and climax
**soluō 3 *soluī solūtum* I release, loosen, dissolve;
pay, perform
Teucri-a ae 1f. land of Teucer; Teucer was one of the
first kings and founders of Troy
lūctū = ā longō . . . lūctū (cf. 12, and on **21**)

***

2.21–30: Aeneas describes the decline of Tenedos (23) to explain how the Trojans were duped. The Greeks needed to be hidden very near the coast, for speed of access to Greeks inside the horse when they came out of the horse and opened the gates of Ilium (see comment on **2.250–67**). Tenedos (just south of Troy) was the only possible option for a fleet that size, but it was in such a dreadful condition because of the war that no one could ever have imagined a fleet putting in there (note *tantum* and *male fida*, 23, and *dēsertō*, 24, in contrast to its earlier flourishing status at 21–2). So the Trojans are

panduntur portae, iuuat īr_e_ et Dōrica castra
dēsertōsque^ uidēre ^locōs lītusque relictum:
hīc Dolopum manus, hīc saeuus^ tendēbat ^Achillēs;
classibus hīc locus, hīc aciē certāre solēbant.'   30

2.31–9: 'Minerva's gift attracted special attention. Some welcomed it, others wanted it thrown into the sea, burned or opened up'

'pars stupet innūptae^ dōn_um_ exitiāle ^Mineruae

27 *pandō* 3 I open; here the gates are being freely
and joyfully (*iuuat*) flung open – a sign of peace
(S.), in strong contrast to what is to come
*port-a ae 1f. gate
Dōric-us a um Greek
*castr-a ōrum 2n. camp
29–30: there is a sense of excited wonder about the
four short clauses with their fourfold anaphora of
hic that make up these lines, recording what the
Trojans said to each other as they viewed the
scene (for surveying the field of battle after it is all
over – irony – cf. Tacitus *Annals* 1.61–2 and
Histories 2.70)
**saeu-us a um savage, cruel, vicious (because he
dragged [the dead] Hector [round Patroclus'
tomb], says S.)
tendēbat: here intrans., 'used to pitch his tent', 'made
camp', of which both *manus* and *Achillēs* are the
subjects. *V. often uses a s. vb where we would
expect pl.
30 **class-is is 3m. fleet; here dat. pl. (ellipsis of
est)
locus: *-us* scans short becaue the following *h* does
not count as a consonant for scansion purposes
(see p. 42 above)
**aciē = in aciē* (another 'unmarked' abl.)
**cert-ō 1 I fight

Learning vocabulary

castr-a ōrum 2n. camp
cert-ō 1 I fight
class-is is 3m. fleet
condō 3 *condidī conditum* I hide; found, build; bury
cōnspect-us ūs 4m. sight
dēsert-us a um deserted, lonely, abandoned
fīd-us a um faithful, trustworthy
līt-us lītor-is 3n. coast, coast-line
Mycēn-ae ārum 1f. pl. Mycenae, home of Greek
king Agamemnon
nōt-us a um well-known, famous
port-a ae 1f. gate
Priam-us ī 2m. Priam, king of Troy
saeu-us a um savage, cruel, vicious
sin-us ūs 4m. inlet, gulf; ripple
soluō 3 *soluī solūtum* I release, loosen, dissolve; pay,
perform
s. for pl. verb
absence of preps. with acc. and abl. nouns, e.g. *in, ex,
ab, ad* etc.

31 **stupeō 2 I am stunned, astonished (at)
innūpt-us a um virgin; but her horse was heavily
pregnant (see 20)
dōn-um ī 2n. gift, offering; present (and **36)

convinced that the Greeks really have gone (25), and *nōs* indicates that Aeneas agreed.
The sense of the Trojans' relief (26) and excitement (27–30) are well caught: places once
seething with hostilities are free of enemy troops and their ships (28), and Trojans can
now walk freely where once Achilles raged (29) and battle was joined (30). They turn
past events into historical memory as they go, selecting what to highlight about the war.
This is all Aeneas' 'take' on the consequences of the Greeks' departure.

Crunch: 26–30

2.31–9: Aeneas does not associate himself with any of the responses to this 'fatal gift': he
simply reports the reactions. Some do nothing but gape in astonishment and amazement (31–2). But others demand action. Some want to accept it (32–4), for reasons
Aeneas can now see might have been perfidious or simply fated (34); others, seeing it
not as a gift but as a trap and suspicious (36, S.), want to get rid of it somehow, or

et mōlem mīrantur equī; prīmusque Thymoetēs
dūcī intrā mūrōs hortātur et arce locārī,
sīue dolō, seū iam Troiae sīc fāta ferēbant.
at Capys, et quōrum melior sententia mentī,   35
aut pelagō Danau<u>m</u> īnsidiās suspectaque dōna
praecipitāre iubent subiectīsqu<u>e</u>^ ūrere ^flammīs,
aut terebrāre cauās^ uter<u>ī</u> et temptāre ^latebrās.
scinditur incertum^ studi<u>a</u> in contrāria ^uulgus.'

exitiāl-is e deadly; *dōnum exitiāle* makes for a powerful oxymoron (an after-the-event comment? One that Trojans at the time were making? Or 'proleptic', i.e. foreshadowing what it would actually be?)

*Mineru-a ae Minerva (Greek Athena). *innūptae . . . Mineruae* is Aeneas' comment *ex post factō*, in the light of later events (lit. 'from what was done afterwards') – he obviously did not know whose horse it was at the time. There may be a hint here of a *tradition* that the horse had a dedicatory inscription – but it obviously does not in V., since it would render the whole Sinon episode irrelevant (and cf. *fāma* 17)

32 **mōl-ēs is 3f. huge structure; mass, lump; undertaking, burden

mīror 1 dep. I wonder, am amazed at; note the pl., though *pars* controls the s. *stupet* in **31

prīmus . . . hortātur: 'is the first to urge', a common idiom

Thymoetēs: nom s., Thymoetes, whose son and wife were put to death by Priam because Priam had received an oracle that on a certain day a child would be born through whom Ilium would be destroyed. On that day Thymoetes' wife bore a son; on the same day Priam's wife Hecuba also bore a son – Paris (S.)

33 *dūcī . . . locārī*: understand 'the horse'. The inf. is common after *hortor*, which also takes *ut* + subjunc. (cf. **RL**134, **W**36, **M**89–91)

intrā inside

**mūr-us ī 2m. wall

arce: ellipsis of *in*

**locō 1 I place

34 *sīue/seū* if, whether, or

**dol-us ī 2m. trick, treachery; Aeneas speculates,

with some justification, that Thymoetes may have been in on the Greek plan

iam: 'by now'

sīc ferēbant: 'were tending that way'

35 *Capys*: nom. s., Capys, a Trojan (he is in Carthage with Aeneas, 1.183, cf. 511)

quōrum mentī: understand '[those] to whose mind' (*mentī* dat. of possession, **RL**48.2, 88.1(b), **W**Suppl. syntax, **M**10); *Capys* and '[those] to whose mind' are subject of *iubent* (**37**)

sententia: ellipsis of *est/erat*

36 **pelag-us ī 2n. (note n.!) sea, dat. of motion towards, i.e. = *in pelagus*

Danaum: case?

*īnsidi-ae ārum 1f. ambush

suspiciō 3 *suspexī suspectum* I suspect

37 *praecipitō 1 I throw headlong (into + dat.); speed/drive (on); hurry (down from + abl.); understand 'the Trojans' as object of *iubent*

subiciō 3 *subiēcī subiectum* I place under (here abl. of instrument with *flammīs*, 'by . . .'). In the 3rd and 4th p.p.s the first *i* = *y*, as if *subyectum*. Hence the scansion

ūrō 3 I burn

38 *terebrō* 1 I bore through. Note the second *e* scans light. See p. 42(d) above

**cau-us a um hollow

*temptō 1 I check, test, explore

latebr-a ae 1f. recess, hiding-place

39 **scindō 3 *scidī scissum* I divide, cut, split

**incert-us a um uncertain, doubtful, i.e. *incertum* in these circumstances, not because crowds are always uncertain

contrāri-us a um opposing (whether to bring the horse in or destroy/investigate it)

**uulgus 2n./m. crowd, rank and file; mob; herd

investigate further (38). With hindsight (35) Aeneas can now see both of these latter alternatives were more judicious, but at this stage no decision could be reached (39). The Trojans are reasonable people, open to suggestions, still waiting to be persuaded.

Horsfall (1995: 110) raises the question how far Aeneas is actively involved in the picture of events that he paints. Does he include himself among those he describes at 35, for example? Aeneas does not say. Should we assume it? Or does silence speak louder than

2.40–9: 'The priest Laocoon was adamant that, as you would expect from Greeks, it was all a trick'

'prīmus^ ibi, ante omnīs, magnā comitante cateruā,   40
^Lāocoōn ārdēns summā^ dēcurrit ab ^arce,
et procul "ō miserī, quae tanta̲ īnsānia, cīuēs?
crēditis āuectōs hostīs? aut ūlla^ putātis
^dōna carēre dolīs Danaum? sīc nōtus Vlixēs?
aut hōc^ inclūsī* ^lignō̲ occultantur *Achīuī,   45
aut haec^ in nostrōs* ^fabricāta̲ est ^māchina *mūrōs,

Learning vocabulary

cau-us a um hollow
dol-us ī 2m. trick, treachery
dōn-um ī 2n. gift, offering; present
incert-us a um uncertain, doubtful
īnsidi-ae ārum 1f. ambush
locō 1 I place
Mineru-a ae 1f. Minerva (Greek Athena)
mīror 1 dep. I wonder, am amazed at
mōl-ēs is 3f. huge structure; mass, lump; undertaking, burden
mūr-us ī 2m. wall
pelag-us ī 2n. sea
praecipitō 1 I throw headlong (into + dat.); speed/drive (on); hurry (down from + abl.)
scindō 3 *scidī scissum* I divide, cut, split
stupeō 2 I am stunned, astonished (at)
subiciō 3 *subiēcī subiectum* I place under
temptō 1 I check, test, explore
uulgus 2n. (m.) crowd, rank and file; mob; herd

40 *ante omnīs*: i.e. 'in the sight of everyone' (S., though some way off, *procul* **42**). Note the sense of urgency about 40–3
**comitor* 1 dep. I accompany (abl. abs. with *cateruā*)
cateru-a ae* 1f. crowd, throng (abl. abs., **RL150–1, **W**24, **M**79–80); Laocoon is a man with a following
41 **Lāocoōn* nom. s. Laocoon, a Trojan priest and son of Priam and Hecuba
***ārdeō* 2 *ārsī ārsum* I burn, am keen/fiery; S. finds

ārdēns exemplified in the speed (**41**) and explosive passion of Laocoon's outburst. Does *ārdēns* also 'look forward' to Ilium's burning? If so, with what literary significance? See on **2.199–208**

dēcurrō 3 I run down (from)
42 *procul* far off; ellipsis of 'he shouts'
īnsāni-a ae 1f. madness, lunacy
43 *āuehor* 3 *āuectus* I carry myself off (middle usage, cf. on *prōuectī* 24); understand *esse* as the inf. in an acc. and inf.
44 *careō* 2 I lack, am free of (+ abl.)
Danaum: (case?) take with *dōna* (alliteration)
nōtus: ellipsis of *est*
Vlixēs: a splendid climax to these frantic questions. Laocoon did not *know* that the horse was Ulysses' idea, but he was a seer, knew Ulysses' reputation and (irony) lights on the truth. V. leaves us to wonder, deliciously, if Ulysses was listening inside; according to Menelaus in the *Odyssey*, he was (4.269–89)
45 *lign-um ī* 2n. wood (i.e. the horse); note the omission of *in* and the contemptuous tone of *hōc lignō* – no 'offering' in Laocoon's eyes (S.)
occultō 1 I keep hidden, conceal
***Achīu-us a um* Greek; *Achīu-ī ōrum* 2m. pl. Greeks
46 *in*: i.e. against
fabricō 1 I construct
**māchin-a ae* 1f. machine, contraption – Laocoon perhaps envisages it as some sort of scaling-ladder or siege engine

---

words? If Aeneas from time to time remains at something of a distance from the events, it is worth pointing out that he made clear at the start the pain their recall would bring him.

Crunch: 35–8

2.40–9: So *ārdēns* (**41**) is Laocoon to deliver his message that he runs down and shouts *procul* (**42**), even before he has joined the crowd. Note the four frantic, incredulous questions (as if any people could be so blind as not to realise what was going on),

^īnspectūra domōs ^uentūraque dēsuper urbī,
aut aliquis^ latet ^error; equō nē crēdite, Teucrī.
quidquid id est, timeō Danaōs^ et dōna ^ferentīs." '

47 *īnspiciō* 3 *īnspexī īnspectum* I inspect, peer into;
the fut. part. (like *uentūra*) often expresses
purpose, 'to . . .' (**RL**81, **W**32, **M**78). A sort of
early spy-satellite
**dēsuper from above
urbī: i.e. *in urbem*
48 *aliquis:* 'some or other'
**lateō 2 I lie hidden
error -is 3m. deception, trick. Even if he does not
know the real explanation, Laocoon asserts that
there must be a trick somewhere. He is, of course,
right (irony)
nē (+ imper.) don't (an archaic construction,
commonly used in poetry but quite rare in Virgil;
see *Intro* [9] footnote 20; cf. **RLL**–**V**(a)3, **W**28, **M**89)
**Teucr-ī ōrum 2m. pl. Trojans (see on 1.38)
49 *timeō . . .*: this is a famous line: never trust an
enemy
et: even [when]; perhaps 'especially' [when]
dōna: surely sarcastic. Williams (1972) claims this

means 'religious offering(s) to Minerva as a
goddess of Troy'. But Laocoon has made it clear
that he does not know what it is, and nor does
anyone else. It is simply a 'present' from the
Greeks. All he knows is that it is a trick of some
sort, probably devised by Ulysses
ferentīs: agreeing with *Danaōs*

Learning vocabulary

Achīu-ī ōrum 2m. pl. Greeks
Achīu-us a um Greek
ārdeō 2 *ārsī ārsum* I burn, am keen/fiery
cateru-a ae 1f. crowd, throng
comitor 1 dep. I accompany
dēsuper from above
lateō 2 I lie hidden
Lāocoōn nom. s. Laocoon, a Trojan priest
māchin-a ae 1f. machine, contraption
Teucr-ī ōrum 2m. pl. Trojans

moving from Trojan obtuse blindness to Greek duplicity, climaxing with the terse reference to Ulysses. He then provides his analysis (45–8), admitting he does not know what
the trick might be but arguing it would be fatal either to bring it inside the city (45) or
leave it outside (46) and ending with a now famous line – never trust enemies, even
when they send you presents. He probably means 'especially when . . .' Note that, priest
though he is, V. does not introduce him as such, and Laocoon is not claiming any divine
insight into the matter. The whole argument is one based on human probability, i.e. we
know how Greeks, Ulysses most of all, traditionally behave (treacherously), so it is
probable/likely that they are behaving similarly in this case.

There are various sources for Aeneas' tale that V. had at his disposal. Four of these are
reproduced in the *Appendix*. It is, for example, interesting that V. uses Laocoon for this
scene and not Cassandra, perhaps because it is essential that this warning be taken seriously (tragic irony), while Cassandra was fated never to be believed (Austin), cf.
Appendix **12**. But it is equally likely that V. chose Laocoon because he had children, and
was dispensable – and will be dispensed with, along with his children, in the most dramatic fashion imaginable, 'proving' in the process that his analysis here was misguided,
cf. *Appendix* **1**. Myth had it that Cassandra was taken back to Greece by the victors.

Laocoon was a priest of Apollo, and Apollo was also a champion of the *gēns Iūlia* and
the Augustan regime (see *Intro* [28–9]). But Laocoon offended Apollo by making love to
his wife on sacred ground, and had therefore been punished by the god. So V. covers up
Laocoon's connection with Apollo, and instead makes him act more in a private capacity. When we return to Laocoon at 201ff., he will be a priest of Neptune, sacrificing to the
god of the sea (presumably to urge Neptune to smash the Greek fleet?).

See: Clausen (2002: 47–74) for V.'s handling of this whole episode.

Crunch: 40–4

2.50–6: 'Laocoon threw a spear into it, making the horse echo. Had the fates not been contrary, Troy would still stand'

<blockquote>

'sīc fātus, ualidīs^ ingentem* ^uīribus *hastam   50

in latus inque^ ferī ^curuam compāgibus ^aluum

contorsit. stetit illa tremēns, uterōque recussō

īnsonuēre cauae^ gemitumque dedēre ^cauernae.

et, sī fāta deum, sī mēns nōn laeua fuisset,

impulerat ferrō Argolicās^ foedāre ^latebrās,   55

Troiaque nunc stāret, Priamīque arx alta manērēs.'

</blockquote>

50 *******ualid-us a um* strong; *ualidīs . . . uīribus* goes with *contorsit* (52)

**hast-a ae 1f. spear

51 *fer-us a um* savage, cruel; supply 'horse'

*curu-us a um curved, crooked (with + abl.)

compāg-ēs is 3f. joint, structure

alu-us ī 2f. belly (with *latus*, a typical example of expansion, see on **53** below)

52 *contorqueō* 2 *contorsī* I fling with a twist

illa = hasta (*ille* is often used to mark a change of subject)

**tremō 3 *tremuī* I tremble

recutiō 3 *recussī recussum* I make vibrate

53 *īnsonō* 1 *īnsonuī* I resound (form? Cf. *dedēre*)

**gemit-us ūs 4m. groan

cauern-a ae 1f. a hollow, (by extension) ship's hold. This line rings with assonance (note *cau- cau-, -ae, -ēre* in particular), *cauernae* seeming to fade hollowly away (Austin (1964)). Note the typical Virgilian repetitions of basic ideas in **50–4** (see discussion at **2.132–44**)

54 *fāta*: S. says that this derives from *for fārī fātus 'I speak, say' and means 'what the gods say' (see on 777)

deum: case?

mēns: i.e. of the gods – or Trojans?

laeu-us a um unfavourable; adverse; blind; left (referring to both *fāta* and *mēns*)

55 **impellō 3 *impulī impulsum* I drive, force ('[us] to *foedāre . . .*'); after *fuisset* (54), one would have expected *impulisset* rather than the plupf. indic. Austin rightly suggests the indic. is used to indicate that Laocoon nearly succeeded (**RL**S2(c)6, 173, S2(c), **W**33)

*Argolic-us a um Greek (lit. 'from Argos')

*foedō 1 I despoil, disfigure, disgrace

latebr-a ae 1f. recess, hiding-place

56 *stāret . . . manērēs*: the *nunc* shows that these subjuncs. refer to the here and now: hence the impf. (**RL**139, **W**33, **M**115–17). Note the person of *manērēs*: Aeneas vividly turns aside to address the *Priamī arx alta* ('apostrophe')

Learning vocabulary

Argolic-us a um Greek (lit. 'from Argos')

curu-us a um curved, crooked

foedō 1 I despoil, disfigure, disgrace

gemit-us ūs 4m. groan

hast-a ae 1f. spear

impellō 3 *impulī impulsum* I drive, force

tremō 3 *tremuī* I tremble

ualid-us a um strong

2.50–6: Laocoon is as powerful physically as he is verbally. In a tremendous gesture of defiance and contempt, he uses his *ualidae uīrēs* to show what he thinks of this *dōnum* and hurls a huge spear (50) at the horse. The spear's reaction (*tremēns* 52) and the horse's (53) demonstrate the force of the throw. What did he hope to achieve? V. does not say, but if nothing else Laocoon has shown how exposed and vulnerable the horse is. It is there for the taking, and Aeneas immediately reflects – Aeneas' personal comment – on the consequences of the Trojan failure to take it. Scholars argue whether *mēns* refers to the divine or human mind (54). Surely, with S., the latter. First, it is otiose to say that it was the fate of the gods and the mind of the gods too. Second, it is typical of Homer to explain events as 'doubly determined', i.e. by gods and man at the same time, indistinguishably. For example, at *Iliad* 9.702–3, Diomedes says that Achilles will return to the fighting 'when his heart tells him and the god gets him going'. This increases our sense of the tragedy of events. Men could have done something about it. They did not. If everything were driven by the divine will, men would be nothing but puppets, and there is nothing tragic about puppets. As it is, men and gods are both 100 per cent responsible for what happens on earth. See *Intro* [48–50].

Crunch: 54–6

Learning vocabulary for Section 2.1–56

Achiu-ī ōrum 2m. pl. Greeks
Achīu-us a um Greek
Aenēās (acc. *Aenēān*, gen. *Aenēae*) Aeneas
ārdeō 2 *ārsī ārsum* I burn, am keen/fiery
Argolic-us a um Greek (lit. 'from Argos')
armāt-us a um armed
caec-us a um blind, hidden, dark
castr-a ōrum 2n. camp
cateru-a ae 1f. crowd, throng
cau-us a um hollow
cert-ō 1 I fight
class-is is 3m. fleet
comitor 1 dep. I accompany
condō 3 *condidī conditum* I hide; found, build; bury
cōnspect-us ūs 4m. sight
curu-us a um curved, crooked
Dana-ī ōrum 2m. pl. Greeks
Danaum = Dana(ōr)um
Dana-us a um Greek
desert-us a um deserted, lonely, abandoned
dēsuper from above
Dolop-es (-ēs) um 3m. pl. Dolopes, Pyrrhus' (Achilles' brutal son) men
dol-us ī 2m. trick, treachery
dōn-um ī 2n. gift, offering
ductor -is 3m. leader
ēruō 3 *ēruī* I overthrow
fāt-um ī 2n. fate, destiny
fīd-us a um faithful, trustworthy
foedō 1 I despoil, disfigure, disgrace
for fārī fātus I speak, talk, say
frangō 3 *frēgī frāctum* I break, smash
gemit-us ūs 4m. groan
hast-a ae 1f. spear
horreō 2 I shudder
hūc (to) here
impellō 3 *impulī impulsum* I drive, force
incert-us a um uncertain, doubtful
incipiō 3 *incēpī inceptum* I begin
inde from there, then
īnfand-us a um unspeakable, past words; monstrous, accursed
īnsidi-ae ārum 1f. ambush
lacrim-a ae 1f. tear

Lāocoōn nom. s. Laocoon, a Trojan priest
lateō 2 I lie hidden
latus later-is 3n. side
līt-us lītor-is 3n. coast, coast-line
locō 1 I place
lūct-us ūs 4m. grief
māchin-a ae 1f. machine, contraption
Mineru-a ae 1f. Minerva (Greek Athena)
mīror 1 dep. I wonder, am amazed at
mōl-ēs is 3f. huge structure; mass, lump; undertaking, burden
mūr-us ī 2m. wall
Mycēn-ae ārum 1f. pl. Mycenae, home of Greek king Agamemnon
Myrmidon-es (-ēs) um 3m. pl. Myrmidons, Achilles' soldiers
nōt-us a um well-known, famous
ōs ōr-is 3n. face, mouth, speech
Pallas Pallad-is/os 3f. Pallas (Athena) = (Roman) Minerva
pelag-us ī 2n. sea
penitus (deep) within; far away
port-a ae 1f. gate
praecipitō 1 I speed/drive (on); hurry (down from + abl.); throw headlong
Priam-us ī 2m. Priam, king of Troy
rēgin-a ae 1f. queen
rēgn-um ī 2n. kingdom
saeu-us a um savage, cruel, vicious
scindō 3 *scidī scissum* I divide, cut, split
simulō 1 I imitate, pretend
sin-us ūs 4m. inlet, gulf; ripple
soluō 3 *soluī solūtum* I release, loosen, dissolve; pay, perform
stupeō 2 I am stunned, astonished (at)
subiciō 3 *subiēcī subiectum* I place under
temperō 1 I refrain, restrain, soothe
temptō 1 I check, test, explore
Teucr-ī ōrum 2m. pl. Trojans
tremō 3 I tremble
Troi-a ae 1f. Troy, the region where Ilium was located
Troiān-us a um Trojan
ualid-us a um strong

-ue or
uter-us ī 2m. womb, belly

uulgus 2n. (m.) crowd, rank and file; mob; herd
Vlix-ēs ī/is/eī 3m. Ulysses (Greek Odysseus)

Study section for 2.1–56

1. What picture of Greek and Trojan mentality does Aeneas create?
2. How does Aeneas build up our sympathy for the Trojans?
3. What sense of Aeneas the man emerges in this *Section*?
4. Scan 50–7.
5. Compare 3–13 with the way in which Odysseus begins the story of his travels to the listening Phaeacians. Odysseus too is being entertained at a feast, but his hosts do not know his identity. A minstrel has just sung about the Trojan horse, Odysseus bursts into tears and the Phaeacian king asks him why the tears and who he is:

To him in reply the resourceful Odysseus answered:
'King Alcinous, admired of all men,
this is certainly a fine thing to listen to a minstrel
such as this one, like the gods in voice.
I declare that there is no object in life that gives greater pleasure   5
than when good spirits prevail among the whole people,
and feasters throughout a house listen to a minstrel
as they sit in rows with tables next to them full
of bread and meat and, drawing pure wine from the mixing bowl,
a wine-pourer carries it and pours it into goblets.   10
This seems to me in my mind the finest thing.
But for you, your heart has turned to asking about the sorrows that make me sigh
– for me to weep and groan over even more!
What then shall I tell you first, and what last?
– for many are the sorrows which the Olympian gods have given me.   15
Now first I shall tell you my name, so that you
may know it too, and I hereafter, escaping the pitiless day,
may be your friend even when I am living in my palace far away.
I am Odysseus, son of Laertes, who, for my tricks,
am on the minds of all men and my fame reaches heaven.'   20

Homer, *Odyssey* 9.1–20 (Dawe 1993)

2.57–198: Sinon's tale

In this Section, *the captive Sinon is brought in, pretending to be a helpless victim of Greek treachery, and spins a false tale about the wooden horse, persuading the Trojans to bring it into the city.*

2.57–66: *'Then herdsmen brought in a young man, hands bound, primed to trick the Trojans or die – if they but knew it'*

'ecce, manūs iuuen<u>em</u>^ intereā post terga ^reuīnctum
pāstōrēs^ magn<u>ō</u>* ad rēgem *clāmōre trahēbant
^Dardanidae, quī s<u>ē</u> ignōtum uenientibus ultrō,
hoc ips<u>um</u> ut strueret Troiamqu<u>e</u> aperīret Achīuīs,   60
obtulerat, fīdēns anim<u>ī</u> atqu<u>e</u> in utrumque parātus,
s<u>eu</u> uersāre dolōs seu certa<u>e</u>^ occumbere ^mortī.
undique, uīsendī studiō, Troiāna iuuentūs

---

57 *ecce*: S. comments that this interjection almost lays the action out before the reader's eyes

manūs: acc. pl., an acc. of 'respect' ('in respect of') after *iuuenem . . . reuīnctum*, lit. 'bound in respect of his hands', 'with his hands bound'. This is a 'true' acc. of respect, because the young man (Sinon) is an unwilling victim of the binding. See p. 39 ((d)) and compare ((c)(i), (ii))

*terg-um ī 2n. back

reuinciō 4 reuīnxī reuīnctum I bind

58 *pāstor -is* 3m. shepherd, herdsman

**clāmor -is 3m. cry, shout

trahō 3 trāxī tractum I draw, drag. This is a heavily spondaic line, suggestive of the shepherds dragging him unwillingly along, when he was all too willing (*ultrō*, **59)

59 **Dardanid-ae um* m. pl. Trojan(s) (lit. 'sons of Dardanus', an early founder of Troy)

quī: picks up *iuuenem*; the vb governed by *quī* is *obtulerat*

**ignōt-us a um unknown; *sē* (i.e. Sinon) *ignōtum* is the object of *obtulerat*

uenientibus: i.e. to the shepherds who came upon him; they knew nothing about him

*ultrō willingly (i.e. it was all part of Sinon's scheme); it goes with *obtulerat*. *ultrō* often means 'willingly beyond the call of duty, in addition'

60 *hoc ipsum*: 'this very thing', (i.e. being brought before Priam), obj. of *ut . . . strueret* (**RL**145, **W**28, **M**96). **For the scansion of *hoc* as *hocc*, see on 1.539

struō 3 I achieve, devise

61 **offerō offerre obtulī oblātum* I offer, hand over; bring before, exhibit

*fīdō 3 semi-dep. *fīsus* I trust, am confident

animī: gen. of reference, 'in his mind'

uter- utra- utrum-que both, either; here 'both possibilities, to . . . (+ inf.)'

62 *seu* either/or

uersō 1 I keep turning, practise

occumbō 3 I meet with (+ dat.)

63 **undique* from all sides

uīsō 3 I go and look at, view; *uīsendī* is a gerund,

2.57–66: *ecce*: with that one word, Aeneas vividly diverts our attention from Laocoon to the villain of the piece; and whatever spell Laocoon may have held over the Trojans is

[194]

circumfūsa ruit, certantque inlūdere captō.
accipe nunc Danaum īnsidiās et crīmine^ ab ^unō   65
disce omnīs.'

after *studiō* (**RL**175, N, **W**39, **M**109). They are all
keen to have a look at the captive
****iuuentūs iuuentūt-is* 3f. youth, young
people
64 *circumfundō* 3 *circumfūdī circumfūsum* I pour
round, surround
****ruō* 3 *ruī rutum* I rush; drive ahead; churn up.
Note s. *ruit*, but pl. *certant* (cf. on 32) – a
distinction between people rushing up in a body,
but individuals insulting the captive?
inlūdō 3 I mock, insult (+ dat.)
captō: as the Trojans fondly imagine (S.).
Understand *Sinōnī*
65 *īnsidiās*: as Dido had specifically requested, 1.754;
hence *accipe* (s.), addressed to her
crīmen crīmin-is 3n. charge, crime; *ūnō* means 'of
one man'
66 *disce omnīs*: this is an unfinished line. This book
has ten such lines, more than any other (233, 346,
468, 614, 623, 640, 720, 767, 787). See on 1.534,
and cf. *Intro* [7–9]

discō 3 I learn (about), understand
omnīs: understand *Danaōs*

Learning vocabulary
clāmor -is 3m. cry, shout
Dardanid-ae um m. pl. Trojans (lit. 'sons of
Dardanus', an early founder of Troy)
fīdō 3 semi-dep. *fīsus* I put my trust in
(+ gen.)
hic, hoc as *hicc, hocc* (for scansion purposes)
ignōt-us a um unknown
iuuentūs iuuentūt-is 3f. youth
offerō offerre obtulī oblātum I offer, hand over;
bring before, exhibit
ruō 3 *ruī rutum* I rush; drive ahead; churn up
terg-um ī 2n. back
trahō 3 *trāxī tractum* I draw, drag
ultrō willingly (often beyond the call of duty); in
addition
undique from all sides

---

broken (indeed, he must have returned to the citadel at this point, where we find him at
201. Virgil clearly could not have him around while Sinon was spinning his tale). Enter,
then, Sinon, his entry timed to perfection, since he seemed to have intended his capture
at that time (59). Aeneas now analyses in outline what Sinon was doing and why (59–
62). Given the moment of his capture – at exactly the right time to prevent Laocoon
doing any more damage – Aeneas could easily assume he had engineered it intentionally
(59 *ultrō*); and Sinon's state of mind and motives were easy to construct after the event
(60). But in Aeneas' eyes (Aeneas' personal observation) it was not death or glory for
Sinon – it was death or treachery (62). The rush of Trojans to see what was going on
(63–4) takes us back to *ecce* – it was all so quick and unexpected – and with a deep
breath, one feels, Aeneas prepares to describe how the Trojans were utterly deceived –
quae tanta īnsānia (42) indeed, as Laocoon had tragically foreseen only minutes before-
hand. But we are agog: what could Sinon actually *do* or *say* that would persuade the
Trojans to bring the horse inside the city? Whatever it was, Aeneas personally interjects,
it was typically *Greek* (65–6).

One feature needs emphasising: Sinon is not some experienced, worldly-wise, man-
about-town. He is *young* (57), and therefore all the more likely (if he plays his cards
properly) to disarm the Trojans' suspicions about him.

See: Gransden 'The Fall of Troy' in McAuslan and Walcot (1990: 121–33) for this
episode.

2.67–75: 'The captive wondered where he was, an enemy of Greek and Trojan alike. We were immediately interested in his story'

'namque ut cōnspectū^ in ^mediō turbātus, inermis
cōnstitit, atque oculīs Phrygia agmina circumspexit,
"heū quae^ nunc ^tellūs," inquit, "quae^ mē ^aequora possunt
accipere? aut quid iam miserō^ ^mihi dēnique restat,   70
^cuī neque apud Danaōs usquam locus, et super ipsī^
^Dardanidae ^īnfēnsī poenās cum sanguine poscunt?"
quō gemitū conuersī animī, compressus et omnis
impetus. hortāmur fārī quō sanguine crētus,
quidue ferat; memoret quae sit fidūcia captō.'   75

67 *ut*: here + indic.
**turbō 1 I confuse, confound; scatter
inerm-is e unarmed, defenceless
68 *cōnstitit*: one word, one dactyl – the effect is to create a natural pause
*Phrygi-us a um Trojan (see on 1.182)
**agmen agmin-is 3n. rank, (battle-) line
circumspiciō 3 *circumspexī* I look around at; note the rare fifth-foot spondee, to add a sense of – what?
69 *heū alas. There is a heavy spondaic tread about this line
**tellūs tellūr-is 3f. land
**aequor -is 3n. (calm) sea, ocean
70 **restō 1 I remain, am left over; survive from
71 *cuī*: *note scansion *cuī*
**usquam anywhere
locus: supply *est*
*super moreover (adverbial); (+ acc.) above, over
ipsī: with *super*, clever acting from Sinon. It implies that he is *surprised* at the hostility of the Trojan reception – an odd thing to suggest, given the war, but surely calculated to arouse their curiosity
72 *īnfēns-us a um* hostile
***sanguis sanguin-is* 3m. blood (*cum* 'along with'); at 74, family, line
**poscō 3 *poposcī* I demand, beg
73 *quō gemitū*: it is common in Latin to begin sentences with a relative, picking up an idea from the previous sentence, lit. 'by which lament'. In English we use the demonstrative and translate 'by *this* lament'
*conuertō 3 *conuertī conuersum* I change, convert, turn round (understand part of *sum* with *conuersī* and *compressus*, and understand *nostrī* with *animī*)
animī: pl. 'anger'

comprīmō 3 *compressī compressus* I repress, check; take in order *et compressus*
74 *impet-us ūs* 4m. hostility, attack, i.e. urge to kill Sinon (S.)
hortāmur: ellipsis of *eum*. S. comments that this indicates their sympathy for him, whereas e.g. *iubēmus* would not
quō sanguine: abl. of origin. See p. 40 ((g)(vii)) above
crēscō 3 *crēuī crētum* I grow, arise, spring (ellipsis of *sit*, in indir. q., RLR3, W30, M94) i.e. the Trojans want to know about his parents, since they know he is Greek (S.)
75 *quidue*: i.e. or what news (S.)
**memorō 1 I say, tell, narrate, mention, address; subjunc. of indir. command after *hortāmur*, RL134, W36, M89–91
**fidūci-a ae 1f. trust, confidence, faith (in), i.e. what (self-)confidence he could entertain, being *captō*, that the Trojans would spare him (S.)

Learning vocabulary
aequor -is 3n. (calm) sea, ocean
agmen agmin-is 3n. rank, (battle-) line
conuertō 3 *conuertī conuersum* I change, convert, turn round
fidūci-a ae 1f. trust, confidence, faith (in)
heū alas
memorō 1 I say, tell, narrate, mention, address
Phrygi-us a um Trojan (see on 1.182)
poscō 3 *poposcī* I demand, beg
restō 1 I remain, am left over; survive from
sanguis sanguin-is 3m. blood; family, line
super moreover; (+ acc.) above, over
tellūs tellūr-is 3f. land
turbō 1 I confuse, confound; scatter
usquam anywhere

2.67–75: Sinon's play-acting begins at once – he is (to Aeneas' eyes) *turbātus*, when we know he is nothing of the sort (67, S.). His slow, spondaic survey (*circumspexit* 68) of all

2.77–87: 'He admitted to being a Greek, Sinon, and said he was a close friend and relative of Palamedes, put to death for opposing the war'

"'cūnct<u>a</u>^ equidem tibi, rēx, fuerit quodcumque, fatēbor   77
^uēr<u>a</u>," inquit; "neque m<u>ē</u> Argolicā^ dē ^gente negābō.
hoc prīmum. nec, sī miserum^ Fortūna* ^Sinōnem
finxit, ^uān<u>um</u> etiam ^mendācemque improba* finget.   80
fand<u>ō</u> aliquod* sī forte tuās^ peruēnit ad ^aurīs

77: line 76, which is not in the chief manuscripts, has been omitted
**cūnct-us a um all
**equidem [I] for my part
**rēx rēg-is 3m. king
fuerit quodcumque: lit. 'whatever will have been [at the end of all this]', 'come what may' (i.e. whether you let me live or not). Here is a man apparently happy to contemplate death (S.)
fateor 2 dep. *fassus* I confess, acknowledge
79–80: the sentiment is: 'my luck may make me miserable, but it will never make me a liar'
*Sinōn -is 3m. Sinon, the Greek sent to trick the Trojans (acc. *Sinōnem*). He was a distant relation of Ulysses. Introducing himself with 'Sinon' rather than 'me' adds a certain 'force' (S.), making

Sinon sound like a man of high principle who has been mortally traduced (sportsmen play this 'injured merit' card all the time, as in 'You'll never see Joey Moron elbowing someone intentionally in the teeth' when that is precisely what Joey Moron has just done). The name sounds as if it has a connection with the Greek *sin-* stem meaning 'hurt', 'harm'
80 *fingō* 3 *finxī fictum* I make, form, shape; invent, pretend. Subjunc. or indic? See **RLS**2(c), **W**33, **M**115
**uān-us a um deceived, empty, illusory, i.e. Sinon
mendāx mendāc-is false, lying
improb-us a um ill-disposed, malicious, immoral (a fine hypocrisy from this 'helpless victim')
81–7: a complex sentence. The *sī* clause (**81**) covers

---

the Trojans standing around him, shouting and gesticulating (64), was surely calculated to fix audience attention on himself. His opening appeal is powerful: excluded from land (which the Trojans hold) and sea (held by the Greeks, S.), he has nowhere else to go (69–70), and he expresses no surprise that the Trojans will torture and kill him (72). Too true they would, if only they knew! (Irony.) This is designed to capture Trojan sympathy, but it also raises the question in Trojans minds: what on earth is this young man going on about? Why should we *not* kill him? The gambit works. The Trojans are already fascinated, losing all hostility, and ask for more details (73–5). In other words, a *relationship* is being forged, and the Trojans are being gradually drawn into *Sinon*'s view of things – the key to all successful negotiation, and deception. Note further: the relationship is being forged with the reader too. We do not know what Sinon's tactics are, or his end-game. The effect he has on us will be the same sort of effect V. is imagining he would have on the Trojans – except that we are there as distant observers, enjoying the rhetoric. Our lives are not at stake.

From now on till the end of Sinon's speech, a 'score-card' will be appended to each discussion, analysing what Sinon says as 'true' or 'false' and suggesting the image he is trying to create of himself in the eyes of the Greeks. Sinon's ultimate aim is to create in the Trojans *a complete dependency upon him*, helpless captive though he is, so that they trust him utterly, no questions asked, when he tells them what to do about the horse.

Crunch: 69–72

2.77–87: 'I shall tell the truth, come what may.' They all say that, but Sinon goes one better – he does in fact tell a truth, confessing he is a Greek (77–8), the worst possible crime (in

Bēlīdae^ *nōmen ^Palamēdis et incluta^ fāmā
^glōria, quem^ falsā* sub *prōditiōne Pelasgī
^īnsontem īnfandō indiciō, quia bella uetābat,
dēmīsēre necī, nunc ^cassum lūmine lūgent,   85
illī mē^ ^comitem et cōnsanguinitāte ^propinquum
pauper^ in arma ^pater prīmīs^ hūc mīsit ab ^annīs." '

81–3 up to *glōria*; the *quem* clause covers the rest of **83–85** up to *lūgent*; *quem* is then picked up by *illī* 'to that man' (i.e. to Palamedes, **86**); and we finally reach the main clause *pauper pater, prīmīs ab annīs, hūc mīsit mē, comitem et propinquum cōnsanguinitāte, in arma*

fandō: i.e. in talk, conversation; *aliquod* (= 'any [mention of the]') *nōmen* and *incluta . . . glōria* are the subject of *peruēnit*

**forte by chance

*aur-is -is 3f. ear

82 *Bēlīdae*: gen. s. (with *Palamēdis*) 'son of Belus' (father of Danaus)

Palamēdis: gen. s. of Palamedes, a Greek warrior at Troy

inclut-us a um famous

83 *quem*: picks up Palamedes. Follow closely the linking devices; *quem* and its epithets are ultimately the object of *dēmīsēre necī* and *lūgent* (**85**), whose subject is *Pelasgī*

**fals-us a um treacherous, false

sub: on a charge/pretext of (*OLD* A 14b)

prōditiō -nis 3f. charge of treachery. The real story: Ulysses, angry that Palamedes had revealed the trick by which he (U.) tried to avoid going to Troy, forged a letter from Palamedes to Priam, saying he (Palamedes) would betray the Greeks. Ulysses then planted gold in Palamedes' tent to 'prove' it. But Sinon has a different version, 'spun' to fit his cause (see *uetō* below)

*Pelasg-ī ōrum 2m. pl. Greeks (the Pelasgi were an ancient people living in northern Greece); *Pelasg-us a um* Greek

84 *īnsōns īnsont-is* guiltless

indici-um ī 2n. information, evidence. Page notes the 'indignant, hammerlike emphasis of the *in*, combined as it is with a double elision' of this line

quia: 'that', explaining the *real* reason for persecuting Palamedes

uetō 1 I forbid, object to; *bella* = the Trojan war (pl. for s., as often). Palamedes had done nothing of the sort (see **83** above), but this motive would appeal to the Trojans and, by associating Sinon with a 'stop the war' movement, increase their sympathy for him

85 **dēmittō 3 *dēmīsī demissum* I hand/pass/send/ cast down. What form is *dēmīsēre*?

nex nec-is 3f. murder, violent death. After *necī*, understand *sed* before *nunc cassum*

cass-us a um deprived of (+ abl.), referring to the *nunc* dead Palamedes, obj. of *lūgent*

**lūmen lūmin-is 3n. light (here = 'life')

lūgeō 2 grieve for. Note the mournful sound of this pathos-filled line

86 *illī*: i.e. to/of Palamedes

*comes comit-is 3m. companion

cōnsanguinitās cōnsanguinitāt-is 3f. blood-relationship, kinship

propinqu-us a um close, related (a complete lie, of course)

87 *pauper*: Sinon's father, being poor, sent Sinon as a young man to seek his fortune in battle

prīmīs: i.e. of the war, or Sinon's manhood? Probably the latter

Trojan eyes) to which he could admit. If he confesses to that, he will surely confess to anything! So his listeners are already predisposed to believe him. Note *nōn negābō* – as if he could have denied it, but is too honest to – and the subsequent protestations about his *fortūna* (79–80, i.e. nothing is his fault) which will never make *him* (heaven forbid!) a liar (irony: *fingō* twice in 80 is exactly what he is doing, unbeknownst to the Trojans). *fandō aliquod . . .* (81) is a cleverly diffident way of starting his hard-luck story. Even cleverer is the tactic of inserting himself into the (true) story of Ulysses' treachery against Palamedes (81–5), because it draws the listener away from questioning his (non-existent) part in it (86, S.) and enables him to win further sympathy by showing up the wickedness of the Greeks and associating himself (falsely) with the anti-war faction (83–4). His protestations about his father's 'poverty' and 'orders to join the army' prove his filial loyalty (every

2.88–96: 'He said his standing was now lost, and in his grief threatened to take revenge if ever he returned to Greece'

'"dum stābat rēgnō incolumis rēgumque uigēbat
conciliīs, et nōs aliquod nōmenque decusque
gessimus. inuidiā postquam pellācis Vlixī   90
(haud ignōta loquor) superīs^ concessit ab ^ōrīs,
adflīctus uītam in tenebrīs lūctūque trahēbam,
et cāsum īnsontis^ mēcum indignābar ^amīcī.
nec tacuī dēmēns, et mē*, fors^ sī ^qua tulisset,

Learning vocabulary

aur-is -is 3f. ear
comes comit-is 3m. companion
cūnct-us a um all
dēmittō 3 *dēmīsī demissum* I hand/pass/send/cast
  down
equidem [I] for my part
fals-us a um treacherous, false
forte by chance
lūmen lūmin-is 3n. light
Pelasg-ī ōrum 2m. pl. Greeks (the Pelasgi were an
  ancient people living towards the north of Greece)
Pelasg-us a um Greek
rēx rēg-is 3m. king
Sinōn -is 3m. Sinon, a Greek sent to trick the Trojans
uān-us a um deceived, empty, illusory

88 *stābat*: the subject is Palamedes, as too of
  concessit (91)
incolum-is e safe, secure ([*in*] *rēgnō*)
uigeō 2 I flourish, have authority
89 *concili-um ī* 2n. council (= *in conciliīs*)

et nōs = 'I too . . .' (note the 'royal' *nōs*, pl. for s.)
**decus decōr-is* 3n. honour, distinction, standing;
  ornament, decoration
90 *inuidi-a ae* 1f. jealousy (abl. of cause)
pellāx pellāc-is glib, smooth-talking
91 *ignōta*: n. pl., obj. of *loquor*
concēdō 3 *concessī* I depart
**ōr-a ae* 1f. shore (+ *superīs* = 'life on earth above',
  Hades being *below* the earth)
92 *adflīgō* 3 *adflīxī afflīctum* I crush
tenebr-a ae 1f. shadow
93 *īnsōns īnsont-is* innocent
indignor 1 dep. I brood over
94 *dēmēns dēment-is* mad, foolish, i.e. I was foolish
  enough not to hold my peace
mē: acc. after *prōmīsī* (**96**)
fors fort-is 3f. luck, chance (cf. *forte*), with which *qua*
  (= *quae* [indef.] 'any') agrees; *tulisset* is plupf.
  subjunc. in indir. speech beginning with *prōmīsī*
96, responding to Sinon's proposed 'actual words'
  in the fut. perf., 'if any chance brings (= will have
  brought) it about, I shall take revenge . . .' (**RLR4**)

honest son obeys his father, S.) and, even more important, his innocent involvement on the Greek side (87); further, he claims to have gone as a *comitem*, not as a *mīlitem*, as S. notes. It was not as if he had any special grudge against the Trojans.

Score

True: (i) Sinon is Greek (ii) there was a conspiracy against Palamedes, launched by Ulysses
False: (i) Sinon was related to Palamedes (ii) Sinon joined Palamedes as a fellow-fighter at his poor father's bequest (iii) Palamedes wanted to stop the war
Sinon's image: (i) always tells the truth (77–80) (ii) his plight not his fault (87) (iii) obedient to his father (87) (iv) no innate hostility to Greeks

Crunch: 77–80

2.88–96: Since Palamedes was one of the Greek 'kings' (that is, leaders of a contingent of men to Troy), he had some status, which Sinon as a 'relative' also claims to have enjoyed (88–90; this further 'explains' and justifies his anger against the Greeks). Sinon now fingers Ulysses as the prime mover of the plot against Palamedes (90), winning yet

sī patriōs^ umquam remeāssem uictor ad ^Argōs,   95
prōmīsī *ultōre̲m, et uerbīs odi̲a aspera mōuī.'"

2.97–104: 'He described how Ulysses spread rumours about him, determined to do away with him – but he then broke off, wondering why he should waste time telling the Trojans this, since they hated all Greeks'

'"hinc mihi prīma^ malī ^lābēs, hinc semper Vlixēs*
crīminibus^ terrēre ^nouīs, hinc spargere uōcēs^
in uulgu̲m ^ambiguās et quaerere *cōnscius arma.
nec requiēuit enim, dōnec Calchante ministrō –   100
sed quid eg̲o haec^ autem nequīqua̲m ^ingrāta reuoluō,

95 **patri-us a um* paternal, ancestral
remeō 1 I return; *remeāssem = remeā(ui)ssem*
**Arg-ī ōrum* 2m. Argos, an important Greek city, Sinon's place of birth (if he is to be believed); otherwise, regularly used for 'Greece'
96 *prōmittō* 3 *prōmīsī* I promise, vow; construe *mē* (**94**) as an *ultōrem*
ultor -is 3m. avenger
uerbīs: i.e. by speaking out
**odi-um ī* 2n. hatred, i.e. hatred in Ulysses
mōuī: 'I stirred up'

Learning vocabulary
Arg-ī ōrum Argos, an important Greek city; Greece
decus decōr-is 3n. honour, distinction, standing; ornament, decoration
odi-um ī 2n. hatred
ōr-a ae 1f. shore
patri-us a um paternal, ancestral

97 *hinc*: i.e. as a result of this
prīma: i.e. where it all began
lāb-ēs is 3f. sign, mark (*malī* 'of trouble'); stain on reputation (ellipsis of part of *sum*)

98 *crīmen crīmin-is* 3n. charge, accusation
terrēre: historic inf., 'he began to . . .'; so *spargere* and *quaerere* (**99**)
spargō 3 I scatter, spread
99 *ambigu-us a um* double-edged
**cōnsci-us a um* consciously, with deliberate intent; knowingly (of his own guilt?)
arma: i.e. any weapons he could use against me (S.)
100 *requiēscō* 3 *requiēuī* I rest
enim: here 'indeed'
**Calchante*: abl. s. of *Calchās*, the Greek army's chief priest, and therefore a figure of some authority
minister ministr-ī 2m. accomplice, servant (in apposition to *Calchante*, 'with Calchas . . .'; the whole phrase is an abl. abs.). Note the irony: Calchas is portrayed as wholly in Ulysses' pocket
101 *sed quid*: breaking off in mid-sentence is called 'aposiopesis', cf. on 1.135
**nequīquam* in vain, pointlessly
ingrāt-us a um ungrateful (here n. pl.)
reuoluō 3 I turn over, go over

further Trojan understanding (you know all the details, he suggests, flattering them, 91); he romanticises Palamedes' death (*superīs . . . ōrīs* is very grand, 91); and describes his own 'deep mourning' and 'growing anger' (92–3). All this again 'explains' how he foolishly promised revenge (94–6). He agrees this was mad (*dēmēns* 94), but mad in such a noble cause, the honour of an innocent friend (93)!

Score
False: everything
Sinon's image: (i) loyal to the memory of a close friend and relative (92–3) (ii) impulsive in support of friends (94)

2.97–104: That Ulysses should be said to have adopted such underhand, slippery tactics to do away with Sinon (note *nouīs, uōcēs, ambiguās*) would appeal to the prejudices of a Trojan audience. Sinon now seems about to reveal what Ulysses 'actually' did – and with

quidue moror? sī omnīs^ unō ōrdine habētis ^Achīuōs,
idque audīre sat est, iamdūdum sūmite poenās:
hoc Ithacus uelit, et magnō mercentur Atrīdae.'"

2.105–13: 'This made us all the keener to hear his story, and he told how the Greeks wanted to leave Troy, but winds prevented them. So, Sinon said, they built the wooden horse – but it was greeted with a thunderstorm'

'tum uērō ārdēmus^ scītārī et quaerere causās,   105

102 *moror 1 dep. I delay

habētis ūnō ōrdine: 'you hold/judge/consider in one rank, i.e. all alike'

103 *idque*: i.e. 'that name' ('of a Greek', from the previous line), obj. of *audīre*

sat = satis, i.e. 'for you'

iamdūdum lit. 'some while ago now', but with an imper., 'as you should have done long ago!'

sūmō 3 *poenās* I exact a penalty

104 *Ithac-us a um* Ithacan, from (the Greek island of) Ithaca (i.e. Ulysses) – said with (bogus) contempt

uelit . . . mercentur: note conditional subjunc., **RL**139, **W**33, **M**115

magnō: abl. of price, **RLL**(f)4(v), **M**14

mercor 1 dep. I trade, buy

*Atrīdae: nom. pl. the sons of Atreus; see on 1.458

Learning vocabulary

Atrīdae nom. pl., the sons of Atreus

Calchās (abl. *Calchante*) Calchas, the Greek army's chief priest

cōnsci-us a um consciously, with deliberate intent, knowingly

Ithac-us a um Ithacan (i.e. Ulysses)

moror 1 dep. I delay

nequīquam in vain, pointlessly

105 *scītor* 1 dep. I inquire, seek to know

causās: i.e. why the Greeks wanted Sinon dead

the authoritative 'help' of the chief priest Calchas, too – when he stops, as if he is boring the audience with a pointless (*nequīquam*) long story that will do nothing for him or them (*ingrāta* 101, S.), and invites them to do away with him, pointing out that the Greeks (their hated enemies) would applaud, inviting the as yet unanswered question – why would the Greeks applaud? The break is well-judged, of course, to whip up yet further enthusiasm in the audience (S.) to hear more about the horrible Greeks and their cruel, unjust treatment of this kindly, innocent man – and to encourage them to believe the rest of his story all the more wholeheartedly (S.). Observe that Sinon has said nothing yet of the slightest relevance to his ultimate purpose – persuading the Trojans to bring the horse inside the city. First he must win their sympathy, understanding and most of all trust.

Score

False: everything

Sinon's image: (i) innocent victim of Ulysses' plotting (97–100) (ii) though innocent, resigned to his fate

Crunch: 97–9

2.105–13: It works: the Trojans long to hear more. Their state of dependency is growing. Aeneas here associates himself with the foolish (*ignārī* 106) Trojan desire for more (*ārdēmus* 105), and Sinon both raises the emotional temperature and moves closer to his goal by setting the background to his story in the *Greek desire to leave Troy* – a subject of surpassing interest to every Trojan, and one with which Sinon immediately

^ignārī scelerum tantōrum artisque Pelasgae.
prōsequitur pauitāns, et fictō pectore fātur:
"saepe fugam Danaī^ Troiā* cupiēre *relictā
mōlīrī et longō* ^fessī discēdere *bellō;
fēcissentque utinam! saepe illōs^ aspera* pontī   110
interclūsit *hiems et terruit Auster ^euntīs.
praecipuē, cum iam hic^ trabibus* ^contextus *acernīs
stāret ^equus, tōtō^ sonuērunt ^aethere nimbī.'"

106 ***ignār-us a um** ignorant (of + gen.); S. comments 'either because they did not know or were thoughtless'
107 *prōsequor* 3 dep. I follow up/on
pauitō 1 I tremble, am fearful (all part of the act, of course, [S.], as Aeneas now realises, cf. on *pectus* below)
fingō 3 *finxī fictum* I invent
***pectus pector-is** 3n. chest, breast, heart (the seat of the emotions: hence *fictō*, Aeneas' after-the-event comment)
108 *Troiā*: i.e. *ā Troiā*
cupiēre = cupiuērunt
109 ***mōlior** 4 dep. I construct, build; strive, labour at
***fess-us a um** tired
110 *utinam* + subjunc. would that . . .! **RL**153.1
***pont-us -ī** 2m. sea (with *hiems*), lit. 'of the sea', i.e. from the sea
111 *interclūdō* 3 *interclūsī* I shut in
***hiems hiem-is** 3f. storm, winter
***Auster Austr-ī** 2m. south wind (no good for Greeks sailing predominantly south down the Aegean from Troy to Greece)

112 ***praecipuē** especially
***trabs trab-is** 3f. beam, timber, tree-trunk
contexō 3 *contexuī contextum* I join by weaving
acern-us a um of maple (in fact the horse was made of a number of types of wood, cf. 16, 258)
113 ***sonō** 1 *sonuī* I sound, echo, thunder
***aether -is** 3m. upper air, heaven; places described with *tōtus* often omit a preposition, e.g. 'over, in'
***nimb-us ī** 2m. cloud

Learning vocabulary

aether -is 3m. upper air, heaven
Auster Austr-ī 2m. south wind
fess-us a um tired
hiems hiem-is 3f. storm, winter
ignār-us a um ignorant (of + gen.)
mōlior 4 dep. I construct, build; strive, labour at
nimb-us -ī 2m. cloud
pont-us -ī 2m. sea
pectus pector-is 3n. chest, breast, heart
praecipuē especially
sonō 1 *sonuī* I sound, echo, thunder
trabs trab-is 3f. beam, timber, tree-trunk

associates himself (110). Note the flattery of the Trojans implicit in *fessī* (109) – the Greeks can have been *fessī* only because of the courage and tenacity of the Trojans. But the weather also, Sinon lies, played its part – note the effective anaphora *saepe* (108, 111) – and this leads innocently into the real object of Sinon's mission: the horse, its unexplained presence casually mentioned in passing in a discussion of the weather (112–13). Both we and the Trojans ask – what had this horse to do with the Greeks' *departure*? And what to do with the *weather*? Had they built it, perhaps, to try to get good weather for the sailing? One remembers that the Greeks were unable to get to Troy in the first place because of the bad weather which could be ended only by Agamemnon's sacrifice of his daughter Iphigeneia (see note on 116). Note that Sinon's hint here chimes with the Trojan rumours of the horse's purpose at 17.

Score

True: the Greeks often wished to leave Troy
False: (i) the weather prevented them (ii) the wooden horse had something to do with the weather
Sinon's image: he is quite out of sympathy with the Greeks (110)

2.114–21: 'Eurypylus was sent to the oracle, which said they must sacrifice a Greek if they were ever to return'

"'suspēnsī Eurypylum scītāt<u>um</u> ōrācula Phoebī
mittimus, isqu<u>e</u> adytīs haec trīstia dicta reportat: 115
"'sanguine plācāstis uentōs et uirgine caesā,
cum prīm<u>um</u> Īliacās^, Danaī, uēnistis ad ^ōrās;
sanguine quaerendī reditūs, animāque^ litandum
^Argolicā.'" uulgī quae uōx ut uēnit ad aurīs,
obstipuēre animī, gelidusque^ per īma* cucurrit   120
*ossa ^tremor, cūī fāta parent, quem poscat Apollō.'"

114 ***suspendō* 3 *suspēnsī suspēnsum* I keep in suspense; suspend, hang up; *suspēnsī* is nom. pl., with *mittimus*

Eurypyl-us ī 2m. Eurypylus, a Greek

scītātum = 'to consult' (*scītor* 1 dep.); supine of purpose, **RL**118.2, **M**97.8

ōrācul-um ī 2n. oracle

**Phoeb-us ī* 2m. Phoebus Apollo, god of Delphi (see also **121)

115 ***adyt-um ī* 2n. innermost shrine of a temple, sanctuary (only priests went there); supply *ab*

****dict-um ī* 2n. word

reportō 1 I bring back

116 *plācō* 1 I placate, mollify; *plācāstis* = *plācāuistis*; see p. 39 ((b)(ii))

uirgine: Agamemnon's daughter Iphigeneia was sacrificed to appease the goddess Artemis, thus ensuring the winds blew to take the fleet to Troy; note the hendiadys of *sanguine . . . uirgine* (see on 20), and enjoy the masterful positioning in the line of *sanguine* 116, *sanguine* 118 and *Argolicā* 119

***caedō* 3 *cecīdī caesum* I kill

117 ****Īliac-us a um* of Ilium

118 *quaerendī . . . litandum*: gerundives ('requiring to be -ed'), also requiring parts of *sum*; **RL**161, **W**39, **M**111

redit-us -ūs 4m. return

anim-a ae 1f. soul, life, spirit

litō 1 I obtain a favour by a sacrifice; here impersonal gerundive, lit. 'a favour must be obtained'; **RL**O2, **M**112

119 *uulgī*: construe with *aurīs*

quae uōx ut: 'As which/this voice . . .'

120 ****obstipēscō* 3 *obstipuī* I am astounded, dumbfounded. What form is *obstipuēre*?

gelid-us a um cold

****īm-us a um* deepest, bottom-most

****currō* 3 *cucurrī cursum* I run

121 *os oss-is* 3n. bone

tremor -is 3m. trembling, shivering

cūī . . . parent: note *parent*, subjunc. of *parō* 1. This, like *quem poscat Apollō*, is an indir. q. (**RL**R3, **W**30, **M**94) telling us what they were shivering (to think) about (cf. **123**), against Horsfall (2008) who reckons the subjuncs. are those of a 'fearing' clause implicit in *tremor*, **RL**S2(d), **W**40, **M**102–3. But the sense of the *cūī* clause depends on whether *fāta* is subject or obj. If obj., it means 'for whom they (understand the gods) were preparing *fāta* (of death)'; if subject, it means 'for whom the fates were preparing (understand *mortem*)'. The latter is the solution of Horsfall (2008), but I find it unconvincing. If one does not like either, two emendations are possible: replace *cūī* with *quid*, as obj. of *fāta*; or replace *parent* with *paret*, with Apollo as subject from the *quem* clause

Apollō: god of the oracle at Delphi and of prophecy

2.114–21: The horse has crept out of the bag, but is now hurriedly stuffed back in again as if there never had been a horse (or a bag) – a good tactic to maintain audience interest. We shall return to it. Sinon immediately moves on to the 'oracle' which, he fabricates, the Greeks consulted to help them with the weather. It is very persuasive to claim that you have your instructions from an oracle; and it makes it even more credible to relate its response to the well-known story of Agamemnon having to sacrifice his daughter Iphigenia in order to get the winds for Troy in the first place (116–17). So Sinon's 'oracle' – if the Greeks want a wind for home, blood is required (118–19) – perfectly matches the previous one. But whose blood? An animal's? No: *animā* (118), i.e. a human's – pause – *Argolicā* (119, emphatic position). No Trojan captive will do: it must be *Greek* blood. No

2.122–31: 'Ulysses sent for the prophet Calchas who, after a long silence, said Sinon should be the victim'

'"hīc Ithacus uātem^ magnō* ^Calchanta *tumultū
prōtrahit in mediōs; quae sint ea nūmina dīuum
flāgitat. et mihi iam multī^ crūdēle* canēbant
artificis *scelus, et ^tacitī uentūra uidēbant.   125
bis quīnōs^ silet ille ^diēs, tēctusque recūsat
prōdere uōce suā quemqu<u>am</u> aut oppōnere mortī.
uix tandem, magnīs^ Ithacī ^clāmōribus āctus,

Learning vocabulary

adyt-um ī 2n. innermost shrine of a temple, sanctuary
caedō 3 cecīdī caesum I kill
currō 3 cucurrī cursum I run
dict-um ī 2n. word
Īliac-us a um of Ilium
īm-us a um deepest, bottom-most
obstipēscō 3 obstipuī I am astounded, dumbfounded
Phoeb-us ī 2m. Phoebus Apollo, god of Delphi
suspendō 3 suspēnsī suspēnsum I keep in suspense; suspend, hang up

122 uāt-ēs is 3m. prophet
Calchanta: acc. of Calchas, priest and prophet of the Greek army, but 'secretly' in league with Ulysses (see 100), as Sinon wants the Trojans to believe
tumult-us ūs 4m. uproar; this is an abl. of accompanying or attendant circumstances RLL(f)
123 prōtrahō 3 I drag forward
quae sint: indir. q. after flāgitat. As S. says, they knew what the oracle said; they wanted to know who was to be sacrificed

124 flāgitō 1 I demand, ask repeatedly
mihi: 'for me', i.e. as directed at me (dat. of disadvantage)
canō 3 I detect, divine; here impf., 'began to . . .'
125 artifex artific-is 3m. schemer, trickster (Ulysses)
scelus: exactly the way Sinon would represent what Ulysses was planning to do to him
**tacit-us a um silent; probably 'though keeping silent [about it]'
uentūra: n. pl. acc., 'things-about-to-come' for Sinon
126 **bis twice, two times
quīn-ī ae a five each
**sileō 2 I fall silent, keep quiet
ille: Calchas
diēs: acc. of time throughout RL71, W37, M71
tēctus: i.e. in his tent
*recūsō 1 I fight against, refuse, decline to (+ inf.)
127 **prōdō 3 prōdidī prōditum I betray, unmask
*oppōnō 3 opposuī oppositum I expose (X acc.) to; object; oppose
128 **uix scarcely, hardly

wonder Sinon invents a terrified response across the Greek army as they wonder – who (S.)? This is quite brilliant story-telling, everything completely plausible (and complete lies).

Score
False: everything

Crunch: 118–121

2.122–31: *Ithacus*: it had to be him, of course. Sinon persuasively elaborates a picture of a huge, shouting rabble (122) and the priest being *dragged* in (123). Why? Because he wants to convince the Trojans that the whole thing was set up by the evil Ulysses, i.e. that the oracle gave Ulysses a golden chance to finger *him*. Ulysses' 'demand' (123–4) relates not to the meaning of the oracle, of course, but to the identity of the victim; and Sinon describes how many soldiers already 'foresaw' where the fickle finger was pointing, but said nothing (125 *tacitī* – a lovely touch. They, he implies, knew their Ulysses and had no intention of crossing him). The artifice, as Sinon claims it is, is continued by Calchas, who retires for ten days to 'consider' his verdict, as if to make it all the more credible (S.)

compositō rumpit uōc<u>em</u> et mē dēstinat ārae.
adsēnsēr<u>e</u> omnēs et, quae^ sibi quisque timēbat,   130
ūnius* in *miser<u>ī</u> exitium ^conuersa, tulēre.'"

2.132–44: 'Sinon was prepared for sacrifice but escaped; knowing that he now stood no chance of ever returning home, he asked us to take pity on him'

"'iamque diēs īnfand<u>a</u> aderat; mihi sacra parārī

129 *compositō* by agreement (with Ulysses); i.e. the long silence is simply part of the act that Sinon claims Ulysses and Calchas have got up against him

*rumpō 3 *rūpī ruptum* I break (+ *uōcem* 'into'); burst forth

dēstinō 1 I mark out

130–1 *adsēnsēre* = *adsēnsērunt, adsentiō* 'I agree'

quae ... quisque: 'what every man' (subject) [*sibi timēbat*], *tulēre* 'they accepted, [when it was] conuersa in exitium ...*' Sinon claims that he is to act as the 'scapegoat', relieving everyone else of what they 'feared' would 'befall' them

Learning vocabulary

bis twice, two times

oppōnō 3 *opposuī oppositum* I expose (X acc.) to; object; oppose

prōdō 3 *prōdidī prōditum* I betray

recūsō 1 I fight against, refuse, decline

rumpō 3 *rūpī ruptum* I break (into), burst forth

sileō 2 I fall silent, keep quiet

tacit-us a um silent

uix scarcely, hardly

132 *sacra*: n. pl. 'rituals'

parārī: historic inf., cf. on 98 above

(126–7). *prōdere* (127) is elegant: Sinon 'knew' that it was all a set-up and he was their man. Ulysses again is made to act the part to demand an answer to a foregone conclusion from a 'reluctant' Calchas (128), and Sinon is named. With a sigh of relief, everyone agrees – not, Sinon implies, because they hated him (S.), but because *someone* had to die, and they could put up with any man's death as long as it was not their own (130–1). What a brilliant display of the art of lying – every little detail of the whole, completely fictional, conspiracy against Sinon carefully engineered to draw Trojans into its web.

To re-emphasise: the whole story is an invention. There was no Ulyssean plot against Sinon, no oracle, no earnest debate among the soldiers, no 'reluctant' Calchas, no pointing fingers. The only 'plot' was the Greeks cooking up this brilliantly persuasive pack of lies for Sinon to spin. Observe that it is especially effective for Sinon to claim that he was the helpless subject of a conspiracy, engineered by the Trojans' great hate-figure, Ulysses. A dupe of Ulysses, how could Sinon, this poor, wronged man, possibly deceive anyone else? No wonder the Trojans warm to him; Sinon's story feeds Trojan prejudices to perfection, confirming everything they have ever believed, or wanted to believe, about Greeks, and especially about Ulysses. They themselves, of course, are the real victims of this elegant deception.

Score

False: everything

Sinon's image: (i) a badly wronged, innocent victim of Ulysses' plotting (128–31) (ii) fellow soldiers sympathetic to him (124–5, 130–1)

2.132–44: With a bound, he was free! And in the nick of time too (156)! This is all a little glib, but Sinon gets away with it. Note how careful he is to assert that he had no idea how

et salsae frūgēs et circum tempora uittae.
ēripuī, fateor, lētō mē et uincula rūpī,
līmōsōque lacū per noctem obscūrus^ in uluā   135
^dēlituī dum uēla darent, sī forte dedissent.
nec mihi iam patriam antīquam spēs ūlla uidendī
nec dulcīs nātōs exoptātumque parentem,

133 *sals-us a um* salted
frūx frūg-is 3f. crops, fruits; here 'corn, meal'. This
    was sprinkled on the victim's head
tempor-a um 3n. pl. temples (of head)
*uitt-a ae 1f. woollen headband ('fillet'), worn
    by priests and featuring in many religious
    rituals
134 *fateor* 2 dep. I admit (a nice pseudo-apologetic
    touch)
*lēt-um ī 2n. death ('from', either abl. or dat. after
    ēripuī); note that he does not say 'sacrifice' (S.)
*uincul-um ī 2n. chain, bond
135 *līmōs-us a um* marshy
lac-us ūs 4m. lake (here local abl.); Marius, outlawed
    by and fleeing from Sulla, took refuge in the
    marshes at Minturnae in 88 BC
**obscūr-us a um thick, obscuring, dark
ulu-a ae 1f. water-side reeds/grasses, sedge
136 *dēlitēscō* 3 I go into hiding
dum: here + subjunc., meaning . . .? The clause

indicates what Sinon said he was thinking at the
time ('I'll wait till *uēla dent*, if ever they will have
[*dederint*, fut. perf.]'), which, converted into
reported speech in past time, becomes *daret* and
dedissent. See **RL**165.2, **M**119, 124–5 for *dum*; and
RLR4, **W**Suppl. syntax, **M**83–4 for subordinate
clauses in indir. speech
**uēl-um ī 2n. sail, canvas (with *dare*, 'set sail')
137 ***antīqu-us a um* ancient (often with overtones
    of 'noble, 'venerable', S.)
spēs: understand *est*
uidendī: gerund, **RL**175, N, **W**39, **M**109
138 ***nāt-us a um* born (from + abl. of origin/
    source); as noun, *nātus*, son (m.) or *nāta*,
    daughter. These children appear quite suddenly
    and unexpectedly; there was no indication of
    them when he claims his father sent him to Troy
    (86–7)
exoptō 1 I long for, hanker after. Sinon is racking up
    the emotion

the Greeks would react to his escape, i.e. whether, no sacrifice having been offered, they
would sail or not (136). This is further dodgy ground for him. His story is that the oracle
had demanded a sacrifice so that the Greeks could get good weather and sail back to
Greece. But the sacrifice had not happened. So how could the Greeks sail off, the god
unappeased? Sinon therefore keeps it vague, as if he does not know. How could he
know, he implies, lying hidden in a lake? (S. comments that it is always a clever move to
fudge the issue when the argument becomes tricky.) So he moves quickly on to the consequences of his escape for himself and his (non-existent) family (always a sympathy-
winner, S.; but see on 138) back in Greece (137–40) – who, he says, would have to pay
for his escape from death (because he violated the dues owed to gods) with their own
blood. Tragic! What a home-loving, pious fellow Sinon is, and how, by implication,
utterly dependent on the Trojans (S.), who are all he has left. Sinon at once reinforces
the image of himself that he has constructed by screwing the emotion up to an even
higher pitch and calling on heavenly powers of truth and trust (if any still resides anywhere, he says – a rich irony) to back up his appeal for pity.

An important feature of Virgil's style emerges in the course of the opening of Book 2,
i.e. Virgil's love of repeating ideas in different forms, e.g. 10–11, *cāsūs . . . labōrem*, 18–20
inclūdunt . . . complent, 56 *stāret . . . manērēs*, 92 *tenebrīs lūctūque*, 108–9 *fugam . . .
relictā . . . discēdere*, 139–40 *poenās . . . culpam*, 141 *superōs . . . nūmina*. If the main
purpose of this repetition is to look at matters from a different perspective, the challenge
is to identify that perspective. Might it be mere 'ornamentation' (cf. Ovid)?

See: O'Hara 'Virgil's Style' in Martindale (1997: 248) for Virgilian repetition.

quōs illī fors et poenās ob nostra^ reposcent
^effugi_a_, et culp_am_ hanc miserōrum morte piābunt.   140
quod tē, per superōs et cōnscia nūmina uērī,
per, sī qua^ est quae restet adhūc mortālibus usquam
^intemerāta ^fidēs, ōrō, miserēre labōrum
tantōrum, miserēr_e_ animī^ nōn digna ^ferentis.'''

2.145–61: 'We pitied him, and Priam made him one of us, before asking what the wooden horse was for. Sinon said he would tell us, it being no crime now for him to break an oath of allegiance to the Greeks'

'hīs lacrimīs uītam damus et miserēscimus ultrō.   145
ipse^ uirō ^prīmus manicās atqu_e_ arta* leuārī

139 _quōs_ ('from whom') . . . _poenās_: double acc. after _reposcō_
illī: subject, 'the Greeks'
fors perhaps
_et_ = 'even'
_ob_ on account of (+ acc.)
nostra: i.e. my ('royal' we)
reposcō 3 I demand X (acc., _poenās_) from Y (acc., here _quōs_)
140 _effugi-um_ _ī_ 2n. flight, escape
hanc: i.e. my
miserōrum: i.e. of my children and father
piō 1 I expiate, wash away
141 _quod_: 'in relation to which', 'wherefore'
per: in the name of; this controls _superōs . . . nūmina_ . . . **142** '[and] if there is any _intemerāta fidēs quae_' etc.
_tē_: object of _ōrō_ (**143**)!
142 _restet_: an 'indefinite' subjunc. (**RL**140.1, **Q**2(a), **W**38), implying a vagueness to the possibility and so adding 'a new touch of pathos to Sinon's [bogus] despair' (Austin)
adhūc up to this point, so far
*_mortāl-is e_ mortal
143 _intemerāt-us a um_ pure, undefiled
144 *_misereor_ 2 dep. I take pity on (+ gen.); here 2s. imper. (twice)

nōn digna ferentis: here _ferō_ means 'endure', but might Sinon also be _bringing_ 'things they do not deserve' to the Trojans, cf. 49 _et dōna ferentīs_?!

Learning vocabulary
antīqu-us a um ancient (often with overtones of 'noble', 'venerable')
lēt-um ī 2n. death
misereor 2 dep. I take pity on (+ gen.)
mortāl-is e mortal
nāt-us a um born (from + abl.)
nāt-us ī 2m., _nāt-a ae_ 1f. son, daughter
obscūr-us a um thick, obscuring, dark
uēl-um ī 2n. sail, canvas (with _dare_, 'set sail')
uincul-um ī 2n. chain, bond
uitt-a ae 1f. woollen headband, worn by priests and in many religious rituals

145 _hīs lacrimīs_: causal abl., referring to Sinon's tears
miserēscō 3 I pity, have compassion
ultrō in addition (S.)
146 _uirō_: dat., 'from the man'
manic-a ae 1f. handcuff; Sinon had arrived with hands bound (57)
**_art-us a um_ tight
**_leuō_ 1 I lever up, lift, lighten

Score
False: everything
Sinon's image: (i) patriotic and family-loving (137–40) (ii) pious (140) (iii) worthy of pity and undeserving of his fate (143–4)

Crunch: 141–4

2.145–61: The pack of lies Sinon has told so far has been directed at winning Trojan trust by showing himself to be a right-minded, devout, loyal and honest Greek, foully

*uincla iubet ^Priamus dictīsque^ ita fātur ^amīcīs:
"quisquis es, āmissōs^ hinc iam oblīuīscere ^Graiōs
(noster eris) mihique^ haec ēdissere uēra ^rogantī:
quō mōlem hanc immānis equī statuēre? quis auctor?   150
quidue petunt? quae rēligiō? aut quae māchina bellī?"
dīxerat. ille^, dolīs ^īnstrūctus et arte Pelasgā,
sustulit exūtās^ uinclīs ad sīdera ^palmās:

---

147 *uincla* = *uincula* (see also **153**)

148 *quisquis es*: Sinon had not told them who his
father was (cf. 74, Horsfall (2008)). S. notes that
the formula *quisquis es noster eris* was used by
Roman generals welcoming a deserter from the
other side – good (anachronistic) Roman
language

āmissōs: i.e. to whom you will never go back

oblīuīscor 3 dep. I forget. *oblīuīscere* is an imper.;
analyse it carefully and compare/contrast it with
ēdissere (**149**)

**Grai-us a um* Greek; *Grai-ī ōrum* 2m. pl. the
Greeks (also **157**)

149 *haec*: obj. of *rogantī* ('to [me] asking'); *uēra* is
obj. of *ēdissere*

ēdisserō 3 I expound, explain

150 *quō* to what end?

**immān-is e huge, vast; savage, brutal. S. records
that the horse was 120 foot long and 30 foot broad,
and its tail, knees and eyes moved! The
measurement, apparently, goes back to the epic
poet Arctinus (seventh century BC, cf. *Appendix* **1**)

**statuō 3 *statuī statūtum* I establish, found; resolve,
decide (*statuēre* = *statuērunt*)

auctor -is 3m. inventor

151 *rēligiō -nis 3f. sacred offering, religious awe,
conscience, ritual

152 *dolīs . . . et arte*: hendiadys? (See **Glossary of
literary terms**)

**īnstruō 3 *īnstrūxī īnstrūctum* I prepare, ready,
draw up

153 *exuō* 3 *exuī exūtum* I put off, unbind, strip (+
abl. of that of which one is stripped)

**palm-a ae 1f. palm (of hands)

---

ill-treated and tricked by Ulysses, as a result of which he has come within an inch of
being sacrificed. The strategy has worked (145): the Trojans have given him his life and
taken pity on him. So he has them in the palm of his hands from which they have
removed the bonds (146). Now comes the crunch – his real purpose, which is to persuade the Trojans to bring the horse into the city.

   We remember that Sinon has mentioned the horse already (112–13), but just once,
quite casually. That was a tempter, designed to make the Trojans wonder why it was
there, and Sinon had implied that it could be a devotional object of some sort, to help
the Greeks get a wind for home. The reason Sinon left the topic was because he did not
want to raise it himself. That might look too obvious ('Now, er, let me tell you all about
that, er, horse there, um . . .'). *He wanted the Trojans to raise it.* Now Priam, telling him
to forget the Greeks and regard the Trojans as his new best friends (148–9), steps, all
unknowing, into the trap with an unparalleled volley of short, sharp questions, that he
has clearly been bursting to ask (150–1: note *rēligiō* 151 – he had taken Sinon's hint).
dīxerat says the text, baldly (152). He had indeed. The trap silently shuts. Trojan
dependency on Sinon is complete. No wonder he turns to holy powers to see him
through this final stage of the deception: a prayer of blackest hypocrisy, from one
point of view, and of potential glorious triumph – the capture of Troy itself – from
another.

   To take an oath is to invoke higher powers to uphold its truth, and to bring curses on
oneself if it turns out to be false. Sinon here calls on the Sun and Moon (154–5), the altar
and swords where he was to be sacrificed and the headbands he was wearing at the time
(*ēnsēs* apart, these are sacred objects). In their name, he claims, he has a right (*fās* 157–8)
to break his oath of loyalty to the *Greeks*, and so tell the Trojans the (apparent) 'secret' of

"uōs, aeternī ignēs, et nōn uiolābile^ ^uestrum
testor ^nūmen," ait, "uōs ārae ēnsēsque nefandī,   155
quōs fūgī, uittaeque deum, quās hostia gessī:
fās mihi Graiōrum sacrāta^ resoluere ^iūra,
fās ōdisse uirōs atque omnia ferre sub aurās,
sī qua tegunt, teneor patriae nec lēgibus ūllīs.
tū modo prōmissīs maneās seruātaque seruēs,   160
Troia, fidem, sī uēra feram, sī magna rependam.'"

---

154 **aetern-us a um* eternal; with *ignēs* = the
heavenly bodies, i.e. the Sun and the Moon, which
see everything and therefore know everything, to
whom Sinon is raising his hands: *uestrum nūmen*
boils down to the same thing, 'your godhead'
uiolābil-is e that may be violated
155 *testor* 1 dep. I call on (to bear witness)
ait: scans as two syllables
**ēns-is is* 3m. sword
nefand-us a um impious, wicked (because they
threatened him with unjust death)
156 *hosti-a ae* 1f. sacrificial animal (in apposition to
'I')
157 **fās* 3n. duty, divine law; S. suggests *sit* should
be supplied rather than *est*. More Roman
anachronism, like the rest of the appeal to *iūra*
and *lēgēs* (**159**)
**sacrāt-us a um* hallowed, set apart, sacred
resoluō 3 *resoluī resolūtum* I break
**iūs iūr-is* 3n. law, ordinance, justice, right
158 *ōdī ōdisse* I hate
**aur-a ae* 1f. open air, breeze; *ferre sub aurās* =
'bring into the open'
159 *qua*: 'anything' (= *quae*, indef., n. pl. acc.)
**tegō* 3 *tēxī tēctum* I cover, hide, protect
teneor: begin with clause with *nec*
160 *tū*: referring to *Troia* **161**!
prōmiss-um ī 2n. promise

maneās . . . seruēs: jussive subjuncs. **RL**152, **W**28,
M34, 89
seruātaque: agreeing with *Troia*, the subject of *seruēs*
161 *Troia*: far more dramatic and binding than
appealing merely to Trojans
rependō 3 I pay in return

Learning vocabulary

aetern-us a um eternal
art-us a um tight
aur-a ae 1f. open air, breeze
ēns-is is 3m. sword
fās 3n. duty, divine law
Gra-ī ōrum 2m. pl. the Greeks
Grai-us a um Greek
immān-is e huge, vast; savage, brutal
īnstruō 3 *īnstrūxī īnstrūctum* I prepare, ready, draw
up
iūs iūr-is 3n. law, ordinance, justice, right
leuō 1 I lever up, lift, lighten
palm-a ae 1f. palm (of hands)
rēligiō -nis 3f. sacred offering, religious awe,
conscience, ritual
resoluō 3 *resoluī resolūtum* I break
sacrāt-us a um hallowed, set apart, sacred
statuō 3 *statuī statūtum* I establish, found; resolve,
decide
tegō 3 *tēxī tēctum* I cover, hide, protect

---

the horse (this oath is an anachronistic touch, presumably the contemporary Roman
oath of military loyalty, the *sacrāmentum*, 'that a soldier, going out to battle, should
swear to do nothing against the interests of the state', S.). At first sight, this looks like a
dreadful thing to do: publicly announcing that you were going to break an oath would
surely result in instant divine condemnation. But as S. points out, this is all elegantly
ambiguous. Sinon is breaking no 'oath of loyalty' (whether he took one or not) to the
Greeks. Quite the reverse. He keeps any oath of loyalty to them very firmly, by ensuring
the Trojans are led straight into the trap. Further, when he says he is no longer subject to
Greek law (159), he is (for once) telling the truth, since he has been made an honorary
'Trojan' (149). Again, his demand that they repay him for his information by swearing
to save him, if he keeps them safe (160–1), is meaningless: for if he does not save them
(i.e. the Greeks take Ilium), there will be nothing they can do about him anyway, but if
he accidentally does save them (i.e. the plan to take Ilium goes catastrophically wrong),

2.162–79: 'Sinon said the Greeks had lost the confidence of Minerva because they stole the Palladium, her image, from her temple in Ilium. When the image started acting strangely, Calchas said they had to take it back to Greece, consult the omens and then return with it to Troy'

"'omnis spēs Dana<u>um</u> et coeptī^ fidūcia ^bellī
Palladis auxiliīs semper stetit. impius^ ex quō
^Tȳdīdēs sed enim scelerumqu<u>e</u> inuentor Vlixēs,
fātāl<u>e</u>^ adgressī sacrāt<u>ō</u>* āuellere *templō   165
^Palladium, caesīs^ summae* ^custōdibus *arcis,
corripuēre sacr<u>am</u> effigiem, manibusque cruentīs
uirgineās^ ausī dīuae contingere ^uittās:
ex illō fluer<u>e</u> ac retrō sublāpsa^ referrī
^spēs Danaum, frāctae uīrēs, āuersa^ deae ^mēns.   170

162 *coeptī*: i.e. the war they had begun
163 *Palladis*: gen. s.; note the emphatic position
stetit: (note s. for pl.) 'stood firm on' + abl.
**impi-us a um unholy, godless; begin the sentence
with *sed enim* 'but indeed'
ex quō 'from what time/the time when . . .', picked
up by *ex illō*, 'from that time' (**169**). The *ex quō*
clause involves Diomedes and Ulysses entering
(*adgressī* **165**), killing (*caesīs* **166**), seizing
(*corripuēre* **167**) and daring to touch (*ausī . . .
contingere* **168**)
164 *******Tȳdīdēs* nom. s. Diomedes (see on 1.97)
sed enim: 'but [it did not always stand firm] for . . .',
'but the fact is . . .'
inuentor -is 3m. inventor
165 *fātāl-is e* fateful
adgredior 3 dep. *adgressus* I set about, undertake
āuellō 3 I tear away
166 ******Palladi-um ī* 2n. the Palladium, a sacred
image of Minerva in her temple on the citadel of
Ilium

167 *******corripiō* 3 *corripuī correptum* I snatch up,
seize; speed along
effigi-ēs ēī 5f. image
**cruent-us a um bloody, bloodthirsty. S. says there
are three reasons for the god's anger: guards
killed, statue taken and headbands touched with
bloody hands
168 *uirgine-us a um* virgin
ausī: understand *sunt*
**contingō 3 *contigī contāctum* I touch, reach,
influence; happen
169 *******fluō* 3 *flūxī flūxum* I flow, ebb (away) (here,
historic inf., like *referrī*; see on 1.423. The image is
tidal). **169–70** contain a typical run of roughly
similar ideas
*retrō back(wards)
sublābor 3 dep. *sublāpsus* I slip back
***referō referre rettulī relātum* I bring/carry back,
return; recall, recount
170 *******āuertō* 3 *āuersī āuersum* I divert; turn back/
away/round

---

he is dead meat. The whole oath is formally and solemnly uttered – another impressive, and at the same time, if you are Aeneas, indescribably vile and sickening, performance.

Score
Sinon's image: a man you can trust (145–61)

Crunch: 145–7

2.162–79: Sinon begins, as usual, with a sprinkling of facts sparkling alluringly over the web of lies (S.): Greek hopes were indeed pinned on Minerva's continuing help (162–3), and (as the Trojans well knew) Ulysses and Diomedes had indeed stolen their Palladium (163–8), a sort of talisman which, an oracle said, the Greeks had to seize if Ilium were to fall. This is typical of Sinon's tactics: (i) begin with an incontrovertible truth to establish your credentials as an honest man; (ii) spin off from it a new story of gripping interest to

nec dubiīs^ ea signa dedit Trītōnia ^mōnstrīs.
uix positum^ castrīs ^simulācr<u>um</u>: ārsēre coruscae^
lūminibus* ^flamm<u>ae</u> *arrēctīs, salsusque^ per artūs
^sūdor iit, terqu<u>e</u> ipsa solō (mīrābile dictū)
ēmicuit, parmamque ferēns hastamque trementem.   175
extemplō temptanda^ fugā canit ^aequora Calchās,
nec poss<u>e</u> Argolicīs^ exscindī Pergama ^tēlīs,
ōmina nī repetant Argīs nūmenque^ redūcant
–^quod pelag<u>ō</u> et curuīs^ sēc<u>um</u> āuēxēre ^carīnīs.'"

171 **dubi-us a um* doubtful
ea signa: i.e. signs of this
Trītōni-a ae 1f. = Minerva; S. suggests *Trītōnia*
   might derive from 'terrifying' (Greek *treō* 'I fear':
   typically hopeless ancient etymologising), or be
   connected with the river Trito in Boeotia, or
   because Minerva was born near lake Tritonis in
   north Africa
mōnstr-um ī 2n. sign, portent
172 *castrīs*: ellipsis of *in*
**simulācr-um ī* 2n. image, statue. Supply 'when'
   before *ārsēre*
****corusc-us a um* tremulous, shimmering; flashing;
   the statue seems to come to life
173 ***arrēct-us* raised; pricked up. Minerva is lifting
   up her flashing eyes in fury
sals-us a um salty
****art-us ūs* 4m. limb
174 *sūdor -is* 3m. sweat; Roman portents regularly
   involve an object sweating (anachronism)
****ter* three times (a ritual number)
ipsa: i.e. the statue, meaning the divinity inside it;
   perhaps 'of its own accord'
****sol-um ī* 2n. ground (here '*from* the ground')
****mīrābil-is e* miraculous
dictū: 'to relate'. See on 1.111
175 *ēmicō* 1 *ēmicuī* I spring forth (i.e. the goddess
   leapt into sight)

parm-a ae 1f. shield; the statue is wearing full
   armour
trementem: emphatic position; presumably Minerva
   meant business
176 *extemplō* suddenly
**temptō* 1 I attempt, try out (ellipsis of *esse* in indir.
   speech after *canit*; *posse* is inf. for the same
   reason)
canō 3 I prophesy
177 *exscindō* 3 I demolish
****Pergam-a ōrum* 2n. the citadel of Ilium
178 ***ōmen ōmin-is* 3n. omen
****nī = nisi*
****repetō* 3 *repetīuī repetītum* I repeat; begin from,
   return to, recall. This is subjunc., like *redūcant*,
   because it reports in indirect speech what Calchas
   said ('if you will not . . .'), **RL**71, **W**37, **M**71
nūmen: here = the Palladium, envisaged as the spirit
   that dwells within it that needed appeasing
179: the dash in the text indicates that this line is a
   statement by Sinon on what the Greeks are now
   doing – taking the Palladium back to Greece. It is
   no part of what Calchas is claimed to have said,
   and therefore the vb is not in the subjunc.
**curu-us a um* curved
āuehō 3 *āuēxī auectum* I carry off
**carīn-a ae* 1f. ship (lit. 'keel')

the Trojans, which (iii) is designed to further your ultimate end, whatever lies it involves. The vital thing, he knows, is to keep the audience's keenest attention. So give them only what they want to hear, but (just as important) keep it new. Reach your goal with a variety of different tales from different angles. This helps maintain audience interest, but more important does not allow them to think too hard about the details. You are, after all, lying through your teeth: short, sharp lies spread over a range of disparate topics are less easy to see through than lies which have to remain consistent throughout the course of a long, single narrative.

Sinon continues to feed Trojan prejudices about impious (cf. 163–4) Greeks by claiming that the Palladium had been violated (167–8) and reacted accordingly (171–5). The result was the decline of Greek fortunes (169–70). Hence Calchas' warning: take it back to Greece, take the omens afresh there and then return to Troy with the newly

2.180–98: 'Sinon said the Greeks had now left for home, leaving the horse to atone for their sin against Minerva. He said that if the Trojans did not violate it, but took it into the city, it was fated that Troy would take the battle to Greece'

'"et nunc quod patriās^ uentō petiēre ^Mycēnās,   180
arma deōsque parant comitēs, pelagōque remēnsō

Learning vocabulary

arrēct-us raised, pricked up
art-us ūs 4m. limb
āuertō 3 *āuersī āuersum* I divert; turn back/away/round
carīn-a ae 1f. ship
contingō 3 *contigī contāctum* I touch, reach, influence; happen
corripiō 3 *corripuī correptum* I snatch up, seize; speed along
corusc-us a um tremulous, shimmering; flashing
cruent-us a um bloody, bloodthirsty
curu-us a um curved
dubi-us a um doubtful
fluō 3 *flūxī flūxum* I flow, ebb (away)
impi-us a um unholy, godless
mīrābil-is e miraculous
nī = nisi
ōmen ōmin-is 3n. omen
Palladi-um ī 2n. the Palladium, a sacred image of Minerva

Pergam-a ōrum 2n. the citadel of Ilium
referō referre rettulī relātum I bring/carry back, return; recall, recount
repetō 3 *repetīuī repetītum* I repeat; begin from, return to, recall
retrō back(wards)
simulācr-um ī 2n. image, statue
sol-um ī 2n. ground
temptō 1 I attempt, try
ter three times
Tȳdīdēs nom. s., Diomedes, a Greek warrior

180 *et nunc quod* 'now as to the fact that', 'the reason they have . . . [is because] *parant* . . .' Horsfall (2008) wonders if V. in fact wrote *quī* for *quod* 'those who . . .'
181 *comitēs*: in apposition to *deōs*; the gods having deserted them, the Greeks must win their support again back in Greece in order to be able to 'return' with their blessing to Troy
remētior 4 dep. *remēnsus* I go back over (here abl. abs. with pass. sense)

appeased goddess and Palladium. This was good Roman practice (more of V.'s anachronism): as S. says, to ensure that any expedition had set out with the gods' favour in the first place, 'if they had taken to the field and fought badly, they returned to take the auspices again'. Some commentators get worried that this whole story is 'inconsistent' because it is not what the tradition said happened – but of course it isn't! Sinon is lying about the violation and its aftermath; he is feeding the Trojans exactly what they want to hear about sacrilegious Greeks, so persuasively, indeed, that he has taken in the commentators too.

Score
True: (i) Greek reliance on Minerva (ii) Ulysses and Diomedes stole the Palladium
False: (i) the violation of the Palladium (ii) Minerva's hostility (iii) the Palladium's behaviour (iv) Calchas' insistence that, if the Greeks are to take Ilium, they return with it to Greece and then bring it back (v) the Greeks are now taking it back to Greece.
Sinon's image: shocked by Greek impiety (163–8)

Crunch: 167–70

2.180–98: Sinon moves in for the kill with a tightly woven argument, pointing in one direction only:

imprōuīsī aderunt; ita dīgerit ōmina Calchās.
hanc^ prō Palladiō monitī, prō nūmine laesō
^effigiem^ statuēre, nefās* ^quae *trīste piāret.
hanc^ tamen ^immēnsam Calchās attollere ^mōlem   185
rōboribus textīs caelōque ēdūcere iussit,
nē recipī portīs aut dūcī in moenia posset,
neū populum antīquā^ sub ^rēligiōne tuērī.
nam sī uestra manus uiolāsset dōna Mineruae,
tum magnum exitium^ (quod* dī prius *ōmen in ipsum   190

182 **_imprōuīs-us a um_ unexpected, sudden (irony!
  They will indeed)
dīgerō 3 I arrange, analyse, expound (the _ōmina_ refer
  to the Palladium, cf. 171). The fact that Calchas is
  expounding an omen allows Sinon to get away
  with a certain vagueness at this point
183 _prō_: 'in place of' and 'in compensation for' (the
  latter referring to _nūmine laesō_)
monitī: by (the Trojans are expected to think)
  Calchas
**_laedō_ 3 _laesī laesum_ I damage, injure, offend,
  wrong
184 _effigi-ēs ēī_ 5f. statue
statuēre = _statuērunt_ (the inf. would be _statuere_)
*_nefās_ 3n. crime against divine law
piō 1 I expiate; note subjunc. in rel. clause expressing
  purpose, RL145.3, M97.5
185 *_immēns-us a um_ huge
attollō 3 raise, build
186 *_rōbur rōbor-is_ 3n. oak (see on _abiēs_, 2.16)
texō 3 _texuī textum_ I weave
caelō: dat. 'to the sky'

ēdūcō 3 I build up
moeni-a um 3n. (defensive) walls; fortified town
187 _nē_: introducing a neg. purpose clause,
  understood subject 'the horse', whose main vb
  posset controls three infs., _recipī, dūcī_ and _tuērī_
  188, RL145, W28, M96–8
188 _neū_: not _nec_, because it is in a purpose clause
  introduced by _nē_ 187 (M97)
tueor 2 dep. I protect, shelter
189 _nam sī . . . nepōtēs_ (194): acc. and inf., as Sinon
  reports what Calchas said. Begin 'For Calchas
  said that if . . .'; _uestra_ refers to the Trojans (and
  192)
uiolō 1 I violate; _uiolāsset_ is a reported fut. perf.;
  Calchas said 'If you will have . . .' Calchas is now
  imagined to go on to say that if the Trojans
  violate the horse, that will be the end of their
  empire; but if they bring it into the city
  (_ascendisset_ 192) . . .
190 _quod . . . ōmen_: 'which/this omen/augury'. Here
  Sinon interrupts his account of Calchas' 'words'

(i)   The Greeks will soon be back (181–2), i.e. the Trojans had better act fast, while they
      are safe from the Greeks (!) and still can (S. comments 'Sinon extremely skilfully
      plays on Trojan fears for the future: his revelation of the Greeks' secret plans seems
      to demonstrate the [future] danger they are in, and to that extent makes them feel
      secure about the present – to encourage them to throw caution to the winds');
(ii) the horse was specifically designed to be too big to be brought into Ilium (187–8),
      raising in Trojan minds the question they had already been asking, 'Why so big?' (cf.
      150);
(iii) now comes the reason – because if you do not violate it (by e.g. treating it as
      Laocoon wanted) but bring it into the city, the Trojans will take the war to Greece
      itself (192–4), i.e. there is nothing to fear about its size. Calchas wanted it built that
      large to prevent the unthinkable (as far as Greeks were concerned) happening. As S.
      comments, 'since it was necessary for the Greeks to build a horse that size to contain
      the soldiers, Sinon emphasises the virtual impossibility of bringing it into the city in
      order to increase their desire to do so'.

The horse has now become an offering to a god, and its size has been explained. It
never occurs to the Trojans that this new story does not fully square with Sinon's initial

conuertant!) Priamī imperiō Phrygibusque ^futūrum;
sin manibus uestrīs uestr<u>am</u>^ ascendisset in ^urbem,
ultr<u>ō</u> Asiam^ magnō* Pelop<u>ēa</u>^ ad ^moenia *bellō
^uent<u>ūram</u>, et nostrōs^ ea fāta manēre ^nepōtēs.'"
tālibus īnsidiīs periūrīqu<u>e</u>^ arte ^Sinōnis   195
crēdita rēs, captīque dolīs lacrimīsque coāctīs
quōs neque Tȳdīdēs nec Lārīsaeus Achillēs,
nōn annī domuēre decem, nōn mīlle carīnae.'

191 *conuertant*: jussive subjunc. expressing a wish, RLL–V(a)4, **M**34
ipsum: i.e. on Calchas' head
futūrum: ellipsis of *esse*. This passage continues to report what Calchas said; hence *uentūram (esse)* and *manēre* **194**
192 *ascendō* 3 *ascendī* I ascend, climb, rise
193 *Asiam*: the land in which Troy is located
Pelopē-us a um of Pelops, grandfather of Agamemnon; the Peloponnese is the island (Greek *nēsos*) of Pelops
194 *nostrōs*: i.e. the Greeks
*nepōs nepōt-is 3m. descendant. Calchas is 'saying' that the fate (*ea fāta*) of destruction that could be visited on Troy – *magnum exitium,* **190** – was in fact *now* awaiting – *manēre* (note pres. tense) – the descendants of the Greeks, i.e. *uentūram* is all too certain. There is an irony here. Sinon is lying when he says there is an oracle that Trojans will conquer Greece if they take in the horse. But the Trojans, in the shape of Romans (!), will in fact come to Greece and conquer it in the second century BC (irony). See **1.278–88** and *Intro* [18]
195 **periūr-us a um* false, lying
196 *crēdita . . . captīque*: ellipsis of *est/sunt* respectively; for *captī*, tr. 'and the [men, i.e. we]

were captured *quōs* (acc., 'whom') neither T. nor A. nor . . . could conquer'
197 *neque . . . nec* (**198**) . . . *non . . . non*: Aeneas lets his true feeling show with this intense, resounding, pathos-filled roll-call of the mighty forces ranged against the Trojans that achieved nothing over ten long years. It took trickery and treachery to defeat them
Lārīsae-us from Larisa (N. Greece), Achilles' home territory. S. comments 'Aeneas honours the fighting abilities of Diomedes and Achilles, by both of whom he was defeated in battle' (see *Iliad* 5.297ff. (see on 1.97), 20.318ff.)
198 *domō* 3 *domuī* I tame, conquer; this vb controls all four subjects in **197–8**
mīlle: Homer's count is 1,186 ships (the total found in *Iliad* 2.494–759), but a round 1,000 had already been proposed by Aeschylus (*Agamemnon* 45). Thucydides went for 1,200 (1.10.4)

Learning vocabulary
immēns-us a um huge
imprōuīs-us a um unexpected
laedō 3 *laesī laesum* I damage, injure, offend, wrong
nefās 3n. crime against divine law
nepōs nepōt-is 3m. descendant
rōbur rōbor-is 3n. oak

mention of the horse, which seemed to imply it had been built much earlier to help the dejected Greeks get a favourable wind for home (110–13). Most important of all (psychologically), Sinon has (apparently) kept his side of the bargain by breaking the oath of loyalty he swore to the Greek army and revealing all about Greek plans (as he said he would, 157–8). Here, then, is a man who keeps his word, at whatever risk to himself from men or gods.

Aeneas' summary (195–8) is tragically apt: deceit, perjury, tricks and tears achieved what Diomedes and Achilles, ten years of war and a thousand ships never could. Pride and pain are mingled here. Greek efforts on the battlefield never brought the Trojans low; it took just one man spinning a pack of lies to do that. Trusting, gullible Trojans against one foul, treacherous Greek: no contest.

Score
False: everything

Sinon's image: (i) respects the gods (184) (ii) hates the Greeks (190–1) (iii) keeps his word, come what may.

Crunch: 195–8

Learning vocabulary for Section 2.57–198

adyt-um ī 2n. innermost shrine of a temple, sanctuary
aequor -is 3n. (calm) sea, ocean
aetern-us a um eternal
aether -is 3m. upper air, heaven
agmen agmin-is 3n. rank, (battle-) line
antīqu-us a um ancient (often with overtones of 'noble', 'venerable')
Arg-ī ōrum Argos, an important Greek city; Greece
arrēct-us raised, pricked up
art-us a um tight
art-us ūs 4m. limb
Atrīdae nom. pl., the sons of Atreus
āuertō 3 *āuersī āuersum* I divert; turn back/away/round
aur-a ae 1f. open air, breeze
aur-is -is 3f. ear
Auster Austr-ī 2m. south wind
bis twice, two times
caedō 3 *cecīdī caesum* I kill
Calchās (abl. *Calchante*) Calchas, the Greek army's chief priest
carīn-a ae 1f. ship
clāmor -is 3m. cry, shout
comes comit-is 3m. companion
cōnsci-us a um consciously, with deliberate intent, knowingly
contingō 3 *contigī contāctum* I touch, reach, influence; happen
conuertō 3 *conuertī conuersum* I change, convert, turn round
corripiō 3 *corripuī correptum* snatch up, seize; speed along
corusc-us a um tremulous, shimmering; flashing
cruent-us a um bloody, bloodthirsty
cūnct-us a um all
currō 3 *cucurrī cursum* I run
curu-us a um curved
Dardanid-ae um m. pl. Trojans (lit. 'sons of Dardanus', an early founder of Troy)
decus decōr-is 3n. honour, distinction, standing; ornament, decoration
dēmittō 3 *dēmīsī dēmissum* I hand/pass/send/cast down
dict-um ī 2n. word
dubi-us a um doubtful

ēns-is is 3m. sword
equidem [I] for my part
fals-us a um treacherous, false
fās 3n. duty, divine law
fess-us a um tired
fīdō 3 semi-dep. *fīsus* I put my trust in (+ gen.)
fidūci-a ae 1f. trust, confidence, faith (in)
fluō 3 *flūxī flūxum* I flow, ebb (away)
forte by chance
Gra-ī ōrum 2m. pl. the Greeks
Grai-us a um Greek
hēū alas
hiems hiem-is 3f. storm, winter
ignār-us a um ignorant (of + gen.)
ignōt-us a um unknown
Īliac-us a um of Ilium
immān-is e huge, vast; savage, brutal
immēns-us a um huge
impi-us a um unholy, godless
imprōuīs-us a um unexpected
īm-us a um deepest, bottom-most
īnstruō 3 *īnstrūxī īnstrūctum* I prepare, ready, draw up
Ithac-us a um Ithacan (i.e. Ulysses)
iūs iūr-is 3n. law, ordinance, justice, right
iuuentūs iuuentūt-is 3f. youth
laedō 3 *laesī laesum* I damage, injure, offend, wrong
lēt-um ī 2n. death
leuō 1 I lever up, lift, lighten
lūmen lūmin-is 3n. light
memorō 1 I say, tell, narrate, mention, address
mīrābil-is e miraculous
misereor 2 dep. I take pity on (+ gen.)
mōlior 4 dep. I construct, build; strive, labour at
moror 1 dep. I delay
mortāl-is e mortal
nāt-us a um born (from + abl.)
nāt-us ī, nāt-a ae son, daughter
nefās 3n. crime against divine law
nepōs nepōt-is 3m. descendant
nequīquam in vain, pointlessly
nī = nisi
nimb-us -ī 2m. cloud
obscūr-us a um thick, obscuring, dark
obstipēscō 3 *obstipuī* I am astounded, dumbfounded
odi-um ī 2n. hatred

offerō offerre obtulī oblātum I offer, hand over;
bring before, exhibit

ōmen ōmin-is 3n. omen

oppōnō 3 *opposuī oppositum* I expose (X acc.) to;
object; oppose

ōr-a ae 1f. shore

Palladi-um ī 2n. the Palladium, a sacred image of
Minerva

palm-a ae 1f. palm (of hands)

patri-us a um paternal, ancestral

pectus pector-is 3n. chest, breast, heart

Pelasg-ī ōrum 2m. pl. Greeks (the Pelasgi were an
ancient people living in north Greece)

Pelasg-us a um Greek

Pergam-a ōrum 2n. the citadel of Ilium

Phoeb-us ī 2m. Phoebus Apollo, god of Delphi

Phrygi-us a um Trojan

pont-us -ī 2m. sea

poscō 3 *poposcī* I demand, beg

praecipuē especially

prōdō 3 *prōdidī prōditum* I betray

recūsō 1 I fight against, refuse, decline

referō referre rettulī relātum I bring/carry back,
return; recall, recount

rēligiō -nis 3f. sacred offering, religious awe,
conscience, ritual

repetō 3 *repetīuī repetītum* I repeat; begin from,
return to, recall

resoluō 3 *resoluī resolūtum* I break

restō 1 I remain, am left over; survive from

retrō back(wards)

rēx rēg-is 3m. king

rōbur rōbor-is 3n. oak

rumpō 3 *rūpī ruptum* I break (into), burst forth

ruō 3 *ruī rutum* I rush; drive ahead; churn up

sacrāt-us a um hallowed, set apart, sacred

sanguis sanguin-is 3m. blood; family, line

sileō 2 I fall silent, keep quiet

simulācr-um ī 2n. image, statue

Sinōn -is 3m. Sinon, a Greek sent to trick the
Trojans

sol-um ī 2n. ground

sonō 1 *sonuī* I sound, echo, thunder

statuō 3 *statuī statūtum* I establish, found; resolve,
decide

super moreover; (+ acc.) above, over

suspendō 3 *suspēnsī suspēnsum* I keep in suspense;
suspend, hang up

tacit-us a um silent

tegō 3 *tēxī tēctum* I cover, hide, protect

tellūs tellūr-is 3f. land

temptō 1 I attempt, try

ter three times

terg-um 2n. back

trabs trab-is 3f. beam, timber, tree-trunk

trahō 3 *trāxī tractum* I draw, drag

turbō 1 I confuse, confound; scatter

Tȳdīdēs nom. s., Diomedes, a Greek warrior

uān-us a um deceived, empty, illusory

uēl-um ī 2n. sail, canvas (with *dare*, 'set sail')

uincul-um ī 2n. chain, bond

uitt-a ae 1f. woollen headband, worn by priests and
in religious rituals

uix scarcely, hardly

ultrō willingly (usually beyond the call of duty); in
addition

undique from all sides

usquam anywhere

Study section for 2.57–198

1. To what extent does Sinon's speech read like Aeneas' *personal* account of the matter? How revealing is it of Aeneas?

2. The salesman wants to persuade his customers that *his* idea is *their* idea. How does Sinon set about doing this?

3. How successfully does Sinon build up his image of himself?

4. Do we know who invented the pack of lies that Sinon tells? Is there any reason to believe that Ulysses had anything to do with it?

5. Scan 145–51.

6. The *Greek* epic poet Quintus from Smyrna (probably c. AD 250, i.e. much later than V.) offers the following version of the Sinon story. Compare and contrast it with V.'s handling. On whose 'side' is Quintus?

[The Trojans see that the Greeks have gone]
'Joyfully they all ran to the shore,
but wearing their armour. Fear still haunted them.
They saw the well-made horse. They stood around it,
wondering, since it was indeed a mighty work.
Nearby they saw hapless Sinon.   360
Each of them began questioning him,
standing round him in a circle. First,
they began with gentle questions, then with terrible
threats. Then they began to torture that guileful man
for a very long time. Firm as a rock   365
he held his ground, limbs unshaking. Finally
they tore off his ears and nose,
disfiguring him all they could, so he would tell the truth,
where the Greeks had gone with their ships, or what the horse
held inside. He, resolute in mind,   370
ignored their hideous abuse but endured
in heart, though horribly wracked by flogging
and fire; for Hera (Juno) breathed strength into him.
Guilefully he told them this tale:
"The Greeks have fled by sea in their ships,   375
exhausted by this long war and its pains.
At Calchas' orders they built the horse
for wise Triton-born [Minerva] to propitiate her wrath
at the theft of the Palladium. To win their return,
the Greeks wanted to kill me at Odysseus' [Ulysses'] bidding   380
and sacrifice me by the resounding sea
to the gods of the sea. But I knew their plan, and escaping
before they made sacrificial libations or scattered the grains,*
with the gods' help I seized the feet of the horse.
They, though unwilling, had to leave me there,   385
fearing the anger of the stern daughter of great Zeus."**
So cunningly he spoke, his heart untamed by the torture.
It is the mark of a brave man to endure dreadful necessity.
Some of the army believed him, others said
he was a lying fraud, and among them was   390
Laocoon. He wisely spoke up and said
he was a trickster, put up to it by the Greeks,
and told them all to burn the horse to the ground
and find out if there was anything hiding inside.'
[Laocoon is promptly driven mad, blinded and attacked by sea monsters who kill his sons, but
not him; he continues prophesying doom while the Trojans joyfully bring the horse into the
city. Cassandra then joins him in foretelling disaster, to be equally mocked by the Trojans.]
          Quintus Smyrnaeus, *Sequel to Homer* 12.356–94

* accompaniments of a sacrifice

** Sinon was in contact with a sacred object and therefore inviolate

2.199–267: The fate of Laocoon

In this Section, *Laocoon and his sons are killed by serpents emerging from the sea, and the Trojans demand that the horse be brought into the city. They celebrate, and in the dead of night, as they sleep it off, Sinon lets the Greeks out of the horse. They kill the guards and open the gates of the city.*

2.199–208: 'Then another sign: as Laocoon sacrificed, two huge serpents emerged from the sea'

'hīc aliud^ ^māius miserīs multōque ^tremendum
obicitur magis atque imprōuida pectora turbat.   200
Lāocoōn, ductus^ Neptūnō sorte ^sacerdōs,
sollemnīs^ taurum ingentem mactābat ad ^ārās.
ecce autem geminī^ ā Tenedō tranquilla* per *alta

199 *hīc*: i.e. at this point

aliud māius: n.; presumably 'prodigy', or some such thing. The horse was already seen as a prodigy. Here comes another one, even bigger and (for all the anxieties associated with the horse, 189–94) one much more obviously terrifying (*tremendum*)

miserīs: dat. after *obicitur*, '[us] *miserīs* [ones]'; a 'proleptic' usage, i.e. they are not currently *miserī* but soon will be – another personal interjection by Aeneas

multōque: 'much' with the comp. *magis* (very emphatic position, so far from *multō*) 'much more', lit. '(more) by much' (adv. of 'measure of difference'). See **RLL**(f)4(iv), **W**Suppl. syntax, **M**14

tremendum: a gerundive, **RL**161, **W**39, **M**111

200 *obiciō* 3 I lay in front of, expose to (+ dat.); treat the first syllable for scansion purposes as if the vb is *obyiciō* (it is also found as *obiiciō*)

imprōuid-us a um unwary, thoughtless, i.e. blind to its significance (Aeneas' comment). Note the

solemn alliteration of these lines, especially *m* and *d/t*

201 *ductus*: 'drawn/selected [as]'

Neptūn-us ī 2m. Neptune, god of the sea, who had built the walls of Ilium but, cheated of payment by the then king Laomedon (see on 1.643), renounced it. *Neptūnō* here is dat. 'for/in honour of Neptune'. See on **2.40–9**

sors sort-is 3f. lot(tery), chance

sacerdōs sacerdōt-is 3m. priest

202 *sollemn-is e* ceremonial, traditional; the altars are on the shore, as they would be for a sacrifice to Neptune

taur-us ī 2m. bull

mactō 1 I sacrifice; note impf., 'began to'

203 **gemin-us a um** twin – but twin *what*? The tension rises . . .

Tenedō: abl. of Tenedos, the island where the Greek fleet was hiding

tranquill-us a um peaceful, calm

alta: cf. English 'the deep'

2.199–208: the dramatic, appetite-whetting opening two lines – *tremendum* indeed – lead to the setting of the scene on the beach: a sacrifice (201–2). Why Laocoon is sacrificing we are not told – how could Aeneas know? – but see on **2.40–9**. The scene is immediately intensified by *ecce*, a call to attention (Aeneas the picture-painter at work), followed by a slowly unfolding, cinematic tracking shot – two somethings, setting out

[218]

(horrēscō referēns) immēnsīs orbibus ^anguēs
incumbunt pelagō pariterque ad lītora tendunt;   205
pectora^ quōrum inter flūctūs ^arrēcta iubaeque
sanguineae superant undās, pars cētera pontum
pōne legit sinuatque immēnsa^ uolūmine ^terga.'

2.209–27: 'As we fled in terror, they made for Laocoon, attacked his sons and then turned on him as he tried to save them. The snakes then took refuge in Minerva's temple'

'fit sonitus, spūmante salō; iamque arua tenēbant

204 *horrēscō* 3 I shudder
**orb-is is 3m. coil; globe, world; orb
angu-is is 3m. serpent, snake
205 **incumbō 3 *incubuī incubitum* I lean (forward) on, fall on, breast
**pariter equally, side by side, abreast
206 *pectora quōrum*: reverse order, 'whose breasts/ fronts'
**flūct-us ūs 4m. wave
iub-a ae 1f. crest
207 *sanguine-us a um* bloody
superant: here 'overtop', 'rise above', as also 219
**und-a ae 1f. wave
pars cētera: i.e. as opposed to the heads and breasts of the snakes
208 *pōne* behind
legit: here 'traverse, skim'

sinuō 1 I arch, writhe
uolūmen uolūmin-is 3n. fold, coil, spiral; here abl. of manner

Learning vocabulary
flūct-us ūs 4m. wave
gemin-us a um twin
incumbō 3 *incubuī incubitum* I lean on, fall on
orb-is is 3m. coil; globe, world; orb
pariter equally
sacerdōs sacerdōt-is 3m. priest
sors sort-is 3f. lot(tery), chance
und-a ae 1f. wave

209 **sonit-us ūs* 4m. sound
**spūm-ō 1 I foam
sal-um ī 2n. sea, waves
**aru-um ī 2n. field; land (here = shore)

---

far off in Tenedos in a calm sea (203), eye-witness comment, huge coils – *anguēs*! (204) and making for the shore (205). Details become clearer as they approach: breasts and crests first, *making* waves (206; the sea seemed calm at 203) – blood red – rising above those waves (207), coils now seen to be writhing (208).

A disclaimer: in a much-lauded paper, B.M.W. Knox argues that images of snakes and flames permeate Book 2 as a 'dominant and obsessive metaphor'. There are certainly lots of the latter, and more than a few of the former. But is quantity alone sufficient? Try as I might, I cannot see any intelligible metaphorical connection between, for example, Laocoon's snakes here and the snake to which Aeneas and his men are likened in a simile when the Greek Androgeos accidentally comes across them (376–82), or e.g. the flames of Troy with the flame that plays round Ascanius' head at 682–7. So I shall not refer to it. Nevertheless, it makes a useful test-case for this sort of approach.

See: Knox 'The Serpent and the Flame: The Imagery of the Second Book of the *Aeneid*' in Commager (1966: 124–42).

Crunch: 203–5

2.209–27: As the snakes get nearer, the Trojans hear the sound (*ssss*, 209), and already they are on the shore. Now they can see the eyes – bloodshot – and the flickering tongues

ārdentīsque oculōs suffectī sanguine et ignī   210
sībila^ lambēbant, linguīs uibrantibus, ^ōra.
diffugimus uīsū exsanguēs. illī agmine certō
Lāocoōnta petunt; et prīmum parua^ duōrum*
^corpora *nātōrum serpēns amplexus uterque
implicat et miserōs^ morsū dēpāscitur ^artūs;   215
post, ipsum^ auxiliō ^subeuntem ac tēla ^ferentem
corripiunt spīrīsque^ ligant ^ingentibus; et iam
bis medium amplexī^, bis collō squāmea* circum
*terga ^datī superant capite et ceruīcibus altīs.

210 *ārdentīs oculōs*: dir. obj. of *suffectī*, the part. used
   here not in its pass. sense, but as if it were act.; see
   p. 39 ((c)(ii)) above
sufficiō 3 *suffēcī suffectum* I imbue
ignī: the usual form of the abl. s. of *ignis*, a 'pure'
   i-stem of the 3rd decl.
211 *sībil-us a um* hissing
lambō 3 I lick
uibrō 1 I vibrate, flicker
212 *diffugiō* 3 I scatter, disperse
*uīs-us ūs 4m. sight, vision
exsangu-is e bloodless, pale
agmine certō: 'in a straight line'? To S. it suggests the
   smooth flow of a river (cf. 782) or a tail dragging
   along the ground (*Georgics* 3.423). But *agmen* also
   has military connotations
213 *Lāocoōnta*: acc. s. of Laocoon (five syllables)
214 *serpēns serpent-is* 3m. serpent
*amplector 3 dep. *amplexus* I wrap up, embrace (and
   218)

uter- utr-a- utr-um-que each of two
215 **implicō* 1 *implicuī* I enfold, twine round, wrap up
mors-us ūs 4m. bite
dēpāscor 3 I feed on
216 *post*: adverbial, 'next'
ipsum: i.e. Laocoon, obj. of *corripiunt* (**217**)
auxiliō: 'for a help', 'to help' (dat. of purpose,
   RL88.6, WSuppl. syntax)
**subeō subīre subi(u)ī subitum I come to rescue; put
   in; seek shelter
217 *spīr-a ae* 1f. coil, spiral
ligō 1 I bind
218 *medium*: '[him] round/by the middle'
squāme-us a um scaly
circum . . . 219 *datī*: treat as one word. Tmēsis
   (Greek 'cutting') is the term used to describe a vb
   separated from its prefix, a very common feature
   of Homeric language. *circumdatī* is used in the
   active sense (see on **210**), 'circling' *squāmea terga*
   round *collō*

(210–11). Transfixed to start with, the Trojans (including Aeneas, *diffugimus*) turn and run before this purposeful assault (212). There is something pathetic about *miserōs morsū* and rather crunchy about the sound of *dēpāscitur artūs* (215). The small, helpless children are soon finished off, but Laocoon who comes to help them (216) puts up strong resistance. So they wind their coils round him (217), twice round his middle and twice round his neck (218–19). Gore- and poison-stained (221), screaming (222), he tries to tear off the coils, but all he can use is his hands (220). He does not stand a chance – even the holy headbands, *uittās* (221), do not protect him. The simile is apt. A priest knows all about bulls at sacrifice that are not killed with a single, decisive stroke, and Laocoon was making such a sacrifice at the time (202). His death (V. does not actually *say* he is killed, but cf. 229) is similarly slow and lingering, and the noise he makes is like a bull in its death throes (223–4) – himself a sacrificial victim. As Laocoon, so (soon) Troy. Their job done, the snakes take refuge in Minerva's shrine. So it was Minerva's doing . . .?

For the possible further significance, and other versions, of this scene, see **Study section for 2.199–267**.

Crunch: 212–15

ille^ simul manibus tendit dīuellere nōdōs, 220
^perfūsus saniē uittās ātrōque uenēnō,
clāmōrēs^ simul ^horrendōs ad sīdera tollit:
quālīs mūgītūs, fūgit cum saucius^ āram
^taurus et incertam^ excussit ceruīce ^secūrim.
at geminī^ lāpsū dēlūbra* ad *summa ^dracōnēs 225
effugiunt, saeuaeque^ petunt ^Trītōnidis arcem,
sub pedibusque deae clipeīque sub orbe teguntur.'

2.228–40: 'Assuming that this omen was the punishment for Laocoon attacking the horse, people shouted for the horse to be brought into the city. We celebrated as we did so'

'tum uērō tremefacta^ nouus* per ^pectora cūnctīs

220 ***simul** at the same time, together
dīuellō 3 I prise apart
nōd-us ī 2m. knot, coil
221 *perfundō* 3 *perfūdī perfūsum* I soak, drench; here a true pass. part., with *uittās* an acc. of respect, **RLL**(f)4(vi)
sani-ēs ēī 5f. gore, pus (presumably Laocoon's, from the snakes' venomous bites – not that the snakes *need* venom, but it all adds to the horror)
uittās: worn by those engaged in religious ritual – whether as priest (as Laocoon here) or victim (as Sinon claimed 133). Having been priest, Laocoon is about to change roles and become a victim
***āter ātr-a um** black
uenēn-um ī 2n. poison
222 *horrend-us a um* fearful, terrifying (a gerundive, lit. 'to be shuddered at', 'shuddersome')
223 *mūgīt-us ūs* 4m. bellow; *quālis* here introduces a simile: 'of what sort is/like the bellowing *cum* . . .' 'The comparison is made because of Laocoon's role [as priest]' (S.)
sauci-us a um wounded
224 ***excutiō** 3 *excussī excussum* I throw/shake off/out, evade
secūr-is is 3f. sacrificial axe
225 *lāps-us ūs* 4m. glide, gliding escape
***dēlūbr-um ī** 2n. shrine, temple
dracō -nis 3m. snake, serpent
226 *Trītōnidis*: gen. s. of *Trītōnis*, Minerva (see on 171)
227 ***clipe-us ī** 2m. shield; a dactyl-filled line,

suggesting the speed of the serpents' retreat? Minerva is pictured with her shield on the ground in front of her. The serpents hide between it and her feet
teguntur: note the 'middle' use, 'hide themselves', see p. 39 ((c)(i)) above

Learning vocabulary
amplector 3 dep. *amplexus* I wrap up, embrace
aru-um ī 2n. field
āter ātr-a um black
clipe-us ī 2m. shield
dēlūbr-um ī 2n. shrine, temple
excutiō 3 *excussī excussum* I throw/shake off/out, evade
implicō 1 *implicuī* I enfold, twine round
simul at the same time, together
sonit-us ūs 4m. sound
spūm-ō 1 I foam
subeō subīre subi(u)ī subitum I come to rescue; put in; seek shelter
uīs-us ūs 4m. sight, vision

228 ***tremefaciō** 3 *tremefēcī tremefactum* I cause to tremble
cūnctīs: dat., 'for/in all [of us]'; S. comments that, after Laocoon's death, everyone (not just these who had seen the snakes attack) agreed that Laocoon had paid the price for his crime, **229–31**

2.228–40: Whichever divinity was responsible for the serpents' assault (if a divinity *was* involved), Aeneas describes how the Trojans, terrified at what they have just seen and its implications (228–9), draw the inevitable conclusion that Laocoon was being punished *merentem* for his attack (see 50–3), now converted into a *scelus* (229), on what is no

īnsinuat *pauor, et scelus expendisse merentem^
^Lāocoōnta ferunt, sacrum* ^quī cuspide *rōbur   230
laeserit et tergō scelerātam^ intorserit ^hastam.
dūcendum^ ad sēdēs ^simulācrum ōrandaque^ dīuae
^nūmina conclāmant.
dīuidimus mūrōs et moenia pandimus urbis.
accingunt omnēs operī, pedibusque rotārum   235
subiciunt lāpsūs, et stuppea uincula collō
intendunt; scandit fātālis māchina^ mūrōs
^fēta armīs. puerī circum innūptaeque puellae
sacra canunt, fūnemque manū contingere gaudent.
illa subit mediaeque^ mināns inlābitur ^urbī.'   240

229 *īnsinuō* 1 I creep, work into (+ dat.)
pauor -is 3m. fear, terror
expendō 3 *expendī* I pay the price for; observe how
  the people now think that Laocoon's earlier action
  was a 'crime', presumably against them (because
  of Sinon's assurances about what the horse could
  do for them) and Minerva (whose horse they had
  been told it 'was')
mereō 2 *meruī meritum* I am worthy, deserve
230 *ferunt*: 'they say'
cuspis cuspid-is 3f. spear, point
231 *laeserit . . . intorserit*: the *quī* clause reflects
  what the people actually say (*ferunt*); hence
  these are perf. subjuncs. of past action in
  primary sequence, with a strong causal bias
  ('*in that* he had . . .'), RLR4, WSuppl. syntax,
  M83–4
scelerāt-us a um wicked, sinful
intorqueō 2 *intorsī* I hurl
232 *dūcendum . . . ōranda*: gerundives. Note the
  ellipsis of *esse*, after *conclāmant*
sēdēs: i.e. of Minerva (see on 229), also referred to in
  dīuae
simulācr-um ī 2n. image
233 *conclāmō* 1 I shout (in unison, together);
  another unfinished line (see on 1.534)
  234 *dīuidō* 3 I open up, breach (i.e. by breaking
  through the wall above the top of the gate)
moenia: can = buildings or houses of a town (S.) as
  well as 'walls'

pandō 3 I reveal, lay open, open a way into
235 **accingō* 3 *accīnxī accinctum* I prepare (myself)
  for (+ dat.); get down to (+ dat.); gird myself with
rot-a ae 1f. wheel
236 *subiciunt*: for scansion, see on 2.200
laps-us ūs 4m. smooth movement (take with
  rotārum). The Greeks would hardly have fitted
  with wheels something which (according to
  Sinon) was not to be moved!
stuppe-us a um of flax
237 *intendō* 3 I draw tight. Note the steady,
  relentless tread of the spondees *intendunt . . .
  armīs*
scandō 3 I climb (cf. *ascendō*) – not literally, but
  figuratively. Soldiers attacking a wall did this
  literally, and the first to do it was decorated
fātāl-is e fateful
238 *fēt-us a um* pregnant (usually the sign of
  impending life)
circum: adverbial, 'around about'
innūpt-us a um unmarried (a touch full of pathos, cf.
  503; the 'horse' is pregnant, but these young girls
  will never produce Trojan children)
239 *sacra*: n. pl.; presumably songs, or hymns
canō 3 I sing
fūn-is is 3m. rope
gaudeō 2 semi-dep. I rejoice
240 **minor* 1 dep. I threaten
inlābor 3 dep. I slide into

longer a horse but, significantly, a *sacrum . . . rōbur* (S., 230), *sacrum* to Minerva, as
Sinon had lied to them (183–9). So they busy themselves – note the volley of active verbs
in 234–40 – about bringing it inside (observe that Aeneas again involves himself in 234).
V. Romanises (anachronism) a scene reminiscent of those where gods are welcomed
and pulled into cities on trolleys, to songs from the young (see Austin). Aeneas,
however, seems to be holding himself back at this point, intent on describing as dispas-
sionately as he can the entrance of this *fātālis māchina* (237), with few emotionalising

2.241–9: 'We ignored the signs as we brought it in, ignored Cassandra's prophecies and instead adorned the gods' shrines'

'ō patria, ō dīuum domus Īlium et incluta^ bellō
^moenia Dardanidum! quater ipsō^ in ^līmine portae
substitit, atque uterō sonitum quater arma dedēre;
īnstāmus tamen immemorēs, caecīque furōre,
et mōnstrum īnfēlīx sacrātā^ sistimus ^arce.   245

Learning vocabulary

accingō 3 *accīnxī accīnctum* I prepare (myself) for (+ dat.); get down to (+ dat.); gird myself with
minor 1 dep. I threaten
tremefaciō 3 *tremefēcī tremefactum* I cause to tremble

241 ***Īli-um ī* 2n. Ilium, the town besieged by the Greeks
inclut-us a um famous, renowned
242 *Dardanidum*: gen. pl.
quater four times (and 243)
**līmen līmin-is 3n. threshold; it was counted unlucky to trip on a threshold (anachronism: brides were once, perhaps still are, lifted over it)
243 *subsistō* 3 *substitī* I stop; the pause at the end of this, the first word of the line, seems to bring the horse lurching to a halt. It was a bad omen to stumble over a threshold. The Trojans pay no attention

244 **īnstō 1 I press on [with], urge on
immemor -is mindless, thoughtless. 'Gods, make them fearful, terrified, forgetful' was part of a formula uttered by the Roman army before attacking a city (anachronism), comments S., pointing out that *immemorēs, caecīque furōre* sound like the words of a people whom the gods have deserted
furōre: abl. of cause, explaining *caecī*
245 *mōnstr-um ī* 2n. monster, portent (defined by the grammarian Festus as 'things that exceed the limits of nature, like a snake with feet'); and often acting as a warning too
**īnfēlīx īnfēlīc-is* accursed (a comment made in hindsight, S.)
sistō 3 I stop, halt; enjoy the finality of this heavy, slow, spondaic line, with its contrast of *īnfēlīx* with *sacrātā*, climaxing in *arce*, where the *mōnstrum* comes to a juddering halt

---

additions (to *fātālis* add *fēta* [238], dramatically delayed to the start of the next line, and *mināns* [240]), though with dreadful irony at *sacra canunt* and *gaudent* (239). This restraint will not last.

Was the action of the serpents all part of the divine plan? S. (on 199) thinks not: 'it must not seem that Ilium fell to superior strength or that Aeneas willingly fled. By this episode Aeneas shows that accidental events conspired to support the Greeks' tricks.' Commentators rightly point out that V. himself does not specifically point the finger at any divine intervention (cf. 54–6), but fail to observe that V. is not speaking: Aeneas is. How could he know whether the gods had done this or not? V., like Homer, tends to distinguish between what the characters know at any time and what the omniscient narrator is privy to, greatly increasing the readers' sense of the ironic and tragic dimensions of human life.

See: Jones (2003) on 15.461 for an example of Homer's distinctions between levels of divine and human understanding.

Crunch: 237–40

2.241–9: Aeneas can hold himself in no longer. In a passionate outburst, reminiscent of the reflections of a Greek tragic chorus or hero seeing the truth 'too late' (a typical tragic theme), he goes back over the entrance of the horse again at 242–3 and finally sees it

tunc etiam fātīs^ aperit Cassandra ^futūrīs
ōra^, deī iussū nōn umquam ^crēdita Teucrīs.
nōs^ dēlūbra deum ^miserī, quibus ultimus^ esset
^ille diēs, fēstā^ uēlāmus ^fronde per urbem.'

2.250–67: 'As we slept, the Greek fleet left Tenedos, Sinon opened up the horse and the city's gates. The Greeks killed the guards and joined forces'

'uertitur intereā cae<u>lum</u> et ruit Ōceanō nox,   250

246 *tunc etiam:* then again/too

**aperiō 4 I open (up), reveal

*Cassandr-a ae 1f. Cassandra, a prophetess fated always to tell the truth but never to be believed because, having agreed to make love to Apollo (god of prophecy), she turned him down at the last minute. S. comments that Aeneas saves the Trojans from a charge of stupidity by saying that it was on the god's orders (**247**) that they would never believe. Aeneas' explanation at **244** is probably sufficient

247 *ōra:* 'lips' gets the pl.

Teucrīs: dat. of agent; RLL(e)1(iv), **W**24, **M**111

248 *dēlūbra deum:* obj. of *uēlāmus* (**249**)

*ultim-us a um last, final

esset: ellipsis of *futūrus*; either causal subjunc., explaining *miserī* (**RLR**4, **W**Suppl. syntax, **M**83–4) or concessive ('although') modifying **249** (**RLV**)

249 *fēst-us a um* festal, celebratory

uēlō 1 I garland

frōns frond-is 3f. garland, leaf (myrtle, laurel and so on, the traditional decoration for statues and altars on festal occasions) – a little detail, full of pathos

Learning vocabulary

aperiō 4 I open (up), reveal

Cassandr-a ae 1f. Cassandra, a prophetess fated always to tell the truth but never to be believed

Īli-um ī 2n. Ilium, the town besieged by the Greeks

īnfēlīx īnfēlīc-is accursed

īnstō 1 I press on [with], urge on (+ dat.)

līmen līmin-is 3n. threshold

ultim-us a um last, final

250 *Ōcean-us ī* 2m. Ocean, the deep (here abl. '*from* Ocean' – it is not yet midnight). The heavens were thought to be two hemispheres, one bright (with the sun) and one dark. They moved across the sky, and as the sun in the west sank into the sea, the dark hemisphere in the east sped up (*ruit*) from it

placed on the citadel (**245**). He calls on fatherland, gods, walls (**241–2**) – all now gone, nothing but a memory (see **Study section for 2.402–505**, 5.) – and recalls with dreadful clarity the Trojan inability to register what was really happening (**242–3**, the great crashes from inside the horse as it ground to a halt when it was hauled over the threshold). He blames their (note 'we' *īnstāmus, sistimus*) blind madness in pressing on (**244**: note *furōre*; cf. **42, 54, 200**). We had our chances. We did not take them. After all that, there is hardly any surprise in Cassandra being ignored (**246–7**) – that was inevitable (note on **246**). All Aeneas can do is remark, with remorse and bitter irony, yet again, on the religious zeal and rejoicing with which the Trojans (note *nōs* **248**) celebrated their own doom, imagining they were pleasing Minerva (**248–9**, cf. **239–40**) and laying the groundwork for a glorious future (**192–4**) – tragic irony indeed. Aeneas does not try to hide his feelings or distance himself from the events he describes in these lines – note that insistent 'we'.

Crunch: 241–5

2.250–67: It is not surprising that the Trojans have celebrated the night away (**252–3, 265** *uīno*): they have brought the Greek talisman inside the walls, so 'know' that they have nothing to fear and, indeed, will soon be launching an attack on Greece itself (**192–4**). But

inuoluēns umbrā magnā terramque polumque
Myrmidonumque dolōs; fūsī^ per moenia ^Teucrī
conticuēre; sopor fessōs^ complectitur ^artūs.
et iam Argīua phalanx^, īnstrūctīs nāuibus, ībat
ā Tenedō, tacitae* per amīca silentia *lūnae,   255
lītora nōta ^petēns, flammās cum rēgia puppis
extulerat, fātīsque^ deum dēfēnsus* ^inīquīs
inclūsōs^ uterō ^Danaōs et pīnea^ fūrtim
laxat ^claustra *Sinōn. illōs patefactus^ ad aurās
reddit ^equus, laetīque^ cauō* sē *rōbore prōmunt   260

251 *inuoluō* 3 I envelop
***pol-us ī* 2m. pole, sky
252 ***fundō* 3 *fūdī fūsum* I pour out, shed, scatter; rout
253 *conticeō* 2 *conticuī* I am silent
sopor -is 3m. weariness
***complector* 3 dep. *complexus* I embrace
254 ***Argīu-us a um* Greek
phalanx phalang-is 3f. troop of soldiers. But how did the Greeks *know* Sinon had been successful in persuading the Trojans to bring the horse into the city? Presumably because (somehow) they could see the Trojans taking it in; or were ready to sail hastily back if they saw the Trojans waiting for them. At any rate, V. indicates no means of communication to inform them (but the Greeks use a fire signal to contact Sinon at **256–7**)
ībat: inceptive, 'began to move'
255 *Tenedō*: abl. of the off-shore island Tenedos (see 21–5)

silenti-um ī 2n. silence: a famously lovely line, vowels and consonants harmoniously playing off against each other, but oddly within a lively, dactylic rhythm. Yet it works. That's a poet for you
256 *cum*: 'inverted' *cum* clause, **RL**T(e)3, **M**122, cf. **W**31
rēgi-us a um royal
***pupp-is is* 3f. ship, stern, poop
257 ***efferō efferre extulī ēlātum* I raise/lift up, bring out; carry off
inīqu-us a um cruel, unfair; further comment by Aeneas
258 ***inclūdō* 3 *inclūsī inclūsum* I enclose, shut in
pine-us a um of pine
fūrtim secretly
259 *laxō* 1 I unfasten, release
***claustr-a ōrum* 2n. bolts, bars; cage, prison
illōs: i.e. the Greeks inside the horse
patefaciō 3 *patefēcī patefactum* I open
260 *prōmō* 3 I bring out/into view

Virgil is preparing for the denouement: the shadow cast by night seems to conspire against the Trojans (252–3), while the *amīca*, silent moon (255) somehow seems to side with the Greeks. How? Ancient warships do not try to dock at night: they cannot see where they are going. But by the light of the moon, they can. So off the Greeks go with some chance of success, under such a light, of *lītora nōta petēns* (256: *nōta* because they have just left them, S.). The signal reaches Sinon who – Aeneas contributes another bitter comment about the gods' protection of the Greeks (*inīquīs*, 257) – opens up the horse (258–9). Enjoy the delayed subject *Sinōn* at 259 – that man again, putting the finishing touches to his foul deception. No wonder Aeneas assumes the Greeks inside were *laetī* ('focalisation') – the trick had worked and the city was virtually defenceless, with guards easily overcome (266), presumably because they were looking out of the city, not into it (even if they too had not been partying). That the Trojans were sound asleep and drunk (265) lessens the credit the Greeks could take for their capture (S.). The men in the horse link up with those from the ships (266–7), and the scene is set. Were there only nine Greeks inside it? That is what V. says. At least it is a sensible number, given a horse of feasible size that would not attract suspicion; and all they have to do is kill the guards and open the gates (other traditions fill the horse with anything from 22 to 3,000 men! See note on 2.150). S., ever keen to find examples of Aeneas downplaying Greek courage or skill, says this shows how terrified the

∧Thessandrus Sthenelusque ducēs et dīrus Vlixēs,
dēmissum∧ lāpsī per ∧fūnem, Acamāsque Thoāsque,
Pēlīdēsque Neoptolemus, prīmusque Machāōn
et Menelāus et ipse∧ dolī fabricātor ∧Epēos.
inuādunt urbem∧ somnō uīnōque ∧sepultam;   265
caeduntur uigilēs, portīsque patentibus, omnīs∧
accipiunt ∧sociōs atque agmina cōnscia iungunt.'

261 *Thessandrus* Greek warrior (unknown to the Iliad)

Sthenelus Greek warrior

262 *******dēmitto* 3 *dēmīsī dēmissum* I hand/pass/send down, cast down

**lābor 3 dep. *lāpsus* I slip, glide, pass by, fall down; make a mistake

fūn-is is 3m. rope, cable

Acamās nom. s. Greek warrior (unknown to the Iliad)

Thoās nom. s. Greek warrior

263 *Pēlīdēs* nom. s. grandson of Peleus, father of Achilles

Neoptolemus (also called Pyrrhus), son of Achilles

Machāōn nom. s. Greek warrior; *prīmus* here means 'distinguished/unrivalled' or 'important' (he was the Greek doctor)

264 *Menelāus* husband of Helen

fabricātor -is 3m. maker

Epēos nom. s. Greek warrior

265 *inuādō* 3 I invade

somnō uīnōque: hendiadys (see **Glossary of literary terms** 20) for 'drunken sleep'?

sepeliō 4 *sepelī(u)ī sepultum* I bury

266 *uigil uigil-is* 3m. guard, sentry

**pateō 2 I am accessible, lie open; am revealed

267 **iungō 3 *iūnxī iūnctum* I join, unite; *cōnscia agmina* refers to the bands of troops arriving from the ships and linking up with those inside, all in on (*cōnscia*) the plot ('He elegantly identifies their complicity in the ambush', S.)

Learning vocabulary

Argīu-us a um Greek

**claustr-a ōrum 2n. cage, prison; bolts, bars

complector 3 dep. *complexus* I embrace

dēmitto 3 *dēmīsī dēmissum* I hand/pass/send down, cast down

efferō efferre extulī ēlātum I raise/lift up, bring out; carry off

fundō 3 *fūdī fūsum* I pour out, shed, scatter; rout

inclūdo 3 *inclūsī inclūsum* I enclose, shut in

iungō 3 *iūnxī iūnctum* I join

lābor 3 dep. *lāpsus* I slip, glide, pass by, fall down; make a mistake

pateō 2 I am accessible, lie open; am revealed

pol-us ī 2m. pole, sky

pupp-is is 3f. ship, stern, poop

Greeks were of the Trojans, because they first killed the guards who could have raised the alarm! Pretty sensible thing to do, one would have thought.

It is hard to see how Aeneas could possibly have known about the event, let alone named the names, of 254–67, since he was asleep at the time. Here and elsewhere in Book 2, Aeneas is occasionally used as if he were Virgil, the third-person master-narrator.

Learning vocabulary for Section 2.199–267

accingō 3 *accīnxī accīnctum* I prepare (myself) for
(+ dat.); get down to (+ dat.); gird myself with
amplector 3 dep. *amplexus* I wrap up, embrace
aperiō 4 I open (up), reveal
Argīu-us a um Greek
aru-um ī 2n. field
āter ātr-a um black
Cassandr-a ae 1f. Cassandra, a prophetess fated
always to tell the truth but never to be believed
**claustr-a ōrum 2n. cage, prison; bolts, bars
clipe-us ī 2m. shield
complector 3 dep. *complexus* I embrace
dēlūbr-um ī 2n. shrine, temple
dēmittō 3 *dēmīsī dēmissum* I hand/pass/send down,
cast down
efferō efferre extulī ēlātum I raise/lift up, bring out;
carry off
excutiō 3 *excussī excussum* I throw/shake off/out,
evade
flūct-us ūs 4m. wave
fundō 3 *fūdī fūsum* I pour out, shed, scatter; rout
gemin-us a um twin
Īli-um ī 2n. Ilium, the town besieged by the Greeks
implicō 1 *implicuī* I enfold, twine round
inclūdō 3 *inclūsī inclūsum* I enclose, shut in

incumbō 3 *incubuī incubitum* I lean on, fall on
īnfēlix īnfēlīc-is accursed
īnstō 1 I press on (with), urge on (+ dat.)
iungō 3 *iūnxī iūnctum* I join, unite
lābor 3 dep. *lāpsus* I slip, glide, pass by, fall down;
make a mistake
līmen līmin-is 3n. threshold
minor 1 dep. I threaten
orb-is is 3m. coil; globe, world; orb
pariter equally
pateō 2 I am accessible, lie open; am revealed
pol-us ī 2m. pole, sky
pupp-is is 3f. ship, stern, poop
sacerdōs sacerdōt-is 3m. priest
simul at the same time, together
sonit-us ūs 4m. sound
sors sort-is 3f. lot(tery), chance
spūm-ō 1 I foam
subeō subīre subī(u)ī subitum I come to rescue; put
in; seek shelter
tremefaciō 3 *tremefēcī tremefactum* I cause to
tremble
uīs-us ūs 4m. sight, vision
ultim-us a um last, final
und-a ae 1f. wave

Study section for 2.199–267

1. What is the significance of Laocoon's role?
2. It has been suggested that the Laocoon scene – itself a 'sign' – foreshadows the fall of Troy: the snakes are the Greek ships coming from Tenedos, their red crests the fire signal that the ships are on their way (2.256–7), the death of Laocoon and his sons the fall of Troy, and the snakes' residence in the citadel the activity of Minerva from the citadel against Troy at 615. Do you agree?
3. Scan 241–9.
4. In the *Appendix*, read the versions of Arctinus (**1–2** '. . . fire-signal to the Greeks') and Apollodorus (**10** 'The others burned . . .' to **14** '. . . to guide their way'). What are the differences from V.'s version of this part of the story? Can you see advantages in V.'s way of handling the story, or any special purposes he may have had in mind?

2.268–401: From a dream of Hector to the battle for Ilium

In this Section, *the dead Trojan hero Hector appears to Aeneas in a dream, telling him to escape at once with Troy's gods. Aeneas wakes up, sees what is happening and prepares to fight for the city, with some initial success. Coroebus suggests they swap their Trojan armour for Greek.*

(Note: from now on till the end of Book 2, elisions will not be marked, and linking devices will be more sparingly used. You can also choose your own passages to *crunch*.)

2.268–86: 'As I slept, Hector, still mutilated from Achilles' assault on him, appeared to me in a dream. I asked why he had come'

'tempus erat quō prīma quiēs^ mortālibus aegrīs
incipit et, dōnō dīuum, ^grātissima serpit.
in somnīs, ecce, ante oculōs maestissimus Hector^   270
^uīsus adesse mihī largōsque effundere flētūs,
^raptātus bīgīs, ut quondam, ^āterque cruentō
puluere, perque pedēs ^trāiectus lōra tumentīs.
ēi mihi, quālis erat, quantum mūtātus ab illō

---

268 *quō*: at which, when
aegrīs: 'weary, anxious' rather than 'sick'
269 *grātissima*: 'most welcome' and 'most pleasing', cf. 265 for a very different image. Is Aeneas suggesting he was not one of those in a drunken slumber? Or is it just a general comment on the blessings of sleep, in contrast to the nightmare to come?
serpō 3 I creep
270 *******maest-us a um* tearful (and **280**)
**Hector -is 3m. Hector, greatest Trojan fighter, killed by Achilles
271 *uīsus*: ellipsis of part of *sum* (regularly used of people dreaming)
mihī: like *tibi*, this can scan with short or long last syllable (see p. 42 above)
larg-us a um copious

effundō 3 *effūdī effūsum* I pour out
flēt-us ūs 4m. tears
272 *raptō* 1 I drag. When Achilles killed Hector, he pierced his heels and passed leather straps through them which he tied to the chariot and then drove off, dragging him through the dust; he also dragged Hector's body round the tomb of his beloved Patroclus, whom Hector had killed. See *Iliad* 16.818–67; 22.395–404; 24.14–18
bīg-ae ārum 1f. two-horsed chariot
273 *trāiciō* 3 *trāiēcī trāiectum* I pierce, pass through; the meaning is 'passing the *lōra* through (*per*)'; cf. p. 39 ((c)(ii))
lōr-um ī 2n. strap, thong
tumeō 2 I swell
274 *ēi* alas, woe

2.268–86: The blessed gift of sleep is the last gift of the gods (268–9) that most of the Trojans are to enjoy: the calm before the storm. Aeneas now recalls the dream when,

Hectore quī^ redit, exuuiās ^indūtus Achillī,   275
uel Danaum* Phrygiōs ^iaculātus *puppibus ignīs,
– squālentem barbam et concrētōs sanguine crīnīs
uulneraque illa ^gerēns, quae circum^ plūrima ^mūrōs
accēpit ^patriōs. ultrō flēns ipse uidēbar
compellāre uirum et maestās exprōmere uōcēs: 280
"ō lūx Dardaniae, spēs ō fīdissima Teucrum,
quae tantae tenuēre morae? quibus Hector^ ab ōrīs
^exspectāte uenīs? ut tē post multa tuōrum
fūnera, post uariōs hominumque urbisque labōrēs
dēfessī aspicimus! quae causa indigna serēnōs   285
foedāuit uultūs? aut cūr haec uulnera cernō?'"

275 *exuui-ae ārum* 1f. pl. spoils (of war); here dir.
obj. of *indūtus* used as if an act. vb; see p. 39 ((c)
(ii)) above
induō 3 *induī indūtum* I dress, clothe myself
Achillī: gen. s. Patroclus was wearing Achilles'
armour, which Hector stripped off and wore
himself after he had killed him (*Iliad* 17.125–31,
188–97). Aeneas compares Hector on that return,
in triumph, with this one (though in Homer he
never actually returned *home* if that is what *redit*
means). Note that Aeneas does not say Hector
had got the armour off Patroclus: he omits that in
order to increase Hector's glory (S.)
276 *iaculor* 1 dep. I throw, hurl. Hector hurled fire
on the Greek ships at *Iliad* 16.112–24, which
caused Achilles to send Patroclus back into battle
(16.124–9) – to his death
277 *squāleō* 2 I am covered in dirt
barb-a ae 1f. beard
concrēscō 3 *concrēuī concrētum* I congeal, clot;
Hector was (apparently) famous for his hair (S.)

278 *gerēns*: agreeing with *Hector* in the previous
sentence. S. comments that Hector is said to
'wear' his wounds as if they were badges of
honour collected from his many battles for his
fatherland
279 *fleō* 2 I weep
280 *compellō* 1 I address
exprōmō 3 I express
281 *Dardani-a ae* 1f. Troy
283 *exspectāte*: not the 2s. imper., but voc. of the
perf. part.!
ut: how ('gladly' implied) . . .!
284 **uari-us a um* various
285 **dēfess-us a um* exhausted
**aspiciō* 3 *aspexī aspectum* I see, observe, catch
sight of
indign-us a um shameful
serēn-us a um calm, serene
286 **uult-us ūs* 4m. face, look
**cernō* 3 *crēuī crētum* I see

weeping (*flēns*, 279–80), he came face to face with a tearful Hector (270–1). Note that
mihi 271 – Aeneas is now fully and *personally* engaged, rather than merely part of the
larger crowd. Hector's past – a life of glorious success (274–6) followed by death and
disfigurement at Achilles' hands (272–3, 277–9) – maps the fate that Troy is on the point
of suffering. It may seem bewildering that Aeneas, who knew exactly what had happened to Hector, should appear not to realise that Hector is dead, but this is a *dream*. It
is psychologically astute of V. to understand that in dreams we are not in contact with
reality; and Aeneas inserts an 'editorial' comment to show that he now understands this
(*ut quondam*, 272). It is therefore entirely reasonable for Aeneas to be baffled by
Hector's absence and bewildered by his ghastly appearance, calling him Troy's greatest
hope, come so late (281–3; S. comments on the paradox that *spēs* is always uncertain,
but in Hector it was *fīdissima*). Even in this sweet sleep, when in 'real' time Aeneas had
every reason to believe that the Greeks had departed and the Trojans had 'won', he is
still churning over the battles of the past, still fighting and exhausted by them, especially
in Hector's apparent absence (283–5). It takes this nightmare vision of Hector to alert

2.287–97: 'He ignored my questions and told me Troy was no more: I was to flee, taking the city's sacraments and household gods with me'

'ille nihil, nec mē quaerentem uāna morātur,
sed grauiter gemitūs īmō dē pectore dūcēns,
"hēū fuge, nāte deā, tēque hīs" ait "ēripe flammīs.
hostis habet mūrōs; ruit altō ā culmine Troia.   290
sat patriae Priamōque datum: sī Pergama dextrā
dēfendī possent, etiam hāc dēfēnsa fuissent.
sacra suōsque tibī commendat Troia penātīs;
hōs cape fātōrum comitēs, hīs moenia quaere
magna, pererrātō^ statuēs quae dēnique ^pontō."   295

Learning vocabulary

aspiciō 3 aspexī aspectum I see, observe, catch sight of
cernō 3 crēuī crētum I see
dēfess-us a um exhausted
exuui-ae ārum 1f. pl. spoils (of war)
Hector -is 3m. Hector, greatest Trojan fighter, killed by Achilles
maest-us a um tearful
uari-us a um various
uult-us ūs 4m. face, look

287 ille nihil: ellipsis of 'said' qualified by nec . . . morātur, i.e. Hector ignored Aeneas' questions
morātur: = 'he pays attention to mē quaerentem uāna' (acc. n. pl.)
290 *culmen culmin-is 3n. top, peak, height
291 *sat = satis; sat datum (est) lit. 'enough has been given to . . .' This is a financial idiom, meaning 'the account is squared with', i.e. 'you have fulfilled all your obligations to . . .'

292 possent . . . fuissent: try to bring out the impf./plupf. differentiation of the subjuncs. in this conditional; **RL**139, 173, S2(c), **W**33, **M**115–16
etiam hāc: i.e. dextrā, by this (hand of mine) etiam 'as well' (sc. 'as yours'). Neither of them, says Hector, could save Troy; no shame, therefore, attaches to either
293 sacra: n. pl.; presumably the sacred fire (which must never go out) referred to at 297
commendō 1 I entrust; note that Hector says not 'I' but Troy entrusts its gods to Aeneas (S.) – Aeneas and the future of Troy are linked for the first time
294 hōs . . . hīs: referring to the penātēs; comitēs is in apposition to hōs, hīs dat. 'for [the advantage of] these'
295 magna: the great walls (of the new city) quae statuēs, pererrātō . . . pontō (abl. abs.), i.e. you will construct great walls, you will not find them waiting for you (S.); and it will be a long, hard journey
pererrō 1 I roam through

Aeneas to the nightmare that is to come, when he will have to become the lūx Dardaniae, the spēs fīdissima Teucrum.

This is a justly famous passage, heavy with pathos. But, like Homer, Aeneas here does not invite us to feel sorry or sympathise or react in any particular way ('It was so sad, wasn't it?'). He simply depicts what he saw, heard and said and how he reacted to it. He leaves our reaction up to us.

2.287–97: One might imagine Hector had been crying over his dreadful treatment at Achilles' hands, as Aeneas was. Far from it: his tears (271, cf. gemitūs 288) are for Troy and for the need for a great hero like Aeneas to flee (S.). Aeneas, after the event, now knows that his questions were uāna (287) and relates Hector's sharp, unvarnished, clear, rhetorically organised commands: (i) run for it (289), because (a) Troy is done for and (b) they have done all they honourably can (sat . . . datum, 291: 'it is agreed that no one can fight fate', affirms S.); (ii) take Troy's gods with you, which Hector (still in the dream) hands over to him: the penātēs (293) and Vesta, goddess of the hearth (296) with

sīc ait, et manibus uittās Vestamque potentem
aeternumque adytīs effert penetrālibus ignem.'

2.298–317: 'As the noise of battle grew, I made for the top of the house to witness the scene, like a shepherd watching a fire or flood. Destruction was widespread; foolishly I armed myself for battle'

'dīuersō intereā miscentur moenia lūctū,
et magis atque magis, quamquam sēcrēta^ parentis
Anchīsae ^domus arboribusque ^obtēcta recessit,   300

296 *manibus*: this is all a *dream*: the sacred objects are not *physically* handed over till 320–1 (see **2.318–35**)

uittās Vestamque: i.e. the Vesta *with* the headbands (hendiadys? See **Glossary of literary terms**), presumably an image so adorned

**potēns potent-is powerful (over + gen.)

297 **penetrāl-is e* innermost; *penetrāle* 3n. inner shrine

ignem: the 'eternal fire' of Troy was transferred to the altar of Vesta in Rome and burned there, thus ensuring (it was hoped) the city's security for ever – a powerful, symbolic link between past and present

Learning vocabulary

culmen culmin-is 3n. top, peak, height
penetrāl-e is 3n. inner shrine
penetrāl-is e innermost
potēns potent-is powerful (over + gen.)
sat = *satis*

298 **dīuers-us a um scattered
**misceō 2 *miscuī mistum/mixtum* I mix, scatter, disturb, confuse
299 *sēcrēt-us a um* secluded, remote
300 **Anchīs-ēs -ae* Anchises, Aeneas' father
obtegō 3 *obtēxī obtēctum* I protect, screen
*recēdō 3 *recessī* I stand apart; depart, leave

its eternal flame (297); and (iii) re-establish Troy somewhere else (294–5) – which Aeneas will eventually do when he brings these gods into Latium (1.5–6).

This scene, which is never referred to again, is of the utmost importance. Heroes do not run for it, nor will Aeneas – at least to start with. He has his heroic duty to do. But he also has his instructions from Hector, and when he finally realises where his destiny lies, i.e. not in Ilium but somewhere else (559ff.), he can leave it, head held high: '. . . this desertion needs to be presented not as the faint-hearted flight of a man concerned to save his own skin, but as a way of carrying out an act of pious duty towards the sacred images, the *penātēs* of Troy, for whom he must provide a new, secure home'. After all, if the great Hector and Aeneas could not have saved Troy (291–2), who could? In other words, Troy falls because of Sinon's treachery and Trojan innocence – not because of any failure in heroism on Aeneas' part. In this V. is ensuring that Aeneas, who in Homer's *Iliad* is something of a minor figure, is seen on the same footing as Troy's greatest Iliadic hero, Hector, whose death in Homer 'stands for' the death of Ilium (*Iliad* 22.410–11). Aeneas is to 'stand for' Ilium's resurrection as Rome.

See: Heinze's comments on this scene at 33–5/21–2 and 26/16–17.

2.298–317: Aeneas begins by explaining why he had not been awoken by the battle in the town: his father's house was well set back and screened by trees (298–300). Nevertheless, as the noise encroached more and more (301) – presumably 298 refers to his drowsy awareness of some sort of crying from different quarters – he shook himself out of his dream (302); a sharp observation of the way in which, asleep or dreaming, one

clārēscunt sonitūs, armōrumque ingruit horror.
excutior somnō, et summī fastīgia tēctī
ascēnsū superō, atque arrēctīs auribus astō:
in segetem uelutī cum flamma, furentibus Austrīs,
incidit, aut rapidus montānō flūmine torrēns   305
sternit agrōs, sternit sata laeta boumque labōrēs
praecipitīsque trahit siluās; stupet īnscius∧ altō*
∧accipiēns sonitum saxī dē *uertice ∧pāstor.
tum uērō manifesta fidēs, Danaumque patēscunt
īnsidiae. iam Dēiphobī dedit ampla∧ ruīnam,   310

301 *clārēscō* 3 I sound clearly
ingruō 3 I advance threateningly
*horror -is 3m. terror, alarm
302 *excutior*: in 'middle' reflexive sense, 'I shake myself free'; see p. 39 ((c)(i)) above
**fastīgi-a ōrum 2n. pl. outlines; roof, heights, tips
303 *ascēns-us ūs* 4m. ascent, climb
superō: 'I climb over' (OLD 1)
a(d)stō 1 I stand (upright)
304 *segēs seget-is* 3f. corn-field, crop
**uelut(ī) just as
**furō 3 *furuī* I rage
305 *incidō* 3 I fall on
**rapidus violent, swift, consuming
montān-us a um in a mountain, mountain
torrēns torrent-is 3m. rushing stream
306 **sternō* 3 *strāuī strātum* I flatten
sat-a ōrum 2n. pl. crops
bōs bou-is m./f. ox, bull; cow (gen. pl. *boum*); their *labōrēs* are the *fruits* of their labours

307 **praeceps praecipit-is* headlong; sheer, steep
īnsci-us a um ignorant, bewildered; he can see the flood but has no idea why it has occurred (S.) or what to do about it
308 ***uertex uertic-is* 3m. peak; whirlpool
pāstor -is 3m. herdsman
309 *manifest-us a um* clear, plain, manifest
fidēs: = proof (ellipsis of *est*) i.e. of what Hector told him? Or rather, ironically, 'the good faith (sc. of the Greeks)', explained in the next clause (S.'s choice)?
patēscō 2 I am revealed
310 *Dēiphob-us ī* 2m. Deiphobus, brother of Hector. Tradition had it that his house was attacked first, because he had married Helen when Paris was killed in battle
ampl-us a um great
**ruīn-a ae 1f. wreck, ruin, collapse; *ruīnam dō* lit. 'I give a crash', i.e. collapse

can be vaguely aware of some external intrusion before waking with a start. He races up to the roof (302–3) – there is an urgency about *superō* – and tries to catch what is happening (it was the sound that awoke him).

V., like Homer, tends to introduce similes at moments of high drama, and this is one: Aeneas' first awareness of what is happening to his city, just as Hector had told him. The simile of the shepherd, baffled and helpless (*īnscius* 307) as, from a high rock (308), he hears a fire raging through crops (304–5) or a burst river flattening fields and country-side (305–7), is based on Homer: 'As two mountain rivers in winter, fed by their great springs higher up, meet in full spate in some deep ravine, while far off in the mountains a shepherd hears the thunder, such were the yelling and turmoil as the two armies came to grips' (Rieu-Jones, *Iliad* 4.452–6). The central feature of both similes is that there is nothing man can do in the face of the irresistible violence of nature, which is what the Greek assault on Ilium adds up to. As Hector said, nothing more could be done. The simile demonstrates it. But in Homer's simile, the shepherd is more of a bystander, and only the natural world is at risk. V.'s simile, however, puts a human at the centre of it, and a bewildered, apprehensive one too, observing from his high rock, like Aeneas from the top of the house, the work of *men* (304, 306) being destroyed as well as of the natural world: and the city was above all the work of men.

Volcānō superante, ^domus, iam proximus ārdet
Vcalegōn; Sīgēa ignī freta lāta relūcent.
exoritur clāmorque uirum clangorque tubārum.
arma āmēns capiō; nec sat ratiōnis in armīs,
sed glomerāre manum bellō et concurrere in arcem   315
cum sociīs ārdent animī; furor īraque mentem
praecipitat, pulchrumque morī succurrit in armīs.'

311 *Volcān-us -ī* 2m. Vulcan, god of fire; here the name of the god stands for his attribute (metonymy)
312 *Vcalegōn* nom. s. Ucalegon, a Trojan counsellor
Sīgē-us a um of Sigeum, a headland near Troy
fret-um ī 2n. strait, narrow, sea
relūceō 2 I shine out
313 *exorior* 4 dep. I arise
clangor -is 3m. clangour, shriek
tub-a ae 1f. trumpet
314 **āmēns āment-is* mindless, mad, frantic
315 ***glomerō* 1 I gather; throng round; the inf., like *concurrere*, controlled by *ārdent animī* (**316**)
bellō: dat. of purpose; **RL88.6, WSuppl.** syntax
concurrō 3 I run together
317 *succurrit*: 'it occurs/seems (to me to be)'

dīuers-us a um scattered
fastīgi-a ōrum 2n. pl. outlines; roof, heights, tips
furō 3 *furuī* I rage
glomerō 1 I gather; throng round
horror -is 3m. terror, alarm
misceō 2 *miscuī mistum/mixtum* I mix, scatter, disturb, confuse
praeceps praecipit-is headlong; sheer, steep
rapid-us a um violent, rapid, consuming
ruīn-a ae 1f. wreck, ruin, collapse
recēdō 3 *recessī* I stand apart; depart, leave
sternō 3 *strāuī strātum* I flatten
uelut(ī) just as
uertex uertic-is 3m. peak; whirlpool

Learning vocabulary

āmēns āment-is mindless, mad, frantic
Anchīs-ēs -ae 3m. Anchises, Aeneas' father

Aeneas now reflects on the meaning of it all – the truth revealed at last of Greek treachery (309–10; contrast *manifesta* with *īnscius* and note the ironical *fidēs*). He observes the violent destruction of houses (310–12) and the flames illuminating the straits well out to sea (312), hears the noise of conflict (313). This inflames him and makes him lose all grip on reason (314), as he freely admits (S., keen to save Aeneas' reputation, comments 'he wanted to show that his first thought was for his fatherland, but that there was nothing rational about coming to its aid with weapons, since it was on fire – and how could he defend a city in flames?'). Desperate to link up with fellow men and fight (315–16), he admits that he was driven by *furor* and *īra* (316), a potentially fatal combination for a warrior, and thinks only of the beauty of death in battle (317).

But what of Hector's unambiguous assessment of the situation that Troy is done for and Aeneas is the future? Aeneas admits it played no part in his thoughts. It was all forgotten. And, after all, the encounter with Hector *was* simply a dream. Further, Aeneas has now awoken to the devastating reality of the situation – the brutal destruction of his own people. How could any man be expected to react to that? Does not a man of *pietās* owe a duty to his community? The shepherd in the simile was *īnscius*: so was Aeneas, but now he will find out what the truth of the matter really is. The eventual consequences, did he but know it, will involve him in changing the world for ever.

Commentators argue endlessly about whether, after Hector's unambiguous warning, Aeneas' actions here are to be condemned or not. They signally fail to take into account

2.318–35: 'I asked the priest Panthus, escaping with grandson and holy objects, what was happening and he said all hope was lost – the Greeks had taken the city'

'ecce autem tēlīs Panthūs ēlāpsus Achīuum,
Panthūs Othryadēs, arcis Phoebīque sacerdōs,
sacra manū uictōsque deōs paruumque nepōtem   320
ipse trahit, cursūque āmēns ad līmina tendit.
"quō^ rēs summa ^locō, Panthū? quam prendimus arcem?"
uix ea fātus eram, gemitū cum tālia reddit:
"uēnit summa diēs et inēluctābile tempus
Dardaniae. fuimus Trōes, fuit Īlium et ingēns   325

318 *Panthūs* nom. s. a Trojan priest of Apollo, son of Othryas (**319**); voc. *Panthū* (**322**). V. may have transferred the role of priest of Apollo from Laocoon to Panthus (see on **2.40–9**). Since Apollo was a strongly pro-Trojan god, it is right that a priest of his should be attempting to save the city's gods

**ēlābor 3 dep. *ēlāpsus* I escape, slip away from *Achīuum*: gen. pl.

320 *uictōsque deōs*: if a city was conquered, its gods must have been as well (cf. on 351 below)

321 *trahit*: parents, with their longer legs, always need to hurry along small children, cf. on 457/724

322 *quō . . . locō*: 'in what condition?' (S. comments

'the useful citizen elegantly makes the republic his first concern')

rēs summa: = main/brunt of the battle

prendō 3 I hold, occupy; it could be present or perfect – any preference? *arcem* means 'position of strength', 'strong point'

323 *cum*: see on 256

324 *inēluctābil-is e* insurmountable, inescapable

325 *Dardaniae*: gen. or dat. – any preference?

fuimus . . . Teucrōrum (**326**): wonderful triplet (note position of *glōria*, **326**). **324–6** are a fine example of V.'s supreme simplicity. See *Intro* [9] footnote 20

** *Trōes* 3m. pl. Trojans

(as often) the main point, that *it is Aeneas who is speaking*, making his own honest assessment, as narrator, of his behaviour many years after the event. He admits that, at the time, he was driven by anger and rage. But that is not the master-narrator V.'s judgement. It is his own, and we should accept it as it stands. We may conclude that he is to be applauded for his honesty. Is there not such a thing as justifiable anger? (See *Intro* [43], **2.526–43**, **2.589–603**; and for the powerful attachment to one's home, *Intro* [39].)

Austin (1964) points out that V. probably invented the notion that Ilium was set ablaze as soon as the Greeks emerged from the wooden horse (in other traditions, it was fired only as the Greeks left: see e.g. *Appendix* 22). The flames and night-time setting certainly provide a magnificently dramatic backdrop to the Greek assault. The flames equally ensure that (ultimately) there is nothing Aeneas can do to save Ilium (*fuit Īlium*, as Panthus is about to say, 325). Aeneas' attempts are, indeed, madness – heroic madness?

See: Stahl (1981: 165ff.), who argues strongly that this fighting is designed to bring out the heroic side of Aeneas-as-warrior. See *Intro* [38, 43].

2.318–35: Panthus, like Aeneas (314), is frantic (*āmēns* 321). He is a priest and carries with him the sacraments of Troy (320), described by Hector in Aeneas' dream at 293–7. He is bringing them to Aeneas' house (*ad līmina* 321), and we must assume that at this point they are handed over (otherwise Aeneas cannot give them to his father for safe-keeping at 717). But at this crisis Aeneas reasonably has no time to worry

glōria Teucrōrum; ferus omnia Iuppiter Argōs
trānstulit; incēnsā Danaī dominantur in urbe.
arduus^ armātōs mediīs in moenibus ^astāns
fundit ^equus, uictorque Sinōn incendia miscet
īnsultāns. portīs aliī bipatentibus adsunt,   330
mīlia quot magnīs^ umquam uēnēre ^Mycēnīs;
obsēdēre aliī tēlīs^ angusta uiārum
^oppositīs; stat ferrī aciēs^ mucrōne coruscō
^stricta, ^parāta necī; uix prīmī^ proelia temptant
portārum ^uigilēs et caecō Mārte resistunt."'   335

326 *fer-us a um* savage, wild; S. notes that Virgil ensures that Aeneas, unlike Panthus the priest, never rushes into criticising the gods like this, but cf. 428

omnia: all the gods have gone over to Greece, taking everything the Trojans had with them, cf. 351–2

327 *trānsferō trānsferre trānstulī* I transfer, give over. Gods abandoned a defeated city. Troy is destitute of divine help in any form, it seems

*incendō 3 incendī incēnsum I set fire to

**dominor 1 dep. I rule over (+ dat.)

328 *ardu-us a um* high, towering

astō 1 I stand

329 **incendi-um ī 2n.* fire

330 *īnsultō 1* I gloat, prance

bipatēns bipatent-is double, i.e. both halves of the city's double gates are open

331 *mīlia quot*: 'as many thousands as', in apposition to *aliī* **330**, as if none had been killed in the previous ten years

Mycēnīs: 'from Mycenae'

332 **obsideō 2 obsēdī obsessum* I besiege

angust-us a um narrow (here n. pl., i.e. parts of the street)

333 **oppōnō 3 opposuī oppositum* I interpose

mucrō mucrōn-is 3m. sword-point

334 *stringō 3 strīnxī strictum* I draw (of swords)

nex nec-is 3f. slaughter, murder

335 *uigil -is* 3m. guard, sentry (cf. 266, so some survived, even if only a few, implied by *uix* **334**)

**Mārs Mārt-is 3m. Mars, god of war/battle; *caecō Mārte* = 'blind resistance' (one of S.'s suggestions, among 'in a battle at night', 'in the uncertainty of battle' and 'in the confusion of battle')

See: on **318**, E. L. Harrison 'Divine Action in *Aeneid* Book 2' in S. J. Harrison (1990: 53) for a discussion of Apollo's role.

Learning vocabulary

dominor 1 dep. I rule over (+ dat.)

ēlābor 3 dep. *ēlāpsus* I escape, slip away from

incendi-um ī 2n. fire

incendō 3 incendī incēnsum I set fire to

Mārs Mārt-is 3m. Mars, god of war/battle

obsideō 2 obsēdī obsessum I besiege

oppōnō 3 opposuī oppositum I interpose

Trōs pl. *Trōes* 3m. Trojans

about them – he does not recall Hector's instructions anyway, and currently has other priorities – and urgently asks Panthus what the situation is. Panthus repeats what Hector said in the dream: it is the end. Note especially the mournful pathos of 324, sounding like a death-knell (that wonderful Virgilian invention *inēluctābile*: you cannot even *struggle* to avoid it), sinking under the weight of *Dardaniae* in the next line; the bald, bleakly repeated *fuimus . . . fuit* (325) – not *erāmus* or *erat*, because the end *has* happened and it is *now* all over – and the impact of *glōria*, first word of 326. It has all gone. Their past is *now* past, whether Dardanian, Trojan, Iliadic or Teucrian (the four terms indicating 'Trojan', all with different historical associations, used at 325–6). Even Jupiter, now *ferus*, is against them, having already transported (perf.) everything across (and across the hexameter too) to Greece (326–7). The run-over lines draw out the agony, closing only with the (end-stopped) Greeks triumphant in the city inferno (327).

Panthus now draws the more detailed picture: the horse pouring out soldiers (328–9), a triumphant Sinon (329–30), the gates open (330), streets blocked (332–3) and Greeks

2.336–54: 'I joined other Trojans and urged them to be ready to die in defence of a lost cause'

'tālibus Othryadae dictīs et nūmine dīuum
in flammās et in arma feror, quō trīstis Erīnȳs,
quō fremitus uocat et sublātus ad aethera clāmor.
addunt sē sociōs Rhīpeus et maximus armīs
Ēpytus, oblātī per lūnam, Hypanisque Dymāsque   340
et laterī adglomerant nostrō, iuuenisque Coroebus^
Mygdonidēs – illīs ad Troiam forte diēbus
uēnerat īnsānō Cassandrae ^incēnsus amōre
et ^gener auxilium Priamō Phrygibusque ferēbat,
^īnfēlīx quī nōn spōnsae praecepta furentis   345
audierit!
quōs ubi cōnfertōs audēre in proelia uīdī,

336 *Othryadae*: i.e. of Panthus (see on 318)
nūmine dīuum: S. glosses 'with the god instilling evil
  desires [in me]', with reference to 396. Whether
  the god did or did not, that is Aeneas' account of
  his feelings. Some prefer to avoid the problem by
  glossing as e.g. 'under the impulse of misguided
  desires'
337 *feror* (pass. of *ferō*) I rush
Erīnȳs nom. s. Fury of war, war frenzy (a Greek god
  of vengeance). 337–8 is another typical Virgilian
  triplet, cf. 169–7
338 *fremit-us ūs* 4m. groan, yell
339 ** *addō* 3 *addidī additum* I add, receive
Rhīpeus nom. s. a Trojan
armīs: abl. of respect
340 *Ēpytus* nom. s. a Trojan
Hypanis nom. s. a Trojan
Dymās nom. s. a Trojan

341 *laterī*: i.e. the band at our side
adglomerō 1 I join (myself to + dat.)
Coroebus nom. s. a Trojan
342 *Mygdonidēs* nom. s. son of Mygdon (a king of
  Phrygia)
343 *īnsān-us a um* crazed, deranged
344 *gener -ī* 2m. (prospective) son-in-law (in
  apposition, 'as . . .')
Phryg-ēs um 3m. pl. Phrygians, i.e. Trojans
345 *quī . . . audierit*: causal subjunc., 'in that/because
  he . . .', see **RL**140.2
spōns-a ae 1f. (intended) bride
praecept-um ī 2n. warning
346 *audierit*: for unfinished lines, see on 1.534
347 *quōs*: i.e. these soldiers
cōnfert-us a um standing side by side, packed
audēre in: to be bold for (would *ārdēre* be
  better?)

ready for the kill (333–4) – impossible therefore to consolidate the Trojans into a single fighting unit – and few offering resistance (334–5). In other words, the sheer number of Greeks in the city and their hold on the main routes of communication make any prospect of effective defence out of the question. It is going to be every man for himself.

2.336–54: Aeneas has the picture, from both Hector and Panthus: resistance is pointless. It makes no difference. At Panthus' words, Aeneas is carried off by some supernatural impulse (note *nūmine dīuum* 336 – Aeneas' explanation – and *feror* passive) into battle. His blood is up: he is not his own man. Since he cannot see where the fighting is, he follows the noise of battle (337–8), gathering men in ones and twos as he goes (339–42; S. comments that Aeneas does not have to look for them but is actively sought out by them, i.e. he is a natural leader, cf. 797).

Coroebus gets a special mention. He had come to Troy out of crazed love for the prophetess Cassandra (341–3), stupidly paying no attention to her warnings (345–6).

incipiō super hīs: "iuuenēs, fortissima frūstrā
pectora, sī uōbīs audentem extrēma cupīdō
certa sequī, quae^ sit rēbus ^fortūna uidētis: 350
excessēre omnēs,^ adytīs ārīsque relictīs,
^dī quibus imperium hoc steterat; succurritis urbī
incēnsae. moriāmur et in media arma ruāmus.
ūna salūs uictīs, nūllam spērāre salūtem.'"

348 *super* in addition (i.e. to make them more eager); *hīs* refers to the words he spoke

349: a difficult line. Translate as: *sī extrēma cupīdō [est] uōbīs sequī [me] audentem certa* (n. pl., i.e. certain death)

cupīdō cupīdin-is 3f. desire

351 **excēdō* 3 *excessī excessum* I depart (from + abl.); cf. 326–7. Austin quotes a tradition that on the night Ilium fell, the gods were seen carrying their images out of their temples. S. suggests that the gods have been 'called out' of the city by the enemy, who do not wish to commit sacrilege by attacking it (and therefore the gods) while they are still there (another anachronistic Roman tradition, cf. on 320 and *Intro* [23])

352 *quibus*: 'with whose help'

353 *moriāmur . . . ruāmus*: note subjunc., in comparison with *succurritis* (**352**)

354 *ūna . . . uictīs*: understand *est*: a crisp, brilliantly paradoxical *sententia* of the sort with which orators were encouraged to end their harangue. It expands on Aeneas' thoughts at 317. S. comments that desperation increases firmness of resolve, but they are already *uictīs*, so there is no hope: only death awaits

Learning vocabulary

addō 3 *addidī additum* I add, receive
Coroebus nom. s. a Trojan
Dymās nom. s. a Trojan
Ēpytus nom. s. a Trojan
excēdō 3 *excessī excessum* I depart (from + abl.)
Hypanis nom. s. a Trojan
Rhīpeus nom. s. a Trojan

This is a typically Homeric touch. Homer often added brief thumb-nail sketches of warriors who come to Troy despite warnings that they will never return. In this scene V. combines two such Homeric sketches: specifically, (i) of Othryoneus: '[Idomeneus] struck panic into the Trojans by killing Othryoneus, an ally who had joined them from Cabesus. Drawn by news of the war, this man was a newcomer to Troy who had asked Priam for the hand of Cassandra, the most beautiful of his daughters . . . he had promised to do great things and drive the Greeks from his shores' (Rieu-Jones, *Iliad* 13.362–5); and, more generally, (ii) of the sons of Merops: 'A chariot and two leaders of the people then fell to [Odysseus and Diomedes]. They were the two sons of Merops of Percote, the ablest prophet of his day. He had forbidden his sons to go off to the killing fields, but these two, led on by the demons of death, had not listened to him' (Rieu-Jones, *Iliad* 11.328–32). The effect is to add pathos to their entry into a fight which they are certain to lose.

The battle-fury is on Aeneas. Like a good leader, he senses his men's mood (347), does not try to deceive them about what lies ahead (350) or the reason for it (351–2), and encourages them to be ready to die (*moriāmur* 353, *uictīs* 354). (Cf. Mustafa Kemal to his Turkish troops at the defence of Gallipoli against an attacking Australian and New Zealand force in April 1915: 'I am not ordering you to fight. I am ordering you to die.') This is the epic hero at his most extreme and defiant.

See: Heinze (28–33/18–20), and cf. *Appendix* **8** for the many traditions uncomplimentary to Aeneas.

2.355–69: 'We attacked like wolves; the city was on its knees, bodies everywhere (Greek and Trojan), grief, fear and death universal'

'sīc animīs iuuenum furor additus. inde, lupī cēū   355
raptōrēs ātrā in nebulā, quōs^ improba* uentrīs
exēgit ^caecōs *rabiēs, catulīque relictī
faucibus exspectant siccīs, per tēla, per hostīs
uādimus haud dubiam in mortem, mediaeque tenēmus
urbis iter; nox ātra cauā circumuolat umbrā.   360
quis clādem illīus noctis, quis fūnera fandō
explicet aut possit lacrimīs aequāre labōrēs?
urbs antīqua ruit, multōs domināta per annōs;
plūrima perque uiās sternuntur inertia passim
corpora, perque domōs et rēligiōsa deōrum   365
līminā. nec sōlī poenās dant sanguine Teucrī;
quondam etiam uictīs redit in praecordia uirtūs,
uictōrēsque cadunt Danaī. crūdēlis ubīque
lūctus, ubīque pauor et plūrima mortis imāgō.'

355 *lup-us ī* 2m. wolf
*****cēū* like (take before *lupī*). V. is imitating Homer's common description of warriors attacking *lukoi hōs* ('like [*hōs*] wolves'), always at the end of the line
356 *raptor -is* 3m. robber, ravager, plunderer
*******nebul-a ae* 1f. cloud
improb-us a um shameless, uncontrollable
uenter uentr-is 3m. belly, stomach
357 *exigō* 3 *exēgī exāctum* I drive (on)
rabi-ēs ēī 5f. hunger
catul-us ī 2m. cub
358 *fauc-ēs ium* 3f. jaws; here abl. abs., abl. of 'attendant circumstances' (**RL**150–1, **W**24, **M**79–80)
sicc-us a um dry
359 *uādō* 3 I advance
mediae . . . urbis: i.e. into the middle of the city (S. comments 'This refers to their bravery', and compares 736–7 where, fearfully, they keep off the main paths)
360 *circumuolō* 1 I hover round
361 *clād-ēs is* 3f. slaughter

362 *explicō* 1 I unfold, list in full; note the 'potential' subjunc., **RL**153.2
aequō 1 I match; *lacrimīs* is abl. of means, like the gerund *fandō* **361** (cf. on 6)
364 *iners inert-is* lifeless, resistless
*****passim* far and wide
365 *rēligiōs-us a um* hallowed, sacred, awe-filled
366 *poenās dant*: one may ask 'what penalty, to whom and why?', but this is how Aeneas sees the situation with hindsight
367 ***quondam* at times; formerly; some day; note the assonance of *uictīs . . . uirtūs . . . uictōrēs* in **367–8**
praecordi-a ōrum 2n. pl. breast, heart
368 *****ubīque* everywhere
369 *pauor -is* 3m. fear, terror; note that *-or* is metrically lengthened (it was once *pauōs*)
*******imāgō imāgin-is* 3f. image, likeness, appearance, ghost; S. prosaically suggests *plūrima mortis imāgō* means different types of death (sword, fire, jumping from a height), or death 'full on'. Perhaps 'death in every shape'?

2.355–69: Aeneas was driven by *furor īraque* (316). Now he fills his men with *furor* too (355), beaten though they are before they begin (*haud dubiam in mortem* 359, *uictīs* 367). A wolf simile accompanies their entry into battle (a typical place for similes to occur in Homer). The wolves are reckless (*improba* 355, *rabiēs* 356), cf. the Trojan's *furor*; they attack in the dark (*ātra nebula* 356), cf. *nox ātra . . . umbrā* 360; and they leave

2.370–85: 'We killed the Greek Androgeos and his men, who did not recognise us as Trojans'

'prīmus sē Danaum, magnā comitante cateruā,   370
Androgeōs offert nōbīs, socia agmina crēdēns
īnscius, atque ultrō uerbīs compellat amīcīs:
"festīnāte, uirī! nam quae tam sēra morātur
sēgnitiēs? aliī rapiunt incēnsa feruntque
Pergama: uōs celsīs nunc prīmum ā nāuibus ītis?"   375
dīxit, et extemplō (neque enim respōnsa dabantur

Learning vocabulary	371 *Androgeōs* nom. s. Androgeos, a Greek soldier
cēu like	(unknown to Homer; also **382**)
imāgō imāgin-is 3f. image, likeness, appearance,	*socia agmina*: i.e. 'our ranks [to be] *socia*'
ghost	**372** *īnsci-us a um* unaware
nebul-a ae 1f. cloud	*ultrō*: i.e. without any approach from us
passim far and wide	*compellō* 1 I address
quondam at times; formerly; some day	**373** *sēr-us a um* late, too slow
ubīque everywhere	**374** *sēgniti-ēs ēī* 5f. sluggishness
	375 *cels-us a um* high, lofty
370 *prīmus . . . Androgeōs*: take in order *prīmus*	**376** *extemplō* suddenly
Danaum, Androgeōs, offert sē nōbīs. cateruā refers	*rēspōns-um ī* 2n. reply
to his accompanying troops	

their young behind (357–8), as the Trojans are leaving their families behind and taking to the streets. Some see a problem: wolves are not normally taken to be noble creatures. Does that matter? On the other hand, they do show valour. Should we question the 'ethical and moral evaluation' which such a simile lends to the narrative? But Aeneas is speaking; the action is being 'focalised' through his eyes. That is how he sees himself and his men at that moment; that is what he perceives as the only spirit in which to enter such a battle against such a treacherous and deadly enemy. He does not shirk from being honest about his feelings (see on **2.298–317**).

Trojan courage is illustrated by their route straight into the middle of the city (359–60) – at which point Aeneas, in tragic Greek chorus mode, inserts emotionalising questions and personal, mournful reflection at 361–3 (on 363, S. comments 'an utterance typical of one grieving, not stating the facts') which lead him to develop harrowing images of the dead strewn across streets, homes and temples (364–6; S. notes the careful gradation, climaxing in the dead in temples, an insult to the gods) and to remember occasional Trojan triumphs (367–8). He closes the scene with a striking, abstract picture of savagery, terror and death (368–9). Aeneas seems to be struggling to present a composite picture of the whole horrifying experience before he ventures into the details – his audience must be made to know *and feel* what it was really like and how dreadful the consequences – but he cannot forget or distance himself from his feelings. He chops and changes between narration, reflection, question and comment as his own emotions keep on intruding.

See: Horsfall (1995: 113–14) on the wolf simile; but Horsfall (2008: 293–4) changes his mind slightly.

2.370–85: Aeneas and his men are making for the middle of the city (359–60), and the first Greek they encounter is Androgeos, who mistakes them for Greeks (370–2).

fīda satis) sēnsit mediōs dēlāpsus in hostīs.
obstipuit, retrōque pedem cum uōce repressit.
imprōuīsum^ asprīs uelutī quī sentibus ^anguem
pressit, humī nītēns, trepidusque repente refūgit   380
^attollentem īrās et caerula colla ^tumentem,
haud secus Androgeōs, uīsū tremefactus, abībat.
inruimus dēnsīs et circumfundimur armīs,
ignarōsque locī passim et formīdine captōs
sternimus; aspīrat prīmō Fortūna labōrī.'   385

377 *dēlābor* 3 dep. *dēlāpsus* I descend, fall among
   (here *sēnsit dēlāpsus*, lit. 'he sensed having fallen
   among' means 'he sensed that he had fallen
   among', imitating a common Greek nom. + part.
   construction)
378 *reprimō* 3 *repressī* I check
379 *asprīs = asperīs*: *uelutī quī* is the subject 'just as
   one who . . .'
sent-is is 3m. bramble, bush
angu-is is 3m. snake
380 *premō* 3 *pressī* I tread on
humī on the ground (-*ī* was always the Roman
   locative form; thus *Rōmae* 'at Rome' was once
   Rōmāī, Carthāgine Carthāginī, etc.)
nītor 3 dep. I rest my weight, tread; the firm tread of
   spondaic *nītēns* is followed by the sudden dactylic
   jump back of *trepidusque repente refūgit*, with
   repeated *re-* (Page 1894)
trepid-us a um fearful
refūgiō 3 *refūgī* I retreat
381 **attollō* 3 - - I raise, lift up

caerul-us a um dark blue
tumeō 2 I swell
382 *secus* differently
tremefaciō 3 *tremefēcī tremefactus* I cause to
   tremble
abībat: impf., as of one *on the point of* retreating or
   trying to retreat (S.); or *beginning*
383 *inruō* 3 I charge in
**dēns-us a um* in a pack; thick, frequent (here abl. of
   means)
circumfundor 3 I surround; used in a 'middle' sense,
   taking an understood dir. obj. 'them'. See p. 39
   ((c)(ii))
384 *ignarōsque . . . captōs*: ellipsis of 'them /
   Androgeos' men'
formīdō formīdin-is 3f. fear, terror
385 *aspīrō* 1 I am favourable to

Learning vocabulary
attollō 3 - - I raise, lift up
dēns-us a um in a pack; thick, frequent

Brusquely addressing them, he clearly thinks they are not making the necessary speed from the ships into the city, which he describes as being on fire and looted (373–5). Too late, he realises his mistake. Aeneas greets this exciting moment – the first action – with a simile. Note that the man in the simile finds himself unexpectedly in danger and tries to escape (379–80), and the snake is angry (381). The Trojans are the angry party, as Aeneas is happy to admit (316–17), though it is the simile that contains the information that they are angry; this is not specifically expressed outside it (unless one goes back to e.g. 355). In other words, similes can themselves add to the narrative picture as well as describe it.

V. again finds his model in Homer. Menelaus and Paris have agreed to fight a duel to settle the outcome of the war, but 'When godlike Paris saw Menelaus emerging through the ranks, his heart failed him completely and he retreated into his own contingent of warriors to avoid death. Like a man who catches sight of a snake in a wooded ravine and sharply recoils, knees trembling, and retreats, pale-faced, so godlike Paris disappeared back into the mass of proud Trojans' (Rieu-Jones, *Iliad* 3.30–6). The 'anger' element in the simile (*īrās* 381) could have occurred to V. from the simile describing how Hector decided to stand and face Achilles: 'As a mountain snake waits for a man beside its hole: it has swallowed poisonous herbs, its anger is dreadful and intimidatingly it stares at

2.386–401: '*Coroebus suggested disguising ourselves as Greeks, and we began by enjoying great success*'

'atque hic successū exsultāns animīsque Coroebus
"ō sociī, quā prīma^" inquit "^Fortūna salūtis
mōnstrat iter, quāque ostendit sē ^dextra, sequāmur:
mūtēmus clipeōs, Danaumque īnsignia nōbīs
aptēmus. dolus an uirtūs, quis in hoste requīrat?   390
arma dabunt ipsī." sīc fātus deīnde comantem^
Androgeī ^galeam clipeīque īnsigne decōrum
induitur, laterīque Argīuum accommodat ēnsem.
hoc Rhīpeus, hoc ipse Dymās omnisque iuuentūs
laeta facit: spoliīs sē quisque recentibus armat.   395
uādimus immixtī Danaīs, haud nūmine nostrō,
multaque^ per caecam congressī ^proelia noctem
cōnserimus, multōs Danaum dēmittimus Orcō.
diffugiunt aliī ad nauīs et lītora cursū

---

386 *success-us ūs* 4m. good result
exsultō 1 I jump about, exult; S. comments 'with joy – a mark of stupidity'
387 *quā prīma . . . Fortūna . . . quāque dextra*: 'where the first [stroke of] Fortune . . . and where favourable/on the right [strokes of Fortune]'
salūtis: construes with *iter* (388)
388 *sequāmur*: mood? So too *mūtēmus* (389) . . . *aptēmus* (390). See on 75
389 *īnsign-ia ium* 3n. pl. insignia, distinguishing marks
390 **aptō 1 I prepare, fit
dolus an uirtūs: ellipsis of *sit*; note the mood of *requīrat* (see on 8)
391 *comāns comant-is* plumed
392 *Androgeī*: gen. s. of Androgeos
gale-a ae 1f. helmet
īnsign-e is 3n. s. device, blazon

decōr-us a um fine, handsome
393 *induor* 3 I clothe myself in, don ('middle' reflexive use)
accommodō 1 I fit X (acc.) to Y (dat.)
394 ***iuuentūs iuuentūt-is* 3f. youth, young men
395 **spoli-a ōrum 2n. pl. spoils, booty, plunder (often enemy weapons captured in battle)
**recēns recent-is fresh, new
396 *uādō* 3 I advance
immisceō 2 *immiscuī immixtum* I mix in, mingle
haud nūmine nostrō: as if, by putting on Greek armour, they were left under the protection of alien, hostile gods? S. comments on *haud nostrō* 'not useful to us'. See also on 336
397 *congredior* 3 dep. *congressus* I join battle
398 *cōnserō* 3 I join
Orc-us ī 2m. Orcus, Hades
399: *aliī*: i.e. other Greeks

---

him, wreathing its coils round its lair – so Hector, his determination unquenchable, refused to retreat' (Rieu-Jones, *Iliad* 22.93–6). See further on **2.199–208**.

The Trojans taste blood (383–5). Aeneas characterises the Greeks as fearful (384), and comments that fortune favoured the Trojans' *first* effort. This does not bode well for the future.

2.386–401: Aeneas reports that the enthusiastic Coroebus, claiming fortune is on their side, urges them to follow up the initial success (386–8). His stratagem is an exchange of armour (389–90), on the grounds that no *enemy* (*in hoste*: presumably, no *Greek* enemy in particular) would worry about whether it was *dolus* or *uirtūs*. But that suggests the choice of *dolus* might be a problem for the Trojans. Is it the sort of thing expected of men who will in time become upstanding, principled Romans (as they liked to see

fīda petunt; pars ingentem^ formīdine turpī   400
scandunt rūrsus ^equum et nōtā conduntur in aluō.'

400 *formīdō formīdin-is* 3f. fear	**Learning vocabulary**
turp-is e shameful, disgraceful	*aptō* 1 I prepare, fit
401 *scandō* 3 I climb (into)	*iuuentūs iuuentūt-is* 3f. youth, young men
*rūrsus again	*recēns recent-is* fresh, new
conduntur: a 'middle' (reflexive) usage; see p. 39 ((c)	*rūrsus* again
(i)) above	*spoli-a ōrum* 2n. pl. spoils, booty, plunder (often
alu-us ī 2f. belly	enemy weapons captured in battle)

themselves)? There are reasons for believing that Coroebus' plan may not be a matter for 'automatic condemnation', e.g. Romans' regular use of trickery in battle (like burrowing under fortifications) – *dolus*, in other words, in a noble cause, for all its potential moral ambiguity. Whatever the answer, while the *dolus* of the wooden horse worked, this *dolus* will turn out very differently.

It may be significant that Aeneas says nothing about this trick, nor about whether he personally changed armour, though *omnis iuuentūs* (394) does. But he certainly joins in the fighting (*uādimus* 396), battling it out with the Greeks with great success (397–8). The result is that Greeks they encounter flee back to their ships, the shore or even into the wooden horse (! 399–401). Aeneas comments on the Greek performance, *fīda* and *nōtā* uttered with sarcasm, and *turpī* with disgust. Second round to Aeneas and his men.

See: Horsfall (2008: 303–6, 314) on Coroebus' deception.

Learning vocabulary for Section 2.268–401

addō 3 *addidī additum* I add, receive
āmēns āment-is mindless, mad, frantic
Anchīs-ēs -ae Anchises, Aeneas' father
aptō 1 I prepare, fit
aspiciō 3 *aspexī aspectum* I see, observe, catch sight of
attollō 3 - - I raise, lift up
cernō 3 *crēuī crētum* I see
cēū like
Coroebus nom. s. a Trojan
culmen culmin-is 3n. top, peak, height
dēfess-us a um exhausted
dēns-us a um in a pack; thick, frequent
dīuers-us a um scattered
dominor 1 dep. I rule over (+ dat.)
Dymās nom. s. a Trojan
ēlābor 3 dep. *ēlāpsus* I escape, slip away from
Ēpytus nom. s. a Trojan
excēdō 3 *excessī excessum* I depart (from + abl.)
exuui-ae ārum 1f. pl. spoils (of war)
fastīgi-a ōrum 2n. pl. outlines; roof, heights, tips
furō 3 *furuī* I rage
glomerō 1 I gather; throng round

Hector -is 3m. Hector, greatest Trojan fighter, killed by Achilles
horror -is 3m. terror, alarm
Hypanis nom. s. a Trojan
imāgō imāgin-is 3f. image, likeness, appearance, ghost
incendi-um ī 2n. fire
incendō 3 *incendī incēnsum* I set fire to
iuuentūs iuuentūt-is 3f. youth, young men
maest-us a um tearful
Mārs Mārt-is 3m. Mars, god of war/battle
misceō 2 *miscuī mistum/mixtum* I mix, scatter, disturb, confuse
nebul-a ae cloud
obsideō 2 *obsēdī obsessum* I besiege
oppōnō 3 *opposuī oppositum* I interpose
passim far and wide
penetrāl-e is 3n. inner shrine
penetrāl-is e innermost
potēns potent-is powerful (over + gen.)
praeceps praecipit-is headlong; sheer, steep
quondam at times; formerly; some day
rapid-us a um violent, rapid, consuming
recēdō 3 *recessī* I stand apart; depart, leave

recēns recent-is fresh, new
Rhīpeus nom. s. a Trojan
ruīn-a ae 1f. wreck, ruin, collapse
rūrsus again
sat = satis
spoli-a ōrum 2n. pl. spoils, booty, plunder (often enemy weapons captured in battle)

sternō 3 *strāuī strātum* I flatten
Trōes 3m. pl. Trojans
uari-us a um various
ubīque everywhere
uelut(ī) just as
uertex uertic-is 3m. peak; whirlpool
uult-us ūs 4m. face, look

Study section for 2.268–401

1. Is there any rational point to Aeneas' desire to fight? (See on **1.92–101**.)
2. Can you justify Aeneas' refusal to obey Hector's instructions?
3. To what extent is Aeneas the narrator in control of his emotions?
4. Scan 348–54.

2.402–505: The siege of Priam's palace

In this Section, *after the disastrous losses incurred by the Trojans because of Coroebus' effort to save Cassandra, Aeneas makes his way to Priam's palace, where Trojans are trying to prevent the Greeks from forcing the palace doors. He joins the Trojans fighting from the palace roof. He can only watch as Achilles' brutal son Pyrrhus/Neoptolemus smashes his way through.*

2.402–12: 'Coroebus saw Cassandra being dragged away by the Greeks, and led a ferocious assault; but Trojans mistook us for Greeks, and the slaughter was great'

'heu nihil inuītīs fâs quemquam fidere dīuīs!
ecce, trahēbātur passīs^ Priamēia* *uirgō
^crīnibus ā templō *Cassandra adytīsque Mineruae,
ad caelum *tendēns ārdentia lūmina frūstrā,   405
lūmina, nam tenerās arcēbant uincula palmās.

402 *nihil . . . fâs*: '[there is] in no way (*nihil* is a limiting accusative, **RLL**(c), especially 6) divine justification for *quemquam* to . . .' Aeneas' ominous comment looks forward, with hindsight, to what is to come

403 *trahēbātur*: the Greek soldier Ajax (son of Oileus) dragged Cassandra away from the shrine of Minerva in Ilium (**404**), where she was taking refuge, to rape her. Since she is now being dragged from the temple, she has already been raped (S. suggests that Aeneas uses *trahō* to draw a veil over the term 'rape'; not having witnessed it, he cannot comment anyway). No wonder Coroebus loses all self-control at the sight. This violation of Minerva's sanctuary had dreadful repercussions for the Greek fleet when it sailed for home: Minerva wrecked it (1.39–45)

*pandō 3 pandī passum I spread (out); it was not uncommon for women to untie their hair when begging deities for help (e.g. Livy 3.7.8, in time of plague in Rome). Knots in anything (rope, hair, clothes) were thought to impede divine powers, perhaps because they were bindings and could therefore 'bind', i.e. prevent or hinder, divine interventions (anachronism)

Priamēi-us a um (offspring) of Priam; S. comments that *uirgō* is much more relevant at this point than *fīlia*

406 *tener -a -um* tender, delicate

**arceō 2 arcuī I confine; keep at a distance, ward off

palmās: one normally stretched one's hands to heaven in prayer; all Cassandra can do is turn her eyes to heaven (**405**, S.), the moving, emphatic repetition of *lūmina* in **406** followed by the explanation

---

2.402–12: The almost involuntary cry of anguish (*heu* 402) comments not on human fallibility but on divine *im*providence: for Aeneas now knows that all his efforts were in vain from the very start. *ecce* (403) does not 'disrupt action in progress' (Austin 1964) but explains the exclamation *heu*. Note how the picture of the seizure of Cassandra

nōn tulit hanc speciem furiāta mente Coroebus,
et sēse medium iniēcit peritūrus in agmen;
cōnsequimur cūnctī, et dēnsīs incurrimus armīs.
hīc prīmum ex altō dēlūbrī culmine tēlīs   410
nostrōrum obruimur, oriturque miserrima caedēs
armōrum faciē et Graiārum errōre iubārum.'

---

407 *speci-ēs ēī* 5f. sight
furiāt-us a um maddened: Coroebus had come to
   Troy to marry Cassandra (343)
408 *iniciō* 3 *iniēcī* I hurl; see on 37 *subiciō* for
   scansion
peritūrus: intention, or inevitability? **RL**81, **W**23,
   M77–8
409 *cōnsequor* 3 dep. I join in following
dēnsīs . . . armīs: 'closing ranks' (Cong.)
incurrō 3 I charge
411 *nostrōrum*: gen. pl. of *noster nostr-a um* (the
   gen. pl. of *nōs* is *nostrum* or *nostrī*), after *tēlīs*
   (understand 'men' with *nostrōrum*)
**obruō 3 *obruī obrutum* I overwhelm, bury, sink;

note that the final syllable of *obruimur* scans long
   (cf. on 1.308)
*caed-ēs is 3f. slaughter
412 *faci-ēs ēī 5f. look, appearance (abl. of cause, as
   too *errōre*)
error -is 3m. mistake (i.e. the mistake we made with
   reference to *iubārum*)
iub-a ae 1f. helmet

Learning vocabulary

arceō 2 *arcuī* I confine; keep at a distance, ward off
caed-ēs is 3f. slaughter
faci-ēs ēī 5f. look, appearance
obruō 3 *obruī obrutum* I overwhelm, bury, sink
pandō 3 *pandī passum* I spread (out)

---

unfolds from *trahēbātur*: dragged – by the hair – Cassandra – innermost sanctuary (usually entered only by priests, S.) – temple – to heaven – burning eyes – yes, eyes – hands bound. The position of *frūstrā* (405), the image conjured up by *ārdentia* (405), the repetition of *lūmina* (405, 406) and *tenerās* all add to the passion and pathos of the scene. Cassandra was a prophetess: the gods will not save even her. Nor will Coroebus, seized by *furor* as he is (407). Without a word (S. comments 'he rightly prefers fighting to talking', contrasting 386–91), Coroebus plunges into battle, followed by Aeneas and his men ('we' 409). But, disguised as Greeks, they are mistaken by the Trojans for the real thing (412) – not surprisingly, since the Trojans are not in close contact with them but hurling missiles at them from the top of the temple roof (410). *Miserrima caedēs* (411) indeed, as Trojan slaughters Trojan (S.); this is another passage in which Aeneas' feelings run high. One advantage of the Coroebus episode is that it enables V. to deal with the rape of Cassandra, referred to by Juno at 1.39–41.

Given that there were traditions in which Aeneas was thought to have *betrayed* Troy, one could argue that V. created this rather odd exchange of armour to explain why Aeneas – who on this theory must have exchanged his armour – had been seen going round Troy apparently fighting on the Greek side.

See: Heinze (36–9/22–3) on Cassandra and Coroebus; Stahl (1981: 167) on
   explanations for Aeneas' 'betrayal' of Troy.

2.413–34: 'The Greeks too, seeing through our disguise, attacked us. It was like adverse winds clashing; despite my efforts, most of my companions were killed'

'tum Danaī,^ gemitū atque ēreptae uirginis īrā,
undique ^collēctī inuādunt, ācerrimus Aiāx
et geminī Atrīdae, Dolopumque exercitus omnis: 415
aduersī ruptō^ cēū quondam ^turbine uentī
cōnflīgunt, Zephyrusque Notusque et laetus Eōīs^
Eurus ^equīs; strīdunt siluae, saeuitque tridentī
spūmeus^ atque īmō ^Nērēūs ciet aequora fundō.
illī^ etiam, sī quōs obscūrā nocte per umbram   420
fūdimus īnsidiīs tōtāque agitāuimus urbe,
^appārent; prīmī clipeōs mentītaque tēla
agnōscunt, atque ōra sonō discordia signant.
īlicet obruimur numerō, prīmusque Coroebus

413 *gemitū . . . īrā*: both abl. of manner
ēreptae: 'at the snatched-away virgin', i.e. at the
seizure of the virgin. So did Coroebus (briefly)
rescue Cassandra? S. assumes he did
414 *inuādō* 3 I attack; there is a solid 'thump' to the
metre and sound of the first half of this line
Aiāx Ajax, son of Oileus, known as a swift runner,
Cassandra's rapist
415 *geminī*: Agamemnon and Menelaus were
brothers, not twins. They attract this epithet
presumably because they often fight as a pair
416 *cēū quondam*: begin with these words
introducing a simile
turbō turbin-is 3m. whirlwind
417 *cōnflīgō* 3 I clash
Zephyr-us ī 2m. west wind
Eō-us a um eastern
418 **Eur-us ī* 2m. east wind
***strīdō* 3 *strīdī* I howl, shriek, creak; whirr. Note the
alliterative *s* sequence to *spūmeus* in 419
saeuiō 4 I rage, am violent
***tridēns trident-is* 3m. trident, the traditional
implement of gods of the sea (and also of
Britannia, who rules – or used to – the waves.
'Rule, Britannia!' was lustily played by bands on
board Nelson's twenty-seven ships eagerly
waiting to obliterate the thirty-three of

Napoleon's admiral Villeneuve at Trafalgar, 19
October 1805)
419 *spūme-us a um* covered in foam
Nērēūs nom. s. a sea-god (father of the Nereids)
cieō 2 I stir up
fund-us ī 2m. bottom
420 *illī*: i.e. Greeks
sī quōs: 'if [there were any] whom (object) we had
. . .', RL139.1, M134
421 *īnsidiīs*: i.e. their disguise
agitō 1 I pursue, hunt, hound
422 ***appāreō* 2 *appāruī appāritum* I appear (as if
like ghosts!)
prīmī: i.e. they were the first to
clipeōs: i.e. *our* shields
mentior 4 dep. *mentītus* I deceive, give a false
impression
423 *ōra*: i.e. speech
son-us ī 2m. sound (abl. of respect, referring to the
Trojans' accent or dialect)
discors discord-is different
signō 1 I mark, note
424 *īlicet* instantly; that's that (this word is a
contraction of *īre licet*, used in legal cases to
indicate the case was over, and it was time to go)
numerō: S. comments 'in case they seem to have
been overcome by superior ability'

2.413–34: The Trojans are up against, first, a formidable force of the Greeks' best soldiers who come from everywhere to help (414–15); second, being disguised as Greeks, the Trojans find themselves up against their own men too (410–11); and third, those Greeks whom they had earlier tricked (420–2, cf. 399–401) recognise them as Trojans by their strange accents (one wonders why the other Greeks did not). This is all slightly messy – perhaps intentionally. That is what it was like for Aeneas from what he, as

Pēneleī dextrā, dīuae armipotentis ad āram,   425
prōcumbit; cadit et Rhīpeus, iūstissimus ūnus
quī fuit in Teucrīs et seruantissimus aequī
(dīs aliter uīsum); pereunt Hypanisque Dymāsque
cōnfīxī ā sociīs; nec tē^ tua plūrima, Panthū,
^lābentem pietās nec Apollinis īnfula tēxit.   430
Īliacī cinerēs et flamma extrēma meōrum,
testor, in occāsū uestrō nec tēla nec ūllās
uītāuisse uicēs Danaum, et sī fāta fuissent
ut caderem, meruisse manū.'

425 *Pēneleī*; gen. s. of Peneleus, a Greek
dīuae: i.e. of Minerva
armipotēns armipotent-is powerful in arms, warlike
  ('and expressing her hostility to the Trojans, since
  even he who had tried to save her priestess
  [Cassandra] is said to have been killed at her
  altar', S.)
426 **prōcumbō* 3 *prōcubuī prōcubitum* I collapse,
  sink down (a 'thud' to the word)
427 *seruantissim-us a um* most protective
428 *dīs*: dat. pl. of *deus*
aliter differently; cf. on 326
uīsum: ellipsis of *est* (note: neuter)
429 *cōnfīgō* 3 *cōnfīxī cōnfīxum* I pierce
Panthū: voc. of Panthus (see 318–20)
430 *Apollinis*: gen. s. of Apollo
īnful-a ae 1f. priest's headband (flocks of white wool
  tied round a *uitta* and hanging down each side of
  the head)
431: this whole line is in the voc., Aeneas calling
  them to witness (*testor*) that . . .

cinis ciner-is 3m. ashes; S. comments that it is right
  to swear by what you hold the dearest
flamma extrēma meōrum: i.e. final flames/funeral
  pyre of my [people]
432 *testor* 1 dep. I call (you) to witness that; followed
  by acc. and inf., [*mē*] *uītāuisse* (**433**) . . . *meruisse*
  (**434**)
occās-us ūs 4m. setting-sun; ruin; death
433 *uītō* 1 I avoid (understand *mē* as subject)
uic-ēs 3f. hazards, vicissitudes, changing fortunes (of
  [battle with] *Danaum*)
fuissent: **RL**173, **W**33, **M**115
434 *ut caderem*: i.e. '*fāta* that I . . .' (result clause, cf.
  RL135, **M**105). This is *not* a half-line
meruisse: i.e. 'I [*mē* understood] earned the right
  because of (what I achieved) *manū*.' Here we have a
  mixed condition. With *fuissent* it looks as if it is
  going to be an unfulfilled 'would have' condition;
  but *meruisse* in indir. speech is the equivalent of the
  perf. ind., i.e. 'I did in fact earn the right . . .', nothing
  unfulfilled or conditional about it. See **RLR**4(b)

narrator, remembers in the heat of the battle. Anyway, the result is that Aeneas' band is
picked off one by one (424–30).

    The triple assault is likened to triple winds coming from different directions and
causing havoc by land and sea (416–19: note the alliteration of *s*). A simile of clashing
winds at sea features in *Iliad* 9.4–8 'As the north and west winds suddenly descend from
Thrace to whip up the teeming sea; white horses cap the darkening rollers, and seaweed
piles up all along the beach – so Greek morale was shattered'; a simile of clashing winds
in the woods occurs at *Iliad* 16.765–71 'Like the east and south winds tussling with one
another in a mountain glen, setting the dense wood heaving, beech and ash and smooth-
barked cornel: their long boughs lash each other with a terrifying sound, and the
branches snap noisily – so the Trojans and Greeks leapt at one another and destroyed'
(both Rieu-Jones). Only winds from all directions (cf. *undique* 414) and *cōnflīgunt* in the
simile relate specifically to the action.

    The Trojan victims are each given brief descriptions (as in Homer), emphasising how
undeserving they were of death. Coroebus is (ironically) killed next to Minerva's altar,
from which Cassandra, whom he was trying to save, had been so sacrilegiously torn
(425). Aeneas' comment *dīs aliter uīsum* (428) of Rhipeus is particularly bitter. Note the

2.434–52: 'I and two others reached Priam's palace; while the Greeks tried to storm it, the Trojans from above hurled down on them whatever they could tear from the building, while massed Trojans defended the entrance. I rushed to join them'

'[ut caderem, meruisse manū.] dīuellimur^ inde,
Īphitus et Peliās mēcum (quōrum Īphitus aeuō   435
iam grauior, Peliās et uulnere tardus Vlixī),
prōtinus ad sēdēs Priamī clāmōre ^uocātī.
hīc uērō ingentem pugnam, c̄ēū cētera^ nusquam
^bella forent, nūllī tōtā morerentur in urbe,
sīc Mārtem indomitum Danaōsque ad tēcta ruentīs   440

Learning vocabulary

appāreō 2 appāruī appāritum I appear
Eur-us ī 2m. east wind
prōcumbō 3 prōcubuī prōcubitum I collapse, sink
  down
strīdō 3 strīdī I howl, shriek, creak; whirr
tridēns trident-is 3m. trident (Neptune's traditional
  implement)

434 dīuellō 3 I wrench, pull away; the pass. explained
  by uocātī (437)
435 Īphitus nom. s. a Trojan
Peliās nom. s. a Trojan
*aeu-um ī 2n. age (abl. of cause)

436 grauior: rather burdened, weighed down
Vlixī: gen. s., i.e. a wound inflicted by Ulysses
437 prōtinus immediately
438 ingentem pugnam: the obj. of cernimus 441!
cēū: introduces the conditional forent and
  morerentur clauses, 'as if there were . . .' These
  clauses indicate that this is a battle overshadowing
  all others
439 forent = essent, impf. subjunc., RL130.2
nūllī: understand et 'and no others' (a rare plural)
  morerentur 'were dying'
440 Mārtem: tr. '[the mother of all] battle[s]'?
indomit-us a um untameable, ferocious

unexpected change to the 'sympathetic' second person ('apostrophe') to describe the pious Panthus (429), who had earlier been trying to rescue the gods of Troy (320–1). Aeneas presents himself as feeling a close personal attachment to him. Homer uses this device of Patroclus in the *Iliad*, increasingly as he nears death in Book 16, e.g. 'But when he [Patroclus] leapt in like something superhuman for the fourth time, then, Patroclus, the end was in sight. In the heat of the battle, Phoebus encountered you, Phoebus most terrible' (Rieu-Jones, *Iliad* 16.786–9). Do we assume (with Austin) that Panthus, like Hypanis and Dymas, was killed by his own comrades? Aeneas ends by claiming that his deeds earned him the right to die a heroic death at this point (cf. 1.94–8; *uicēs* [433] implies that he gave as good as he got). Note that he swears before the Carthaginians in the name of what he holds most dear – Ilium and its dead, now dust and ashes (431) – to establish once and for all that he was no coward (ancients freqently swore in the name of their parents and children). This is, in fact, the last hand-to-hand fighting in which he will engage. The passage is rich in personal observation and reflection.

See: Stahl (1981: 167–8) for his argument that *testor* (432) suggests Aeneas is on the defensive, i.e. V. is clearing his name of treachery or cowardice and bringing out 'a positive, valuable feature in the character of Aeneas'. Cf. Stahl's views at **1.92–101, 2.298–317, 402–12**.

2.434–52: *dīuellimur* (434) vividly indicates the reluctance with which Aeneas left the fighting to heed what must have sounded almost like a summons to Priam's palace

cernimus obsessumque āctā testūdine līmen.
haerent parietibus scālae, postīsque sub ipsōs
nītuntur gradibus, clipeōsque ad tēla sinistrīs
prōtēctī obiciunt, prēnsant fastīgia dextrīs.
Dardanidae, contrā, turrīs ac tōta^ domōrum   445
^culmina conuellunt; hīs^ sē, quandō ultima cernunt,
extrēmā iam in morte parant dēfendere ^tēlīs,
aurātāsque trabēs, ueterum decora alta parentum,
dēuoluunt; aliī, strictīs mucrōnibus, īmās
obsēdēre forēs, hās seruant agmine dēnsō.   450
īnstaurātī animī rēgis succurrere tēctīs,
auxiliōque leuāre uirōs uimque addere uictīs.'

441 *testūdō testūdin-is* 3f. roof of shields (lit.
'tortoise') – another Roman anachronism
442 ***haereō** 2 *haesī haesum* I am entangled with,
cling/stick to; linger, am unable to move
pariēs pariet-is 3m. wall (of a house); note the
scansion here, as if four-syllable *paryetibus*
scāl-a ae 1f. ladder
**post-is is* 3m. door, door-post
sub: + acc. = close by
443 *nītor* 3 dep. I struggle/force my way up (by); the
subject is 'Greeks'
grad-us ūs 4m. rung, step
ad tēla: i.e. *contrā tēla*
sinistr-a ae 1f. left arm
444 *prōtegō* 3 *prōtēgī prōtēctum* I guard, protect
(here in a 'middle' reflexive sense)
obiciō 3 I shove X (acc.) forward; for scansion, see
on 200
prēnsō 1 I grasp
445 *contrā* on the other side
turr-is is 3f. tower
446 *conuellō* 3 I tear down. As will soon appear, the
Trojans are ripping up the whole roof in their
defence (*tōta* 445)
hīs: 'with these as *tēlīs*'
quandō since

ultima: i.e. the end, final outcome; it has been
argued that *cernunt* here means 'decide' (*OLD* 3)
rather than 'see' (a sense of 'now or never',
requiring desperate measures)
448 *aurāt-us a um* gilded
parentum = parentium
449 *dēuoluō* 3 I roll down
stringō 3 *strīnxī strictum* I draw (of swords)
mucrō -nis 3m. sword (point)
īmās: i.e. the doors on the ground floor
450 *obsēdēre*: form? Note that this refers to Trojans
'blocking' the doors from the inside
for-ēs um 3f. pl. doors (and 453); *hās* refers to 'these
[doors]'
451 *īnstaurō* 1 I renew (ellipsis of *sunt*), followed by
three infs. ('renewed *to . . .*')
animī: i.e. my spirit/courage (subject): Aeneas is
now alone

Learning vocabulary
aeu-um ī 2n. age
haereō 2 *haesī haesum* I am entangled with,
cling/stick to; linger, am unable to
move
post-is is 3m. door, door-post

(437). The age of Iphitus hints at how desperate the Trojans were for fighters of any
description (435–6) and, with Pelias wounded, explains why Aeneas is soon on his own.
Aeneas now describes two areas of action where the fighting was so fierce that fighting
elsewhere (e.g. 411) might not seem to qualify for the term (438–9) and where, indeed,
Mars himself seemed to be present (440): (a) where the Greeks were attempting to scale
the walls of the palace (440, developed at 441–9), and (b) where the Greeks were
attempting to force their way through the doors of the palace at ground level (441,
developed briefly at 449–50). Aeneas will describe the action on both fronts in more
detail in the next two passages.

The assault on the roof is daring. The Greek ladders are placed right by the doorway

2.453–68: 'I entered the palace by a back entrance and made for the roof; there we collapsed a tower onto the Greeks below, but still they came'

'līmen erat caecaeque forēs et peruius ūsus
tēctōrum inter sē Priamī, postēsque relictī,
ā tergō īnfēlīx^ quā sē, dum rēgna manēbant,   455
saepius ^Andromachē ferre ^incomitāta solēbat
ad socerōs, et auō puerum Astyanacta trahēbat.
ēuādō ad summī fastīgia culminis, unde
tēla manū miserī iactābant inrita Teucrī.
turrim^ in praecipitī ^stantem summīsque sub astra   460
^ēductam tēctīs – unde omnis Troia uidērī
et Danaum solitae nāuēs et Achāica castra –

453 *caecae*: here 'hidden, secret'
perui-us a um for passing through (presumably
   tēctōrum, **454**)
ūs-us ūs 4m. 'right' of way
454 *inter sē*: i.e. between the two *tēctōrum*
relictī: i.e. ignored/left alone by the enemy (which is
   why Aeneas could get in that way)
455 *ā tergō*: punctuated as in Horsfall (2008), i.e. *ā
   tergō* is taken with the Andromache clause (not
   with *postēsque relictī*), emphasising
   Andromache's discretion
sē: object of *ferre* **456**
456 *Andromachē* nom. s. Andromache, wife of (the
   dead) Hector
incomitāt-us a um unaccompanied. S. comments
   that this passage enabled Andromache and her
   son to visit Priam without being encumbered
   with servants. So *saepius . . . solēbat* refers to
   earlier, happier, domestic days (a typical
   'Homeric' flashback), and *īnfēlīx* becomes Aeneas'
   sympathetic comment on what had happened
   subsequently (the death of Hector and, soon, of
   her son, see **457**). *dum rēgna manēbant* (**455**),
   primarily a comment on the immediate
   destruction of the palace, may also suggest 'before

Hector died', since the death of Hector seemed to
   mark the end of Ilium (see 289–92, and cf. on
   2.526–43)
457 *socer -ī* 2m. in-law
au-us ī 2m. grandfather (Priam); here dat. of
   person concerned, e.g. 'for his grandfather's
   pleasure'
Astyanacta: acc. s. Astyanax, son of Andromache
   and Hector. When Ilium had been captured, the
   Greeks, fearing what a son of Hector might do to
   them in the future, sensibly threw him off the
   battlements. 'Astyanax' means 'city (Greek *astu*)
   chieftain (Greek *anax*)'
trahēbat: a nice domestic touch, the small child
   being bustled along by mother, cf. on 321
458 **ēuādō* 3 *ēuāsī ēuāsum* I climb up, evade, escape
   from
459 *inrit-us a um* pointless, in vain
460 *turr-is is* 3f. tower; the object of *adgressī* (**463**)
   . . . conuellimus (**464**)!
in praecipitī: i.e. on the edge of the roof, poised over
   the drop
astr-um ī 2n. star; note *sub* + acc.
461 *uidērī*: inf. after *solitae* (*sunt*) **462**, the main verb
   of the *inde omnis . . . castra* clause

(442), where the Trojan defence was gathered (450). The only way the Trojans on the roof can hold them off is, ironically, by destroying the very palace and everything precious in this ancestral home that they are trying to protect (445–9); but then they are at death's door themselves, and know it (446–7). Meanwhile, at ground level (*īmās*, 449), the Greeks lay siege to the palace entrance, and the Trojans mass inside to protect it (449–50). This courageous defence inspires Aeneas to do all he can to help the *uictīs* (452) – a comment made with hindsight, or did he sense it at the time?

2.453–68: If Aeneas is to help his fellow Trojans on the roof, he has to get up there. But he informs us that he was aware of a door unknown to the Greeks at the back of the

adgressī^ ferrō circum, quā summa* labantīs
iūnctūrās *tabulāta dabant, ^conuellimus altīs
sēdibus impulimusque; ea lāpsa repente ruīnam   465
cum sonitū trahit et Danaum super agmina lātē
incidit. ast aliī subeunt, nec saxa nec ūllum^
tēlōrum intereā cessat ^genus.'

2.469–90: 'The snake-like Pyrrhus (son of Achilles) and other Greeks hacked into the door into the palace and observed the confusion and terror inside'

'uestibulum ante ipsum, prīmōque in līmine, Pyrrhus^

463 *adgredior* 3 dep. *adgressus* I assault
circum: adverbial
labō 1 I am loose, shaky (and 492)
464 *iūnctūr-a ae* 1f. joint, i.e. this tower has been
   built onto the palace roof, and its base therefore
   provides points/joints at which it can be levered off
tabulāt-um ī 2n. floor, storey
dabant: i.e. provided, offered
*conuellō 3 *conuulsī conuulsum* I pull, wrench
465 *sēdibus*: i.e. from the place where it was fixed
impulimusque: i.e. gave it a final shove
ea: i.e. the tower
ruīnam . . . trahit: as the tower falls, it seems to take
   the rest of the building with it, like an avalanche
   (Austin)
467 *incidō* 3 I fall; the metrical and grammatical
   break after this word, which runs over from the

previous line, creates a sense of expectancy –
dashed by *ast aliī*
saxa: but whose? Surely the Trojans', whose only
   form of defence has been to hurl anything they
   can lay their hands on (*ūllum / tēlōrum . . . genus*)
   down onto the Greeks below
468 *cessō* 1 I stop, cease. For unfinished lines, see on
   1.534

Learning vocabulary
conuellō 3 *conuulsī conuulsum* I pull, wrench
ēuādō 3 *ēuāsī ēuāsum* I climb up, evade, escape
   from

469 *uestibul-um ī* 2n. front entrance
*Pyrrh-us ī 2m. Pyrrhus (also called Neoptolemus),
   son of Achilles

---

besieged building, linking Priam's palace with the residence of his son Hector and family (453–5). Aeneas explains this by informing us that Hector's wife Andromache used it to visit Priam with her son (455–7). There is no hint of any such feature in Homer, but the introduction of Andromache and memories of a time of peace are very Homeric (see on 456).

Aeneas describes himself emerging on the roof (458), where Trojan missiles are achieving nothing (458–9). So – whether on his advice or not: Aeneas is not yet presenting himself as a great leader – the Trojans change tactics and decide to lever up a steep tower/turret, built on the top of the roof (460–1) and used as an observation post (461–2), and tip it onto the Greeks below. They hack away at it with crowbars, axes etc. (*ferrō*) at the points where the tower/turret had been joined to the roof, lever it up and give it a final shove (463–5). Down it crashes (465–7 are rhythmically dramatic), crushing Greeks – but to no avail. Other troops replace them, and the Greek assault and Trojan defence continue (467–8). With that half-line, V. moves the camera from the roof back to the attack on the palace doors below. From now on Aeneas will be simply a reporter of, not a participant in, the fighting.

2.469–90: Aeneas sets the scene with a picture of a young warrior prancing about in glittering armour (470). Pyrrhus runs the risk of being taken for nothing but a show-off (see

exsultat, tēlīs et lūce ^coruscus aēnā: 470
quālis ubi in lūcem coluber^ mala grāmina ^pāstus,
frīgida* sub terrā tumidum quem *brūma tegēbat,
nunc, positīs ^nouus exuuiīs ^nitidusque iuuentā,
lūbrica* conuoluit, sublātō pectore, *terga
^arduus ad sōlem, et linguīs micat ōre trisulcīs.   475
ūnā ingēns Periphās et equōrum agitātor Achillis,

---

470 *exsultō* 1 I prance about

aēn-us a um bronze; i.e. his armour gave off a
  bronze gleam (*tēlīs . . . lūce* – hendiadys (see
  Glossary of literary terms)?)

471 *quālis ubi . . . coluber*: 'of what sort a snake/like
  a snake, when . . .'

in lucem: it is not precisely clear with what vb this
  phrase construes; perhaps it is best to say that it
  prepares the way for the general picture of a snake
  emerging after winter (**472**) *ad sōlem* (**475**)

coluber colubr-ī 2m. snake; follow the links to make
  the agreements down to **475**

grāmen grāmin-is 3n. grass, herb

**pāscor 3 *pāstus* I graze, feed (on)

472 *frigid-us a um* cold; begin this verse with *quem*
  (the *coluber*) with *tumidum* in agreement, obj. of
  tegēbat

tumid-us a um swollen; it was believed that snakes
  were swollen with poison, generated by the *mala*
  herbs (**471**) they had been consuming during the
  winter, cf. Homer's description of Hector

awaiting Achilles' attack at **2.370–85**. See **Study
  section for 2.402–505**, 4. for some other sources

brūm-a ae winter

473 *exuui-ae ārum* i.e. its old skin

nitid-us a um shining

iuuent-a ae 1f. youth; S. comments 'it is agreed that
  once snakes shed their skin their capabilities are
  renewed'. Should one see in the old skin the dead
  Achilles, and in the new skin his son Neoptolemos ('new [in] war')?

474 *lūbric-us* slithering

conuoluō 3 I coil

475 *ardu-us a um* rearing/arching up

micat: i.e. flickers, darts (used of lightning, like
  coruscus 470)

trisulc-us a um three-forked (poetic imagination,
  perhaps suggesting the blur of the flicker)

476 *ūnā*: with *ūnā* **477**, 'all together'

Periphās nom. s. a Greek

agitātor -is 3m. driver

Achillis: gen. s.

Study section for 2.402–505). Aeneas quickly corrects that impression: young and glit-
tery the son of Achilles may be, but he is as evil and poisonous as a snake (cf. on 472), the
glitter of his armour (470) like the glitter of a snake that has shed its skin (473), and
the elation (*exsultat* 470) matched (perhaps) by the snake's writhing and rising up to the
warm sun, flickering its tongue as if hungry for prey (474–5). Aeneas' loathing is clear.
Other named troops (476–7) reach the palace and fire the roof which Aeneas has just left
(468).

Meanwhile, Aeneas sees Pyrrhus smashing through the door and trying to rip it out of
its sockets (479–81). He finally manages to hack a hole in it (481–2) to view the scene
inside. The result is breathtaking: *appāret* (483) and *appārent* (484) seem to 'open up'
(*patēscunt*) to the whole world the most intimate and holy interior (*penetrālia* 484) of
Priam's palace. Trojan soldiers are ready to defend it to the last (485, cf. 491–2) but the
screams of the women echo round the long halls (487–8), as they cling to and kiss farewell to their homes (490) – captive women were regularly sold into slavery – and
perhaps to their lives. Again, it is not at all clear how Aeneas could have witnessed *all* of
this in such detail – though he will insist he did at 499ff.

See: West 'Multiple-correspondence Similes in the *Aeneid*' in S. J. Harrison (1990: 432)
  on the simile; Kenney in West and Woodman (1979: 103–20) for an appreciation of
  469–505.

armiger Automedōn, ūnā omnis Scӯria pūbēs
succēdunt tēctō et flammās ad culmina iactant.
ipse inter prīmōs correptā dūra^ bipennī
^līmina perrumpit postīsque^ ā cardine uellit   480
^aerātōs; iamque excīsā trabe, firma cauāuit
rōbora et ingentem lātō dedit ōre fenestram.
appāret domus intus, et ātria longa patēscunt;
appārent Priamī et ueterum penetrālia rēgum,
armātōsque uident stantīs in līmine prīmō.   485
at domus interior gemitū miserōque tumultū
miscētur, penitusque cauae plangōribus^ aedēs
^fēmineīs ululant; ferit aurea sīdera clāmor.
tum pauidae tēctīs mātrēs ingentibus errant
amplexaeque tenent postīs atque ōscula fīgunt.'   490

477 *armiger -ī* 2m. armour-bearer
Automedōn nom. s. Automedon
Scӯri-us a um from Scyros (a Greek island), where
  Pyrrhus' grandfather Lycomedes was king
***pūb-ēs is* 3f. manpower, youth
478 *succēdō* 3 I come up to, attack (+ dat.)
479 *ipse*: Pyrrhus. Note the spondees: this is a
  determined attack (Austin)
dūr-us a um hard, tough (they are bronze-plated,
  481)
bipenn-is is 3f. axe
480 *līmina*: here, 'doors'
perrumpō 3 I break though (pres. continuous, 'is in
  the process of'); cf. the perfs. of **481–2**, where
  Pyrrhus has achieved his ends
cardō cardin-is 3f. door-socket (and 493); *postīs* here
  are door-jambs. Unlike our doors, ancient ones
  were not fitted onto the door-frame at the side
  ('door-jamb') by hinges. The side of the door itself
  had a post fixed onto it, the protruding top and
  bottom of which fitted into sockets in the
  horizontal lintel above and threshold below,
  allowing the door to swing open and shut
uellō 3 I pluck, tear (also present continuous)
481 *aerāt-us a um* bronze-plated
***excīdō* 3 *excīsī excīsum* I cut, hack out
trabs: here, one of the solid beams/planks (*OLD* **3**)
  out of which the door was made
firm-us a um tough
cauō 1 I hollow out

482 *fenestr-a ae* 1f. opening (window)
483 ***intus* inside
ātri-um ī 2n. main room; house, palace
patēscō 2 I am revealed
486 *interior is* interior
tumult-us ūs 4m. chaos
487 *cauae*: because vaulted?
plangor -is 3m. wail, scream
488 *fēmine-us a um* of women
ululō 1 I echo, resound
***feriō* 4 I strike, hit; S. dryly comments 'many refer
  aurea sīdera to the decorated ceiling. Which is
  stupid.' Too true
489 ***pauid-us a um* fearful, terrified, panic-stricken
tēctīs . . . ingentibus: local abl., 'in, around'

See: West 'Multiple-correspondence Similes in the
  Aeneid' in S. J. Harrison (1990: 432) for the
  argument about the old and new skin of the
  snake.

Learning vocabulary
excīdō 3 *excīsī excīsum* I cut, hack out
feriō 4 I strike, hit
intus inside
pāscor 3 *pāstus* I graze, feed (on)
pauid-us a um fearful, terrified, panic-stricken
pūb-ēs is 3f. manpower, youth
Pyrrh-us ī 2m. Pyrrhus (also Neoptolemus), son of
  Achilles

2.491–505: *'Breaking through the door, the Greeks butchered the occupants, as destructive as a river in spate. All hope was gone. The Greeks were the masters'*

'īnstat uī patriā Pyrrhus; nec claustra nec ipsī
custōdēs sufferre ualent; labat ariete crēbrō
iānua, et ēmōtī prōcumbunt cardine postēs.
fit uia uī; rumpunt aditūs prīmōsque trucīdant
immissī Danaī et lātē loca mīlite complent.   495
nōn sīc, aggeribus ruptīs, cum spūmeus amnis
exiit oppositāsque ēuīcit gurgite mōlēs,
fertur in arua furēns cumulō, campōsque per omnīs
cum stabulīs armenta trahit. uīdī ipse furentem^
caede ^Neoptolemum geminōsque in līmine Atrīdās,   500
uīdī Hecubam centumque nurūs Priamumque^ per ārās
sanguine ^foedantem quōs ipse sacrāuerat ignīs.

492 *sufferō sufferre* I withstand
labō 1 I am loose
ariēs ariet-is 3m. battering, hammering (scan as if *aryete*)
493 *ēmoueō* 2 *ēmōuī ēmōtum* I move out, shift
cardine: i.e. from their sockets (take with *ēmōtī*). Once the internal structure of the great beamed door had been smashed, it simply fell out of its sockets
494 *fit uia uī*: a condensed, powerful utterance, the logical outcome of Pyrrhus' *īnstat uī* (**491**)
adit-us ūs 4m. entrance
trucīdō 1 I slaughter
495 *immittō* 3 *immīsī immissum* I send in
loca: *locus* occasionally adopts the n. form in the pl.
compleō 2 I fill
496 *nōn sīc . . . cum* 'not thus i.e. not with such violence, when . . .', introducing a simile
agger -is 3m. bank, barrier

spume-us a um foaming
amn-is is 3m. river; subject of all the vbs up to *trahit*
499
497 *exeō exīre* I come out
*oppōnō 3 *opposuī oppositum* I put in the way
ēuincō 3 *ēuīcī* I overpower
gurg-es gurgit-is 3m. flood
498 *cumul-us ī* 2m. surge (here modal abl., 'in a surge', with *fertur*)
camp-us ī 2m. plain
499 *stabul-um ī* stable, pen
arment-um ī 2n. herd, cattle
500 *Atrīdās*: acc. pl.
501 **Hecub-a ae* 1f. Hecuba, wife of Priam
nur-us ūs 4f. daughter, daughter-in-law (she had fifty of each)
ārās: s. for pl.
502 *foedantem . . . ignīs*: take in order *foedantem ignīs quōs*
sacrō 1 I sanctify

2.491–505: Aeneas now reports on Pyrrhus, with the scent of easy blood in his nostrils, attacking the door again with all his father Achilles' might (491). The inner bolts give way, and the door is smashed down, falling out of its sockets (491–3). The brutal assault begins (494). Greeks burst in, slaughter all in front of them and fill the *loca* (these magnificent rooms are now simply 'places') with soldiers (494–5). There is a cold, merciless ruthlessness to this assault – everything that Greeks, in Aeneas' eyes, stand for. A simile accompanies the moment, the surge of soldiers being likened to a torrent which bursts its banks and overwhelms everything in its path (496–99) – or rather, not likened to a torrent (*nōn sīc* 496), whose effects were far less severe. The broken palace entrance (494) is the broken *agger* (496); the Greeks (495) are the *spūmeus amnis* (496); the guards are the *oppositās . . . mōlēs* (497); the fields and their animal contents (498–9) are

quīnquāgintā illī thalamī, spēs tanta nepōtum,
barbaricō postēs^ aurō spoliīsque ^superbī
prōcubuēre; tenent Danaī quā dēficit ignis.'   505

503 *quīnquāgintā* fifty
thalam-us ī 2m. bed-chamber; cf. on 238
504 *barbaric-us a um* barbarian, eastern, non-Greek.
  This may seem an odd thing for Aeneas to say,
  especially accompanied by *superbī* (with its
  potentially disdainful overtones). But might
  barbaricō imply *Roman* distaste for eastern
  luxury, i.e. Aeneas is (anachronistically) aligning
  Trojans with Romans-to-be?
postēs: it was customary to hang up the spoils of war
  around the palace; here they are hung
  (presumably) on the doors of the bedroom?

aurō spoliīsque: hendiadys (see **Glossary of literary
  terms**)?
505 *tenent*: its obj. is effectively *quā dēficit ignis*
  dēficiō 3 I fail (of the *ignis*, i.e. to catch hold)

See: Reed (2007: 101–9) on *barbaricō*.

Learning vocabulary
oppōnō 3 *opposuī oppositum* I put in the way
Hecub-a ae 1f. Hecuba, wife of Priam

---

the palace with its men and women. The Greeks have as much feeling for those in the
palace as does the river for the countryside it flattens and the animals it carries off.

All this is witnessed by Aeneas from his location on the top of the palace. How? It is
hard to see, for example, how from that position both Aeneas *and* Pyrrhus could have
peered through the hole Pyrrhus had made in the door (i.e. 482–90). V. does not give us
any solid clues. The story is all, and here, as occasionally elsewhere, he seems to forget
that it is not he but Aeneas who is telling the story. We must just assume that Aeneas
was, first, peering down from the palace roof onto Pyrrhus and his men assaulting the
door (Aeneas had just helped lever the turret/tower down on top of the attackers there),
and then, second, looking down either through the atrium or into an open courtyard
(512) to see what was happening inside. The result is that – in tragic mode again, rather
like a messenger – he can see the berserk Pyrrhus/Neoptolemus and the sons of Atreus
on the attack (499–500), Hecuba, Priam dead at the altar (501–2: note the pathos of the
repeated *uīdī* 499, 501), the huge house and all its wealth flattened (503–5), and Greeks
holding everywhere that the fire has not (yet) reached (505). There is further pathos
about Aeneas' simple, unadorned comment *spēs ampla nepōtum* (498): what progeny,
what a future, those bedrooms all promised, now nothing but the ashes and flames
which Aeneas had earlier called to witness to his courage (431) and which he can now do
nothing but watch as they consume everything. Such hopes for the future will now rest
with Aeneas and *his* offspring – and what a (Roman!) future it will be.

See: Heinze (40–1/24) for the question of Aeneas' view of the scene from the roof.

Learning vocabulary for Section 2.402–505

aeu-um ī 2n. age
appāreō 2 *appāruī appāritum* I appear
arceō 2 *arcuī* I confine; keep at a distance, ward off
caed-ēs is 3f. slaughter
conuellō 3 *conuulsī conuulsum* I pull, wrench
ēuādō 3 *ēuāsī ēuāsum* I climb up, evade, escape from
Eur-us ī 2m. east wind
excīdō 3 *excīsī excīsum* I cut, hack out
faci-ēs ēī 5f. look, appearance
feriō 4 I strike, hit
haereō 2 *haesī haesum* I am entangled with, cling/ stick to; linger, am unable to move
Hecub-a ae 1f. Hecuba, wife of Priam
intus inside

obruō 3 *obruī obrutum* I overwhelm, bury, sink
oppōnō 3 *opposuī oppositum* I put in the way
pandō 3 *pandī passum* I spread (out)
pāscor 3 *pāstus* I graze, feed (on)
pauid-us a um fearful, terrified, panic-stricken
post-is is 3m. door, door-post
prōcumbō 3 *prōcubuī prōcubitum* I collapse, sink down
pūb-ēs is 3f. manpower, youth
Pyrrh-us ī 2m. Pyrrhus (also Neoptolemus), son of Achilles
strīdō 3 *strīdī* I howl, shriek, creak; whirr
tridēns tridnt-is 3m. trident (Neptune's traditional implement)

Study section for 2.402–505

1. How persuasively does Aeneas justify his survival?
2. What image of Aeneas does this *Section* conjure up?
3. Scan 469–75.
4. Discuss V.'s use of the sources in his construction of the similes at 471–5 and 496–9:

471–5

(a) See on **370–85** for two Homeric snake similes
(b) From Nicander's *Theriaca*, a poem on poisonous creatures (Kenney 'Indicium transferendi' in West and Woodman (1979: 106–8):
   (i) '... at the time when the snake sloughs the withered scales of age, moving feebly forward, when in spring he leaves his den, and his sight is dim; but a meal of fenny's sappy shoots makes him swift and bright of eye' (31–4)
   (ii) 'Beware too when the viper, having doffed the wrinkled scales of age, comes abroad again exulting in his new-found youth' (137–8)
   (iii) 'Nor at spring's oncoming, after it has quitted gully and hollow cleft in the season when earth brings reptiles to light, does it browse upon the waving shoots on the fennel's branch, when it clothes its limbs with their new skin beneath the sun' (389–92)
   (iv) 'Yet when it hears some strange noise or sees a bright light, it throws off from its body dull sleep and wreathes its coil in a circular ring upon the ground, and in the midst it rears its head, bristling in deadly fashion' (164–7)

496–9

V.'s simile is based on Homer's, of the Greek hero Diomedes rampaging through the Trojan ranks:

(v)   'Diomedes . . . stormed across the plain like a winter torrent in spate, bursting dykes as it races along; when the skies open, neither close-packed embankments nor walls built to protect fertile gardens can contain its sudden onslaught, and far and wide it flattens the good work of industrious farmers – so the dense ranks of the Trojans were thrown into confusion by Diomedes, unable for all their numbers to withstand him' *Iliad* 5.87–94 (Rieu-Jones)

It also has associations with Lucretius, who pictures the effect of a river bursting its banks as follows (Kenney 'Indicium transferendi' in West and Woodman (1979: 110–12):

(vi)   'In no other way do [winds] flow and cause havoc than when water, soft though it naturally is, suddenly turns into a rising torrent. The great flood of water, swollen by heavy rains, surges down from the mountain heights, tossing up wreckage from woods and whole trees. Solid bridges cannot stand up to the sudden assault of the onrushing waters, such is the sheer power with which the seething, storm-flushed torrent smashes against the piers. With a tremendous roar it flattens them, rolls huge rocks under its waves and sweeps aside whatever stands in its path' (*Dē rērum nātūrā* 1.280–9)

5. V. often adapts material from the earlier poet Ennius (*Intro* [20–2]). See Reed (2007: 100–9) and compare 241–2 and 499–505 with Andromache's lament at the fall of Troy from Ennius' tragedy *Andromache*:

Ō pater! Ō patria! Ō Priamī domus!
saeptum altisonō cardine templum!
uīdī ego tē, astante ope barbaricō,
tēctīs caelātīs, laqueātīs,
aurō, ebore īnstrūctum rēgificē.   5
haec omnia uīdī īnflammārī,
Priamō uī uītam ēuītārī,
Iouis āram sanguine turpārī.
'O father, O fatherland, O house of Priam,
O temple closed by a door that sounds in the heavens!
I have seen you, your eastern armies at hand,
[royally fitted] with engraved and panelled ceilings,
with gold and ivory, royally fitted.   5
All this I have seen in flames,
Priam's life by violence unlifed,
Jove's altar by blood polluted.'

Cicero, whose quotation of these lines resulted in their survival, implies that they were extremely famous and thought them a superb evocation of fallen greatness, the last three lines 'full of melancholy in content, diction and rhythm' (see *Tusculan Disputations* III.xix.44–5). The rhyming of the last three lines is very rare.

2.506–58: The death of Priam

In this Section, the old king Priam arms himself, only to see his son Polites cut down by Pyrrhus. He attacks Pyrrhus, only to be brutally cut down himself at the altar.

2.506–25: 'Old Priam buckled on his armour, but his wife Hecuba told him to seek refuge with her at the altar'

'forsitan et, Priamī fuerint quae fāta, requīrās.
urbis utī captae cāsum conuulsaque^ uīdit
^līmina tēctōrum et medium in penetrālibus hostem,
arma diū sēnior dēsuēta trementibus^ aeuō
circumdat nequīquam ^umerīs, et inūtile ferrum   510
cingitur, ac dēnsōs fertur moritūrus in hostīs.
aedibus in mediīs, nūdōque sub aetheris axe,
ingēns āra fuit, iuxtāque ueterrima laurus^

506 *forsitan* perhaps (this takes the subjunc.)
Priamī . . . requīrās: take in order *requīrās* (addressed to Dido) *quae fuerint fāta Priamī* (hinted at in 501–2 but not taken further). *quae* introduces an indir. q. **RLR3, W**30, **M**94
507 *utī* = *ut* (the vb is *uīdit*, so it means . . .?)
508 *līmina*: doors (cf. 480)
penetrālibus: this sometimes refers to the innermost sanctuary of a temple, or the place in the home where the *penātēs* were kept. So while it basically means 'the house' here, it has (as S. points out) something 'sacred' about it – as will shortly become apparent (**513–14**)
509 **sēnior -is* older (perhaps 'too old'), in one's later years
dēsuēt-us a um unaccustomed
aeuō: abl. of cause with *trementibus*

510 *circumdō* 1 I put X (acc.) round Y (dat.)
inūtil-is e useless (he could not use it properly, anyway, and will not, anyway)
511 *cingor* 3 I gird on ('middle' usage with dir. obj.). Contrast *fertur* here, a 'middle' reflexive usage, as is *cingī* at **520**. Revise p. 39 above
moritūrus: with an overtone of purpose, or inevitability
512 *nūd-us a um* naked, open i.e. in a courtyard open to the air (S., assuming V. has a Roman house in mind, suggests the *impluuium*)
ax-is is 3m. vault (of the sky)
513 **iuxtā* nearby
laur-us ī 2f. laurel-tree (a sacred tree, with strong Augustan associations; two grew outside the entrance to his palace on the Palatine)

2.506–25: At 501–2 Aeneas prepared his listeners for his account of the death of Priam (who was of particular interest to Dido, 1.750). Aeneas now describes how he saw the old king, who had helplessly watched the destruction of his city and the entrance of the enemy into his palace (507–8), deciding on a final, futile gesture of defiance. There is no one to help him arm, so he does it himself (510–11). *sēnior . . . dēsuēta trementibus aeuō* (a superb triplet: no longer used to arms he once wielded, he trembled, not from fear,

^incumbēns ārae atque umbrā ^complexa penātīs.
hīc Hecuba et nātae nequīquam altāria circum,   515
praecipitēs ātrā cēu tempestāte columbae,
condēnsae et dīuum amplexae simulācra sedēbant.
ipsum autem sūmptīs Priamum iuuenālibus armīs
ut uīdit, "quae mēns tam dīra, miserrime coniūnx,
impulit hīs cingī tēlīs? aut quō ruis?" inquit.   520
"nōn tālī auxiliō nec dēfēnsōribus istīs
tempus eget; nōn, sī ipse meus nunc adforet Hector.
hūc tandem concēde; haec āra tuēbitur omnīs,
aut moriēre simul." sīc ōre effāta recēpit
ad sēsē et sacrā longaeuum in sēde locāuit.'   525

514 *incumbō* 3 *incubuī incubitum* I lean over/onto
  (+ dat.)
complector 3 dep. *complexus* I embrace (with
  umbrā, 'shade')
515 *nātae*: daughters and daughters-in-law (501)
altār-ia ium 3n. pl. altar (with *circum*)
516 *praecipitēs*: in the sense 'driven headlong to
  earth'; *praecipitēs . . . columbae*: take in order *cēu*
  praecipitēs columbae ātrā tempestāte
tempestās tempestāt-is 3f. storm
columb-a ae 1f. dove
517 *condēns-us a um* wedged, crowded together
518 *ipsum . . . Priamum* is the object of *ut uīdit*
  (**519**), whose subject is Hecuba (understood)
iuuenāl-is e youthful
519 *ut uīdit*: the subject is Hecuba
**coniūnx coniug-is* 3f., m. wife, husband

521 *dēfēnsor -is* 3m. defender
istīs: 'like you'
523 *tandem*: in commands and qs., often = 'please, I
  beg you'
concēdō 3 I withdraw, yield (used of inviting
  someone companionably aside)
524 *moriēre*: = *moriēris* 2s. fut. of *morior*
simul: = 'with us'
effor 1 dep. *effātus* I speak out
525 *longaeu-us a um* old, aged (i.e. man)

Learning vocabulary

complector 3 dep. *complexus* I embrace
coniūnx coniug-is 3f., m. wife, husband
incumbō 3 *incubuī incubitum* I lean over
iuxtā nearby
senior -is older, in one's later years

merely age, S.) and . . . *nequīquam . . . inūtile*, with the inevitable consequence *moritūrus* (his death is a stone-cold certainty, and he knows it), emphasise Aeneas' sense of the pointlessness and pathos of it all. But then, Ilium had been captured and his palace stormed. The whole place was about to be ransacked. What was its king to do? Sit and watch? What further purpose did his life serve? Note that Aeneas does not accuse Priam of *furor* and *īra* as he had himself at 314–17 (cf. **2.298–317**, and *Intro* [43]); Hecuba gently reprimands him for pointless bravado instead (519–22).

   An altar was a place of refuge in the ancient world, sacred (cf. 525) to its god who would be offended by anyone who violated its sanctity and so insulted the deity. Ajax son of Oileus had already done just that in order to rape Cassandra, who was taking refuge at the altar to Minerva in her temple (403–6), and Minerva punished him for it (1.39–45). It is here, at a shrine sacred to the *penātēs*, gods of the household, that Hecuba and her daughters had gathered – *nequīquam* (515). They clutched the altar (517) as they were required to in order to remain unharmed (contact was essential). V. likens them, all huddled together, to doves escaping a storm (516) – vulnerable, harmless, innocent creatures (note the light dactyl of *praecipitēs* followed by the heavy spondees of the storm). Seeing Priam heaving on his *iuuenālibus* armour (518) – a dreadful pathos to that adjective – Hecuba calls him *miserrime coniūnx* (she is full of pity for him) and summons him to take shelter at the altar too, pointing out that everything is up for

2.526–43: 'Priam's son Polites tried to escape Pyrrhus, but was killed near the altar. Priam rounded on Pyrrhus, accusing him of being no true son of his father Achilles'

'ecce autem ēlāpsus Pyrrhī dē caede Polītēs,
ūnus nātōrum Priamī, per tēla, per hostīs,
porticibus longīs fugit, et uacua ātria lūstrat
saucius. illum ārdēns īnfestō uulnere Pyrrhus
īnsequitur, iam iamque manū tenet, et premit hastā.   530
ut tandem ante oculōs ēuāsit et ōra parentum,
concidit, ac multō uītam cum sanguine fūdit.

---

526 *Pyrrhī*: 'at the hands of . . .' (with *caede*)
Polītēs nom. s. Polites, a son of Priam
528 *portic-us ūs* 4f. colonnade; here the local abl.
   means 'by way of, along'
ātri-um ī 2n. room; house, palace (an anachronistic
   Roman term, of course). Why *uacua*, asks S.:
   because everyone was at the altar? Because the
   Trojans had deserted the place? Because the
   palace was so vast? The first seems likeliest.
   Camps (1969: 65) suggests that *longīs* and *uacua*
   'identify emotive features in the special situation
   . . . they lead the imagination to supply the
   suspense of the onlookers, the echoing footsteps
   of the runners, and so on'. It is hard to credit that
   Aeneas could actually *witness* this chase through
   the palace, though see **2.526–43**
**lūstrō 1 I move through, traverse; survey, study

529 *sauci-us a um* wounded
illum: obj. of *īnsequitur* (**530**)
īnfest-us a um poised to kill
uulnere: i.e. with a wound-delivering weapon (S.)
530 *īnsequor* 3 dep. *īnsecūtus* I follow closely on,
   pursue
iam iamque: 'at any moment now'
premit: i.e. presses closely on him. *premit* could
   mean 'overpower', but *iam iamque* surely applies
   to *premit* as much as to *tenet*
531 *ut*: + indic.
tandem: it is a long chase
532 *concidō* 3 I fall, collapse; do we conclude with S.,
   who wonders if the *multō . . . fūdit* clause suggests
   Polites is hit again at this point, that Pyrrhus now
   delivers the death-stroke? It is possible. On the
   other hand, Polites is already *saucius* (**529**)

---

them, and would still be even were *meus Hector* (note the maternal affection, S.) alive (519–23: implication – you cannot be a Hector). There is surely no scorn (Page 1894) in *istīs* (521) – simply '[defenders] like you'. Hecuba ends by acknowledging the reality: this is the only place where we have any chance of survival (poetic irony). Lyne (1987: 54–5) points out the 'gentle humanity' in Hecuba's questions at 519–20 and the colloquiality of *hūc tamen concēde* (523); and there is tenderness in *recēpit ad sēsē*, and further pathos in *longaeuum* (but for how long?).

We have already noted one place where V. takes over the role of primary narrator from Aeneas (**2.250–67**). The death of Priam must now be added, e.g. *utī . . . uīdit* (507: how could Aeneas know?), though V. does his best to maintain the fiction (506!). The convention V. is adopting is that of the 'messenger speech' in Greek tragedy, reporting off-stage action – painting the complete picture, human motives and all, however impossible it would have been for the messenger to have been acquainted with it.

See: West 'Multiple-correspondence Similes in the Aeneid' in S. J. Harrison (1990: 342) for the dove simile.

2.526–43: Our immediate reaction is – oh no. Anyone but Pyrrhus. Aeneas sees him chasing down the wounded Polites (527–9), and the blood-lust is on him (*ārdēns* 529). In Homer, Polites is characterised as very fast (*Iliad* 2.791–4), which is how he has managed

hīc Priamus, quamquam in mediā iam morte tenētur,
nōn tamen abstinuit nec uōcī īraeque pepercit:
"at tibi prō scelere," exclāmat, "prō tālibus ausīs   535
dī, sī qua est caelō pietās quae tālia cūret,
persoluant grātēs dignās et praemia reddant
dēbita, quī nātī cōram mē cernere lētum
fēcistī et patriōs foedāstī fūnere uultūs.
at nōn ille, satum quō tē mentīris, Achillēs   540
tālis in hoste fuit Priamō; sed iūra fidemque
supplicis ērubuit, corpusque exsangue sepulcrō
reddidit Hectoreum, mēque in mea rēgna remīsit."'

533 *in mediā . . . morte*: i.e. death was all around him
534 *abstineō* 2 I hold back
uōcī īraeque: hendiadys (see **Glossary of literary terms**)?
535 *exclāmō* 1 I cry out
aus-um ī 2n. crime, outrage (*audeō*)
536 *dī*: subject of *persoluant* and *reddant* (**537**); note they are subjunc. (jussive: see **RL**152, **W**28, **M**34, 89). So too is *cūret* (of characteristic: **RL**140.1, Q2(a), **W**38, **M**100)
caelō: local abl.
537 *persoluō* 3 I pay off/in full
grātēs 3f. pl. thanks (to a god), thanksgiving
538 *quī*: understand *tibi* [Pyrrhus] *quī fēcistī mē cernere lētum nātī cōram et foedā(ui)stī . . .*
**cōram face to face
539 *******fūnus fūner-is* 3n. death
540 *sat-us a um* born (from + abl.) Ellipsis of *esse* and take in order *quō tē satum (esse) mentīris*

541–3 *in hoste . . . Priamō*: 'in the case of his enemy Priam'. Priam refers to himself, powerfully, in the third person – as if he were worth killing (S.)?
sed . . . (**543**) *remīsit*: Priam remembers how he went by night to Achilles' tent to supplicate (beg) for the return of Hector's body, how Achilles respected the laws of good faith to a suppliant, returned the body and ensured he and his dead son got safely back. The incident is narrated at *Iliad* 24.468–691
542 *supplex supplic-is* 3m. suppliant
ērubeō 2 I blush at, respect
exsangu-is e lifeless (*sanguis*)
sepulcr-um ī 2n. grave, tomb; here 'for burial'
543 *Hectore-us a um* of Hector

Learning vocabulary
cōram face to face
fūnus fūner-is 3n. death
lūstrō 1 I move through, traverse; survey, study

to escape so far, wounded though he is. Page takes *premit hastā* as the final strike, so that Polites is cut down before Priam's eyes; but only after *premit hastā* does Polites *euāsit* (531) i.e. get out of the *porticūs* and *ātria* where he had been running (528) and emerge *tandem* into the courtyard at the altar in front of his parents (531). (Perhaps V. is maintaining the narratorial fiction by suggesting that Aeneas' view was impeded at this point?) Note that 538–9 does not imply that Priam had seen the death-stroke, but only his son die. That is why the *quamquam . . . tenētur* clause (533) is important: death is everywhere – Priam is surrounded by it – but this death is different not because his own son has died (that is what happens in war) but because he died *before his very eyes* (emphatic 531, S.).

Priam cannot restrain his *righteous* anger at this (534; he wants to die honourably, says S. Cf. on **2.506–25** above, and especially *Intro* [43]). Not that there is anything to indicate that Pyrrhus actually engineered Polites' death at that spot, let alone that he delivered the death-blow there (unless we want to read that into *concidit*). Far from it. It was Polites who 'led' him there; Pyrrhus was merely in hot pursuit. But rational analyses of that sort count for little in this sort of situation. A son's death had taken place in front of the eyes of a father who had seen his world collapsing and who knew his end was near.

2.544–58: 'Priam threw a feeble spear at Pyrrhus, who told him to report his actions to Achilles in Hades, then slaughtered him, leaving his headless corpse on the shore'

'sīc fātus sēnior, tēlumque^ ^imbelle sine ictū
cōniēcit, raucō ^quod prōtinus aere ^repulsum,   545
et summō clipeī nequīquam umbōne pependit.
cūi Pyrrhus: "referēs ergō haec et nūntius ībis
Pēlīdae genitōrī. illī mea trīstia facta,
dēgeneremque Neoptolemum nārrāre mementō.
nunc morere." hoc dīcēns, altāria ad ipsa trementem^   550
trāxit et in multō ^lāpsantem sanguine nātī,
implicuitque comam laeuā, dextrāque coruscum^

544 *fātus . . .* **545** *repulsum*: ellipsis of *est*
imbell-is e feeble
ict-us ūs 4m. strength, penetration
545 *rauc-us a um* rattling, ringing
aere: i.e. bronze shield
repellō 3 *reppulī repulsum* I reject, repel. This means
  that it did not get through the shield, only far
  enough into its top layer to be able to hang
  uselessly from it (**546**)
546 *umbō -nis* 3m. (shield) boss
547 *nūntius*: in apposition, 'as a messenger'
548 *Pēlīdae*: dat. s. Pelides, son of Peleus, i.e.
  Achilles (dat. after *referēs* and *nūntius*)
trīstia facta: obj. of *nārrāre*; so too the acc.

and inf. **549** *dēgeneremque [esse]*
  Neoptolemum
549 *dēgener -is* of inferior breed, not up to his
  father's standards (S.)
Neoptolemum: Neoptolemus was Pyrrhus'
  alternative name
mementō: imper. of *meminī*
550 *morere*: imper. of *morior*, cf. *moriēre* 524
altār-ia ium 3n. pl. altar – the one place where
  Priam might expect help (S.)
trementem . . .
551 *lāpsantem*: i.e. Priam
552 *lāpsō* 1 I (keep on) slithering, slipping
  ('frequentative' of *lābor*)

Pyrrhus' one foul action simply epitomises in Priam's eyes everything that Greeks stand for (note Aeneas' interpolations in 533–4). So his outburst at 535–9 is at heart a cry to the gods for vengeance against *all* the Greeks for their treacherous destruction of Troy (remember Sinon?). It is at 540–3 that Priam becomes personal, accusing Pyrrhus of being not a bastard but unworthy of such a father, and proving it by comparing Pyrrhus' treatment of his son Polites with Achilles' of himself and his son Hector. Priam points out that Achilles also allowed him (Priam) to return to his own kingdom (543) with Hector's body, when Achilles could easily have won the war at a stroke by refusing to release Priam and Hector until Helen was returned (S.).

There are many recollections of *Iliad* 22 (the death of Hector) and *Iliad* 24 (Achilles returns Hector's body to Priam) in this episode, i.e. the death of Priam in V. signals the end of Ilium as clearly as the death of Hector did in Homer ('It was as if the whole of frowning Ilium were smouldering from top to bottom' *Iliad* 22.410–11, Rieu-Jones).

See: Heinze (43–4/25–6) on Priam's heroic death; Bowie (1990) on *Iliad* 22 and 24.

2.544–58: The sense of helplessness and despair that has increasingly characterised Aeneas' account of the battle reaches its climax with the ghastly death of Priam. *sēnior, imbelle, sine ictū* (544), *repulsum* (545), *nequīquam* (546) tell their own story, as does the description of Priam's throw: it hit the shield, Aeneas observes, but all it could do

extulit, ac laterī capulō tenus abdidit ^ēnsem.
haec fīnis Priamī fātōrum, hic exitus illum^
sorte tulit Troiam incēnsam et prōlāpsa ^uidentem   555
Pergama, tot quondam populīs terrīsque ^superbum
^rēgnātōrem Asiae. iacet ingēns lītore truncus,
āuulsumque umerīs caput, et sine nōmine corpus.'

---

553 *laterī*: i.e. in his side
capul-us ī 2m. handle, sword-hilt
tenus + abl. as far as (controls *capulō*)
*abdō 3 *abdidī abditum* I hide, conceal
554 *haec*: f., agrees with *fīnis*, which is normally m. S.
    explains that it is f. if used to signify a long period
    of time
exit-us ūs 4m. conclusion, end, departure
555 *prōlābor* 3 dep. *prōlāpsus* I collapse, fall to ruin
556 *Pergama*: strictly, the citadel of Ilium
tot quondam populīs terrīsque: abl. of cause,
    explaining *superbum*
superbum: with its overtones of 'disdain',
    'haughtiness', is this V.'s comment? If V. is the
    narrator, it is easier to understand: that is how he
    might think of an eastern monarch. But it may be
    (anachronistically) Aeneas' comment. See on
    2.544–58
557 *rēgnātor -is* 3m. ruler

trunc-us ī 2m. trunk, body. Note *ingēns* and see
    on *ingēns/magnus* in **2.544–58**
558 *āuellō 3 *āuellī/āuulsī āuulsum* I tear/wrench
    off
sine nōmine: implying 'without acknowledgement or
    respect' (S.), i.e. ingloriously thrown out onto the
    beach and abandoned, unburied. It would be
    typical of someone like Pyrrhus, i.e. (in Aeneas'
    eyes) all Greeks, to do something like that

See: Jenkyns (1998: 413–14) for the view that Asia
    may seem 'alien, oriental and remote' but there is
    something Wagnerian and romantically tragic
    about the collapse of a whole, immense
    continent.

Learning vocabulary
abdō 3 *abdidī abditum* I hide, conceal
āuellō 3 *āuellī/āuulsī āuulsum* I tear/wrench off

---

was make the shield ring (545), while its power was just sufficient for it to stick into the surface and hang limply there (546). Pyrrhus' bitterly sarcastic, joking (S.) response to Priam's effort sums him up to perfection (he calls himself Neo-ptolemus here: it means, significantly, 'new (in) war, young fighter'): Priam's job in death is to be a *nūntius* (547) and deliver a message to Achilles (548 – note the grand, sonorous naming), which he must get word-perfect (*mementō*, 549) – that Pyrrhus is indeed no son of his father (cf. 540–1). He seems to rejoice in associating Achilles with his own savage behaviour (*trīstia facta*, 548). Here is a man who values the reputation of his dead father as little as he does his own or anyone else's. Priam's accusation at 535–6 is proved at every point.

The words of this snake (remember 472–5) are matched by actions. There is an unbearably clinical precision about Aeneas' description. One could not imagine that even Pyrrhus was going to demonstrate how *dēgener* he was by ensuring that he butchered Priam at the altar, defying every sanction of man and god. He *drags* him there (551), this old, trembling man (550, cf. on 509), not because he could not walk but because he was slipping in his own son's blood (551); humiliatingly winds his hair in his left hand (552, to hold his head up and force him to watch?); draws a flashing sword – flashing as he uses it; and *buries* it (no more flashing) into Priam's side (553). V. makes Aeneas add no moralising or tear-inducing comment. He describes what he *sees* and no more – classical, tragic restraint at its most overwhelming.

Aeneas adds a moving epilogue, as if Priam's death were still fresh in his mind. As Austin points out, the *hic exitus* (554) formula 'brings V. very close to the historian's manner' – here, the death of Priam signifying the end of an epoch. Among others,

Austin compares Livy 39.51.12. *hic uītae exitus fuit Hannibalis . . .* He also cites the epitaph of Pompey the Great (*Magnus*) by the post-Virgilian historian Velleius Paterculus (ii.53.3): 'After three consulships and three triumphs, conquering the whole world, and reaching a peak of fame beyond which it is impossible to rise, the *uītae fuit exitus* of that upright and illustrious man in his fifty-eighth year, the day before his birthday. Such was the inconstancy of his fortune, that he who shortly before had no more lands to conquer now found none for his burial.'

The reference to Pompey is important. In the bare, almost abstract 557–8, V. shifts focus from the altar where Priam was slaughtered, watching his world collapse around him (555–6), to the beach where (presumably) his body was taken and left. *Pompeius Magnus* too had conquered much of Asia (66–62 BC), and the description *superbum rēgnātōrem* (556–7) would fit him, a proud man, very well. Like Priam, he too was left a headless corpse, stabbed to death on a beach in Egypt, unburied, where he had arrived in flight from Caesar during the civil war in 48 BC. S. says 'he touches on the history of Pompey, when he says *ingēns* [557] not *magnus*'. Had Velleius been reading his *Aeneid*?

There is no account of the fall of Ilium that makes the death of Priam the climax of events, bar V.'s – the climax and turning-point (though it does not finally collapse till 624–31). The death of the king, with its moving epilogue, summarises in a single paragraph how godless and corrupt the Greeks were, how hopeless the whole battle had been, how inevitable Ilium's end – and, by extension, how pointless Aeneas' efforts to save it had been. Aeneas finally realises this bare truth, and from now on, escape is all that he will have in mind. But that is not all. In Homer, Aeneas was predicted to survive the war and rule Troy (see *Intro* [18]). The king of Troy is now dead. Long live the king . . .? And the new Trojans/Romans? (See *Intro* [23].)

See: Heinze (39/23ff.) on the climax of Priam's death.

Learning vocabulary for Section 2.506–58

abdō 3 *abdidī abditum* I hide, conceal
āuellō 3 *āuelli/āuulsī āuulsum* I tear/wrench off
complector 3 dep. *complexus* I embrace
coniūnx coniug-is 3f., m. wife, husband
cōram face to face
fūnus fūner-is 3n. death

incumbō 3 *incubuī incubitum* I lean over
iuxtā nearby
lūstrō 1 I survey, study; move through, traverse
nequīquam in vain
sēnior -is older, in one's later years

Study section for 2.506–58

1. How does Aeneas generate pathos in this episode?
2. In what sense might one call this episode 'tragic'?
3. The narrative is spoken by Aeneas in his capacity as a personal witness to events. Has V. successfully maintained this convention here?
4. Is Priam's death 'futile bravado' (Lyne (1987: 55))?
5. Scan 547–53.

6. Does Quintus from Smyrna's description of the death of Priam have anything to recommend it?

When he saw the son of Achilles,
Priam recognised him and did not tremble, since he
Desired to lose his life among his sons.
So, craving death, he spoke to him: 225
'Fierce-hearted son of the great warrior Achilles,
Kill me and do not have pity on me in my misery, since I,
Having suffered so much, no longer wish to look upon
The light of the all-seeing sun, but now
wish to die with my children and forget my deadly   230
Anguish and the dreadful fighting. Would that
Your father had killed me before I saw Ilium
In flames, when I brought him the ransom for the dead
Hector, whom your father killed. As for that, I suppose
The Fates decreed it. But you glut with my blood   235
Your fierce heart, so that I may forget my pain'.
As he spoke the fierce son of Achilles addressed him:
'Old man, you order me to do what I am keen and eager to,
For I shall not leave you my enemy among the living.
For nothing is dearer to men than life.'   240
So speaking he sliced off the head of the grey old man
Easily, as if some reaper were chopping off an ear
In the time of harvest in a parched cornfield.
Still murmuring it rolled over the earth a long way
From the other limbs which quivered on him.   245
He lay amid the black blood and slaughter of other men . . .
[missing lines]
In wealth and lineage and many children.
Not for long will a man's glory grow,
But somewhere unforeseen shame leaps on him.
So fate seized him. and he forgot all his troubles.   250

        Quintus Smyrnaeus, *Sequel to Homer* 13.222–50

2.559–633: Helen and Venus

In this Section, as Aeneas' thoughts turn to his family (and he is tempted to kill Helen whom he sees in hiding, a passage whose authenticity is doubtful), Venus appears to him and shows him the gods destroying Ilium and the whole city collapsing in flames.

2.559–66: 'I suddenly thought of my father, wife and family, and found myself alone'

'at mē tum prīmum saeuus circumstetit horror.
obstipuī; subiit cārī genitōris imāgō,   560
ut rēgem^ ^aequaeuum crūdēlī uulnere uīdī
uītam ^exhālantem, subiit dēserta Creūsa
et dīrepta domus et paruī cāsus Iūlī.
respiciō et quae sit mē circum cōpia lūstrō.
dēseruēre omnēs dēfessī, et corpora^ saltū   565
ad terram mīsēre aut ignibus ^aegra dedēre.'

559 *circumstō* 1 *circumstetī* I stand round, surround
560 *subiit*: 'there came to mind'; so too **562**, 575
561 *aequaeu-us a um* of the same age (i.e. as my father)
562 *exhālō* 1 I breathe out
*Creūs-a ae 1f. Creusa, Aeneas' wife
563 *dīripiō* 3 *dīripuī dīreptum* I plunder
domus: note the necessary metrical lengthening of the last syllable; cf. on 1.308
Iūl-us ī 2m. Iulus/Ascanius, Aeneas' son. For the significance of the name, see on **1.267–77
564 *respiciō* 3 I look back

mē circum = *circum mē*
cōpia: i.e. of men
565 *salt-us ūs* 4m. jump, leap (i.e. jumping down to escape Greeks who had made it to the roof)
566 *aegra*: 'suffering'? 'fainting'? 'weary'?

Learning vocabulary

Creūs-a ae 1f. Creusa, Aeneas' wife
Iūl-us ī 2m. Iulus/Ascanius, Aeneas' son

2.559–66: *tum prīmum* (559): up till now Aeneas has been all courage, even if despairing courage (e.g. 316–17, 353–4, 367, 451–2). Now, as he sees Priam's dying body (561–2), he remembers that he has abandoned his family for the fight, and a *saeuus horror* surrounds him. (The ancients often express feelings as if they are visited upon them from some external source. Observe too the physicality of the feelings: *horror* comes from *horreō*, 'I shudder'.) Further, he has been so gripped by events in the palace, especially the death of Priam, that he has not even noticed he is now alone, his allies on the roof having jumped for it (564–6). S. observes how Aeneas does not blame them but grieves for them; they are *dēfessī* and *aegra*.

2.567–88: *('Then I saw Helen; she was trying to hide from Trojans as well as Greeks. I thought of her returning home to Greece in triumph and longed to kill her there and then and take revenge for all she had done')*

('Iamque adeō super ūnus eram, cum līmina Vestae
seruantem^ et ^tacitam sēcrēta in sēde ^latentem
^Tyndarida aspiciō; dant clāram incendia lūcem
errantī passimque oculōs per cūncta ferentī.   570
illa^ sibi īnfestōs ēuersa ob Pergama Teucrōs
et Danaum poenam et dēsertī coniugis īrās
^praemetuēns, Troiae et patriae commūnis Erīnȳs,
abdiderat sēse atque ārīs inuīsa sedēbat.
exārsēre ignēs animō; subit īra cadentem   575
ulcīscī patriam et scelerātās sūmere poenās.
"scīlicet haec Spartam incolumis patriāsque Mycēnās

567 *super . . . eram*: by tmēsis (see 218) = *supersum superesse* I survive. Note that Aeneas is still on the palace roof
568 *seruantem*: 'keeping close to'. It is not clear how Aeneas should now be able to see someone prowling around the temple of Vesta, let alone hiding there but also wandering about it (**570**)
sēcrēt-us a um remote, separate
569 *Tyndarida*: acc. s. Tyndaris, daughter of Tyndareus, i.e. Helen of Troy
570 *errantī . . . ferentī*: ellipsis of *mihi*
571 *illa*: Helen (change of subject)
sibi: with *praemetuēns* (**573**), 'for her own sake'
īnfest-us a um hostile
** *ēuertō 3 ēuertī ēuersum* I churn up; overthrow
572 *poenam*: (cf. *inuīsa* **574**) – but at *Aeneid* 6.515–29 she is said to have been in league with the Greeks
573 *praemetuō 3* I fear (in advance of what might happen)
Erīnȳs nom. s. Fury (in apposition to *illa*, Helen)
574 **inuīs-us a um hated, loathed, despised (it could also mean 'unseen', but *abdiderat sēse* means that). Helen seems to have moved from the threshold of the temple of Vesta (**567**) to the altar

575 *exārdēscō 3 exārsī* I catch fire, am inflamed, fired; that *ignēs* should 'catch fire' or 'be inflamed' is slightly odd
animō: i.e. Aeneas' mind
īra: 'anger *to* . . .' + inf.
576 *ulcīscor 3* dep. *ultus* I avenge
scelerāt-us a um wicked to inflict, criminal. This is odd: one feels Aeneas ought to be saying 'punishment for her crime' but it does not mean that. Instead, he seems to be questioning the deed he is contemplating. Austin thinks it does mean 'punishment for her crime' (as if *scelerātās* means *sceleris*) and is 'a true Virgilian invention'. Or is this rather a 'transferred epithet' (common in V., see on 1.101), and *scelerātās* refers to Helen, i.e. it means 'penalty exacted from the criminal Helen'?
577 *scīlicet* doubtless, naturally, to be sure. It is very strange for Aeneas, who is telling the story, to break out here into a soliloquy, as if V. were telling it. Austin thinks V. has '[broken] the rule brilliantly'
Spart-a ae 1f. Sparta (where Helen originally lived as wife of Menelaus; Helen brings gifts from Mycenae at 1.650)
incolum-is e safe, secure

It is at this point that the direction of Aeneas' account changes, from his (as he now knows) futile efforts to save the city to his determination to escape with his family. He descends from the roof at 632.

2.567–88: This is a famously controversial passage. The main reason is that these lines do not appear in any of the major mss. and are preserved only by the commentator Servius *auctus* (see *Intro* [51]), who says of 567–88 'these verses come after this verse

aspiciet, partōque ībit rēgīna triumphō?
coniugiumque domumque patris nātōsque uidēbit
Īliadum turbā et Phrygiīs comitāta ministrīs?   580
occiderit ferrō Priamus? Troia ārserit ignī?
Dardanium totiēns sūdārit sanguine lītus?
nōn ita. namque etsī nūllum memorābile nōmen
fēmineā in poenā est, nec habet uictōria laudem,
exstinxisse nefās tamen et sūmpsisse merentis   585
laudābor ^poenās, animumque explēsse iuuābit
ultrīcis flammae et cinerēs satiāsse meōrum."
tālia iactābam et furiātā mente ferēbar . . .')

---

578 *pariō 3 peperī par(i)tum* I get, produce, bear
rēgīna: in apposition to *haec*, Helen
triumph-us ī 2m. triumph. It is not clear exactly
  what 'triumph' Helen gained
579 *coniugi-um ī* 2n. marriage, husband
580 *Īliad-es* 3f. pl. women from Ilium
minister ministr-ī 2m. slave
581 *occiderit*: fut. perf., like *ārserit* and *sūdārit*
  (582). The tone is one of despair and disgust:
  '[Will Helen get home safe and sound, when]
  Priam/Troy will have . . .?'
ignī: abl; see on 2.210
582 **Dardani-us a um* Dardanian/Trojan
  (Dardanus was a founding father of the
  Trojans)
totiēns so often
sūdō 1 I sweat
583 *memorābil-is e* memorable
584 *fēmine-us a um* of a woman
nec habet: the argument goes: 'although there's no
  glory in punishing a woman and winning (that
  victory) does not bring praise, nevertheless
  (*tamen*) I shall be praised to have . . .'
585 *exstinguō 3 exstinxī* I blot out, extinguish (after
  laudābor, 'I shall be praised to have . . .')

**nefās* 3n. crime against divine law (this is
  supposed to mean 'criminal woman')
mereō 2 meruī meritum I am worthy, deserve (here
  gen. s. part., 'relating to the one [Helen] deserving
  it', with *poenās*)
586 **expleō 2 explēuī explētum* I complete, fulfil,
  satisfy X (acc.) with Y (gen.)
587 *ultrix ultrīcis* 3f. vengeful, i.e. the flames of my
  vengeful feelings (an odd phrase)
cinis ciner-is 3m. ashes
satiō 1 I appease
588 *furiāt-us a um* maddened. This line will be
  repeated (in the interests of continuity) at the
  start of the next passage

On *scelerātās* **576**, see Horsfall (2008: 576); on the
  strange soliloquy **577**, see Heinze (46–7/27)

Learning vocabulary
Dardani-us a um Dardanian/Trojan
ēuertō 3 ēuertī ēuersum I churn up;
  overthrow
expleō 2 explēuī explētum I complete, fulfil,
  satisfy
inuīs-us a um hated, loathed, despised
nefās 3n. crime against divine law

[i.e. 566], and were deleted by Tucca and Varius' (editors of the *Aeneid*: see *Intro* [8]).
Servius passes over them in silence. The commentator Donatus likewise moves from 566
to 589 without mentioning them. Meanwhile, on 592 Servius *auctus* comments 'As we
have said, it is agreed that some verses were removed from here, not without justification. For it is offensive for a powerful male to become angry against a woman; and it is
contradictory that Helen should have been in Priam's house, because in Book 6 [495] it
is said that she was discovered in the house of Deiphobus.' It is surely even more offensive for a *pius* hero to consider slaughtering a woman in cold blood (575–6), let alone a
woman taking refuge at an altar (567, cf. Priam!), and think he will feel satisfied by, and
be congratulated on, it (584–7).

So that leaves the question: what is the status of these lines? Are they not by V. at all
(i.e. they are a later addition by some other writer)? Or are they an early draft which did

2.589–603: 'Suddenly Venus appeared to me, telling me to look for my family and forget about Helen or Paris – the gods were responsible for Troy's fall'

['tālia iactābam et furiātā mente ferēbar,]
cum mihi sē^, nōn ante oculīs tam clāra*, ^uidendam
obtulit et pūrā per noctem in lūce refulsit   590
*alma parēns, cōnfessa deam quālisque uidērī
caelicolīs et quanta solet, dextrāque prehēnsum

589 *ante* previously
uidendam/obtulit: '[she] provided *sē* to be seen', a
    common idiom, **R**161.1, **M**110.4
590 *pūr-us a um* pure, undefiled, radiant
refulgeō 2 *refulsī* I shine out
591 ** *alm-us a um* kindly, fostering
cōnfessa deam: i.e. revealing her divinity (cf. her
    earlier disguise, 1.314ff.)

quālisque . . . **592** *quantaque* . . . *solet*: 'of
    what looks and . . . of what stature she was
    accustomed', i.e. of the same looks and
    stature as
592 *caelicol-a ae* 1m./f. dweller in the sky
prehendō 3 *prehendī prehēnsum* I seize, take (i.e. *mē*
    prehēnsum)

not make it to V.'s final draft because he was not satisfied with them as they stood (cf. *Intro* [4, 7–8])? There could be a case for that, if one argued that Virgil wanted his hero, driven (perhaps) by rage and an overwhelming sense of guilt after all he had experienced, and entirely forgetting his future responsibilities, to yield to a blind desire for vengeance at any cost, even against a woman.

The problem will be discussed in more detail in the next passage, but it ought to be pointed out here that it is ultimately the *language* that makes the case against Virgilian composition. A commentary on this scale cannot deal with that issue, but I quote Horsfall's conclusion (2008: 565) 'the author (of the Helen episode) . . . has identified correctly numerous characteristics of Virgilian writing, only to employ them with heavy-handed abandon . . . such at times uncaring excess is not to be attributed to V. even in his roughest drafts'. One example: while V. regularly begins and ends a line with participles (e.g. 381, 771, and for an extreme example 12.903–4!), there is usually some special sound or effect in mind. To have two such lines 'framed' in such close proximity with no such effect (568 and 570) suggests the work of an author who has spotted the Virgilian quirk, but does not know how to use it.

But do we have any of V.'s 'roughest drafts'? No.

See: Austin (1964) *ad loc.* for the 'early draft' theory; Goold 'Servius and the Helen Episode' in S. J. Harrison (1990: 60–126) that the passage is not Virgilian. Heinze (45–51/26–30) also believes that, as does Gransden 'The Fall of Troy' in McAuslan and Walcot (1990: 130–1).

2.589–603: If Goold (1990) is right that 567–88 are not by V., it must still be the case that V. was planning something that would, as Venus says, excite in Aeneas grief leading to anger (594), making him rage and forget all about his family (595). Goold reckons that (i) in his first draft V. moved straight from 566 to 624 (1990: 115); (ii) he then decided to expand this passage and added 589–623 (116); (iii) but he did not live long enough to compose the passage prior to that (118); with the result that (iv) 567–88 were interpolated into the text by a later composer (117) who (v) picked up the idea for it

continuit roseōque haec īnsuper addidit ōre:
"nāte, quis^ indomitās ^tantus ^dolor excitat īrās?
quid furis? aut quōnam nostrī tibi cūra recessit?   595
nōn prius aspiciēs ubi fessum^ aetāte ^parentem
līqueris ^Anchīsēn, superet coniūnxne Creūsa
Ascaniusque puer? quōs omnīs undique Graiae^
circum errant ^aciēs et, nī mea cūra resistat,
iam flammae tulerint, inimīcus^ et hauserit ^ēnsis.   600
nōn tibi Tyndaridis faciēs inuīsa Lacaenae
culpātusue Paris, dīuum inclēmentia, dīuum,
hās ēuertit opēs sternitque ā culmine Troiam.'"

593 *contineō* 2 *continuī* I stop, hold back
rose-us a um rosy; S. comments that some think this epithet inappropriate in such a scene of destruction, 'not knowing that this is a constant epithet for Venus'
īnsuper in addition
594 *indomit-us a um* fierce, untamed
excitō 1 I arouse
dolor: does Aeneas feel guilty about his failure to save the city?
595 *quōnam* wherever
nostrī tibi cūra: lit. 'the care in you for us', i.e. your care for our family (S., as becomes clear in the next two lines)
597 *līqueris . . . superet*: subjuncs. in indir. q. after *aspiciēs*
superō 1 I remain alive, survive
coniūnxne: take *ne* with *superest*, 'and whether . . .'
598 **Ascani-us ī 2m. Ascanius or Iulus, son of Aeneas
quōs omnēs: controlled by *circum* (**599**)
599 *resistat . . .* **600** *tulerint . . . hauserit*: conditional subjuncs. ('were [now] . . . would [by now] have . . . would have', the vivid primary sequence perf. subjuncs. replacing the more usual plupf. in this construction, **RL**139, **W**33, **M**115–17

600 *hauriō* 4 *hausī haustum* I consume, drink, devour
601 *tibi*: an 'ethic' dative, calling attention to the fact that the person involved should have a keen interest in the matter. In Welsh, 'look you'; in English, the 'look' beloved of politicians, **RL**88.4, **W**38, **M**10
Tyndaridis: gen. s. of *Tyndaris* 'daughter of Tyndareus', i.e. Helen
faciēs . . . Paris . . . (**602**) *inclēmentia*: three subjects of **603** *ēuertit . . . sternit*
Lacaen-us a um Spartan
602 *culpātus* blamed; note *-ue* 'or'
Paris nom s. Paris, Helen's Trojan lover. Note that Venus here is blaming the gods; so there is no absolute *necessity* for any reference to Paris or Helen in the 'Helen' episode
dīuum: understand *sed*; note the passionate repetition of *dīuum*
inclēmenti-a ae 1f. mercilessness

See: on **602** *Paris*, Horsfall (2008) on 601.

Learning vocabulary
alm-us a um kindly, fostering
Ascani-us ī 2m. Ascanius or Iulus, son of Aeneas

from the reference to 'Helen's hateful face' at 601. Goold guesses that V. was perhaps thinking that the passage now filled by 567–88 would describe Aeneas' climactic onset of rage against Helen and Paris for innocent Trojan suffering and resolution 'to launch one last demonic attack upon the foe' (118). See **Study section for 2.559–633** for a different view, and cf. *Intro* [4] for V.'s method of composition.

Whatever one believes about the problem, V.'s purpose in 589–603 is for Venus to impress on Aeneas the true seriousness of the situation (it is the gods' doing) and his responsibility for his family to which he had been alerted by Hector (289–97) and which he seemed to have finally realised at 559–63 before being led astray again (whether by the Helen episode or something else). So Venus appears unambiguously before him, without disguise or deception (589–93), to point out how far he has allowed himself to be ruled by his (freely admitted, 2.314–17) emotions (*īrās* [594],

2.604–23: 'Venus showed me Neptune, Juno and Minerva at work destroying the city, and told me to escape'

'"aspice (namque omnem^, ^quae nunc ^obducta tuentī*
mortālīs hebetat uīsūs *tibi et ^ūmida circum   605
cālīgat, ^nūbem ēripiam; tū nē qua parentis
iussa timē, nēū praeceptīs pārēre recūsā):
hīc, ubi disiectās mōlēs āuulsaque saxīs
saxa uidēs, mixtōque undantem puluere fūmum,
Neptūnus mūrōs magnōque ēmōta tridentī   610
fundāmenta quatit, tōtamque ā sēdibus urbem
ēruit. hīc Iūnō^ Scaeās ^saeuissima portās
^prīma tenet, sociumque furēns ā nāuibus agmen,

604 *namque . . .* **606** *ēripiam*: take in order *namque ēripiam omnem nūbem^ ^quae nunc ^obducta hebetat mortālīs uīsūs tuentī tibi et ^ūmida circum cālīgat*

obdūcō 3 *obdūxī obductum* I spread over (+ dat., *tuentī . . . tibi*)

605 *hebetō* 1 I blunt, dull

ūmid-us a um dank, misty

circum: adverbial, 'round about'

606 *cālīgō* 1 I am dark

nē qua do not in any way; *nē* + imper. 'don't' is a (rare) archaic construction, cf. **RLL–V**(a)3, **W**28, **M**89 and *Intro* [9] footnote 20

parentis: word-play with *pārēre* **607** (see on 1.261)

607 *praecept-um ī* 2n. advice

pārēre: note the long *ā*

608 *hīc*: Venus (with a gesture) directs Aeneas' gaze

to the divinities about their work of destruction; cf. *hīc* **612**, *iam . . . respice* **615**

disiciō 3 *disiēcī disiectum* I scatter, shatter, disperse. For scansion, see on *subiciō* 37

609 *undō* 1 I surge, billow

puluis puluer-is 3m. dust

fūm-us ī 2m. smoke

610 **Neptūn-us ī** 2m. Neptune, god of the sea. He and Apollo had built the walls of Ilium but been cheated of payment for the work by the then king Laomedon

ēmoueō 2 *ēmōuī ēmōtum* I remove, dislodge

611 *fundāment-um ī* 2n. foundation

quatiō 4 I shake

612 **Iūnō Iūnōn-is** 3f. Juno, wife of king of the gods Jupiter; she was bitterly hostile to the Trojans (see *Intro* [16, 25])

Scae-us a um Scaean, one of the gates of Ilium

furis . . . cūra recessit [595]), and how desperate the plight of his parents and son is (596–9). To anticipate the possible objection that S. (on 602) suggests Aeneas might have raised ('you're a fine one to lecture *me* about the situation we are in, especially since you started the whole thing by rewarding Paris with Helen after he had given you the golden apple'), Venus points out that she *has* been looking after his family so far (599–600), but that the real culprits are not the human agents but the merciless gods (i.e. there is a limit to what Venus can achieve on her own when all the other gods are against her – note the emphatically repeated *dīuum* at 602; cf. *Intro* [48–50] and Juno at **1.34–41**, who blames fate for her inability to keep the Trojans away from Italy). At all events, Aeneas has no option: if the gods are united in their action against Troy, there is nothing he can do.

2.604–23: Venus must now prove to Aeneas that it is the gods who are at work (602–3) and there is nothing to be done to save the situation. As a result, Aeneas witnesses something to which no human was ever privy – the gods ruthlessly tearing down a city. Note how V. piles up words indicating the blindness of normal mortal perception (604–6) to prepare him for this dreadful revelation. It is a unique scene, a horrifying vision of

ferrō ^accīncta, uocat.
iam summās arcēs Trītōnia, respice, Pallas   615
īnsēdit, nimbō effulgēns et Gorgone saeua.
ipse pater Danaīs animōs uīrīsque secundās
sufficit, ipse deōs in Dardana suscitat arma.
ēripe, nāte, fugam, finemque impōne labōrī;
nusquam aberō, et tūtum patriō tē līmine sistam."   620
dīxerat et spissīs noctis sē condidit umbrīs.
appārent dīrae faciēs inimīcaque Troiae
nūmina magna deum . . .'

614: this is an unfinished line (see on 1.534)

615 *Trītōni-us a um* Tritonian (see on 171). Pallas (Minerva) was, like Juno, a god rejected by Paris for the golden apple

**respiciō 3 *respexī respectum* I look back (Aeneas really *can* see what is going on)

616 *īnsīdō* 3 *īnsēdī* I settle on, possess

nimbō: i.e. from a storm-cloud

effulgeō 2 I flash, gleam

Gorgō -nis 3f. Gorgon-shield, with which Minerva is *saeua* (Minerva's shield bore a head of the original Gorgon, Medusa, a snake-haired woman whose look turned you to stone)

618 *sufficiō* 3 I provide

Dardanus a um Trojan

suscitō 1 I arouse, whip up X (acc.) *in* against

619 *ēripe . . . fugam*: lit. 'snatch your flight', i.e. get away while you still can

**impōnō 3 *imposuī impositum* I lay, place (on)

620 *nusquam* nowhere (an essential promise, because the Greeks hold the city (505), S.)

patriō . . . līmine: i.e. your father's house

sistō 3 I plant, station

621 *spiss-us a um* thick

623: another unfinished line (see on 1.534), romantically punctuated in this text as if V. meant it, and Aeneas found himself lost for words at this dreadful vision

Learning vocabulary

disiciō 3 *disiēcī disiectum* I scatter, shatter, disperse

impōnō 3 *imposuī impositum* I lay, place (on)

Iūnō Iūnōn-is 3f. Juno, wife of king of the gods Jupiter

Neptūn-us ī 2m. Neptune, god of the sea and earthquakes

puluis puluer-is 3m. dust

respiciō 3 *respexī respectum* I look back

merciless divinities at their work of vengeful destruction. Neptune (the earthquake god) takes care of the buildings at ground level, ripping them apart stone by stone (608–9), levering them up from the foundations with his trident (610), tearing the city up by its roots (611–12); Juno furiously urges the Greeks through the gates (612–14; *saeuissima* to the Trojans because she thereby hinders their escape, S.); Minerva occupies (*īnsēdit*) her own citadel, flashing out destruction from the top of the city (615–16); and, climactically, Jupiter himself (note *ipse*, twice, 617–18) both endows the Greeks with courage and strength and encourages the gods in their work.

But no gods are seen supporting Troy. There is nothing for it, says Venus: Aeneas must go. He has, in other words, served the demand of *pietās* as far as the community goes; he must now turn to protect his family and look to the new community of the future. But she will protect him – though only as far as seeing him safely home (619–20). The reason for this modified help is that V. is preparing episodes that will threaten to frustrate the whole escape from Troy, i.e. Anchises' refusal to leave and the loss of Creusa. But he cannot play these cards if Venus has total control, let alone develop Aeneas as the new leader of the Trojans by exploring how he reacts to them.

As Venus disappears into the night, V. describes the appearance of vague, ghastly

2.624–33: 'I saw Troy toppling like a ancient ash tree'

'tum uērō omne^ mihī ^uīsum cōnsīdere in ignīs
^Īlium, et ex īmō uertī Neptūnia Troia: 625
ac uelutī summīs antīquam^ in montibus ^ornum
cum ferrō ^accīsam crēbrīsque bipennibus īnstant
ēruere agricolae certātim, illa^ usque minātur
et ^tremefacta comam concussō uertice nūtat,
uulneribus dōnec paulātim ^ēuicta, suprēmum   630
congemuit trāxitque iugīs ^āuulsa ruīnam.
dēscendō ac, dūcente deō, flammam inter et hostīs
expedior: dant tēla locum flammaeque recēdunt.'

624 *uīsum [est]*: *Īlium* and *Neptūnia Troia* are the
  subjects; *uīsum [est]* controls the infs. *cōnsīdere*
  and *uertī*
cōnsīdō 3 I subside, sink into
625 **uertō 3 *uersī uersum* I turn (round), turn
  upside down, overthrow
Neptūni-us a um of Neptune, who had been
  responsible for building its walls (see on 610)
626 *orn-us ī* 2f. ash-tree; it is the obj. of *agricolae*
  īnstant ēruere (**627–8**)
627 *accīdō* 3 *accīdī accīsum* I cut nearly through
bipenn-is is 3f. axe
628 *ēruere*: here 'bring down'
certātim in competition
illa: i.e. the ash-tree
usque: to be picked up by *dōnec* (**630**)
629 *comam*: here = tree-top (acc. of respect after
  tremefacta)
concutiō 3 *concussī concussum* I shake violently
nūtō 1 I nod
630 *paulātim* gradually
ēuincō 3 *ēuīcī ēuictum* I overcome
suprēm-us a um final, last; here adverbial acc. 'for
  the last time'
631 *congemō* 3 *congemuī* I groan (here the 'gnomic'

perf. of what happens continually or proverbially;
  it is translated as a present tense, as too *trāxit*)
**iug-um ī 2n. ridge, yoke; take *iugīs* either with
  āuulsa ('from the ridge') or locally ('along the
  ridge'). *trāxit ruīnam* describes the agonisingly
  slow collapse of the tree and crash onto the
  ground (cf. on 465)
632 *dēscendō* 3 I come/get down (Aeneas has been
  on the palace roof since 458)
deō: it is very probable that V. wrote *deō*, but
  would you like to propose a different reading
  which many manuscripts prefer? S., however,
  comments that divine powers are not
  necessarily distinguished by sex; and there
  is no reason 'divine power' should not be
  meant
inter: construes with *flammam* and *hostīs*; so also
  681
633 *expediō* 3 I free, extricate; the passive here
  means 'I am given a free path'

Learning vocabulary
iug-um ī 2n. ridge, yoke
uertō 3 *uersī uersum* I turn (round), turn upside
  down, overthrow

images and mighty forces at work – an image of almost gothic power and intensity
(622–3). It is hard to see how V. could have improved on the astonishing half-line at 623
(see on 1.534), with its mysterious assonance. Whercof man cannot speak, thereof he
must be silent (Wittgenstein). See *Intro* [47].

2.624–33: Ilium seems to settle into the flames (624–5, like a corpse on a funeral pyre?)
and to be cut down (625) like a tree (626). The tree, like Ilium, is (i) venerable (626), (ii)
built high up and visible (626), (iii–iv) being attacked with blades (627), by men
attempting to outdo each other in their enthusiasm (628), (v) on the brink of collapse
for a long time (628–9), (vi) and finally falls with a tremendous crash (631). It is also
virtually personified, as if it were human (trembling, nodding, wounds, groans – does it
bring Priam to mind?). Note that fallen warriors were often likened to fallen trees, e.g.

Iliad 13.178–80 'Imbrius fell like an ash-tree that has stood as a landmark on a high hill-top, until it is cut down by an axe and brings its delicate foliage to the ground'; 13.389–91 'Asius crashed down as an oak crashes down or a poplar or a towering pine, which woodsmen cut down in the mountains with their newly sharpened axes to make timbers for a ship' (Rieu-Jones). If there was any doubt in Aeneas' mind that Ilium is done for, there is none now. There is something almost matter-of-fact about *dēscendō* and Aeneas' instant departure from the scene. No fury, no tears, no regrets. It is the gods' will. The iron has entered his soul. Off.

This is the great turning-point of Book 2: from duty to old Troy to duty to his family and the Troy of the future. It has been proposed that the controversial *deō* (632) suggests Jupiter is now centrally involved in Aeneas fulfilling his mission (as Jupiter will be again at 2.679ff., cf. 779).

See: West 'Multiple-correspondence Similes in the *Aeneid*' in S. J. Harrison (1990: 431–2) on the simile: 'the personification of the tree, its trembling hair, its shuddering and nodding head, its wounds, its gradual weakening and its death cry heighten our emotional reaction to the Trojan narrative'; and E. L. Harrison 'Divine Action in *Aeneid* Book 2' in S. J. Harrison (1990: 48–9) on the *deō* argument.

Learning vocabulary for Section 2.559–633

alm-us a um kindly, fostering

Ascani-us ī 2m. Ascanius or Iulus, son of Aeneas

Creūs-a ae 1f. Creusa, Aeneas' wife

Dardani-us a um Dardanian/Trojan

disiciō 3 *disiēcī disiectum* I scatter, shatter, disperse

ēuertō 3 *ēuertī ēuersum* I churn up; overthrow

expleō 2 *expleuī explētum* I complete, fulfil, satisfy

impōnō 3 *imposuī impositum* I lay, place (on)

inuīs-us a um hated, loathed, despised

iug-um ī 2n. ridge, yoke

Iūl-us ī 2m. Iulus/Ascanius, Aeneas' son

Iūnō Iūnōn-is 3f. Juno, wife of king of the gods

Jupiter

nefās 3n. crime against divine law

Neptūn-us ī 2m. Neptune, god of the sea

puluis puluer-is 3m. dust

respiciō 3 *respexī respectum* I look back

uertō 3 *uersī uersum* I turn (round), turn upside down, overthrow

Study section for 2.559–633

1. Do you find Aeneas' decision to kill Helen 'heroic'? Or just comprehensible? What difference do his circumstances make?

2. Why does Virgil not choose to make Aeneas catch sight of and kill Sinon? Would that have made a better climax than the current 'Helen' episode?

3. What image of the gods emerges in this *Section*?

4. (a) Conte (1986: 196–207) argues that the notorious Helen passage above (567–88) is Virgilian in concept if not in finish, suggesting it is based on Homer. Agamemnon has insulted Achilles so badly that Achilles draws his sword to kill him:

So he spoke, and his words infuriated Achilles.
In his manly chest, his heart was torn
whether to draw the sharp sword from his side,   190
thrust his way through the crowd and disembowel Agamemnon,
or to control himself and check his angry impulse.
These thoughts were racing through his mind,
and he was just drawing his great sword from his sheath when Athena came down
from the skies. The goddess white-armed Hera had sent her   195
because she felt equally close to both men and was concerned for them.
Athena stood behind Achilles and seized him by his auburn hair.
No one but Achilles was aware of her; the rest saw nothing.
Achilles was amazed. He swung round, recognised
Pallas Athena at once – so wonderful was the light from her eyes –   200
and spoke winged words . . .
[and persuades him to desist.]

(Rieu-Jones, Iliad 1.188–210)

In what ways do the Helen–Venus episode and this passage compare?

(b) Reckford in *Arethusa* (1981: 85–99) points to parallels with Euripides'
Orestes 1131–9, where Orestes' chum Pylades is trying to persuade
Orestes to kill Helen. Pylades argues:

. . . My scheme is honourable.
If against a chaster woman
we were aiming our swords, that would be dishonourable murder.
As it is, Helen will be punished on behalf of all Greece,
whose fathers she killed, whose children she destroyed,   1135
whose brides she made widows.
There will be shouts, fires lit to the gods,
they will call blessings on you and me
for shedding a wicked woman's blood . . .

Compare Pylades' justification for killing Helen with Aeneas'. Can you draw
any conclusions about Virgilian authorship from these passages?

2.634–734: Anchises

In this Section, Aeneas' father Anchises refuses to leave with the rest of the family, but an omen and a sign from Jupiter convince him. The party scatters when Anchises sees Greeks approaching.

(Note: from now on there will be no more **Learning vocabularies**. Vocabulary not listed in the *Total learning vocabulary* will be glossed in the text.)

2.634–49: 'I found my father, but he refused to leave; he had been useless for too long and wanted to die in Troy'

'atque ubi iam patriae peruentum ad līmina sēdis
antīquāsque domōs, genitor, quem tollere in altōs^   635
optābam prīmum ^montīs prīmumque petēbam,
abnegat excīsā^ uītam prōdūcere ^Troiā
exsiliumque patī. "uōs ō, quibus integer aeuī
sanguis," ait, "solidaeque suō stant rōbore uīrēs,
uōs agitāte fugam.   640
mē sī caelicolae uoluissent dūcere uītam,
hās mihi seruāssent sēdēs. satis ūna^ superque
uīdimus ^excidia et captae superāuimus urbī.

---

634 *peruentum*: ellipsis of *est*, an impersonal passive, lit. 'it was come', i.e. I came, **RL**155, **M**106
635 *genitor*: i.e. Anchises
636 *prīmum . . . prīmum*: S. suggests 'especially'; probably adverbial with *optābam* and *petēbam*, but could be adjectival
637 *abnegō* 1 I refuse (and 654)
excīdō 3 *excīdī excīsum* I raze, destroy
prōdūcō 3 I extend, spin out
638 *quibus integer aeuī sanguis*: ellipsis of *est*, lit. 'to whom there is . . .'
integer: i.e. undiminished
aeuī: gen. of reference, 'as regards old age'
639 *solid-us a um* unwavering, strong, firm
suō rōbore: S. glosses 'without anyone else's help, which Anchises needs'

640 *agitō* 1 I plan, intend (an unfinished line, 1.534)
641 *caelicol-a ae* 1m./f. dweller in the sky
dūcere = spin out, prolong
642 *super*: more than (enough, after *satis*)
643 *excidi-um ī* 2n. destruction
superō 1 I survive (+ dat.); the reference is to Hercules' sack of the city after its king Laomedon cheated him. Laomedon had offered up his daughter Hesione as a sacrifice to a sea-monster, and asked Hercules to save her. In return, Laomedon promised Hercules the famous horses that Jupiter had given him (L.) in compensation for abducting L.'s beautiful son Ganymede. Laomedon never paid up, and Hercules returned with a force to sack the city and put Priam on the throne

---

2.634–49: Aeneas is now expecting to locate his family in his beloved home (note the affectionate *antīquāsque* 635) and to escape from Troy with them and anyone else he can

sīc ō sīc positum adfātī discēdite corpus.
ipse manū mortem inueniam; miserēbitur hostis   645
exuuiāsque petet. facilis iactūra sepulcrī.
iam prīdem inuīsus dīuīs et inūtilis annōs
dēmoror, ex quō mē dīuum pater atque hominum rēx
fulminis adflāuit uentīs et contigit ignī.'''

2.650–70: 'No one could persuade Anchises otherwise; I decided I had to stay and fight'

'tālia perstābat memorāns, fīxusque manēbat.   650
nōs contrā, effūsī lacrimīs, coniūnxque Creūsa
Ascaniusque omnisque domus, nē uertere sēcum

644 *positum*: Anchises has long since made his decision to stay: he feels himself to be laid out as a corpse already
adfor 1 dep. I say farewell to (as one did at a funeral with the words *auē, uale*)
645 *manū*: not by suicide, but (like old (561) Priam, 544ff.) by charging the enemy (who will look to strip him of his armour, *exuuiās* (**646**))
miserēbitur: an ironic paradox from a man tired of life – the pitiless enemy will unknowingly be doing me a kindness in killing me
646 *iactūr-a ae* 1f. loss, jettisoning
sepulcr-um ī 2n. tomb. No ancient wanted to remain unburied; Anchises is emphasising the desperate nature of their situation. Cf. Aeneas at ll. 94–101
647 *inūtil-is e* useless
648 *dēmoror* 1 dep. I delay (+ acc. *annōs*, i.e. he has been foiling the passage of time by living too long)

ex quō: 'from the time when'. Jupiter was said to have punished Anchises for boasting that he had made love to Venus (the youthful Anchises had already been warned of the consequences if he did. But he was young and male and . . .); the thunderbolt, however, was diverted by Venus so that Anchises was scorched, not killed, leaving him crippled for life. S. tells us that some writers claimed that any great leader struck by a thunderbolt and surviving was guaranteed a glorious posterity
649 *fulmen fulmin-is* 3n. thunderbolt
adflō 1 I breathe on

650 *perstō* 1 I stand firm, persist
651 *effūsī* (*sumus*): as if melted in tears
652 *nē*: understand '[begging] that (**653**) *pater* [should] not *uellet* to . . .', i.e. an indir. command, **RL**134, **W**36, **M**89–91

find. But he had not reckoned with his old father, Anchises. His father comes first (635–6), but Anchises will have none of it. Since, however, as Anchises knows very well, no Roman son could conceivably leave his father to die at enemy hands, he has to produce a string of reasons why his case is different. He begins by saying that he could not endure exile (638). But that sounds like simple weakness. So he turns to the facts of the situation as it is *now* and argues that it is only those with the strength to do so who should consider flight (639); the gods clearly agree to his death (641–2); he has seen one sack already and that is quite enough (642–3); he is effectively a corpse laid out for burial, eager to die at enemy hands (644–6); the loss of proper burial is trivial (646: '*iactūra* is an act of jettison, voluntarily performed, to save what really matters': Austin 1964); he has outlived his usefulness and is hated by the gods of old (647–9). Weak, useless, the object of divine disfavour, dead already and careless of memorial – what more can he say?

2.650–70: Aeneas reports that the whole family's tearful pleas have no effect on the stubborn Anchises, who seems to them intent on making the situation even worse than it is

cūncta pater fātōque urgentī incumbere uellet.
abnegat, inceptōque et sēdibus haeret in īsdem.
rūrsus in arma feror, mortemque miserrimus optō.   655
nam quod cōnsilium aut quae iam fortūna dabātur?
"mēne efferre pedem, genitor, tē^ posse ^relictō
spērāstī, tantumque nefās patriō excidit ōre?
sī nihil ex tantā superīs placet urbe relinquī,
et sedet hoc animō, peritūraeque addere Troiae   660
tēque tuōsque iuuat, patet istī iānua lētō,
iamque aderit multō Priamī dē sanguine Pyrrhus,
nātum ante ōra patris, pātrem quī obtruncat ad ārās.

653 *urgeō* 2 I press hard
incumbere: i.e. add (yet more)/lend (his own) weight
to + dat.
654 *incept-um ī* 2n. intention
655 *in arma feror*: Aeneas does get his weapons
(671–2) but does not actually rush into
battle
657 *mē-ne*: an exasperated first word – so you really
expected (**658**) *me . . .*!
pedem efferre: lit. 'carry out a foot', i.e. leave
658 *spērā[ui]stī*: here meaning 'expect', with pres.
inf.
tantumque . . . ōre: i.e. could a father say anything so
sacrilegious?
excidit: note that the first *i* is short. Aeneas uses
excidit, says S., to suggest that Anchises was not
thinking about what he was saying – it just
slipped out
659 *nihil . . . relinquī*: i.e. not even humans
should be left; *placet . . .* **660** *sedet . . .* **661** *iuuat*

form another typically Virgilian trio; see on
2.132–44
660 *hoc*: 'this [idea]', subject
peritūraeque: again, with a sense of inevitability, cf.
on 511
661 *tē tuōsque*: obj. of *addere*; the subject of *iuuat* is
tē (understood)
istī . . . lētō: 'to that death of yours' (*istī* spat out
emphatically, i.e. which you seem to be so
desperately keen on)
662 *aderit*: from *adsum*. The subject is still *iānua lētō*
dē: i.e. fresh/straight from
663 *obtruncō* 1 I cut down; take in order (*Pyrrhus*)
*quī obtruncat nātum ante ōra patris, pātrem ad
ārās* (526–58). Note the different scansion of
patris/patrem! Aeneas suggests that, if it is death
Anchises wants, there is no need to rush out to
battle (cf. 645–6). It will come soon enough in the
shape of Pyrrhus – and will take the rest of them
too

(651–3). But this selfish old man can do nothing but think of himself (654). Aeneas is
now in an impossible position – no wonder he is *miserrimus* (655): he had (at last) a
cōnsilium other than fighting, but Anchises has ruined it; so only *fortūna* is left, and
everyone knows which way that is pointing (656). He describes his final plea, which
becomes more desperate as he speaks. First, he accuses his father of unintentional
(*excidit*) but wicked resistance to the divine will (*nefās*, 658), the result of which will be
the destruction of everyone in Troy, themselves included (659–61). The example of
Pyrrhus' recent behaviour (of which Anchises knows nothing) makes the point (662–3).
Increasingly panic-stricken, Aeneas appeals to Venus, picturing the family slaughtered
in each other's blood (664–7; *mactō* 667 is used of animal sacrifice at the altar, where he
has just witnessed Priam slain). His words are directed as much at Anchises, who knows
nothing of Venus' interventions, as they are at Venus. The staccato 668 and desperate
669–70 are the final throw of the dice. But Anchises remains unmoved. The obstinate
old man's determination to commit suicide will take the rest of the family, and the
whole line, down with him. So be it. The Roman *paterfamiliās* had to be obeyed. *Pius
Aeneas* – expressed here in his duty to his father – will set an example (670), if that is

hoc erat, alma parēns, quod mē per tēla, per ignīs
ēripis, ut mediīs hostem in penetrālibus utque   665
Ascanium patremque meum iuxtāque Creūsam
alterum in alterius mactātōs sanguine cernam?
arma, uirī, ferte arma; uocat lūx ultima uictōs.
reddite mē Danaīs; sinite īnstaurāta reuīsam
proelia. numquam omnēs hodiē moriēmur inultī.'"   670

2.671–91: 'As I armed, Creusa begged me to think of the family. At that moment a supernatural flame appeared on Iulus' head, a sign greeted joyfully by Anchises who begged Jupiter for confirmation'

'hinc ferrō accingor rūrsus, clipeōque sinistram
īnsertābam aptāns, mēque extrā tēcta ferēbam.
ecce autem complexa^ pedēs in līmine ^coniūnx
haerēbat, paruumque patrī tendēbat Iūlum:
"sī peritūrus abīs, et nōs rape in omnia tēcum;   675
sin aliquam^ expertus sūmptīs ^spem pōnis in armīs,
hanc prīmum tūtāre domum. cūī paruus Iūlus,
cūī pater et coniūnx quondam tua dicta relinquor?"
tālia uociferāns, gemitū tēctum omne replēbat,

---

664 *hoc erat quod . . .* **665** *ut . . .* **667** *cernam*?: 'was this why . . . so that . . . I should see?' *hostem . . .* (**666**) *Ascanium patremque meum . . . Creūsam* are all objects of *cernam*, agreeing with *mactātōs* (**667**)
alma parēns: note gender of *alma*; Aeneas has turned to appeal to Venus
667 *alterum in alterius*: 'each in the *sanguine* of the other'
mactō 1 I sacrifice
669 *sinō* 3 I allow, permit ('that I . . .' + subjunc., *reuīsam*)
īnstaurō 1 I renew, repeat
reuīsō 3 I revisit, return to
670 *inult-us a um* unavenged

671 *accingor*: 'middle' reflexive usage
clipeōque: i.e. 'through [the strap in the middle of] my shield' before graspng the handle at the shield's edge

sinistr-a ae 1f. left arm
672 *īnsertō* 1 I insert, fix; the impf. tenses in this line indicate that Aeneas was beginning to carry out these actions ('inceptive' use of the vb)
extrā + acc. outside
674 *patrī*: meaning Aeneas; Creusa is appealing to Aeneas' paternal feelings, cf. **678** where *pater* = Anchises
675 *peritūrus*: that form again, cf. 660, 511
676 *experior* 4 dep. *expertus* I have experience of
677 *tūtor* 1 dep. I guard, protect. For the Roman's strong attachment to his home, see *Intro* [39]
cūī: i.e. to what fate; note the emotional repetition in **678**
678 *dicta*: i.e. said to be (but *quondam* indicates that Creusa soon expects *not* to be)
relinquor: this refers to all the subjects in this sentence, not just Creusa
679 *uōciferor* 1 dep. I cry out, yell

---

what Anchises wants. But what sort of example of *pietās* is Anchises setting? Aeneas' honesty and courage are evident in his reporting of his father's obstinacy, his efforts to fight it, his failure to do so and despairing call to die.

2.671–91: Aeneas is preparing to put words into action (671–2), when *ecce autem* (673) stops him. At the threshold of the house, Aeneas reports Creusa supplicating him; that

cum subitum dictūque^ oritur ^mīrābile mōnstrum.   680
namque manūs inter maestōrumque ōra parentum,
ecce leuis^ summō dē uertice ^uīsus Iūlī
fundere lūmen ^apex, tāctūque innoxia^ mollīs
lambere ^flamma comās et circum tempora pāscī.
nōs pauidī trepidāre metū crīnemque flagrantem   685
excutere et sānctōs restinguere fontibus ignīs.
at pater Anchīsēs oculōs ad sīdera laetus
extulit, et caelō palmās cum uōce tetendit:
"Iuppiter omnipotēns, precibus sī flecteris ūllīs,
aspice nōs – hoc tantum – et sī pietāte merēmur,   690
dā deīnde augurium, pater, atque haec ōmina firmā.'"

---

680 *dictūque*: take with *mīrābile*; see on 1.111

mōnstr-um ī 2n. warning, omen

681 *inter*: controls both *manūs* and *ōra*

682 *leu-is e* light, thin

uīsus [*est*]: the subjects are *apex* (**683**) and *innoxia* . . . *flamma* (**683–4**)

683 *apex apic-is* 3m. point, top, crown, i.e. tongue of flame

tāct-us ūs 4m. touch (here abl. of respect)

innoxi-us a um harmless

moll-is e soft

684 *lambō* 3 I lick

com-a ae 1f. hair

tempor-a um 3n. pl. temples

685 *trepidō* 1 I am alarmed, nervous; historic inf., as the two other vbs in this sentence, indicating urgent action (see on 1.423)

crīn-is is 3m. hair

flagrō 1 I blaze

686 *excutere*: i.e. shake the fire out of his hair

restinguō 3 I quench, put out

fōns font-is 3m. spring, water

688 *caelō*: i.e. to the heavens

689 *omnipotēns omnipotent-is* all-powerful

prex prec-is 3f. prayer

flectō 3 I sway, persuade (tense? voice?)

690 *hoc tantum* just this once (and no more)

merēor 2 dep. I deserve well, have a claim to kindness (because of + abl.)

691 *auguri-um ī* 2n. sign, augury

firmō 1 I confirm

---

is, from a position of helplessness and self-subjugation (conventionally, crouching down and seizing the knees, though here Creusa seizes his feet, 673) she makes a life-or-death appeal, reinforced emotionally by her holding up the *paruus* Iulus to him (674). Her point is that, if he dies, they all die, so he may as well take them all with him (675) and get it over with (*rape*, of instant, even violent action); but her alternative suggestion is that, if he is to resort to arms, his first duty is to protect the home (676–7). An emotional rhetorical question centred round the family – note *paruus* (677) again and the foreboding *quondam tua dicta* (678) – ends her appeal on a high note. The home, or revenge in the name of a fallen Troy – which does the man of *pietās* choose?

But as lamentation breaks out – reinforcing the emotional pressure on Aeneas – a miracle occurs (679–80), giving Aeneas no time to reply to her. The child is in his parents' hands at eye-level (681, cf. 674) when – *ecce* (again) – his hair seems to catch fire (682–4). It is harmless – a miracle – but they are not to know that at that time, and desperately try to put it out (685–6: can we assume that *sānctōs* is Aeneas' comment after the event? Or that they had begun to realise there was something supernatural about the flame?). Anchises, however, sees its significance. Recently a recalcitrant corpse, he now looks up, stretches his arms to heaven and *laetus* (687–8, cf. his earlier gloom) asks for an omen from Jupiter himself (689–91). The point is that a miracle has occurred: but what does it actually mean? What course of action does it portend? A further sign is needed.

2.692–704: 'When a shooting star flashed across the sky, Anchises agreed to leave'

'uix ea fātus erat sēnior, subitōque fragōre
intonuit laeuum, et dē caelō lāpsa^ per umbrās
^stēlla, facem ^dūcēns, multā cum lūce cucurrit.
illam,^ summa super ^lābentem culmina tēctī,   695
cernimus Īdaeā ^clāram ^sē condere siluā
^signantemque uiās; tum longō līmite sulcus
dat lūcem et lātē circum loca sulphure fūmant.
hīc uērō uictus genitor sē tollit ad aurās,
adfāturque deōs et sānctum sīdus adōrat.   700
"iam iam nūlla mora est; sequor et quā dūcitis adsum.
dī patriī, seruāte domum, seruāte nepōtem.
uestrum hoc augurium, uestrōque in nūmine Troia est.
cedō equidem nec, nāte, tibī comes īre recūsō."'

692 *subit-us a um* sudden	**697** *signō* 1 I indicate, leave a trail to show (*uiās* i.e.
fragor -is 3m. crack, rumble	our path)
693 *intonō* 1 *intonuī* I thunder (here impersonal)	*līmes līmit-is* 3m. path, track
laeuum: acc. of respect	*sulc-us ī* 2m. furrow, trail
694 *stēll-a ae* 1f. star	**698** *sulphur -is* 3n. sulphur (a smell commonly
fax fac-is 3f. torch; with *dūcēns* = 'shooting-star'	accompanying such celestial phenomena in the ancient world)
facem dūcēns: note that the Greek for a shooting star, leaving a trail like hair, was *komētēs* ('comet'); and *komē* is Greek for 'hair'. This second sign is therefore firmly linked to the first, which was fire playing in Ascanius' *comae* (684). See O'Hara (1996) and cf. 1.261	*fūmō* 1 I smoke
	700 *adfor* 1 dep. I address
	adōrō 1 I worship
	701: *nūlla mora*: i.e. on *my* part (as his next words show)
	702 *dī patriī*: punctuated not with *dūcitis* but with *seruāte*, Horsfall (2008)
696 *Īdae-us a um* of Mount Ida, a mountain range south of Troy	**703** *auguri-um ī* 2n. sign

This is an important passage. If Anchises cannot be brought to see that the family must survive somehow, and Aeneas can see no other way to respond to the *paterfamiliās* than to charge straight into battle, someone else must intervene on the family's behalf. Creusa takes this responsibility on herself by pointing out that Aeneas can, and should, best use his military skills defensively; and it cannot be mere coincidence that it is the child Iulus – the future of the family, indeed the future of Rome – who is the subject of the miraculous fire playing round his hair. But, given Anchises' behaviour so far, is there a degree of irony in Aeneas reporting his hint that the gods might be favourable because of his *pietās* (690)?

2.692–704: Immediately, Aeneas reports hearing a clap of thunder on the left (692–3) – favourable when it was a *divine* sign in the Roman (not the Greek) world – and seeing a shooting star (693–4). Its path, swooping over the house, takes it to Mount Ida, where it disappears into a wood (695–7); its long tail remained, marking out the route which Aeneas and his family must take (697–8). Anchises, once so obstinate, seated (654), almost prostrate (644), had lifted arms and eyes to heaven at the first sign (687); now he acknowledges he was wrong (*uictus*, 699, cf. 704 *cēdō*) and lifts himself up to stand,

2.705–20: 'I said I would carry Anchises; everyone was to meet by an ancient cypress tree; Anchises would bring Troy's sacraments and ancestral gods'

'dīxerat ille, et iam per moenia clārior ignis 705
audītur, propiusque aestūs incendia uoluunt.
"ergō age, cāre pater, ceruīcī impōnere nostrae;

705 *moenia*: here meaning 'town'
clārior: Aeneas' house is set back and surrounded by
   trees (299–300), through which the flames are
   becoming brighter
706 *propius* nearer
aestūs: acc. pl.
707 *ergō* therefore, so
age come, now; S. points out that this is not an

imperative but rather an encouragement to
   action
cār-us a um dear
ceruīcī: i.e. shoulders. Anchises is not having a
   'piggy-back', but is riding on Aeneas' shoulders,
   leaving Aeneas' arms free for fighting. Cf. Fig. 3!
impōnere: 2s. pass. imper., with a middle sense,
   'place/set yourself on' + dat.

presumably hands raised (699), to worship the star (700). That is the usual position for prayer to the gods above and, further, a sign of his readiness to depart (Page 1894). He recognises that they are in the hands of the gods of the fatherland; the survival of family and especially of Iulus (*nepōtem*), is now the priority (702); and indeed that *Troia* (! the 'Troy' of the future) is in divine hands (703). He cannot refuse to leave.

It was first Aeneas, but then Anchises, who had threatened the whole Trojan 'mission' to which Hector had pointed (294–5). Anchises had claimed that the gods aquiesced in his desire to stay and die (641–2, cf. 647–9). So it is Anchises who must now be convinced that it is his divine duty to go, and the gods respond accordingly (this family needs pushing, hard). Which gods? Presumably Jupiter, to whom Anchises prayed at 689–91. Jupiter may be urging on gods hostile to Ilium to destroy it (617–18), but he has plans for Aeneas' family which Anchises looked set to wreck. No longer. So Aeneas, having ignored everything Hector said at 289–97, can now have no doubts where his duty lies. But will his new resolve last?

It was the Roman tradition that the first auspices were taken by Romulus, but there were other traditions that put the institution earlier. V. in this episode puts it earlier still – for nothing as dramatic as the departure from Troy, the first step in the founding of Rome, could conceivably have happened without any indication of divine approval. The whole incident is modelled on features of a traditional Roman augury. An unexplained sign is given, so Anchises asks for a confirmatory sign from Jupiter (all signs came from Jupiter); Anchises is head of house, and the chief magistrate in Rome took the auguries; it is dawn, the best time for taking them; Anchises is seated, watching the skies, as was the magistrate; and as soon as Anchises sees it, he rises, as did the magistrate, to ensure another sign did not cancel it out.

The confirmatory sign may nod to Julius Caesar/Augustus. The 'Julian star' had appeared at Julius Caesar's funeral games and was thought to be his soul being received into heaven. It was featured by Augustus on statues of Julius Caesar and is referred to elsewhere in V. (for the Julius–Iulus/Ascanius connection, see 1.288).

See: Heinze (55–7/32–4) for the Roman augury; Zanker (1988: 34–5) for the Julian star on statues.

2.705–20: Now that Anchises is on board, the tone of the relationship between him and

ipse subībō umerīs, nec mē labor iste grauābit;
quō rēs cumque cadent, ūnum et commūne perīclum,
ūna salūs ambōbus erit. mihi paruus Iūlus   710
sit comes, et longē seruet uestīgia coniūnx.
uōs, famulī, quae dīcam animīs aduertite uestrīs.
est urbe ēgressīs tumulus templumque uetustum
dēsertae Cereris, iuxtāque antīqua^ ^cupressus
rēligiōne patrum multōs ^seruāta per annōs;   715
hanc ex dīuersō sēdem ueniēmus in ūnam.
tū, genitor, cape sacra manū patriōsque penātīs;
mē, bellō ē tantō dīgressum et caede recentī,
attrectāre nefās, dōnec mē flūmine uīuō
abluerō.'"   720

708 *subeō subīre* I support (understand 'you')
umerīs: abl. of means
iste: i.e. that you impose
grauō 1 I weigh down
709 *quō . . . cumque* = *quōcumque* 'however', lit. 'to
wherever' (tmēsis). *cadent* suggests an image of
dice 'falling (out)'
710 *ambōbus*: dat. pl., *ambō* (i.e. father and son)
711 *sit*: note jussive subjunc., as too *seruet*
longē at a distance. S. comes up with a practical
reason for this: too big a crowd would look
suspicious, cf. **716**, where Aeneas suggests
everyone gets to the shrine of Ceres by different
routes. The narrative purpose, however, is that
Creusa will be 'lost' from the story. The reason is
that Jupiter plans for the new Roman race to be a
mixture of Trojan and Italian blood (2.783ff., cf.
7.98ff., 12.835ff.). Her loss will bring
consequences, however: Aeneas will be free to
have a disastrous affair with Dido (in Book 4),
with all the dreadful repercussions that spring
from the relationship
seruō: here 'I pay attention to, note'
uestīgi-um ī 2n. footprint
712 *famul-us ī* 2m. slave
aduertō 3 I pay attention (to *quae dīcam*)
713 *ēgressīs*: 'for those having departed *urbe*'

tumul-us ī 2m. (burial) mound (and 742)
uetust-us a um ancient
714 *Cer-ēs Cerer-is* 3f. Ceres (and 742). She is a god
of grain, and therefore associated with the
countryside; hence her shrine outside the city. S.
suggests (among other reasons) that it may be
dēserta[e] because Ceres was always in mourning
for her lost daughter Proserpina, snatched from
her for six months of the year by the underworld
god Pluto; or it may be a transferred epithet, i.e. it
is the temple which is abandoned (Horsfall
(2008)). The cypress is the tree of mourning in the
Roman world
cupress-us ī 2f. cypress tree
716 *dīuersō*: i.e. by different routes
718 *mē . . .* **719** *nefās* [*est*]: 'it is/would be sacrilege
for me to . . .'
dīgredior 3 dep. *dīgressus* I depart from, leave
719 *attrectō* 1 I touch (understand 'the holy objects',
which Aeneas presumably took over from Panthus;
see on 2.318–35); cf. 167 where (Sinon claims)
Odysseus and Diomedes incur divine wrath by
touching the Palladium with blood-stained hands
uīu-us a um living, flowing
720 *abluō* 3 *abluī* I wash, purify. Note the fut. perf.
(not subjunc.) – there is no doubt that this is what
Aeneas will do – and the unfinished line

Aeneas changes. He is *cāre* (707); his weight will be no problem (708); they are all in this
together, and Aeneas' words imply that this is an advantage – all for one and one for all
(709–10). Here is true *pietās* in perfect action – the duty one owes to the family and to
the gods. Aeneas splits the party up and tells them to find their own separate ways to the
shrine of Ceres (see note on *longē* 711) and its ancient tree – a place rich in religious significance over many years (714–15: their best chance of protection lies in a holy place
they have protected so faithfully? *Pietās* again). And the final act of *pietās*: the gods of
Troy are to be taken with them (cf. Hector's instructions at 293–5), carried by the
paterfamiliās (717). See notes on 719, 720.

2.721-34: 'Now fearful of everything, I set off with Anchises, Creusa and Iulus, but Anchises heard foot-steps and told me to run for it'

'haec fātus, lātōs umerōs subiectaque colla
ueste super fuluīque īnsternor pelle leōnis,
succēdōque onerī; dextrae sē paruus Iūlus
implicuit, sequiturque patrem nōn passibus aequīs;
pōne subit coniūnx. ferimur per opāca locōrum,   725
et mē,^ ^quem dūdum nōn ūlla iniecta mouēbant
tēla neque aduersō glomerātī ex agmine Grāī,
nunc omnēs terrent aurae, sonus excitat omnis
^suspēnsum, et pariter comitīque onerīque ^timentem.

721 *subiectaque*: for scansion, see on *subiciō* 37 and cf. 726	**724** *patrem*: Aeneas refers to himself in the third person
lātōs: heroic boasting? Or statement of fact, i.e. Aeneas is up to the task?	*pass-us ūs* 4m. step; cf. on 321, 457, but nothing 'domestic' about this moment
722 *ueste . . . pelle*: 'with a covering and a skin', i.e. 'of a skin' (hendiadys – see **Glossary of literary terms**)	**725** *pōne* behind
super: adverbial 'above'	*opāc-us a um* dark, shadowy (n. pl., ellipsis of e.g. 'parts')
fulu-us a um tawny	**726** *dūdum* previously
īnsternor 3 I cover + acc. ('middle' reflexive usage)	*iniciō* 3 *iniēcī iniectum* I throw in
pell-is is 3f. skin, hide	**727** *Grāī = Graiī*
leō leōn-is 3m. lion	**728** *son-us ī* 2m. sound
723 *succēdō* 3 I bend down to	*excitō* 1 I arouse

The family had been on the point of self-destruction, and therefore of the ultimate betrayal: for the whole future of Troy lay in their hands. So everything was at stake in Anchises' refusal to leave, the family's *pietās* most of all. The sense of relief that floods this passage indicates how close a call it was. The very last man who should have threatened that breakdown, the *paterfamiliās*, is now on the shoulders of his son, carrying the gods of Troy with him into whatever the future holds (709). That said, the family will not be saved in its totality: Creusa (as we have seen) will be lost in the panicky scramble to get away. Commentators worry about Aeneas' apparent coldness at 711 (and see also on **2.671-91**, where he is in fact *unable* to reply to Creusa). They are wrong. There is no coldness there. Time is short. Aeneas knows and trusts his wife. She does not need to be lectured, as the slaves do (712); she has no objections to his scheme, nor does anyone else. These are the practical instructions of a man of action not wasting his words on the midnight air but making instant decisions at a critical moment, and *admitting* to them – even though he now knows what the dreadful consequences were.

2.721-34: With Anchises on his shoulders and young Iulus clinging tightly to his hand (*implicuit* 724) – Iulus' *nōn passibus aequīs,* scampering to keep up, is a nice touch – Aeneas describes himself setting off and Creusa following, the position and order of *pōne subit coniūnx* (725) matching the reality. (See Figure 4, cf. Fig. 3, p. 182.) There is nothing demeaning or thoughtless about this. Iulus is a young child, needing male protection in the heat of battle. Of course the man will feel he has to lead the way. Creusa makes no complaint at being asked to bring up the rear. It is the logical thing for her to do: family security fore and aft. What other order should they go in?

Figure 4 Aeneas and his family escape from Troy

iamque propinquābam portīs omnemque^ uidēbar   730
ēuāsisse ^uiam, subitō cum crēber^ ad aurīs
^uīsus adesse pedum ^sonitus, genitorque per umbram
prōspiciēns "nāte," exclāmat, "fuge, nāte; propinquant.
ārdentīs clipeōs atque aera micantia cernō.'"

730 *propinquō* 1 I approach; note the quickening   **733** *exclāmō* 1 I shout out
dactylic rhythm of the end of **731** into **732** –
suggesting footsteps?

They keep to the shadows (725), and Aeneas admits, for the first time, to experience fear (728–9). This is a brilliant touch. He did not fear battle when he was doing what heroes do, risking his own life but in control of his own destiny and confident of fighting and winning (726–7). But the situation is entirely different when his new mission is to *avoid* battle and lead his whole, otherwise helpless, family to safety and through them win the future of the new Troy. This is a massive responsibility compared with mere self-preservation, and not one of which he can feel in complete control and therefore be confident of fulfilling. No wonder he confesses to seeing danger everywhere, in every *aura* and *sonus* (728) – and refers to his beloved father Anchises as an *onus* (729).

And they so nearly make it. But near the gate they hear the tramp of feet (731–2) and Anchises, from his vantage point on Aeneas' shoulders and alert to the danger (i.e. now fully engaged with the escape – no useless *onus*!), warns with a terse, urgent command that the enemy are approaching (733). This is real danger: Anchises can now *see* the glinting bronze of weapons and armour (734).

Study section for 2.634–734

1. To what extent does Anchises demonstrate *pietās* in this *Section*?
2. How does Aeneas justify his decision to return to the fight? What does it tell you about Aeneas?
3. Does Aeneas present himself as a good leader in this *Section*?

2.735–804: Creusa

In this Section, *Creusa is lost in the panic. Aeneas goes back to look for her, but is met by her ghost who assures him all will be well. He returns to his followers and, as day breaks, they depart.*

2.735–51: 'I ran off wildly and, meeting up at the tree, found Creusa missing. I armed and went back to find her'

'hīc mihi^ nescio quod ^trepidō male^ nūmen ^amīcum   735
cōnfūsam ēripuit mentem. namque āuia cursū
dum sequor, et nōtā excēdō regiōne uiārum,
hēu miserō, coniūnx – fātōne ērepta Creūsa
substitit? – errāuitne uiā sēu lassa resēdit? –
incertum; nec post oculīs est reddita nostrīs.   740
nec prius āmissam respexī animumue reflexī
quam tumulum antīquae Cereris sēdemque sacrātam
uēnimus: hīc dēmum, collēctīs omnibus, ūna
dēfuit, et comitēs nātumque uirumque fefellit.

735 *nescio quod*: lit. 'I don't know what', agreeing with *nūmen*, i.e. 'some *nūmen* or other'
trepid-us a um fearful
736 *cōnfundō* 3 *cōnfūdī cōnfūsum* I bewilder, cause turmoil
āui-us a um out of the way (n. pl. 'places'), cf. on 359
738 *hēu miserō*: i.e. 'alas for me *miserō*' and 'from me *miserō*' (after *ērepta*). **738–40** break out into an extraordinary staccato, guilt-laden series of questions, that Aeneas is scarcely able to articulate, about what might have happened to Creusa. **740** *incertum* [*est*] (to which the rest of the sentence 'should' have been grammatically attached, i.e. with the three verbs in **739** in the subjunc., as indir. qs.) completes the sense of Aeneas groping hopelessly for an answer, a reason, and finding none

739 *subsistō* 3 *substitī* I stop
lass-us a um exhausted, tired. Austin comments that this is the 'everyday' word for 'tired', used regularly in the comic playwrights Plautus and Terence (who never use *fessus*) – she just could not put one more step in front of the other. V. is a master of combining the homely with the epic
resīdō 2 *resēdī* I sit down
741 *āmissam*: '[that she had] been lost'
reflectō 3 *reflexī* I turn (*animum*, ellipsis of 'to her')
743 *dēmum* at last, i.e. here and here only
744 *dēsum dēesse dēfuī* I am missing
fallō 3 *fefellī* I deceive, cheat, fail. The word contains the idea that she was expected, but never turned up, and therefore both cheated her companions of their hopes and left them baffled as to why: 'was missing, to the bewilderment of . . .'?

2.735–51: Aeneas makes it clear that he cannot explain what happened next (*nescio quod* 735). Whatever it was, he panicked, ran for it without thinking where he was going (736–7), did *not* look back and so lost Creusa (cf. Orpheus who *did* look back and lost

quem nōn incūsāuī āmēns hominumque deōrumque,   745
aut quid in ēuersā uīdī crūdēlius urbe?
Ascanium Anchīsēnque patrem Teucrōsque penātīs
commendō sociīs et curuā ualle recondō;
ipse urbem repetō et cingor fulgentibus armīs.
stat cāsūs renouāre omnīs, omnemque reuertī   750
per Troiam, et rūrsus caput obiectāre perīclīs.'

2.752–70: 'Despite Greek control of the city and its treasures, I searched everywhere, even calling her name'

'prīncipiō mūrōs obscūraque līmina portae,
quā gressum extuleram, repetō et uestīgia retrō
obseruāta sequor per noctem et lūmine lūstrō:

745 *incūsō* 1 I accuse
deōrumque: the final *-que* needs to be elided with the
   next line's *aut* in order to scan; Aeneas' emotions
   getting the better of him?
746 *crūdēlius*: form?
747 *penātēs*: see 293
748 *commendō* 1 I entrust
uall-is is 3f. valley
recondō 3 I hide, i.e. 'all of them'. That they had to be
   hidden in a *uallis* shows how many of them there
   were (S.)

749 *cingor* 3 I arm myself with (middle 'reflexive'
   use)
750 *stat*: 'it is my fixed resolve'
renouō 1 I risk again
reuertor 3 I go back through
751 *caput*: i.e. my life
obiectō 1 I expose X (acc.) to Y (dat.)

752 *prīncipi-um ī* 2n. beginning
754 *obseruō* 1 I watch, attend to

Eurydice, *Georgics* 4.485–98 – a wonderful passage). Note that at 735–6, Aeneas blames a *male nūmen amīcum*. It is typical of ancient thought to ascribe feelings and actions, especially irrational ones, to an external power, without necessarily removing the responsibility from oneself. Aeneas here as good as admits he got it wrong, under the pressure of an instant reaction to Anchises' sharp orders (733–4) – and a son always obeys his father.

The moving 738–40 (see note) do not assign blame to anyone. How could they? Aeneas does not *know*, any more than we do, how Creusa came to be lost. But the lines show a distraught man openly describing how he took full responsibility for what had happened and torturing himself as he tries to understand it. He clearly blames himself at 741–2 – what *was* he thinking about to have missed her? – but the truth dawns only when they are all together – all, that is, bar one (743–4). His confessed mindless outburst (745–6; note that *āmēns*, cf. 314–17) turns to cool decision-making (*commendō* 748, *stat* 750): he will go back for her. Once again, the whole mission is put at risk: family vs. public duty again for the man of *pietās*.

Aeneas cannot forgive himself for Creusa's loss. When he said he did not know how things would turn out (709), he could hardly have expected this blow so soon. It is the first of many he will have to learn to endure in his search for a new home. Will Carthage go some way to healing that wound? Remember that Aeneas is recounting his tale to Dido. S. comments on 746 'the future husband (i.e. Aeneas) puts in a good word for himself by demonstrating in front of the woman (Dido) that he had loved his former wife'. See *Intro* [44].

2.752–70: Aeneas is looking for his wife who became lost in the panic-stricken flight from an approaching Greek contingent just as they were about to leave the city by a gate

horror ubīque animō, simul ipsa silentia terrent.   755
inde domum, sī forte pedem, sī forte tulisset,
mē referō: inruerant Danaī et tēctum omne tenēbant.
īlicet ignis edāx summa ad fastīgia uentō
uoluitur; exsuperant flammae, furit aestus ad aurās.
prōcēdō et Priamī sēdēs arcemque reuīsō: 760
et iam porticibus uacuīs Iūnōnis asȳlō
custōdēs lēctī, Phoenix et dīrus Vlixēs,
praedam adseruābant. hūc undique Trōia gāza
incēnsīs ērepta adytīs, mēnsaeque deōrum
crātērēsque aurō solidī, captīuaque uestis   765

755 *silenti-um ī* 2n. silence
756 *sī forte . . . sī forte*: emotional repetition of the
    '[to see] if only' formula; Aeneas was hoping
    against hope (cf. **770**)
pedem . . . tulisset: i.e. Creusa
757 *inruō* 3 *inruī* I charge in; *inruerant* comes as a
    shock. Venus had earlier prevented this (599, (S.))
758 *īlicet* at once
edāx edāc-is all-consuming, devouring. These two
    lines offer another example of Virgilian
    repetitiveness (**2.132–44**)
759 *exsuperō* 1 I reach the top
760 *prōcēdō* 3 I move, advance; Aeneas does not
    decorate this moment with any emotional
    outpourings about the destruction of his ancestral
    home; he at once moves on to see if Creusa (a
    daughter of Priam) is at her parental home
reuīsō 3 I revisit, return to
761 *portic-us ūs* 4f. colonnade
asȳl-um ī 2n. shrine, sanctuary (in apposition to
    porticibus). An *asȳlum* is a place 'from which no

one can be removed' (S.). Normally such a place
was a refuge for those unjustly treated; here the
captives from the sack are (ironically) forcibly
imprisoned (with almost all of Troy's
treasures)
762 *Phoenix* nom. s. Phoenix, guardian of Achilles
    as a child
763 *adseruō* 1 I guard
Trōi-us a um Trojan (three syllables)
gāz-a ae 1f. treasure (a Persian word, redolent of
    eastern luxury). Not all Trojan treasure was lost,
    since the Trojans were able to take some with
    them (e.g. 1.647–56); they lost some more at sea
    (1.119)
764 *adyt-um ī* 2n. sanctuary
mēnsaeque deōrum: the tables on which offerings
    etc. to the god were placed (a Roman custom),
    described in **765**
765 *crātēr -is* 3m. mixing-bowl
solid-us a um solid
captīu-us a um captured

through the walls. Since it was reasonable to assume that Creusa had tried to follow, the walls and the darkened parts of the gate through which he had fled were therefore the first places to look; and he is guided by the footprints left from his flight (752–4). In his imagination he admits to finding threats everywhere (755, cf. 728–9). Having found nothing on the path, he makes his way back to his house, hoping against hope she had gone there (756–7). If she had, she was certainly done for: it was in flames, Greeks everywhere (757–9). Had she sought refuge in the palace, or Juno's temple (760–1)? That was being used for a purpose for which it was not designed, as a storehouse for the stolen treasure (762–5). One can imagine Aeneas scanning the long line of helpless refugees (766–7). Having searched the obvious places where Creusa might have hidden herself, all he can now do is wander aimlessly about, miserably (769) calling her name, again and again. There is great pathos in the vain repetitions of 770. Throughout, Aeneas movingly depicts his increasing despair, guilt and helplessness. But it is significant that he now accepts the destruction of his public world – Ilium, the royal family, the Trojan people – as fact. It is the prospect of the loss of his wife that creates this agonised outpouring (cf. **2.624–33**).

congeritur. puerī et pauidae longō ōrdine mātrēs
stant circum.
ausus quīn etiam uōcēs iactāre per umbram,
implēuī clāmōre uiās, maestusque Creūsam
nequīquam ingemināns iterumque iterumque uocāuī.'   770

2.771–89: 'Then Creusa appeared as a ghost, telling me it was the gods' will and predicting the Trojan future in Hesperia'

'quaerentī^ et tēctīs urbis sine fīne ^ruentī,
īnfēlīx simulācrum atque ipsius umbra Creūsae
uīsa ^mihi ante oculōs, et nōtā māior imāgō.
obstipuī, steteruntque comae et uōx faucibus haesit.
tum sīc adfārī et cūrās hīs dēmere dictīs: 775
"quid tantum īnsānō iuuat indulgēre dolōrī,

766 *congerō* 3 I heap up
766–7: an all too accurate image of the fate of refugees: terrified women and children – their men all dead or fled – standing helplessly around in long lines
767: an unfinished line (1.534)
768 *quīn etiam* nevertheless
iactō 1 I throw, hurl
769 *impleō* 2 *implēuī* I fill
770 *ingeminō* 1 I redouble, increase in intensity

771 *tēctīs* = *per tēcta*
fīn-is is 3m. end
ruentī: furentī occurs in some manuscripts. Do you have a preference? Is Aeneas a *furēns* warrior at this point? Otis (1964: 250–1) thinks he is; does **776** make a difference?

772 *īnfēlīx:* but in whose eyes? S. rightly suggests Aeneas', since Creusa herself calmly accepts her fate
umbra: cf. *per umbram* 768
773 *nōtā:* abl. of comparison after *māior*. The dead always appear larger than life-size at such moments
774 *steterunt:* note the irregular short second *e*
com-a ae 1f. hair
fauc-ēs ium 3f. pl. throat
775 *adfor* 1 dep. I address; historic inf., as *dēmere*, with Creusa as subject
dēmō 3 I remove
776 *īnsān-us a um* mad, crazy
indulgeō 2 I give way to. Creusa's restraint of Aeneas may remind us of Hecuba's of Priam (518–25)

2.771–89: In such a large city as Ilium, speed is of the essence if Aeneas is to find Creusa. As he rushes from house to house (771), her ghost emerges before him, in a form Aeneas slowly comprehends: a likeness, *simulācrum*, then a shade, *umbra*, and finally (confirmation) a larger-than-life *imāgō* (772–3). Her moving speech is a combination of farewell, *cōnsōlātiō* to assuage Aeneas' guilt (not sharpen or prolong it) and *dīuīnātiō*, to point his way ahead. There is no need for him to grieve, she says (775–6); this was the gods' doing (776–8, cf. Aeneas at 738, 745), Jupiter's will most of all (778–9). So it was destiny; Aeneas is not to blame. Then, in oracular tone – the dead, their spirit freed from the body (S.), regularly see into the future – she outlines what is to happen to him: a long period of travel till he reaches a western land and its river (780–2), where he will found a kingdom and find a new wife (783–4). Dido . . .? Creusa further consoles him by assuring him that she is not in enemy hands, but under the care of the great goddess Cybele (786–8). She ends by telling him not to fail in his love for their son (789). S. comments 'As a concerned mother [would], because she had said he would find another wife.' The

ō dulcis coniūnx? nōn haec sine nūmine dīuum
ēueniunt; nec tē hinc comitem^ asportāre ^Creūsam
fās, aut ille sinit superī rēgnātor Olympī.
longa tibi exsilia, et uastum maris aequor arandum,   780
et terram Hesperiam ueniēs, ubi Lȳdius^ arua
inter opīma uirum lēnī fluit agmine ^Thybris.
illīc rēs laetae rēgnumque et rēgia coniūnx
parta tibī; lacrimās dīlēctae pelle Creūsae.
nōn ego Myrmidonum sēdēs^ Dolopumue ^superbās   785
aspiciam aut Graīs seruītum mātribus ībō,
Dardanis et dīuae Veneris nurus;

777 *ō dulcis coniūnx*: no question, then, about
  Creusa's feelings for Aeneas
sine nūmine dīuum: S. comments 'As Statius says,
  fāta sunt quae diī fantur', i.e. *fatum* is
  etymologically connected with what the gods
  fantur, say (*for fārī*). This may, for a change, be
  the case
778 *ēueniō* 4 I turn out, happen
asportō 1 I carry away
779 *sinō* 3 I allow
super-us a um above, upper
rēgnātor -is 3m. ruler
Olymp-us ī 2m. Olympus
780 *uast-us a um* huge, vast (transferred epithet, see
  on 1.101)
arō 1 I plough, cross; a gerundive, **RL**161, **W**39, **M**111
781 *Hesperi-a ae* Hesperia, western land
Lȳdi-us a um Lydian. The Tiber is so called because
  (S.) it flowed through the territory of the
  Etruscans, who were thought to come from Lydia
  (Asia, i.e. modern western Turkey)
aru-um ī 2n. field
782 *opīm-us a um* rich

uirum = *uirōrum*
lēn-is e gentle
agmen agmin-is 3n. stream
Thybris nom. s. m. river Tiber
784 *pariō* 3 *peperī partum* I win, gain
dīlēctae . . . Creūsae: a magnificent phrase. Creusa
  refers to herself in the third person (cf. **778**) – that is
  all she can be for Aeneas now. But she was *dīlēctae* –
  even at this moment, when resentment could have
  been her main reaction, she knew Aeneas loved her
  (cf. *dulcis* 777). Her name occurs nine times, each
  time at the end of the line, and 'echoes . . . through
  the stricken city, as Aeneas calls it again and again'
  – Jenkyns (1998: 405–6)
pellō 3 I dismiss
786 *seruītum*: 4th p.p. of *seruiō* 'I work as a slave' (+
  dat.), indicating purpose after the vb of motion
  ībō. See **RL**118.2, **M**97.8
787 *Dardanis* nom. s., daughter of Dardanus, royal
  Trojan ('[I, as a] . . .')
nur-us ūs 4f. daughter-in-law; an unfinished line
  (see on 1.534). S. says some suggest *et tua coniūnx*
  as a filler

positive tone of the speech is worth comparing with the unsympathetically negative
tone of Anchises' at 634–49.

   Hard lessons here for Aeneas, scarcely alleviated by the news that this was all the gods'
will – information that does nothing to explain why it was the gods' will, or what
purpose they had in mind. Aeneas simply has to accept it, buckle down and slog on. The
future Creusa sketches for him does not sound immediately tempting either. The goal of
Hesperia, its rich farmland (781–2) and a prosperous new kingdom (783–4) is all very
well, but at the expense of an immense amount of time and effort (780). After his experience of divine help in Troy, Aeneas may well be wondering whether it is a goal he will
ever attain. Certainly Creusa's words do not burn themselves into his brain, because he
will keep on forgetting or ignoring them. As S. comments, 'Why does Aeneas not
remember these words, but settle in Thrace and other places?'

   Jenkyns (1998: 402–9) deals with this passage with exemplary sensitivity and feeling.
Here is part of it (408–9):

sed mē magna deum genetrīx hīs dētinet ōrīs.
iamque ualē et nātī^ seruā ^commūnis amōrem." '

2.790–804: 'I tried in vain to embrace her, rejoined my family and companions and set off for the hills'

'haec ubi dicta dedit, lacrimantem et multa uolentem   790
dīcere dēseruit, tenuīsque recessit in aurās.
ter cōnātus ibī collō dare brācchia circum;
ter frūstrā comprēnsa manūs effūgit imāgō,

788 *genetrīx genetrīc-is* 3f. mother, i.e. Cybele, a goddess associated with Mother Earth and much venerated in the region of Troy, i.e. where the *gēns Iūlia* had its origins. Augustus included her temple in his restoration programme (and had himself depicted as being crowned with a laurel wreath by her). By Virgil's day, the festival named after her, the Megalesia, was one of the most important in the Roman calendar. See E. L. Harrison 'Divine Action in *Aeneid* Book 2' in S. J. Harrison (1990: 55ff.).
dētineō 2 I detain, keep

790 *lacrimō* 1 I weep; ellipsis of *mē* with *lacrimantem . . . uolentem.* Creusa may have removed his *cūrās* (775) but this does nothing to alleviate Aeneas' sense of loss

791 *dēserō* 3 *deseruī* I desert, abandon; Creusa is the subject
tenu-is e thin
792 *ter* three times; this scene is beautifully adapted from Homer's *Odyssey* 11.206–8, where Odysseus in the underworld tries to embrace the ghost of his mother: 'Three times I started towards her, my spirit telling me to hold her, / and three times from my hands, like a shadow, or rather a dream, / she flew. In my heart the sharp pang of grief grew more' (Dawe (1993)); cf. Achilles trying to embrace the ghost of Patroclus, *Iliad* 23.99–101
cōnātus: ellipsis of *sum*
brācchi-um ī 2n. arm
793 *comprehendō* 3 *comprehendī compr(eh)ēnsum* I grasp

Virgil's language hints at the mysterious connection between the soil and the people who dwell upon it: good land, good men. It is a note that has been heard in the *Georgics,* and in Lucretius, and it will be heard again later in the *Aeneid.* Here it counterbalances the strangeness and elegance of *Lydius . . . Thybris* with the sentiment of tradition, solidity, patriotism, and deep roots.

Even the sound of the verse helps to shape Virgil's meaning. Up to the end of line 780 Creusa has a severe message to impart, and the prophecy of Hesperia that follows can have little emotional appeal in itself to a Trojan. And yet the gentle tones in which the Tiber is depicted – especially the limpid sounds of *l* and *y* – begin to give the new land a certain charm; we are indeed lapped in soft Lydian airs. Then comes a climax with the glad tidings of line 783, the firm slow rhythm reinforced by the strong but not excessive alliteration of the letter *r*, before the lapse back to the delicate lyric pathos of *lacrimās dīlēctae pelle Creūsae.* The description of Tiber and Hesperia stands between defeat and success, and its complex ambivalence makes the transition between the two. The episode as a whole fluctuates between hope and sorrow; its elusive mood is epitomised in the lines on Italy, with their blend of exile and enchantment, home and far romance.

See: Lyne (1987: 170), who does not think Creusa's words exculpate Aeneas: 'did she have to be lost *in that way*?'

2.790–804: Aeneas has seen Ilium captured, his home destroyed, and now the ghost of his dead wife, whom he has three times tried in vain to embrace (790–4), slip through his hands for ever. Jenkyns (1998: 404) writes:

pār leuibus uentīs uolucrīque simillima somnō.
sīc dēmum sociōs, cōnsūmptā nocte, reuīsō.   795
atque hīc ingentem^ comitum adflūxisse nouōrum
inueniō admīrāns ^numerum, mātrēsque uirōsque,
collēctam exsiliō pūbem, miserābile uulgus.
undique conuēnēre, animīs opibusque parātī,
in quāscumque uelim pelagō dēdūcere terrās.   800
iamque iugīs summae surgēbat Lūcifer Īdae
dūcēbatque diem, Danaīque obsessa tenēbant
līmina portārum, nec spēs opis ūlla dabātur.
cessī, et sublātō montīs genitōre petīuī.'

794 *leu-is e* light
uolucr-is e fleeting
795 *dēmum* at last, finally
cōnsūmō 3 cōnsūmpsī cōnsūmptum I spend, use up
reuīsō 3 I revisit, return to
796 *adfluō 3 adflūxī adflūxum* I flow in
797 *admīror 1 dep.* I wonder at
798 *exsiliō*: dat., 'for [the purpose of going into] exile', RL88.6, WSuppl. syntax
miserābil-is e pitiable
799 *conueniō 4 conuēnī conuentum* I meet, assemble

800 *uelim*: subjunc. of implied indir. thought in *animīs* (**799**)
pelagō 'by sea'
dēdūcō 3 I lead away (technical term for colonisation)
801 *Lūcifer -ī* 2m. the morning star, the planet Venus, also known as Hesperus
Īd-a ae 1f. Mount Ida, where the shooting star had directed them (696), c. 40 miles south-east of Troy

---

The pathos of Aeneas' situation is that he seems briefly to be so close to her; like the scene with Venus in the first book [1.402–10], this is an encounter which at the last moment fails to be an encounter. There is speech, but no reciprocity: just as Aeneas is about to answer, *multa uolentem dīcere*, Creusa is no longer there, and the joy of touch and solid flesh denied. So near and yet so far; the ambivalence, and even the contradictoriness, of Aeneas' account is of the essence.

Creusa is the one person with whom Aeneas has had an intimate relationship. All we see of that side of it is its demise. It is worth pointing out here that, if the taciturn man of action had few words to say when he asked Creusa to follow behind him (711) – how many words did he need? – his emotional reaction to her loss is overwhelming. Taciturnity does not extend to absence of feeling when personal tragedy strikes.

'*sīc* (795) marks a very abyss of sorrow' (Austin 1964): but the night is over, day is dawning (801) and Aeneas is not for giving up. So back he goes to his companions (795). To his surprise and delight (*admīrāns* 797), he reports finding a huge number of followers gathered waiting for him, 'willing and able' (*animīs opibusque parātī*, 799, S.) to go wherever he leads them (800), apparently signalling, as S. says, 'as though the kingship had passed [from Priam] to Aeneas with everyone's consent', cf. 339–42, where soldiers suddenly appear to join Aeneas' charge into battle. He is a man who attracts followers. (Heinze 62–3/37 finds this 'improbable', but the point is that Aeneas is not an authorised head of state. He is gathering together any he can, to set off into the unknown *as though* he is their leader. See *Appendix* 7.) Further, Aeneas observes *Lūcifer* 'light-bringer', the star that appears with the new dawn (801) – i.e. Venus, who had promised never to desert him (620, S.). New dawn, new start; and since, with the Greeks in complete control (802–3), there is no prospect of doing anything for Troy (803), Aeneas yields to fate and all it might bring, shoulders Anchises ('Aeneas wants to take every opportunity to demonstrate his *pietās* in relation to his father', S.) and heads for the woods of Mount Ida (804), where he will find refuge and the timber to build the fleet that he will need for the journey he must now undertake.

See: *Intro* [39–44] and, by contrast, Lyne (1987: 146–51, 168–71), who suggests that Virgil is employing a 'too late' aspect to Aeneas' character, against Heinze (401–14/314–19) who felt Virgil simply wanted to hurry the action forward, come what may.

Study section for 2.735–804

1. Is it in character for Aeneas to panic when Anchises sees soldiers? (Consider 721–34.) What does this tell you about Aeneas' self-presentation?
2. Can you blame Aeneas for the loss of Creusa?
3. Read Diodorus' account of Aeneas' departure (*Appendix* 18) and discuss why Virgil did not follow this version of the story. In particular, consider the effect of Virgil's version on our understanding of Aeneas.

Topics for extended essays on Book 2

1. 'In his own narration in Books 2 and 3 [Aeneas] often seems to miss the chance to impress us with his own view of things' (Reed (2007: 181)). Discuss.

2. In Book 2, Aeneas' 'whole character is dominated by *furor*' (Otis (1964: 242)). Do you agree? If you do, why does Virgil make Aeneas present himself in this light?

3. What picture of divine activity does Aeneas present in Book 2?

4. If you were Dido, how would you react to Aeneas' self-presentation?

5. To what extent does Aeneas in Book 2 show himself to be the man to re-found a nation?

6. Write an appreciation of any scene in Book 2 that particularly appeals to you.

7. Take any of the sources in the *Appendix* relevant to Book 2 and show how and why Virgil uses them (or not) as he does.

8. What do you make of Aeneas' account of the Trojans?

9. The poet Ovid said *expedit esse deōs et, ut expedit, esse putēmus* ('It is useful that the gods exist and, as it is useful, let us suppose they do', *Ars amatōria* 1.637). Discuss in relation to the story of Rome as Virgil presents it.

10. If you were Virgil, what changes would you have made to Book 2 of the *Aeneid* during your three-year sojourn in Greece (*Intro* [7])?

Some views for general discussion

1. 'Aeneas never has freedom of action. Every act of his is conditioned by the presence of his people, his son, and by the *public*, not private, destiny marked out for him' Anderson (1969: 15).
2. 'The heroic has become magnified to the point that the hero himself has become faceless' Ross (2007: 9).
3. 'Virgil's narrative style is . . . *subjective* or, more accurately, *empathetic-sympathetic*. Virgil not only reads the minds of his characters; he constantly communicates to us his own reactions to them and to their behaviour' Otis (1964: 88).
4. 'Despite the help and inspiration afforded him, [Aeneas] is left to discover largely for himself the role he must play in the vast drama of Roman history just beginning to unfold' Hunt (1973: 80).
5. 'While Virgil glorified Roman power and presented it as a great historical development presided over by Jupiter and Fate, he could not pretend that this often terrible process had any regard for the deserts of individual people' Rudd (2005: 42–3).
6. 'Virgil's politicisation of epic for the ends of empire demanded the curbing of the Homeric heroic will, and the flatness and passivity of Aeneas became the virtuous traits . . . As opposed to the wandering Odysseus and the rebellious Achilles, the hero of empire became an executive type who places duty over individual desire' Quint (1993: 95).
7. 'The gulf between human and divine understanding creates resources of irony which contribute powerfully to the tragic atmosphere of the poem' Feeney (1991: 182).
8. '[Aeneas] has all the old-style heroic fighting spirit and scorn of death but, in addition, he must learn to accept submission to the far-reaching purposes of heaven' Griffin (2001: 79).
9. The 'pain' surrounding the 'strangely impeded' figure of Aeneas implies 'nothing less than the creation by Virgil of a truly moral world' Nuttall 'Virgil and Shakespeare' in Martindale (1984: 79).

Appendix:
Other versions of the sack of Ilium

Summary of *The Sack of Ilium* (Arctinus from Miletus, c. ?650 BC)

1. The Trojans, deeply suspicious of everything to do with the wooden horse, stood round it debating what they ought to do. Some thought they ought to throw it over the cliff, others to set fire to it, while others said they ought to offer it up to Athena. This last opinion finally prevailed, and they turned to joyful feasting, as if the war were over. But at this very moment two serpents appeared and destroyed Laocoon and one of his two sons. Aeneas' followers, deeply concerned at this omen, left for Mount Ida.

2. Sinon, having already got into the city under false pretences, raised the fire-signal to the Greeks. They sailed in from Tenedos, and those in the wooden horse emerged, attacked their enemies, killed many and took the city by force. Neoptolemus killed Priam who had taken refuge at the altar of Zeus god of the hearth; Menelaus killed Deiphobus and marched Helen back to the ships. Aias (Ajax) the son of Ileus (= Oileus) tried to drag Cassandra by force away from the image of Athena, tearing it away in the act. The Greeks, incensed, decide to stone Aias to death, but he escaped the danger by fleeing for protection to Athena's altar . . . Finally the Greeks sailed away, and Athena planned their destruction on the high seas.

From the summary of the *Little Iliad* (Lesches, c. ?650 BC)

3. The Trojans were besieged, and on Athena's instructions Epeius constructed the wooden horse. Odysseus disfigured himself and went in to Ilium as a spy. He was recognised there by Helen and plotted with her for the capture of the city. He killed some of the Trojans and returned to the ships. After that, with Diomedes' help, he removed the Palladium from Troy. Then the Greeks put their best men into the wooden horse, burnt their huts and sailed to Tenedos. The Trojans, assuming their troubles were over, destroyed a part of their walls, welcomed the wooden horse into their city and feasted as though they had defeated the Greeks.

Dionysius of Halicarnassus, *The Roman Antiquities* (c. 7 BC)
Book 1 46–8 (Loeb translation)

(Note: the references in brackets are to the sections of the original text)

4. [46] When Troy had been taken by the Greeks . . . the greatest part of the Trojans and of their allies then in the city were surprised and slain in their beds; for it seems that this calamity came upon them in the night, when they were not upon their guard. But Aeneas and his Trojan forces . . . while the Greeks were taking the lower

town, fled together to the stronghold of Pergamus, and occupied the citadel, which was fortified with its own wall; here were deposited the holy things of the Trojans inherited from their fathers and their great wealth in valuables, as was to be expected in a stronghold, and here also the flower of their army was stationed. Here they awaited and repulsed the enemy and . . . were able . . . to rescue the multitude which was seeking to escape at the taking of the city; and thus a larger number escaped than were taken prisoner . . .

5. But . . . [Aeneas] reasoned very properly that it would be impossible to save a city the greater part of which was already in the possession of the enemy, and he therefore decided to abandon the wall, bare of defenders, to the enemy and to save the inhabitants themselves as well as the holy objects inherited from their fathers and all the valuables he could carry away. Having thus resolved, he first sent out from the city the women and children together with the aged and all others whose condition required much time to make their escape, with orders to take the roads leading to Mount Ida . . . when Neoptolemus and his men gained a foothold on part of the acropolis and all the Greeks rallied to their support, Aeneas abandoned the place; and opening the gates, he marched away with the rest of the fugitives in good order, carrying with him in the best chariots his father and the gods of his country, together with his wife and children and whatever else, either person or thing, was most precious.

6. [47] In the meantime the Greeks had taken the city by storm, and being intent on plunder, gave those who fled abundant opportunity of making their escape. Aeneas and his band overtook their people while still on the road, and being united now in one body, they seized the strongest parts of Mount Ida . . . The Greeks, having reduced to slavery the people who were left in the city and in the places near by and having demolished the forts, were preparing to subdue those also who were in the mountains. When, however, the Trojans sent heralds to treat for peace and begged them not to reduce them to the necessity of making war, the Greeks held an assembly and made peace with them upon the following terms: Aeneas and his people were to depart from the Troad with all the valuables they had saved in their flight within a certain fixed time, after first delivering up the forts to the Greeks; and the Greeks were to allow them a safe-conduct by land and sea throughout all their dominions when they departed in pursuance of these terms. Aeneas accepted these conditions, which he looked upon as the best possible in the circumstances . . .

7. [48] This, then, is the most credible account concerning the flight of Aeneas . . . There are different accounts given of the same events by some others, which I look upon as less probable than this. But let every reader judge as he thinks proper. Sophocles, the tragic poet, in his drama *Laocoon* represents Aeneas, just before the taking of the city, as removing his household to Mount Ida in obedience to the orders of his father Anchises, who recalled the injunctions of Aphrodite and from the omens that had lately happened in the case of Laocoon's family conjectured the approaching destruction of the city. His iambics, which are spoken by a messenger, are as follows:

> Now at the gates arrives the goddess' son,
> Aeneas, carrying on his shoulders his father,
> The linen mantle falling down his back, that back
> Once struck by the thunderbolt of Zeus.
> A crowd of household slaves surrounds them.
> There follows a multitude beyond belief
> Who long to join this Phrygian colony.

8. But Menecrates of Xanthus says that Aeneas betrayed the city to the Greeks out of hatred for Alexander [–Paris] and that because of this service he was permitted by them to save his household. His account, which begins with the funeral of Achilles, runs as follows: 'The Greeks were oppressed with grief and felt that the army had had its head lopped off. However, they celebrated his funeral feast and made war with all their might till Ilium was taken by the aid of Aeneas, who delivered it up to them. For Aeneas, being scorned by Alexander and excluded from his prerogatives, overthrew Priam; and having accomplished this, he became one of the Greeks.'

Apollodorus, *The Library of Greek Mythology* (c. AD 100??), tr. by Robin Hard (World's Classics) *Epitome* 5.13–23

9. [13] Odysseus went up to the city with Diomedes by night. Leaving Diomedes waiting outside, he assumed a mean appearance and put on shabby clothing, and entered the city undetected in the guise of a beggar. He was recognised, however, by Helen, and with her assistance he stole the Palladion, and then, after killing many of the guards, he took it to the ships with the aid of Diomedes.

10. [14] Odysseus later had the idea of constructing a wooden horse, and he suggested it to Epeios, who was an architect. Using timber felled on Mount Ida, Epeios constructed a horse that was hollow within and opened up at the side. Odysseus urged fifty – or according to the author of the *Little Iliad* three thousand – of the bravest men to enter this horse; as for all the rest, they were to burn their tents when night fell and put out to sea, but then lie in wait off Tenedos, ready to sail back again the following night. [15] Persuaded by his plan, the Greeks put their bravest men inside the horse, making Odysseus their commander; and they carved an inscription on it reading, 'For their return home, a thank-offering to Athena from the Greeks.' The others burned their tents, and leaving Sinon in place to light a beacon for them, they put out to sea at night and lay in wait off Tenedos.

11. [16] When day came and the Trojans saw the Greek camp deserted, they thought that the Greeks had fled. Overjoyed, they hauled the horse to the city, stationed it beside the palace of Priam, and debated what they should do.

12. [17] When Cassandra said that there was an armed force inside it and she received support from the seer Laocoon, some proposed that they should burn it, and others that they should throw it down a cliff; but the majority decided that they should spare it because it was an offering sacred to a deity, and they turned to sacrifice and feasting.

13. [18] A sign was then sent to them by Apollo; for two serpents swam across the sea from the islands nearby and devoured the sons of Laocoon.

14. [19] When night fell and all were fast asleep, the Greeks sailed over from Tenedos, and Sinon lit a fire on the grave of Achilles to guide their way. And Helen walked around the horse and called out to the heroes within, imitating the voice of each of their wives; but when Anticlos wanted to answer, Odysseus covered his mouth.

15. [20] When they judged that their enemies were asleep, they opened up the horse and climbed out with their weapons. Echion, son of Portheus, the first to emerge, was killed by the leap, but the others lowered themselves on a rope, made their way to the wall, and opened the gates to let in the Greeks who had sailed back from Tenedos.

16. [21] Advancing into the city fully armed, they entered the houses and killed the Trojans as they slept. Neoptolemos killed Priam, who had taken refuge at the altar of Zeus of the Courtyard . . . Aeneas picked up his father Anchises and fled, and the Greeks allowed him to pass because of his piety [cf. Diodorus, below].

17. [22] . . . The Locrian Aias saw Cassandra clinging to the wooden image of Athena and raped her; and for that reason, they say, the statue looks up towards the sky. After killing the Trojans, they set fire to the city and divided up the spoils.

Diodorus Siculus ('from Sicily'), *Library of History* (c. 30 BC), 7.4

18. [4] When Troy was taken, Aeneas, together with some other Trojans, seized a part of the city and held off the attackers. And when the Greeks let them depart under a truce and agreed with them that each man might take with him as many of his possessions as he could, all the rest took silver or gold or some other costly article, whereas Aeneas lifted upon his shoulders his father, who was now grown quite old, and bore him away. For this deed he won the admiration of the Greeks and was again given permission to choose out what he would of his household possessions. And when he bore off the household gods, all the more was his virtue approved, receiving the plaudits even of his enemies; for the man showed that in the midst of the greatest perils his first concern was piety toward parents and reverence for the gods. And this was the reason, we are told, why he, together with the Trojans who still survived, was allowed to leave the Troad in complete safety and to go to whatever land he wished.

Total learning vocabulary

This list contains all the words that are *shared* between the learning vocabularies of *Reading Latin* and *Wheelock* (see p. 37), plus all the vocabulary set to be learned in *Aeneid* 1 and 2.

A

ā tergō in the rear, from behind
ā/ab (+ abl.) from, away from
abdō 3 *abdidī abditum* I hide, conceal
abeō abīre abiī abitum I go/come away, depart
ablāt-; see *auferō*
absēns absent-is absent, away
abstul-; see *auferō*
absum abesse āfuī I am away from, am absent; I am distant
ac (or *atque*) and
accēdō 3 *accessī accessum* I approach, come near, reach
access-; see *accēdō*
accingō 3 *accīnxī accīnctum* I prepare (myself) for, get down to (+ dat.); gird myself with
accipiō 3 *accēpī acceptum* I receive, accept, take, welcome; learn; obtain, get; sustain; meet with
accūsō 1 I accuse (X acc. of Y gen.)
ācer ācr-is e keen, sharp, eager, spirited, severe
acerb-us a um bitter, harsh, grievous
ācerrim-us a um sup. of *ācer*
Achill-ēs is/ī 3m. Achilles
Achīu-ī ōrum 2m. Greeks; *Achīu-us a um* Greek
aci-ēs ēī 5f. battle-line; sharp edge, point; keenness (of sight)
āct-; see *agō*
ad (+ acc.) towards; at, up to, near; for the purpose of; *usque ad* right up to
addō 3 *addidī additum* I add, receive
adeō adīre adiī aditum I go/come to, approach
adferō adferre attulī allātum I bring to
adiuuō 1 *adiūuī adiūtum* I help, aid
adsum adesse adfuī I am present, am at hand, am near, assist
aduers-us a um hostile; facing, opposite; unfavourable, adverse
adulēscēns adulēscent-is 3m. youth, young man
adyt-um ī 2n. innermost shrine of a temple, sanctuary
aeger aegr-a um sick, ill; sorrowful; weary, anxious
aegrē with difficulty, hardly, scarcely
Aenēās (acc. *Aenēān*, gen. *Aenēae*) Aeneas

aēn-us a um bronze
Aeol-us ī 2m. Aeolus, lord of the winds
aequō 1 I equal, divide up equally
aequor -is 3n. (calm) sea, ocean
aequ-us a um fair, balanced, even, equal, level, favourable, just
āēr āer-is 3m. air
āēs āēr-is 3n. bronze
aest-us ūs 4m. swell, tide; heat
aetās aetāt-is 3f. age; lifetime, life; generation, time
aetern-us a um eternal
aether -is 3m. upper air, heaven
aetheri-us a um ethereal, high in the heavens, of heaven
aeu-um ī 2n. age
ager agr-ī 2m. land, field, farm, territory
agmen agmin-is 3n. battle-line, line
agnōscō 3 *agnōuī agnōtum* I recognise
agō 3 *ēgī āctum* I do, act; drive, lead, direct; spend, pass; (*dē* + abl.) discuss; *gratiās agō* I thank
aiō irr. I say, assent *ait* (s)he says, *aiunt* they say
Albān-us a um Alban, from Alba
aliēn-us a um someone else's, foreign, strange, alien
aliī . . . aliī some . . . others
aliquis aliqua aliquid someone, something (pron.)
aliquis aliqua aliquod some (adj.)
aliter ac otherwise than
ali-us a ud other (two different cases in same clause = 'different . . . different')
ali-us ac different from; other than
alm-us a um kindly, fostering
alō 3 *aluī altum* I feed, nourish, rear; support, sustain, cherish; strengthen
alter alter-a um one (or other) of two
alt-us a um high; deep; (as a noun) deep sea
ambō (nom.) both (*ambōbus* dat. pl.)
ambulō 1 I walk
āmēns āment-is mindless, mad, frantic
amīciti-a ae 1f. friendship
amīc-us ī 2m. friend, ally
āmittō 3 *āmīsī āmissum* I lose, let go
amō 1 I love, like
amor amōr-is 3m. love; pl. girl-friend, sexual intercourse

amplector 3 dep. *amplexus* I wrap up, embrace

an = ne = ? (in direct questions); whether, if, or (in indirect questions; + subjunc. *= num*); (on its own) or, it can be that

Anchīs-ēs -ae 3m. Anchises, Aeneas' father

anim-us ī 2m. mind, spirit, heart, soul; pl. *anim-ī* high spirits, pride, courage

ann-us ī 2m. year

ante (+ acc.) before, in front of; (adv.) earlier, before

anteā (adv.) before, formerly

antīqu-us a um ancient (often with overtones of noble, venerable)

aperiō 4 I open (up), reveal

appāreō 2 *appāruī appāritum* I appear

appellō 1 I address; name, call

appropinquō 1 (+ dat.) I approach, draw near to

aptō 1 I prepare, fit

apud (+ acc.) at the house of, in the hands of, in the works of

aqu-a ae 1f. water

ār-a ae 1f. altar

arbitror 1 dep. I think, consider; give judgement

arbor arbor-is 3f. tree

arceō 2 *arcuī* I keep at a distance, ward off; confine

ārdeō 2 *ārsī ārsum* I burn, am keen/fiery

argent-um ī 2n. silver; silver-plate; money

Arg-ī ōrum 2m. pl. Argos, an important Greek city; Greece

Argīu-ī ōrum 2m. pl. the Greeks

Argīu-us a um Greek

Argolic-us a um Greek (lit. 'from Argos')

arm-a ōrum 2n. pl. arms; armed men

armāt-us a um armed

arrēct-us a um raised, pricked up

ars art-is 3f. skill, art, accomplishment

art-us a um tight

art-us ūs 4m. limb

aru-um ī 2n. field

arx arc-is 3f. citadel, stronghold

Ascani-us ī 2m. Ascanius, son of Aeneas (also known as Iulus)

Asi-a ae 1f. Asia Minor

asper asper-a um rough, harsh

aspiciō 3 *aspexī aspectum* I see, observe, catch sight of

at but; mind you; you say

āter ātr-a um black, dark

atque (or *ac*) and, and also, and even

Atrīd-ae -ārum 2m. pl. sons of Atreus, Agamemnon and Menelaus

attollō 3 I raise, lift up

attul-; see *adferō*

auctōritās auctōritāt-is 3f. weight, authority

audāci-a ae 1f. boldness, cockiness, daring

audāx audāc-is brave, bold, daring, resolute

audeō 2 semi-dep. *ausus* I dare

audiō 4 I hear, listen to

āuellō 3 *āuulsī āuulsum* I tear/wrench off

āuertō 3 *āuertī āuersum* I divert X (acc.) from Y (abl.), turn back/away/round (trans. and intrans.)

auferō auferre abstulī ablātum I take away, carry off (X acc. from Y dat.)

aur-a ae 1f. open air, breeze

aure-us a um golden

aur-is -is 3f. ear

aur-um ī 2n. gold

aus-; see *audeō*

Auster Austr-ī 2m. south wind

aut . . . aut either . . . or

aut or

autem but, however, moreover (2nd word)

auxili-um ī 2n. help, aid

B

bellum gerō 3 I wage war

bell-um ī 2n. war

bell-us a um pretty, beautiful, handsome, charming

bene well, thoroughly, rightly; good! fine! (comp. *melius*; sup. *optime*)

bibō 3 *bibī* - I drink

bis twice

bon-us a um good, brave, fit, honest (comp. *melior*; sup. *optimus*)

breu-is e short, brief, small; shallow

C

cadō 3 *cecidī cāsum* I fall; die

caec-us a um blind, hidden, dark

caed-ēs is 3f. slaughter

caedō 3 *cecīdī caesum* I kill

caelest-is e in the heavens

cael-um ī 2n. sky, heaven

calamitās calamitāt-is 3f. disaster, calamity, misfortune

Calchās (abl. *Calchante*) Calchas, the Greek army's chief priest

candid-us a um white; bright, shining, beautiful

capiō 3 *cēpī captum* I take, capture, seize, get

caput capit-is 3n. head; source, fount

cardō cardin-is 3f. door-socket; turning-point

carīn-a ae 1f. ship

cār-us a um dear, beloved; loving

Cassandr-a ae 1f. Cassandra, a prophetess fated always to tell the truth but never to be believed

castr-a ōrum 2n. camp

cās-us ūs 4m. outcome; event, occurrence; accident, chance; disaster, death

cateru-a ae 1f. crowd, throng

caueō 2 *cāuī cautum* I am wary, beware, avoid

caus-a ae 1f. case, situation; reason; cause; *causā* (+ gen. – which precedes it) for the sake of

cau-us a um hollow

cecid-; see *cadō*

cēdō 3 *cessī cessum* I yield; go

celer celer-is celer-e swift, quick, rapid

celeritās celeritāt-is 3f. speed, swiftness

celeriter quickly

cēn-a ae 1f. dinner

centum hundred

cēp-; see *capiō*

Cer-ēs -is 3f. grain, corn (Ceres was god of grain)

cernō 3 *crēuī crētum* I see

certē without doubt, certainly

certō 1 I contend, fight

cert-us a um sure, certain, definite, reliable

ceruīx ceruīc-is 3f. neck

cēter-ī ae a the rest, the others

cēū like, as if

cingō 3 *cīnxī cīnctum* I surround, encircle, block in

circum + acc. around; (adv.) round about

circumdō 1 *circumdedī circumdatum* I surround, enclose

cīuis cīu-is 3m. and f. citizen

cīuitās cīuitāt-is 3f. state, citizenship

clāmor -is 3m. cry, shout

clār-us a um famous, well-known, renowned, illustrious; clear, bright

class-is is 3m. fleet

claudō 3 *clausī clausum* I close, shut in

claustr-a ōrum 2n. cage, prison; bolts, bars

clipe-us ī 2m. shield

coepī (perf. form; past part. act./pass. *coeptus*) I began

cognit-; see *cognōscō*

cognōscō 3 *cognōuī cognitus* I get to know, examine, become acquainted with, learn, recognise (perf. tense = I know, plupf. = I knew, fut. perf. = I shall know)

cōgō 3 *coēgī coāctus* I force, compel; gather

colligō 3 *collēgī collēctus* I collect, gather; gain, acquire

coll-um ī 2n. neck

colō 3 *coluī cultus* I worship; cherish; cultivate, till; inhabit

com-a ae 1f. hair

comes comit-is 3m. companion

comitor 1 dep. I accompany (+ abl.)

committō 3 *commīsī commissus* I commit, entrust

commūn-is e shared in, common, general, universal

comparō 1 I prepare, provide, get ready, get

compellō 3 *compulī compulsum* I force, drive

complector 3 dep. *complexus* I embrace

compōnō 3 *composuī compos(i)tum* I settle, arrange, adjust; put to rest

condō 3 *condere condidī conditum* I found, build; bury, hide

cōnfiteor 2 dep. *cōnfessus* I confess, acknowledge

cōniciō 3 *cōniēcī cōniectum* I throw, hurl; put together, conjecture

coniūnx coniug-is 3f., m. wife, husband

cōnor 1 dep. I try, attempt

cōnsci-us a um conscious, with deliberate intent; knowingly; inwardly aware of (+ gen.)

cōnseruō 1 I keep safe, preserve, maintain

cōnsili-um ī 2n. plan, purpose; advice; judgement

cōnsistō 3 *cōnstitī* - I stop, rest, stand my ground; depend on

cōnspect-us ūs 4m. sight

cōnspiciō 3 *cōnspexī cōnspectum* I catch sight of, see

cōnstit-; see *cōnsistō*

cōnsul cōnsul-is 3m. consul

contingit (impersonal) 3 *contigī* it comes to pass for X (dat.) (with the idea of a happy chance)

contingō 3 *contigī contāctum* I touch, reach, influence; happen

contrā (+ acc.) against, in reply; (adv.) in reply/ return

conuellō 3 *conuulsī conuulsum* I pull, wrench, shatter

conueniō 4 *conuēnī conuentum* I meet, assemble, agree

conuertō 3 *conuertī conuersum* I change, convert, turn round

conuertor 3 *conuersus* I turn round, am converted, changed

conuocō 1 I summon, call together

cōpi-ae ārum 1f. pl. troops

cor cord-is 3n. heart

cōram face to face

corn-ū ūs 4n. wing (of army); horn

Coroebus nom. s. a Trojan

corpus corpor-is 3n. body

corripiō 3 *corripuī correptum* I snatch up, seize; speed along

corusc-us a um tremulous, shimmering

cotīdiē daily

crēber crēbr-a um frequent, numerous; thick, close

crēdō 3 *crēdidī crēditum* I believe in (+ dat.); entrust (X acc. to Y dat.)

crīn-is is 3m. hair

crūdēl-is e cruel

cruent-us a um bloodthirsty, bloody

cūī dat. s. of *quī/quis*

cūī scans as one long syllable

cūīdam dat. s. of *quīdam*

cūīquam dat. of *quisquam*

cūīus gen. s. of *quī/quis*

cūīusdam gen. s. of *quīdam*

culp-a ae 1f. fault; blame

cum (+ abl.) with; (+ subjunc.) when; since; although

cūnctor 1 dep. I delay; hesitate (+ inf.)

cūnct-us a um all

cupiditās cupiditāt-is 3f. lust, greed, avarice, passion, desire, longing

cupiō 3 *cupīuī cupītus* I desire, wish, long for, yearn for; want desperately

cūr why?

cūr-a ae 1f. care; attention; worry, concern, anxiety, caution

cūrō 1 I look after, care for, attend to; heal; see to it that

currō 3 *cucurrī cursum* I run

curr-us ūs 4m. chariot

curs-us ūs 4m. running; course; direction; voyage

curu-us a um curved, crooked

custōs custōd-is 3m. and f. guard, guardian

D

Dana-ī ōrum 2m. pl. Greeks

Danaum = Dana(ōr)um

Dardanid-ae um m. pl. Trojans (lit. 'sons of Dardanus', an early founder of Troy)

Dardani-us a um Dardanian/Trojan (Dardanus was a founding father of the Trojans; see on 2.582)

dat-; see *dō*

dē (+ abl.) about, concerning; from, down from

dēbeō 2 I ought, must (+ inf.); owe

decim-us a um tenth

dēcipiō 3 *dēcēpī dēceptus* I deceive

decus decor-is 3n. ornament, decoration; honour, distinction

ded-; see *dō*

dēfendō 3 *dēfendī dēfēnsus* I defend, ward off, protect

dēfess-us a um exhausted

deinde then, next

dēleō 2 *dēlēuī dēlētus* I destroy, wipe out, erase

dēlūbr-um ī 2n. shrine, temple

dēmittō 3 *dēmīsī dēmissum* I hand/pass/send down; cast down

dēnique finally; in a word

dēns-us a um in a pack; thick, frequent

dēserō 3 *dēseruī dēsertum* I desert, abandon

dēsert-a ōrum 2n. wilderness

dēsert-us a um deserted, lonely, abandoned

dēsuper from above

de-us ī 2m. god (nom. pl. *deī* or *dī*) god

dexter dextr-a um right; favourable

dextr-a ae 1f. right hand

dī nom. pl. of *deus*

dīc imper. s. of *dīcō*

dīcō 3 *dīxī dictus* I speak, say, tell, name

dict-um ī 2n. word, order

Dīdō Dīdōn-is 3f. Dido, queen of Carthage

diēs diē-ī 5m. and f. day

difficil-is e difficult, hard, troublesome

diffīdō 3 *diffīsus* I mistrust, distrust

dignitās dignitāt-is 3f. distinction, position; honour; rank, high office

dign-us a um worthy; worthy of (+ abl.)

dīligēns dīligent-is careful, diligent

dīligenti-a ae 1f. care, diligence

dīligō 3 *dīlēxī dīlēctus* I love, esteem

dīmittō 3 *dīmīsī dīmissus* I send away/off

dīr-us a um fearful, horrible

discēdō 3 *discessī discessum* I depart, go away

disiciō 3 *disiēcī disiectum* I scatter, shatter, disperse

diū for a long time; comp. *diūtius*; sup. *diūtissimē*

dīuers-us a um scattered

dīu-ī ōrum 2m. gods (also s., e.g. *dīu-a ae* goddess)

dīuiti-ae ārum 1f. pl. riches, wealth

dō 1 *dedī datus* I give

doceō 2 *docuī doctum* I teach, inform

doct-us a um skilled (in X; abl.); learned, taught, skilled

doleō 2 I suffer pain, grieve

Dolop-ēs um 3m. pl. Dolopes, soldiers of Achilles' brutal son Pyrrhus

dolor dolōr-is 3m. pain, anguish, grief

dol-us ī 2m. trick, treachery

domī at home

dominor 1 dep. I rule over (+ dat.)

domin-us ī 2m. master, lord

domō from home

domum to home, homewards

dom-us ūs 4f. (irr.) house, home

dōnec until

dōn-um ī 2n. gift, offering; present

dormiō 4 I sleep

dubitō 1 I doubt; hesitate (+ inf.)

dubi-us a um uncertain, doubtful, ambiguous

dūc imperative s. of *dūcō*

dūcō 3 *dūxī ductus* I lead; think, consider; prolong

ductor -is 3m. leader

dulc-is e sweet, pleasant, agreeable

dum (+ ind.) while; (+ ind./subjunc.) until; (+ subjunc.) provided that (also *dummodo, modo*)

duo duae duo two

dux duc-is 3m. leader, guide, general

dūx-; see *dūcō*

Dymās nom. s. a Trojan

E

ē (+ abl.) out of, from (also *ex*)

eā abl. s. f. of *is*

ea nom. s. f. or nom./acc. pl. n. of *is*

eādem abl. s. f. of *īdem*

eadem nom. s. f. or nom./acc. pl. n. of *īdem*

eae nom. pl. f. of *is*

eam acc. s. f. of *is*

eandem acc. s. f. of *īdem*

eārum gen. pl. f. of *īdem*

eās acc. pl. f. of *is*

eāsdem acc. pl. f. of *īdem*

ēdūcō 3 *ēdūxī ēductus* I lead out, extend up

efferō efferre extulī ēlātum I raise/lift up, bring out; carry off

efficiō 3 *effēcī effectus* I bring about (*ut* + subjunc.); cause, make; complete

effugiō 3 *effūgī* I escape, fleeing from, away

effundō 3 *effūdī effūsum* I pour out

ēg-; see *agō*

egeō 2 I lack, need, am in want of (+ abl. or gen.)

ego I

ēgredior 3 dep. *ēgressus* I go/come out, depart

ēgress-; see *ēgredior*

eī dat. s. or nom. pl. m. of *is*

eīs dat./abl. pl. of *is*

eius gen. s. of *is*

ēlābor 3 dep. *ēlāpsus* I escape, slip away from

enim for, in fact, truly (2nd word)

ēns-is 3m. sword

eō īre iī itum I go/come

eōdem abl. s. m. or n. of *īdem*

eōrum gen. pl. of *is*

eōs acc. pl. m. of *is*

eōsdem acc. pl. m. of *īdem*

epul-ae ārum 1f. pl. feast

Ēpytus nom. s. a Trojan

eques equit-is 3m. horseman; pl. cavalry; 'knight' (member of the Roman business class)

equidem [I] for my part

equitāt-us ūs 4m. cavalry

equus ī 2m. horse

ergō therefore

ēripiō 3 *ēripuī ēreptus* I snatch away, rescue

errō 1 I am wrong; wander

ēruō 3 *ēruī* I overthrow

et and; also, too; even; *et . . . et* both . . . and

etiam still, even, as well; yes indeed

etsī although, even though, even if

ēuādō 3 *ēuāsī ēuāsum* I climb up, evade, escape from (safely)

ēuertō 3 *ēuertī ēuersum* I churn up; overthrow

Eur-us ī 2m. east wind

ex (or *ē*) (+ abl.) out of, from

excēdō 3 *excessī excessum* I depart (from + abl.)

excidō 3 *excidī* I fall from (+ abl.) I escape, slip out

excīdō 3 *excīsī excīsum* I cut, hack out

excipiō 3 *excēpī exceptus* I sustain, receive; welcome; catch; make an exception of

excutiō 3 *excussī excussum* I throw/shake off, shake out; evade

exercit-us ūs 4m. army

exiti-um ī 2n. death, destruction

expleō 2 *explēuī explētum* I complete, fulfil, satisfy

exsili-um ī 2n. exile

exspectō 1 I await, wait for

extrēm-us a um furthest, outermost, last, extreme

exuui-ae ārum 1f. pl. spoils (of war)

F

fābul-a ae 1f. story; play

fac imperative s. of *faciō*

faci-ēs ēī 5f. look, appearance

facil-is e easy, agreeable, affable; prosperous (sup. *facillimus*)

faciō 3 *fēcī factus* I make, do, accomplish

fact-; see *fīō*

fact-um ī 2n. deed, act, achievement

fals-us a um deceitful, treacherous; deceived, deluded

fām-a ae 1f. rumour, report, hearsay; reputation (good or bad)

famili-a ae 1f. household

fās n. duty, divine law

fastīgi-a ōrum 2n. pl. outlines; heights, tips

fāt-um ī 2n. fate, destiny

fēc-; see *faciō*

fēmin-a ae 1f. woman

fer imper. s. of *ferō*

ferē almost, nearly, generally

feriō 4 I strike, hit

ferō ferre tulī lātus I bear, suffer, endure; bring, carry; lead

feror (pass. of *ferō*); I am said (to + inf.); I rush

ferr-um ī 2n. sword; iron

fess-us a um tired

festīnō 1 I hurry

fēt-us a um teeming, fertile, pregnant

fidēs fid-ēī 5f. loyalty, honour; trust, faith; promise; protection

fīdō 3 semi-dep. *fīsus* I put my trust in (+ gen.)

fidūci-a ae 1f. trust, confidence, faith (in + gen.)

fīd-us a um faithful, trustworthy

fīgō 3 *fīxī fixum* I fix, skewer

fīli-a ae 1f. daughter

fīli-us ī 2m. son

fīn-is is 3m. end; (pl.) boundary, limit

fīō fierī factus I become; am done, am made (passive of *faciō*)

flamm-a ae 1f. flame

flūct-us ūs 4m. wave

flūmen flūmin-is 3n. river

fluō 3 *flūxī flūxum* I flow, ebb (away)

foedō 1 I despoil, disfigure, disgrace

for 1 dep. *fātus* speak, talk, say

fore = futūrum esse to be about to be; *fore ut* (+ subjunc.) that it will/would turn out that

for-ēs um 3f. pl. doorway
fōrm-a ae 1f. beauty, shape, form
fōrmāt-us a um p.p. of *fōrmō* 1 I shape, form, mould
fortasse perhaps
forte perhaps, by chance
fort-is e brave, courageous, strong
fortūn-a ae 1f. fortune, luck; pl. wealth
fortunāt-us a um fortunate, lucky, happy
for-um ī 2n. forum (main business centre)
foueō 2 *fōuī fōtum* I nurture, nourish, grow
frangō 3 *frēgī frāctum* I break, smash
frāter frātr-is 3m. brother
fremō 3 *fremuī fremitum* I roar, howl, rage
fret-um ī 2n. seas, straits
frūstrā in vain
fu-; see *sum*
fug-a ae 1f. flight
fugiō 3 *fūgī fugitūrus* I escape, run off, flee, avoid, shun
fugō 1 I put to flight, rout
fulgeō 2 *fulsī* I shine, flash
fundō 3 *fūdī fūsum* I pour out, shed, scatter; rout
fūnus fūner-is 3n. death
furō 3 *furuī* I rage
furor furōr-is 3m. rage, fury; passion; madness
fūs-us a um sprawled, spread

G

gaudi-um ī 2n. joy, delight
gemin-us a um twin
gemit-us ūs 4m. groan
genitor -is 3m. father
gēns gent-is 3f. tribe, clan; race; family; people, nation
genus gener-is 3n. family; stock; tribe; type, kind
germān-a ae 1f. sister
germān-us ī 2m. brother
gerō 3 *gessī gestus* I do, conduct, carry on, manage; accomplish, perform; show, display, wear, carry
gladi-us ī 2m. sword
glomerō 1 I throng round; gather
glōri-a ae 1f. glory, renown, fame
gradior 3 dep. *gressus* I walk, step
Graec-us a um Greek
Grā-ī ōrum 2m. the Greeks
Grai-us ī 2m. Greek
grāti-a ae 1f. thanks, favour, recompense
grātiās agō (+ dat.) I thank
grāt-us a um pleasing (to X, dat.)
grau-is e serious, important, weighty; heavy; severe
grauitās grauitāt-is 3f. seriousness; solemnity; importance, authority
gress-us ūs 4m. steps, feet

H

habeō 2 I have; hold, regard
haereō 2 *haesī haesum* I am entangled with, cling/stick to; linger, am unable to move
harēn-a ae 1f. sand
hast-a ae 1f. spear
haud not, not at all (strong negative)
Hector m. Hector, greatest Trojan fighter, killed by Achilles
Hesperi-a ae 1f. Hesperia, western land
hēū alas
hic haec hoc this; this person, thing; pl. these; he/she/it, they; *hic, hoc* often scan long, as if *hicc, hocc*
hīc here
hiems hiem-is 3f. storm, winter
hinc from here
hodiē today
homo homin-is 3m. human being; man; fellow
honor (honōs) honōr-is 3m. respect, esteem; public office; honour, offering
hōr-a ae 1f. hour
horrēns horrent-is quivering, awe-inspiring; bristling
horreō 2 I shudder
horror -is 3m. terror, alarm
hortor 1 dep. I urge, encourage
hospes hospit-is 3m. host; friend; guest; connection
hospiti-um ī 2n. welcome, hospitality, entertainment
hostis host-is 3m. enemy (of the state)
hūc to here
Hypanis nom. s. a Trojan

I

ī imper. s. of *eō*
i-; see *eō*
iaceō 2 I lie, lie prostrate/dead
iact-ō 1 I throw/toss about; throw/hurl out
iam now, by now, already; at present
iānu-a ae 1f. door
ibi there
īdem eadem idem the same
igitur therefore
ignār-us a um ignorant (of + gen.)
ignis ign-is 3m. fire
ignōscō 3 *ignōuī ignōtum* I forgive, pardon, overlook (+ dat.)
ignōt-us a um unknown, incalculable
Īliac-us a um of Ilium
Īlionēī gen. s. of *Īlioneus*, a ship's captain
Īli-um ī 2n. Ilium; the town besieged by the Greeks; *Troia* is the *region*
ille ill-a illud that; that person, thing; pl. those; former; the famous; he/she/it, they
imāgō imāgin-is 3f. image, likeness, appearance, ghost
imitor 1 dep. I imitate

immān-is e huge, vast; savage, brutal
immēns-us a um huge
impedīment-um ī 2n. hindrance
impediō 4 I prevent, impede, hinder
impell-ō 3 *impulī impulsum* I drive, force
imperātor imperātōr-is 3m. leader, general,
    commander
imperi-um ī 2n. order, command; power (to
    command), authority; control; dominion
imperō 1 I give orders (to), command (+ dat.; often
    followed by *ut/nē* + subjunc. 'to/not to')
impi-us a um unholy, godless
implicō 1 *implicuī* I enfold, twine round
impōnō 3 *imposuī impositum* I lay, place (on)
imprīmīs; see *in prīmīs*
imprōuīs-us a um unexpected
īm-us a um deepest, bottom-most
in (+ acc.) into, onto; (+ abl.) in, on; (+ acc.) against
in prīmīs especially
incēdō 3 *incessī incessum* I enter, arrive
incendi-um ī 2n. fire
incendō 3 *incendī incēnsum* I set fire to
incert-us a um uncertain, doubtful
incipiō 3 *incēpī inceptum* I begin
inclūdō 3 *inclūsī inclūsum* I enclose, shut in
incumbō 3 *incubuī incubitum* I lean on/over, fall on
inde from there, then
īnfand-us a um unspeakable, past words, accursed
    (gerundive based on *for*); horrible, monstrous
īnfēlīx īnfēlīc-is accursed
ingeni-um ī 2n. talent, ability
ingēns ingent-is huge, large, lavish
inimīc-us a um hostile, personal enemy
inquam I say (*inquis, inquit; inquiunt*)
īnsequor 3 dep. *īnsecūtus* I follow closely on, pursue
īnsidi-ae ārum 1f. ambush
īnsign-is e famous, distinguished (for/in + abl.)
īnstituō 3 *īnstituī īnstitūtus* I begin, establish;
    construct; resolve
īnstō 1 *īnstitī* I press on [with], urge on (+ dat.)
īnstruō 3 *īnstrūxī īnstrūctum* I prepare, ready, draw
    up
integer integr-a um whole, untouched
intellegō 3 *intellēxī intellēctus* I perceive, understand,
    comprehend, grasp
inter (+ acc.) among; between
intereā meanwhile
interficiō 3 *interfēcī interfectus* I kill
intrō 1 I enter
intus inside
inueniō 4 *inuēnī inuentum* I find
inuideō 2 *inuīdī inuīsum* I envy, begrudge (+ dat.)
inuīs-us a um hated, loathed, despised
inuīt-us a um unwilling
ioc-us ī 2m. joke, joking, fun

Iou-; see *Iuppiter*
ipse ips-a ips-um very, actual, self
īr-a ae 1f. anger, wrath
īrāscor 3 dep. *īrātus* I grow angry (with X; dat.)
īrāt-us a um angry
is e-a id that; he/she/it
iste ist-a istud that of yours
it-; see *eō*
ita so, thus; yes
Ītali-a ae 1f. Italy
itaque and so, therefore
iter itiner-is 3n. journey, route
iterum again
Ithac-us a um Ithacan (i.e. Ulysses)
iubeō 2 *iussī iussus* I order, command, tell
iūcund-us a um pleasant, agreeable, gratifying
iūdex iūdic-is 3m. judge, juror
iūdicō 1 I judge
iug-um ī 2n. ridge, yoke
Iūl-us ī 2m. Iulus
iungō 3 *iūnxī iūnctum* I join, yoke, unite
Iūnō Iūnōn-is 3f. Juno, wife of king of the gods
    Jupiter
Iuppiter Iou-is 3m. Jupiter, Jove
iūs iūrand-um iūr-is iūrand-ī 3n. oath
iūs iūr-is 3n. law, ordinance, justice, right
iuss-; see *iubeō*
iussū by the order (of X; gen.)
iuss-um ī 2n. order
iuuat it pleases
iuuen-is iuuen-is 3m. young man
iuuentūs iuuentūt-is 3f. youth, young men
iuxtā nearby

L

lābor 3 dep. *lāpsus* I slip, glide by, pass by, fall down;
    make a mistake
labor labōr-is 3m. toil, hard work; trouble; job,
    business
lacrim-a ae 1f. tear
lacrimō 1 I weep
laed-ō 3 *laesī laesum* I damage, injure, offend, wrong
laetiti-a ae 1f. joy, happiness
laet-us a um happy, abundant
laeu-a ae 1f. left hand
Lāocoōn nom. s. Laocoon, a Trojan priest
lātē far and wide, broadly (*lāt-us a um* broad, wide)
lateō 2 I lie hidden; escape the notice of
Latīn-us a um Latin, from Latium
Lati-um ī 2n. Latium
lāt-us a um broad
latus later-is 3n. side
lect-us ī 2m. couch, bed
lēgāt-us ī 2m. commander, ambassador, deputy
legiō legiōn-is 3f. legion

legō 3 *lēgī lēctum* I read; select, choose; traverse
lēt-um ī 2n. death
leu-is e light
leuō 1 I lever up, lift, lighten
lēx lēg-is 3f. law, statute
līber līber-a um free
līber-ī ōrum 2m. pl. children
līberō 1 I free, release
lībertās lībertāt-is 3f. freedom, liberty
lībō 1 I graze, touch lightly; pour (a libation)
Liby-a ae 1f. Libya (= north Africa)
Libyc-us a um Libyan
licet 2 it is permitted (to X dat. to Y inf.)
līmen līmin-is 3n. threshold
lingu-a ae 1f. tongue; language
litter-ae ārum 1f. pl. letter(s); literature
lītus lītor-is 3n. coast, coast-line
locō 1 I place
loc-us ī 2m. place; passage in literature; pl. *loc-a ōrum* 2n.
locūt-; see *loquor*
longē far (off)
long-us a um long
loquor 3 dep. *locūtus* I am speaking, say
lōr-um ī 2n. whip, rein
lūct-us ūs 4m. grief
lūdō 3 *lūsī lūsum* I play (with); deceive
lūmen lūmin-is 3n. light; eye
lūn-a ae 1f. moon
lūstrō 1 I survey, study; move through, traverse
lūstr-um ī 2n. sacred season
lūx lūc-is 3f. light

M

māchin-a ae 1f. machine, contraption
maest-us a um tearful
magis more, rather
magnopere greatly (comp. *magis*; sup. *maxime*)
magn-us a um great, large, important (comp. *maior*; sup. *maximus*)
māior māiōr-is greater, bigger
mālō mālle māluī I prefer (X *quam* Y)
mal-um ī 2n. trouble, evil
mal-us a um bad, evil, wicked (comp. *peior*; sup. *pessimus*)
maneō 2 *mānsī mānsum* I remain, wait, continue, stay
man-us ūs 4f. hand; band
mare mar-is 3n. sea (abl. *marī*)
Mārs Mārt-is 3m. Mars, god of war
Maximus; see *magnus*
mē acc. or abl. of *ego*
meditor 1 dep. I think, ponder on; practise
medi-us a um middle (of)
melior meliōr-is better (see *bonus*)

meminī (perf. form) I remember
memor memor-is remembering (X; gen.); unforgetting; mindful of (X; gen.)
memori-a ae 1f. remembering, memory, recollection; record
memor-ō 1 I say, tell, mention, narrate, address
mēns ment-is 3f. mind, thought, intention
mēns-a ae 1f. table, meal
metuō 3 *metuī metūtum* I fear, am afraid of
met-us ūs 4m. fear, terror
me-us a um my, mine (voc. s. m. *mī*)
mī = mihi (dat. s. of *ego*)
mī voc. s. m. of *meus*
micō 1 I flash, sparkle
mihi dat. s. of *ego*
mīles mīlit-is 3m. soldier
mīlitār-is e military
mīlle thousand (pl. *mīlia*)
Mineru-a ae Minerva (Greek Athena)
minim-us a um smallest, fewest, least (see *paruus*)
minor 1 dep. I loom up; threaten
minor minōr-is smaller, fewer, less (see *paruus*); descendant
mīrābil-is e wonderful
mīror 1 dep. I wonder, am amazed at
mīr-us a um amazing, wonderful
mīs-; see *mittō*
misceō 2 *miscuī mistum/mixtum* I mix, scatter, disturb, confuse
miser miser-a um miserable, unhappy, wretched
misereor 2 dep. I take pity on (+ gen.); here 2s. imperative
miss-; see *mittō*
mittō 3 *mīsī missus* I send; throw; dismiss
modo now, just now; only
mod-us ī 2m. way, fashion, manner; measure, bound, limit
moeni-a um 3n. pl. defensive walls; fortified town
mōl-ēs is 3f. undertaking, burden; huge structure; mass, lump
mōlior 4 dep. I construct, build; strive, labour at
moneō 2 I advise, warn
monit-a ōrum 2n. pl. advice, warning, precepts
mōns mont-is 3m. mountain
mōnstrō 1 I show, point (out)
mor-a ae 1f. delay
morior 3 dep. *mortuus* I die, am dying
moror 1 dep. I delay
mortāl-is e mortal, human
mōs mōr-is 3m. way, habit, custom; pl. character
mōt-; see *moueō*
moueō 2 *mōuī mōtus* I remove (from; abl.); move; cause, begin
mox soon
mulceō 2 I calm

mulier mulier-is 3f. woman, wife

multum (adv.) much

mult-us a um much, many

mūnus mūner-is 3n. gift; duty, function, office

murmur -is 3m. murmuring, humming

mūrus ī 2m. wall

mūtō 1 I change, alter, exchange

Mycēn-ae ārum 1f. pl. Mycenae, palace of Agamemnon, brother of Menelaus

Myrmidon-ēs um 3m. pl. Myrmidons, Achilles' soldiers

N

nam for

nārrō 1 I tell, relate

nāscor 3 dep. *nātus* I am being born

nātūr-a ae 1f. nature

nāt-us a um born of (+ abl.); *nātus* = son, *nāta* = daughter

nāuigō 1 I sail

nāuis nāu-is 3f. ship

naut-a ae 1m. sailor

nē (+ subj.) 'not to', 'that x should not . . .'; 'lest', 'in order that not', 'in order not to . . .'; 'that', 'lest'; (+ perf. subjunc.) 'don't'

-ne (added to the first word of a sentence) = ?

nē . . . quidem not even (emphasising the enclosed word)

nē quis 'that no one'; 'in order that no one . . .'

nebul-a ae 1f. cloud

nec and . . . not; neither; nor

necesse est it is necessary, inevitable (for X dat. to Y inf.)

necō 1 I kill

nefās 3n. crime against divine law

neglegō 3 *neglēxī neglēctus* I ignore, overlook, neglect

negō 1 I deny, say that X is not the case (acc. + inf.)

nēmo nēmin-is 3m. no one, nobody

nemus nemor-is 3n. grove

nepōs nepōt-is 3m. descendant

neque and . . . not; neither; nor (also *nec*)

nequīquam in vain, pointlessly

nesciō 4 I do not know

neu = *nēue*

nēue (+ subjunc.) 'and not to', 'and that X should not . . .'

nī = *nisi*

niger nigr-a um black

nihil (indecl. n.) nothing

nimb-us ī 2m. cloud

nimis too much (of X; gen.)

nisi unless, if . . . not; except

noceō 2 I harm, injure (+ dat.)

nōd-us ī 2m. knot

nōlī (+ inf.) do not

nōlō nōlle nōluī I refuse, am unwilling (+ inf.)

nōmen nōmin-is 3n. name

nōn not

nōndum not yet

nōnne surely?

nōnnūll-us -a um some, several

nōn-us a um ninth

nōs we

nōscō 3 *nōuī nōtus* I get to know (perf. tenses = I know)

nōt-us a um well-known, famous

Not-us ī 2m. south wind

nōu-; see *nōscō*

nou-us a um new

nox noct-is 3f. night

nūb-ēs is 3f. cloud

nūll-us a um no, none, not any (gen. s. *nūllīus*; dat. s. *nūllī*)

num surely . . . not?; (+ subjunc.) whether (indir. q.)

nūmen nūmin-is 3n. divine power, godhead, majesty

numer-us ī 2m. number

numquam never

nunc now

nūntiō 1 I announce, proclaim

nūnti-us ī 2m. messenger

nymph-a ae 1f. young woman, nymph

O

ob + acc. on account/because of

obdūrō 1 I am firm, hold out, persist

obruō 3 *obruī obrutum* I overwhelm, bury, sink

obscūr-us a um thick, obscuring, dark

obsideō 2 *obsēdī obsessum* I besiege

obstipēscō 3 *obstipuī* I am astounded, dumbfounded

occāsiō occāsiōn-is 3f. opportunity

occidō 3 *occidī occāsum* I fall, die, set (of the sun)

occīdō 3 *occīdī occīsum* I kill, cut down, slay

occupō 1 I seize

ocul-us ī 2m. eye

odi-um ī 2n. hatred

offerō offerre obtulī oblātum I offer, hand over; bring before, exhibit

offici-um ī 2n. duty, service, job

ōlim one day; at some time; long ago

ōmen ōmin-is 3n. auspices (taken in the course of any serious business)

omittō 3 *omīsī omissum* I give up; let fall; omit, leave aside

omnīnō altogether, completely, wholly, altogether

omn-is e all, every; *omnia* everything

onerō 1 I load, stow

onus oner-is 3n. load, burden

oper-a ae 1f. attention; service, work, help

opēs, op-um 3f. pl. power, resources, wealth

oportet 2 it is right/fitting for X (acc.) to Y (inf.), X (acc.) ought to Y (inf.)

oppōnō 3 *opposuī oppositum* I expose (X acc.) to; object; oppose; interpose

opportūn-us a um strategic, suitable, favourable, advantageous

oppress-; see *opprimō*

opprimō 3 *oppressī oppressus* I surprise; catch; crush, overpower

oppugnō 1 I attack, assault

optim-us a um best (see *bonus*)

optō 1 I wish, desire, want

opus oper-is 3n. job, work, task, deed; fortification

ōr-a ae 1f. shore

ōrātiō ōrātiōn-is 3f. speech

orb-is 3m. globe, orb, world; coil

ōrdō ōrdin-is 3m. rank, class (i.e. section of society or line of soldiers); order

orīgō orīgin-is 3f. stock, source, origin

orior 4 dep. *ortus* I rise, proceed; begin, spring from, originate

ōrō 1 I beg, pray, entreat

ōs ōr-is 3n. face, mouth, speech

ostendō 3 *ostendī ostēnsus* (or *ostentus*) I show, reveal, exhibit, display

ōti-um ī 2n. cessation of conflict; leisure, inactivity

ouis ou-is 3f. sheep

P

palam openly, plainly

Palladi-um ī 2n. the Palladium, a sacred image of Minerva

Pallas Pallad-is/os 3f. Pallas Athena, (Roman) Minerva

palm-a ae 1f. palm (of hands)

pandō 3 *pandī passum* I spread (out)

pār par-is equal, like

parcō 3 *pepercī parsūrus* I spare, am lenient to (+ dat.)

parēns parent-is 3m. father, parent; f. mother

pāreō 2 I obey (+ dat.)

pariō 3 *peperī partus* I bring forth, bear, produce; obtain, acquire

pariter equally, on an equal footing

parō 1 I prepare, get ready; provide, obtain

pars part-is 3f. part; side

paru-us a um small (comp. *minor*; sup. *minimus*)

pāscō 3 *pāuī pāstum* I feed

pāscor 3 *pāstus* I graze, feed (myself)

passim far and wide

patefaciō 3 *patefēcī patefactus* I reveal, expose, disclose, throw open

pateō 2 I am accessible, lie open; am revealed

pater patr-is 3m. father

patior 3 dep. *passus* endure, suffer; allow, permit

patri-a ae 1f. fatherland

patri-us a um paternal, ancestral

pauc-ī ae a a few

pauid-us a um fearful, terrified, panic-stricken

pauper pauper-is 3m. poor man; (adj.) poor

pāx pāc-is 3f. peace

pectus pector-is 3n. chest, breast, heart

pecūni-a ae 1f. money

peior peiōr-is worse (see *malus*)

pelag-us ī 2n. sea

Pelasg-ī ōrum 2m. pl. Greeks (the Pelasgi were an ancient people living in northern Greece)

Pelasg-us a um Greek

penat-ēs um 3m. *penates*, household gods

pendō 3 *pependī pēnsum* I hang

penetrāl-is e innermost; *penetrāl-e is* 3n. inner shrine, parts

penitus (from) deep within, far away

peper-; see *pariō*

per (+ acc.) through; in the name of

perdō 3 *perdidī perditus* I lose; destroy, ruin

pereō perīre periī peritum I perish, die

perferō perferre pertulī perlātus I endure (to the end); complete; carry to; announce

perficiō 3 *perfēcī perfectus* I finish, complete, carry out; *perficiō ut* (+ subjunc.) I bring it about that

Pergam-a ōrum 2n. pl. Pergama, the citadel of Ilium, or Ilium itself

peri-; see *pereō*

perīcul-um ī 2n. danger

perit-; see *pereō*

perscrībō 3 *perscrīpsī perscrīptus* I write in detail, put on record

persequor 3 dep. *persecūtus* I pursue, follow after, take vengeance on

persuādeō 2 *persuāsī persuāsum* I persuade (+ dat.) (to/not to *ut/nē* + subjunc.)

peruēniō 4 *peruēnī peruentum* I reach, arrive at, come to (*ad* + acc.)

pēs ped-is 3m. foot

pessim-us a um worst (see *malus*)

petō 3 *petīuī petītus* I beg; seek; proposition, court; attack, make for; stand for (public office)

pharetr-a ae 1f. quiver

Phoeb-us ī 2m. (Phoebus) Apollo

Phrygi-us a um Trojan

pietās pietāt-is 3f. respect for gods, men and family; sense of duty; piety; goodness

pi-us a um pious, god-fearing

placet 2 *placuit placitum* it is pleasing (to X dat. to Y inf.); X (dat.) votes (to Y inf.)

placid-us a um peaceful, calm, cool

plānē clearly

plēn-us a um full (of) (+ gen. or abl.)

plūrim-us a um most, very much (see *multus*)

plūs plūr-is 3n. more

poen-a ae 1f. penalty

Poen-ī ōrum 2m. Carthaginians

pol-us ī 2m. pole, sky

pōnō 3 *posuī positus* I place, position; lay aside (= *dēpōnō*)

pōns pont-is 3m. bridge

pont-us ī 2m. sea

popul-us ī 2m. people, a people, nation

port-a ae 1f. gate

port-us ūs 4m. harbour

poscō 3 *poposcī* I demand, beg

posit-; see *pōnō*

possum posse potuī I am able, can; am powerful, have power (+ adv.)

post (adv.) afterwards, later; (+ acc.) behind, after

posteā afterwards

post-is is 3m. door, door-post

postquam (conjunction) after

posu-; see *pōnō*

pot-; see *possum*

potēns potent-is powerful

potior 4 dep. I control (+ gen.); gain control of (+ abl.)

potius quam rather than

potu-; see *possum*

praeceps praecipit-is headlong; sheer, steep

praecipitō 1 I speed/drive (on); hurry (down from + abl.); throw headlong

praecipuē especially, in particular

praeclār-us a um very famous, outstanding, brilliant

praed-a ae 1f. game, booty

praeficiō 3 *praefēcī praefectus* I put (X acc.) in charge of (Y dat.)

praemi-um ī 2n. reward, prize

praesum praeesse praefuī I am in charge of (+ dat.)

praetereā moreover, further

praetereō praeterīre praeteriī praeteritus I pass by; neglect, omit

premō 3 *pressī pressus* I press, chase; oppress; repress, check

Priam-us ī 2m. Priam, king of Troy

prīmō at first

prīmum (adv.) first

prīm-us a um first

prīnceps prīncip-is 3m. leader, chieftain; (adj.) first

prior -is first, earlier, former

prius (adv.) before, earlier; first

prius quam before (+ subjunc.)

prō (+ abl.) for, in return for; on behalf of; in front of; instead of; in accordance with

prōcumbō 3 *prōcubuī prōcubitum* I collapse, sink down

prōdō 3 *prodidī proditum* I betray

proeli-um ī 2n. battle

proficīscor 3 dep. *profectus* I set out

prohibeō 2 I prevent, restrain, inhibit, hinder, keep X (acc.) from Y (abl. /ā (ab) + abl.)

prōiciō 3 *prōiēcī prōiectus* I throw down, forward

prōpōnō 3 *prōposuī prōpositus* I set before; imagine; offer

propter (+ acc.) on account of

prōspiciō 3 *prōspexī prōspectum* I look out, see

prōuideō 2 *prōuīdī prōuīsus* I take care of (that), foresee

proxim-us a um nearest, next

pūb-ēs is 3f. manpower, youth

pudor pudōr-is 3m. modesty, sense of shame

puell-a ae 1f. girl

puer puer-ī 2m. boy

pugn-a ae 1f. battle, fight

pugnō 1 I fight

pulcher pulchr-a um beautiful; (sup.) *pulcherrimus a um*; (comp.) *pulchrior*

puluis puluer-is 3m. dust

pūniō 4 I punish

pupp-is is 3f. stern, poop; ship

putō 1 I reckon, suppose, judge, think, imagine

Q

quā where, by which route; somehow, by any route

quadrāgintā forty

quaerō 3 *quaesīuī quaesītus* I seek, look for; ask

quam how! (+ adj. or adv.); (after comp.) than

quam prīmum as soon as possible

quamquam although

quamuīs (+ subjunc.) although; (+ adj.) however

quandō since, when

quant-us a um how much, how great

quārē why?; therefore

quārt-us a um fourth

quasi as if, like

quater four times

quattuor four

-que (added to the end of the word) and

quemadmodum how

queror 3 dep. *questus* I complain

quī quae quod which? what?; who, which; (+ subjunc.) since (also with *quippe*); (+ subjunc.) in order that/to

quīcumque quaecumque quodcumque whoever, whatever

quid what?; why? (see *quis*)

quīdam quaedam quid-/quod-dam a, a certain, some

quidem indeed, certainly, at least, even (places emphasis on the preceding word)

quiēs quiēt-is 3f. sleep, rest

quippe quī (quae quod) inasmuch as he (she, it)

quis qua quid (after *sī, nisi, nē, num*) anyone, anything

quis quid who, what?
quisquam quicquam (after negatives) anyone
quisque quaeque quodque (quidque) each
quisquis quidquid (or *quicquid*) whoever, whatever
quō to where?; whither, to where
quod sī but if
quondam at times; formerly; some day
quoque also, too
quot how many

R

rapid-us a um violent, swift, consuming
rapiō 3 *rapuī raptus* I snatch, seize, carry away, plunder
ratiō ratiōn-is 3f. plan, method; reason; count, list; calculation, judgement, consideration
recēdō 3 *recessī recessum* I depart, leave, go to; stand apart
recēns recent-is fresh
recēp-; see *recipiō*
recipiō 3 *recēpī receptus* I welcome, receive, take in, regain, admit; *mē recipiō* I retreat
recūsō 1 I fight against, refuse, decline
reddō 3 *reddidī redditus* I return, give back, restore
redeō redīre rediī reditum I return, go back (intrans.)
redūcō 3 *redūxī reductus* I lead back
referō referre rettulī relātum I bring/carry back, return; recall, recount, report
refulgeō 2 *refulsī refulsum* I shine out
rēgīn-a ae 1f. queen
regiō regiōn-is 3f. region, area
rēgnō 1 I rule
rēgn-um ī 2n. kingdom, kingship, control, dominion, territory
regō 3 *rēxī rēctum* I rule, control
relict-; see *relinquō*
rēligiō -nis 3f. sacred offering, religious awe, conscience, ritual
relinquō 3 *relīquī relictus* I leave behind, leave, abandon
remaneō 2 *remānsī remānsum* I remain, stay behind, continue
repente suddenly
reperiō 4 *repperī repertus* I find, discover, learn, get
repetō 3 *repetī(u)ī repetītum* I begin from, return to, recall; repeat
requīrō 3 *requīsīuī requīsītus* I seek out; ask for/after/about; miss, need
rēs pūblic-a rē-ī pūblic-ae state, republic
rēs rē-ī 5f. thing, matter, business, affair; property; affair
resistō 3 *restitī -* I resist (+ dat.); stand back; halt, pause
resoluō 3 *resoluī resolūtum* I break
respondeō 2 *respondī respōnsum* I reply, answer

restō 1 I remain, am left (over); survive from
retrō back(wards)
reuīsō 3 I return
reuocō 1 I call back, ask, ask for, summon up
rēx rēg-is 3m. king
Rhīpeus nom. s. a Trojan
rōbur rōbor-is 3n. oak
rogō 1 I ask (*ut* + subjunc.)
Rōm-a ae 1f. Rome (*Rōmae*, locative, at Rome)
Rōmān-us a um Roman
ruīn-a ae 1f. wreck, ruin, collapse
rūmor rūmōr-is 3m. rumour, (piece of) gossip, unfavourable report
rumpō 3 *rūpī ruptum* I break (into), burst forth
ruō 3 *ruī rutum* I drive ahead, churn (up); rush
rūp-ēs -is 3f. cliff
rūrsus again

S

sacer sacr-a um holy, sacred
sacerdōs sacerdōt-is 3m./f. priest(ess)
sacrāt-us a um hallowed, set apart, sacred
saecul-um ī 2n. age
saepe often
saepiō 4 *saepsī saeptum* I enclose, surround
saeu-us a um savage, cruel, vicious
sal -is 3m. salt, sea
salūs salūt-is 3f. safety, salvation; health; greeting
salu-us a um safe, sound
sānct-us a um sacrosanct, sacred, holy, blessed, upright, pure
sangu-is -inis 3m. blood
sapienti-a ae 1f. wisdom
sat = satis
satis enough (of) (+ gen.)
Sāturni-a ae 1f. daughter of Saturn(us), i.e. Juno
Sāturni-us a um of Saturn
sax-um ī 2n. rock, stone
scelus sceler-is 3n. crime, villainy; criminal, villain
scēptr-um ī 2n. sceptre, rod (i.e. rule, power)
scindō 3 *scidī scissum* I divide, cut, split
sciō 4 I know
scopul-us ī 2m. rock
scrībō 3 *scrīpsī scrīptus* I write
sē himself, herself, itself/themselves
sēcum with/to himself/herself
secund-us a um second, willing
secūt-; see *sequor*
sed but
sēd-ēs is 3f. seat
semel once
semper always
senāt-us ūs 4m. senate
senex sen-is 3m. old man
sēnior -is older, in one's later years

sēns-; see *sentiō*

sententi-a ae 1f. opinion; judgement; sentence, vote; maxim

sentiō 4 *sēnsī sēnsus* I feel; understand; perceive, realise

septem seven

sepulc(h)r-um ī 2n. tomb, grave

sequor 3 dep. *secūtus* I follow

sermō sermōn-is 3m. conversation, discussion

seruō 1 I keep safe, preserve, guard

seru-us ī 2m. slave

sēsē = sē

sēū, sīue whether/or

sī + impf. subjunc., impf. subjunc. 'if X were happening (now), Y would be happening' (sometimes; 'if X had happened, Y would have happened')

sī + plupf. subjunc., plupf. subjunc. 'if X had happened, Y would have happened'

sī + pres. subjunc., pres. subjunc. 'if X were to happen, Y would happen'

sī if

sīc thus, in this way, so

sīdus sīder-is 3n. star

sign-um ī 2n. seal, signal, sign; figure; statue; standard; trumpet-call

sileō 2 I fall silent

silu-a ae 1f. wood, forest

sim pres. subjunc. of *sum*

simil-is e alike, similar, like (+ gen.)

simul at the same time, together

simulācr-um ī 2n. image, statue

simulō 1 I imitate, pretend

sin but if

sine (+ abl.) without

singul-ī ae a individual, one by one

Sinōn -is 3m. Sinon, a Greek sent to trick the Trojans

sin-us -ūs 4m. inlet, gulf, ripple (?)

soci-us ī 2m. ally, friend

sōl sōl-is 3m. sun

soleō 2 semi-dep. *solitus* I am accustomed, am used (+ inf.)

solit-; see *soleō*

sollicitō 1 I bother, worry, stir up, incite

sōlum (adv.) only; *nōn sōlum . . . sed etiam* not only . . . but also

sol-um ī 2n. ground

soluō 3 *soluī solūtum* I loosen, dissolve, release; pay, perform

sōl-us a um (gen. s. *sōlīus*; dat. s. *sōlī*) alone; lonely

somn-us ī 2m. sleep

sonit-us ūs 4m. sound

sonō 1 *sonuī* I sound, echo, thunder

soror -is 3f. sister

sors sort-is 3f. lot(tery), chance

spērō 1 I hope; expect

spēs spē-ī 5f. hope(s); expectation

spoli-a ōrum 2n. pl. spoils, booty, plunder

spūmō 1 I foam

statim at once

statuō 3 *statuī statūtum* I establish, found; resolve, decide

sternō 3 *strāuī strātum* I flatten

stet-; see *stō*

stil-us ī 2m. stylus (for writing in wax)

stō 1 *stetī statum* I stand

strīdō 3 *strīdī* I howl, shriek, creak; whirr

studi-um ī 2n. enthusiasm, zeal

stult-us a um stupid, foolish, a fool

stupeō 2 I am stunned, astonished

sub (+ abl.) beneath, under, up under, close to

subeō subīre I put in, seek shelter

subiciō 3 *subiēcī subiectum* I place under

subitō suddenly

subitus a um sudden

sublāt-; see *tollō*

succurrō 3 *succurrī succursum* I run to help, assist (+ dat.)

sum esse fuī futūrus I am

summergō (submergō) 3 *summersī summersum* I sink, submerge X (acc.) under Y (+ abl.)

summ-us a um highest, top of; main, principle

sūmō 3 *sūmpsī sūmptus* I take; put on; eat *supplicium/poenam sūmō (dē + abl.)* I exact the penalty (from)

sūmpt-; see *sūmō*

sūmpt-us ūs 4m. expense(s)

super moreover; (+ acc.) above, over

superb-us a um proud, fine; haughty, glorying in

super-ī ōrum 2m. pl. gods, powers above; note *superum* = gen. pl. *super(ōr)um* 'of the gods'

superō 1 I conquer, overcome; get the upper hand; rise above, tower over

supplex supplic-is 3m. suppliant, one coming to supplicate/beg help from

supplici-um ī 2n. punishment *summum supplicium* the death penalty

supplicium sūmō (dē + abl.) I exact the penalty (from)

surgō 3 *surrēxī surrēctum* I rise, arise, get up

suspendō 3 *suspendī suspēnsum* I hang; keep in suspense

sustineō 2 *sustinuī sustentus* I withstand, endure; support; hang up

sustul-; see *tollō*

su-us a um his, hers/theirs

Syrācūs-ae ārum 1f. pl. Syracuse (*Syrācūsīs* at Syracuse)

T

tabell-ae ārum 1f. pl. writing-tablets

taceō 2 I am silent, leave unmentioned

tacit-us a um silent

tāct-; see *tangō*

tāl-is e of such a kind

tam so, to such a degree

tamen however, but (second word)

tamquam as though

tandem at length

tangō 3 *tetigī tāctus* I touch, lay hands on

tant-us a um so great, so much, so important

tard-us a um slow

taur-us ī 2m. bull

tēct-um ī 2n. building

tēcum with you/yourself

tegō 3 *tēxī tēctus* I cover, hide, protect

tellūs tellūr-is 3f. land

tēl-um ī 2n. spear, weapon

temperō 1 I restrain, soothe; refrain

tempestās tempestāt-is 3f. storm, tempest

templ-um ī 2n. temple

temptō 1 I attempt, try; check, test, explore

tempus tempor-is 3n. time

tendō 3 *tetendī tentus* (or *tēnsus*) I stretch (out); offer; direct; travel; strive, fight

teneō 3 *tenuī tentus* I hold, possess, keep, restrain

tenuēre = tenuērunt

ter three times

terg-um ī 2n. back, hide (also *tergus tergor-is* 3n.)

terr-a ae 1f. land

terreō 2 I frighten

terti-us a um third

tetig-; see *tangō*

Teucr-ī ōrum 2m. Trojans

timeō 2 I fear, am afraid of; (*nē* + subjunc.) am afraid that/lest

timor timōr-is 3m. fear

tollō 3 *sustulī sublātus* I lift, remove, take away, destroy

torqueō 2 *torsī tortum* I twist, rotate, hurl, bend

tot so many

tōt-us a um (gen. s. *tōtīus*; dat. s. *tōtī*) whole, complete, entire

trabs trab-is 3f. tree-trunk, beam, timber, girder

trādō 3 *trādidī trāditus* I hand over, transmit

trahō 3 *trāxī tractum* I drag, draw

trāns (+ acc.) across

trēdecim 13

tremefaciō 3 *tremefēcī tremefactum* I cause to tremble

tremō 3 *tremuī* I quiver, tremble

trēs tri-a three

tridēns trident-is 3m. trident (Neptune's traditional implement)

trīgintā thirty

trīs = trēs

trīst-is e sad, gloomy, unhappy, baleful

Troi-a ae 1f. Troy, the region where Ilium, destroyed by Greeks, was located

Troiān-us a um Trojan

Trōs Trojan (Greek declension; *Trōes* nom. pl., *Trōas* acc. pl.)

tū you (s.)

tueor 2 dep. I watch over, protect; view, scan; preserve

tul-; see *ferō*

tum then

turb-a ae 1f. crowd, mob, uproar, disturbance

turbō 1 I scatter, confuse, confound

turbō turbin-is 3m. whirlwind

turp-is e disgusting, filthy, outrageous, ugly

tūt-us a um safe, protected, secure

tu-us a um your(s) (s.)

Tȳdīdēs; nom. s. of Tydides, son of Tydeus, i.e. Diomedes

Tyri-us a um Tyrian, from Tyre

U

uacu-us a um empty; free (from; + abl. or *ā* (*ab*) + abl.)

uad-um ī 2n. shallow(s), sea-bed, depth(s), ford

ualē(te) goodbye!

ualeō 2 I am strong; am well, am powerful; am able (cf. *ualē* = 'Farewell!' 'Goodbye!')

ualid-us a um strong

uān-us a um empty, illusory, vain

uari-us a um diverse, various

uast-us a um huge, vast

ubi where?; when?

ubīque everywhere

-ue or

uehemēns uehement-is impetuous, violent, emphatic

uehō 3 *uēxī uectum* I carry, bear, transport

uel . . . uel either . . . or;

uel even

uēla dō 1 I set sail

uelim pres. subjunc. of *uolō*

uellem impf. subjunc. of *uolō*

uēl-um ī 2n. sail, canvas (often pl. *uēl-a ōrum*)

uelut(ī) just as

ueniō 4 *uēnī uentum* I come, arrive

uent-; see *ueniō*

uent-us ī 2m. wind

uerber uerber-is 3n. blow; whip

uerb-um ī 2n. word

uērō indeed, in truth, to be sure

uers-us ūs 4m. verse; pl. poetry

uertex uertic-is 3m. peak, head, summit; whirlpool, eddy

uertō 3 *uersī uersum* I turn (round), turn upside
   down, overthrow
uertor 3 *uersus* intrans. of above
uēr-us a um true real, genuine; right, proper
uester uestr-a um your(s) (pl.)
uest-is is 3f. dress, clothes; tapestry; covering
uetus ueter-is old; long-established
ui-a ae 1f. way, road
uīc-; see *uincō*
uīcīn-us ī 2m. neighbour
uict-; see *uincō*
uictor -is 3m conqueror, winner
uictōri-a ae 1f. victory
uīct-us ūs 4m. way of life; provisions, food
uideō 2 *uīdī uīsus* I see, observe, understand
uideor 2 pass. *uīsus* I seem; am seen
uinc(u)l-um ī 2n. chain, binding, bond
uincō 3 *uīcī uictus* I conquer
uīn-um ī 2n. wine
uir uir-ī 2m. man, husband, hero
uirgō uirgin-is 3f. young girl, virgin
uirtūs uirtūt-is 3f. manliness, courage; goodness
uīs 2nd s. of *uolō*
uīs irr. force, violence (acc. *uim*; abl. *uī*); pl. *uīrēs*
   uīr-ium 3f. strength; military forces
uīs-; see *uideō/uideor*
uīs-us ūs 4m. sight, vision
uīt-a ae 1f. life
uitt-a ae 1f. woollen headband, worn by priests and
   in many religious rituals
uīuō 3 *uīxī uīctum* I am alive, live
uix scarcely, hardly
ūll-us a um (gen. s. *ūllīus*; dat. s. *ūllī*) any (cf.
   nūllus)
ultim-us a um last, final
ultrō willingly (usually beyond the call of duty); in
   addition
umbr-a ae 1f. shadow, darkness; shade, ghost
umer-us ī 2m. shoulder
umquam ever
ūnā all together, as one
und-a ae 1f. wave

unde from where, whence
undique from all sides
ūn-us a um (gen. s. *ūnīus*; dat. s. *ūnī*) one, single,
   alone
uōbīscum with you (pl.)
uocō 1 I call, summon
uolō uelle uoluī I wish, want, be willling
uoluntās uoluntāt-is 3f. will, wish
uolu-ō 3 *uoluī uolūtum* I cause to roll through; set in
   motion; unfold, relate
uōs you (pl.)
uōx uōc-is 3f. voice; word
ūs-; see *ūtor*
usquam anywhere
usque ad (+ acc.) right up to
usque continually, without a break
ut (+ indic.) how!; (+ indic.) as, when; (+ subjunc.)
   to, that . . . should; (+ subjunc.) that (after *accidit*,
   perficiō etc.); (+ subjunc.) that (result); (+
   subjunc.) in order to/that (purpose); (+ subjunc.)
   that . . . not (after verbs of fearing)
uter-us ī 2m. womb, belly
ūtor 3 dep. *ūsus* I use, make use of; adopt (+ abl.)
utrum . . . an (+ subjunc.) whether . . . or (indir. q.;
   neg. *necne*)
utrum . . . an (double q.) A or B? (neg. *annōn* = or
   not?); (+ subjunc.) whether . . . or (indir. q.) (neg.
   necne = or not)
utrum . . . an = double question, i.e. A or B? (neg.
   annōn)
uulg-us -ī 2n. (m.) crowd, mob, herd
uulnus uulner-is 3n. wound
uult 3rd s. of *uolō*
uultis 2nd pl. of *uolō*
uult-us ūs 4m. face, look, features
uxor uxōr-is 3f. wife

V

Vest-a ae 1f. goddess of the hearth and family
Vlix-ēs ī/is/eī 3m. Ulysses (Greek Odysseus),
   renowned in the *Aeneid* for his mercilessness and
   deceitfulness

Index

References marked with square brackets [ ] are to the *Introduction*; references in **bold** are to the discussion passages; all other references are to the notes.